HOUSEBOAT CHRONICLES

HOUSEBOAT CHRONICLES

NOTES FROM A LIFE IN SHIELD COUNTRY

JAKE MacDONALD

THE LYONS PRESS
Guilford, Connecticut
An imprint of The Globe Pequot Press

10   9   8   7   6   5   4   3   2   1

Printed in the United States of America

ISBN 1-59228-553-8

Library of Congress Cataloging-in-Publication Data is available on file.

For Ann

HOUSEBOAT CHRONICLES

A blank landscape.

My hand, holding a Laurentien coloured pencil in Emerald Green, pauses at the lower right-hand corner of the page. What should I draw? All around me, kids are hunched over their desks. Grumbling, furtively farting, whispering to each other, humming softly as they work at their own pieces of art.

It's hard to concentrate because the teacher is somewhere in the back of the room. This is Sister George Mary's Grade 6 class, and there's no tomfoolery permitted. When Kenny Richard catches my eye from across the aisle, pulls a booger from his nose, and pretends to flick it in my direction, Sister George launches towards him.

Sister George wears a hooded head cowling and floor-length black skirt, and glides up the aisle like a condor. Bending over, she hisses in Kenny's ear and writes his name on her clipboard. He's earned another five points in The Minute Club. Ha ha. He gives me that look, like he's gagging. Every time one of us gets caught communicating with a classmate, Sister George fines us five minutes. Every two weeks, you have to stay after school and work off the fine. After four detentions, you get the strap. When someone takes the long walk down to the principal's office, accompanied by the teacher, the entire school gets as quiet as Sing Sing prison during an electrocution. Everyone sits there, exchanging anticipatory monkey grimaces, waiting for the sound of the leather belt to come echoing up the waxed hallway.

St. Ignatius School is in the south end of Winnipeg, at the corner of Stafford Street and Corydon Avenue. Just a few blocks north of the school is the genteel, wooded neighbourhood of River Heights, where the large century-old homes are occupied by lawyers, doctors, and judges, many of whom are Anglican or United Church and are unfortunately going to Hell. South of the school is the poorer, working-class neighbourhood of Fort Rouge, where the crooked old wood-frame houses are filled with large Italian immigrant families, many of whom are rosary-clutching church-goers going to Heaven. Or at least the women are.

When it's my turn to serve 6:45 mass I walk to church in the bitter cold, sharing that desolate time of morning with the frozen elms, a million stars, and perhaps a furtive wild creature or two – a cottontail rabbit darting through the fresh snow, pausing to perk its ears and look back at me – and when I get to church those Italian mothers are always there in their black veils, kneeling. They're praying, no doubt, for their wayward sons, my enemies. Their sons tend to be thin sulky boys who smoke cigarettes and fight with their feet, dancing around like fighting cocks. One of the worst is Raymond Cantafio, who weighs about eighty pounds, stands about four foot ten, and has hair like a matinee idol. Many times I've seen Raymond Cantafio slap the faces of boys twice his size, slap their faces back and forth, trying to goad them to fight. And once, while walking home, I had the grave misfortune of running into Raymond Cantafio in a back lane. For an entire city block I edged along backwards, walleyed with terror, while Raymond hissed and feinted at me like a ferret.

Boys like Raymond and his friends make certain streets into no-go zones. But like the cagey citizen of some bombed-out European city, I know safe routes through the various enclaves. Some of my friends are rich, from Yale Avenue, and some are poor, from Garwood. Some are feeble and some are tough. Some are good in school and some are so dumb that you have to wonder if they're retarded. (Danny Barton, for example, shot himself in the leg with a .22 pistol to impress a girl.) I'm sort of in-between. I'm not the most uncoordinated boy in the school yard, nor am I an athlete who gets picked first for baseball teams. My father is a senior bureaucrat with the city, so he makes a good salary. But my parents are raising a family of seven kids, so we're kind of poor anyway. We live in a tract-house neighbourhood seven blocks west of the school. The post-war economy is humming, and my street, Mulvey Avenue, is sort of a suburban battery farm – long rows of temperature-regulated boxes churning out small human beings like me.

It's Sister George's task to whip us into shape, but art class is not high on her list of educational priorities. Art class can only encourage us to screw open the lids of our fetid little minds, and what good can come of that? She'd rather have us do something useful, like long division. Or, if she's in a good mood, she'll permit a spelling bee. Today, she's definitely not in a good mood. I have a bruised lip to attest to that. At lunch hour, when we were all stampeding back to class, I stopped for a drink at the water fountain. Sister George glided up and whacked me in the back of the head, driving my upper lip into the chromium steel of the spigot. "Woe betide," she exclaimed, "if you're not back to class in one second." I should have known better, trying to drink water after the bell had rung. But Sister George's bloody willingness to always ratchet up the tension one more notch fills most of us with a fearful respect. This is a woman who, without too much provocation, would probably drive spikes through our heads and cook us for dinner.

On Sister George's desk at the front of the room, a plastic desk radio issues the rackety piano music of the CBC's weekly Manitoba School Broadcasts. The announcer has the sweet maternal voice of Miss Roma Harpell, the hostess of a television show called *Romper Room*. I don't think it's actually Miss Roma, but it sounds like her. She sounds like the sort of woman who thinks that children are bunnies, full of bright ideas and sweet affections. As Kenny would have it, she's fucked in the head. But I'd rather spend the next hour listening to Miss Roma than Sister George. So I cooperate with all of Miss Roma's instructions. As the piano murmurs gently in the background, her cooing voice issues our marching orders. *Now children, put your heads down on your desks and close your eyes. That's right, nice and tight! Now just be very quiet . . . and dream that we're drifting in the vast darkness of space. Look at that lovely blue planet over there! How pretty it is! Look at the many green continents, so magical and different! What faraway lands will you visit today?*

Somewhere behind me a yardstick whacks a desk. "Close your eyes!" bellows Sister George.

It's the same battle in every art class. The girls close their eyes. The boys refuse. We cooperate to the extent of laying our heads on our arms, but closing your eyes is for sissies. If Sister George prowls past, I scrunch my eyes shut, but open them again as soon as she's past. Sneakily, with my head down, I peer out the window and try to decide what faraway land I'm going to visit today. Outside, the snow is falling, a grey winter afternoon somewhere in the long march from Christmas to Easter. As long as Sister George doesn't catch me, I can spend long minutes thinking up my magical land, lulled into a dream by the hypnotic motion of the falling snow.

You're allowed to sit up straight when you're ready to start drawing. Having selected my destination, I draw a green wavy line across my blank sheet of paper. Using the sides of the pencil, I fill in the contours with olive greens and smoky blues, creating a prospect of distant hills. Above the hills, a hazy sky. With a check mark I create a cruising eagle. I'm fairly serious about art class. If I had my choice, this is what I would do all day. All my textbooks are disfigured with little sketches. With the money that my aunt gave me for Christmas, I sent away for a book called *Learn to Draw with Jon Gnagy*. I've learned some tricks from Jon Gnagy. For example, he's got this trick where you can draw any animal with a series of interlocking circles. But constructing animals from circles is not as interesting as dreaming up a picture – staring at a blank page, then scrawling a horizon line, a pale sky, a drifting eagle. You feel as if a new world is coming to life under your fingertips. It's like being God.

Actually, it's not like being God. You can burn in Purgatory for thinking like that. In my desk I have a comic book called *Chuck White, Catholic Boy*. Each issue tells a story about a dilemma in Chuck's life and how he solved it. The latest issue talks about Purgatory, and all the good works Chuck performs whenever he catches himself thinking sinful thoughts, like comparing himself to God. As every Catholic knows, there are two types of punishments awaiting sinners in the afterlife. Purgatory is the penalty for venial sins, like coveting your neighbour's bicycle or thinking impure thoughts. If you act on your thoughts – steal your neighbour's bicycle, for example, or feel up a girl – you commit a different class of offence, a mortal sin, and get sent to Hell, which is a maximum security institution from which there is no escape. *Chuck White, Catholic Boy* doesn't talk much about Hell, because what's to say? Hell is like a big penitentiary, full of screaming people who are on fire. Hell is a conversation-stopper. The only insurance against going there, after committing a mortal, is to get yourself immediately to Confession. But that doesn't always work. Chuck had a friend who French-necked with a girl, and on their way to church they were run over by a cement truck.

Chuck reduces his earned time in Purgatory by performing good works, which earn rewards, called indulgences. Indulgences can be applied to one's own Purgatory sentence or transferred to someone else's. They're like Old Dutch points. The black-veiled Italian ladies who attend 6:45 mass every morning are earning major indulgences, which they transfer to their no-good sons. The biggest indulgence of all is called a Plenary Indulgence, and it pretty much buys you a permanent licence to commit mortals. Whenever Chuck feels a gnawing worry that he's building up a lot of Purgatory time, he performs good works and keeps track of his indulgences with an easy-to-use reward schedule at the back of his Holy Catechism book. Let's say he attends first Friday mass for a year. Right away, he can look it up on the chart – *One Year of Attending Mass on First Friday* – *412 years off.*

Still, it's probably easier to avoid blaspheming God in the first place by comparing your art-class drawings to His mighty works. Choosing a pencil of Mediterranean Blue, I grind the tip in my little pencil sharpener and set to work creating a lake in the foreground, and a red canoe. Two people are paddling the canoe across the lake, a boy and a girl. They're not thinking impure thoughts; they're just paddling a canoe. Choosing my trusty green pencil again I create a foreshore, and a yellow cottage. From force of habit I draw a ribbon of white smoke slanting up from the chimney. The CBC lady has conducted her invocation well. Scribbling madly with the coloured pencil, I'm no longer sitting in Sister George's class. It's not winter any more. It's a warm summer afternoon, and I'm walking through the meadow to our cottage. I can feel the prickly grass under my bare feet, and I can smell the lake.

∿

My father built the cottage a few years ago. He built it at Laclu, a small community by a lake that played an important role in the romance between him and my mother.

When he was young, my dad studied graduate level economics at the University of Toronto. He roomed on Spadina Avenue with his buddy Frank Pickersgill. It was the late 1930s, and the Spanish Civil War was underway. My dad and Pickersgill were fellow Winnipeggers and avid lefties. They would spend their weekends sitting in swanky restaurants in hotels like the Royal York, arguing about politics and ordering crusty rolls and coffee. They would eat crusty rolls for about two hours, then leave without ordering dinner. As they walked out, they'd wave at the head waiter. Sorry, we changed our minds! For fun, they'd sneak into examination halls and try to pass the tests for courses they weren't enrolled in.

After university, my dad got a job with the Winnipeg Electric Company, a utility that ran the streetcars. There weren't a lot of people in the office with postgraduate degrees from the U of T, so he was groomed as senior management material. He stood six foot two, had blue eyes and an athlete's graceful saunter, and the secretaries liked him. But he was awkward around women and wasn't suited to small talk. He could talk for hours with men, but couldn't think of three words to say to a woman. He told the secretaries he had a fiancée in Toronto named Frances, meaning Frank.

One of the clerks in the payroll department was an Irish Catholic girl named Peggy Monahan. With her shoulder-length dark hair and dark eyes, she looked like the teenaged Elizabeth Taylor in *National Velvet*. My father kept dropping by her desk to scrutinize memos, and finally confided that he didn't really have a fiancée, and would she like to go to a movie? They went to the Capitol theatre and watched *The Light That Failed*, starring Ronald Colman. On their second date he showed up at her front door with a cardboard box containing a puppy. Her mother was infuriated at his nerve, but Peggy christened the collie pup Eubie, after the Baltimore jazzman, and kept it at the foot of her bed. When the puppy fell ill with distemper a few weeks later, her mother knit him a yellow sweater and nursed him through the crisis.

Donald Ian MacDonald and Peggy Christine Monahan were married in June 1941 and went on their honeymoon to Laclu – a pretty lake in the Canadian Shield, a hundred miles from Winnipeg, in the western part of Ontario. They rented a cottage and explored a different uninhabited lake every day, hiking the portage trails with a canoe and Eubie galloping up the path to check for bears. It was an unusually cold and stormy June, and the lakes were so rough they had to be careful traversing the big stretches, keeping to the lee shores and making Eubie lie down when they headed into the heavy waves. At night, they curled up in the cottage and listened to the radio, and caught up with the bad news coming from Europe. Swastika flags were flying above Paris. The Americans hadn't joined the war yet, and Britain was preparing to make a last stand against Operation Sea Lion, a massive German invading force that was expected to arrive on their beaches during the next full moon.

At the same time they were exploring the lakes around Laclu, a crew of German sailors was ploughing a monstrous new German battleship named the *Bismarck* through the heavy seas of the Denmark Strait. The *Bismarck*'s battle plan was to cruise down into the shipping lanes of the north Atlantic and prey on Canadian convoys hauling supplies to the doomed England. An RAF Spitfire spotted the *Bismarck*, and warships of the King's Royal Navy set off to engage the battleship. In the murky predawn light of May 24, a British heavy cruiser named the *Hood* caught sight of the *Bismarck* and challenged him (the Germans referred to their warships as males) from sixteen miles away. The *Bismarck* swung broadside, fired one salvo from its terrible huge guns, and hit the *Hood* amidships. The explosion literally blew the *Hood* out of the water, and it sank in less than a minute. Three English sailors survived; 1,415 died.

The *Hood* had been the pride of the Royal Navy, and the news that she'd been destroyed delivered yet another devastating blow to British morale. With bulletins like this coming over the CBC radio (courtesy of the announcer Lorne Greene, whose grave delivery earned him the title "the voice of doom"), my father knew that it was just a matter of time until he wound up in uniform, so after their honeymoon at Laclu he volunteered, and ended up a lieutenant in the Royal Canadian Navy. His friends all volunteered too. His best buddy, Frank Pickersgill, spoke fluent French, so he volunteered for the intelligence service and parachuted into occupied France. As soon as he arrived, he was caught by the Nazis, thanks to an informant, and was sent to Buchenwald, where he was tortured with piano wire at Block 17, then hung on a meat hook cemented into a wall. According to German camp documents that became available after the war, the only words his torturers could extract from him were "Long live free France, long live Canada." After the war, my father kept his war stuff and Pickersgill's letters in the top of his closet. My brother and I would take out my father's Navy gas mask, a rubbery-smelling thing with squid-like eyes, and chase each other around the bedroom.

Laclu therefore held a special place in the hearts of both my father and mother, and in 1954 they bought two acres of land on the north shore of Laclu lake. When summer came, we all piled into the car and went to see the property. We had seven kids in the family by then, plus my parents, plus my beloved white-haired grandmother, so we needed a big car, and a big car we had. My dad was a General Motors man, and his latest car was a lime-green Buick with chromium exhaust ports and doors as big as the loading bays on a Halifax bomber. Ten people, however, made a full load even for a car that size, so it was a long ride. That particular day, it was fantastically hot, as only southern Manitoba can be in July. I drank too much grape juice and fell asleep with my head tilted drunkenly askew in the direct blast of the sun. When I awoke, with a wretched gurgle of the stomach, a purple column of vomit spewed out of my mouth and arced across the back seat onto my brother Danny, who looked at the vomit on his shirt and immediately threw up on Sally, who threw up on Babe, and so forth. In short order, the crowded back seat was a vomitorium, and we all had to change into fresh clothes on the side of the road. But somehow we made it to Ontario, turned off the highway, drove along a winding gravel road for a few miles, and parked in the middle of nowhere.

We got out of the car and milled around in confusion, blinking in the heat. Where are we? Where's the lake? Can we go home now?

We were surrounded by nothing. On the right side of the road was a thick forest. On the left side of the road was a rolling hayfield. The sky was empty and there wasn't a building anywhere. Led by our intrepid parents we hiked through the hayfield, over a knoll, and down towards the lake. There wasn't much to look at, really. Just high grass, and a few wooden stakes pounded into the ground to mark our property line. We walked around for a while, looking at the stakes, then one of my sisters screamed – wood tick.

Back at the car, we had to strip down to our underwear and pick off the ticks. My brother and I wanted to burn them to death but my mother wouldn't allow it. My mother is the sort of human being who won't kill even a bee. She traps them alive in a wad of tissue paper and releases them outside. So that was our first visit to the vacant lot that would soon become our cottage site. The following summer, we returned to Laclu and rented a cottage at Webbs' Camps. My father worked on the cottage and we hung around Webbs'. There was an enormous amount of work to do, but that wasn't our problem. Our job was having fun. Every day my mother would do her laundry, her cooking and cleaning, and every day my father would build the cottage. When he came back at night, he'd be all filthy and banged up from the construction work, and we'd exclaim, "Show us your splinters!" He'd sit down and display his big hands, impressively damaged by the day's work.

It couldn't have been much fun for either of them, but they kept at it. Over the next couple of summers the cottage began to take shape – a big wooden box on stilts. It had a stepladder for front steps and no roof. The site was strewn with scrap lumber, and the hayfield was full of bloodthirsty ticks. But every time we arrived the place looked a little better. The farmer who sold us the land came and mowed the hay, using his tractor to pull the hay-rake, a scary-looking contraption with scissor-action teeth. When he was finished, the lawn was as spiky as tooth-picks. But at least it no longer harboured wood ticks, and after a few days, the grass got softer and we could walk on it bare-foot without mincing.

Finally my mother decided to spend a whole summer there, with us kids. My dad worked in the city, and every Friday night he drove up to the lake. We walked down the road to meet him. My brother and I wanted to toughen our feet so we walked bare-foot. The whole family made a game of estimating how far we would make it along the road before my dad's lime-green Buick came gliding over the hill.

Danny and I met some other kids. Every morning, we convened for the purpose of adventure. Some mornings we walked to Webbs' and went swimming. Other mornings we caught frogs, snakes, and turtles and gathered them in large menageries. Sometimes we armed ourselves with hatchets and home-made spears – hunting knives lashed with twine to the end of a pole – and went off to explore the woods. We'd cross the big hayfield and venture into the deep woods. We never went very far. Maybe a hundred yards, close enough to the road that we could still hear the rip of cars going past, but far enough that we could feel the great palpable Presence of the wilderness.

∾

Towards the end of summer the cottage was roofed in, plumbed, and wired. And one Saturday morning my father announced that he was taking the day off.

People who don't own vacation properties might assume that the whole point of owning a cottage is to have a place where you can relax, enjoy nature, and take the day off. But there were seldom moments when my parents weren't working. The drone of a lawn mower, the swish and gurgle of the wringer washer, the distant growl of my dad's curse as he whacked his thumb with the hammer – this was the sound track that should have accompanied my drawing. Every day, my mother was either making meals, cleaning up after meals, or getting ready for the next meal. Every morning, my dad would eat his standard breakfast of bacon and eggs, then go out into the yard and set up his sawhorses, unfurl his extension cords, and get to work. Their days consisted of work, dawn to dusk, seven days a week. But every once in a while, perhaps twice during the summer, they'd take a day off to enjoy themselves.

In northwestern Ontario, something quite dramatic occurs around the fifteenth day of August. The mornings are still lush and warm, but there's something in the air, or more accurately, something missing from the air. You wake up one morning, step outside, take a curious look at the lake, the emerald dew-covered lawn, and realize with a vague uncertainty that something has changed. The sun is still strong, but it seems hazy and fixed at an odd angle in the sky. And the forest seems different. What is it? You can stand there for minutes before you realize what it is – the birds have stopped singing.

All the various flowers, insects, and songbirds go through intense, dramatic breeding cycles that last only weeks, or even hours. Once the birds have raised their young, their chatter ceases. And you realize, with a surge of sadness, that summer is ending. Undoubtedly, it was a recognition like that that caused my father to announce one day over breakfast, "Mother, let's take the day off."

It always surprised me to discover that my parents had lives of their own. Sometimes they expressed their independence by going for long car drives together or, in Winnipeg, going to the monthly Sneak Preview at the Gaiety Theatre. We didn't mind when they went out on these dates. It gave us the chance to have the house to ourselves. We could eat what we wanted, jump on the beds if we wanted, and if our older sisters, who were in charge of us, ended up in a hair-pulling brawl, so much the better. On nights when they announced their intention to go out on a date, my mother would have a bath, change into her slip, then sit at the vanity table in their bedroom, powdering her cheeks, putting on her lipstick, and taking the better part of an hour to get ready. Her emollients and creams filled the room with the scent of flowers, and my brother and I would sit on the edge of the bed, watching her brush her hair.

We hadn't yet developed any real routines at the cottage, so when my father made his announcement that he was taking the day off, we weren't sure if that included us. I don't think he was sure either, because he and my mother conferred in the kitchen for a while, then came out and suggested that we all go fishing. My sisters had been hoping that we'd go to Kenora, and they didn't seem much interested in a fishing trip. That left my little brother Danny and me. So we packed a lunch, went to the Webbs' store, and bought some fishing tackle. (I knew every lure by heart. The Mud Puppy had a beautifully illustrated cardboard box that showed an enormous gape-jawed muskie bearing down on the hapless Puppy. The yellow Five of Diamonds spoon cautioned buyers to "stand behind a tree" when fastening the lure to their fishing line, lest the fish jump right out of the lake and grab it out of their hand. To my distress, my father ridiculed these advertisements, telling me they were "meant to catch fishermen, not fish.")

After stocking up on lures, minnows, and soft drinks, we drove up the winding gravel road, heading north. The road was an offshoot of the Trans-Canada Highway that passed through Laclu, then wound through heavy forests and swamp country. I loved driving up this road, because it got narrower and rougher as you went, and you never knew when you might see an animal. My father was in a good mood, and he drove with his window down and listened to the news on the radio. It was 1960, and John Diefenbaker was the prime minister of Canada. In Hamburg, Germany, the Indra Club was rocking every night to the tunes of a teenage band called the Beatles. And in Canada, the farthest north you could drive, in this part of Ontario, was a muddy little parking lot at Rosena Lake. From Rosena Lake onward, if you wanted to keep going, you had to climb in a canoe or a float plane, or start walking. There wasn't another road or power line all the way to the North Pole. So in effect, when we pulled into the parking lot, we'd arrived at the edge of civilization, the edge of the world.

Here lived a trapper named Carl Mueller. A rusty old pick-up truck was parked next to his ramshackle cabin, and his backyard was filled with scrap lumber, discarded appliances, plywood hide stretchers, bed frames, rotting boats, stacks of mouldy firewood, and half-dismantled outboard motors. Past the beach, the blue waters of Rosena Lake glittered in the sun. I knew that my dad had fished here with his buddies prior to the war. I'd seen the old black and white photographs – young men in leather jackets and tweed motoring caps, holding up impressive stringers of fish. So my brother and I were excited. Clambering out of the car, we dashed down to the lake to explore the shoreline.

The half dozen boats pulled up on the shore were flat-bottomed rowboats, full of scummy water that swarmed with tiny waterbugs. After making a rental agreement with Carl, my parents came down to the shore toting tackle boxes and fishing rods. My dad bailed out one of the boats and got its little Johnson Sea Horse running. He put some dry boards in the boat so that we didn't have to walk on the slimy bottom. We climbed in and headed off on our adventure.

When we reached the fishing spot, my father shut off the motor, opened his tackle box, and assembled an intricate series of swivels, lead weights, clips, and something he called a June Bug spinner, which was a red and white blade that fluttered in the breeze like a bangle earring. Reaching into the metal bait bucket, he extracted a live minnow and threaded the hook through its mouth, out its gills, and through its midriff. He then rigged up rods for my brother and me. Starting the motor again, he trolled slowly along the shoreline while we paid out line from each of our rods, careful not to let out too much line lest we snag our lures on the bottom.

A few minutes later my brother shouted the alarm. His rod began dancing and we all shouted conflicting instructions. He avidly cranked at the handle of his reel and soon a fish appeared at the side of the boat. My father scooped it up with the landing net and laid it, flipping crazily, in the bottom of the boat.

I'd never seen such a fish. Its skin was textured like hammered brass, and its jaws snapped open and shut as it writhed in the wet net. Sharp spikes protruded from its back and its white eyes were as large as marbles. My father said that it was a pickerel, the best type of fish, and we'd save it for dinner. He clipped a chain stringer onto its jaw, lowered it into the water, and smiled. "All right, let's catch another one."

He explained that pickerel travel in schools, so once you catch one, you should troll back over the same spot. This time it was my father who caught one. After catching a few more – which my father released because they were too small – we carried on, and the lake got wilder and more desolate-looking. On one island we heard dogs barking, and as we drew closer we saw some huskies chained up along the shore. They looked like slant-eyed, half-starved wolves, and they yelped angrily at us as we puttered past. "Those are the sled dogs for Carl's trapline," my father said. "He keeps them here all summer, and throws them a fish now and then."

"It's so cruel to keep them chained up," my mother said. "Look at their ears."

My father nodded in agreement. We could see the bloodied stumps of their ears. Each dog had a halo of tiny flies buzzing around its head. My dad liked people well enough, but he saved his unconditional affection for dogs. Even hostile dogs rated a kind word. If a chained-up dog barked at him, he would scold it for being such a grump, let the dog sniff his hand, and soon enough it would wag its tail. These huskies looked like they hadn't eaten in weeks. I half-expected my father to go ashore and give them our lunch.

A little farther on, we trolled into a bay that was full of lily pads and sunken trees. From inside the long grass, a blue heron suddenly popped open like an umbrella, croaked, and laboured away with great wing-beats. Looking down into the murky water, I could see schools of minnows darting through the down-slanting rays of light. Near the shore, a snapping turtle sunned itself on a rotted log. The monstrous creature's shell was as large as a slab of rock, covered with bony ridges and dried algae, and as we trolled past, its snakelike head swivelled towards us.

Just after we passed the turtle, I felt a violent jerk at my lure and the rod doubled over. Realizing that I'd hooked a whopper, my father ordered my mother and brother to reel in their lines. He instructed me to let it run, but I didn't have any choice in the matter. I was using a nickel-plated Pflueger Akron reel, loaded with black line, and the hub of the reel was spinning so quickly that it burned my thumb. In no time, the fish peeled off so much line that my father had to chase it with the boat.

When we got into deeper water, the fish headed straight down. If we'd been a group of Nantucket whalers in Melville's novel, we'd have said that the fish had "sounded." The momentum was brutal and irresistible. It was like my fishing lure was attached to an anvil. I wasn't worried about losing the fish as much as by the possibility that I would never see it. I devoutly wanted to see it. I knew that it had to be a fish, but I kept imagining that it was something else, I didn't know what. This was such a wild, spooky place – this weedy bay, this desolate lake with its pre-historic turtles and crazed dogs – I wondered if it was possible that I'd hooked onto something else: something nameless, an underwater creature that would amaze us when it surfaced.

With so little line left on my reel, I clamped both thumbs down on the spool and held on with all my strength. My father shouted a warning, but I wasn't about to let the beast escape. The rod bent terrifically, then the line snapped.

What?

I couldn't believe that the fish was gone. Hoping against hope, I cranked the reel until the frayed end finally emerged from the water. "What did I do wrong?" I whined.

"Nothing," my father said.

"Do you think it'll come back?"

He just chuckled, as if such foolishness didn't deserve an answer.

"How big do you think it was?"

"Who knows," he said. He started the motor and shifted into gear. No one could accuse my dad of coddling his kids. He came from a long line of jocular but unsentimental Scots. His solution to bad luck was simple – take it on the chin and move on.

We motored to another spot and caught more pickerel. Some we kept, and some we released. By mid-afternoon, we had nine or ten fish on the stringer. I'd caught a few keepers myself, which had helped me to recover from the loss of my big one. As we trolled back to the trapper's place, my dad pointed out a winding marshy creek that led, he said, to the next lake to the north. He said that Rosena was part of a chain of lakes that went on forever. There were thousands of lakes, so many lakes that most of them didn't even have names. I thought this was amazing. "What do they call this place?"

"It's called the Precambrian Shield."

"Why do they call it that?"

He shrugged.

"But why do they call it that?"

"Because scientists aren't very good at naming things."

"But really, why do they call it that?"

"Because it's a big plate of rock, shaped like a shield."

I looked at the broken cliff along the shore. It didn't look much like a shield to me. "But if it's made of rock, why is it covered with so much water?"

He gave the rod a twitch. He was wearing a white T-shirt and his big arms were resting on his knees. He was so accustomed to boats that he drove them with a kind of detached air, steering with a nudge of his knee or elbow. He wasn't a man who relished conversations conducted at the Grade 5 level. It wasn't that he was bored by my questions. He had an encyclopaedic mind and enjoyed talking about things. But I had a short attention span, and often he'd get halfway through an explanation and I'd interrupt him with another question. On long car trips, I'd stand in the back seat of the car, elbows propped against the seat back, interrupting him with questions until he refused to answer.

So when I asked him about the Precambrian Shield, he was quiet for a minute, as if hoping I would lose interest in the subject. But I really wanted to know the answer. I wanted to explore this place. It felt both mysterious and forbidding, two qualities that were near irresistible to my ten-year-old brain.

"Answer him, Don," my mother said. She believed we would all become brilliant scientists one day.

"In a country called Wales," he said, "they once discovered rocks that came from a very ancient time, when life on earth was just beginning. The nearest town was called Cambria, so they named the period the Cambrian period. Precambrian rock is even older. It comes from a time before there was life on earth. You see that smooth rock along the shore? That's Precambrian granite, and it's almost as old as the sun."

This seemed incomprehensible, and I was silent for a moment, absorbing it.

"The Shield is covered with lakes," he continued, "because granite doesn't soak up water. When the rain falls, it gathers in these big pools, these lakes."

"So is this water really old too?"

He thought about this for a moment. "I'll show you a book about the water cycle sometime. In the meantime, there's the trapper's house. So reel in your lines."

I reluctantly brought my lure in, reeling slowly, hoping that some big fish would take advantage of one final opportunity to gobble my bait. When the lure came up beside the boat, I leaned over the gunwale and watched the gold blade spinning lazily in the water. This was the part I loved, the nose-to-nose examination of the big mystery. Below the lure, columns of sunlight slanted through the water and disappeared into the purple depths. Rippling on the surface of the water was the reflection of my face.

ꙮ

The Spanish essayist Ortega y Gasset once wrote, "Tell me where you live and I'll tell you who you are."

If a substitute teacher had come into our class one day and asked us to write a paragraph introducing ourselves, I probably would have written down my name, my height and weight, and the names of my family members. I would have described the house where I lived, the bedroom that I shared with Danny, the paint-by-numbers portraits on the wall of the two dogs we called Inky and Stinky, and the view from our bedroom window of the white houses, freshly laid streets, and skinny trees of our neighbourhood. I would have described the seven-block walk to school, the back alleys where the bullies lurked, the stores where you could buy licorice whistles, and the classroom where I spent most of my waking hours. I would have described the wet-sheepdog smell of the cloakroom where we kept our coats and boots, and the gravel school yard where Kenny and I spent recess, running back and forth like dogs liberated from a kennel.

That was all I knew. My entire world was defined by the ten square blocks where I lived. Years later, when I grew up, I acquired an Econoline camper van and used it to explore far-flung parts of Canada. I clambered hand over hand down a crumbly red-sand cliff in Prince Edward Island, stripped off my clothes, and swam in the cold Atlantic. On the west side of Vancouver Island, I clambered down yet another precipitous cliff, stashed my clothes, and swam in the cold Pacific. Along the arctic sea coast of northern Manitoba, I walked the ice-scoured granite shoreline and wondered if I was going to blunder into a polar bear. And one time, in the wooded valley of the Battle River in Alberta, I cooked dinner over a fire and watched a big harvest moon rise in the east while distant coyotes yipped and howled.

These experiences weren't exceptional in any general sense. But I regarded them as exceptional because they happened to me. When you see a place, when you walk its roads and listen to its birds and crickets, when you kneel down on its earth and smell the aroma of its mouldy topsoil and feel its wind on your face, it leaves an impression that never goes away. The land becomes part of who you are. In the same way, thanks to the woods and the fields around Laclu, my brothers and sisters and I developed an expanded sense of the possibilities that the world offered. We went Indian, as they say. We became water babies. We swam all day, built rafts, explored the lake by canoe, and played on the beach at Webbs'. There was a rickety swimming raft at Webbs' with a three-level diving tower. There was deep water all around the diving raft and it was kind of scary, swimming out to it, feeling the slippery weeds brush your legs. We'd cannon-ball off the top tower or swim underneath the raft. It was dark and creepy underneath. There were vacant compartments with no flotation barrels and the sunlight bladed down through the floorboards, illuminating the water with a green glow and making our voices echo as we ducked under the greasy planks, wondering if we could make it back out again without drowning. The scariest part was feeling the cold water beneath you. The lake was so deep, so mysterious and frightening and beautiful at once. If you could move through this environment without flinching, it was like defying death.

When summer finally ended, we weren't happy about returning to our old selves. We pulled into the city on a Sunday night. It was a beautiful late-August evening, and the melodramatic sunset made it seem even crueller that we were going home. The suburban homes looked neat and well-kept. Sprinklers chattered on the lawns, and the sweet aroma of new-mown grass hung in the air. My siblings and I were disgusted. "Look at all these cars!" my sister Wendy exclaimed, holding her nose. "Can you stand this pollution?"

Back at school, my new teacher was Mrs. Laviolette, a civilian teacher who had a metal brace attached to her leg and walked with a limp. She seemed to like kids, so I liked her more than the nuns. But I wasn't pleased to be cooped up in her classroom. I kept to myself and spent the day drawing. In the margins of my school books, I drew pictures of birds and animals. My textbooks didn't have a single patch of habitat that wasn't occupied by a turtle or red-winged blackbird. In my imagination, I was still at the lake.

At home, my father had fixed up the basement and filled the shelves with books and long-playing records of music from America's jazz age. Prior to the post-war housing boom of the 1950s, our neighbourhood hadn't existed. Meadowlarks and jackrabbits had populated the wide-open prairie, and horses grazed in the alfalfa field across the road. Now our neighbourhood was a warren of tract housing, and our particular home was a two-storey, stucco-covered white box that looked like every other house on the street. But my father turned the basement into a sort of shrine, or museum, filled with old stuff that counteracted the newness and sameness of the neighbourhood. He covered the walls with varnished pine half-log siding that made you feel like you were in a log cabin. There was a brick fireplace in the centre of the room, and an ancient wooden cabinet clock that marked the hour with heavy, London-style echoing bongs. There were oil paintings of Brittany hunting dogs, two or three shotguns hanging on the wall, and an antique piano. Not very often, perhaps once a month, my mother would go down to the basement and play the piano. She liked playing when no one else was in the room, and we'd hear the sweeping melodies of her favourite composer, Hoagy Carmichael, come echoing up the basement stairs.

My best friend, Kenny, didn't have a cottage at the lake, and he'd never been to Laclu. But he'd somehow latched on to the

same obsession with the wilderness. He lived in a small bunga-
low deep within Little Italy, and since he was lucky enough to
come from a small family, he was often alone in the house. On
Friday nights I would buy a large bag of potato chips and bicycle
down to Kenny's house, keeping a weather eye peeled for
Raymond Cantafio and his merry band of foot-fighters.

When I arrived at Kenny's house, we'd heat the potato chips
in the oven – a recipe we'd devised ourselves – then retire to the
living room, where there was a low-slung, walnut-panelled
Eatonia hi-fi along one wall of the living room, and if you pushed
on the front panel, it swung open to reveal a record compartment
inside. The long-playing albums all belonged to his father, so we
had to be careful about leaving no evidence. Wiggling his fingers
like a safecracker, Kenny would delicately withdraw a record and
hold it up for my approval. His dad had good records – Bobby
Darin, Duane Eddy, Carl Perkins, and of course our favourite,
Johnny Horton, the Singin' Fisherman from Noonday, Texas.[*]

---

[*] They called Johnny Horton the Singin' Fisherman because he made up his
songs while he was out by himself for weeks on end, fishing in the Everglades.
He was at the peak of his career, that year, and he'd just married Billie Jean
Williams, the capricious beauty who'd driven Hank Williams into an early
grave and had been the subject of many of Hank's songs ("Hey, Good
Lookin'"). Like so many other young singing stars of that era, Johnny Horton
was marked for death. On November 5, 1960, he was scheduled to drive to
Dallas in the pre-dawn darkness and meet his buddy Claude King ("Wolverton
Mountain") for an early-morning duck hunt. After the hunt, he planned
to carry on into Dallas and have lunch with Ward Bond, who wanted him to
appear in an upcoming episode of *Wagon Train*. But a drunk driver crossed the
centre line of the highway and collided with Horton's car, killing him instantly.
Later that morning, on his way to meet Johnny Horton for lunch, Ward Bond
died of a heart attack. So it was a bad day all around for people who like
cowboy hats.

After removing the glassine sleeve, Kenny would lay the Johnny Horton record on the turntable, turn on the power, and delicately lower the needle onto the opening grooves. A thunderous hissing filled the room, followed by the whack of a drum and a male choir hooting the ghostly refrain "Way up north."

In no time, Kenny and I were up on our feet, marching around the room and singing "North to Alaska." The carpet became a field of snow, the walls a forbidding range of mountains. Wolves howled, the northern lights flamed overhead, and the spooky chanting of the back-up singers completed the hallucination. My favourite part was crossing that huge expanse of frozen lake, popping our whips at the labouring dogs. Like all great singers, Johnny Horton had vocal techniques that he only hinted at, and when the song warranted, when the lyric rose to dramatic summits that called out, indeed begged, for some kind of passionate emphasis, he threw in a slight yodelling, glottal yip that made our blood run cold.

The movie *North to Alaska* had also just been released, so we eagerly rode the bus down to the Lyceum to see it. We paid our twenty-five cents, took our usual seats in the front row, and completed the usual security precautions with our popcorn (each of us sticking a kernel up our nose, smearing it with nasal fluid, then shaking it in with the rest of our box to ensure that the other guy wouldn't snatch a handful when he'd finished his own).

The movie starred John Wayne and Fabian, and it was the usual overblown star vehicle, with the Duke sauntering into every scene, reciting his lines, then grinning at the audience as if to let us know that he didn't take it seriously either. The movie's version of Alaska didn't look like our version. There were no frozen lakes and jagged mountains, no glittery-eyed timber wolves baying at the cruel stars. These prospectors spent most of their time in some red-velvet saloon, slurping down mugs of beer and fighting over the waitresses. By the end of the picture John Wayne had cowed the bad guys, taught Fabian a few lessons about life, and walked off with the sexy starlet on his arm. But as disappointing as the story was, it was reassuring, somehow, to see that Hollywood had gotten it wrong. The ghostly wind of the north still muttered through Kenny's living room. And I could continue to dream about the secrets buried at Rosena without worrying that someone had already taken them.

∾

I realized that if I was going to explore the Precambrian Shield, I was going to need equipment.

Since we were now cottage people, my mother enrolled me in Saturday morning swimming classes at the downtown YMCA. But after taking a swing through the locker room at the Y, I decided that it wasn't my kind of place. There are probably all kinds of ten-year-old boys in this world who don't mind spending their Saturday mornings in a locker room full of fat guys with hairy asses, but I wasn't one of them.

Instead of going to my swimming class I surreptitiously hung around a store called Sydney I. Robinson, which was right across the street from the YMCA. Sydney I. Robinson was a wilderness store. It didn't cater to the fashionable urban nature-lover crowd. It catered to rustic people who lived in the woods. Besides being a prairie city, Winnipeg is also a gateway to the north. For centuries, northern firms have been based here. The Hudson's Bay Company, which was once the largest company in the world, is headquartered in Winnipeg. And because of its ongoing association with modern resource industries – commercial fishing, mining, pulp and paper – Winnipeg was the perfect location for a store like this: a bustling, crowded warehouse where you could see guys with plaid shirts and work boots shopping for peavey poles, snowshoes, and beaver traps.

I could easily dispose of an hour walking around Sydney I. Robinson. There was a fur-buying section in the back, hung with racks and racks of fresh animal pelts, and nobody seemed to mind if I strolled up and down the aisles, running my fingers through the silky pelage of timber wolves, mink, and otter. The fur was plush and aromatic. Unlike people, animals don't seem to develop bad body odour, although you'd think they would. They smell great, even when they're dead. The red fox smelled like ginger, and the black bear hide, which was stiff as plywood and hung on the rack from its eyehole, smelled like wild hay.

Instead of hanging around the Y, learning to tread water, I spent my time watching trappers haul their wares through the loading door, carrying in bundles of fur they'd brought down from the north. A grader in a leather apron took charge of the pelts and laid them out on the table for pricing. Trappers kill animals by the thousands, so you'd expect them to be unsavoury types. In Hollywood movies they're always unshaven thugs with French-Canadian accents and whisky on their breath. But the trappers at Sydney I. looked kind of pleasant to me. You'd see some strong-looking sixty-year-old Metis guy come walking in with his plaid shirt, suspenders, wool logging pants, high-top leather boots, and a bundle of muskrat pelts. He would have an old-style pencil-thin moustache, and he'd flash a big smile as he joshed with the fur grader. Watching him, I would be tempted to ask a few questions, He'd no doubt learned a few things, spending his life in the bush. But I never summoned the courage to walk up and introduce myself.

The tools of his trade were displayed in the next aisle. Sheaves of steel traps hung from the wall. Most of them were Oneida Newhouse long spring leg-hold traps, a type invented in a backwoods commune over a hundred years ago. The members of the Oneida commune renounced private property and marriage, and vowed to share all work, assets, child-rearing, and sex. Since there was no welfare or unemployment insurance in those days, they had to rely on their own wits for making money. After experimenting with various types of small manufacturing, they decided to make steel traps and sell them to local woodsmen. They recruited a local trapper named Robert Newhouse, built a metal forge and a steel fabrication shop, and began experimenting with trap designs.

In 1852, Robert Newhouse stumbled upon a scientific tempering process that made his trap resistant to temperature change. Until then, most of the traps on the market stiffened up in extreme cold weather. But the new mainspring on the Oneida Newhouse trap worked fine in bitter cold, and within five years, the commune's leg-hold steel trap captured the market in Russia and Canada, where the cold climate produced the richest furs in the world. The commune eventually split up over bickering and sexual jealousy, but their patented steel trap dominated the Canadian fur industry for over a century. Hanging in bunches by their chains, the Oneida Newhouse traps at Sydney I. Robinson were displayed according to size, ranging from No. 2 muskrat traps, which cost only $1.50 and were small enough to put in your pocket, to huge forty-five-pound bear traps, which had steel fangs welded onto their jaws and were powerful enough to break a man's leg.

Next to the trap display, shelves were stacked with skinning tools and hide stretchers and bottles of obscure potions, lures, and scents. Each scent was brewed up for a different animal. I knew that asafoetida was apparently so awful-smelling that if I opened the lid for even a second, I could probably clear the store. Other bottles contained female wolf urine, skunk scent, and extract of beaver testicle. Animals themselves may not smell bad, but they relish foul odours. A bottle of fish entrails, left to cook in the sun for several weeks, produces a violent and horrific-smelling residue that supposedly spells sheer lust to bobcats and lynx. As a substitute, trappers sometimes use Chanel No. 5 perfume, which you wouldn't think would have much in common with the oily residue of fetid beaver testicles, but in the deep woods, they supposedly both connect to the same primitive nerve in the limbic brain.

In other parts of the store there were rows and rows of axes, tents, ice augers, dog sleds, and guns. There were so many guns that I may as well have been walking through the armoury of the Royal Winnipeg Rifles. The guns weren't sequestered up on walls behind the salesman's desk or locked up with lengths of plated chain. They were stacked in the open, row upon row, and everywhere you looked, men were testing their heft and balance as they might hockey sticks, racking the authoritative actions and pointing them across the store at a moose head on the wall.

I knew that some people regarded guns as nasty things. But in Winnipeg even non-hunters tended to regard them as symbols of the outdoorsy life that everyone wished to have. In the pine-panelled basements of my friends' homes, they were displayed as a rustic design motif, like a dartboard or beer sign. Usually their owners didn't even use them. They regarded them as conversation pieces, or symbols of a rural life that their grandfathers lived, many years ago, and to which, in daydreams, they imagined returning one day. There were no legal restrictions on buying guns, and most people would have thought it downright unpatriotic to imagine that there ever would be. It wasn't really a crime issue, because criminals knew better than to use guns in Winnipeg. If they did, the city's cops – most of whom were gigantic, foul-tempered Scotsmen – would seize them by the scruff of the neck and given them a licking they wouldn't soon forget.

The current law stipulated that you had to be only fourteen years old to buy a gun. But I was just ten, so I had to content myself with browsing the air rifles. The best air rifle in the store was a Daisy Scout BB gun. It looked like the lever-action Winchester that the cowboys use. And it was powerful enough to punch a hole in a can, break a bottle, or do other kinds of damage, which I felt was important. Lifting one off the rack, aiming it at the poor old moose on the wall, I could easily imagine keeping it handy while I canoed up the winding creek that leads north out of Rosena. I knew I would need a lot of things when I eventually made that trip. I would need a BB rifle, a good compass, a hatchet, and a few bear traps. And to get them, I would need money.

To that end, I acquired a paper route. My bundle drop was at the corner of Cambridge and Corydon. Every night after school, my chain-smoking district manager pulled up in his *Winnipeg Free Press* panel van and threw down a hefty bundle of eighty papers, my allocation, for which I signed my contract. Stuffed into my canvas bag, the papers made a heavy load; heavier still on Thursdays, when they included flyers, and on Saturdays, when they included comics and classifieds. Most days, the bag weighed about forty pounds, and since it was a good seven-block hike to the beginning of my route, I ran the strap across my forehead, like the "tumpline" employed by voyageurs to haul massive bundles of pelts across the old portage trails that connected one lake to the next.

Bent over, with my load balanced on the small of my back, I could walk a long way without tiring. And it wasn't so bad, in any case, to surrender to the pure mindlessness of a long walk, to soak in the world without really looking at it; to walk out of summer's end and into autumn's beginning. I saved my money in a hollow Porky Pig, and with each passing month the pig filled up with more dimes, quarters, and crumpled dollar bills. I had no idea what it cost to buy a compass, axe, belt knife, BB gun, or a grizzly bear trap. But I was beginning to feel rich. My mother was impressed because I was doing so well with my swimming lessons. And my father was impressed because I was a news-paper carrier. It was a job that he seemed to idealize, given the long perspective of adulthood and the fact that he was an ex-newspaper boy himself.

During Sunday dinner, he sometimes hinted that I was fulfilling an important social task. After all, I wasn't delivering junk mail; I was delivering the news, hauling not just a bunch of paper but forty pounds of the truth. He admired newspapers, and people in the newspaper business. One night after Sunday dinner he asked me if I knew who John Dafoe was. "John Dafoe is the editor of the *Free Press* and probably the best journalist in North America," he said. "And he's your boss." He retrieved a book from his library and thrust it into my hands. "Read this."

The book was called *The Unknown Country*, by a journalist named Bruce Hutchison. It was a book about Canada. In it, the author devoted a chapter to Dafoe, the "huge roughcast figure, the shaggy head of reddish hair, the carved-stone face."

> For nearly fifty years Dafoe has been doing a large part of Canada's thinking. Day in, day out, he has sat down in his littered office and slowly, with the stub of a pencil, has scrawled his closely reasoned and documented editorials. What Mr. Dafoe said today will be said all over Canada tomorrow, echoed in other newspapers, stolen by scores of journalists, voiced in Parliament, often denied by the government and quietly incorporated in government policy. In his own field, Dafoe has been more influential than any corresponding journalist in the British Commonwealth.

Hutchison liked Winnipeg too, which made me hopeful, since I was stuck here.

> This was the ideal place for him. Winnipeg largely gave him his character. His character has largely made the mental climate of Winnipeg. . . . The spirit of Winnipeg is the true hope of Canada – the forward look, the broad, world-wide feeling, the pioneer spirit, the willingness to gamble. It is no accident, therefore, that Canada's best thinking in the last twenty years has come out of such a place.

The newspaper's publisher, Sir Clifford Sifton, was no slouch either. He owned both *The Winnipeg Free Press* and *The Toronto Globe and Mail*, and for many decades, one covered the east and the other covered the west. You couldn't follow national affairs without reading both. He was also smart in the way he structured his business dealings with his front-line troops – the paper carriers. Under Sifton, we weren't employees; we were "contractors." We bought our newspapers on consignment and resold them to our customers. It was our job to collect our bills. If we couldn't collect from a certain troublesome customer, it came out of our share, not the newspaper's. We never questioned the arrangement. We thought it was the way of the world, and it was.

My route stretched along five blocks of Grosvenor Avenue. It was an old neighbourhood, with big trees and large turn-of-the-century homes, and my customers were reasonably affluent. But collecting my money was sometimes like going through one of those trials of character from medieval literature. There were three or four dogs on my route that came after me the moment I entered the yard. One of them was a monstrous German shepherd. It wore a leather muzzle, so it couldn't actually bite, but it made little whining sounds as it thumped its snout against my legs – a display of impotent fury that the owner watched from the window with amusement.

Another one of my customers was a middle-aged woman who was missing half her hair. The entire front portion of her head was bald. I didn't know much about cancer or chemotherapy, but I knew there was some terrifying problem here. And every time I showed up at her door, I prayed that she wouldn't invite me in to share her story. I also ran into problems at 1123

Grosvenor. It was a big stone house with the faint whine of an electric guitar coming from inside. I would ring the doorbell over and over again, shifting back and forth to keep warm in the winter darkness. Finally a lanky, mop-haired teenager would come to the door with his Gretsch guitar strung over his shoulder and a slightly peeved look on his face.

"Collecting," I said, showing him my little receipt book.

"Mum's not home," he mumbled. You could barely hear him. He was one of those teenagers who mumbled not because he was shy, but because he was sixteen years old and couldn't be bothered wasting valuable time talking to people.

"When will she be home?"

"I dunno."

"Later on tonight?"

"I dunno."

This was a recitation we conducted every two weeks at his doorstep. He sometimes played with his rock band at our CYO* dances. This, and the fact that his mum was a minor celebrity on CBC television, made me hesitant to press the issue, and to this day, I believe Neil Young owes me $2.40.

Along with the paper route, I earned money shovelling snow or working as a bartender. My bartending job was not a real job. My dad belonged to a poker club that sometimes convened at our house. They played in the pine-panelled room in the basement, where they guffawed at their own jokes and filled the house with cigar smoke. My dad's circle of chums included a man who ran the neighbourhood Esso, the mayor of the city, a biologist who spent his life studying mosquitoes, a hard-drinking Irishman

---

* Christian Youth Organization.

who lived in a half fallen-down barn and rented riding horses for three dollars an hour, and a man whose line of paperback romance books had made him the largest publisher in Canada. For Danny and me, poker night was a major event. Dressed in our pyjamas, we loitered in the kitchen, periodically nipping downstairs to take orders. Playing bartender wasn't complicated, because my dad's friends always ordered the same drink – "I'll have another rye and Seven there, junior." In eastern Canada, men drink scotch. But on the prairies, the patriotic liquor was rye whisky, made from number one western wheat.

When we delivered the drinks, the men generally passed us a quarter and ignored us, this being the contemporary and normal way to treat children. Grown men of that era didn't like to get too friendly lest it erode the sense of deference children needed to become good citizens. Even after my dad's chums had a few drinks, they never did much more than wink at us or crack a joke at our expense. No matter how rowdy the party became, my brother and I never addressed them by their first names or spoke to them without being spoken to first.

The only one whom we addressed by his first name was Ned Jordan. Physically, Ned was an imposing figure – a tall, broad-shouldered gypsy with a swarthy face and a hooked nose. He worked part-time at the racetrack, which you could tell by his sheepskin coat, which exuded a strong aroma of whisky and cigars and horse manure. My dad was working his way up the ladder at the city bureaucracy, and Ned was one of his right-hand men, a supervisor at the Transit Department. Ned drove around in a Transit patrol car and kept an eye on the buses, making sure there were no foul-ups moving citizens from one end of the city to the other. It was probably a mundane job, but

Ned made it look dire and mysterious. He wore an old cowboy hat, and whenever he happened to cruise past in his Transit patrol car, he lifted his paw in a stately wave, and my brother and I shouted a fervent greeting.

During the poker games, Ned always asked Danny and me how we were doing in school, how many goals we'd been scoring in hockey, and so on. During one of these conversations, I mentioned that the clutch of quarters in my hand was going straight upstairs to my piggy bank, to be hoarded for the eventual purpose of acquiring a tent, axe, compass, hunting knife, and of course a BB gun. Ned must have listened with some amusement because a few weeks later, with no advance warning, his Transit car pulled up to the house and he climbed out with two long cardboard packages under his arm.

My mother rose from the dinner table and greeted him at the door. She liked Ned and this excused him from a variety of missteps. So even though she probably knew what the packages contained, she smiled and thanked him. Without pausing to visit, Ned raised his arm in his trademark cowboy salute and walked back to his car.

Ripping open the boxes, my brother and I howled in ecstasy. Daisy Scout lever-action BB guns! We were armed! Cocking one of the guns, I raised it to my shoulder and aimed at a vase. The gun made a *whap* and fragments of glass flew in all directions. My sisters screamed. Oh brother, I thought, I didn't know it was loaded. My father roared in dismay and seized the guns on the spot, promising to keep them until we learned to use them safely. Later, when he cooled down, he explained that he wasn't blaming us. We just needed to learn the basics, which he would teach us next summer, at the lake.

This was cruel punishment. I couldn't believe that we had to wait until next summer to use our new guns. So I gave him a few days to cool off, then brought up the case of my friend Kerry, who owned not only a gun, but a real gun, a Mossberg .22 rifle. And he was allowed to shoot it in the city. In fact, he was not only allowed to shoot it in the city, he was instructed to shoot it in the city, by his dad, who hated squirrels. The squirrels nested in their attic and chewed the insulation. Sometimes Kerry's dad even shot the squirrels himself. On Sunday mornings, when the squirrels woke him up with their chewing, he would go out into the backyard in his pyjamas, swearing his head off, and shoot at the squirrels. One time he winged a squirrel and followed it halfway down Oxford Street, blasting away at it while it scrambled along the trees and did flying Tarzan leaps between the telephone wires.

I used this story to demonstrate to my dad that the city provided excellent hunting opportunities, as long as you exercised reasonable caution. But my dad wasn't impressed. He told us we couldn't shoot our BB guns until we got to the lake, and that was final. Anyway, he pointed out, Kerry's dad had a special permit to discharge a firearm inside the city limits from his golfing buddy, George Blow, the chief of police.

∾

People who grow up on the prairies usually display a few subtle quirks, one of them being a preoccupation with the weather. They know what sundogs are, and they know what kind of winds presage the arrival of a cold front. Our local TV sports commentator, Cactus Jack Wells, opens his newscast in typical fashion. "Well, folks, it turned out nice again."

Like the landscape, the local weather gets inside us, and becomes part of who we are. Coexisting with twelve months of prairie weather is like living in a family of twelve strong-willed individuals. There's no choice but to try to get along. January has the worst reputation, but in my opinion, January in Winnipeg is not as bad as everyone thinks. January has a stillness that comes with stable weather. The polar air mass has established itself over the northern Great Plains, and there are few storms or even cloudy days. The air is fiery cold, but the snow is pure white and the noon-hour sky is as blue as a flag. After a fresh snowfall, it's so silent that the only sound is the steamy huff of your breath and the squeaking of the snow underfoot.

February feels different.

At sunrise it might be twenty-six below zero, but when you walk to school you can feel the tentative but noticeable warmth of the early sun on your face. Sunrise comes a few minutes earlier every day. And if you have a daily routine as I do, trudging down Jessie Avenue with schoolbooks and my frozen peanut butter sandwiches under my arm, the sun is higher each morning above the smoking chimneys. Nobody talks about spring yet. After all, the hockey and curling seasons are in full swing. But the faint warmth of the sun in early February is the first palpable hint that this winter, too, will pass.

My dad has probably felt the difference in the weather, because he's taken on a new project. On cold February nights, after dinner, he puts on his coat, hefts his toolbox, and goes outside. If you peer out the frosted windows, you can see a light burning in the garage. Intrigued, my brother and I go out to spy on him.

A little baseboard heater grumbles in the corner. The wires on the convex face of the heater glow fiery-red in the dark, but it's still so cold in the garage that my father's breath rises like smoke as he saws, hammers, drives the long brass screws into the oak brackets. The muscles of his forearm jump as he turns the massive screwdriver. The project sits propped up on two sawhorses. It's sixteen feet long and resembles the skeleton of an upside-down beluga. The ribs are frayed with wood splinters that need to be sanded off, and the spine is caked with drops of malodorous red glue. Watching him drive the screws into the skeleton's pelvis, we ask no questions, and he offers no explanation. The noticeable thing about fathers is not what they tell you, but what they keep to themselves. We don't know where he got the plans, or how he learned to do any of this. All we know is that he's building a boat.

By early March the blue skies and doldrums of midwinter give way to unsettled winds from the south. The sky turns white and the high prairie wind begins to blow. This is humid air from the south, and nights are turning mild. The sidewalks are caked with frozen slush, and the wind, as I'm walking to the hockey rink at night, carries a pungent reek that evokes rain and dreams, faraway places. It smells like the ocean. If they didn't put so much salt on the streets of Winnipeg and Regina, maybe all those prairie boys wouldn't be so quick to join the navy.

Now that spring is in the air, I'm collecting other critical items for my survival kit. I've purchased a beautiful brass compass, with a flip-up crosshair sight. And I've bought a book called *I Live in the Woods*: an excellent Canadian manual filled with techniques for building rudimentary shelters, cleaning swamp water with sand, and starting a fire with nothing but dry sticks. You can't study this stuff without developing an enormous respect for the Indians. They're the masters of the wilderness.

They were authentic hunter-gatherers. Each native hunter carried about twenty-five pounds of stuff with him. Anthropologists have studied hunter-gatherer societies all over the world and discovered that they all stick to the twenty-five-pound rule. If they exceed the limit, they throw something away. It explains why they didn't own a lot of things. Who wants to carry a Spanish Colonial bedroom suite over a three-mile portage? They perfected the use of the natural materials around them. If they put a hole in a birch-bark canoe, they fixed it in a few minutes with materials from the forest. If you had given them a modern, expensive aluminum canoe, they probably would have thrown it away. What good is a boat you can't repair?

When I grew up, I met a man named Tommy Duck[*], a Chipewyan hunter from northern Manitoba. Tommy is one of the most impressive human beings you could ever meet. In his hockey jacket, baseball hat, and heavy-framed Masters of the Universe sunglasses, Tommy resembles a swarthy Anthony Quinn going incognito.

In the bitter cold of a January afternoon in Churchill, Manitoba, I once stood on a street corner talking to Tommy Duck. No matter where you travel in the north, you'll run into Tommy Duck. He's everywhere, like Zelig. I asked him what was new in his life, and he mentioned that he was leaving for Yellowknife the next day. I asked him how he was getting there. "I just walk," he said.

I thought he was pulling my leg. Yellowknife was almost 1,000 miles to the west, across a trackless wilderness riddled with frozen lakes. It was minus 34 with a stiff wind. Walking

---

[*] Who has a relative, no surprise, named Donald.

from the Seaport Hotel to Penny Rawlings' Trading Post was like getting your face massaged by a belt-sander. But Tommy Duck wasn't pulling my leg. The arctic landscape didn't frighten him. He said he made the journey often, with a small backpack, a sleeping bag, and a .22 rifle. "But what if you get lost?" I asked.

He shrugged. "How can an Indian get lost when he's already home?"

ॐ

My birthday comes in the month of April, so the weather on that day is cemented like a survey stake into my memories of spring.

On the morning of the big day there's usually a bit of snow in the shade of the house, and the sodden lawn has frozen overnight. But the sidewalks are bare, the streets are covered with sand, and the flag-blue sky echoes with the beagle-like yelping of migrating geese. The polar air mass is falling back, falling back, retreating to its refuge in the high north, and the tropical air mass is sweeping into southern Manitoba. By the end of April, the days are sunny and warm and mint-green leaves are emerging from the elm trees. By early May, we're making plans to return to the lake.

My dad has finished the boat. With its broad rear end and deep midsection it's designed for hauling a family, but it has a dashing aspect too. It's red and white and there's a bold lightning strike down its side. Just as the invention of the airplane opened up a whole new world of the sky, this boat will take us on into a new state of evolution. We'll become emperors of the water.

Once spring arrives, there isn't a person in the city who isn't walking with a bounce in their stride. The citizens of "Winterpeg" tend to feel defensive about their city, as if the sub-zero temperatures were their idea. But when the month of May arrives, everyone feels vindicated. Winter is over, and now this prairie outpost is on its way to becoming one of the best places in Canada instead of one of the worst.

With the bush country only an hour's drive away, there are thousands of pristine wilderness lakes where city people can go camping and canoeing. And because of the abundance of inexpensive vacation property, Winnipeggers have the highest rate of cottage ownership in the country. When the Victoria Day weekend arrives, it's generally assumed that anybody with an ounce of sense will be heading "down to the lake." Two days before the appointed day, my mum has already done the shopping, my dad has filled the boat with freight and tied it down under a tarpaulin, and Danny and I have packed our clothes, comic books, and BB guns. On the morning of Friday, May 18, my parents issue strict instructions – come straight home from school, no dawdling, so we can get a jump on rush hour.

Everyone in the city has the same plan. Once we load the car and get underway, it takes half an hour to creep through heavy traffic into St. Boniface, where the great slaughterhouse and its awful smell mark the edge of the city. The highway is so choked with vehicles that we might as well be refugees fleeing Budapest with the Germans blowing up bridges behind us. My mother sits in the front seat of the Buick with Mary Kate, the squalling baby, on her lap. Nanny sits beside her, with Peter the toddler squished in between her and my dad.

Our family has gradually somehow become what Zorba the Greek described as "the full catastrophe." Despite all the theories about kids being products of their environment, every human being in this car is different. When he grows up, Peter will become an orthopaedic surgeon, with hands as graceful as a blackjack dealer's, but right now he can't seem to get a glass of orange juice anywhere near his mouth without dumping it all over his shirt. Mary Kate will become a judge when she grows up, but right now she is having a major fit because she's lost her pacifier. The other five – my brother Danny and I and our three older sisters – are crammed into the back seat, threatening each other in furious whispers. When Sally grows up she will become a pediatrician, but right now she is acting like a bit of a child herself, elbowing Babe, the future ethics professor, who is unethically sitting on a paperback copy of *Bonnie Prince Fetlar, The Story of a Pony*. The missing book belongs to her sister Wendy, who is frantic, because she loves the book and loves horses more than anything else on earth, even though she is allergic to them. We have to fight silently, because only one person in this car is allowed to make a sound, and that's my father who, as he creeps through traffic, regularly thumps the steering wheel with the heel of his hand and grumbles about the "bloody idiots" he's sharing the road with.

We arrive at Laclu at sundown. The cottage looks a bit faded and neglected after the long winter. Some of the young apple trees have died, and the soggy lawn smells like a collie. After hauling our bags into the cottage and dropping them beside the fold-out couch on the veranda, my brother Danny and I sprint down to the shoreline to look at the lake. It's always the first item on the work list when we arrive at the cottage – we have to run down the hill and look at the lake.

The water looks the same, black and cold, and the dock has survived the winter. My dad built the dock with timbers, rocks, and rough lumber. The challenge around here is building a dock that will make it through the spring, when big rafts of ragged ice come drifting down the lake, tearing out buoys and docks, and pushing big rocks up onto the shore. Ice-out usually happens in a few hours, and if the wind is from an unfavourable direction, the ice destroys everything in its path. It's a final pointless gesture of hostility from winter. Our dock is bent and heaved slightly, but it escaped major damage. Walking up and down, testing it with our weight, we judge it sound. My brother elbows me and points across the darkening lake to a necklace of delicate yellow lights moving along the far shore. It's the Canadian!

Every Friday night the Canadian arrives and stops at the little railway station alongside the lake. I've never ridden on a train. With so many kids in our family we can't afford it, but Danny and I love watching the Canadian stop, toot its whistle, and then slide off again. Its dome cars and myriad lights reflecting on the glassy water evoke some romantic postcard image of old-time Canada.

When it's gone we continue our inspection. The water is tea-coloured and barren, devoid of life; not even a minnow has survived the winter. We skip a few stones, then explore the tangled woods along the shore, where we discover a dead thing secreted in the underbrush, a great malodorous sodden hump of black and white feathers. It's probably a duck, or perhaps a loon. It's been lying under the snow all winter, and now it's rotting like a thawed mammoth. We poke it with sticks a few times, then walk back to the dock, where we listen to a celebratory yodel echoing across the lake. Another loon has evidently survived and is announcing to the world that it's ready to take a go at life.

∾

The next day my father puts the new boat in the water. We kids have been exchanging whispered speculation about whether it will actually float, and when my father backs the trailer into the lake at Webbs' beach we're horrified to see water flooding into the scuppers. Our new boat is sinking!

My father is unconcerned. He says that all wooden boats leak for the first couple of days until the wood joints swell up. The outboard motor, a 10-horse Johnson, sits in the trunk of the car. My dad lifts the motor out of the car and climbs into the boat.

The combined weight of a motor and a two-hundred-pound man makes the boat tremble, but my dad steps lightly down the row of seats and lowers the motor onto the transom. Now comes the start-up procedure. He opens the air vent on the gas cap, clips the fuel line onto the motor, and squeezes the rubber bulb until it's full. Then he flips out the choke and yanks the cord effortlessly, yanks it again, and again, with the engine coughing and sputtering as if in alarm. Then suddenly a concussive report detonates inside the motor and it bursts into life. He fiddles with some settings, closes the choke switch, adjusts the Lean-Rich dial, and a great cloud of delicious smoke pours out across the clean water. What excitement! My sisters are applauding. My brother and I are exchanging punches. And Spike the cocker spaniel, a local mutt who doesn't really belong to us but hangs out at our cottage anyway, barks in agreement.

At my dad's order, we all climb into the boat and grab a seat. My dad gives the motor some gas, and moments later we're roaring down the lake with big waves unfurling off the transom. Spike stands wide-legged on the prow of the boat, with his chest puffed out and his ears flapping in the wind.

Since this is the boat's maiden voyage, none of us have the nerve to ask my dad if we can drive it. But the following weekend my sisters start lobbying for permission. Soon enough, they're moving the boat from one side of the dock to the other, using it to pick up a life jacket that has accidentally blown into the lake, or volunteering to take the boat to the store to pick up a quart of milk for my mother – an errand that seems to require the better part of an afternoon. By the beginning of summer holidays Danny and I have launched our own lobbying campaign, and my father is growing increasingly grumpy about the subject. He takes the position that he put a lot of effort into building the boat. And the more kids start using it, the more likely it is that someone will crash into a rock and wreck it.

It's a good point. But this is a large family, with the kids spaced only two years apart, and the sheer number of siblings produces a random, ever-evolving fog of disinformation that works in our favour. My parents almost need a chart on the wall to keep track of curfew times, allowances, and the types of movies each of us is allowed to attend. This is complicated by the fact that my dad is a libertarian who doesn't like rules and likes obeying them even less. So when he's obliged to issue a decision, he assumes that we'll respect the reasonableness of his point of view and conduct ourselves accordingly. He doesn't realize that we're going to come at him with one appeal after another. And when that happens, he can't quite remember what he said in the first place.

After my older sisters have been driving the boat for a few weeks, Danny and I try appealing to the notion that it's inherently unfair to let Sally drive it when she's just a girl. This doesn't sway him, so we try arguing that most of the kids our age are driving boats, which is hard to respond to when he doesn't know if it's true.

So he meets us halfway and permits me to drive, by myself, and Danny when he's with his older sisters. After a couple of lessons, he decides I'm qualified to take the boat to Webbs' for a carton of milk. It's exciting to have such a powerful vessel under your personal control. But sometimes I wonder if my dad is right, and this is too dangerous for someone my age. When I walk to the dock and sit down to face the motor, my gut twists with apprehension. The green Johnson Sea Horse has a lurking, hostile quality. The muscular bulges of its cowling are smeared with grease. And its many mysterious dials carry labels that I don't understand. What, for example, is the High Speed Mixture Adjustment? Does it make the boat go faster? I'm particularly shocked by the faded label stuck to the faceplate of the motor – *Failure to Comply With Operational Guidelines May Result in Serious Injury or Death.*

There's no going back, so I take a deep breath and grasp the pull cord. Some people prefer to start the motor from a sitting position. My sister uses both arms and plants her foot against the motor. I prefer to stand wide-legged so that I can exert full body force. But when the motor backfires, the cord yanks so hard it almost pulls my arm off. After two or three unsuccessful pulls, my gut begins to fill with dread. What if I flood the motor? My father always cautions me against flooding it. I don't know what flooding the motor means, but if the smell of gasoline begins to penetrate the air I know I'm in trouble. When you flood it, you have to unhook the fuel line and pull the cord fifty or sixty times, then hook up the gas line and start all over again. I'm strong enough for only a couple of dozen pulls. So the smell of gas is like the smell of fear.

If I screw up, I can always walk up the hill and get my dad to help. But when I'm at the store, flooding the motor would be a disaster. Girls my age are often suntanning on the dock there. They wear feline dark glasses and maintain an air of haughty scientific detachment as they watch the boats come and go. They're in charge of determining who's a loser and who isn't. If the motor defeats me while they're watching, I might as well go back to the cottage and spend the rest of the summer curled up on the couch sucking my thumb. So whenever I sit down like this to prepare the boat for a quick trip to the store, the fear inside me is not only fear of personal injury, but also fear of the total collapse of my worth as a human being.

Even if I manage to start the motor and get it running, dangerous things can happen. Once, when I was coming back from the store by myself, it suddenly issued a wild, terrifying roar, as if it had abruptly decided to destroy me in an act of ritual sacrifice. I frantically shut the motor off. And since the cottage was only a few hundred yards away, I paddled back to the dock where, thankfully, no one had witnessed the incident. It never happened again, and I had to assume it was just another one of those unexplained, bizarre things that machines do when you lower your guard for a moment.

One day at Webbs' our friend Larry climbed into the boat to "give her a try." For some reason Larry felt that his casual friendship with Danny and me entitled him to drive our dad's boat. And for some reason we agreed with him. Untying the ropes, Larry got into the boat and neglected to check the throttle grip on the motor. It was set at full-speed, and as soon as he pulled the cord the boat lunged forward. This is the precise scenario by which numerous fishermen, every year, get thrown overboard and killed. It's a curious fact that an empty boat will inscribe a near perfect circle. If the steering handle is tilted over at a gentle angle, the circle will be a large one. If the steering handle is tilted acutely, the circle will be tight and ferocious. But either way, the boat eventually comes back over the same spot and strikes the person in the water. The victim can sit there treading water for a full minute, watching the far-off boat go through the clubhouse turn, knowing that it's coming back to get him. What's the best thing to do? Ducking underwater at the last minute takes coolness and athletic coordination, two qualities that aren't common to situations of primal terror. Fully dressed, in boots and maybe a life jacket, you won't find it easy to get far enough underwater to avoid the charging propeller. So if you ever get thrown out of your boat, good luck. You probably have only a few moments to live.

In Larry's case, the steering handle was tilted all the way over. So the boat slewed around and started cutting crazy tight circles with its bow pointed straight up and its engine roaring. Larry lay upside down in the back of the boat, his hands clawing for purchase, his eyes white with shock. The boat went around and around, making extraordinary gyrations. And although we were only a few steps away, standing on the dock, we were powerless to stop it. For perhaps twenty or thirty seconds the boat tore around in tight circles, flinging Larry back and forth like a kid strapped into a Tilt-o-Whirl. Then the boat suddenly straightened out and rammed into the shore, stalling the motor. We pushed it off the rocks and Larry climbed out, tearfully swearing. In situations of stress, Larry usually blamed his older brother ("That goddamn Brian . . ."). But we weren't worried about him. We were worried about the boat.

Fortunately, my dad had built the boat with a hefty strip of brass on the prow, which absorbed most of the impact. We never mentioned it to him, but it was a good lesson anyway – preadolescent self-confidence getting to know billion-year-old granite.

∞

Gun training takes place at a gravel pit down the road.

My mother comes along. She stands in the background, saying nothing as my dad lectures us on the responsibilities of gun ownership. My brother and I stand straight as soldiers. My dad, with the Daisy BB gun in his hand, walks us through the rules. What's the first thing you do when you pick up a firearm?

"Point it in a safe direction," my brother recites. "And check to see if it is loaded."

"Once you're sure that it is unloaded, how do you handle it?"

"It's always loaded," I respond.

"What do you mean?"

"You always assume it's loaded, and keep the muzzle pointed in a safe direction."

My father nods. He's throwing us trick questions, and it's a good thing that we're catching them. Every couple of minutes he reiterates that if he catches us handling our guns in an unsafe manner, he'll take them away.

It's a clear Saturday morning in May, with new leaves fluttering in the poplar trees and ravens arguing in the woods. A good day for establishing dominance over Mother Nature. The sun is cold, and my mother is holding her white cardigan sweater to her throat. If this country plans on producing a summer, it's got a lot of work to do. My dad searches around in the dead weeds and finds an empty Rothmans package. He mounts it in the fork of a sapling and steps back, loads the BB gun, and holds it up to his shoulder. He pulls the trigger and the gun issues a sharp asthmatic *thup*.

We walk up to the tree and look at the package. Wow. He hit it dead-centre!

My brother and I are next. We take turns shooting at the package and missing it. Every once in a while the cardboard flinches, registering a hit. Normally my brother and I would be razzing each other, but today we're on our best behaviour. No crude comments in the presence of my mother. We're responsible gun owners.

On subsequent weekends we get more training. My father walks us along the lake, drilling us with the rules. The rules are complicated, with innumerable clauses and sub-sections dealing with everything from gun etiquette to ballistics. If we break the rules, he'll take the guns away.

Once we've passed the safety module, he teaches us which living creatures we're allowed to shoot and which we're not allowed to shoot. Birds are definitely off limits. We probably could have figured this out on our own – the walls of our cottage are covered with framed bird pictures, and the yard is full of birdhouses. All winter long he builds birdhouses, and once we're at the lake, he nails them up in the crooks of trees. Needless to say, if we shoot a bird, he'll take our guns away.

We know that Dad goes duck hunting in the fall, so we diplomatically introduce the notion that we could perhaps use our BB guns to bag a mallard or two.

"You can't shoot a duck with a BB gun," he says. "You'd just wound it."

"What if we shoot it in the eye?"

My father pauses for a long moment. Maybe he's sending a mental note to Ned Jordan. "Look . . ." he says. "You don't hunt ducks in the summer. They're raising their young. What if you crippled a mother duck?"

This seems a bit melodramatic. Does he really think we're going to provide child support for every duck in the neighbourhood? But we don't debate the point, or he might take our guns away.

He also prohibits us from shooting hawks, on the grounds that they control mice; barn swallows, on the grounds that they control insects; and frogs, on the grounds that it's just a stupid idea. "Why in god's name would you shoot a frog?"

"Okay, rats," my brother proposes.

"There are no rats in Laclu."

"But if we find a rat, can we shoot it?"

We agree to all his rules, and the next morning he allows us to take our guns when we go exploring. Soon we run into some boys who also have BB guns. Without a word of discussion we immediately understand that we have to form a gang – five or six rebel boys in bathing suits and flip-flops. We master the art of waving at our parents, looking boyish and harmless as we walk away. As soon as we meet our fellow gang members, we get down to the gunplay proper.

Adults have rules, but gangs have rules too. One of our rules is "If it flies, it dies." We shoot at crows, hawks, blackbirds, or anything that moves. A hundred BBs cost only a nickel, and we shoot so much, day in, day out, that soon we're handling our guns with an offhand and lackadaisical expertise. We speed-load our guns by pouring a whole package of BBs into our mouths, like Apaches, and spitting them into the magazine. Cocking the gun with a quick stroke of the lever, we can hit a dragonfly on the wing or shoot a thrown soup can without even raising the gun to the shoulder. In a good breeze, we know how much

windage you need to hit and shatter the glass insulator on a telephone pole. And we know the various distances at which it is
acceptable to shoot a human being. If your brother is wearing
jeans, for example, you can put one into his rear end at sixty
paces without actually injuring him. He'll just wheel around and
give you the thumb – a gesture that we've accepted as the ultimate put-down. But if you shoot him at that distance when he's
wearing a wet bathing suit, the sting of the BB will be wicked
enough to make a welt, which will cause him to yell in pain, and
maybe even threaten to tell Mum, who will then tell Dad, who
will take our guns away.

∽

All winter long I have been looking forward to exploring the
wilderness. Now that school has adjourned and we've moved to
Laclu for the summer, I'm keen to get back to Rosena Lake. I've
decided that I want to be an Indian. My father has given me
Ernest Thompson Seton's book *Two Little Savages*, and I can't
wait to make a bow and arrow, a buckskin vest, and a birch-
bark canoe.

I've told the other members of my gang about the
Precambrian Shield. I've told them about the snapping turtles,
the giant fish that broke my line, and all the thousands of nameless lakes that lie just beyond it. I've told them we could do some
serious hunting up there. We could build a teepee.

"Where are we gonna get a teepee?"

"I've got the plans. We'll use my dad's tarpaulin."

"Okay, so what's this lake look like?"

"Lots of dead trees, cliffs, and swamps."

"Cool. Is there quicksand?"

For some reason, quicksand plays a big role in our determination of whether a place is interesting. I didn't see any quicksand at Rosena, but I tell the boys I'm pretty confident that we could find some if we put our minds to it.

"Okay, this columbian shield of yours," says Dennis, sucking thoughtfully on an ice cube. "What's the best way to get there?"

"We'll take canoes," I say. "We'll take the creek from Laclu into Bell Lake, and then take another creek into Rosena."

Dennis points out that Danny and I are the only gang members with a canoe. "One canoe won't carry all five or six guys."

"I could get my mum to drive us," says Randy.

Dennis groans. He's a bit older than we are and thinks that getting driven places by someone's mother defeats the whole purpose of being in a gang.

I tend to agree with him. Now that my dad has shown me the way to the Shield, I want to try exploring it without the benefit of parental supervision. "Why don't we walk?" I suggest.

"How far is it?"

"About four miles." I have no idea how far it is, but four miles sounds about right.

So it's agreed – we'll hike to Rosena. Once we get there, we'll do some scouting and find a good campsite. After a preliminary scouting trip we'll return with pup tents, fishing rods, hatchets, and gasoline. With a good campsite, we'll be independent of adult interference. We'll stay up late, play poker, and smoke Cameos. During the day we can shoot things and roll giant boulders off the cliffs. We can go around smeared with soot from the fire, wearing feathers in our hair and animal skins for loincloths. We can build an Apache war drum and use the gasoline for making torches. Soaked in gas, held aloft, a burning cattail will illuminate the eyes of any hostile predators circling our stronghold.

For the next few days we refine our plan. Our general meeting place is Webbs'. People come to Webbs' to buy groceries or gas. We like to watch them buy gas. Sometimes the gas pump is the most interesting show in town. It's an archaic contraption with a glass fuel globe on top. When motorists fill their tanks, air wobbles up through the clear brown gasoline like murderous thought-bubbles rising in a Martian's brain. When they're finished buying gas, they purchase groceries inside the store, which is a large rustic building divided into two sections. One half of the building makes up the store, and the other half is a large dance hall with varnished log walls. High on the wall of the dance hall there's a stuffed bull caribou that was shot on the lake in the winter of 1923. A moth-eaten northern pike the size of a railway tie hangs above the fireplace. There's a bandstand at the back end of the room, and a lunch counter at the front. After our afternoon swim, in which we furtively try to overturn the diving platform, we gather at the lunch counter. Johnny Webb, the owner of the place, never seems particularly happy to see us, perhaps because he suspects that we're the unknown parties who have been releasing garter snakes in his store. But he tolerates us enough to accept our grimy fistfuls of warm change, which we barter for chocolate bars and packages of BBs.

While we sit at the counter, we debate various aspects of the trip and make lists of the things we're going to need. Because I've been to the Precambrian Shield already, and because I'm basically the promoter of the trip, I more or less chair the meetings. My fellow gangsters are full of questions, and although I don't necessarily have the answers, I use my experience based on an afternoon of fishing and a winter's worth of book research. In our planning sessions, Rosena Lake gradually rises to grandiose stature. It's not just a picturesque lake where we plan to camp out and do a little hunting. It's a place where we will unravel the mysteries of life and become men.

We spend so much time planning that I begin to worry we're going to spend the whole summer talking about it instead of actually doing it. Every morning, I wake up in a general condition of optimism, wondering if this is going to be the day for our wild trek. Danny and I sleep on the eastward-facing veranda, and our bed is flooded with sunlight by five-thirty in the morning. We thrash around a bit, clamp pillows over our heads, but by six o'clock it's so bright we can't sleep, and we're stumbling outside to take a pee in the grass. Being a kid, I'm not formulating what you'd strictly call a "plan" for the day. But I'm thinking about it. Once you get half a dozen boys together, then add in weather, family chores, and the chaos theory, it's quite an accomplishment that we're even planning something.

After breakfast we fill our backpacks with apples and peanut butter sandwiches and set out to meet the boys. Will this be the day we go to Rosena? It's hard to know, because there are many temptations between there and here. Two boys walking barefoot along a dewy gravel road with Daisy Scout lever-actions have no trouble finding distractions. It's an absorbing world, in the early morning, with the hieroglyphics of tiny animal footprints in the sand, the incessant chatter of unseen birds in the woods, and the macabre spiders spinning their gossamer webs in the cool gloom of the undergrowth. Our meeting place is a derelict wooden church that stands at a crossroads a little way north of our cottage. When we approach the church early in the morning, I sometimes feel like it's an emblem of my fallen religion, a ruined building with the morning sunlight playing on its blanched siding and broken windows. Just beyond it is the backdrop of the wilderness, the dark swamps and forbidding woods.

The roadside ditch alongside the church is filled with stagnant water, and the high grass beside the ditch is filled with leopard frogs, good-sized ones, which leap into the water with a loud splash when you stalk through the grass. Once a frog jumps into the water, it thinks it's safe, and it floats there, its arms akimbo, staring up at you. The other boys like to shoot frogs, and I shot a few myself the first time I carried my BB gun – just to see how it worked on them – but it feels mean, to kill them for no reason. My affection also extends to turtles, with their general all-around helplessness and their good-natured willingness to trudge for hundreds of yards on crooked legs. Snakes I like too. Cold and unblinking, they're like living strings of code. And while I understand why people might recoil from snakes, it seems craven and sissified to snap their backbones in jest, as I've seen my buddies do.

So while Danny keeps a lookout for the other boys, I usually check out the interior of the church. The churchyard is overgrown with hip-high weeds and Russian thistle. Making your way around to the back stairway, you have to watch your step because of all the old boards with nails sticking out of them. If you step on a rusty nail you get lockjaw, and they have to pull out your teeth in order to pipe water into your mouth so you won't die of thirst. The stairs themselves are rotted and falling apart. Climbing up the stairs, you enter a porch and then a little office. It's probably the Lutheran equivalent of what Catholics call the sacristy, where the priest dons his vestments and pre- pares for mass. It's a little room with old wine bottles on the floor and rain-buckled girlie magazines in the drawers. When I first arrive in the sacristy I spend a little time looking for hidden contraband or new writings on the wall. Because of my reason- able fear of rabid animals, I never go into the church until my gang arrives.

How many dark winter mornings have I spent in rooms like this? The priests I always worked for never spoke while they dressed. Their glittering rayon vestments rustled in the silence. The only sound came from the main hall of the church, where you'd hear an occasional cough or the bang of a kneeler as the old Italian ladies filed into the pews. I'd pull on a black cotton cassock, and over that, a blowsy white surplice with short sleeves. The priest never talked when I prepared his candles and filled his glass wine cruets. Some priests wanted only a dollop of wine. Others wanted the chalice full to the brim, and we had to know the difference. While preparing for mass, you knew there were things you could touch and things you couldn't. It was like working in a laboratory. Touch the Host, for example, and you were doomed. My friend Kenny once got the flesh of Christ stuck to the roof of his mouth and pried it off with his finger. It was a spur of the moment decision, but he's probably going to Hell for it.

Above the cheap little plywood desk with its cupboards, there's a church service schedule and some ancient birth and death notices pinned to the wall. The names are mostly Swedish. Or maybe they're Icelandic. Whoever they are, they arrived in

Canada late, after the best agricultural land had already been taken, and the Federal Land Office convinced them to try farming in northwestern Ontario. The rolling hills, lakes, and verdant forests around Laclu must have looked attractive when they first arrived, and quite a few farmers – including Gunnar Sigurdson, the man who sold us our cottage property – slaved half their lives trying to make their farms work. They cleared forests, built barns, and raised pigs and dairy cattle. Their kids went to a one-room schoolhouse just up the road, and on Sunday mornings, the families gathered here for church. But this country is hell on livestock. The winters are so cold that animals have to be kept inside, like prison inmates. The sweltering hot and thunderstormy summer days produce hordes of biting flies that can drive a thin-skinned dairy cow mad. So eventually the farmers lost everything. And the only reminder that Laclu was once a bustling little farming community is this derelict church with its old announcements pinned to the wall.

Once my crew finishes up with the frogs and comes up the stairs into the sacristy, we move into the church proper, cocking our guns and keeping an eye peeled for hydrophobic skunks. You can tell a skunk with hydrophobia because it trails long gobs of drool from its fangs as it staggers towards you, wanting to accomplish just one last thing in its miserable life and that's to kill, kill. We've already got a tactical plan worked out for our first encounter with a rabid skunk – who shoots first, who shoots backup, etc. – but if one of us gets bitten we know what happens next. Our parents would never admit it but we know the truth: they chain you to a stout tree. Doctors arrive, but they don't actually touch you. They push food and water towards you with a stick until they find out if you're going to turn rabid.

That's all right. If you're going to venture into the woods, you have to take the good with the bad. We know that during any one of these patrols one of us might get caught in quicksand, step in a rusty old Oneida Newhouse bear trap, or get attacked by a crazed furbearer. Still, a ruined church is too powerful a lure to pass up. This is a place where adult society has no writ, and it fills us with reverent silence. We communicate in whispers as we pad up the aisles, past the shattered stained glass windows and empty pews, stepping over the animal turds and broken glass with our guns at the ready.

Near the back of the church I spot the skeleton of a dead animal lying on the buckled linoleum floor. Kneeling down, I examine the skeleton, probing it with the muzzle of my gun. It's the remains of a bird, I think. The bones are slender and delicately tethered, like the ribs of a broken kite. Above me is the stained glass window where the bird beat itself to death, trying to escape. If it had had a larger brain, it could have flown right up through the roof. High overhead, there's a rent in the ceiling, a hole laced with rafters where you can see the blue sky. A big puffy white cloud drifts across the opening. Its escape route was right there. It's like what the life-saving manuals always advise. When you're drowning, kick free and head for the light.

∽

After we satisfy ourselves with a thorough exploration of the church, we descend the stairs and get moving again.

The morning is well advanced by now, and the sun is hot on our bare arms as we move up the road. Cars occasionally roar past us, stirring up clouds of dust, and we wave at them with our thumbs out.

No one seems interested in picking up six barefoot boys with BB guns. I've calculated that it's probably about a two-hour walk to Rosena Lake, and it's a constant challenge to keep my fellow hoods focused on the mission. Squirrels lope across the road, provoking fruitless pursuit. Glass insulators need to be shot. Or sometimes it's a big wasp nest. Wedged in the crook of a tree, like a lady's hat, a wasp nest is a provocation that can't be ignored. When the first BBs hit the nest, the wasps come boiling out. It takes them a few moments to determine why little holes are being punched in their structure. But then they send out scouting parties, and even if you're a hundred feet from the nest, you're going to be sorry when they find you.

Farther on, there's a bend in the road where, many years ago, someone spilled a trailer load of rotted lumber or plasterboard. Instead of loading it back onto the trailer, he just flung the trash into the ravine. Eventually that particular bend in the road became an accepted place to jettison garbage and is now known as the dump. There's no official sign indicating that this place is a dumping site. But when you get within about fifty yards, the bad smell floating up from the ravine lets you know you've arrived.

The dump is such a compelling spot that our mission to Rosena gets delayed while we check it out. It's usually deserted, with no signs of life except a few ravens flapping around in the pit. With our guns resting in the crooks of our arms we stand in silence on the lip of the pit for a few moments, soaking up the atmosphere. A few garbage bags are lying on the very edge, left there by people who are too frightened of bears to walk to the edge and throw them in. We throw the bags two-handed to get maximum destruction as they crash down the slope. Then we climb down after them. The sun is high overhead by now, and the motionless, super-heated air of summer is so fouled with the smell of decomposition that we have to screw up our faces to breathe.

Down in the ravine the ground is drenched with chemicals, pools of green fluid scummed with dead insects. Ravens fly overhead, croaking in alarm. Walking around, we look for things to shoot. The dump is a target-rich environment, littered with unbroken windows, whisky bottles, and tin cans. The best target of all is the Franklin's ground squirrel. The Franklin's is a tough and resilient little animal, and a direct hit in the body isn't enough to disable one. They know us, and it's hard to get a shot at them because their sentries issue a shrill warning call as soon as they spot us. As we stalk through the ravine, the gophers scold us from their hiding places, making high-pitched hysterical titters.

All summer we've been trying to bag a gopher. Sometimes we encircle the dump in a pincer movement, communicating with each other with birdy whistles and hand gestures. The suspense heightens as we draw closer, belly-crawling through the rusted cans and straggly weeds. At the very edge of the crater, we mount our guns and scrutinize the detailed walls of the pit, watching for any tell-tale movement that might, with the blink of an eye, magically transform itself into the slinky body of a foraging gopher.

Inevitably, something goes wrong. In the relationship between hunter and prey, the odds overwhelmingly favour the prey. According to my library books, wolves have the devil of a time bringing down a moose. African lions fail nine times out of ten. Human hunters are even less effective, and feminist anthropologists like Adrienne Zihlman have proven that hunter-gatherer cultures relied less on hunting, which is done by men, than on gathering, which is done by women. The Indians who used to live around here probably wouldn't have wasted their time hunting at all if an occasional kill didn't yield such a bounty of protein. Five hundred pounds of moose meat, cut into thin strips and dried in the sun, would feed an extended family for months.

Even gophers exceed our ability as hunters, and most of the time a snapped twig or an incautious whisper triggers a mad chorus of warning calls. Our stalks fail in curious and hard-to-predict ways, and the manner in which they fail is almost as interesting as the stalk itself. On one occasion, for example, we make it all the way to the garbage pit without triggering a warning call. With anxious hearts, we take up sniper positions on the edge of the pit and lie in silence, waiting for an unsuspecting gopher to show itself.

Finally, on the garbage slope below me, a gopher slinks out from underneath a broken railway tie. Standing upright in that oddly serpentine way, it searches the area for danger. As I carefully take aim and squeeze the trigger, a paper wasp – probably one of the same wasps whose nest we destroyed a week ago – lands on my neck and decides to sting me. As the wasp pumps venom into my skin, I'm slowly pulling the trigger. The BB is already travelling down the barrel at 450 feet per second when the pain receptors in my neck light up. The barrel twitches and the BB flies a few inches astray and strikes the railway tie head-on. The tiny metal spheroid pushes into the tar-saturated fibre of the railway tie for a millisecond or two, rebounds, then flies back towards me at near-full velocity, striking me in the centre of the forehead.

Yelping in pain, I clutch at both injuries, on my neck and forehead. The forehead wound is worse and produces a wee spot of blood. If the pellet had hit me an inch or two lower, it would have embedded itself in my eye and blinded me for life, a fact that everyone in the gang finds hilarious, including me.

∾

Finally, we make a kill.

My sniper's position is down in the bottom of the dump, behind a tipped-over refrigerator. It's a humid mid-summer after-noon and my underarms are slick from the heat. The silence is threaded by the steady oscillating drone of hornets and bluebot-tles. Above me, the steep rumpled slopes of garbage and heaped grass clippings are trapping the sun's heat like a solar panel. The flattened mud beneath my sandals is saturated with some kind of lime-green engine fluid, and its molecular formula is rising in my nostrils. As the minutes pass, there's ample time to sink into non-thinking awareness. This is what hunters spend most of their time doing – nothing. Everyone thinks that hunting is aggressive, but actually it's passive. You sit and wait, and wait. All the white noise of civilization – interior monologues and radio chatter and annoying snippets of the latest songs – gradually fade out, giving way to the awareness of your steady breathing and the complex texture of the physical world.

To relax my eyes, I occasionally cut my gaze off towards the far end of the dump where the strewn garbage gradually gives way to grass and foliage. A few plastic bags flutter from the low willows. Beyond that is a forest of aspen trees, then a high dark jungle of evergreens. That's the edge of the northern forest, right there, and it's one of the reasons this dump is such an intriguing spot. It's a two-hearted kind of place in between civilization and the wilderness. Black bears come here. We've seen their blue-berry-speckled crap, and sometimes even a footprint. Bear tracks add a whiff of danger, and we're regularly checking the forest fringe to make sure that one of them doesn't come walking up behind us.

Shifting my focus back to the garbage heap, I'm startled to see a large gopher emerge from a gutted sofa and perch on the armrest. It's just a few yards away, and it doesn't see me. I take careful aim at its head. We've learned that a lightweight metal BB can't penetrate their furry skin. On past occasions, when we've managed to hit one in the body, it's just taken off, bucking up and down like a bronco whacked with a lariat. This time I squeeze the trigger carefully and the BB hits it right in the fore-head. What happens next is a bit horrifying.

Every mammal's legs and arms are controlled by spinal reflexes. They're called "reflexes" because they're capable of independent action. If you step on a sharp piece of glass or get stung by a hornet, your muscles don't wait for instructions. They automatically jerk your limb away from the pain stimulus. The next time you're walking barefoot through your house and you step on a discarded staple, notice how your leg automatically buckles, refusing to accept your full weight. That's a reflex deci-sion. The limbs of the body are like remote provinces, with their own local powers, and sometimes they choose to run the show on their own. The whole system seems to work just fine until you remove the central governance of the brain.

When my BB strikes the gopher in the forehead, the animal's brain temporarily shuts off, and in the sudden absence of neural guidance, all the various squabbling reflexes take control. This results in what a scientist – if we'd had a scientist in our gang – would call "inappropriate motor response," that is, scrambling, back-flipping, frantically running on the spot, and so on. Even the hard-core members of our group are shocked by this performance. Right before our eyes, the gopher starts flipping, whirling, and somersaulting through the garbage, looking like it's possessed by demons. At moments like this, we realize that we're staring deep into a world that's scarier than we imagined.

Dennis, however, is more seasoned than the rest of us. He has an inky coil of Bobby Curtola hair dangling from his forehead, and keeps a pack of Cameos stuffed down the front of his pants. He's seen some things, in his day, and doesn't let a little thing like a freaked-out gopher bother him. While I just stand there, stunned, watching the gopher doing its dervish-dance, Dennis sprints down into the garbage pit, grabs a stick, and whacks the gopher until it's dead.

He lifts it by the tail and shows it to the group. Everyone cheers. It was a team effort, and now we're the proud owners of one dead gopher. Once we realize it's dead, a subtle mood of anticlimax settles on the group. We like to think of ourselves as subversives, but now that we've succeeded in killing an animal, we can't remember why we did it. Dennis hands me the gopher, and I examine the little feller. It has neat black claws and a tiny drop of blood oozing from the tip of its lacquered nose. It has tiny footpads. Under different circumstances, we might have been friends, this gopher and I. Stroking its handsome fur, I reflect that it could have perched on my hand, eating the crusts of my sandwiches. But it's too late now. Holding it up by the tail for one last admiring glance, flicking off the tiny red lice that are trying to climb my wrist, I pass the gopher to the next guy.

Being a fallen Catholic, I'm always trying to keep the boys cognizant of the various ethical dimensions of our crimes, and since I've killed this gopher myself, I feel duty-bound to treat the corpse in some kind of ceremonial way. We devote a considerable amount of time arguing about what we're going to do with the body. Everyone has an opinion. One of the boys suggests that we tie a rock to the gopher's tail and drown it in the lake. A dissenter points out that you can't drown something that's already dead. Grant suggests that we douse the corpse in gasoline and set it on fire. But Grant is going through a phase where his solution to everything is to set it on fire. I'm in favour of skinning it. I argue that we can collect a number of hides and sell them at Sydney I. Robinson. Everyone thinks this is a good idea, so we head for the tree house.

Our tree house is located in the woods behind the church. It's a rickety platform of lumber and plywood nailed into the crotch of a big tree. We borrowed our dads' tools to build it and scavenged old lumber from the ruined church. Nailing stubs of two-by-four to the bole of the big poplar tree, we built a ladder that allows us to easily climb up to the platform, which sways minutely in the breeze and affords a distant, foliage-screened view of the church steeple with its old rugged cross.

With the boys gathered around me in the tree house, I conduct an autopsy. Slicing open the gopher's belly with my dull pocket knife, I draw out the spaghetti entrails and tiny multi-coloured organs, and organize them in neat rows on the sun-lit plywood floor. Observing this, my colleagues argue over which is the stomach and which is the heart. Cutting off its feet, removing its tiny claws for a necklace, I carefully skin the animal and nail its hide to a board. One of these days we'll have to return these tools. The other day my dad was in quite a temper, looking for this hammer.

Once the hide is stretched out it looks official and satisfying, like a miniature bear rug. It's not always pleasant, killing things, but a man has to make a living. Once the skin is properly converted into leather by the sun, I'll take it back to Winnipeg, to Sydney I. Robinson, and do some haggling with the fur buyer. If they don't offer me a fair price, I'll keep it for a trophy. With a border of red felt, it would look nice up on my bedroom wall.

Propping the little board up so that the gopher skin absorbs the direct rays of the sun, I follow the boys back down the ladder. We then adjourn to Webbs', to celebrate our victory with a 7-Up float. There's an old kerosene tank behind Webbs' store, with high grass growing up beneath it. We always hide our guns under the tank. Like a frontier saloon keeper, Johnny Webb has a no-guns policy in his establishment.

A few days later, I return to the tree house to retrieve my gopher hide. Unfortunately, the bluebottles have found it, and the fur is seething with maggots. To dispose of it, I have to climb down the ladder and toss it in the bush, holding my nose to stave off the gag reflex.

∾

Summer is drawing to a close.

The early part of August has delivered two solid weeks of rain and thunderstorms, and now the wind has turned around to the north. The sky is low and shaggy. The lake is corrugated with whitecaps. Every morning when we wake up there's rain drumming on the roof, and nobody feels like going exploring.

My dad has been trying to dig a septic field. But with all the rainy weather, he's running out of time, so he decides to hire a contractor to help finish the trench. My dad doesn't usually seek outside help. He comes from a tradition of self-sufficiency, where men own their own tools and solve their own problems.

But every once in a while he encounters something he can't handle by himself, and that's when he calls Cliff Harrison.

Cliff lives year-round at Laclu and drives a ramshackle '49 Fargo pick-up truck. His truck has so many loose parts that after breakfast, we can hear it clapping and banging long before it comes into sight. Cliff is a jack-of-all-trades. He does plumbing, wiring, carpentry, and garbage hauling. He drives your honey-wagon and he traps your nuisance skunks. He has a backhoe for digging holes, and when his truck comes into sight, his orange backhoe is bounding along behind it.

Climbing out of his truck, Cliff spits a wad of tobacco into the grass and greets us with a modest wave. He wears a striped railway engineer's hat and tattered coveralls, and his face is as dark as an old leather boot. Johnny climbs down from the tractor and swats away the various neighbourhood dogs. Johnny and his dad are a physical mismatch, the two of them. Whereas Cliff is thin and tall, Johnny is chubby and tragically short. He's short enough that it's easy to imagine that when he grows up his shortness will become a sort of infirmity. As Cliff would have it, they built the sidewalk too close to Johnny's ass.

Climbing up into the back of the truck, Cliff organizes his tools. Johnny doesn't say anything. He just leans against the truck. While we wait for my dad to come up from the dock and direct the project, Danny and I grill Cliff about his tractor, his truck, his trapline, his hunting dogs, his guns, and whether he's shot any bears lately. "Just that one the other day," he allows.

Ah yes, that one. Johnny Webb had spotted a bear on his property and called Cliff. Everyone in Laclu knows what to do when bears venture onto the property – you blow them to kingdom come. Cliff showed up an hour later and drove around looking for the bear. Finally a kid on a bicycle flagged Cliff down and told him the bear was just down the road, dismantling a garbage bin. When Cliff showed up, the bear was standing in the driveway with a milk carton in its mouth. Without even getting out of the truck, Cliff rolled down the window and put a bullet in its chest.

When the gun went off, Danny and I were swimming at Webbs' beach about three hundred yards away. A few minutes later we spotted Cliff pulling up to the pump in his old Fargo truck. We grabbed our towels and ran up to see him. "What's going on, Cliff?"

"Just shot a bear," he casually remarked, gesturing towards the back of the pick-up.

We scrambled to the back and looked inside. It was the first time I'd seen a dead bear. I've always expected that a real bear, close-up, would be some enormous beast with slobbery jaws and a head the size of a sofa. But the animal in Cliff's truck didn't look much bigger than a badger. It had small ears and a narrow wedge-shaped head, and it was slumped face down on the hard metal. The leathery nose was no bigger than a dog's, and its front legs were splayed stupidly akimbo, as if it had been whacked on the head. There was a slick of syrupy blood on the ribbed metal truck bed. Carrion flies with green jewel-like tails had somehow already found it, and were crawling all over its face. "Is it a baby?" my brother finally asked.

"Hell no," said Cliff. "Three or four years old, probably."

"What are you going to do with it?"

He shrugged. "Throw it in the dump."

This seemed like a waste, throwing away a perfectly good dead bear. I considered asking him if we could have it. It seemed to me that if you had a dead bear, you should keep it around for a while and give everyone a chance to enjoy it. I reasoned that Danny and I could borrow a wagon and pull it back to the cottage, and keep it in the tool shed for a few days. But I knew that my parents would think it was a dumb idea. We asked Cliff if we could join him the next time he shot a bear. But he pointed out that bears don't keep to a schedule. Still, we decided to keep tabs on Cliff's activities. And when he showed up in our yard that morning, I asked him what jobs he'd planned for the day.

"I'm gonna dig this trench."

"Then what are you going to do?"

"I'm going up to Rosena Lake to check on some minnow traps."

Danny and I looked at each other. "Can we hitch a ride?"

"Why?"

"We want to go camping."

"Well . . . ask your father."

We ran down to the dock, where my dad was gathering his tools. We asked him if we could go camping overnight at Rosena.

"Ask your mother."

&

An hour later, we're speeding down the gravel road in the back of Cliff's pick-up truck.

What an adventure! My dad offered to drive us in the Buick, but we've leapt at the chance to go in Cliff's truck, which not only affords a better view of the passing countryside but has the added benefit of being dangerous. Five of us are in the truck – Dennis, Larry, Randy, my brother Danny, and I – and we've loaded so much gear into the back that we have to perch on the rails, grasping at whatever handholds we can find to avoid being thrown out.

My dad has agreed to let us take the red canoe, and it's among us, tied down with a cat's cradle of yellow ropes. Alongside the canoe there are piles of sleeping bags, life jackets, fishing rods, BB guns, Coleman coolers full of soft drinks and wieners, and various cardboard boxes stuffed with chocolate chip cookies, ripple chips, marshmallows, and other survival gear.

We couldn't have picked a better day for our expedition. It's a warm day in mid-August with signs everywhere that summer is ending. The hayfields are high and ripe, tawny now instead of green and powdered with dust from the passing traffic. The aspen trees alongside the road are showing patches of yellow. In another week we'll all be heading home, to the dreaded prospect of a new school year. We couldn't be happier than to be swooping down this gravel road in the back of this old Fargo truck. But our happiness is informed by the knowledge that our days of freedom will soon be over.

With each passing mile, the road gets narrower and rougher, as if the contractors gradually lost enthusiasm for pushing much farther north. By the time we arrive at Rosena the foliage is leaning overhead and slapping against the fenders of the truck. Cliff pulls up to the boat launch next to the trapper's cabin, and although there's a dog barking inside the house there are no other signs of life on the property. For us this is an adventure, but for Cliff it's just another chore. He's always got lots of work to do, so we hurriedly remove our stuff from the truck.

Finally the supplies are laid out on the beach. Cliff makes sure that the truck is empty, and pauses to take one last look at us. "So you're all right? When is your dad coming to pick you up?"

"Tomorrow at four o'clock," I answer. We wanted to stay out here for a week, but it took some lobbying just to persuade our mothers to agree to a single overnight. My mother was disappointed that we preferred to catch a ride with Cliff, rather than my dad. But the whole point of going camping is to do it on your own.

"You sure you got enough stuff?" he asks, glancing at the mountain of supplies on the shore. He's kidding us, I know, but it's remarkable how much equipment you can assemble when you're trying to keep things to a minimum. "Is your tent rain-proof?"

"Yep, but the forecast is for nice."

He scowls and looks up at the sky, which is starting to look a little hazy. "Looks like rain to me. But anyway . . . good luck." He waves and climbs into his truck.

We get busy loading the canoe. The shores of Rosena Lake are fairly easy walking, a long open expanse of granite lightly wooded with jackpine, and our plan is to conduct a two-pronged foray into the wilderness. We'll use the canoe as a sort of freight barge for our supplies. One guy will paddle it, loaded to the brim, along the shoreline while the exploration party pushes forward on foot.

This seems like a good idea, in theory, but after we launch the canoe, with me paddling and the others proceeding on foot, the foot patrollers soon run into a swampy bay that's fringed with cattails and marsh grass. They can't get across it, so I come ashore and ferry them across the bay, one guy at a time, with the canoe so overloaded that I can barely move without tipping it over. The deerflies are bad today, and the guys who are waiting on the shore keep yelling at me to hurry up. It's an arduous process, going back and forth. But finally we're on the other side of the inlet, pushing on, pushing on past the island with its barking huskies, past the bay where I hooked and lost my monstrous fish, past the lily-pad bay where we saw the big snapping turtle, and towards the creek mouth which leads farther north, into the secret heart of the wilderness.

Just as Cliff predicted, it's getting cloudy. We're not afraid of a little rain, but we'd like to find a campsite and get our stuff inside. So at the mouth of the creek, I beach the canoe and we get organized. While we're unloading the canoe and hauling stuff up to the campsite, the first serious mishap occurs.

Along with the firecrackers and potato gun, we've brought along a gallon jug of gasoline. Gasoline is essential for making bonfires, bottle bombs, cattail torches, and other camping equipment. An average cattail fits snugly into the mouth of the jug, and once you've soaked five or six of them with gasoline and mounted them in a circle around the tents, it makes the campsite look like a village in a Boris Karloff movie. But while Dennis is carrying stuff up to the campsite, the glass jug slips out of his grip and smashes on the rocks. The gasoline runs down through the undergrowth to the lake, where it produces a rainbow-hued slick on the water. This is rotten luck, but there's nothing we can do. So after grumbling a bit, we continue unloading the canoe. Then we encounter another problem – how are we going to pound plastic tent stakes into bare granite?

Various solutions are proposed. Can we anchor the tent with big rocks? This doesn't seem workable. What if we use big logs and some nails? This sounds a little more promising, but we forgot to bring nails. So we stand around for a few moments, thinking it over. Dennis fishes a Cameo out of his pocket and lights it, tosses the wooden match over his shoulder. It lands on the moss and the hillside explodes.

The fire is ferocious and silent. The flames are chin-high and stretch all the way down to the water's edge. For a moment we stand frozen, then come to the same instant conclusion. Let's get the hell out of here! Grabbing our tent, groceries, and sleeping bags, we run down to the shore and toss them into the canoe. I leap in and madly paddle after the boys, who are wasting no time galloping down the shore, through the woods, up and down granite humps and ledges, putting space between them and the fire. We're not afraid of being burned alive. We're afraid of getting in trouble.

Paddling like a man possessed, I feverishly review excuses – it wasn't us; it was an accident; some big kids made us do it, etc. Deep in my heart, however, I know we're sunk. We've just started a forest fire. In another twenty minutes this whole place is going to look like a preview from *Walt Disney Presents* – towering flames, stampeding animals, and teams of forest rangers swooping down in helicopters. The other boys have out-distanced me by now. They're about two hundred yards ahead of me, waving and shouting. I'm paddling as fast as I can. But they keep pointing, so I pause to look back.

The fire has gone out.

Is it possible? I can see a faint wisp of white smoke rising from the campsite, but even now it drifts on the wind and dissipates. Turning the canoe around, I paddle back to the campsite, where we all review the damage. The moss is scorched and blackened. The willow bushes along the hillside are denuded of their leaves, but the fire has gone out. All the rain we've been having for the last few weeks has apparently rendered the woods uninflammable. Walking up and down the hill, we stomp on a few wisps of smoke and pour water on anything that looks like it might start burning again. But if flames taller than our heads won't do the job, I don't think we have to worry much about embers.

What now? If we stay here, an adult might come along. If he sees all these charred bushes, he'll probably try to blame it on us. So we decide that we'd better find a new spot. Just down the shoreline we find a little peninsula covered with scrubby oak trees. The ground is rough and knotted with roots. There aren't many places large enough to pitch our big tent. But at least there's enough dirt to hold tent pegs. So we get to work.

Erecting the tent takes about half an hour, and involves the usual bickering and Laurel and Hardy teamwork, tripping each other with guy ropes, etc. But finally we step back and admire our work – a sway-backed hump of canvas that actually resembles a tent.

We're still covered with soot, so we decide it's time for a swim. It's always a bit intimidating, swimming in an unfamiliar lake when you happen to know that snapping turtles and other flesh-eating creatures swim in its depths, so after changing into my suit, I stand on the shore for a while, gazing down at the chilly-looking water for signs of trouble. Finally I decide there's no point in drawing out the torture, and I suck in a deep breath and jump. The water erupts all around me, as I sink into the shocking cold and darkness. Planting my feet on the greasy rocks of the lake floor, I push upwards, break into daylight. The other guys are looking at me from the shore, waiting for my report. With an effort to keep my voice steady, I say, "You're not going to believe how warm it is."

As they run towards the water and take flying leaps, I shout, "Suckers!"

ॐ

As we're cooking dinner, someone shouts an alarm.

I'm down on one knee, tending the fire. Looking towards the east, I see a dome of red light bulging up through the trees – a full moon.

We're making a dinner of roasted wieners, marshmallows, and Kool-Aid. After dinner we retire to the tent for an evening of poker, with wooden matches of various lengths representing ten-, twenty-, and hundred-dollar poker chips.

The moon floods the tent like a headlight. Whenever I go outside to take a pee I'm unprepared for the brightness of the night landscape. The lake is paved with hammered silver and the granite shoreline is creamy pale. It reminds me of the night scenes in the old cowboy movies. While I pee, I keep hearing crackly noises in the forest. I can't imagine camping in these woods alone. Frankly, it's not bears I'd be worried about, but tall frog-men with clawed hands and seaweed dripping off their shoulders. Inside the tent, I feel safe. There's courage in numbers. We've got belt knives, hatchets, and machetes, and any creature short of a legionnaire of the damned is going to have his work cut out, tackling us.

Dennis has brought along a little transistor radio, and it's hanging from the tent pole. As the walls of the tent luff and sway in the wind, the little radio turns minutely on its strap, rotating like a radar dish. It's difficult to pick up radio stations around here. The nearest town, Kenora (pop. 15,000), has a radio station that supposedly plays the Top 40. But you can't pick up its signal from more than a few miles away. Radio stations from the United States are more powerful. One of the best is WLS in Chicago, the power station, 890 on your dial. Call in and win, baby; WLS is gonna make you a rich bitch. Thanks to the full moon, WLS is coming in strong tonight, bringing us songs that come drifting through the crackle and static like messages from an alien planet. Right now the radio is playing Del Shannon's "Runaway." I love the opening scene in the song, where he's walking down the road in the rain. And I like it when he loses it and starts stuttering and the organ takes over and does the singing for him, erupting into the wild chorus that sounds like the howling of a ghost.

Sitting cross-legged in the circle, slapping my bets down and drumming my fingers to the baying organ, I feel liberated from my grim future, at least for tonight. As soon as I get back to the city, it'll be time to face another school year. It'll be time to face newer and crueller schoolteachers (I'm probably going to get Sister George, the dragon slayer), bigger school-yard thugs, colder winter nights, tougher homework assignments, and better-looking girls who are even less interested in me than they were last year.

The other guys are facing the same fate. We're a bunch of rejects, every one of us. I have such a sore back that I could barely lift the canoe. Randy stutters. And Larry has a dick the size of a peanut. It probably wouldn't hurt to talk things over. But that would be unmanly. We just let Del Shannon's organ do the talking for us.

∾

In the early morning the lake is a mirror. With my fishing rod I walk along the rocky shoreline, feeling the stiffness in my back dissipate as I move around a bit. When I come to a little rocky point, I tie a River Runt on my line and cast it towards some off-shore lily pads.

As I reel it in, the lure swims brightly, wagging its sexy rear end from side to side. Suddenly the water erupts in a boil and the lure disappears. It's a fish! I've got a fish! The rod bends over, and a strange power comes vibrating up the line. A second later a three-pound bass leaps out of the lake, shaking its head furiously. The boys come running out of the tent. "Don't horse him!" they yell. "Don't horse him!"* After a valiant battle, the bass weakens, and I drag it onto the rocks and the boys cheer. They run and get their own rods, and within an hour, we've caught three bass, two pike, and a small pickerel. We've filleted them, lit a fire, heated the frying pan, and the delicious aroma of birch smoke, fried fish, and sizzling bacon is floating on the morning air.

After breakfast we fill our backpacks with supplies and strike off on a hike. Dennis carries the potato gun – a bazooka-like weapon we built in his tool shed, and Larry carries the ammunition. Larry's mother didn't have any potatoes, which make the best ammo, so he brought a sack of onions instead. We hike along the shoreline to a high cliff at the end of the lake, where everyone decides to set up the cannon and do some artillery practice. I'd prefer to keep moving. I want to do some serious exploring, but Dennis is insistent upon setting up the cannon

---

* It's an accepted fact among us that you're guaranteed to lose a fish if you "horse" it, whatever that means.

and firing off a few volleys. "I see an enemy force headed our way," he says, gesturing towards a group of seagulls riding the waves perhaps two hundred yards away.

Larry gathers some good-sized rocks and builds an emplacement for the cannon. The potato cannon is a piece of plastic pipe three feet long, two inches in diameter. We learned how to make it from Richard Johnson, the local hot-rodder. The day we learned about the potato gun, Danny and I were walking barefoot down the gravel to Webbs', and Richard Johnson came thundering past with his buddies. He hit the brakes and backed up. "Hey . . . where's your sister?"

"Don't know."

"Where are you going?"

"Nowhere."

"Have a smoke," he said. Richard had been influenced by the thoughts of Duane Eddy and kept a pack of Pall Malls rolled up in the sleeve of his T-shirt.

Danny and I each accepted a cigarette.

Richard reached out the window with one muscular arm and flipped the top off his Zippo. Holding the flame to each of our cigarettes, he watched as we lit up. "You have to inhale."

I inhaled a big lungful of smoke and coughed so hard I almost retched. Inside the car there was a chorus of laughter from Richard's hoodlum buddies.

When we finished coughing, Richard pulled a piece of plastic drainpipe out of the back seat and brandished it in our faces. "Want to see something?" He aimed it at a road sign, pushed a red button, and the pipe banged like a gun. An object of some kind caromed off the road sign.

"Holy cow," Danny exclaimed. "What's that?"

"Potato cannon," Richard Johnson said. "Play your cards right, I'll show you how to make one."

It was an idle promise, intended most likely to enhance his standing with our older sisters. But we took him at his word. And whenever we saw him at the gas pump at Webbs', we badgered him for instructions. Finally he whipped out a pencil and drew us the plans on the hood of his car. We knew the basic stuff. Like most boys, we already had a working familiarity with most types of home-made artillery. In Winnipeg, we'd built light, practical cannons from dismantled bicycle pumps. The explosive charge was a four-inch blockbuster, dropped down into the tube. The projectile was a crab apple, a rounded slug of modelling clay (which made an impressive blue splatter when it hit a stucco wall), or a jumbo marble. Loaded with a big cat's eye marble, that baby kicked like a shotgun.

Richard Johnson's potato cannon, however, opened up a whole new world of personal artillery. We built the barrel and combustion chamber out of plastic pipes, elbows, and screw-off drain caps that we scrounged from our dads' tool sheds. Instead of using expensive firecrackers for propellant, we used WD-40, a common lightweight lubricant easily liberated from any tool shed. Instead of using a flammable wick, we used the standard push-button igniter found on any barbecue. And instead of crab apples, we used cooking potatoes for ammo, which we rammed down the muzzle with a stick.

Our first prototype didn't work. We discovered that you have to take care while ramming the projectile home, or you push the potato down into the combustion chamber and the charge of WD-40 doesn't have the correct fuel-to-air ratio required to make an explosion. You can't use too much WD-40 either, or you flood the combustion chamber and you have to take the whole thing apart. But we experimented, built a ramrod with a notched marker that drove the potato to the perfect depth, and toyed with varying concentrations of WD-40 until we found the perfect mixture (three careful squirts, left to vaporize inside the combustion chamber for the count of ten). Finally, after many failures, we tried firing it and to our shock the gun barked like a tailpipe. The shell, a hefty white sebago, shot skyward with such velocity that we couldn't even pick it out with the naked eye until it was two hundred yards distant, a miniature dot curving down from the bright blue like a golf ball whacked by Gary Player.

We used a vacant hayfield for a firing range, and stacks of cardboard boxes for targets. After lots of practice, we could visualize the potato's soaring trajectory even before we fired the trigger. Once the various complexities of muzzle velocity and distance wore a groove into our neural pathways, it became difficult to see the world in the same way. I could no longer look across an expanse of driveways and private yards and see a barbecue standing alone without thinking, hmm, nice target. I couldn't watch a speedboat go past without calculating the windage and elevation required to drop an Idaho red into its cockpit. Potato artillery was fascinating at first. But as soon as you acquire a new body of expertise, you quickly lose respect for it. So I'm feeling a bit impatient about interrupting our hike while the gang nestles the cannon among the rocks and makes ready to fire on the hostile gulls.

Selecting an onion, Dennis rams it home, then squats down and peers along the barrel, making tiny adjustments by shifting the rocks supporting it. He unscrews the plastic cap and injects three squirts of WD-40. Silently counting to ten, he nods towards Larry. "Fire in the hole."

Larry pushes the button and it clicks. Nothing happens. He pushes it again. Click, click, click. It's a misfire.

Dennis unscrews the cap of the combustion chamber and trouble-shoots the system, wiping off the lighter switch, cleaning out the residue of WD-40, and screwing the whole thing together again. This time, the cannon makes a healthy *whack*, and the projectile soars out in a faint arc and throws up a plume of spray fifty yards shy of the enemy birds. "Who brought these stupid onions?" Dennis asks, scowling at Larry, his gunnery corporal. "We might as well be shooting bran muffins."

Dennis tries a larger onion, but it jams in the barrel, and Larry declines to push the button, a cowardly refusal which Dennis feels is rather selfish, given that we're supposed to be working towards a common goal. No one else is willing to take the risk of having the gun blow up in his face, so Dennis has to take the cannon apart again. This is getting a bit tedious, so I make some impatient noises in the background. Dennis probably shares my feeling that all this bluster, tomfoolery, and ineffectual fist-shaking in the direction of Nature is starting to look a bit pathetic, because after fussing with the cannon for a few minutes he suddenly stands up, holds the length of plastic tubing in his hands as if seeing it for the first time, then flips it over his shoulder and says, "Fuck it. What's next?"

I hook my thumb over my shoulder. "Let's head north."

We forge on, following an old portage trail that winds through the woods. For half an hour we follow the trail, which may have been pioneered by buckskinned Montrealers two hundred years ago, or maybe even stone-age Indians a thousand years before that. We enter a spruce bog, a place that even in daylight seems spectral and gloomy, full of gnarled spruces shaped like medieval candle sconces draped with cobweb. The muskeg underfoot is so yielding and bosomy that we hop warily from hump to hump, fearing that we'll get caught in the warm muck, burdened with heavy backpacks, and get horribly sucked down while the others shout advice and offer flimsy sticks. On the other side of the bog the trail zigzags up the flank of another cliff. And when we reach the crest we have to cast around, looking this way and that, until we find some trees with healed-over axe cuts that mark the trail.

Now we're on a high ridge, heavily wooded, and the trees around us are great tall monsters that creak like rigging in the wind. The ground is carpeted with pine needles, and as we follow the faint imprint of the trail I feel that we're making progress, advancing the quest, following this pathway into the past, into our childhood dreams, back into the dreams, too, of the voyageurs, ancient hunter-gatherers, and rough ice-age beasts that must have slouched down this path thousands of years ago.

Sometime in the last few years – I don't know exactly when – I lost my belief in religion. I've come to the conclusion that the stories in the Bible are just fables, like the adventures of Sinbad the Sailor. I don't believe that the Red Sea actually divided in two when Moses raised his staff, or that it rained frogs in Egypt, or that the Apocalypse will be announced by four skeletal riders on pale horses galloping out of the clouds. I've decided that my school-age religious instruction was just a package of far-fetched scary stories to make us behave. Now that I've thrown away my religion, I've got nothing to replace it.

It's like being lost and having no compass. I no longer know where to go, or what the truth is. But by a process of elimination, I've worked my way through the places where the truth isn't. I know, by now, that you won't find it inside a priest's sacristy at six-thirty on a winter morning. I know that you won't find it with a piece of home-made plastic artillery, or inside a gopher's multicoloured entrails. So far, the only place that seems promising is this pathway into the wilderness.

Finally we arrive at a lake that is too big to walk around. Standing on the crest of a huge granite promontory, we gaze out at a great vista of wrinkled water and islands, and a faraway opening that might be the mouth of a river or a creek.

"Looks like a dead end," announces Dennis.

The wind is filled with the peaty scent of the lake, and the water is green and rough, slopping against the rocks far below. That far-off narrows might be a river mouth, in which case it would be worthwhile to bring the canoe next time.

"We should climb a tree," I suggest. "Get a look at the far end of the lake."

Dennis sits down. "You climb one, major."

We have a rotating system of command. The others guys criticize you until you get crabby, and then someone else takes over. I'm not a very good climber. But sometimes doing the dirty work is the price of holding office.

The big white spruce has stout branches that are spaced like ladder rungs. And without much strength or climbing expertise, I am able to climb to a frightening height. I climb so high that I can feel its monstrous trunk stirring in the wind. The branches open like windows on the lake, and I can see that the far-off opening is definitely a creek mouth. Bordered with lime-coloured marsh grass, it winds sinuously out of sight. With a stout branch serving as a seat, I sit up there for several minutes, feeling the tree sway, and feeling the clean wind. I can hear the boys shouting at me but I ignore them.

They can climb up here and see for themselves. Maybe someday I'll come back here without them. Maybe when I get older I'll have a girlfriend, and she'll enjoy exploring the wilderness too. We can paddle up that river and find out where it leads.

∾

Three drawings are completed now.

I've got them in a neat pile on the corner of my desk. There's one portrait of our yellow cottage on a summer day, one of a giant snapping turtle hauled out on a log, and one of Big Sam crossing a treacherous, half-frozen river with his dog team.

When we're finished with our drawings, Sister George will stuff them in the garbage. Schoolteachers haven't yet become "educators," and they're not in the habit of praising their little darlings' work and mounting it on the walls. My parents have been better supporters of my artwork, and last year my dad took me to meet Dick Sutton, the curator of the Manitoba Museum. Dick Sutton is quite a wildlife artist, and he showed me some of his own pencil sketches, and some paintings in the museum by different artists. My favourite Canadian painter is a guy named A.Y. Jackson, whose cold lakes, rocky ridges, and gnarled jack-pines remind me of the landscape around Rosena. Sister George isn't quite as keen on art, and she usually throws our stuff away as soon as the class is over. So Kenny and I usually try to compare our pictures when her back is turned.

Catching Kenny's eye, I display my portrait of Big Sam and carefully pass it over to him. Kenny scrutinizes the picture. He'll probably add something, like a wolverine crouching in the branch of a tree, getting ready to pounce on Big Sam's head. We sometimes do this – pass the same picture back and forth, layering on plot twists like dime novelists complicating a mystery. We're not defacing each other's work. We're trying to work within the realistic possibilities of the scene. If Kenny challenges me with a wolverine, I'll have to counter the threat. Perhaps I'll sketch Fabian into the background, bringing up the rear in his own dog sled, drawing his Colt revolver as he spies the looming threat from the pugnacious little member of the weasel family.

Kenny shoulder-checks, then shows me his own picture, a fine landscape of a clear morning on an island in the south Pacific, circa August 1942. In the foreground is a flat sandy beach and some ratty palm trees. It looks like an island in the Solomons, perhaps Guadalcanal. We attend a lot of war movies, and we're pretty much up to date on our Pacific battle sites and aircraft recognition. He's drawn a Japanese Zero dive-bombing out of the sun, hosing hot lead at a squad of American Marines. They're galloping down the beach, but they can't outrun a pair of drum-fed Mitsubishi wing cannons. Body parts are flying in all directions, smeared with lurid Crayola splashes of blood and liquefied brain matter. Walking past Kenny's desk, Sister George looks at his drawing and just shakes her head. Miss Roma would probably be shocked by the mayhem that issues from our imaginations, but Sister George, in her discouraging way, knows us better than anyone.

There's still ten minutes left in the class, enough time for me to create one more scene. Sharpening my blue pencil, I stare across the room, watching the snowflakes feather past the windows. Where should I go? Mathematics class comes next, so this is our last few minutes of happiness. While I ponder my choices, Sister George opens the door and walks across the hall, confers with Sister William, who teaches the adjoining class. Both doors are open, and I can see into the other room.

This gives me an opportunity to catch a side view of Teresa, a pretty blond girl who sits in the other Grade 6. Like us, they're listening to the CBC Manitoba School Broadcast, and Teresa's face is clenched with concentration as she works at her sketch. Upright as a quail's topknot, her blond ponytail quivers as she leans over her page, scribbling furiously. I can't see what she's working on, but it seems to be a large piece, with paper drooping off the sides of her desk. She's wearing a bulky turtleneck sweater, a pleated skirt, and her long thin legs are all intertwined beneath her desk.

Teresa is a good subject, so I begin planning a wilderness scene in which she's a central figure. For me, human beings are difficult to draw. I can produce an excellent sketch of a leaping fish or a galloping horse. But my human beings end up looking like they were drawn by Picasso during his eye-in-the-forehead phase. Faces, in particular, defeat me. There are dozens of muscle packages in a person's face, and with every nuance of thought and feeling, the average face goes through changes that are as subtle as the movement of wind on water. If you get the slightest detail wrong, the tilt of the nose or the clench of the jaw, your portrait suddenly becomes a caricature. So the only way I can draw Teresa is by copying her profile, bit by bit.

I'll draw a scene in which we're paddling a canoe. We'll paddle a canoe up that wilderness river at the top end of Rosena.

With scrupulous care, I draw the prow of the canoe curving down to the waterline, a ripple coming off the hull, and then Teresa's figure in the front seat. After a few minutes I've got her blocked in, sitting in the front of the canoe, graceful and straight-backed, drawing a bow and arrow to aim at some distant target. The canoe is a birch-bark type, and she's dressed like an Indian. I like conceiving of the two of us as Indians, because Indians are pure of heart and they wear fewer clothes. As I study her facial profile she raises her head, glances across the hall, and catches me looking at her. This is potentially embarrassing. But she evidently assumes that our eyes have met only by coincidence, and subtly wiggles her fingers in greeting. I nod, and we both return to our work.

I'll keep drawing her, but I'll have to sneak glimpses. I have some kind of relationship with Teresa, but I'm not sure what it is. It's difficult to evaluate the relationship because we've exchanged only about a dozen words all year. At the beginning of the school year, she moved here from England, and she speaks with a musical English accent that only deepens my suspicion that she's some kind of fairy princess who's flown all the way across the ocean with the sole mission of breaking my heart.

The fact that we've barely spoken all year makes me suspect that she likes me too. In Grade 6, the rules of romance are well understood. If you have no particular affection for someone, you talk openly with each other. But if you have a crush on someone, you never talk to one another – not a word. You look away when you run into each other in the hall, ride your bike in the other direction if you encounter each other in the neighbourhood, and leave the table, immediately, if you happen to end up sitting together at lunch time. You finally come to identify each other by a process of elimination.

The only time Teresa and I ever had a conversation was on a Sunday night when we ran into each other at the skating rink. My father is a good skater who plays inter-office hockey and is urging me to play organized hockey with the various teams at Crescentwood community club. But I've never really enjoyed the high seriousness of those Saturday afternoon games, where all the kids suit up like little gladiators, and the spectators scream for blood. Like most of my buddies, I prefer the pick-up hockey games we organize by ourselves, at night, when the adults aren't around, and where we can all pretend to be the legendary Andy Bathgate, Gordie Howe, or the regal Jean Beliveau.

On savagely dark Manitoba nights, when my single-paned bedroom windows are rimed with frost, and Ed Russenholt the TV weatherman is predicting overnight temperatures of 32 degrees below zero, I can't wait to finish Sunday dinner so that I can sling my hockey bag over my shoulder and head for the rink. Usually when I arrive, a gang is already there. Some kids will be wearing pads, and some won't. Some can't even afford skates and will be galloping around in rubber boots. But there's a rough egalitarianism to our games. Left to our own devices, we make difficult decisions on our own, and there's never a fight or even an argument during our dire scrimmages.

On the Sunday night when I had my conversation with Teresa, it was so cold that my mother wanted me to stay home. But I had important work to do – I had to practise my slapshot. For anyone who doesn't pay attention to hockey, I should provide some background. It's 1962, and the Montreal Canadiens are unbeatable. They've won five straight Stanley Cup titles, and there's no longer any doubt that they are the greatest team in history. Beliveau is the captain, the slight graceful Dickie Moore is the league's top stickman, and Rocket Richard chases the puck so intently that when William Faulkner attended his first hockey game a few years ago, he described Richard's fierce dark eyes as reminiscent of the "passionate glittering fatal quality of snakes."

Among them is Bernard "Boom Boom" Geoffrion, a hockey idol who has devised a whole new way of shooting the puck. Traditionally, there have been only two ways to shoot the puck – a wrist shot or a backhand shot. When Bernie Geoffrion was twelve years old, playing hockey at a local rink in Montreal, he missed an easy goal one day and took a frustrated golf swing at the puck, sending it sailing over the boards. He was so impressed by the speed and loft of the unintentional shot that he started secretly practising it. He worked on it for years, and when he signed on with the Montreal Canadiens in 1951, he brought a new and fearsome weapon with him – the slapshot. It changed the game of hockey forever.

Sports writers wax poetic about the slapshot's blistering 100-mph speed and the terrible roar it makes when it strikes the boards. But for me, the slapshot is a thing of beauty. A slapped puck floats the length of the rink in slow motion, as if suspended from the laws of gravity, and enters the goal with such vehemence that the net billows like a flag. Word on the street has it that you can pull off a cheater slapshot if you slice open a soda straw and tape it along the bottom edge of your stick. And I've tried that, tried everything in fact, but the magic of Boom Boom's slapshot still eludes me. For that reason, dangerous wind chills or not, I go to the rink every Sunday night to practise.

That Sunday evening, as I got within sight of the rink, I saw that the big mercury vapour lights above the hockey rink were turned off and the clubhouse was dark. Normally you saw little shadows racing back and forth, and heard the warlike boom of the puck striking the boards. But tonight, all I heard was the whisper of the night wind, and a distant, bell-like sound that was like a child singing. Singing?

I paused at the edge of the wide-open field and listened. Yes, it was certainly a voice. So I trudged closer and saw that it was Teresa. She was cutting loops and figure-eights, and singing to herself as she whirled. I knew the song, and liked it. I'd heard it a few times on Bob Burns' *Top 10 Countdown*. It was called "I Told Every Little Star." The way Teresa sang it, in a proper English accent, the song sounded inadvertently comical, like Julie Andrews singing Brenda Lee.

When Teresa became aware of my presence, she waved. I approached the rink and asked her if any of the guys had been here, playing hockey. She said they'd been here, but the manager never arrived to turn on the lights so they went home. We talked about school a bit, and I laced on my skates and took to the rink, thumping the boards with the puck while Teresa cavorted at the far end of the rink. When I got out of breath I rested for a moment and observed the scene. A winter moon illuminated the ice. Teresa was practising her jumps and twirls. And as she went spinning through the air, scintillae of light flew away from her fingertips.

I returned to my work, shooting the puck. I felt that there was something deeply intimate and weighty about the two of us inhabiting this pool of ice and darkness. This was what I imagined marriage might be like, two people occupying the same silent place, joined by mystic understanding.

Since then, I've felt that Teresa and I have a secret relationship. And my appreciation of her deepens as I draw the line of her back, and the clench of her slender arm as she draws back the bowstring. If I were a sculptor, I'd carve her in white marble or stamp her image on a coin. But I'll do the best with what I have – this sheet of general-purpose mimeograph paper embossed with tiny flecks of mashed bark.

In my drawing, it's a hazy summer evening on Rosena Lake. Ripples of pastel water curve away from the canoe as it slides through the lily pads. The sun is down; the sky is piled with burning clouds. I'm in the stern of the canoe, paddling. At least the guy in the stern of the canoe started out being me. Then he developed a hawk nose, ponytail, and big shoulders. I seem to have put on some weight and acquired a tan. Teresa is wearing a buckskin skirt with a big knife at her waist, and a rawhide sort of brassiere with fringes along the front. She has a quiver of arrows slung over her bare shoulder, and a blue jay feather fluttering from her ponytail. She's holding the wooden longbow at full draw, aiming at something just ahead of the canoe.

Maybe a dog would be a good addition to the picture – a stalwart dog like Eubie, the dog that guarded my parents on their honeymoon. My brown pencil is poised just above the mid-point of the canoe, preparing to sketch in the dog's head, when it occurs to me that Sister George has re-entered the room and is standing behind my desk, looking over my shoulder.

"My goodness," she mutters. "What's this?"

I look over at Kenny's desk. Is Kenny in trouble again?

She seizes the pencil from my hand, leans down, and begins drawing on my picture. "Give the girl some clothes, for heaven's sake!" Using the soft brown pencil she covers Teresa's upper body with brown cross-hatching that looks like fur. Wielding the pencil furiously, she scribbles in a pair of long sleeves and then a long skirt down below Teresa's knees. She hands me back the pencil, mutters in disgust, and moves on.

Kenny looks at me, smirks.

Folding my arms, I lean back in my desk. She's wrecked my picture.

This is what I mean. Last year I was a contented kid. But now I'm angry. I don't want to be here. This classroom is like a jail. One day, I swear to God, I'm going to escape this place. I'm going to climb the wall and head for the wilderness.

It'll be my salvation.

∾

It took twelve years before I made the break.

My twenty-fourth birthday found me enrolled in the University of Manitoba, in a master's program in English literature, and lacking only two more courses for my degree – Old English (*Beowulf*) and Practical Criticism (with an emphasis on semiotics). My plan was to finish those courses in summer school.

When I was a kid, I never imagined that I'd be spending my adulthood in seminar rooms with form-fit plastic chairs and acoustic tile on the ceiling. I never imagined that I'd be spending my evenings hunched over a desk, trying to decipher the turgid prose of Jacques Derrida and Edmund Spenser. I imagined that I'd have some kind of exciting job like bush pilot or forest ranger. I wasn't quite sure what forest rangers did all day, but I thought the duties probably involved having a green truck, a pet timber wolf, and a pretty girlfriend in a checkered blouse. Silly as they might sound, those were my expectations. Everyone has expectations. Mine didn't work out for a variety of reasons, the most important one being that I got sick.

After getting home from my camping trip to Rosena, my lower back became so painful that I could barely walk. My parents took me to the hospital in Kenora, where the doctors looked me over, shrugged, and sent me to Misericordia Hospital in Winnipeg, where I spent three weeks getting X-rayed, probed, and paraded in front of different medical teams. They cut open my chest and chiselled some bone out of my clavicle, sent it to the lab, and found nothing. They conducted every blood test in the book, and checked my heart for viral fever. They stuck periscopes up different bodily openings and had a look. Finally they gave up and sent me to a larger hospital in downtown Winnipeg, where I spent another three weeks going through the same tests and various new ones.

One of them was a bone marrow biopsy, a procedure so crude that it's best compared to the medieval technique of brain trepanning. They wheel you into a room and freeze the skin of your lower back with a horse needle. Assorted broad-shouldered assistants circle the table, murmuring calm reassurance and getting ready to hold you down. Then a doctor uses a power drill to punch a hole into the flat bone of your lower back. Once he's drilled into the inner pelvis, he draws out the marrow with a plastic tube. The vacuum tube makes a festive gurgling noise, and the aching sensation of the marrow drawing out of your body gives you a sudden surge of panic, as if your vital juices were being drained by an enormous spider.

After taping a padded bandage onto my lower back, they sent me back to my room to await results. The results came back the next day and showed the same thing as the other tests – nothing. Medical people with clipboards came to my room and conducted long interviews. Doctors are a bit like cops. They distrust each other's investigative skills and want you to retell your story from the beginning. Eventually too, just like cops, they begin to suspect that you're making it all up. One day an orderly took me to the office of a young psychiatrist. He asked me questions designed to determine whether I was crazy. ("The nurses say that you refuse to take your afternoon nap. Do you resent authority?") After talking to me for a while, the psychiatrist confessed that he had no patience for hospitals, either, and sympathized with anyone who rebelled. "I don't know why they sent you here. But I guess we've got an hour to kill. Do you want to go get a bite to eat?"

The psychiatrist turned out to be a good guy. Like me, he was an aspiring adventurer who hadn't had any adventures, and we ended up swapping tales of our single camping trip. Hospitals, being pressurized environments, tend to reduce people to their essence. For every petty despot, there's some decent soul who is spending his or her whole life trying to help people. Patients are in such distress that the smallest act of generosity can burn itself into long-term memory. I know, for example, that I'll never forget the anonymous nurse who materialized at my bedside in the middle of the night, when a sudden assault of pain snatched me out of the world of dreams and flung me gasping and wide-awake into my hospital bed at three o'clock in the morning. In the dark, while the night-sounds of the hospital and the far-off city murmured around us, she rubbed my bare feet with her warm hands and told me stories about her dog, her dad, and her cottage at the lake. Then there was George, a campy middle-aged homosexual nurse, a man with perfect hair and hands like a jazz piano player, who could whip off a bandage or slip in an IV needle with such deftness that you never felt a thing. I first met George when I was getting ready to go into the O.R. for the shoulder bone biopsy, lying alone on a stretcher with a tube in my arm.

There's a kind of fatal gloom to the décor and lighting of the surgical wing, and as I lay there, I pondered all the things I was going to miss about life. I was going to miss the fact that I was never going to have a girlfriend. I was going to miss riding through Europe in a train with her, or canoeing the Oiseau River in northern Ontario, and sleeping together while the rain pattered on our cozy tent. I was going to miss a lot of things. And I couldn't figure out any way to get them back, because I'd never had them in the first place. Worst of all, there was no one I could summon for help. I had always been raised to believe that in times of crisis, you could go to an adult, who would chuckle and explain that you were mistaken, and there was actually nothing to worry about. But this was the real thing, and no human being could save me from it, not the doctors, not the nurses, not even my father, who knew everything, and was afraid of nothing, and approached all problems with the calm, sauntering purposefulness of Gary Cooper in *High Noon*. This was a bogeyman I had to face alone.

I was therefore searching for a perspective of some kind, a little psychic amulet that I could clutch when it was time to go into the operating room, when a great hulking furry-browed gorilla of a man with a voice like Judy Garland sashayed into the room and spotted me lying there. "How are you doing, chum?" he asked, patting me on the shoulder. He checked my IV line and glanced down at my face. "Are you doing all right?"

What kind of a question was that? Being a homo, he must surely know that I was not doing all right. Like him, and like everyone else in this hospital, I was definitely not doing all right. But he was one of those people who have mastered the knack of taking the tragedy of life and flipping it over into repartee and humour. You could tell by the bounce in his walk. He adjusted my intravenous line and winked at me. "You're going to be fine," he said, with the authority of an old campaigner. He said it with a confidence based on inside knowledge. He promised me I'd be fine, and I believed him. And still do.

The operation, of course, turned out to be no worse than getting a tooth pulled. Every time we go into a hospital we think we're going to die, and we never die. Life goes on and on. It's like one of those films they make in Sweden. The results came back from the lab and showed the usual non-results. This was getting to be a real mystery. Or at least that was the way I preferred to think of it, as a gumshoe investigation, rather than the comic tale of a physical reject. Every night my family would troop into my room, brothers and sisters, cousins, and of course my mother, who would have camped at the foot of the bed if I had let her. But I didn't encourage long visits. They created the impression that I was a mere boy, a wheelchair-bound poster child, rather than some gallant young Hemingway type who'd taken a few slugs in the shins while holding off the fascists. So I usually feigned grumpiness and exhaustion until they left, then spent my evenings talking to my buddies on the payphone. One evening, after another round of tests had produced another round of non-results, my father came to visit and said he'd decided to take me to the Mayo Clinic to see if they could sort it out. It must have been expensive to fly me down to the United States and book me into a first-class American hospital, but my dad didn't seem bothered by it. And I wasn't bothered by it either. I saw it as an opportunity to go for a ride in an airplane. As soon as my dad left, I went down to the payphone and called my pal Kenny to tell him the good news.

"We're flying down to the States!"

"So they don't know what's wrong with you?" Kenny asked.

"Nope, they're stumped."

For some reason Kenny thought this was rich, and between coughing gales of laughter, kept asking me if it was really true that they didn't know what was wrong with me. He acted like this was one of our Johnny Horton Appreciation Nights in his living room, and I'd just told him the funniest story he'd ever heard.

I regarded myself as a fairly seasoned traveller. I'd been to Niagara Falls, for example, and on different occasions I'd taken automobile trips to Swift Current, Saskatchewan, and Fargo, North Dakota. But I didn't ride airplanes every day. In fact I'd never been on one before. So in preparation for the trip I dressed in a suit, necktie, and private eye–style trench coat. At the Winnipeg airport, we boarded a sleek and ultra-modern Trans-Canada Airlines four-engine Vickers Viscount turbo-prop and took off for Minneapolis. The Viscount was a first-rate ship (we seasoned aviators like to use nautical terminology). Her turbine engines were smoother than the radial engines on the old DC-3s she replaced, and in a recent big international air race from London to Christchurch, she had beaten her nearest competitor by nine hours. TCA ran a pilot school in Winnipeg, and Viscounts were always flying over our house. One day my brother Danny and I noticed a Viscount flying over the house with a dead engine, and its propeller spinning lazily. After spotting it, howling in alarm, jumping up and down, we sprinted into the house and grabbed my dad, who knows about these things, and he told us that it was only a training exercise. The pilot was probably practising landings with a dead engine. I'd always been an airplane-fetishist and had a home-built plastic Mustang, a Zero, a Catalina flying boat, and even a scale-model Viscount hung on threads from my bedroom ceiling. The Viscount flew proudly among those warplanes for several months until it became soaked with lighter fluid one day and crashed, full of screaming passengers, into my backyard.

After a month at the Mayo Clinic, they diagnosed me with an obscure condition called anklyosing spondilitis. Its genesis is complicated, but in essence it's triggered when your body gets invaded by a very smart little bacterium. We already have billions of bacteria inside our bodies, and most of them do good work. So when a new bacterium enters our body, our immune system reviews its documents to see if it's a friend or foe. Enemy bacteria are always trying to figure out ways to slip past the guards. In my case, a bacterium called HLA-B27 entered my body wearing the disguise of a human cartilage cell. A patrolling antibody arrested the suspect and, after a bit of confusion, decided to err on the side of caution and destroy it. The antibody dispatched a description of the suspect to the central immune system, and it relayed the information to the other patrols. Antibodies are well intentioned, but they aren't noted for their ability to think outside the box. They just follow orders. Other antibodies soon discovered other cells that resembled HLA-B27 and destroyed them too. Trouble is, they weren't enemy bacteria, they were cartilage cells. This destruction of natural cartilage caused distress and inflammation to my spine, which in turn triggered a more aggressive response from my immune system. After two months in Winnipeg hospitals and a month at the Mayo Clinic, the whole lunatic feedback cycle began to settle down, and I could walk again.

My doctors told me that my prognosis was hard to predict. They told me that I should avoid heavy lifting and overexertion. They said I might totally recover, and on the other hand, I might have recurring episodes and wind up with a stiff back. With most victims (the syndrome occurs in only one of ten thousand people) the prognosis is somewhere in between. I hoped that I'd be one of the lucky ones.

When I got back to Winnipeg, I reviewed my options. It seemed that I wouldn't be able to seek a career as a trapper, lumberjack, or some other type of outdoorsman, so I decided to become a pilot. I figured that it couldn't be a physically arduous job. My new buddy, Chris, had the same ambition, and while we walked the streets of River Heights, we played a game where you had to identify the name and model of airplanes flying overhead by listening to their engines.

Chris was a little older than I was, and by the time he was sixteen he was taking flying lessons. After he soloed, he took me out flying with him. As most people do, he was learning to fly on the Cessna 150, a little trainer that aviation schools rent out to students. On spring evenings, instead of studying for our Grade 11 final exams, we'd go out to the Winnipeg Airport and practise stalls and spins. You weren't allowed to practise over a built-up area, so we'd fly west and level out at 4,500 feet over the great checkerboard of fields beyond the city. Practising stalls and spins is a required part of every pilot's training, and it sounds more dangerous than it really is.* To incite a spin, you first have to incite a stall. Most non-pilots think that when an airplane

---

* Although some planes have a scary plaque riveted to the instrument panel –
Do Not Intentionally Spin This Aircraft.

"stalls" the motor cuts out. But in aviation, the term "stall" refers to a wing that has lost its lift. To stall an airplane, you pull the stick back and commence a steep climb. It's like ascending to the top of the arc on a playground swing. The plane pauses, shudders, and then tips over and nosedives. As it's falling, it begins to corkscrew. With your stomach hovering up in your throat somewhere, you shut off the throttle, push the stick forward, and apply hard opposite rudder, a kind of kicking motion that draws the plane out of the spin. Chris let me try all these manoeuvres too: stalling the plane, spinning it, landing it. It was illegal, but he was my buddy.

As soon as I turned eighteen, I paid $25 and went to have my medical at the CNR station. To loosen up, I gobbled a fistful of aspirins ahead of time, but the doctor was a wise old fellow who sensed that something was amiss. He made me jump up and down and touch my toes until he ascertained that I seemed to have some kind of stiffness in my lowest three or four vertebrae. The stiffness was, of course, working its way up my spine. But I was involved in the full zest of teenage denial and believed that the doctor should just sign his name on that sheet of paper, and I could go off and become a Class One commercial pilot. He flunked me, of course. And the last I heard of Chris, he was an Air Force major, flying Starfighters in Germany.

Once again, I considered my future. In high school, the only course I'd ever excelled at was English. I'd always been an avid reader, and my schoolteachers had sometimes complimented me on my creative writing – stories written in scrupulous longhand, bound in Duo-Tang folders, and illustrated with coloured pencil (*Curse of the Rabid Wolverine*). I wasn't producing these stories out of some long-term ambition to become a writer. I knew that most writers were rich American expatriates who lived in places like Cuba and Paris. I was writing them because it offered the same creative satisfaction that you might get from puttering away on an intricately detailed model airplane. For as long as you focused on the project, you were free. It was just like flying, except you didn't need a pilot's licence.

I therefore began writing stories, and after graduating from high school and starting university, I decided to specialize in English literature. I thought I might eventually become a university professor. I didn't know much about professin' work, but I imagined that a professor's duties involved wearing comfortable old tweed jackets, reading great novelists and poets, and showing a willingness to become the confidant of numerous flaxen-haired young coeds in black turtleneck sweaters.

Over the next few years I discovered that I was misinformed. The leftist intelligentsia had formed a sort of unofficial polit-buro that set the tone on campuses across North America. Under the new regime, nobody studied great poets any more. They studied great theories. Poems about nightingales and graveyards were written by DWEMs (dead white European males) and were therefore passé. To become an English professor under the new order, you had to know your "semiotics" – structuralism, deconstructionism, or one of the many other *isms*, most of which regarded classical literature as a sort of appalling remnant of colonialism. Instead of sitting in my study carrel pondering *Tintern Abbey*, I pondered passages like this:

> Saussure focused on linguistic signs, whilst Peirce
> dealt more explicitly with signs in any medium, and
> noted that the relationship between signifiers and their
> signifieds varies in arbitrariness – from the radical

arbitrariness of symbolic signs, via the perceived simi-
larity of signifier to signified in iconic signs, to the
minimal arbitrariness of indexical signs.

I hung in, thinking that once I got my Ph.D., I could get a
job teaching on Vancouver Island or some place where they
hadn't yet heard about the Death of Literature. I'd buy a rambling old house by the sea, acquire a Jeep and a dog, and settle
into a rustic literary life. During my four-month-long summer
vacations, I'd do some writing and perhaps build a boat with
my own hands. But as I advanced into graduate school, I also
began to notice that everyone avoided one question – would
there actually be jobs available when we graduated? My
professors acted as though the subject of employment was
beneath them. And if I couldn't ask them, who could I ask?
Some of my fellow students might have been studying semiotics
because it was just so darned fascinating. But I wanted to get
something out of my degree, and I was worried that there might
be nothing more than a brown envelope and a diploma waiting
for me when I finally graduated. University enrolments were
dropping, and some of my seminar groups had only a handful
of students. One seminar consisted of exactly one student – me –
and the professor who ran the class made it clear that she'd lose
a third of her income if I dropped out. I had three more years of
this ahead, plus a thesis. And by the time I hit the job market, I
feared that my doctorate in semiotics would qualify me to drive
a cab anywhere in North America.

So that bright green summer morning in June, as I cruised
down the road towards the University of Manitoba, I suddenly
experienced such an intense attack of ambivalence that I

pulled over to the side of the road and sat there with the turn signal blinking.

What should I do? Should I quit school and try something else? Or should I keep a stiff upper lip and finish what I started?

The logical half of my brain suggested that I should carry on, or live forever with the knowledge that I was a craven quitter. I'd signed up for graduate school, and it was my duty to finish it. Apprenticeships in any field are designed to weed out the weaklings. And nothing is easy.

The other half of my brain – the half that always got me in trouble – argued that it wasn't a matter of being a quitter. I'd given university a good shot, and it wasn't working out. The longer I stayed, the worse it was going to be when I finally bailed out.

I felt that I was sitting at a major fork in the road. Each choice seemed equally plausible and unacceptable. At times like this, people tend to fumble around for some tried and true formulaic way of making decisions. And as I sat there, pondering my future, I recalled a tiny bit of allegorical wisdom from my old hardcover wilderness survival book, *I Live in the Woods*. The author, Paul Provencher, had spent his whole life working as a timber cruiser in northern Quebec. He never explained what a timber cruiser does all day. (I guess we're supposed to know that.) But he spent a lot of time explaining how to avoid getting lost in the woods.

People get lost because they get caught up in the details. When you're down in the underbrush, climbing over deadfalls and detouring around thickets, you quickly lose your sense of grand direction. You can't see the forest for the trees. According to him, you have to ignore the immediate environment while you're travelling, and concentrate on following a line, which you maintain by keeping your eye on distant landmarks. You pick a tall, odd-looking tree that's a mile away, for example, and move towards that. At the same time, you maintain a sense of the path behind you. You stop, once in a while, and look back on the distant landmarks you've passed. When you lose sight of where you're going, you have to look back at where you've been.

∾

When I was a boy, I thought I sprang up out of these scruffy Winnipeg sidewalks like a prairie weed. But now that I was in university, studying literature and history, I was beginning to understand that everyone in this country came from somewhere else.

I'd learned that the MacDonalds came from the Scottish Highlands, and that in the old days, the English regarded all Highlanders as illiterate savages who stood in the way of British sovereignty. I'd read about the ethnic cleansing of the Highlands and the royal edict that resulted in "every MacDonald under the age of seventy" being dragged from his bed and put to the sword at Glencoe. And I'd seen the 1747 Act of Proscription, in which the English parliament banned the teaching of Gaelic, the wearing of tartan, and the playing of bagpipes. I'd read that the Scots were gradually harassed and bullied off their lands by wealthy men who wanted to convert their small plots into large sheep ranches. In 1773, a group of 179 of those landless farmers sailed to Nova Scotia aboard a ship called the *Hector*. They were my ancestors.

According to old newspaper clippings and other historical records, the MacDonalds carried on doing what they knew best, working the land. One newspaper obituary, for example, describes my great-grandfather, John MacDonald (who passed away on December 25, 1907), as a man of "sterling and upright character" who spent his entire life farming the same plot of land. His son, my grandfather, drifted down to Halifax and moved west in search of work. He wound up migrating to what Churchill called "the breadbasket of the empire," the western prairies, and found a job in Winnipeg selling farm equipment for John Deere. He must have been good at it, because I've seen photos of his big house on the river, and pictures of his son, my dad, going off to school at the University of Toronto, and then later in his naval officer's uniform, going off to war.

When I got to know my grandfather he was already an elderly man, but a strong and independent one. Every Sunday when he came over for dinner, my brother and I would run to the window and watch him arrive. He stood six foot three and until he was ninety-three moved with the measured saunter of someone athletic enough to shoot his age in golf. He always looked somewhat intimidating in his dark business suit and necktie. Spotting us at the window, he never smiled. His face was like the face of those stone-faced men you see in the framed portraits stacked in dusty piles upstairs in country antique stores. While my mother prepared dinner, my brother and I would sit in the living room and try to talk to him. Those were our marching orders – go and talk to your grandfather. One of the fingers on his right hand was missing. No matter how many times we asked him about his missing finger, he always said the alligator ate it. He wore a Freemason's pin on his lapel, and during dinner, he would often launch into a speech my brother and I had memorized word for word: his personal indictment of the cowardly French under Duplessis. Nobody ever argued with him, not even my dad, who was a lefty and knew his history.

He was, in other words, not one of those twinkly-eyed and kindly old grandfathers you saw on Sunday nights on the Walt Disney show. But he had emotions, buried somewhere under that dark suit. Every year at Easter, he would pull his curtains and take his phone off the hook and remain incommunicado for several days, listening to *Messiah* and weeping. He disliked cities and always mourned the fact that he'd left the Nova Scotia farm and spent his life working in a city. He sometimes told us stories about his childhood, growing up on the family home-stead, and he told us that when we grew up, we should go and find a place in the country, a little house on a river, with trees and birds all around, a place where you could get up every morning and feel God's earth under your feet.

I'd already decided that's what I wanted to do. But his sermons on that subject made me realize there was a continuity of purpose stretching back through the generations. Casting my eye back over a century of family history, I could see that the MacDonald men had always tried to stay connected to the land. The idea of being a farmer didn't appeal to me. But when my grandfather talked about being part of the land, I don't think he was talking about sitting on a tractor driving back and forth all day, chewing on a straw and thinking about hog prices. He was talking, I believe, about being in touch with unbroken earth – wild earth like the plot of woods down at the end of the field where the creek made its turn, and the blackbirds teetered among the bulrushes, flashing their red wings and singing like rusty gate hinges. My dad's favourite poet was Gerard Manley Hopkins, which surprised me, since Hopkins was a Jesuit and my dad never had much time for the church. But some of Hopkins's work summed up nicely what he and my grandfather probably felt about Nature:

What would the world be, once bereft
Of wet and wildness? Let them be left,
O let them be left, wildness and wet;
Long live the weeds and the wilderness yet.

When my grandfather died, he left me a bit of money, which I used to buy a delivery van. I fixed it up with shag carpeting and a fridge and a bed, and whenever I had a bit of time and a few hundred dollars, I went off exploring. I wanted to find my own little piece of wild earth. Several of my friends wanted to do the same thing too. So we hit the road and did the research. On various trips, we drove from Alaska to Florida and back again. We explored California, investigated the offshore islands of the Carolinas, and drove down into Mexico. We combed the Midwest, and we combed Texas. We even combed Wheeling, West Virginia, home of WWVA, the hillbilly radio station that drifted like a spectral fog all through the night skies of the eastern seaboard and once, long ago, convinced a Nova Scotia farm boy named Hank Snow to buy his first guitar.

We had many adventures, but it seemed that we'd arrived late. The music had stopped, and every chair in the United States was taken. You couldn't drive from Boston to Miami and find a single piece of ocean-front real estate that wasn't grabbed up, developed, or fenced off in anticipation of an exciting new condominium project. (That we couldn't afford to buy an exciting new condominium didn't seem relevant. The point was that we didn't want one.) The more I travelled, the more I realized how lucky we were to live in Canada, where the wilderness started an hour's drive outside any major city and sprawled all the way up to the Arctic.

Despite the superiority of American myth-making, it eventually occurred to me that the best country in North America was in fact our own, so I began spending more time exploring the Canadian backwoods. I thought it was a good place to investigate the big mystery that everybody knows is out there. I didn't know what the Big Mystery was, but all those travels, images, and memories felt like pieces of a puzzle, and I was intrigued by the idea that they might eventually add up to something one day – if not an "answer," then perhaps a code to live by, or an insight of some kind into the principles that make the world tick.

In Canada, the challenges are approximately the opposite of what you encounter in the States. In the United States, it's all been explored, and everything is spoken for. In Canada, it's all wide open, and there's so much wilderness you don't know where to begin. I felt the deepest connection to the myriad lakes and sprawling wilderness of the Shield country. It was the great blank space on the Canadian map, the desolate realm studied by painters like Tom Thomson, and mined for symbolism by writers like Hugh MacLennan. ("This anomalous land, this sprawling waste of timber and rock and water . . . this tract of primordial silences and winds and erosions and shifting colours . . .") It was the landscape that first captured my heart when I was a kid, and it was where I always imagined myself building a cabin one day.

But where would I begin? The Shield country is big – very big. It covers about half of Canada, which is an area of land about the size of the Indian subcontinent. If you were looking down at it from outer space, you'd see different zones of vegetation covering it. The southern edge of the Shield is clad with the so-called Great Lakes forest, which is mostly hardwoods, mixed with spruce and pine. A little farther north, the hardwood forests transition into boreal forest, which is dominated by jackpine and black spruce. In the boreal forest, soil is thin to nonexistent and the ground is covered by duff – a thin carpet of matted pine needles and moss. In many places there's not even much duff, just bare rock, weathered granite that has been sanded by so many glaciers that it resembles bleached skull, covered with a ragged scalp of moss and thumbtack trees.

Farther north the boreal forest yields to the taiga zone, a featureless monoculture of bog and stunted spruce. The treeline at the top fringe of the taiga isn't so much a line as a ragged edge, beyond which the bent little spruce trees can't stagger any farther into the north wind. The barrenlands aren't really barren. The landscape explodes to life with berries and flowers in the summer. The rivers swarm with fish and the hills are alive with caribou. It's hard to believe that this is the same geographical region as the heavily wooded Shield country of the south, but what all these habitats have in common is water – lots of water. Impervious granite makes for poor drainage, so everywhere you go on the Shield, north, south, east, or west, you'll see shimmering water. Water is often called an element but it's actually a compound, and it changes constantly. The way it moves, the way it smells, the way it vaults through granite predicaments and tumbles through a rapid: these are filled with enough nuance and subtlety to keep the observer entranced, as if watching a fire. Calm water, too, never stops changing. If you glide over glassy water on a hot day in summer, the slightest zephyr will alter its colour from pastel blue to olive black. And the slow-moving, tea-coloured water of the muskeg zone couldn't be more different from the cold water of Great Bear Lake, which is so transparent you can see the pebbled bottom at fifty feet. But although the water is infinitely various, wherever you go in the Shield it's also the same, in the sense that it's the Shield's defining feature. It's what brings people to its lakes every summer, to fish, to swim, to canoe, or just to sit on the decks of their cottages and stare at the water, as if observing an enigma.

Canada possesses only .05 per cent of the world's population, but our country contains about 30 per cent of the planet's fresh water, and the bulk of it resides in wilderness lakes, most of which don't even have names.* There's so much water that overland transportation is difficult, and highway construction is such an arduous undertaking that roads tend to be nasty and short. In the olden days, the principal means of travel was that unique Canadian invention, the canoe. Nowadays, the main method of getting around is the float-equipped airplane. The DeHavilland Beaver, the Twin Otter, and the Noorduyn Norseman were all designed in Canada specifically for travel on the Shield. And although Canadians tend to regard float planes as mundane transportation, foreign visitors are amazed when they drive through Kenora or Red Lake and see airplanes cruising along on top of what amounts to boxed-in aluminum canoes.

I couldn't afford to explore the Shield by airplane, so I drove the roads. The Trans-Canada Highway heading over the top of Lake Superior is, in places, as spectacular as the more famous Highway One along the coast of Big Sur, and has the added advantage of being deserted, because most trucks go around the

---

* Some lakes are named in honour of Canadian aviators who died in the wars. I met one family that camps out at a wilderness lake in the summer, in honour of their uncle, a Lancaster crewman killed at the age of eighteen.

south side of Lake Superior, through the States, which is a faster but less interesting route. The north shore is A.Y. Jackson country. He spent his formative years painting in rural Quebec, but eventually fell in love with the rugged northern Ontario wilderness. Like the other members of the Group of Seven, he became a lobbyist for the notion that the Canadian landscape is a worthwhile subject for serious art. That might seem like a self-evident proposal today, but his rough, uncultivated landscapes were haughtily dismissed by art critics of the day. I'd read a bit about him, and he seemed the most charismatic of that bunch, except for perhaps Tom Thomson, his pal and room-mate, whose legend, it should be allowed, has been burnished by the fact that he died mysteriously. Like Thomson, Jackson was a loner, an affable but solitary man who'd survived the inferno of the trench campaigns of the Great War and used the tonic of clean air and God's own wilderness to cure his heart. He liked roughing it, sleeping on the ground, and he undertook many explorations here, riding north in an Algoma Central boxcar with his legs hanging out the door, his backpack full of painting supplies on his knees, and the spectacular cliffs rolling past.

I went to visit a friend in Thunder Bay, who took me to a high precipice overlooking Lake Superior. You walk through the woods and come to a clearing where the flat rock just ahead of you drops into nothingness. The wind is so strong that you fall to your knees and crawl the last few yards to the edge, lest vertigo or an errant gust nudge you off. If you threw a penny, it would fall straight down, winking in the sun and drifting in the wind, falling forever. You can see for countless miles across the wrinkled lake, and it's so far down to the water that the tiny flecks of black ash far below are soaring ravens. In northern

Manitoba, in the midst of another road trip, I met a fellow who took me down beneath the Shield, rather than high above it. We donned boots and hard hats, climbed into a rude elevator cage, and descended into a nickel mine. It was a primitive mine, with makeshift equipment, no lights except for our headlamps, and a minimal crew of miners on duty. But still, the shaft went thousands of feet down into the earth, deep enough that when we fumbled our way along the wet, utterly dark tunnel at the bottom of the mine, the rough walls felt warm.

My long-term hope was to get past the reach of roads and rails, and spend the entire summer working in the wilderness.

∾

One spring day at the university I spotted a note on the bulletin board in front of the Canada Manpower Centre. It was only a hand-lettered file card, but it changed my life.

> Remote wilderness fly-in lodge in northern Ontario
> requires fishing guides. Must be skilled in boating and
> the outdoors, and enjoy working with people. Inquire
> within re. Bending Lake Lodge.

It sounded too good to be true. I went inside and scheduled an interview. A few days later I returned with my university chum Fariborz Tajidod, who'd grown up in Iran and had only a basic grasp of English, but shared an interest in nature and the outdoors. The lodge owner, a steely-eyed ex-military pilot named John Hansen, conducted the interview and seemed amused by our apparent willingness to tell him anything we thought he wanted to hear. "We have lots of white water on our river system," he warned us. "Would you be afraid of shooting rapids?"

Fariborz, who with his doe-eyed and slightly apprehensive manner resembled the young Dustin Hoffman, assured John Hansen that he'd seen many rapids and wasn't afraid of them. "In Tehran, my uncle shot a rapid in his garden."

After our final exams, Fariborz and I drove three hundred miles to Ignace, Ontario, where we reported to the local float-plane base to arrange for our ride into Bending Lake Lodge. Our pilot looked like he'd slept in his clothes. His plane, a beat-up old Beaver, had sooty exhaust pipes and dented sheet-metal floors congealed with half a century's worth of fuel oil, powdered milk, and moose blood. We climbed aboard and strapped ourselves into our seats and the engine exploded to life, trembling with a rough and guttural idle that sounded more like a tractor than a lighter-than-air flying machine. But soon enough we were roaring down the lake and lifting off, ascending a bumpy stair-case of thermals into the extraordinary spring sunshine.

Down below the plane the country rolled off to the horizon, a patchy, rumpled mould culture of forest, rock, and hammered lakes glinting in the sun. What an adventure! I pressed my nose against the dirty window and drank it all in. Fariborz was sitting up front with the pilot, and at one point he leaned over and asked the pilot what would happen if the engine failed. The pilot gave him a grim look, reached over, and shut off the engine, and the plane nose-dived like a falling piano. After making his point, the pilot restarted the motor and we carried on. Eventually we arrived at Bending Lake Lodge: a rustic village of buildings on the south end of an otherwise uninhab-ited lake.

We were assigned bunkhouses and put to work. The guide contingent consisted of a few white university boys like us, and a dozen Ojibway men, most of whom had many years of guiding experience. It was early in May, and the fishing season wouldn't open for another few weeks, so the boss's priority was to whip the camp into shape and get the new rookies trained as guides. All day long we chopped firewood, repaired docks and levelled cabins, and went out to learn the river system with our Indian instructors. My teacher was Stewie, a thin young Ojibway man with Beatle boots, a pompadour hairdo, and a bad complexion. Stewie's routine was to pretend to see the cheerful side of any misfortune. Even if it was a cold and miserable morning, he always came hunching through the sleet with the same absurd greeting. "Hey dere, boys! Nice morning dis morning!"

The Turtle River system sprawled off for many miles in several directions, and white-water rapids formed links between the lakes. Stewie took me to fishing spots in the different lakes and paused long enough at each spot to demonstrate to our mutual satisfaction that he could whip my ass anytime when it came to jigging lake trout with a spinning rod. (He could out-fish almost anyone in camp.) He showed me how to run down the rapids and how to get back upstream again – slewing and bounding the boat through the powerful waves, dodging boulders, climbing the muscular chutes of green water, and quickly killing the motor to prevent the boat from capsizing if it suddenly was overcome by the force of a wave and sent caterwauling backwards. Like a kung fu master, he'd stand up on the high, slippery rocks and watch me trying to reproduce his performance, waving and pointing to hazards I couldn't see. When I swerved the boat sideways and filled it with water, he'd clutch his head in theatrical dismay, and when I did it right, he'd clap and grin, shouting inaudible praise across the roaring water.

Learning the rapids was nerve-racking work. Most of the rookie guides and a few of the less experienced Indian guides had close calls. One university student from Winnipeg reared his boat like a horse and flipped it back on himself in Number Six Upstream. He was pulled unconscious from the water and medivacced out to the hospital, where he eventually recovered and decided he didn't want to be a guide after all. Another guide, named Sidney, an Indian but an inexperienced one, swamped his boat and almost drowned. I was sure that my turn was coming up next, and when it came to practising the more difficult rapids, such as the fearsome Number Two Downstream, I was sometimes so apprehensive that I'd go into the bush and retch before climbing into the boat. But gradually I got the hang of it, and by the time the guests arrived on the May 24 long weekend, I was confident enough of my boat-handling skills that the familiar bounce and kick of the rapids felt more like an amusement ride than a toboggan run to hell.

Every night there was a card game in the Swingin' Teepee, the big bunkhouse where the Indians lived, and we white boys gradually got to be friends with the veteran guides, some of whom were walking encyclopaedias of knowledge about fish, animals, weather, and the bush. There was lots of wildlife around – moose were a normal sight along the river, and we had lots of problems with bears interrupting our shore lunches. The Indian guides knew these wild animals in a way that wasn't abstract but specific – based on personal experience: spending long months at a stretch in trappers' cabins with no company but a few squirrels living in the eaves, a car radio hooked up to a

12-volt battery, and the brooding silent forest right outside their door. A scientist might have known the Latin names of the local trees and wild animals, but old guides like Junior Robinson knew practical stuff, such as how a bear of a certain age, size, and gender would likely react if you tried to shoo it away. They weren't reluctant to share the information either, as long as you didn't mind a joke or pun included with the lesson. Spending days on the river with old-timers like Junior was like taking university classes in forest lore. And because the information was applicable to immediate problems at hand – like trying to preserve a campfire in the midst of a sudden downpour[*] – it was like studying French in France.

I guided two summers at Bending Lake Lodge, then managed to get a job doing the same thing up in the Northwest Territories, on Great Slave Lake, where we had to sleep with blankets on our windows because it never got dark, and the great high rocky cliffs along the lake were constructed of the oldest rock on the planet. Great Slave Lake is tremendously deep and cold. The camp was, and still is, one of the most prestigious sport-fishing lodges in the world, with crisp white buildings arranged with military orderliness on the remote east arm of the lake. Except for a few white guys, the guides were mainly Dene, and the lodge's guests were wealthy Americans, whom we took in pursuit of lake trout, which in the north grow to an enormous size. In frigid water, a lake trout grows only half a pound a year, and a fifty-pound trout is conceivably almost a century old. They look it too, ancient brutes with hooked jaws, battered heads, and the blank, stone gaze of a pagan idol. Great Slave is

---

[*] Throw a large rotten stump on the fire.

one of the largest lakes in the world, and we had to cross enormous passages of open water, not a pleasant experience in an open sixteen-foot boat. The water is only a few degrees above freezing, and when the wind started blowing, pushing fifteen-foot-high swells, it was like crossing the north Atlantic.

Sometimes we took the camp Norseman and flew side trips out to the barrenlands, to Artillery Lake, where the trout were black, or Lac Du Gras, a spooky place where the fish had enlarged heads and serpentine bodies, and were so desperate for food they'd almost chase the lure up onto shore. We went to the Thelon River, which is an arctic oasis surrounded by tundra, through which every autumn the tens of thousands of caribou of the Qaminurjuag and Beverly herds pour, and where the English eccentric John Hornby built a log cabin in 1926, determined to become this river's white lord. Like Mr. Kurtz, he was a charismatic loner, and he brought along disciples: two English schoolboys named Edgar Christian and Harold Adlar. Hornby planned to kill enough caribou to get them all through the winter, but the caribou never came. Apparently they usually come, but sometimes they don't. Hornby and the boys spent six months starving to death. Edgar Christian's journal was found with their skeletons the following year, and all three are buried behind the decrepit cabin, their graves marked by three rotted wooden crosses.

Sometimes, while my guests wandered the riverbank and fished, I'd sit on a glassy-smooth hump of granite next to a thundering rapid, soak up the sun, and wonder what I could learn from this primitive landscape. Like most English majors, I was reading a lot of contemporary poets, trying to decide which ones I most wanted to imitate. I favoured the California bunch, particularly Robinson Jeffers, who wrote of ancient tragedies like the Christ and Icarus legends. As a boy he built home-made wings and tried them out by jumping off a roof, and as a grown-up he often wrote of dangerous things – hawks, eagles, and other fierce-eyed flying creatures, symbols of the poetic impulse. He moved to Carmel, California, and on a hill above the ocean he built a stone house and an observation tower, from which he contemplated "the great blue eye of the Pacific," imagining that, like all great bodies of water, it was expressing an eternal truth, and that he needed to learn the ocean's own alien language before he could comprehend it.

These ancient rivers and lakes seemed to emit the same eternal message. But you'd have to be pretty naïve to think that you could decipher the code by bombing into a remote location like this and spending a few hours lounging by the rapids in your sunglasses. I suspected that you needed to slow down and pay attention to the water. You needed to spend some time here alone, like Siddhartha. I liked to kid myself that I was exploring the edges, but remote camps like Great Slave Lodge were just divots of civilization dug up and transplanted to the wilderness. We could drink canned beer as we explored this river, play with million-year-old fish species on ultra-light graphite spinning rods, and know all the time that there was a great dinner waiting for us back at the lodge. It was so comfortable that sometimes it seemed that we weren't in the wilderness at all. We were just looking at it, as if through protective eyewear.

Once I was back at school, cracking the books, I had to confess that my summer in the wilderness hadn't changed me much. How could it? I'd spent the whole summer surrounded by all the comforts of home. I fancied myself to be a woodsman, but the truth was, I'd never even spent a night alone in the forest.

It was just play-acting. And I was getting too old for that kind of thing. If I quit school, I had to roll up my sleeves and get serious about an alternative education. If I stayed in school, it was time to grit my teeth and make a long-term commitment to my Ph.D. program. Either way, I was tired of halfway measures. It was time to make a decision. For a few minutes I sat there. Then I shifted the van into gear and voted with my foot.

∾

For the next few days I gathered supplies – tent, lanterns, sleeping bag, tools, books, fishing rod, gun, boots, rain gear, rope, cooking utensils, and all the hundreds of other things you need to simplify your life. Hunting through the classified ads I found an old square-stern canvas-covered canoe with a 3-horse motor for $200.

Several days later, I pulled out of Winnipeg and headed east on the Trans-Canada Highway, with the wind humming in the guy ropes and the warm June air pouring in the window. Thirty miles east of Winnipeg, the highway climbs out of the old floor of Lake Agassiz and ascends a gentle gravel beach ridge into the great eastern forest. Scrubby poplar bush gradually turned to jackpine forest, and a few miles farther on, the first rocky outcrop appeared in the ditch. I stopped the van and took a look at it, squatted down and scraped away the scalp of dirt. This stub of granite marked the edge of the Shield.

An hour later, I stopped for coffee in a log-and-stone roadside restaurant, where bass and shovel-jawed pike hung from the walls. I ate lunch and browsed my maps, formulating a plan.

In my boyhood days, you couldn't drive any farther north than Rosena Lake. It was the end of civilization. But nowadays the map showed a crooked blue road that led farther north to the village of Minaki. When I was a boy, you could reach Minaki only by train. I liked the idea of driving there, going to the end of the road where you couldn't drive any more, then putting the canoe in the water and heading up the river. I liked the idea of studying the larger world by getting to know one specific place. As it says in the Bible, God is in the details.

Just before the town of Kenora, I took a left turn and headed up the rough gravel road to Laclu. I drove past the road into our family cottage, past the old wooden church and the dump where we used to hunt gophers when we were kids. It was eerie to be driving past these places, my old childhood haunts. Almost by accident, I was picking up where I'd left off. The road was in rough shape, and it took almost two hours before I finally bounced across the CNR tracks and into Minaki, a small community with lots of abandoned cars, dismantled snowmobiles, and crooked little unpainted plywood houses. Above the harbour was a train station, an antique and weathered-looking old building with geraniums in its window boxes, a chalkboard with train schedules on the wall, and a big block-lettered MINAKI sign hanging above the platform.

It was too late to launch the canoe, so I decided to sleep in the van. My best bet was probably to find a public parking lot. After checking out a few places down by the water, and rejecting them because they looked like private property, I drove over the hill and cruised down a long undulant driveway bordered by golf fairways. At the end of the driveway, backlit by a flaming sunset, stood a high castle of log and stone that I deduced to be

Minaki Lodge. My older sister Wendy had worked here as a waitress, years ago, and always described it as the most adventurous summer of her life.

After parking the van next to the golf course, I walked across the fairway to get a closer look at the lodge. The delicious aroma of prime rib and roasting potatoes wafted on the air, and violin music issued from the broad verandas. Walking up the flagstone steps and through the front door, I entered the Grand Rotunda, an immense hall appointed with stuffed elk heads and hanging tapestries. In the bookstore, I browsed through some guidebooks, some maps, and a short history of the lodge. According to the book, during the 1920s both the CPR and the CNR were involved in constructing some of the finest resort hotels in Canada. The president of the CNR, Sir Henry Thornton, got the idea of attracting business by offering plush cross-country railway tours of Canada, with overnight stopovers at grand resorts in each natural region. To showcase the Rockies, he built Jasper Park Lodge. In Nova Scotia, he built Pictou Lodge, and in the Shield country, he decreed the construction of this place.

His crews stripped the topsoil off a farm in Manitoba and shipped three thousand boxcars of earth to Minaki. They blasted away the granite and used the soil to upholster a rolling nine-hole golf course. They built a beautiful hotel that put the CPR to shame, and when it was finished, Sir Henry dubbed it the Minaki Inn. On June 11, 1925, one day before the lawn party marking the grand opening, a summer student employee accidentally set fire to a gallon of linseed oil and burned the place to the ground. Nice move, son.

Sir Henry started over again. This time, he brought in the Scottish stonemasons and Norwegian log builders who'd just finished Jasper Park Lodge. The fire was a cruel setback, but it also provided a unique opportunity for client, architect, and contractors to work out the wrinkles they'd encountered in putting up the first building. The new Minaki Lodge was completed in 1927 and was a masterpiece. Critics of the day described it as "the finest log structure in the world," and I could see why. As I stood reading the little history book, the evening sun poured down through the stained-glass windows and illuminated the high ceiling, which was a sixty-foot-high vault of interlaced blond logs hung with immense iron chandeliers.

Nowadays, Minaki Lodge was ailing. The CNR no longer owned it, and it was limping along from one private owner to another. The clerk in the bookstore said that the construction of the new highway had helped. But judging from the number of muffler pipes I'd seen littering the gravel road on the way, you wouldn't want to be coming here in an expensive car. "We're so far away from everything," he said. "If we had a big city like Toronto within a couple of hours, we'd be the most famous resort in Canada."

Walking down the hill, I checked out the water. You can't really say you've visited a place until you go down and look at the water. There's never anything much to look at, just waves splashing on the shore and a few seagulls flying by, but the water nevertheless seems to be where a resort's ineffable spirit resides. The water is why we're here. The lodge seemed to have a large fishing operation, maybe thirty Lund fishing boats tethered with military precision along the big dock. It was getting late, and the workday was over. But as I was standing there, one last fishing boat glided towards the dock. After manoeuvring his boat into its stall, the tanned young fishing guide snapped a lariat around a dock ring and stepped out. His Kodiak boots were well-scuffed, the collar of his denim jacket was flipped up, and a leather-sheathed knife dangled from his belt. I hadn't driven a boat since last summer and was immediately filled with nostalgia for the life of a guide – no worries, no ambitions. Just fooling around all summer like Tom Sawyer.

Climbing out, he dragged a monstrous fish onto the dock. His guests, a man and his wife, were clumsily trying to stuff film into their camera. Their hands were trembling with excitement. The fish was about four feet long and had gleaming wet skin that transmitted flashes of blue and silver iridescence, and gaping jaws that opened and closed dumbly as the guide hefted it for a photograph. The woman, who'd evidently caught it, stood beside him and smiled bravely while her husband snapped a picture. It was a muskellunge, a fish so mythic and elusive that I'd never even seen one before, although I'd been coming to this country for half my life.

Night was falling quickly, and I renewed my search for a campsite. Finally I pulled into a place called Murray's Camp, which looked like a fishing lodge, albeit one more humble than Minaki Lodge. According to my map, this was the end of the road. There wasn't another road, fence, or hydro line between here and Russia, so I felt like this was the perfect place to launch my exploration, a jumping-off place on the edge of the world.

I went looking for Murray. The river was invisible in the darkness but its scent drifted up through the trees. Bugs whirled around a high mercury vapour lamp. Under the light's glow a dapper old gentleman was walking across the lawn. He was sauntering along with a drinking man's wobbly-kneed walk, each tottery leg deployed as if by remote control. I hailed him and introduced myself.

He shook my hand and said his name was Don Campbell. He said that he owned the place and didn't know anyone named Murray. He said he had no idea how Murray's Camp had got its name, and that no, nobody had ever asked him about it before. He didn't seem surprised that I'd driven into his parking lot with everything I owned. He was Max Yasgur and I was just another hippie. "Just park it back in the trees where it'll be out of the way," he instructed in a Chicago drawl. "If you want to leave it for a while, that's okay. Just give me a couple of bucks whenever."

Moving the van to a quiet corner of the parking lot, I cleared out some space in the back for my sleeping bag. My faithful truck had done a good job today. In fact everything went more smoothly than I expected – no flat tires, no mechanical problems, and no mental breakdowns from my parents. Most of their seven kids were on their way to becoming doctors, lawyers, and prominent professionals of one sort or another, so one black sheep in the mix wasn't a bad average. Anyway, when your twenty-four-year-old son tells you that he wants to quit university, buy a tent, and go searching for the Lost Secret of the Canadian Shield, what else can you do but wish him good luck.

Before I got into my sleeping bag, I gobbled a couple of aspirins to numb the nagging pain in my back. It had been a long day of carrying, packing, loading, and driving, and my vertebrae weren't pleased. For most of my adolescent years, the stiffening of my lower back had been gradual enough that I was able to dismiss it with painkillers and healthy doses of denial. But lately, both tactics had been less effective. When I was working up at Great Slave, some of my guests had made comments ("What's the matter, did you hurt yourself?"). And it was becoming obvious, even to me, that things were getting worse. Oddly enough, this made me want more out of life, rather than less. Illness and the constant background ticking of Time's stopwatch make you greedy. I admired people like Walden Robert Cassotto, who grew up a poor kid in the Bronx, knowing from the age of eight that he had a defective heart that would kill him early. He drove himself to become one of the great singers of his era, Bobby Darin, before he died at the age of thirty-seven. Ditto for the doomed Jim Morrison, who wanted the world and wanted it now.

Tennessee Williams once proposed that there are two planes in life, the realistic and the fantastic. I wanted to find the fantastic plane and stay there. But as I lay in the darkness, listening to the wind, listening to the whisper of the pines, listening to the far-off laughter of someone telling a story in the fish house, I knew that it was entirely possible that I'd just committed the biggest blunder of my life.

ᖰ

In northwestern Ontario, the first white-throated sparrow starts whistling at three o'clock in the morning. It's still utter darkness, but the birds can feel the planet turning. By four o'clock, the eastern sky is growing pale, and by four-thirty, it's another brand-new day.

When I woke up the sun was shining through the windows, and the interior of the van was as hot as an oven. I climbed out of the side door, pulled on a T-shirt and some blue jeans, and peed against the tire, keeping an eye peeled for tourists. It's a great life, being a vagabond, but the open road is skimpy on washrooms.

I boiled some tea on the Coleman stove, made a breakfast of porridge and granola, and started unloading the truck. Using my brain instead of my temperamental back, I managed to get the freighter canoe off the roof, and some kindly American tourists helped me carry it down to the water. The cedar canoe was old and heavy, but once we slid it into the water, it floated like a leaf. With my jeans rolled up, I waded in the cold water and loaded the canoe with camping equipment and supplies. The motor was a museum piece, a 3-horse Evinrude with a built-in gas tank and a toy propeller. But it worked fine, according to the owner.

I locked the van and left the keys on the tire. Goodbye, Minaki, I'll be back when I get back. I pushed the canoe away from shore and primed the Evinrude. On the fourth or fifth pull it erupted into a cranky idle, snarling and coughing out those big clouds of aromatic blue smoke that Canadians always associate with the great outdoors.

I steered the canoe away from shore and opened the throttle. With the motor bawling, I cruised down the channel, and past the stone fountains and opulent gardens of Minaki Lodge. During the next twenty-five years I would see it fall, rise again, fall once more, rise again more glorious than ever, and then finally, as the century ended, crumble once again, like an operatic hero experiencing multiple deaths. Its lawns would run rampant and its beautiful golf course would grow hip-high with thistle. Its verandas would rot and birds would fly among its broken stained-glass windows. But this morning, it looked like an enormous, flower-bedecked symbol of beauty and possibility.

Past the lodge, the river flowed beneath the steel girders of the CN railway bridge. The current was strong, and for a full ten minutes I had to work my way up through its whorls. Finally, the bridge glided overhead and I was moving forward again on the wide-open river.

As I cruised along, I studied the map on my knee. I reflected that several centuries ago this waterway, the Winnipeg River, formed the western leg of what used to be Canada's main highway. Surveying the passing scenery, I wondered how many explorers and voyageurs had cruised along this same channel. Surrounded by primal forest, I found it hard not to think that I was travelling into the past. Rivers like this one formed an unbroken chain from western Canada to the St. Lawrence, which served as the original doorway into the country. Jacques Cartier was one of the first guys to enter the St. Lawrence, back in 1534. Like many European sailors he hoped that Canada's rivers might provide a short cut to the Far East, where he could fill the ship with cinnamon, pepper, and other spices, which were prized in Europe as food flavourings, preservative agents, and aphrodisiacs.

As Cartier cruised down the St. Lawrence, he realized there was no passage to India here, just a "land that God gave Cain," a rocky wilderness full of biting insects and hostile natives. Cartier overwintered in Stadacona (the current site of Quebec City), almost died of scurvy and was almost murdered by Indians, and might have gone back to Europe a complete failure, if he hadn't found his own version of buried treasure – *Castor canadensis*, the beaver. Because of the bitter winters that prevail across the north, Canadian beavers wear the thickest and glossiest pelts of any fur bearers in the world, and back in Europe those furs were worth a lot of money.

When Cartier returned with fresh beaver pelts from Canada, it was big news for the European fashion industry. At the time, there was no greater fashion statement in France than a wide-brimmed hat. Hats in general were *haute couture*, ordered with much ceremony and consultation, and each hat was designed for each particular gentleman, characterizing and even caricaturing his personality. The best hats were made from beaver, not from the actual fur, but from the felt, which produced a lightweight, attractive *chapeau* that was handsome, warm, durable, and waterproof.

Based on the intelligence gathered by Cartier, Samuel de Champlain went over to the St. Lawrence River himself in 1603. Champlain rambled around the Shield country, persuaded the Indian tribes to hunt beavers for him, and gave them steel traps, kettles, axes, guns, blankets, and various other coveted items in return. The beaver industry moved into higher gear in 1670, when the British caught wind of the fur trade and established the Hudson's Bay Company, which laid claim to the Hudson Bay watershed – that is, all the lands draining into Hudson's Bay, which happened to be most of Canada. Backed up by a Royal charter, the HBC became our country's first government.

Over the next century, the HBC made so much money from beaver that it became the most powerful corporation in the world. Its employees were mainly Indians like the Cree and the Ojibway, who like hunter-gatherer peoples all through history avidly participated in the industry that eventually destroyed them. Instead of living off the land, the natives became self-employed fur trappers. They may have known it was the devil's bargain, but they sold out for the same reason that anyone sells out – money. A dozen pelts bought a brass kettle, which boiled water a lot more quickly than a birch-bark tub filled with hot stones, or a gun, which could kill a deer from across a river. Soon enough, the Indians depended on the fur trade, and the fur trade depended on the Indians. The link between them was the "Made Beaver" (MB), or finished beaver pelt, which was Canada's first dollar.*

The London-based HBC conducted a centralized business from fortified trading posts. This created an opportunity for their old rivals, the French, who detoured around the HBC monopoly by going deep into the backcountry and buying directly from the Indians. French fur traders became "runners of the woods": *coureurs de bois* who learned native survival skills, slept in native villages, and took native wives. If the symbol of the British fur trade was the log palisade and snapping flag, the symbol of the French fur trade was the birch-bark canoe and fringed buckskin jacket. Even today, you can see the cultural difference written into Canada's maps. Rather than selecting European names for the country's lakes and rivers (Thompson, Mackenzie, Nelson, Churchill, etc.), the French retained the aboriginal names, which not only are more lyrical (Wapegeesi, Pekagoning, Kinmoapiku) but teach you something about the river itself. This river, for example, is named after *Gitchi Weenipake*, its destination.†

As the nattering Evinrude pushed me ever farther from civilization, I took off my shirt and enjoyed the warm sun. I pulled out a cup and took a drink from the river. From looking at the map I could see that the river system branched out in four directions from Minaki. Each branch was fifteen or twenty miles long and

---

* Along the hem of a Hudson's Bay point blanket or coat, black stripes or "points" indicate its value in MB dollars.

† Weenipake means "sea," and "Gitchi" means "great," as in *Gitchi Manitou* – Great Spirit.

consisted of countless islands, bays, and channels. My plan was to establish a camp and use it as a base for explorations. I didn't have a specific methodology in mind. But I reasoned that in exploring a subject, you can either go wide or go deep. My plan was to go deep: pick one piece of wilderness real estate and get to know it intimately. I'd brought along a box full of natural history guide-books, and I planned to sketch any species I couldn't identify.

Half an hour after leaving Minaki, I experienced the first sign of trouble. The little Evinrude issued a loud *bang*, hacked and sputtered for a second, then quit. I checked the gas tank. It was half full. Removing the cowling, I examined the innards. Except for waves of heat pouring off the cylinder head, every-thing seemed normal. The bolts were all bolted on and the wires were all fastened to their usual wire-places. Despite my years of guiding, I had little experience fixing outboard motors. I yanked the cord a couple of times, but there was no resistance. I believe that a motor is supposed to have a certain quality called com-pression, and this one didn't seem to have any. I was no expert, but it seemed that the engine was definitely broken.

It was a long way to shore. For some reason I had been travelling down the middle of the river. The canoe was badly overloaded, and now that it had swung stern-first into the wind, waves were splashing over the lip of the transom. In a few more minutes, I'd be swamped. I didn't have a life jacket, of course, because real men don't wear them. I wouldn't freeze to death in this water, but it was a long way to shore, and I'm not the world's best swimmer. So moving gingerly, I dug around beneath my now-wet supplies and located the paddle.

The big freighter canoe handled like a waterlogged tree, and it took half an hour of hard paddling to reach the nearest landfall –

three islands, tethered like ships alongside the heavily wooded mainland. The first two islands were scruffy and nondescript, covered with tangled second-growth balsam and poplar. They looked like woodtick farms. But the third island was a beauty, a high, blunt-nosed hump of weathered granite, covered with massive pines. On the lee side of the island, a little bay afforded some shelter from the wind. Minaki was only five or six miles away, but that seemed like a good distance, close enough that I could sneak into town and buy supplies, if needed, and far enough that I could still feel like I was confronting the savage wilderness.

I dragged the canoe onto the beach, climbed the terraced granite, and explored the island. Mostly it was weathered rock, covered with moss, lichen, and carpeted pine needles. When I stopped on a high ledge, the only sound was the faint creak of the huge pines stirring in the wind. I unfolded the federal hydro-graphic chart and found out that this spot was called Tower Island. The map indicated that it was Crown land, which meant that it belonged to the citizenry – in other words, me.

I explored the island and found a patch of flat ground among some big pines, just the right size for my nine-by-twelve prospector tent. I set up the tent, ate some lunch, and sat on the ledge of mossy rock, gazing out at the blue water. So now what? Ah yes – that's always the big question. Back in the city there's never any shortage of things to do. Always lots of homework, errands to run, people to call. My former roommate Paul, when he wasn't ushering women through the turnstile on his bedroom door, was studying Transcendental Meditation, and when he got home from TM class, he was usually all wide-eyed with medita-tive elation. He would open a tin of mushroom soup, spoon it into his mouth in big gelatinous gobs, and talk about nirvana.

His guru explained that our minds are like restless toddlers. They hate inactivity, and they're always daydreaming about sex or trying to remember the words to some inane Top 40 song. The idea is, you have to force yourself to focus on the present, focus on your breathing. You have to gaze at a distant cloud and rid your mind of all restless chatter. You have to imagine you're a flower. You're neither in the past or the future. You're just sitting here in the sun, a living thing. No less than the trees and the stars, you have a right to be here.

I meditated for a while, sitting motionless, breathing in and breathing out. I could feel the breeze on the left side of my face. I could feel the sun on the nape of my neck. I could feel myself breathing in, breathing out. I could sense that time itself was slowing down. I spent a long time avoiding all thought, until my brain ached like a bicep in the middle of an isometric curl. Finally I looked at my watch. I had meditated for a total of ten minutes.

Now what.

I did some exploring. I crept through the woods and discovered many spiderwebs. At the far end of the island, I found an old cabin that looked like it might have once belonged to a mad trapper. The roof had fallen in, the floor was covered with animal droppings, and the door was peppered with bullet holes. It seemed unlikely that the owner would be returning any time soon, so I salvaged a tin cup and a rusty frying pan and walked back to my campsite, which hadn't changed in my absence. The wind gushed through the trees overhead. The sun sparkled on the water, but there were few signs of life. Most coffee-table books about the Canadian wilderness promote the impression that there's a never-ending pageant of wildlife residing in the wilderness – moose standing belly-deep in the lily pads, and bears and beavers and eagles peering from behind every tree. On this island, I seemed to be the only living thing.

In the evening, the sun finally descended behind a bank of low cloud, and the river turned calm. I listened to the silence, a silence so absolute that I could hear the faint spatter of a duck's wings half a mile away. Then, just as dusk descended, a rumbling, keening dynamo-like hum rose in the woods – mosquitoes.

Soon a hostile swarm gathered around me. I hurried into the tent and zipped up the door. Until now, I'd entertained a vague notion that I might paddle back to Minaki and drop off the broken Evinrude at the repair shop – if they had one – and maybe clean myself up a bit and go for a beer at Minaki Lodge. After all, I was here to conduct research. After drinking lots of beer and maybe even smoking a few cigarettes, I could walk over to Murray's Camp and sleep in the van. I was accustomed to the van, and it wasn't as lonely as this place. But now that I was inside the tent, with half a million mosquitoes clustering on the netting of the door and darkness falling on the river, I realized I was stuck here. It was going to be my first night alone in the woods.

For several hours I read a book by the garish light of a pressurized gas lantern. The lantern's pneumatic hissing drowned out the ominous rumble of the mosquitoes. But finally, at midnight, the lantern began to run out of gas, and I wondered if I should refill it or go to sleep. Closing my book, I watched the lantern gasp, flicker, and slowly die. Then the darkness of the night settled all around.

With fingers laced across my chest I lay flat on my back, listening to the sounds of the night – ducks quacking, frogs croaking along the shoreline, and rodents scurrying through the undergrowth. In the interests of taking a positive slant on the situation, I tried to play a sort of nature quiz. What kind of animal is making that odd noise? Is that darned non-stop croaking sound a duck or a frog? It's way too loud to be a frog, but if it's a duck, why didn't I notice any ducks when it was daytime? Is that persistent chewing noise a termite in a nearby tree? Do we have termites here? Or is it a rodent of some kind, a virus-riddled rodent, trying to gnaw a hole in the side of my tent?

Sometimes there was a sound I couldn't identify, like a stick snapping, or the clink of a rock, and my heart would jump. Is that a bear? Or something worse? When I was a kid, sleeping in the woods, I wasn't afraid of animals so much as Frankenstein monsters. Now that I was older, I knew that every little snapped twig didn't necessarily mean that I was about to be attacked by a member of the undead. But oddly enough, this knowledge didn't make the noises any less alarming.

Lying there, I thought of my friend Mark, who rides a Norton motorcycle, works the door at a tough bar, and studies eastern mysticism – Gurdjieff, Krishnamurti, and the Sufi philosophers. If Mark were here, he'd probably say that my nervousness wasn't just a vestige of the days when we were hunted by sabre-toothed tigers. He'd say that here in the Western world, we carry around this self-image that's constructed of our background and upbringing, personal ethics, sexual attachments, scientific beliefs, religious upbringing, and so on.

When someone sneezes, we say, "God bless you." We still adhere to the old folkloric belief that our bodies are evil, and that the loss of our identities, for even a millisecond, allows our fallen animal selves to seize control. Mark would say that going into the wilderness alone is frightening because we don't want to lose our identity. But there's no choice; that's the price of admission. You have to say goodbye to safety. You have to turn away from the known world, sink into this impenetrable darkness, and open yourself to the fear.

I tried to accept it. I tried to accept that in comparison to this land I was nothing, a glitch, a footnote, a two-legged accident whose passing would make no more impression on this island than the death of a day-old gnat. I tried to accept the truth, but the more I accepted it the more desolate I felt. For the next few hours I drifted in and out of sleep, dozing off for a few minutes, then coming awake with a spurt of raw terror. Each time, I was certain that something was about to attack me. But the sounds of the night were always the same, the same quacking ducks and croaking frogs.

Sometime very late in the night, I heard a far-off boom, like distant boxcars. And for the next hour I lay awake and listened to the approaching storm. Gradually the wind strengthened, moving through the high trees with a sound like rushing water. Then a flash of raw light illuminated the tent and thunder crashed overhead. Rain drummed on the canvas, and it occurred to me that these huge pines all around the tent, which seemed so benign in daylight, were dangerous now. It was unlikely that a three-hundred-year-old tree would pick this particular night to blow over. But even a heavy limb, torn off by the wind, could make a jagged and lethal missile if it fell through the tent.

Finally the thunderstorm passed, and a driving rain settled in. When daylight came it was drizzling. One corner of the tent floor had flooded, and water was dripping from the ceiling onto my sleeping bag. I climbed into sodden jeans and hiked barefoot through the jagged woods, looking for a decent place to answer the call of nature. This was one aspect of wilderness living that I could do without. Squatting down among the cobwebs and dripping limbs, I reflected on the sorry state of the human animal, reduced to the basics. If it weren't raining so hard, I'd fetch my tools, cut down some poles, and build a proper biffy. But right now, it was taking all my willpower just to consider spending the day here, let alone the rest of the summer.

I went down to the shoreline, where the canoe was pulled up. It was filled with water and blown leaves. I emptied out the water, hauled it onto shore, overturned it, and stowed the paddles. I noticed a small ragged hole in the underside. During the storm, wave action must have rubbed it against a rock. Now I was stranded here, or at least stranded until I could somehow patch it.

It rained all day and all night, and the next day it rained more. I passed the time reading books and eating crackers and cheese. For three days it poured rain. It seemed impossible that the sky could deliver so much rain. But then again, I could remember times in the city when it rained for ten days straight, and I barely noticed it. It was just a wet spell. In the city, you don't notice the weather as much. You can always get your umbrella and walk down to the corner, and have a coffee, read the newspaper. You can go home and take a hot bath. You can call up some friends and go to a movie. Here, life was boiled down to its miserable essence – avoiding swamp monsters, staying alert, breathing in oxygen, exhaling carbon dioxide, stuffing food in your mouth. It could rain for weeks, or even months, and it would make no impression on this island whatsoever. I could spend my entire summer here, in this tent. I could catch a cold, die, and get eaten by insects, and this island would look exactly the same. Nothing had happened here for ten thousand years.

The next day I did catch a cold, or at least a flu-like malady that I probably got from drinking river water. Along with intestinal distress, I spiked a high fever and spent several days lying in my sleeping bag drifting in and out of dreams that featured giant spiders climbing on my head. I slept most of the day and lay awake most of the night, and it was right in the middle of one of these endless nights that the vermin arrived.

It was some indeterminate hour between midnight and dawn, and the wind was gusting through the trees. The tent was swaying, and I noticed a large moth climbing the canvas wall above my bed. I lifted my hand to brush it away and it fell, with a sharp squeak, onto my face. It wasn't a moth. It was a mouse. With a surge of disgust I slapped it away and yelled, scrambling for the light. With the flashlight in one hand and a shoe in the other, I explored the tent, intending to kill the mouse. But it was gone. I lit the lamp, searched the tent, and found a little hole, which I stuffed with a sock.

I left the light on for a while. But it's impossible to sleep with a gas lantern hissing over your head. So I finally turned it off. The tent was no sooner plunged into darkness when tiny feet skittered across the sleeping bag. The damn mouse was back. There was no time to light the lamp, so I fumbled for the flashlight and yelled, and in the flashlight's faint glow I saw the mouse bolting for cover. But then I saw another flash of movement, and another, and realized that the tent was full of them. They had smelled the food. And they were coming in.

I had no particular fear of mice. But this was like a scene from Edgar Allan Poe. I yelled and threw a shoe at them, but they only darted from one end of the tent to the other. Finally I realized there was no stopping them. My tent was leaking and Nature was pouring in. I grabbed my clothes, stuffed them into the knapsack, and did the best to save myself. I plunged out into the darkness and blowing rain. The night was wild, and the great trees howled and cracked in the wind, swaying like the booms of a dying ship. With the flashlight in my hands, barefoot, I hobbled down across the bare rock to the shoreline. I paused momentarily, to deal with a wave of nausea. My stomach was heaving and I was weak enough to faint. I knelt down and propped one hand against a fallen tree. The tree's bark was damp and ragged under my hand. With a calm scientific part of my brain I took notice of everything that was happening around me, as if the main thing was to keep an accurate record, no matter what happened.

I wondered if I should launch the canoe, fight my way back to Minaki, and sleep in the van. But then I remembered the canoe had a hole in the bottom, which I'd never be able to plug properly in the dark. I could try stuffing the hole with something, but if the plug failed, I'd never make it to shore.

I fumbled through my knapsack and pulled out some dry clothes. I climbed into my rain pants and my waterproof jacket, flipped up the hood, zipped it to my chin, and climbed under the canoe. This is how the voyageurs used to spend their nights. The moss was soft, and although the rain rattled on the hull, it was reasonably dry. I curled up and bunched the knapsack under my head for a pillow. I couldn't imagine doing this in winter. How did the Indians ever survive here, five hundred years ago? Obviously, they were tough. And it wasn't just physical toughness. They needed to be emotionally tough to endure the cruelty of Nature. As far as Nature was concerned, people didn't matter and neither did mice. We could all survive the storm or not survive the storm. Nature didn't care. Nature was managing this island on the four-billion-year plan.

Huddled under the canoe, I hoped only to stay reasonably warm and remain alert for any rodents that might eat my face. But I must have fallen asleep, because one minute it was dark, and the next minute it was light. Mosquitoes were buzzing around my ears. I was stiff from lying on the ground, and it took a few moments to climb out from under the canoe. Mist drifted on the surface of the river, and the trees dripped water. But through the trees I could see the sunrise burning through the shaggy clouds. The rain had stopped.

I gimped up to the campsite and opened the tent. The mice were gone. They were deer mice, and they come out only at night, like vampires. The tent didn't look too bad. Perhaps in the darkness they'd seemed more numerous than they really were. One box of crackers was torn open and crumbs were scattered on the floor. But everything else was just as I'd left it – the sock stuffed in the hole and the sleeping bag thrown open. I cleaned out the tent, emptied the cooler, and spread my wet boots, clothes, and sleeping bag outside to dry off in the sun. I was so dehydrated from being sick that I drank an entire cardboard box of apple juice, and stood there quietly for several minutes, hoping it would stay down. Some of my books were wet, so I put them in the sun too. Finally there was nothing in the tent but the mattress. I stripped off my wet clothes, lay on the mattress, and covered myself with a sheet. Compared to the rocky ground it was as soft as a cloud, and I immediately fell asleep.

I woke up at mid-morning. Outside, wet rocks glistened in the heat and birds chattered in the forest. The river was calm and pale blue. I wondered if I should take advantage of the bright sun by patching the canoe, breaking camp, and paddling back to Minaki. I'd load the van and keep going, maybe head down the highway to the Lake of the Woods and get a motel room for a day or two. I needed to rest up. I needed to lie in bed on a stack of pillows and watch a movie. I needed to get out of here.

But then I'd probably go back to Winnipeg. And with no job, and no courses lined up for the summer, I'd be worse off than when I left. The Cheyenne Indians had a good concept – the dog soldier. A dog soldier always carries his integrity on his belt, in the form of a wooden peg and a ten-foot length of rawhide. When pursued by his foes, the dog soldier drives his stake into the earth, draws his belt knife, and stands there tethered, making his last stand.

As I stood there, thinking about it, I decided I'd be stubborn, like a dog soldier. I was pretty good at being stubborn. I'd been stubborn about deciding to explore this country, even though my aching joints made me ill-equipped for the job. And I'd been stubborn about writing unpublished stories, even though my professors and various others had kindly suggested that it was a waste of time. Even my refusal to finish my M.A. degree in English was arguably a kind of stubbornness. Being stubborn is not particularly exciting. As personality traits go, it's like a Stone Age implement. It's crude and simple, but it was all I had.

I therefore erred on the side of stubbornness and decided to stay. I boiled a bucket of water to make some safe drinking water. I used duct tape to patch the hole in the bottom of the canoe. Paddling the canoe down the shoreline to the trapper's cabin, I dismantled one entire wall. After loading the weathered boards into the canoe, I transported them back to my campsite.

The exertion made me dizzy, so I drank more water, spiked with lemon juice and sugar. I took down the tent and used some old boards to build a solid wooden floor. Then I rebuilt the tent. Now it was waterproof, or at least protected from groundwater. With the rest of the boards, I built a wooden skirt around the base of the tent to repel the mice. With some rusty window screen from the derelict cabin, I made heavy-duty patches for the holes they'd already chewed. The canned food I moved outside, stacked on home-built shelves, and all the chewable foods went into my knapsack, which I hung from a tree. I emptied the water out of the toolbox. The sheepskin gun case had also sopped up some water, and my gun, a little .410 that my dad had given me for Christmas many years ago, had gotten a bit rusty. I cleaned it off with cooking oil and pulled an oily rag through the barrel with a length of fish line. Tomorrow I'd salvage more lumber and build some storage boxes.

I was filthy from all this work – not to mention the last week or so without shaving or bathing. So I stripped naked, waded into the lake, and swam out to where the sun was hitting the water. I floated there for a while, looking at the camp. It was my seventh day on the island. I wasn't much of a creator. But as I floated in the water, gazing at my work, I decided it was good.

The next day my appetite returned. I ate some pasta and went for a paddle. About a mile from the camp, I caught a large walleye, which I took back to camp and cooked for dinner. The next day I went back to the trapper's cabin and scrounged some more boards, then went looking for driftwood planks washed up along the shore. I enjoyed cruising along in the canoe, looking for a telltale glint of blanched wood in the brush along the shore. The boards were like found art, rubbed smooth by years of drifting. I used some of them to build a bed. Next to the bed, where the screened window overlooked the water, I built a small desk to work on my novel (a great walloping heap of scribbled, crossed-out, and re-scribbled foolscap). After years of writing regularly, I was addicted to it.

The mice must have been baffled by my fortifications because they didn't get in that night, and I clocked a solid nine hours of sleep. I felt energized and well rested as I made the morning campfire, and wished that I had a girlfriend to share this experience with. Life comes in fits and starts, and I knew things would probably get difficult again very soon. But that didn't prevent me from relishing the beauty of the quiet morning, going for a long swim, and moving on with the plan.

The days settled into a routine. I went to bed at sundown, got up at daybreak. Had porridge, granola, and tinned fruit for breakfast. Worked on the novel, then went outside and made lunch over the fire, usually walleye, beans, and pan-fried spuds. In the heat of the afternoon, with the river as calm as glass and the big thunderheads piling up in the southwest, I'd paddle the canoe through whatever spooky lily-pad bays and marshes I hadn't explored yet, search for birds and aquatic plants and look them up in my handbooks, cast for pike (a hefty one, caught in deep water, made a delicious dinner, baked with onions in tinfoil), and search for driftwood planks for my little island settlement. Like Robinson Crusoe, I was becoming a compulsive renovator of Nature, and used the planks to build a picnic table, and a bench upon which I could sit and watch the sunset.

The village of Minaki was not far away, and it emanated a sort of invisible energy, like radio waves. I can't pretend that it bothered me to have all those people living just down the river. I knew my Utopia, population One, was essentially an exercise in let's pretend. This island was close enough to civilization that I could always paddle back to town if I ran out of Edwards coffee or got bitten by a squirrel. Sometimes, however, I wished that I was camping on the Thelon River or some place like that in the uninhabited Arctic, facing the wilderness alone. It was hard to contemplate the message of this ancient landscape with so many distractions. At least once a day I'd hear whoops, and water-skiers would go howling by. Float planes flew overhead constantly, and one night, while I was paddling across the river, I almost got cut in half by a huge powerboat.

I was paddling home from an evening of bird-watching. I'd finally learned to tell the difference between a juvenile merlin (*Falco columbarius*) and a juvenile sharp-shinned hawk (*Accipiter striatus*), and I'd drawn sketches of both. My heavy binoculars were hanging around my neck and my guidebooks were stuffed in my pockets. I was paddling hard to keep ahead of the mosquitoes. Halfway across the river, I became aware of the far-off whine of a motorboat. It was unusual to hear boats at night, so I listened absent-mindedly as the sound drew closer. Finally I twisted around and looked in the direction of the noise, and saw a nebula of coloured lights.

It seemed to be coming in my direction. It was making a lot of noise and looked big. It kept coming, and at two hundred yards, I realized it was headed straight for me. I had no flash-light, like an idiot, and since I'd quit smoking I didn't even have a lighter. But a quick search of my jacket pockets produced a book of matches. The first match fell apart as I struck it. The second match adhered to my thumb, cooked the skin for a moment, and went out. The third ignited, but as soon as I lifted it up in the air, the flame petered out. Now the boat was only forty or fifty yards away, coming fast, and I had to make a decision. If I stayed broadside, the skipper might spot me, and swerve out of the way. If I turned head-on, the canoe presented a smaller target, but he'd be less likely to see me.

I decided to turn and face the boat. Digging the paddle into the water, I gave the canoe a violent thrust and swung it head-on. The boat thundered past and soaked me with its rooster tail. It kept going and never slowed or wavered until it was out of sight.

Marvelling at my stupidity and good luck, I took a moment to shake the water off my notebooks. Then I heard the distant noise of the boat again, coming back for another pass. I was probably three hundred yards from shore. But I don't think it took more than a few seconds to paddle that big freighter canoe to the safety of the island.

I'd brought enough food to last five or six weeks. I was managing to gather lots of fresh fish, blueberries, and an occasional male ruffed grouse from the nearby woods (shot illegally; the season wasn't open until October), so my pantry was holding out nicely. And now that I'd settled into the easy life of mid-summer camping – writing every morning, exploring in the canoe every afternoon – the days went by fairly smoothly. For more than a month I never spoke to another human being. I discovered that a hermit's life can be quite idyllic, if you don't mind going a little funny in the head.

When working around the campsite, I'd fallen into the habit of conversing with inanimate objects. "Oh sure, coffee pot, why don't you just *tip over?*" Sometimes fishing boats puttered past the island – a couple of tourists usually, squired by some bored-looking young guide from Minaki Lodge or Murray's Camp – and I'd hide behind a tree, peering out from the undergrowth. One day a pair of canoeists stopped by the island, and I was struck dumb. What should I do? I had *company.*

The guy, whose name was Martin, sported army pants, a cotton rope for a belt, and a ragged goatee. The woman, whose name was Lillian, had tanned, muscular arms, ripped cutoffs, and the lush tangled hair sported by Raquel Welch in the movie *One Million Years B.C.* They told me they'd been in the bush for two months, canoeing the English, the Wabigoon, the Turtle, and other remote waterways of northern Ontario. They said Tower Island was the most beautiful camping spot they'd come across. As we knelt around the fire, brewing coffee, I realized two things: that I'd forgotten how to talk, and that their condition was even worse than mine. They had gone feral, like cats.

That evening, as I prepared dinner, a great storm, tall as a dreadnought, grumbled and shot tracers of fire in the distant west. I had used all the plates preparing the fish, and because I was busy cooking, I assumed that my friends would wash the dishes before we sat down to dinner. But they didn't seem concerned. When I activated my rusty vocal cords and announced that dinner was ready, Martin dug into the frying pan with the flipper and dumped a heap of fried fish, kernel corn, and hash browns onto the bare granite. Then they both reclined on the rock and began eating with their fingers.

I had managed to find out a bit about them. (She was the daughter of a prominent architect. His parents were psychiatrists in Toronto.) They were full-blown urbanites, in other words. But they had gotten right down to the bottom of the bucket and broken through to the other side. As we ate, a whip of lightning lashed across the sky. And Martin, who was propped on his elbow, fingering hot fish in his mouth, looked up at the sky, narrowed his eyes, and issued a low growl.

That night we brewed a pot of tea and took turns with his old guitar, serenading Lillian. Martin sang the "Ballad of Stagger Lee" and I sang "Long Black Veil." This wasn't very interesting, least of all for Lillian, so after a few more tunes we put away the guitar and drank our tea. We stared at the fire, listened to the sounds of the night, and exchanged stories of the north woods. I told them I'd always had the feeling that this big, brutal rocky landscape of the Shield was like a Rosetta stone or a rune. I was sure it contained some deep and inexpressible mystery, if only you could figure it out.

Martin said that the summer before, they'd found a sacred artefact: a birch-bark scroll upon which some Ojibway shaman had written down the ancient teachings. He said, "There were eight levels of the Midewiwin Society, and you had to start studying when you were a child. If you lived to be eighty, you might reach the highest level, called the Sky Lodge. The Sky Lodge priests knew the secret of life, and they wrote it on these scrolls, which they hid in special places, usually a high cliff facing the rising sun."

Lillian nodded. She lit a rolled cigarette from a flaming twig. She exhaled a languorous cloud of smoke. "They're like the Dead Sea scrolls."

I asked, "Where did you find this scroll?"

"It was on another river system, not far from here," said Martin. "But I shouldn't say the exact place. Anyway, I climbed up on this cliff to take a picture and saw something hidden behind some rocks. It was like a long wooden cylinder, very old, with a birch-bark scroll inside. I started pulling it out, then I saw the pictographic writing, and I suddenly felt like, 'Holy smoke, maybe I shouldn't be touching this.'"

"So what did you do?"

"Put it back."

"Don't you think you should tell a museum curator or someone?"

"If I meet the right person, I'll tell them."

I took out my notebook. "How do you spell Midewiwin?"

He told me. I jotted it down. "And what did you say the name of that lake was?"

"Nice try," said Martin.

The next day they decided to move on. I helped them break camp. We would have exchanged addresses, but didn't have any, so I gave them the address of my parents, and Martin gave me the address of his. They were stopping in Minaki to replenish their supplies, so I gave them some postcards addressed to my friends and family, just to tell everyone I was alive and well.

Martin climbed into the canoe. "Take it easy," he said.

Lillian was already in the canoe. She waved and pushed away from shore. Just as she was digging her paddle into the water, she paused and pointed over my shoulder. "Look at the bear," she said.

I didn't see it at first. Then I saw the upright black ears and the inquisitive face peering at us from the underbrush. Yes, a bear.

It didn't look like a big bear. A big bear has small ears, and a small bear has big ones. The ears, of course, stay the same size;

it's the bear's head that keeps growing. It was the first time I'd seen a bear this summer, and it always perks you right up, seeing one close by. "Scat!" I shouted, clapping my hands.

The bear lowered its head but didn't move, as if it assumed that perhaps I was shouting at some other bear.

Martin banged his paddle on the gunwale of the canoe. The bear wheeled and disappeared into the bush.

"You told me bears didn't go on islands," said Lillian.

Martin smiled and looked at me. "Lillian doesn't like bears."

"I like them fine," I said. "I just don't want to share a small island with one."

Martin said, "They live here."

"Thank you for that information."

We concluded our goodbyes and they paddled off. I watched them until they were out of sight. I walked up the hill to the tent, keeping an eye peeled for my furry visitor. I was thinking that when it got dark tonight, I would load my little single-shot .410. Not that it would do any good. Light shotguns are designed for two-pound grouse, not bears.

∾

I cooked dinner and waited for the sun to go down. What I knew about bears was a combination of information from old-timers like Junior Robinson, book research, and some first-hand experience with bears in the bush. They were intriguing animals, and I liked them. But I liked them in daylight.

When the first Europeans arrived in North America they encountered three species of bears. The most abundant species was the blond-haired plains grizzly, *Ursus horribilis*, a behemoth that prowled the plains from Mexico to the Arctic. When Lewis and Clark travelled up the Missouri, they encountered these bears almost daily. Grizzlies have a touchy sense of personal space, and they often attacked the explorers on sight. The expedition members carried only primitive muskets, and sometimes had to fire a dozen balls into an attacking bear before it died.

It's very difficult to visualize the Great Plains of that era. Driving across Manitoba or North Dakota today, through a manicured landscape of roads and geometric cereal farms, you have to make a considerable effort to visualize the Serengeti-like wilderness that once existed on the prairies. You have to imagine a rolling ocean of thick green grass spangled with wildflowers. The dominant species of grass was big bluestem, a magnificent species that grew eight feet tall. A prairie covered with bluestem rolled off to the horizon like a purplish-green ocean, changing colour in the gusts of wind. Big bluestem was tall enough to hide a rider on horseback, and herds of buffalo flowed through it like schools of fish.

No one knows how many buffalo roamed the Great Plains. It was certainly tens of millions. In 1870 Phil Sheridan, who was an excitable boy, saw a herd of buffalo he estimated at 100 million. But only ten years later they were all gone. One autumn day in 1883 a large bull ran through the town of Souris, Manitoba, crashing through fences and clotheslines. A local man named A.S. Barton grabbed his gun and his horse and chased the bull. Here was a chance to bag the last one! Barton lost the bull when it swam the Souris River, and although the *Plain Dealer* notified the public, the bull was never seen again. With the passing of the buffalo the grizzlies also disappeared. Modern-day farmers occasionally dig up a skull, but grizzlies no longer survive on the plains. A few grizzlies still eke out a living on the northern barrens, but most have retreated into the dense forests and mountains of British Columbia.

The second species, polar bears, live in the Arctic and spend most of their lives either hunting on the ice or hanging out on the coast, waiting for the ice to return. They have a Velcro-like coating on their feet, which provides traction on the ice. Polar bears are actually black, but their translucent pelts make them appear white. Each hair is like a hollow fibre-optic cable that pipes sunlight down to their skin. Bears are highly individual animals, and trying to predict a bear's behaviour is like trying to predict a person's behaviour. Some polar bears befriend dogs, their ancient enemy, and spend hours romping with them. Some bears are playful, some are mischievous, and some are grumpy. A good-natured bear will run when it sees a grumpy bear coming. All polar bears retreat when they see a full-grown male coming. A male polar bear is the largest carnivore on earth.

Females spend six months of the year asleep. While they're hibernating, they give birth to two or sometimes three cubs in a snow cave. Moses Alyak, an old hunter from Rankin Inlet, once told me that the third cub usually dies of starvation. There's only so much milk to go around, and its siblings are usually bigger and more assertive. Moses says that if the third cub survives, it will grow up to be embittered and dangerous from the treatment it received when it was young. It sounds a bit like Dr. Spock, but Moses knows what he's talking about. Most modern-day Inuit live in large settlements with schools, hospitals, food stores, and satellite television, but Moses still spends most of his time living out on the land. He's hunted whales with harpoons, slept in igloos during howling arctic blizzards, and on three separate occasions been assaulted by polar bears.

During a four-day layover in Rankin Inlet, weathered in by fog, I heard stories about Moses and thought he sounded like someone worth meeting. I spent several days trying to find him, but it's tricky asking directions in an Inuit community. Everyone is happy to help out. In fact it's considered rude not to give advice. Some people knew for sure that Moses was south of town, at Corbett Inlet, while others were certain that he was out west, or down north. The search finally led to a fishing camp on the Melanine River. Whenever you find someone in this country there always seems to be water nearby. The sun had finally come out and the river looked like spilled sunlight: wide and shallow and ribbed with boulders. The Inuit clan were camped out on a gravel bar alongside the water. Honda dirt bikes were parked among the cabins and wall tents, and rows of fresh-caught char were draped over clotheslines like red stockings.

I was talking to a young woman who spoke fluent English when an elderly man pulled up on a Honda dirt bike. "This is Moses," she said. I gathered that she was either a granddaughter or someone who felt protective of him, because she didn't seem very happy to introduce me to him. She suggested that I was taking advantage of him and asked me to pay him something. "How much?" I asked. She talked to Moses. Moses didn't seem as distrustful as she was, but agreed that he could use some money for gas, perhaps five dollars. I gave him twenty, and we sat on the riverbank and talked, drinking tea and eating whale blubber, while the young woman sat on a plastic crate across from us, translating.

Moses' face was long and narrow, rugged and dignified looking. He wore a wool cap to cover the terrible scars of a bear mauling. He said he grew up with his grandparents in hunting camps. There was no town then, and life was not difficult. There were many animals and they lived in the same way that his people had lived since the beginning. His grandfather taught him to hunt and to use every piece of the animal. It wasn't a matter of practicality; it was a matter of respect. If you take away an animal's life, you must use every part of it. He said this duty was very private. It was between you and the animal. One time he killed a caribou without realizing it had a fawn, and for days afterward he apologized to the spirit of the caribou and asked it to forgive him.

His grandfather was a great hunter and fought Nanuq the old way, with a spear. In the dark of the winter night the dogs would bark and the people would know that Nanuq was coming. If they stayed inside their snow huts, Nanuq would break through the roof, so the hunters would dress quickly and go outside to engage him. Moses said that when Nanuq attacks a man, he first tries to push him down. He won't bite a man until the man is on the ground. So it's important to stay on your feet, to fend him off and back away from him like a man fighting another man. Nanuq is left-handed or right-handed, like a person, and you have to watch him to see which paw he is going to hit you with. Just before he strikes, he will twist his head slightly to one side, and that tells you which paw he favours. You strike him with the spear in the opposite side. While Moses recounted these lessons, he periodically stood up and played the different roles. First he would be the hunter, feinting with the spear, then he would play Nanuq, and it was almost as if he would turn into a bear. He would rear up on his hind legs and hunch over, facing his invisible adversary. Then he would sway back and forth, and twist his head to one side as he cocked a paw. Sitting down again, he would explain that these lessons helped him to survive three attacks.

Moses' ten-year-old grandson Kook must have sensed that he was missing out on something, because he came along and joined us, sitting next to his grandfather. Kook was a good-looking youngster, a silent boy with large brown eyes. Moses said the first time he was attacked, it was his own fault. It was snowing and he was wearing white, and Nanuq charged him, thinking he was another bear. Nanuq struck him once, realized he was a man, and broke off the attack. The second time he was at Whale Cove. He went up on the hill to look across the sea, and when he came back he saw two bear cubs at the cabin, getting into the char. Kook was up on the roof, waving at him, shouting. The mother bear came out of the cabin, saw Moses, and ran up the hill and tried to push him down. He backed away from her, trying to keep his feet. She struck him with her claws, tearing his arm open. He said he didn't want the bear to kill him because he didn't want Kook to have to see that. After hitting him, the mother bear assembled her cubs and left. Moses said he didn't blame her for injuring him. She saw him as an interloper and was trying to keep him away from her cubs.

On July 9 the year before, he and Kook and some other people went to camp out at the place where he grew up, Corbett Inlet. They went up to see the camp, and while they were gone the tide came up and the boat drifted away. His gun was in the boat. A woman named Margaret said she'd swim out and get the boat, but he said, You'll get hypothermia. They went into a tent, made tea, and he called Baker Lake on the radio and told them they'd lost their boat. Then Moses, Kook, and Margaret went outside. As soon as he stepped out of the tent he saw movement and froze. Right next to the tent – right between the tent and the guy ropes – there he was, Nanuq.

The bear started bounding towards him. Moses ran, hoping to draw the bear away from the others. He grabbed for the knife on his belt but the knife was inside the tent. Nanuq chased him and caught him with both arms, hugging him. He yelled for Margaret and Kook to run away. The bear started biting his neck, trying to bite the cervical vertebrae. Moses put his hands over his neck and felt the bear's canine teeth driving through his hands. The bear couldn't get at his neck, so it started biting his head. Moses covered his head with his hands but the bear put one foot on his neck, the other paw on his head, and clawed his hands away, tearing off his scalp. Moses acted it out, becoming the bear again, showing how it pinned his head to the ground and tore away his scalp. He said that in the midst of this, the bear suddenly ran away and he heard someone scream.

Moses lost consciousness for some time. He woke up and crawled fifty yards. The bear came back and attacked him again. Moses felt the bones of his skull breaking as the bear bit his head. He passed out. When he woke up it was quiet, and he could hear Nanuq eating something. He got up and walked to a cabin and found Margaret. He said, "I think I'm the only one who survived." They could hear Nanuq outside somewhere, eating, and Moses said, "I'm sure he's devouring my grandson." Margaret said they should walk over to the other cabin. Moses made the walk, leaning against her, but he fell down many times. When they reached the other cabin, the people splashed water on his wounds. He stayed outside because he was soaked in blood and he didn't want to terrify the children who were cowering inside the cabin. He said he knew that Nanuq would come back, and if he went inside the cabin Nanuq would smell the blood and come into the cabin, so he lay on the ground outside and told the people to block the door.

Suddenly he heard a burst of VHF radio static coming from inside the cabin, then a child's voice. "This is me! This is me! I am scared! I'm in a tent!" It was the voice of Kook. He was still alive. He'd found a hiding place at the other end of the camp and he was calling the RCMP. Soon a helicopter landed outside Kook's tent. A wildlife officer spotted the bear and shot it. The bear was eating an elderly woman named Hattie Amitnak. One of the wildlife officers in the rescue party was Hattie's grandson. Moses took off his hat and showed me the claw marks – deep, wide grooves across the top of his head. He said it was very private, the memory of that day. He said it was terrible to lie there bleeding, listening to the sound of Nanuq eating. He could still hear it. The young woman who was translating this story had been crying for some time now. And while Moses talked about the sound of Nanuq eating, he began weeping too.

When it was time to leave, Moses gave me some *muqtuq* – the blubber from a beluga whale. He cross-hatched the white blubber with a knife to make it easier to chew, which is no easy task even with a small piece. You chew and chew, but it's as resilient as a chunk of inner tube. He said that it sometimes takes a full week to catch a beluga. He and the other hunters comb the ocean all day, then sleep in the boat, anchored in the lee of an island. The whales are plentiful; the problem is getting close enough to get a good shot or throw the harpoon. The whole year is taken up by hunting, and the type of hunting changes every couple of weeks. Goose season segues into whale season. At the end of the summer the caribou arrive. When they migrate in the autumn, it's like a scene from wild Africa, thousands of them pouring through this valley like a visitation from the Old Testament.

The Judeo-Christian ethic proposes a world in which mankind is the Lord of Creation. Down here on the stony arctic seacoast the Inuit know that it's actually the other way around. The pyramid is inverted. The simplest organisms, the algae and phytoplankton, occupy the top. They've survived since the dawn of time and they will endure until the sun exhausts its supply of nitrogen and burns out, approximately 4.5 billion years from now. Beneath them are the protozoa, and beneath the protozoa are the bacteria, about a billion of which inhabit a single litre of seawater. The pyramid becomes narrower and less populated as it descends. Each layer clings by its nails to the one above. Large showy creatures like mammals inhabit the lower apex, and when the climate or environment shifts slightly, they peel away and drop into oblivion. (Woolly camels, mastodons, giant sloths, sabre-toothed cats, and all the rest . . . see you later.) At the very bottom is *Homo sapiens*, a poignant experiment. Moses apologized to the caribou because they're higher in the organization than he is.

Kook wrapped the blubber in some paper towels and I put it in the pouch of my camera bag. I'd borrowed an old pick-up truck from an outfitter in town, and Kook accompanied me to where it was parked. As we walked along, he scanned the faraway hills, looking for something, probably animals. Even though he lived out here, he seemed fixated on this environment, these hills, birds, and distant animals. When they airlifted Moses out to Winnipeg for emergency surgery, Kook went with him. It was mid-summer in the city, green, lush, and hot, and

Kook spent the whole week roaming Winnipeg with his auntie, sightseeing. He'd never been to a city before.

I said, "What was the most interesting thing you saw?"

He considered this for a moment. "Squirrels."

∾

The third species of bear in North America is the black bear, *Ursus americanus.*

Untroubled by pride, the black bear has a long history of working the angles and getting by on leftovers. It came across the land bridge from Asia three million years ago, between ice ages, and arrived on a continent that was already claimed by animals a lot bigger and a lot rougher than it was. Lions, sabre-toothed cats, scimitar-toothed cats (all of them larger than any cats alive today), dire wolves, grizzlies, coastal brown bears, and the biggest bear that ever walked the earth – the short-faced bear or "cave bear" (*Arctodus simus*), a wrecking machine that stood almost twenty feet high.

Faced with this kind of competition, the little black bear kept a low profile. It became an adept climber and learned to scoot up nearby trees when an enemy came along. Pursuing a jack-of-all-trades lifestyle, it took whatever opportunities came its way. Rotted carcasses, birds' eggs, insects, frogs – they all went down the hatch. Sometimes a black bear would run down and kill a young bison or camel, but it wasn't a predator. At the end of the last ice age, the glaciers melted, and the shift in climate was hostile to the mammoths, giant bison, woolly camels, and other huge prey animals. Like one of those Bloody Mondays that occasionally visit the stock market, a mass die-off swept the continent. Nature didn't terminate the black bear, though, because it never really had a job in the first place. If it couldn't eat baby mastodon, it would eat grass. There's something a bit buffoonish about an animal that's willing to do anything for a living. But the same quality that makes the black bear a clownish hustler also, on occasion, makes it dangerous.

Most scientists agree that grizzlies are more dangerous than black bears. But a human is more likely to survive an attack from a grizzly, even though grizzlies are much larger and more ferocious than black bears. When a grizzly charges, it's usually trying to make a point. Grizzlies move around inside an invisible defensive perimeter that's about two hundred yards in diameter. When a human inadvertently wanders into that personal space, the bear either flees or charges. What it does is determined by its age, size, temperament, and so on. But it will almost always do one or the other. The safest response to an aggressive grizzly is passivity. You're supposed to back away, lower your eyes, and demonstrate that you mean no harm. In most cases, the grizzly will make a "bluff charge," then leave the area. If the bear presses the attack, you're supposed to assume the fetal position and take your licking. If you don't fight back, you're less likely to get a severe mauling.

Black bears, on the other hand, almost never approach in such a flat-out aggressive manner. In the same way that a street mugger will often strike up a conversation first or ask for a cigarette, a black bear will take a few moments to measure you up. When you are approached by a black bear, the best response is rude pugnacity. Open your jacket and enlarge your profile like those fringed lizards from Australia. Throw stones, make threatening gestures, yell angrily, and emphasize the point that you're not someone to be trifled with. Black bears are old hands at estimating risk versus gain. And if you convince the bear that you're willing to fight, it'll usually shrug its shoulders and move on.

Still, they're opportunists, always looking for quality protein. In May and June, deer fawns and moose calves lie unattended while their mothers go off and graze. And during those weeks, they're easy pickings. The average moose calf stands a 50 per cent chance of being killed by a black bear before it's six months old. And a black bear stalking its way along a creek on a May afternoon is not looking for nuts and berries. It's looking for meat. It's walking softly and sniffing the wind. If it runs into a boy with a fishing rod, it might very well look at the kid and think, Well, he's not a moose calf, but maybe he'll do.

About forty-five people have been killed by black bears since anyone started keeping records, and the incidents show a pattern. People tend to think that only "sick or starving" animals will attack a human. But killer bears are usually large, healthy males. One spring afternoon in Algonquin Park, four Boy Scouts went fishing along a waterway called Stone Creek. Fifteen-year-old George Halfkenny walked down a trail with his fishing rod, unaware that a 275-pound black bear was following him. The bear rushed him, killed him, dragged him away, and was eating him when the victim's brother, twelve-year-old Mark Halfkenny, came along looking for him. The bear killed Mark, too, and was burying the body under some brush, to secure it from ravens and other freeloaders, when sixteen-year-old Billy Rhindress came along, looking for his friends. The bear killed Billy too. When Billy's older brother came down the trail, the bear crouched in the woods and let him pass. When wildlife officers shot the bear two days later, they found that it was an adult male in good health.

A few years after the Boy Scouts were killed in Algonquin, a middle-aged couple from Toronto went camping in the same area. A black bear observed them from the undergrowth as they unloaded their canoe and set up their tent. Their groceries were sitting in full view on the picnic table. But the bear didn't want their groceries. It wanted them. After a few minutes, the bear sprang from the bush and attacked the woman. When the man broke a paddle over its back, the bear attacked him too. It stayed at the campsite for five days, eating regularly, until the Ontario Provincial Police showed up and killed it.

The newspapers rounded up the usual biologists, who issued the usual statements, that is, that this was "bizarre and highly abnormal behaviour" and the bear was probably sick, starving, or provoked. Some suggested that the campers had done something wrong, by leaving their groceries out in the open. Biologists tend to believe that their job is to defend wildlife, and like dog owners, they sometimes have a hard time admitting that their charges might have bitten someone. But like the man-eater that killed the Boy Scouts along Stone Creek, this bear turned out to be a large male in good health.

This would come as no surprise to Dr. Stephen Herrero, a noted bear expert from the University of Alberta. Like other biologists, Dr. Herrero sees himself as a defender of wildlife. But he's also a defender of seeing the nose on the front of your face, and he insists that predatory attacks on human beings fall within the range of normal black bear behaviour. After all, if a bear will tackle a moose, why wouldn't it tackle a person? Do we really think that humans somehow enjoy special status from the other members of the animal kingdom? All predators tend to focus on traditional prey animals. But that's a practical choice, not an aesthetic one. If a red and white spoon looks enough like a meal, darting through the water, a northern pike will snap at it. And if human beings behave like a potential meal, they run the risk of being snapped at by a meat-eating predator. Of course it's important to balance this against the odds. There are many thousands of human-bear interactions in the bush country every summer, and seldom is anyone injured. The message that emerges from Dr. Herrero's work is that black bears are complex, adaptable animals capable of a whole range of feeding strategies. If you spend enough time in the woods, you may eventually run into the wrong bear in the wrong place. And if that happens, you have a problem.

Usually the culprit bear is a large and self-confident animal that lives in a backcountry wilderness or national park. Bears that live in such pristine wilderness areas have not been hunted, and they haven't learned to be afraid of people. If such a bear meets a person, it may show initial wariness, followed by curiosity. On occasion, anglers and campers have taken films of this sort of black bear following them in the woods. The footage shows the alert, calculating expression of an animal weighing an opportunity. There's none of the snarling and bloody-eyed ferocity depicted by illustrators in outdoor magazines. After all, the bear isn't angry. What's to be angry at? It's just interested in a meal. The bear looks like a cautiously hopeful dog following a kid with a cheeseburger.

Unlike polar bears and grizzly bears, female black bears are not usually aggressive about defending their cubs. Biologists have found that they can inspect black bear cubs and the mother will usually retreat and watch from a distance. It's the males that are dangerous. This has less to do with feminist theory than with the fact that male bears have different nutritional needs than females. Sow bears are smaller, and they're homebodies. They establish a territory and stay within it. The Ontario Ministry of Natural Resources sometimes deals with nuisance bears by catching them in a trap made from a steel culvert, mounted on a trailer. Once trapped, the bear is trucked to a new territory. The conservation officer releases the bear by backing the trap into a lake before opening the door. The bear has to swim a bit before getting to shore, thus allowing the officer time to scramble back into the truck.

Female bears, being homebodies, need to be dropped off at least eighty miles away, or they come straight back home. Once, a three-legged female with cubs was taken 120 miles away from Thunder Bay, and she returned home within a week. When released, female bears swivel their heads for a moment, and then strike off. Biologists suspect that bears find their way around by homing in on familiar smells – the odour of a river, distant pulp mill, or highway. If the transplantation is going to work, the bear has to be taken far enough away that she can't smell her home.

Males, on the other hand, are transients. If you trailer a male thirty miles away from where he was caught, he says thanks for the lift. He's driven by the urge to meet as many females as possible, and he travels incessantly, getting into a lot of territorial squabbles with other males in the process. It's in his interest to "bulk up," which he can do best on a high-protein diet. So the curious bear following a person through the woods is often torn between two opposite urges. Should I try to exploit this opportunity? Or should I play it safe and move on? Usually, his genetic predisposition towards prudence carries the day, and if a prospective victim behaves aggressively, the bear moves on.

Mating season happens in mid-summer, and the males run themselves ragged, looking for sex. By the end of August the party is over, and it's time for all bears to get back to work. The

pregnant females must be in prime condition before they hiber-
nate. They're eating for two (or three) now, and they need lots of
body fat. Their adolescent cubs – having been kicked out of the
house during mating season – also face a tough autumn.
Without a home territory, they wander around, looking lanky
and lost, getting beaten up by other bears, hit by cars, and shot
by homeowners. Big dominant males face the worse odds of all.
Like full-grown males of many species, male bears are viewed by
Nature as nothing more than delivery vehicles for spermatozoa.
A successful boar is a boar that manages to live for a couple of
years in his prime. Once the mating season is over, he has to gain
up to thirty pounds a week before he goes into hibernation. So
late summer is when bears of all ages and sizes become truly
serious about food, roaming twenty-four hours a day.

There's lots of informed opinion about the best ways to co-
exist with black bears in the wilderness. But all the authoritative
books, Ph.D. studies, and back-porch homilies in the world
aren't much help when you introduce food into the picture.

And these were my worrisome thoughts as darkness descended
on my campsite.

∾

After I fastened the flimsy tent door against the mosquitoes, I lit
the gas lantern and kept myself busy with a few chores.

My nonchalance was an act. Just as some airline passengers
are convinced that the plane will remain airborne only if they
stay awake, I operated on the theory that the bear would steer
clear of my camp as long as I remained busy. I knew, of course,
that the bear was probably miles away by now. But I wasn't

so much apprehensive about the bear, as apprehensive about being apprehensive.

At least the food was outside the tent. My larder consisted of some cabinets I'd built along the back wall of the tent. Most of the food was canned, but bears can smell food through a can, and they're quite happy to rip open tins of Libby's beans with their teeth. The cabinet also contained jars of wild rice, dried apricots, granola, and sugar, all of which rate high on a bear's list of favourite foods. If it came back tonight, it would probably hit the cabinets first, which would give me enough time to get out the front door. But what if it pushed against the food cabinets and knocked the tent down?

As I lay in the darkness, thinking over the possibilities, the bear's possible visit began to play out like a bad home movie – the collapsing tent, the dark confusion, the bear, frightened by the kicking motion, biting down on an ankle. I'd slipped the shotgun under the bed. But it's not like in the movies. You don't immediately gain the upper hand just because you display a gun. And this was just a little .410, a Nancy Reagan gun. Bears are durable animals. To kill one, you need to know its anatomy. You need a moment or two to line up a clear shot. You need to be a cool and steady hand, like Atticus Finch. Would the gun be of any use inside a darkened tent in the middle of the night? Not likely.

I began to feel, once again, like the author of my own folly. Probably the only workable use for the gun was to bring it to bed and, at the first sound of a cracking twig, shoot myself between the eyes. Thankfully, that didn't prove necessary because I finally drifted off, and when I opened my eyes it was morning. As the sun grew stronger and filtered through the mosquito netting, I realized that I'd wasted all that time worrying about nothing. Unzipping the door, I walked down to the waterline and threw my sleeping bag on the moss. I took a nap in the sun-dappled morning shade. When I woke up a few hours later, I saw the bear swimming across the river towards me.

Bears don't see as well as people, and it wasn't until the animal was fairly close that it spotted me. It veered away, swam down the shoreline, and vaulted up into the undergrowth. Now that it was daytime, I didn't feel as vulnerable as I had during the night, and I went up to the tent to make sure there wasn't any food left in the open.

About an hour later, I was sitting outside at the picnic table under the big pines, working on my novel, when a flicker of movement caught my eye. The bear was a good distance away, peering from behind a tree like a drug dealer checking the street for cops. I clapped my hands and yelled at it, and it took off. Then an hour later it showed up again, a little closer this time, walking along the outer perimeter of the clearing and swinging its head back and forth. You can determine a bear's gender by the shape of its head. Females have narrow heads and longish noses. Males have broad foreheads and blunter snouts. This one looked like a male. I went into the tent and got the gun, loaded it, cocked the hammer, and walked towards the bear. When he began moving away, I shot him in the rump with a load of bird-shot. It was a quiet afternoon, and the gun boomed like a cherry bomb. He was fifty yards away – just the right distance for the No. 6 pellets to give him a scare rather than an injury – and the detonation of the gun probably had as much effect as the birdshot slapping his rear end.

He ran like a scalded cat. But only five minutes later he was back, shaking his fur and woofing as if in embarrassment. All afternoon, he loitered in the nearby woods. And as time passed, he paid less attention to the noise, the threats, and the warning shots I fired into the foliage over his head. Among my stack of reference books I had a government guidebook called *Safety in Bear Country*. The book recommended a number of bear deterrents, including, as last resort, the "three slug method," a strategy by which you fire a warning shot in the form of a 12-gauge firecracker shell when the bear is three hundred feet away, a non-lethal plastic 12-gauge slug aimed right at his body when he's two hundred feet away, and a lethal lead slug if he's closer than one hundred feet. I didn't have access to such refined munitions, and this bear seemed well past the point of being frightened off by gunfire anyway.

Late in the afternoon, I was kneeling by the campfire cooking fettuccini when I heard a noise and saw him coming. With his head lowered, he advanced towards me, hissing, swinging his head back and forth, and folding his ears back in the universal body language of warning. He wasn't a large bear, perhaps a two-year-old. He might have weighed 150 pounds, about my size. But wild animals are about four times stronger than humans, and with a bear you can probably double that again. No doubt the smell of the bubbling fettuccini was giving him whisky courage, and he'd decided that I was nothing he couldn't handle. When he got within three or four yards, hissing like a punctured tire and waving his head, moving closer, moving closer, I picked up a jagged chunk of granite the size of a grapefruit and threw it at him. It caromed off his forehead. He didn't even blink. When he got within two yards I stood up, took a step back, and ceded him the pasta.

I stepped back a ways and watched him snuffle up my dinner. After a few minutes I went up to the tent and put together an emergency overnight kit – my jacket, sleeping bag, gun, fishing rod, and manuscript. When I came out of the tent the bear was still face-first in the pasta kettle, with cream sauce all over his forehead. Our little dispute had clearly been settled to his satisfaction, and when I walked past he didn't even look up. He was so engrossed in his meal that he might just as well have been a Shetland pony face-deep in a bucket of oats. I went down to the shore and loaded the canoe. If this was a Shakespearean drama, it would be the perfect nadir for the hapless protagonist. *Exit, pursued by a bear.* Launching the canoe, I paddled around to the front of the island and viewed the scene from the water.

The sun was getting low, and it was hard to see the bear among the shadows. The tent began shaking, and his rear end emerged. He was working on the pantry, no surprise. The tent quivered, then the shelving fell onto the rocks with a mighty crash.

I drifted in the canoe, thinking it over. I felt like I was judging a court case, and acting as both prosecutor and defence attorney. If the bear drove me off the island, I had nowhere else to live. And with nowhere to live, I'd probably have to go back to the city.

I could probably devise a way of killing him. It wasn't against the law. The Ministry of Natural Resources was trying to get out of the nuisance bear business. It was too expensive, live-trapping bears and giving them one-hundred-mile rides all over Ontario. So their new policy was destroy the bear if you must, but dispose of the carcass properly. And please stop phoning us.

Eventually, the bear would have to swim back to the mainland. I could paddle up to him while he was swimming. One shot right behind the ear would kill him instantly. Then I'd float him out into the middle of the river, tie a few rocks to his neck, and say goodbye. Maybe I'd slice open his paunch, so he wouldn't pop up a few days later, all tangled up in yellow rope like some bloated Hells Angel. Then I could repair the camp and start over. There was still some fine summer weather left.

On the other hand, you could put forth the argument that this wasn't wholly a dispute between the bear and me. It was more like a dispute between me and Nature. The whole point of going to the wilderness and descending to rock bottom was to accept that you didn't run things. And no matter how attached I was to this island, the bear probably had a more legitimate claim on it than I did.

So after floating quietly for a few minutes, I slipped the paddle into the water and decided to move on.

∾

Minaki's great black railway bridge was silhouetted against a smoky sunset as I paddled into town. Motorboats occasionally sped past me, so I stayed close to shore. As I paddled through the narrows leading to Murray's Camp, I noticed a strange sight.

It was a little cottage that looked like a witch's hut. It seemed, however, to be *floating*. I altered my course slightly to get a closer look. The owner was out on the deck watering his flowers. He waved, and I paddled over to say hello.

His name was Dave. He was a good-looking young guy, bare-chested and tanned, with blond hair tied back in a pony-tail. I didn't recognize him at first. But when he told me he worked as a fishing guide, I realized that I'd seen him at the lodge when I first arrived. He was the guide with the big muskie. He said that he recognized me too. While he'd been out fishing, he'd seen my freighter canoe and my camp, and said he admired me for going "hard core" in the bush. He said that he'd done the same thing when he first moved here. He'd lived in a big tent in the bush, but a bear wrecked it. Then he built a yurt, but a bear wrecked it too. He'd shot the bear, but regretted doing it, because it was "such a waste of a cool animal."

This houseboat was his latest solution. It floated on a pair of twenty-eight-foot-long steel pontoons. The building itself was a charming little shack with curved windows and flowerboxes everywhere. It was clad in rough cedar shakes that overlapped like giant feathers. He showed me the inside, which was decorated like a Victorian curiosity shop, full of antique furniture, glass lanterns, and animal skulls. The sleeping loft was supported by buttresses made from bent tree limbs. The walls were decorated with photographs of Indian renegades. Red Cloud. Poundmaker. Almighty Voice. (What names they had!) The driftwood shelves were stacked with books about aboriginal mysticism – books like *Seven Arrows*, *Black Elk Speaks*, and *Hanta Yo*. Sometimes it seemed like every interesting young white guy I met wanted to be an Indian.

Outside, we walked around the deck and he explained how he'd built the houseboat. As we stood there a raven flew up and, to my surprise, landed on his shoulder. "His name is Gonzo," Dave explained, patting the bird's feathers. "I adopted him when he was a chick, now he's my buddy."

From close up, a raven is larger than you might expect. It preened Dave's hair with its heavy chiselled bill, then squawked, demanding food. Dave told me it lived on a perch at the back of the houseboat and flew after him when he was out in his motorboat, following along overhead like a B-52 bomber. He said that he'd always been fascinated by wild things. He grew up in a tract-house neighbourhood in the south end of Winnipeg. When he was a teenager, he came to Minaki for a weekend and felt like he'd come home. "I'm never going back to the city," he said. He nodded towards the fading sunset and the river, which was glowing like a sheet of rose-coloured glass in the dusk. "How could I ever find a better home than this?"

I climbed into the canoe and paddled over to Murray's Camp. My van had a dead battery and a film of dust on the windows. Unlocking the doors, I dumped my stuff inside, then headed off on foot in the falling dark, looking for a place to eat. Walking up the railway tracks, I crossed a lush fairway towards Minaki Lodge, which was silhouetted against the sunset like a medieval castle. Inside the lodge, I strolled through the main rotunda, admiring the varnished log walls, the big stone fireplace, and the magnificent cathedral ceiling. Downstairs, I found a staff lounge where a group of young men sat at the bar, drinking beer. Because of their tousled hair and dark suntans I guessed that they were fishing guides. At their belts, they wore the guide's trademark long-bladed knife scabbard, minus the knife. (Sign above the cash register – CHECK KNIVES WITH BARTENDER.) In the centre of the room there was a small dance floor, and some girls were twirling and jiving to the thunderous fuzz-tone guitar of "Smoke on the Water."

The music was so loud you could barely talk, but I ordered a cheeseburger and a beer. Soon I was talking to the guide next to me, who told me he'd been in fine arts at the University of Manitoba, but had decided to become a full-time fishing guide instead. I asked him where he lived, and he told me he rented a cabin with a bunch of other guys. "It's a rather modest little abode," he said, with a grim chuckle. "Why don't you come on down and see us sometime? It's called The Swamp."

We talked for a while, but I didn't want to get carried away and spend what little money I had, so I drained my glass and told him I was going to call it a night.

He said, "You're paddling all the way back to Tower Island?"

"How did you know I was staying on Tower?"

"Hey . . . this is Minaki. There are no secrets here. If you're in the Witness Protection Program, you picked the wrong place to hide out."

I slept in the van that night, and the next morning went back to the island to clean up the mess. As I expected, the campsite looked like a bomb had hit it, with shelving, punctured cans, and broken glass flung everywhere. The tent was knocked down and the sidewall was torn open. When I flipped the tent over, I saw that the bear had ripped open an even larger hole on the other wall. I've seen a number of tents destroyed by bears, and for some reason they never use the same hole going out as the one they used going in. It's a matter of principle. They always have to cut two big holes. There was no way of repairing it, so I stuffed the tent into a big garbage bag.

For the next couple of hours I cleaned up the mess, gathering every last piece of broken glass in garbage bags. Then I dismantled and burned my driftwood-plank furniture. It saddened me to watch everything go up in smoke, but it felt good, too, to return the island to its natural state.

By late afternoon, the campsite was so clean that I reckoned an RCMP forensic investigation team would have a hard time determining whether anyone had actually lived here. I needed a souvenir, so I picked up a pine cone and put it in my shirt pocket. Loading the wrecked tent, garbage bags, and defunct little Evinrude 3-horse into the canoe, I pushed away from the shore and paused, for a moment, to look back at the island that had been my idyllic home.

∾

When she was twenty-one years old, Lisa earned $20,000 a week working as a model in New York and Paris. She slept with rock stars, cruised the Mediterranean, and got engaged to the heir to an American breakfast cereal fortune.

One morning she woke up and found her boyfriend dead of an overdose. She wasn't entitled to a cent of his money, so she went back to modelling. But her hard living was starting to show and she wasn't as much in demand. Her next boyfriend was a Saudi playboy who gave her hepatitis C. In an effort to wean herself off the sporting life, she started smuggling Rolex watches between Orly airport and LaGuardia. She got caught and would have gone to jail if it hadn't been for Ray, a grizzle-haired ex-hippie with a pirate moustache who was one of the best organized-crime lawyers in New York.

Ray got her off, and they began dating. He loved her unpredictable brain. She had such a smart mouth, she could entertain an entire dinner party. They eventually got married and moved to Livingstone, Montana, where they built one of those phony *Architectural Digest* log homes and tried to figure out ways to spend Ray's money. Ray took up fly-fishing and dragged Lisa all over North America in pursuit of Alaskan salmon, Bahamian bonefish, and Ontario muskies. When Lisa ended up in my boat, she confessed that she missed those nights in Manhattan, sleeping late, taking long lunches, and going shopping. But she knew that Ray was her last chance at a straight life, and if the price of being together was spending a week, every few months, lounging around in a fishing boat and working on her tan, she figured she could put up with it.

In her sunglasses and blue bikini Lisa was sprawled like a lynx in the front of my boat, smoking a joint and reading a paperback edition of *Dune*. In the other seat, her friend Mickey was tinkering with the ghetto blaster. Mickey, whose bare shoulders were as brown as varnished wood, was tougher, older, and slightly less forthcoming about her personal life. I knew only that she was from Aspen, had been married a number of times, and had lots of money. (One night at the bar in Minaki Lodge, she showed up wearing a necklace that spelled out "Rich Bitch" in diamonds.) Their respective husbands, Ray and Steve, were off somewhere looking for muskies with my partner, Glen.

Lisa, Mickey, and I were ten miles north of Minaki, drifting on the flat calm waters of Big Sand Lake, trying to catch some walleyes. But the fish weren't biting. We'd caught half a dozen earlier in the morning, but nothing for hours, and the day was getting quieter, and hotter – quite unusual weather for the first week of September. At noon, we reeled in our lines and headed off to meet the other boat for lunch. Mickey and Lisa had been feigning indignation about the slow fishing ("Jake, if we don't start catching fish, we're not going to take our tops off"). And when I started the engine and ran the boat across the immense flat, steamy lake, I think they were just as happy to be quitting.

At Skinny Island, Glen's boat was already pulled up on shore and the men were unloading it. I approached the shore and nudged the prow of my own boat onto a granite ledge. The women got out and I unloaded the boat, including the bleached and very dead walleyes we'd caught earlier in the morning. The other guys had spent most of the morning fly-fishing for muskies. After getting the update on their morning (no muskies, Ray cannonballed out of the boat in his underwear, they saw a wolf), Glen and I got busy making shore lunch. We'd been guiding together for four days now, and I liked working with him. He was a better guide than I was, but he treated our partnership as a democracy.

Using the wooden paddle as a work surface, I cut and parried the fish, removed the bones, peeled off the skins and built a pile of fresh fillets, and kept an eye on the guests, making sure that they didn't do anything to hurt themselves. Steve and Ray had fished all over the world, but I kept an eye on them out of habit. It was a normal part of the job. It was like being in charge of a group of youngsters at a lawn party. You never knew when one of them was going to get a bright idea, like sawing at a can of beans with a bowie knife or tossing a tin of gasoline on the fire.

I'd been guiding almost every day for the last month. And that was a good thing, because I was flat broke. Early one sunny morning, not long after the bear banished me from Tower Island, Dave knocked on the door of my van. He knew that I had some guiding experience, and asked if I wanted to come out of retirement. I quickly got dressed and accompanied him to Minaki Lodge, where we gassed up a couple of boats and fitted them out with paddles, life cushions, minnow buckets, and all the other stuff you need to spend a day on the water. I was a bit uneasy, having never guided on this river, but Dave said it wasn't going to be a problem because we had an elderly foursome who wanted to stay together. "Just follow my bubbles."

We had a good day on the water, and I learned some new parts of the river system. Every day, we went to new places, and I began to build up my knowledge of the river and all its attached lakes. The following week I picked up a few days of guiding out of Holst Point, then Murray's Camp, then Minaki Lodge. Soon, I was making money.

Minaki was a road-accessible fishing area, so the tourists weren't quite as wealthy as the ones who patronized fly-in resorts like Great Slave. Some had saved up for years to come fishing in Canada. Even when they flew here, it sometimes took them a day and a half to make the flight connections, rent the car in Winnipeg, and drive to Minaki. It was as hard as travelling overseas, when you added up the hours and the expense. And frankly, I sometimes wondered why they went to so much trouble, just to catch a few little walleyes.

One night in the bar, I ran into a marketing executive from Ontario Tourism. He said that he'd polled twenty-seven thousand American anglers, and it seemed that they weren't just here for the fishing. The survey asked the visitors to name their "top ten" reasons for coming to Canada. It turned out that "catching a big fish" was actually the least important reason, and "catching lots of fish" ranked second-last. The most popular reason was something like "experiencing the beauty of Nature."

Most of them, in other words, were trying to connect with God. All the equipment – the tackle boxes and fishing rods and polarized sunglasses and so forth – were just accoutrements. They needed to have an excuse for being here, and fishing was their cover story. Serious fishermen like Ray and Steve probably would have scoffed at such talk. But they wouldn't have scoffed because they disagreed. They'd have scoffed because as a fishing guide, I was supposed to play along with the game. You couldn't find God by following an agenda. You had to go about your day and hope that you'd catch a glimpse by accident. It was like looking up at the night sky. In order to see those faint constellations, you can't look straight at them. You have to look a few degrees off to one side.

So I knew that even Lisa and Mickey, with their foul mouths and flinty hearts, were keeping their eyes open for some subtle glimpse of beauty that would make their trip worthwhile. And no matter how much they smoked weed and played loud music and nattered on about their self-indulgent lives, I knew they were hoping for a moment of spiritual connection. As their guide, it was my job to help them find it.

When I finished cleaning the fish, I walked up to the fire pit, where Glen was preparing the spuds. He was down on one knee, wielding his razor-sharp filleting knife with a blur of dexterity that reduced eight ultra-large Idaho red potatoes into a bowlful of dice-sized cubes in a few moments. As the fire kicked in, Glen set the huge frying pan on the rolling orange flames, laid out a pound of bacon, and with his other hand, broke eggs and stirred them in a plastic bowl. I prepped the fillets and opened cans of corn and beans. Meanwhile Ray, Steve, Mickey, and Lisa stood around us, watching. Ray had spent most of his life in a courtroom, trying to swing jurors around to his point of view, and he never stopped talking. His specialty was jokes and one-liners. I don't know where he got them from, but he had an inventory of literally thousands of jokes, which he would launch into, unbidden, whenever there was a lull in the conversation. But when Glen and I started cooking shore lunch, even Ray lapsed into silence.

Maybe hunger and anticipation had something to do with it. There was nothing that worked up an appetite like being outside all morning. But shore lunch was also a spiritual ceremony. It took all the elements of angling – the excitement of the quest, the beauty of nature, the sacredness of wild things – and wrapped them all into this ceremony: the meal. Glen and I had done this job so often that it was like a dance routine – batter the fish, start the fire, wash the fillets in the lake, skin the onions, unpack the lunchbox. Don't let them see the tin of Spam in the bottom of the box. (Every guide carries a tin of Spam in his lunchbox, like a trooper's last bullet.) Remove the cans of beans and corn, and nestle them against a rock alongside the fire. Don't forget to open the cans. Sitting in a fire for a few minutes, an unopened can of beans becomes a grenade.

We brewed coffee in a gallon can full of lake water, and laid a green twig across the top of the can to keep it from boiling over. I poured two cups of olive oil into the big frying pan, and tossed a wooden match into the oil – a floating thermostat that would allow us to concentrate on other tasks for a few moments. (When the match ignited, the oil would be ready.) I cracked an egg into a bowl of tinned milk and stirred it up with a fork, filled a paper bag with flour, dipped the fillets into the milk, and dropped them into the bag. Now the fillets were ready to go. I put them where they wouldn't get stepped on. They were tender enough already.

Squatting by the fire, we worked silently, blinking our eyes in the stinging white smoke. It would be pleasant to wear T-shirts and shorts, but most guides dress in the standard bush professionals' outfit of long pants, leather gloves, and Kodiak workboots. With all this boiling oil sloshing around, you don't want to deep-fry your ankles. Shore lunch is one of those undertakings that sounds good as a concept but threatens to fall apart as soon as you begin. Myriad small details conspire to ruin the whole undertaking. Did you forget the spatula? Forget the matches? The week before, I was working with a guide who accidentally ignited a whole clump of wooden matches in his pocket. He jumped up and whacked his head against a coffee pot, spilling hot coffee down his back. He grabbed the kettle and poured coffee into his pocket, extinguishing the fire but scalding his thigh. He was a good fishing guide but was riding an unlucky streak. A few days before that, he'd been making lunch on a deserted rocky point at the top end of Big Sand Lake when his guests noticed an unoccupied boat drifting way out on the lake. "Hey, look at that!" he chuckled. "Some idiot lost his boat!"

There's no such thing as a minor glitch when you're fifteen miles from help. And if you screw up, it's not the weather's fault. It's not the motor's fault. It's your fault, and you have to spend the rest of the day with guests who'd rather be with someone else.

&

Before partnering up with Glen, I worked with some of the other local guides.

George Kelly was a muskie specialist. He was an old-timer with fierce squinty eyes and a rural drawl. (He was an Ojibway, but he'd spent so much time with Americans he talked like them.) He had a collection of several hundred hats and wore a different one every day. He liked baseball caps with golf tees on them, or clownish antlers, or messages (*Instant Asshole – Just Add Liquor*). When George was young, his American guests would take him down to Chicago to attend the big fishing shows, and he would entertain the audience by walking around with eight hundred pounds of flour on his back. He was in his sixties now, but still strong enough to walk a one-mile portage carrying a Mercury 20-horse motor in each hand like a pair of attaché cases.

The rumour was that George knew the location, size, and individual feeding preferences of every large muskie on the river system. He would never divulge his secrets, but he seemed to have some odd methods for catching them. I'd heard that he would pull into a bay and run his boat in crazy circles, revving the motor and whacking his paddle on the water to get the fish's attention. (So much for whispering while you fish.) When anyone asked him about his methods, he would just laugh and wag a finger. "Don't get rowdy!"

As George specialized in muskies, Jimmy Anderson specialized in walleyes. Jimmy weighed about two-fifty and, like George, was a masterful native guide who seemed to know forbidden secrets. Jimmy was so good at catching walleyes that all the other guides would just shrug their shoulders and eliminate him from the argument. He didn't count because he was on another level. I'd watched Jimmy fish, and his method was simple. He would toss a rubber-tailed jig overboard, tighten the line, and right away he'd have a fish.

He'd chuckle, wind in the fish, release it, toss the jig overboard, and do it all over again. He would catch about a hundred fish a day and chuckle every time he did it. You could copy his technique but it didn't make any difference – because he didn't have a technique. It didn't matter whether he twitched the lure, jiggled the lure, or let it sit still. He would even trade rods with you. It didn't matter. He would catch one fish after another, and you'd catch nothing. I wanted to find a scientist who could explain this.

Guiding was so effortless for Jimmy that he had lots of spare time to entertain himself. He and his brother Robert devised nicknames for everyone in Minaki, and the monikers were clever enough that they tended to stick. Jimmy and Robert put a lot of thought into the process, arguing with each other in whispery voices, so a newcomer might not receive his nickname for quite some time. Robert was the younger of the two, and with his great belly and tiny baseball hat he resembled a Samoan prince on a fact-finding tour. He stood around the marina, not saying much, jingling change in his pockets and studying everyone. It was demanding work, and Robert took his work seriously. Whenever he got a chance, he'd slip in a few innocent questions, adopting the mildly uninterested tone of a secret policeman. ("So, uh . . . are they living together, those two?") One day I caught a ride into Kenora with them. Sitting jammed between them in their pick-up truck, I found myself being squeezed, both for space and information. It was quite chatty and pleasant, but they still ended up with all the gossip I knew.

I enjoyed guiding with Jimmy because he knew so much about fishing. But all bets were off if you were working for a different lodge. One hot and dead-calm day, I pulled up near Jimmy, and my guest shouted to his guests, "Are you catching anything?"

The tourists in the other boat smiled. "Oh, we're doing all right."

My guest grumbled, "We haven't caught a thing."

"Do you want a couple of walleyes?" Jimmy asked.

This was a demeaning offer, but my guest was happy because at least now we'd have shore lunch. Jimmy reached into his live well, took out a walleye the size of a French loaf, and threw it. It was a perfect spiral pass, and the walleye drilled into the water a few feet away from my boat. The next fish went over our heads, and the next one went off to one side. He threw half a dozen large fish, each one splattering into the water and disappearing with a flick of its tail. Then he issued a regal wave and drove away.

A lot of corporate groups came to Minaki Lodge for their annual convention. These kinds of outings produced mammoth shore lunches, with sometimes forty people gathered on an island. The guides crouched like galley slaves at a long fire and worked perhaps a dozen frying pans at once. Holding empty plates, the guests lined up like bums at a soup kitchen. Most of the guides were fairly deft comedians, and the banter was incessant and merciless. George Kelly had a son named Johnny who, because of his jet-black ducktail, gravel voice, and habit of playing the guitar for spare change, had been nicknamed Johnny No-Cash by the Anderson brothers. Johnny was a wry storyteller, and while he worked at the fire he sometimes delivered one of his comic monologues, like "Johnny's Trip to Kenora."[*]

By the time the first meals were doled out, the guests would be lining up for a second portion. And by the time the second

[*] "So the judge he says to me he says, 'So do you know why you're here, Kelly? You're here for drinking.' So I says, 'Okay, let's get started.' Everybody in the courtroom starts laughing, eh? So he says, 'Order! Order in the court!' So I says, 'I'll have a rye and Coke, your majesty.'" Etc.

portion was doled out, some of the guests would be expressing deep satisfaction with their lives, rubbing their bellies, lighting cigars, wandering around, and suggesting that maybe it was time to clean up these dishes and get back out on the water. (The sweaty guides, of course, hadn't eaten yet.) One day a fat businessman cleaned off his plate, patted his stomach, and glanced fondly at his buddies. "Well, boys, where are the poor people today?" Squatting by the fire, Johnny No-Cash declared, "They're cooking your lunch."

∾

Towards the end of our week with Lisa and Mickey and Ray and Steve, the wind turned around to the north. The heat had engendered an algal bloom on the lake, and big lime-green waves pounded and thumped against the shore.

On the last day of the party, it was cold and rainy, with squall lines sweeping down the channel like towers of biblical punishment and the peaty smell of the green waves heavy on the wind. As the day progressed the weather worsened. Most tourists would probably have quit at noon. But our party seemed to regard the storm as a sort of survival game, so Glen and I took a short cut across Big Sand Lake, running downwind and side by side through the four-foot waves. Our boats surged like broncos through the rollers and the women yipped with delight. By the time we got back to the Lodge at the end of the day, we were all soaked and frozen.

Glen and I went up to the staff lounge and warmed up while the other guides came in, looking tousle-haired and wild. We sat there eating toast and chili and watching the storm slather the windows. We could see the boats surging as if in slow motion through the whitecaps beneath the bridge. And then a freight train appeared, its orange diesel and black tanker cars rolling slowly across the river. The bridge was the eternal symbol of Minaki, a monstrosity braced with heavy black girders. Sometimes when a train rumbled over it, it was fun to shift the outboard motor into neutral and spin through the turbulent current beneath the girders, looking up through the steelwork at the train's underbelly. Today, I was happy to be watching it from here.

Neither Glen nor I knew it yet, but years from now, on a dark winter midnight, he'd be crossing that bridge on his snowmobile and run into everyone's standard Minaki nightmare, an oncoming freight. He abandoned the machine and tried to get away from the train but didn't make it. The morning after his death I would go looking for some memento of him, searching the snowy girders where he died for a piece of tail light or some scrap of clothing that I could take home to remember my old friend.

Death comes as a surprise to everyone, and a good thing too. Glen and I might not have felt so comfortable, sitting in that log-walled lounge and looking at that rainy bridge, if we'd known it was where his life would end.

After we finished our chili and went down to the shed to clean our fish, Ray came into the shed to give us our tips. Our hands were bloody, so Ray laid the money on the intestine-splattered metal table, slapping down fifties like he was paying for a car. Every time he laid down a few bills he paused and grinned, to tease us, then snapped off a few more. By the time he was finished, there was $600 on the table. He punched our shoulders. "Thanks, boys. You did a great job."

I hadn't made a fortune over the last month, but I'd done all right. In wages and tips, I'd made about $2,500, which would go a long way towards launching my next phase. I didn't know exactly what the next phase was going to be, but I knew it was going to cost money.

∾

The leaves were turning yellow, and the nights were turning cold.

During my long afternoons of guiding, I'd entertained a fantasy about staying in Minaki for the winter, perhaps renting a cottage on the lakefront and fortifying it against the winter. At night, while the north wind scratched and snuffled at the door, I'd sit by my fireplace and work on my novel. By day, I could find some bookish local job (Faulkner was a postmaster) and perhaps learn more about the history of the area, the fur trade, and the traditions of the Indians. I was still trying to establish some kind of working relationship with this country, but I didn't want to put a deadline on it. These projects took time, and they worked best when you went about it indirectly. It was like going fishing. Sooner or later something would happen, as long as you kept your line in the water. But you needed to carry on with your life in the meantime.

Wherever I ended up living, it seemed that I would never escape the universal dilemma of backwoods living – finding a toilet. Like most Canadian bush country hamlets, Minaki is built on bare rock, so houses like The Swamp tended to have no plumbing. The Swamp was nestled in a patch of forest under the bridge. The furnace in the living room had been leaking for so long that the floors and walls were soaked with fuel oil. If you went over there to play cards, you couldn't get the smell of fuel oil out of your cranium for days. But the worst room in The Swamp was the bathroom, with its toilet that consisted of nothing more than a large shit-filled plastic pail with a garbage bag for a liner. The air inside the bathroom was so foul you had to hyperventilate beforehand, as if preparing to duck into a room that was on fire.

One of the guys who lived at The Swamp was a carpenter from Toronto named Tony. He was a broken-nosed ex-hockey player, a thug, but a pleasant guy. He and his wife and kids had discovered Minaki several years before and fallen in love with the place, the lakes, the pristine forests, and had decided to move here. They were tired of the traffic, the lineups, the cost of living, and so here he was, trying to establish himself as a small contractor before he sent for the family.

His bedroom was the only civilized room in The Swamp. He made his bed and hung up his clothes. His wife was always sending him packages of fresh underwear and photographs of the kids. But Tony wasn't having much luck. His construction jobs were always in a state of disaster. He had to drive for hours just to buy lumber. And everything was always going wrong in such cruelly expensive ways that he'd often work a twelve-hour day and come home broker than when he had left in the morning. One night we all played poker and Tony got as drunk as a fifteen-year-old. He wound up crawling into the bathroom and vomiting in the bucket, and when he woke up in the morning discovered that his upper plate was missing.

This wasn't good news. He couldn't afford to lose his dentures. He searched under the bed, under the furniture, and finally summoned the nerve to search in the toilet bucket with a stick, which, as it turned out, was where he'd lost them. I don't know how he cleaned off those teeth; perhaps with bleach? I never had the chance to ask him, because he packed up his van that same afternoon and headed back to Toronto. He was a hard worker, and it was a shame that Minaki lost him. But he was just another of the thousands of people who try to start a new life in the woods and finally give up. There's a common idea that the Big City is the ultimate proving ground for talented and resourceful people. According to people like Frank Sinatra, if you can make it in New York, New York, you can make it anywhere. But it's probably the other way around. If Frank had lived in Minaki, he likely would have ended up selling minnows.

So I lived in the van, took sponge baths, and used public washrooms. I thought about renting a cottage. But the local people told me that winterized cottages were few and far between. And I had certain social aspirations. There was a standard of housing that I wouldn't go beneath. I wanted the kind of place that Jack London or Jack Kerouac might have rented. It could be lacking in class, but it had to lack class in a certain kind of way. Log cabins with rusty woodstoves and squirrels in the walls were okay, but house trailers fitted out with wall-to-wall shag and motel furniture were unacceptable. If I couldn't find a place with a good view of the forest and the lake, I'd go back to the city, which right now didn't seem like such a bad idea. I hadn't written a single paragraph since my departure from Tower Island, and nowadays, the idea of having running hot water and a plug-in typewriter seemed as exotic as any tent camp in the wilderness.

I was sitting in the coffee shop at Holst Point one day, mulling this over, when I looked out the window and saw something out on the river. It was Dave, moving his houseboat. He was pushing it along with his motorboat, and his raven was sitting on the peak of the roof, bobbing its head, squawking, supervising. He was no doubt moving it to some quiet anchorage where it would be safe for the winter. Then it occurred to me, the solution.

∾

Over the next few weeks I made several trips to Winnipeg and purchased several loads of second-hand building supplies – empty forty-five-gallon drums, used planks, second-hand plywood, used windows, and assorted loads of hardware, chimney pipe, insulation, vapour barrier, and roll roofing. I unloaded the whole mountain of stuff on the beach at Murray's Camp, observed by the ever tolerant and solemnly intoxicated Mr. Campbell.

I had no idea what I was doing. But I reasoned that building a home was no different than building an extra-large version of a birdhouse. I felt a bit guilty about copying Dave's idea and believed that I had an ethical obligation to take his original concept and make it better. Late at night, I drew fanciful designs – round windows, ornate swimming ladders, hanging flower baskets, oaken-slab doors with massive iron hinges, and a circular stair leading to a high balcony. I imagined myself sitting up on the balcony in my driftwood easy chair, drinking tea, and surveying the glittering water. I would emulate Sir Henry Thornton and build my very own floating Xanadu:

> In Xanadu did Kubla Khan
> A stately pleasure-dome decree:

Where Alph, the sacred river, ran

Through caverns measureless to man

Down to a sunless sea.

The first step was to decree the foundation, a large square area upon which I could nail up the walls. I considered using a second-hand construction barge for a foundation. But a few phone calls satisfied me that I couldn't afford a barge, not even a second-hand barge, not even a sunken one. In British Columbia they used gigantic cedar logs for flotation, and in Yellowknife they used long sections of heavy-duty petroleum pipe. I didn't have access to either, so I'd decided to use steel barrels.

There were no instruction manuals for this sort of project, so I hauled a bunch of empty barrels into the shallow water off the beach and tried to get them to float in obedient rows while I assembled and hammered together a deck on top of them. This was like herding sixteen toddlers. I'd no sooner get one drum attached when another would bolt from its desk in row number three and wander off. I was working in knee-deep water with my jeans rolled up, and the water was so cold that I could chase drums for only five minutes or so before I had to retreat to the beach to thaw my shins. I didn't know even the basic principles of construction. How did carpenters build a foundation? I crawled underneath one of Don Campbell's rental cabins (observed, with some concern, by the people inside it) and saw that it consisted of two rows of boards – one row of fat boards running one way, and another row of skinnier boards running crosswise on top of them. Every ten feet or so, there was a support post holding up the whole works. Hmm. I could see that there was some logic here. I thought you called the long, fat planks "joyces," but since I was working alone, I didn't worry about terminology. Memorizing the pattern, I lined up eight barrels on shore and built a long set of joyces on top of them. Then I pried and pushed the whole arrangement into the shallow water where, to my delight, it floated.

I then ran a row of long planks across the pontoons, nailed them in place, and began laying down a plywood floor. Once I'd nailed down the plywood, I realized the seams had no support underneath. This was a problem. I foresaw the day when my foot would slip into one of these plywood seams and I'd be caught by the ankle, howling. So I took the floor apart and started over, repositioning the joyces so they corresponded to the sheets of plywood. Then I started building the walls, nailing the two-by-fours in upright rows. The walls were very exciting because they commanded so much space and looked so much like walls. But in no time I ran into the same problem – the seams of plywood didn't match the two-by-four uprights behind them. So again, I tore down and reassembled the walls. It was beginning to occur to me why carpenters always seemed so fussy about measuring things.

Don Campbell seemed interested in my rickety edifice, and now that the tourist season was winding down he occasionally walked down to the beach and offered suggestions. Although he lived alone, he was a bit of a dandy in his own shopworn way, and with his clean-shaven saddlebag jowls and lavish silvery ducktail he looked like he was putting his best foot forward on behalf of the town's elderly widows. "Do you want a bump?" he'd ask, producing a flask of Golden Wedding. I'd unscrew the cap and take a bump, and grimace as the high-octane whisky burned its way into my chest. He'd take the bottle back and study the project. "All right, what's playing today?"

There's something about a floating structure that brings out the Tom Sawyer in people. It seems that everyone has dreamed at one time or another of either writing a novel or living on the water. After watching me work for a while, Don Campbell would often climb onto the deck and offer his expertise. As a carpenter, he felt offended by anything that wasn't fastened with about a dozen spiral nails. Seizing a hammer, he would slash vigorously at the wall until it gleamed with battered nail heads, then he'd give it a satisfied wiggle. "Okay," he'd announce. "That's not going anywhere." His spiral nails made it almost impossible to take anything apart. But he taught me to measure twice before I cut.

The storms of September had settled into the calm, sunny days of October. The water, blue as a flag, was tagged with yellow leaves. It was pleasant to get up in the early morning and see frost sparkling in the grass when I walked up the road for coffee. But my house was going slowly. I'd seen construction projects in which they built a house in a week. I was such an inexperienced carpenter that it took several days to complete the most minor task. At this rate, I wouldn't get the place finished before winter.

One day while I was trying to install a window, I saw a tough-looking Indian guy coming down the road. He was in his early twenties, slanty-eyed and shaven-headed, with a wide-shouldered physique and torn, dirty clothes. He went up to the office and asked Don Campbell if he had any work, but Don told him he was shutting down the camp and didn't need any more help this season. So the young guy came down and watched me work for a while, then climbed onto the deck, unbidden, and began to help out.

I was a little uneasy, because I didn't want to get browbeaten into giving him money. But he was a good worker and didn't ask for anything. His name was Noah Hunter. At one point, I was taking apart a wall with the nail-puller, and thanks to Don Campbell's beloved spiral nails, the wall was fighting me every inch of the way. Noah asked me if he could take a shot at it. I said sure, and handed him the nail-puller. He said he didn't need it. He took a running leap and hit the wall with both feet. There was a frightful bang and the sheet of plywood flew off. I withdrew the nails and fixed the wall in a couple of minutes. After that, we didn't waste time pulling nails or taking boards apart. Noah did the dismantling with his feet. It made me realize that for some people in this world, doors are only a convenience. If you were an executive at Columbia Pictures, and you were trying to duck a meeting with Noah, he'd just come through the wall.

Finally Noah announced it was five o'clock. ("Time to shut her down.") I told him I felt bad about him working for free and offered to give him a few bucks. He said no thanks, a deal was a deal. He said he just wanted to keep busy until he found a job. That evening, in the bar, an off-duty OPP constable approached me and asked if Noah had been causing trouble. I said no, quite the opposite. He said that just the same, be careful, because Noah had just gotten out of the penitentiary, was "extremely dangerous," and that I should call them immediately if he ever showed up with liquor on his breath.

The next day, Noah showed up for work again. He wasn't much interested in fine carpentry, but if there was heavy work to be done, he was your man. He liked manhandling big logs. When he went into the bush to get some firewood (it was getting colder, and we kept a fire in a barrel to warm our hands), he'd disappear for ten minutes. Then I'd see a mountainous tangle of logs coming out of the bush, with Noah's two legs wobbling along beneath. He'd somehow picked up the habit of punctuality in prison and kept an eye on his wristwatch. At twelve o'clock on the nose he'd announce that it was time to "shut her down for lunch." We'd go to Holst Point, and I would buy him two milkshakes and a double order of cheeseburgers and fries. He was an eating machine. You didn't want to get your fingers anywhere near his moving parts. I'd seen enough Jimmy Cagney movies to know better than to ask him why he'd gone to prison. But he said that the penitentiary was "not a bad place." The food was good and the inmates, most of whom were Indians like himself, got along. He'd finished some high school courses, lifted weights, and studied karate. He'd gone to sweat lodge ceremonies and purified himself, learned more about his native heritage. I'd heard that the guards were tough. But Noah shrugged. "Naw . . . they're pretty good guys. This one guard? I borrowed him a smoke? The next day he gave me half a pack."

Meanwhile the houseboat was taking shape. I'd toned down its original fanciful design and had settled on something simpler – your basic wooden box. It's easier to draw turrets, balconies, and widow's walks than to build them. But when it came to building the roof, I was stumped, as was Noah. The typical roof has a ridge down the middle. How do you make the ridge? We didn't know. We considered using a row of support posts. But it seemed like a crude solution. Nobody else's roof had support posts. We pondered the problem, sketched various designs in my notebook, and at one point even considered building a flat roof. Aside from the likelihood that it would spring a leak, I wasn't keen on living in a place that looked like a shipping container.

We called it a day, and Noah asked me if he could borrow my van to drive up to the reserve and visit his family. I could hardly say no, after all he'd done for me. But the next day he didn't come back, and I wondered if I'd made a bad decision. He probably didn't have a driver's licence, which meant that my insurance would be void if he crashed. But the code of the wilderness was to keep your cool, no matter what. Even when it was a matter of life and death, it was incumbent upon the victim to laugh it off. One night at Great Slave Lake, for example, I heard the camp Norseman come droning in for a landing; then suddenly there was a *whack*, like a huge canoe paddle smacking the water. Another guide and I jumped into a boat and sped out to the middle of the lake, where the wreckage of the plane was littered on the water. The boss, the pilot, and the passenger were all treading water among the broken pontoons and boxes of floating groceries. "Sorry to make you guys work overtime," the boss remarked. "Don't apologize to them," said the pilot. "They were probably just worried about the beer." It sounds like bad B-movie dialogue, but it was coming from men who had just finished colliding with rock-hard water at ninety miles per hour, had kicked their way out of a sinking plane, and were trying to stay afloat in water that was only a few degrees above freezing. Maybe people felt obliged to keep their cool under these circumstances because they knew their performance was being observed and would be recounted in bars for years afterward. Whatever the reason, it established a certain rule of decorum, and I wasn't about to get all flustered over a missing vehicle.

I spent the day insulating the walls of my roofless house, and when evening arrived, I got in the boat and went over to Dave's houseboat to ask his advice about building a roof. When I cruised up to his houseboat, I couldn't help noticing the sawed-off head of a bull moose propped on the front deck. He explained that he'd called it by bawling like a cow moose into a birch-bark megaphone ("You pinch your nose and say, 'Ann, Ann . . .' ") and shot it as it came out of the bush fifty steps away. He said it was an old bull, and he felt sorry for it when he saw its scarred head and worn teeth ("He thought he was going to get laid but he got shot"). Now he had four hundred pounds of meat for the winter. He showed me the hindquarters and sliced off a slab of dark meat. "Just fry it up with onions and mushrooms, like a sirloin." He sliced off another one and wrapped them in tin foil. "Give one to Noah, too. I hear he's a pretty interesting guy, been in prison and everything?"

It was the end of a cold October day, so we adjourned to the rustic, pine-panelled pub at Holst Point Resort to discuss the theory and practice of roof construction. The pub stayed open year-round and functioned as the community watering hole. The old-timers sat along the bar, and no one was allowed to take their stools. Johnny Rheault was a former game warden and had a million stories. Connie Gevoga was a train engineer, and when he rolled through Minaki in the middle of the night, he played "Shave and a Haircut" on the locomotive whistle. Another old-timer, a German fellow named Hans, had served as a lance corporal in the Afrika Korps. He was captured by the British, and like thousands of other German soldiers, was brought to Canada and incarcerated in an isolated northern Ontario bush camp.* After the war, Hans was repatriated to Germany and instantly emigrated back here, established a fishing lodge, and started a family. He was a pleasant fellow, and it was hard to believe that such a gentleman could have once fought for Adolf Hitler. But some of the other old-timers in the pub weren't in a big hurry to let him forget it. As Jack Stevens pointed out one night, "I used to get paid fifty cents a day to shoot you bastards."

Most of the younger crowd, my generation, had rolled back and forth across the country like loose pinballs before finally fetching up in this ragged little town at the end of the road. Norman looked like Popeye and came from Liverpool. Evan was a young squash pro from New York. One morning he turned left instead of right, drove north for a thousand miles, and ended up in the yard of Minaki Lodge, where he couldn't go any farther north without driving his van into the lake. Anita was a beautiful girl from Edmonton who'd unrolled a map of Canada one day, closed her eyes, and dropped her finger on Minaki. She had no idea what kind of place it was, but she was ready to take a chance. So she packed everything into her car and drove a

---

* There were six different isolated POW camps on the Lake of the Woods. The prisoners cut wood during the mornings and took the afternoons off. It was a relatively easy life, and no one tried to escape. They built kayaks, held regattas, went fishing, and got paid for their logging work. In the fall, they even borrowed guns from the guards and went hunting. Compared to prisons in Germany, it was like being in a YMCA camp. Sigfried Hauser, a former submariner who spent the war in a POW camp and now lives in Kenora, told me that he fell in love with Canada and Canadians when he was incarcerated here. "Those were the happiest days of my life," he said. His wife, who was serving us coffee at the time, was not amused.

thousand miles. The day she arrived, she met her future husband.

Dave and I sat at a table, sketching roof designs on a cocktail napkin, and our planning session attracted the notice of some of these local folks. Soon, they gathered at the table to talk about the various ways of building a roof. I hoped that Dave, or someone else in this crowd, would actually volunteer to come out and help me build the accursed roof, but they were gracefully ducking the issue. At one point, as Dave sketched a typical truss assembly, I asked him if we could pre-build the trusses on the ground. He looked perplexed. I repeated the question. "What if we just build the trusses on the ground?"

He lifted the flap on my jacket and peered inside. "What . . . have you got a mouse in your pocket?"

"What are you talking about?"

He took a sip of his beer. "You keep saying 'we.'"

Despite their attempts to avoid getting drawn into my little disaster, Dave and the others showed up at the houseboat the following day. The men brought tools and the women brought coffee and sandwiches. It was an old-time barn-raising party. I didn't even know some of the volunteers. Kelly was a big, powerful guy with Harpo Marx hair and a clownish sense of humour. I found out later that he'd been on his way to a serious career in hockey, but had gotten into trouble because he was like Ferdinand the Bull. He refused to fight. His teammates made a few cracks about him being chicken, so he invited them to come at him in the shower room and find out how chicken he was. The hockey career didn't work out, so he moved to Minaki, where he kept law and order in the bar at Holst Point. ("In two years I've never punched anybody.") Long term, he planned to start a canoe-outfitting business with his wife, Sally.

We got to work. Some people sawed and measured. Some nailed down the plywood. I crawled around on the roof, tacking down the shingles. It was a weird feeling up there, with the houseboat canting and shifting in the cold wind, and I kept glancing behind so I wouldn't back off the edge. By four o'clock the roof was finished and we climbed down. Carl Jung once wrote that when we build a house, we're building ourselves. And indeed, as I climbed down the ladder and gazed at the finished roof, I was filled with a new sense of my inarguable status as a human being. I was no longer one of those scoundrels you read about in the police column of "no fixed address." I had a residence, a residence with a roof. And anytime I wanted to change the view, I needed only to rotate the building.

That night I stayed in the houseboat for the first time. As soon as I blew the lantern out it became fiendishly cold. It was hard to get comfortable on my improvised bed of planks laid across a pair of sawhorses. All night long, the houseboat shifted and bumped against the dock, and when I awoke, there was snow on the doorsill. Winter had arrived. My front yard, an immensity of charcoal-dark water, was corrugated by wind. Moving carefully on the icy front deck, I checked the frozen ropes to make sure they had survived the arrival of winter.

While I was checking the ropes, I heard a honk and Noah came coasting down the hill in my van. The van looked fine, and I could tell by his face that he felt bad about showing up late. He parked and climbed out, leapt across the ice-filled culvert, and waded through the snow. He said he'd gotten a flat tire up at the reserve, and it took two days to find the gear to fix it. He said the van was fine now. He'd filled it up with gas and checked the oil. He said he'd decided to move on. He hadn't been able to find any work in Minaki and didn't expect that things would change. "All these goddamn cops," he said.

"Well, good luck, Noah. I know you'll do all right. You're a good man."

"I'll get a job," he said. "There's no way I'm going back to jail."

I didn't run into him again until years later. It was a hot summer day in Thunder Bay, and the streets were jammed with tourists. Turning left, I heard the chirp of a siren and saw flashing lights behind me. Damn, had I made an illegal turn? I shut off the ignition and watched the officer's striped pant legs approach my window. He asked me to step out of the vehicle.

Because of the officer's bulky uniform and dark glasses, it took me a moment or two to recognize Noah's smile. We stood leaning against the cruiser. He told me he'd gone to Aylmer for the training and was now a Special Constable. He took out his wallet and showed me pictures of his wife and kids. He was posted to the same reserve where he'd grown up and got along with everybody, except the local bad boys, who didn't like him because he was a cop. "They throw rocks at my satellite dish."

❧

Long before Noah found a job, long before George Kelly begat Johnny No-Cash, and long before Jacques Cartier bumbled his way along the rocky shores of the St. Lawrence, the village of Minaki was already established.

When I walked along the town at night, I was intrigued by the obscure but undeniable fact that this was an ancient community; older than London, older than Rome. You could walk along canoe portage trails a few miles out of town and crunch your way across thousand-year-old pottery shards. Just north of here, you could climb a high ridge and find a row of mossy boulders arranged in the shape of a gigantic snake. Why was the snake here? Nobody knew, not even George Kelly. Or if he knew, he wasn't saying. I'd met archaeologists who'd told me that this settlement was probably about ten thousand years old. It started when the Pleistocene era ended and the ice sheet that covered most of the northern hemisphere receded and made way for the rise of human civilization and early settlements like this one.

In most modern libraries, the great bulk of historical literature focuses on the rise of humanity in northern Europe and how Europeans brought civilization to the rest of the world. Recently, of course, it has become unfashionable to discuss history in such a lopsided manner. Political niceties must be observed, and smatterings of applause must be offered to the various non-white races that occupied this or that region before the men in leotards and funny hats arrived. But these are token gestures, and most Canadians, let's face it, think that if the aboriginals had been so smart, they would have invaded Europe and figured out some clever way to exploit Europeans, rather than standing by while Europeans invaded their land and exploited them. When the going gets tough, and when government policy gets written, Canadian lawmakers don't take the aboriginals seriously. They sit in Parliament and declare Canada to be a nation of "two founding races," neither of which is the founding one.

In Minaki you could walk along the river at night, where the current rumbled through the black granite under the bridge, and feel the palpable presence of another history, the untold one. Whenever I went to Winnipeg to visit friends and family, I sifted through libraries and government catalogues to acquire whatever materials were available about that untold history. I kept them in a box under my bed and sifted through them each morning, reading them as you'd read the morning newspaper, eating my meals with some faintly photocopied, obscure anthropological journal propped up next to my cereal (*Bear Ceremonialism in the Northern Hemisphere*, 1926).

The publications tended to have low-end production values, and I couldn't find one comprehensive text that gave me an overview of the whole epoch, as did, say, *The Decline and Fall of the Roman Empire*. But that made the investigation more interesting. Each new article prompted a new question. Where were the boundaries between the Indian nations? Who are the Muskego Cree? Who is this man-eater they call the Windigo? What's the Bearwalk? The Shaking Tent? If the Chipewyans live in the Northwest Territories, then why in god's name do they speak the same language as the Navajo?

It was only a hobby, obviously. But just as some readers sharpen their wits on the *New York Times* crossword puzzle each morning, I fiddled with these fragments of confusing and sometimes contradictory history. It was like being a detective or a jungle explorer. Each shard of evidence led down into a deeper and more complicated level than the one before. It was like stubbing one's toe, brushing away the earth to find that the protruding rock was in fact a piece of carved stone, which turned out to be part of a statue, which turned out to be part of a lost civilization.

Minaki was part of the southernmost region of the Shield, occupied by the Ojibway, who were traditionally hunter-gatherers, spending most of the year travelling around in small-ish family groups, living on wild rice, blueberries, smoked fish, and wild game. Their shelter was the birch-bark wigwam and their vehicle was the birch-bark canoe. Each member of the group specialized in different tasks, and being weak or young or old or handicapped was not necessarily an insurmountable problem. Some of the most respected bow and arrow makers were lame or blind. In winter, the group hunkered down and stayed warm by banking snow against their wigwams and sleeping in blankets of woven rabbit fur. It sounds like a hard life. But they worked when the weather cooperated and spent their leisure time playing games, preparing long meals, telling stories, and sewing deer-hide clothing – soft, beautifully beaded shirts and moccasins that for the most part can be found today only in museums. In the summer, the scattered family groups gathered in one large tribal assembly on some windswept point or island for the mid-summer Feast of the Midewiwin.

I'd talked to white people, old people here in Minaki, who remembered summer evenings long ago, when they went to bed listening to the far-off pounding of the Midewiwin drum. The drum was built with much ceremony by a Midewiwin priest. The priest was invariably an old man, because it was impossible to progress to the eighth level, or Sky Lodge, in less than six or seven decades of study. He built the drum over a period of four days. It was important to do it in four days because four was a holy number, corresponding to the circular quadrants of nature, the four winds, the four directions, and the four seasons of the year.

The drum was made of four materials. On the first day he built the body, using a hollowed-out tree, which represented "our plant brothers and sisters with whom we must learn to live in a respectful way." On the second day he attached the head, which was made from deerskin, representing the community of wild animals. (The skin of the deer was also believed to impart an agility and grace to the drumbeat.) On the third day he filled the drum half full with water, to symbolize the blood of Mother Earth. And on the fourth day the old priest opened a plug and blew into the drum, symbolizing the breath of life. He then carved a living root into the shape of a loon's head, and with this drumbeater, he "sounded the drum's voice" four times.

The sound was carried by the wind in four directions and summoned the people to the lodge to begin the healing ceremony. As the singing and the drumming drifted across the water on a mid-summer night, one can imagine the local missionary rolling his eyes in dismay, and the early cottagers thinking that it sounded like a wild party. But the building of the drum was a ritual of what the Catholics call "transubstantiation," that is, a process by which a material object (such as bread) is transformed into the body of Christ. To the Ojibway, the sound of the drum drifting across the lake on a quiet summer night was the thumping of the Creator's heart.

The Midewiwin priests recorded these sacred teachings on birch-bark "instruction scrolls," which prescribed the methods for living a healthy, balanced life, and they stored the scrolls in secret places. The author and artist Selwyn Dewdney (whose son Christopher is likewise an author) became one of the first white people to learn about the scrolls when he visited a man named Jim Red Sky on Lake of the Woods. It was 1960, and Jim Red Sky lived in a remote log cabin accessible only by canoe. According to Dewdney, Jim Red Sky was a large husky man with an "air of serenity I had sensed in many of the elders I had interviewed across the country." Inside that old log cabin he and Jim Red Sky talked about the Midewiwin, a religion about which Dewdney knew very little. Eventually, Red Sky produced seven scrolls from beneath his bed. Jim Red Sky was an educated man, and conversant with the Bible. But he maintained "there's that much and more in the Midewiwin."

Red Sky was one of the very last of the great Midewiwin priests, and after he died, he gave the scrolls to Dewdney, who gave them to the Glenbow Museum. Years later, Dewdney produced a definitive and hard-to-get book on the subject called *Sacred Scrolls of the Southern Ojibway*. I acquired Dewdney's book and hunted down other, more antiquarian texts, like *The Ojibway Indians Observed*, by Fred K. Blessing.

As I studied these books, I sometimes thought about the birch-bark scroll that Martin and Lillian had discovered. I liked the idea that it was written in code, and that it was still out there somewhere, hidden in a crevice on some unnamed cliff facing east.

∾

Meanwhile I was slowly becoming a citizen of Minaki.

I never thought I'd wind up living in a small backwoods community without a single bookstore, library, or even magazine stand. But human beings tend to draw together in like-minded groups, and most of my new friends were young urban people on the lam who, like me, were trying to start their lives again from scratch.

I was enjoying building my house, learning all the things they don't teach in school. I'd insulated the walls and ceiling, and built a kitchen, dining area, and cozy sleeping loft. I was heating it with firewood, and it was so warm inside that even on the most savagely cold winter night, I could rise from bed at three a.m., go outside jaybird naked, tiptoe barefoot across the ice, pry another frozen log from the pile, gaze up at the millions of stars, pause for a moment to listen to the abdominal, never-ceasing grumble of the ice, and then pad back inside. I didn't have to rush, because after tossing the log into the stove, I could climb back into my great fluffy Woods Arctic 5 Star eiderdown flannel-lined survival sleeping bag (a gift from my parents, who, I think, were beginning to vicariously participate in my wilderness adventure) and soon enough, as the log began snapping in the heater, I could drift back to sleep, worried not in the least about the house getting cold, but hoping, perhaps, that it wouldn't get too hot.

I was becoming part of the community too. Once a month there was a town hall meeting, a genuine town hall meeting – not the kind of staged event that has become so popular on CBC television – during which issues of the day were debated. On the matter of the village acquiring its own cemetery, for example, some of the young people proposed that the older folks, the pioneers, deserved a dignified resting place. But the old folks themselves begged to differ. As old Jim Hayward put it, "Those old buggers don't need a cemetery. Just sharpen their feet and pound them into the swamp."

After the issues were resolved, a list of jobs was posted on the wall. Everyone volunteered for something, and if you couldn't find a voluntary job you were expected to devise one. Some people shovelled the hockey rink. Others organized the Saturday night dances, which were crowded, bacchanalian, dance-your-ass-off affairs that took place at the community hall.

I volunteered to work as a roving correspondent for the local eight-page newspaper, *The Minaki News*. I printed up a laminated PRESS identification tag and used it when I wanted to interview a government official or cadge a ride on a Ministry helicopter to the scene of the action (*Forest Fire Charges Minaki!*).

I also managed Classic Cinema Night, a regular Sunday event in which everyone would gather at the town hall, buy a bag of home-made popcorn, and sit on plywood chairs in the dark, watching some hoary classic like *Double Jeopardy* or *King Solomon's Mines*. My duties as movie host were simple – making the popcorn, refrigerating the drinks, doing a little bookkeeping, and drawing the promotional posters and putting them up around town. Every two weeks I'd drive to Winnipeg (which I enjoyed doing anyway), pick up the cases of film, and, theoretically, preview the movies to make sure they were complete. The only part I didn't enjoy was the previewing. Who wants to wreck a movie by watching it ahead of time?

So I avoided that part, and ordinarily it wasn't a problem. Once, however, I rented *Psycho* and designed a series of lurid posters and tacked them up all over town. We managed to get a full house for Sunday night, and at the climax of the film, where Tony Perkins pops up in a flower print dress and goes after the police detective with a huge butcher knife, the reel made a sudden flapping sound and the projector ran out of film. Hmm, obviously a major malfunction. I searched the cases, but there was no more film. Apparently some craven swine had rented this film, ruined it, and not told the agency. Everyone left in disgust, and after they were gone, ten-year-old Pokey Savoyard and a few of her wide-eyed little friends followed me around, earnestly explaining that they didn't understand the ending.

Along with my civic duties, I had to make a living. I'd managed to get an occasional shift at Minaki Lodge, working as night watchman, and all night long I was the sole occupant of the spooky chateau. With a flashlight and time clock, I explored its dark basements and deserted dining halls, observed by fanged bears as I walked through the Trophy Room. My sole duty was to make the rounds every hour, so there was lots of time to write or to read a scary novel. (Stephen King's *The Shining* was considered mandatory on-the-job training.) The shift finished at eight a.m., and I'd walk home through the crisp winter morning, past the bay, parts of which stayed open no matter how cold the weather, past the stands of trees laden with hoarfrost from the mist that incessantly poured off the blue river, and arrive at my houseboat just as the winter sun was topping the trees and swathing the white shoreline with mauve shadows. Inside the houseboat the fire had usually gone out, the floor was cold, and the windows were coated with paisley swirls of frost. I'd split a couple of logs, stuff them in the heater, and get them going with broken kindling and newspaper. The main advantage of cheap sheet-metal woodburners (or "Indian heaters" as they were known hereabouts) was that they threw off a ferocious wall of heat, and in no time the houseboat would be warm again.

I'd sleep all day, and come late afternoon I'd wake up, put the kettle on, and do it all over again. The houseboat had no running water, no electrical hook-up, and no heating except the woodburner. It wasn't as primitive as an Ojibway wigwam, but it was pretty basic, and spending the winter in it gave me an appreciation for the hardships the Indians must have weathered hundreds of years ago. My first winter in Minaki was the coldest in sixty years, with two record-breaking blizzards that piled high pagoda-shaped snowdrifts all along the lee side of the house. But my impressions of that winter weren't so much hard as vivid – the sharp, clean bite of the air; the silence of early morning, a silence so vast that you could hear the creaking of a raven's wings; the orange sunrise spilling across the white lake; the green snow-laden spruces along the shore; and when I got home from my night's work, the happy crude, solid appearance of the houseboat, frozen stubbornly into the lake, blanketed under an immense Bavarian roof of snow.

A dainty ellipsis of tracks near my door would tell me if my buddy, a beautiful red fox, had visited while I was gone. If he came when I was at home, he'd announce his presence with sharp *yap* at the door. When I opened the door he'd shy away, but I'd prop it open with a broom and resume my work inside. Eventually, his face would peer in the doorway. He'd scrutinize the interior, ensuring there were no unfamiliar humans with me, then trot inside, giving me a polite look that said, Got anything to eat?

I was wary of feeding him by hand (childhood memories of catching hydrophobia and being chained to a tree), so at first I wore gloves when I fed him. He had perfect manners though, and soon I was feeding him with my bare fingers. As soon as I relinquished the snack he would wheel around and trot out the door. One night he showed up with two comrades – another red fox and a lovely black cross fox with yellow eyes. They seemed shocked by the first fox's behaviour. But then I began giving him biscuits and they saw his logic. Within minutes they were circling me like trout, darting in to grab a biscuit when they could, and my own fox was getting upset, making little throaty noises and hip-checking them to keep them away from his pet human.

A bit of warm weather during the winter had a remarkable effect on everyone's spirits. Could this mean spring was coming? Even in February a bit of a thaw had everyone cheerfully remarking, "Well, the worst of it's behind us now." Never mind that in this part of the country the month of March usually delivered up some of the nastiest weather of the year. A big pickle jar appeared on the counter next to the cash register at the grocery store, and for one dollar you could buy a ticket and write down your estimate of the precise date and time that the river would break up.

The arrival of spring was a mixed blessing. The locals told me that sometimes the ice went out quietly. And sometimes, pushed by strong winds, it tore up everything in its path. Anyone with buildings or docks along the shore stood to lose everything in a violent breakup, so there was always lots of debate about the signs – the perceived "blackness" of the ice, the predictions of the *Farmer's Almanac*, the rumoured arrival of the first crows, and countless other folkloric indicators that were ordinarily wrong.

In April the weather changed rapidly. The arctic air mass was weakening, and when it fell away in mid-April, a huge southerly flow of warm air gushed into the Shield country. Within days, temperatures shot up and the snow turned to slop, then to puddles, then to sheets of liquid sunlight pouring down the paved hill. The first winter I stayed in the houseboat, I kept a log and recorded the weather every day. The tropical air mass rode into town on the twenty-first in the middle of the night, and by nine in the morning it was warm enough to work outside in a T-shirt. The snow around the houseboat was white and crisp, but the sun was radiant. And when I looked at my shadow on the wall of the building, I could see a blurry mirage pouring off the head, like one of those spirit photographs that purportedly capture the image of a soul leaving a body.

Later in the day I went for a walk along the shoreline, wearing shorts and sunglasses, getting sunburned in the glare. The lake ice was still solid, but had turned black and was as bare as concrete. Boulders as large as overstuffed sofas were lined up along the shore, deposited there in years past by the ice. In the channel near the lodge I tiptoed past "air holes" – spooky cavities that revealed the deep water underfoot. The air holes widened by the hour and were surrounded by "candle ice," supple stuff that jingled like pop bottles in the wind.

A week later, in the middle of the night, the south wind began blowing hard. The trees moaned and creaked outside my bedroom window. At six a.m., I was awakened by the boom and snap of cracking lumber. The ice was going out.

I hopped out of bed. In the predawn light, I could see the neighbour's docks shearing off. Great sheets of crumbled ice were pushing the wrecked docks up into the trees. There was no way to protect the houseboat. All I could do was take my manuscripts, books, and personal effects and load them into the van. At the coffee shop the waitress told me that some people were fighting ice in Town Bay, so I went to watch. The wind was blowing harder now, a warm wind that carried the smells of spruce forest and thawing ground, and a dozen boats and barges were going back and forth like lawn mowers in the shattered ice of the bay, chewing at the front edges of the floes.

I went down to the marina and launched my boat – a wooden one I'd acquired the year before. It was a lapstrake cruiser with a mahogany deck and a windshield. I'd bought it at the end of the summer from the marina manager, who told me that nobody wanted wooden boats any more, and that if I gave him a couple of hundred dollars, it would save him the trouble of burning it. I cleaned it up, sanded it down, and after a few coats of white paint and varnish it looked sharp. It came equipped with an old 40-horse Johnson that ran fine. The motor had been covered by snow all winter, but it started right away. Shifting it into gear, I cruised off to save my houseboat.

The river was choked with ice, and it appeared impossible to make it around the peninsula to Murray's Camp. But I sneaked through by taking long circuitous detours, worming the boat through cracks between the floes. When that didn't work, I broke the ice – not by ramming it, but by running the boat up on top and letting the boat's weight crack the ice underneath. When I reached Murray's Camp, I found the houseboat sitting blessedly intact in an expanse of blue water. A protruding spur of granite had protected it. But if the wind had come from a different direction, it would have been destroyed.

For the next few hours, I butted and steered the drifting floes away with my boat, which was a pleasant job, reminiscent of those boyhood days when you carved drainways in the street to hurry winter on its way. By nightfall, the big southerly was still clocking around to the west and losing its strength. When the sun rose the next morning, the air was balmy and quiet. I untied the houseboat and pushed it away from shore, climbed into the little wooden runabout and swung around behind it. Nosing the prow of my boat against the houseboat's rear end, I gave the motor a shot of throttle and the houseboat moved. Soon the building was budging ponderously forward.

How exciting to have a floating house! Saying goodbye to Murray's Camp, I pushed my home past Minaki Lodge, under the train bridge, and slowly headed off down the river. You couldn't see a single fleck of ice anywhere. The sun was strong, the water was flat and blue, and it was the first day of spring.

ॐ

The longer I lived in Minaki, the more I began to feel the primitive stirrings of something you could almost call a social conscience.

When I first arrived here, unloaded my freighter canoe, and headed down the river, I didn't hesitate to liberate Tower Island for the cause. But lately, it had begun to dawn on me that someone else might want to use it once in a while. After all, it was one of the most beautiful camping spots in the whole area. So I decided to move the houseboat to Virgin Island, where Dave parked his. On the south flank of Virgin Island, a broad shelf of bleached granite sloped into the lake, and I anchored my houseboat down the shoreline a short distance from Dave's. This island didn't have the cathedral pines and hushed magnificence of Tower Island. But it was a sheltered spot, with clear water for swimming, only a few miles from town, and when I stepped outside at night, the only lights I could see were the stars.

Dave and I were still working as guides, and we often carpooled to work. At six-forty-five in the morning, with the sun already high above the mirrored lake, we'd cruise into town in his cedar-strip Peterborough boat, drinking coffee and savouring a few minutes of quiet before launching into the twelve-hour day. Like most young men, I'd had many jobs in my life, most of which could have been performed by a well-trained chimpanzee. Guiding was the hardest job I'd ever had, and the fact that I was only modestly good at it sharpened my respect for the individuals who did it well. There were several dozen fishing guides working the river, and if you drew their abilities on a chart, it might resemble a diagram of the tree of evolution. At the bottom end of the chart you'd find the most primitive skills – the ability to, say, talk without using the f-word more than once in each sentence, and operate a boat without endangering your guests' lives. You had to be able to catch a few fish, cook a shore lunch that didn't have too many ants doing the backstroke in the creamed corn, and find your way around the complexities of the river system without T-boning a reef. The next limb of the tree would feature a more evolved package of skills.

The better the guides, the less they rely on expertise. Deep water is the repository of all the world's secrets, and you can't get at the information with skills you learned from a fishing magazine. Like the subconscious, the lake is a realm of dreams, populated by transient shadows, and after all the techniques of guiding have been practised, you still need to be a bit of a magician to conjure up the fish. Writers have to throw a line into the unconscious and try to come up with an insight, and fishing guides meet the same challenge every day, facing the blank page of the river. Right at the narrows in front of Minaki Lodge, the river system separates off into myriad directions, and when a guide fires up his boat in the morning, he has to review dozens of options for pursuing the quest. He has to consider the weather, water temperature, cloud cover, season, month, and week. He has to think about where the fish are this morning, not where they were yesterday morning. If the walleyes were ganged up on the Rockpile yesterday, he can assume they aren't there today. And he can't afford to drive seventeen miles to a place where the fish were biting yesterday. In the end, all the knowledge in the world produces a guide who is merely competent. The best guides have a mystic gift. Whatever it is, they out-fish the merely competent guides by an embarrassing margin, every day.

I had some of my old guests from the year before, and some new ones besides. Along with the usual array of ordinary tourists, my guest list included four gorillas from Detroit who owned a fleet of garbage trucks ("Hey Angie . . . you hear that? The kid wants to know if the mob's involved in the garbage business!"); a handsome middle-aged former Green Beret who spoke fluent Vietnamese, had spent time in many evil places and done many terrible things, and who spent half an hour in heavy waves one day, trying to revive a dying fish; and a television pitchman who'd invented the Vegomatic and the Miracle Knife (*And look! You can even cut your shoe in half!*).

With such an array of guests, I sometimes felt like I was hosting a floating talk show (*Good Morning, Minaki!*), with swivel boat seats instead of couches and pine trees instead of tropical plants in the background. In the depths of winter, this little northern bush town sometimes felt like the ass-end of the earth. But now that summer was blooming, there wasn't another place in North America where I would rather be. Another armada of university girls had arrived to work at the various resorts and tourist lodges in the area, and the local bachelors were making up for a long winter. (As Dave ruefully noted one morning, "It's not so much a problem of persuading them to come out to the houseboat for a drink, it's a problem of persuading them to go home.") There were bonfires, dances, masquerade nights, scavenger hunts, and late-night screaming parties in hot tubs, with overflowing mobs of people knotted into great garter-snake mating tangles of slithery flesh. In early June, Dave and I bought a piglet for five dollars and set him loose on the island. By the end of the summer he weighed eighty pounds. We shot him in the head and eviscerated him, lashed him to the drive shaft of a Datsun truck, and cranked him over a fire all day.

A hundred people showed up for the party. We had a generator powering the amplifiers and a dance floor in the woods. People were doing the pogo and jumping in the lake naked. Someone slashed his hand open with a machete and had to be evacuated to the hospital in Kenora. Someone else fell in the fire, rolled around, got up on his knees, shook off the flames, and rose to his feet without a mark. ("It's a miracle!") We had amplified dance music and live guitar accompaniment by Sal, another city boy who'd come here looking for God, and who sported a long lush rock star hairdo, knee-high boots, cape, and mystical rings. (The Andersons had named him Quest for Fire.) Sal was not an outdoorsman. He'd had a hard time finding his way out to our island and had an even harder time finding his way home. On the theory that he would simply follow the same route he'd taken on the way out, only in reverse, he drove home looking backwards. He was going wide-open when the boat hit the shore, and the impact threw him forty feet into the woods.

The summer was a great frolic. But when autumn came, and all the university kids went back to school, and the summer resorts nailed plywood on their windows, and the river turned bitterly cold, and yellow leaves skittered down onto the black water, I found myself looking forward to some peace and quiet. I looked forward to cutting up a good supply of firewood, rustling up a freezer full of wild game, hanging out with the old-timers, and settling into another winter in this town, my home.

So the years went past. Calendar leaves ripped off and tumbled away on the wind. I hadn't lost interest in searching for the Big Answer. But in the backwoods, everyday life is complicated. Like a fisherman, I dealt with whatever rewards and frustrations came along, and trusted that sooner or later I'd catch a glimpse of the Almighty. The first sign that the game was once again afoot appeared, one bright spring day, with the arrival at Murray's Camp of a freshly waxed, chrome-bedecked Ontario Provincial Police car.

I was working outside. The sun was beating down on the black ice all around the houseboat, and I'd assembled a rickety catwalk of old boards to provide a gangway to the main dock. The ice was rotting on an hourly basis, and because of its crumbly nature it would have been bad to fall through. I had lots of friends who'd put snow machines through the ice, put trucks through the ice, for that matter, and so many people had drowned around here – since I'd arrived, even – that you needed all your fingers to count them. But thinking about safety all the time is kind of boring. So I was casually trying to figure out how to cross the ice without drowning when the police car swung into the driveway.

I assumed the cops were coming to see Barry Gibson, the new owner of Murray's Camp. (Don Campbell had died over the winter.) Barry was a middle-aged commercial artist from Winnipeg who'd shucked off the city life and moved his wife and kids to Minaki. Being an advertising man and somewhat of a bohemian type, Barry didn't seem to mind having riffraff like me tied up to his dock. He regularly hosted Sunday dinners to which I was invited, as long as I contributed my nasal honkings to the after-dinner sing-along. He and his family had converted

Murray's Camp into a mail-order sweater company, based on Ojibway designs drawn and created by local matriarchs like Pearl Chicago, and it wasn't unusual to see police cars pulling into the driveway at all hours, driven by some cop coming to pick up a skein of wool for his wife.

For some reason Minaki boasted a generous supply of cops. They always looked a bit furtive, doing private errands on company time, but you couldn't blame them. They were waiting for all hell to break loose, and there wasn't much to do in the meantime. They drove around, hung out at the coffee shop, and spent a lot of time sprucing up their neat red-brick detachment building. When you drove by, you'd see them checking and re-checking their equipment, cutting the grass, manicuring the multicoloured flower beds, raising, lowering, and saluting the flag, and monkeying about on the broad driveway with Turtle Wax and soft rags, polishing the patrol cars until bullets of sunlight flashed off the chrome. I didn't mind having them around, nor did anyone else. It made this feel like a real town. And on a muddy April day such as this, with sheets of meltwater running down the roads and the slop, garbage, dead birds, dog shit, and general dross of winter thawing everywhere in the bright sun, it was actually quite cheering to see one of their white-stocking police cars tippytoeing through the puddles, bearing missives from Her Majesty the Queen.

The car stopped and Constable Fred Seyn climbed out. I knew most of the constables, and Fred Seyn was the most imposing – a towering, broad-shouldered, blocky-headed man who looked like he'd been built in someone's basement. Despite his intimidating appearance, Fred had the pleasant voice and doting manner of a kindergarten teacher, and he presented quite a sight at the community dances, where, with his tiny wife, he lurched about the dance floor, wagged his arms, dripped sweat, and rolled his eyes with such abandon that you wondered if he was going through some kind of brain seizure. (The Andersons called him Fred Insane.) I assumed that Fred was here to buy some knitting wool for his wife, but instead, he came down to the dock and asked me if I was interested in part-time work at the police station. He said they needed a civilian employee of "exemplary character" who could work an occasional midnight shift. The responsibilities entailed answering the phone, minding the office, and keeping an eye on prisoners who were held in the lock-up overnight. The pay was good ($19 per hour) and it was usually about a ten-hour shift, starting in the late evening and ending at eight in the morning.

I told him it sounded interesting.

He said, "Can you work tonight?"

For the next few months I worked one or two shifts a week. The cops on the evening shift worked until one or two in the morning, then went home to bed. Until they came back to work at eight in the morning, I was responsible for their prisoners, who were usually local native people who'd been picked up for minor assaults or liquor offences. I knew most of them and had worked with some of them on fishing parties. But they never seemed the least bit confused when I materialized at the door of their cell. ("Hey, Jakes, gimme some water, eh?") They were in jail because they were Indians. And I wasn't in jail because I was white. They understood the system so completely that it bored them to think about it. After guzzling their water, passing a few pleasantries ("Son of a bitch, I got really jagged up, eh?"), they would hand me the plastic pitcher, curl up on the rubber mattress on the floor of their cell, and go back to sleep. I'd lock the main steel door and return to the waxen silence of the brightly lit office, where I'd sit in front of the typewriter and try to remember how my last sentence was supposed to end.

It was a perfect job for a hobbyist writer. The office was equipped with a toll-free telephone, stacks of neat white paper, and ultra-modern IBM typewriters. After I wrote my requisite five hundred words, I would brew up a pot of coffee and recline in the swivel chair and read a book or, failing that, the office's stack of dog-eared law enforcement magazines, ads for ballistic vests, and so on. The nights were long and empty, and obviously I was supposed to remain vigilant, being the eyes and ears of the sleeping town, etc. (One night while I sat with my feet on the desk, reading *The Art of Fiction*, a house across the road burned to the ground.)

The VHF radio crackled monotonously, keeping me company. Most of the radio traffic was from northern Ontario, but sometimes, through the vagaries of atmospheric skip, the monitor delivered snippets of radio chatter from all over North America. Sometimes so many domestic assaults, stolen autos, corner store holdups, and motor vehicle smash-ups were leaking out of the radio at once, it gave me the odd feeling that this small, clean, brightly lit office functioned as a sort of hell-gate for all the bad news in North America. One night, stepping outside in my stocking feet, I stood on the lawn and pulled the cold air into my lungs, shivered, and imagined the curve of the planet, stretching all the way down into the Gulf of Mexico. High above the radio tower on the roof of the police station were the incomprehensible stars. Living in the bush country, so much of your time is spent in distracted awareness of the stars, the daunting abyss of the night sky, knowing that you're not just living in the Canadian Shield but also the Milky Way.

Pondering that sky, and coming up with the usual inconclusive results, I turned to re-enter the office and discovered that I'd goofed. As a security feature, the door locked automatically, and I'd locked myself out. My first concern was for my prisoners. What if there was a fire? It was just a flimsy aluminum door, and I considered finding a rock and breaking the glass, but that seemed a little drastic, given that this was Minaki, so I set off for the sergeant's house, hobbling on the sharp gravel road in my socks.

Sergeant Tom Cooper lived in one of the trailers in Pig Hollow, about half a mile away. I hated to wake him up, given the fact that he'd gone home only a few hours ago. But when I rang his doorbell he stumbled to the door, all rheumy-eyed and dishevelled, and looked relieved when he found out that it wasn't anything more serious. He drove me back to the office and unlocked the door without a word of criticism. His equanimity seemed based not just on his mild temperament, but also on the fact that getting rousted from bed at three in the morning was a normal part of his life.

Tom Cooper supervised the detachment and spent a lot of his off-duty time fishing. Like most of the cops, he wasn't much of an outdoorsman, and he always looked kind of quaint out there on the river, this hound-faced old-timer sitting by himself in his little tin boat. He was a bachelor, and in the evenings, when he was off duty, he would go for dinner at the Filling Station coffee shop. He was a friendly sort and was pleased if you sat at his table and joined him for dinner. Trouble was, he always insisted on buying. And he'd do it sneakily, winking at the waitress when you weren't looking or slipping her his charge card. So there was a kind of invisible circle inscribed around Tom Cooper's table, within which you couldn't venture or he'd buy your meal. I'd sit across the aisle from him, and the other regulars would sit over on the other side of the aisle, and we'd all eat at a safe distance, talking to him from across the room.

One hot summer afternoon at Grassy Narrows First Nation, someone phoned the OPP dispatcher and complained that a gas-sniffer named Tommy Pahpesay was firing random shots with a .22 rifle. In a city, a middle-aged supervisor like Tom Cooper would never be required to handle a firearms complaint. But in the bush, you have to improvise. So Cooper and his young partner, Kevin Orchard, went to check it out. As he approached Pahpesay's house, Cooper didn't even draw his gun. It wasn't his style. He knocked on the door and shouted hello, and from within the darkened interior of the house Tommy Pahpesay stepped out and shot him between the eyes.

Pahpesay then shot Constable Kevin Orchard and took off into the bush. A few days later, during a massive aerial and ground search, Pahpesay popped out of the woods and shot Constable Bill Olynik, an exceptionally pleasant fellow who lived next door to my parents at Laclu and often came over to help them with their heavy chores. Olynik survived, albeit with serious health difficulties, and so did Kevin Orchard, but Cooper was dead when he hit the ground. When Tommy Pahpesay was captured, he gave no reason for the rampage. They were cops; that was the reason. Along with a thousand other people, I went to Cooper's funeral. And nowadays, the big patrol boat on the Lake of the Woods is named after him.

But that particular summer, Cooper hadn't been murdered yet. And one afternoon, while we sat in his office figuring out whether he needed me to work that evening, Constables Jimmy

Calder and Arvinder Parmar came into the office. They were on their way up to the Whitedog reserve, where they usually worked night patrol. Arvy Parmar was a newcomer to Minaki, and he wasn't someone you wanted to stand beside when you were feeling unhappy with your hair. He was the handsome elder son of a Sikh major in the British Army, and with every aspect of his bearing, from his posture to his pressed slacks, he was rigid and sharp as a sabre.

His partner, Jimmy Calder, was a broad-shouldered Ojibway with a wispy Charlie Chan moustache. He'd once played semi-pro hockey and now worked as a special constable in Whitedog. He and Arvy were a relatively new sight around town, and they billed themselves as a sort of super-hero crime-fighting team – the Brown Rice Indian and the Wild Rice Indian.

While they prepared to leave for the reserve, I asked Jimmy Calder if he disliked being called an Indian. Jimmy said it was one of those words that bothered some people and didn't bother others. You had groups like the Saskatchewan Federation of Indians, the Manitoba Indian Brotherhood, the Indian Land Claims Commission. But some leaders, political figures and so on, thought that the word "Indian" was insulting. They preferred the term "First Nations people." He shrugged and sipped at his coffee. "Me, I just call myself an Ojibway."

I asked him if there were still medicine men up at the reserve. He said there wasn't much knowledge of the old ways any more. When the missionaries took the kids off to residential school, they made them speak English and pray to Jesus. If they spoke their own language they got a licking. "I wish I was working in those days," said Jimmy. "I'd have thrown their asses in jail. You imagine that? Taking a kid away from his family? Then every time he talks, hitting him with a yardstick?"

Jimmy said that the residential schools "pretty much broke the circle." He said that the only one who knew much about the old ways was Roy McDonald, the current chief at Whitedog. "He still does the drum ceremony and some other stuff."

I asked him if he could introduce me to the chief sometime.

Jimmy shrugged. "You could probably come up with us tonight, if you want."

I already knew Roy by sight because we often passed each other on the road. Roy drove a blue truck, and you couldn't miss him because he was the only one on the highway who waved with such gusto. Everybody waved, in these parts, but most wavers only extended a couple of grudging fingers, or perhaps resignedly displayed a palm. Roy's wave was a vigorous polishing motion, rendered with such a pronounced twist of the head and merry smile that you had to wonder if you were perhaps a more entertaining fellow than you realized. I'd always wanted to meet Roy and wondered if he'd be a good one to get access to the scroll that Martin and Lillian had found. Tom Cooper told me he could get by without me for the night shift, so half an hour later, I climbed into the police truck with Constables Calder and Parmar and we headed north to Whitedog.

On the way to the reserve, Jimmy Calder told me about his own upbringing. He was lucky enough and young enough to have missed the residential school program and had decided to go into law enforcement because his hockey coach was a well-respected and tough old OPP sergeant. He told me about his dad, who was a trapper, and his grandfather, who lived in the bush and spoke no English. You didn't have to go back too many generations around here to drop right into the culture of Stone Age hunter-gatherers. In his own culture, Jimmy's grandfather would have had an Ojibway name, which was usually a single word about as long as a freight canoe. But at some point, during the last three hundred years, his family had taken on a Scottish surname, which seemed odd unless you happened to know that at the beginning of the fur trade, the Hudson's Bay Company had used Orkney Islanders as trading post managers. At first, the HBC had employed only well-educated young Englishmen, who had seemed like good prospects during the interview process, but once posted to the northern bush had fallen apart under the corrosive drip of loneliness and lust and warehouse rum. So the HBC administrators looked farther afield and finally settled on the Orkneymen, a ruddy-cheeked and uncomplaining breed of Scot who liked rough weather, were handy with boats and tools, and were willing to work for $12 a year. The Orkneymen had names like Scott and Kent and Fobister and Calder. And the native trappers they traded with often adopted their clothing, tools, and surnames.

The reserve was an hour's drive from Minaki, and the rough turnoff was marked by a large and quite beautiful hand-painted plywood billboard that some local art critic had ventilated with a shotgun. Due to the sudden and violent bouncing of the truck, I could tell exactly where the road passed from the provincial highways jurisdiction to the Department of Indian Affairs. After a few miles of violent washboard, we pulled into the community, which wasn't so much a community as a scattering of several hundred prefabricated houses planted on an open muddy hillside above the Winnipeg River. The houses were painted in the queasy colours that seem standard to any government-sponsored undertaking – latrine green, hospital blue, and antacid pink. The yards of the houses were full of weeds, bulldozed mud, pools of water, and derelict car bodies.

The police detachment was a black and white Atco trailer with a stack of pallets for front steps. On the inside it had a battered metal floor, plywood walls, and a couple of rickety desks. Arvy said they'd take me to meet the chief, but they needed to attend to a few chores first. The constables reviewed their paperwork and answered a couple of phone calls. I moved to the far end of the room and sat on a plywood chair, which promptly collapsed. This was probably the northernmost, road-accessible OPP detachment in this part of Ontario, and I could see that Parmar and Calder hadn't been given much in the way of first-class equipment with which to apply the majesty of the law.

Arvy said they had to respond to a complaint about gas-sniffers. We drove across the reserve, parked the Suburban, and climbed out. It was a picturesque spot, a warm summer evening. The river was bright, and far off in the west, the sunset burned. As we walked down the muddy trail, a million dandelion seeds drifted like embers in the low light. We walked in single file towards a low-slung abandoned building with sheets of fresh plywood nailed to the windows. It looked like an old school or hospital, some kind of government centre. We climbed up and down over humps of dried construction mud and descended into a pit where a small hole had been torn in the wall. "I'd like everyone to see this," Arvy said, as if speaking to no one.

He drew the flashlight from his belt, bent down, and slipped into the hole. We followed him. The interior was utterly dark; it looked to be a long hallway strewn with plaster and torn mattresses. The walls were covered with spray-painted obscenities and splatters of flung stuff which, judging from the smell, was dried excrement. We walked down the hall, and the policemen tilted their flashlight beams into the adjoining rooms. Gradually

I became conscious of breathy noises in the darkness – small children, perhaps six or eight of them, barely making a sound. It was eerie, almost frightening, to see them walking beside me. I thought the cops didn't notice until Jimmy, almost absently, reached down and ruffled a boy's hair. "How are ya doing?"

The policemen spent five minutes prowling through the darkness. Arvy climbed across a heap of trash and went into one room, where he pried and poked through overturned furniture, sniffing here, sniffing there, until he finally found a plastic water jug. He screwed off the cap and held it to his nose. "Here's the gas," he said. He looked at the group of kids. "Is this yours?"

One of them nodded.

"Now it's mine," he said.

Another kid was touching Arvy's gunbelt. "Is that for shooting people?"

"Police don't shoot people," he said, in the rote manner of a grammar teacher. "They help people."

"We're going to clear all you kids out of here," said Jimmy. "Come on, let's go."

They herded the kids down the darkened corridor, towards the ragged hole of daylight. Climbing out the hole into the sweet dusk of the summer air was like emerging from some particularly fetid nailed-off corner of your own imagination. Jimmy dragged a big sheet of construction plywood over to the aperture and reapplied it, using a flat rock to pound in the nails. "Don't be coming back here," Jimmy said, glowering at the kids. "You understand?"

"We'll be checking," said Arvy.

Back at the road Arvy opened the tailgate of the truck, put the jug of gas inside. The prisoner's cage in the back of the truck had sheet metal benches and a rail for attaching manacles. Even after quite some time working at the Minaki jail, I still wasn't accustomed to the brute furnishings of the everyday justice system. The kids clustered at the entrance of the cage. They wanted to be arrested. The cops shooed them away. We climbed into the truck and Arvy started it. "They'll be roaming around all night," he said. "Looking for more gas."

"Where are their parents?"

Jimmy said, "Their parents are drunk."

❧

We drove down the road to the band office.

They took me inside, introduced me to Chief Roy McDonald. They said I was "a writer from Minaki." The chief shook my hand. He had a slight limp, not unlike my own, and he looked me up and down and wondered aloud if maybe we were cousins. The cops stayed for a few minutes, making small talk with the chief, telling him about the gas-sniffers at the complex. He seemed to have a cordial enough relationship with the two officers, if a bit standoffish, and after a while they left.

Roy took me into a rather depressing kitchen, with a rusty sink and a dangerous-looking electric hotplate, and tried rustling a pot of coffee. He couldn't seem to find any filters. He was a round-faced and pleasant-looking fifty-year-old, with crinkly eyes and a bemused smile that was more or less his default expression. He wore a white cotton businessman's shirt, rolled up at the sleeves, and black dress slacks that gave no clue as to the source of his limp. It was more of a hitch than a limp, and I wondered if perhaps he'd only hurt himself. When you have an infirmity, you want everyone else to have one too.

We went into his office, which with its rough floors and makeshift furniture suggested a supervisor's office on a back-woods construction project. The windows were spray-painted red, and I could see where someone had been working on them with a scraper, trying to admit some daylight.

"I apologize about the office," Roy said. "We had a break-in last week, and they wrecked the place pretty good."

There was a leatherette swivel office chair with a big splash of hemorrhagic red in the saggy part of the seat. I sat down and told Roy what had brought me to Whitedog. I told him I was studying the history and the native lore of the bush country, which seemed more plausible than saying I was looking for the meaning of life. "I was hoping to meet someone who could tell me about the old Midewiwin religion."

He said the old traditions had been pretty much destroyed by the churches and the residential schools. "Many of our children were sent out for adoption," he added, with gravity. "It hasn't worked out well, for us." He said those upheavals produced much despair and anger. The Ojibways, being a gentle people, turned the anger against themselves. "We have problems with suicide," he said. "I myself couldn't see the way out, so I started drinking. I destroyed everything around me. I was drunk all the time, drunk, drunk. Then one night in Minaki, I walked in front of the train and it cut off my legs."

He stood up and gimped over to a flip chart alongside his desk. He unscrewed the cap from a felt pen and drew a stick man at the top of the chart. "That's when I hit rock bottom," he said. He drew a line down to the bottom of the chart and tapped it with his pen. "Rock bottom."

He sat down again. "I lay in the hospital, thinking that since I hadn't died, the Creator must have had a reason for saving my life. So I stopped drinking, learned to walk again, and learned to raise my family like a proper man."

I took notes while he spoke. He added that he'd been trying to recover the old ways, doing sweat lodges and other ceremonies. I told him about Martin and Lillian's discovery of the old prayer scroll.

Roy listened carefully to my tale and didn't speak until the end. "What's the name of the lake where they found it?"

"They wouldn't tell me," I said. "But they said they would be happy to give the information to someone like you."

He wrote down a few notes. We were both dutiful note takers. The vandals apparently had cleaned out his office and he had only a large felt marker. Or maybe he had only large felt markers at the best of times. He said that these old birch-bark medicine scrolls were exceedingly rare, and it would be terrible if the wrong people found this one and used it to start a campfire or something.

"That's what I thought."

"What's this man's name?"

I gave him Martin's name, and the names of his parents too, who likely wouldn't be hard to track down, given that they were both Toronto psychiatrists.

Roy wrote down the information. The only sound in the office was the squeaking of his felt pen. "I'd like to try and maybe rescue that scroll," he murmured.

"Can I come?"

☙

One rainy afternoon two weeks later five vehicles rolled down the highway towards Vermilion Bay, Ontario, on a mission to find the long-lost scroll.

At the head of the convoy was Roy McDonald, in his blue truck. Behind Roy was a small Subaru wagon with American plates. It was driven by Jim Calumet, a Chippewa native studies professor from Wisconsin. Jim had heard about the mission and had driven all the way from Eau Claire to join us. Behind the Subaru was a big wine-red Lariat pick-up driven by Stan McKay, a Saulteaux elder who taught native spiritualism classes at Stony Mountain Penitentiary. Behind Stan was a low-slung, rust-encrusted Cordoba driven by Trevor Manywounds. Trevor was one of Stan's successful graduates. He'd done time at Stony and now worked with street kids in Winnipeg. Whenever we climbed a slight hill, Trevor's saurian Chrysler unleashed a great cloud of blue smoke, reeking whiffs of which poured in my wind vent. I was low man on the totem pole, playing the role of "back door" as we say in the convoy business. It seemed a bit cumbersome, employing five vehicles to move five people, but no one had volunteered to ride with anyone else.

Around mid-afternoon we pulled into Vermilion Bay. A statue of a huge sasquatch stood on the edge of town, welcoming visitors with a cannibalistic howl. It wasn't apparent why the town would promote itself with the effigy of a monster, but thematically it seemed to fit with the dark rainy afternoon and the mystery that had brought us here. We stopped at the local motel, booked five rooms, and had a planning session in the coffee shop. Roy had telephoned Martin, who was now in medical school out in Vancouver. Martin had mailed him a rough map, which Roy now unfolded and laid out on the table.

Roy seemed to feel that Stan had the upper hand on spiritual authority, and after showing everyone the map, he encouraged Stan to lead the session. Stan was a broad-shouldered sixty-year-old with a baseball hat that advertised Caterpillar Heavy Equipment. He said that he wanted to check in with the local Ojibway elders, just to make sure they had no objection to our mission. But before we did that, the first task was to take Martin's map and determine whether the scroll was still in place.

According to the map, the place that was nearest to the scroll's hiding spot was a fishing camp called Findlay's East Arm. We climbed in our five vehicles and drove over there to try to rent a boat. The lodge owner was clearly curious about the arrival of five stone-faced strangers in city shoes, but he rented us the boat anyway. With Stan McKay at the helm of the eighteen-foot Lund, we navigated down the lake for several miles, worked our way through a tangle of islands, banged along on rough chop down a long windy channel, and went across a wide bay to the base of a tall granite cliff, where great slabs of broken granite were stacked like the remains of a parking garage.

With the hand-drawn map on his knee, Stan trolled along the base of the cliff, scrutinized the high ledges, doubled back, looked at another spot, then folded the map into his pocket and eased the boat into a narrow spot between two shattered boulders. He pointed to a rust-coloured splotch on the rock, six or eight feet above us. It was a petroglyph, a drawing of a four-legged cat with spiky horns. "Misshypishu," Stan murmured.

Misshypishu is one of the more dangerous creatures in Ojibway mythology. He's a horned panther that lives in the bottom of the lake. Out on the west coast the Haida have a similar creature called Skana, whose ever-changing moods produce the storms and squalls on the north Pacific. Misshypishu, his freshwater relative, often lives at the base of a rapids, cliff, or waterfall, and although he doesn't confront people directly, his shadow, according to legend, can sometimes be glimpsed if you find a good set of rapids, gaze down through the crystalline, sunlight-columned upper layers of water, and focus patiently on the depths far below. According to Stewie, my guiding instructor at Bending Lake, you won't see his leg or his head; he's too big. But sometimes you might see the shadow of his huge shoulders as he clambers along the bottom.

Stan asked us to stay in the boat because he didn't want to disturb the site. The mossy rocks looked a bit greasy from the rain, but he climbed out and picked his way up the boulders, moving easily for an older man. He looked behind various rocks, then stiffened as he peered into a crevice. He stood there motionless for a moment, then climbed down again, backwards. He took care placing his feet and half-slid the last part down to the boat. "There's definitely something in there," he said.

We drove the boat back to Findlay's lodge and went off to find the local elders. This turned out to be easier said than done. When we arrived at the local reserve, we discovered that the band office was closed, and there was no sign indicating when it would open again. This was the end of August – the *manomin giizis*, or wild rice moon – and apparently everyone was off harvesting rice. Still, Stan was adamant that we look for someone in authority, so we convoyed up and down a series of gravel roads, looking for encampments of rice pickers. Finally we ran out of daylight and went back to the motel. I was tired from a long day of driving, and it felt good to have a hot shower and flop down in front of the TV.

In the morning we continued with our search for the local elders. It had stopped raining. The morning turned hot and sunny, and a great pall of dust poured off Stan's truck as he forged on ahead of us. We talked to some local Ojibways, and they suggested we talk to a couple of old-timers named Israel and Harriet. We located Israel first, at the end of yet another long gravel road, at an impromptu rice-picking camp of perhaps a dozen wall tents erected next to a river. Israel looked to be in his eighties, a bent and gnarled-looking old fellow with a weathered baseball hat, large bug-eye sunglasses, and a bony face that was as shiny and hard as an axe handle. He didn't seem surprised that we'd shown up to visit him. He didn't seem unsurprised either.

There were sacks of manomin, or rice, stacked in a row next to the canoes, and in his usual folksy way, Roy, our spokesman, made a lot of small talk with the local people. He talked to the old people about the weather, talked to the middle-aged people about the fluctuating price levels of green rice, and asked some nearby kids how each had contributed to the harvesting of so many large and praiseworthy sacks of manomin. A bonfire smoked in the middle of their camp, and the kids dutifully fed it sticks while Roy interviewed them. Roy didn't talk to old Israel, however, who was ignoring us. He was off by himself, unwrapping a brand new pair of Adidas running shoes.

He painstakingly laced up the sneakers, then stood up and signalled to the kids. They seized a sack of rice and dragged it over to a dirt trench next to the fire. With a plastic scoop, Israel picked up a quantity of rice and poured it into the trench, then began carefully padding on the rice with his new shoes. Like some backwoods Minister of Finance, Israel had purchased a new pair of shoes for bringing in the crop. A pole was nailed to a pair of trees on either side of the trench. Like a game but gimpy ballet dancer, he gripped the pole as he moon-walked back and forth on the rice. We stood there watching.

Then Israel nodded towards the kids and said something to them in Ojibway. They each seized a corner of the tarpaulin, hauled the rice out of the trench, and carried it down to the water. Like a bunch of classmates giving their friend the bumps, they tossed the rice up and down, sending clouds of chaff skittering away on the breeze. They continued doing this until most of the chaff was gone. Finally all that remained in the tarp was five or ten pounds of glossy black kernels.

Israel directed them to bring the rice up to the fire, where he heated some cooking oil in a large frying pan. Squatting on his heel, Israel tossed several handfuls of rice into the hot oil. The kernels bubbled and jumped, bursting like popcorn. After a few moments, he scooped the rice out with a strainer and dried it in a paper towel. He seasoned it with butter and salt, then gave each of us a sample, wrapped in tin foil. It was better than the best popcorn I've ever eaten.

"Do you eat a lot of rice in the winter?" I asked him.

"We eat it every day," he said. "Take more." As we stood there on the banks of the river, wolfing down the delicious rice, with the warm sun on our bare arms and the aromatic woodsmoke on the air, Stan lowered himself onto one heel and chatted with Israel in Ojibway. Roy, hampered by artificial legs, couldn't lower himself down next to them. But he stood there in his white shirt and slacks, and fired off an occasional remark anyway, speaking rapid-fire in that many-vowelled language that is so difficult to learn. The two city boys, Trevor Manywounds and Jim Calumet, stood alongside Roy, listening intently. Trevor was a Lakota, not an Ojibway, so he couldn't understand what they were saying. And Jim Calumet, the native studies professor, whose authentic native beaded vest, turquoise jewellery, and melodramatic long, plaited ponytail marked him as the sort of Indian who'd probably never spent a night in the bush in his life, listened to their jabbered conversation with obvious pained incomprehension. Finally Stan stood up and tugged at the brim of his Caterpillar hat. "Okay," he said. "Let's go for a little drive."

Now we had to find Harriet, who was at another rice camp, about forty miles away. Stan drove hard and we arrived there at sundown. This camp consisted of only four tents. An old man was squatting by the campfire, brewing coffee. He told us that Harriet was down by the point. We walked down to a grove of oak trees overlooking the river. Not far away we saw an old lady moving through the woods, bending over, here and there, as if picking objects off the ground. She had her back to us. And in the interest of gently announcing our presence, Stan called out a greeting. "*Boozhoo!*"

Harriet turned and faced us. "*Boozhoo,*" she replied. "*Aaniish na.*"

She was a plump, small, old woman with large eyes, a smooth pretty face, and silvery hair gathered back in a bun. Stan introduced each of us. When it was my turn, I shook her hand, which was soft and warm, and said it was a pleasure to meet her. Harriet said that she was gathering medicinal plants. She held up a willow leaf and handed it to me. "This is *kinnick-kinnick,*" she said, with a tone of gravity and sorrow. "It's for the fever."

She had other plants, folded into a beaded deerhide purse on her shoulder, and she showed us each one of them. I wished that I'd brought along my notebook to make sketches. Harriet said that she wanted to use the last few minutes of daylight, so we walked alongside her, watching her as she stooped and sorted through the undergrowth. Jim Calumet was intrigued and kept stalking through the brush on his long thin legs and returning with plants he'd selected himself, asking Harriet to identify them. He seemed to have a knack for selecting diarrhea remedies.

When you stood beside Harriet, you couldn't accept how tiny she was. She was perhaps only four feet high. Her voice was tiny also, like the voice of a three-year-old girl. But she exuded a presiding matriarchal calmness that made you feel that if you stayed right by her side, it was entirely possible that nothing bad might ever happen to you ever again. In my turn, along with the others, I asked her questions about the plants. But I didn't really care what we discussed. I just wanted to hear her voice.

When I was a small kid in Winnipeg, walking home from school on grey winter afternoons, I would often feel discouraged about my life – the treeless barren of my neighbourhood, the intractable lousiness of my hockey skills, the unattainable per-fection of Teresa, the certainty that I would some day die and go to Hell or at least spend a couple of hundred years burning in Purgatory, and so on. Sometimes, however, when I walked in the back door of my house, the aroma of Player's cigarette smoke filled my nostrils, and I'd realize that my beloved white-haired grandmother was visiting. Kicking off my boots, I would run up the stairs and into the living room, eager to see my nanny and convinced, suddenly, that life was excellent after all. No matter how many things I'd failed at, my grandmother was totally and unequivocally in my corner. And although I didn't know Harriet, she seemed to project that same aura of support.

As we were walking, a tree branch suddenly cracked off in the woods and a black bear appeared behind an oak tree. Standing on its hind legs, the bear looked at us, then climbed the tree. It was a large bear, with a glossy pelt and a hefty rear end, but it went up the tree as lightly as a monkey. It didn't seem afraid of us. Once the bear had gained the crown of the tree, it gathered a limb in its powerful arms and bit at the acorns. It was about forty yards away. "Boy, that's a nice mukwa," said Roy. "I guess he likes acorns."

"We see many mukwa here," said Harriet.

And indeed we saw more bears, about five or six of them. I'd never seen a gathering of bears like this, except in a garbage dump, and judging by the enthusiastic exclamations, I don't think the other guys had either. It was like all the bears that ever there were had gathered here together because there were so many acorns. And until we arrived, Harriet had been here by herself, moving unconcernedly among them.

When it became too dark to gather plants we returned to the tents, where Stan sat down at the campfire next to Harriet and spoke to her in Ojibway for fifteen or twenty minutes. Occasionally we interrupted, firing questions at Stan, which he relayed to Harriet. Apparently she knew about the scroll. She knew it was hidden there. On two different occasions, she'd visited the cliff and burned sweet grass there and studied the scroll. She didn't know how old it was, but she said "those old people" put it there. "What's actually written on the scroll?" I asked.

Stan asked her my question. She answered him in her own language. Stan looked at me. "She says it gives lessons about healing."

"So it's a medical scroll?"

He put the question to her. She talked for several minutes. "She says the scroll is for healing, but not the sort of healing the doctors do, at the hospital. . . ."

Harriet talked some more, and Stan listened. Judging by the way he scrutinized her every gesture, I wondered if he didn't have a full grasp of her dialect. "It's the healing of the chest," he said. "She says there are four levels of nature – the earth mother, the plants, the animals, and the people. They can't exist without each other. If the hoop is broken between the four parts, it causes a sickness in the chest."

"What sort of sickness?"

Stan conveyed the question. I knew that I shouldn't be quite so assertive with my questions, but Stan didn't seem to mind.

Stan finally said, "She says it cures the sickness of the heart."

Roy asked a few questions, then Trevor. Jim finally asked the big question. "Will she let us see it?"

Stan conveyed the question. He listened to her answer, then finally stood up. He looked, if not unhappy, then manfully involved in an effort not to look unhappy. He said we should have a meeting. We thanked Harriet and got back in our trucks. We drove all the way back to Vermilion Bay, went to the Bigfoot Café, ordered some burgers, and sat there for a few minutes before Stan finally gave us the verdict. "Harriet wants the scroll to stay where it is. She says it belongs to her people."

Jim said, "She's not worried about it getting stolen?"

"She says it's been there for many years. Nobody's ever found it before."

Trevor spoke so infrequently that it startled me, hearing his gruff voice. "Did she say if we can look at it?"

Stan chuckled. "Well . . . she says the instruction scroll is like a medicine plant. If you use a medicine too many times, it loses its power. And then some day, when people really need it, the medicine is used up."

Roy was nodding. "I think she's right." He looked around the table. "Don't you think she's right?" Roy always seemed cheered up by bad news. Getting run over by a freight train had made him a hard man to discourage.

"So what are we going to do?" asked Trevor.

Stan said, "I would like to talk to her again tomorrow."

Jim asked, "Do you get the sense she'll change her mind?"

Stan leaned back in the booth, adjusted his beat-up old Caterpillar hat. "No," he said, "but I'd still like to talk to her."

He looked at Roy. "What are you going to do, Chief?"

Roy shrugged. "I'll stay for another day or two."

"Mr. Calumet?"

"I've been going so hard these last few days," Jim confessed. He sounded discouraged. "Maybe I'd better sleep on it."

"I better go home," said Trevor. "I gotta get back to work."

Stan looked at me. "And you?"

I said, "I guess I'll hit the trail too."

Stan nodded. He didn't seem to care. We finished our dinner, paid our bills, and went outside. It was a dark night. There was a smoky scent of autumn in the air. We exchanged handshakes, promised to keep in touch, and went our separate ways. I gassed up the van, found *As It Happens* on CBC radio, and hit the road. After two days of pounding up and down gravel roads, it was a relief to be on a highway again, feeling that smooth asphalt humming under the tires.

I was disappointed about the way the search had concluded. But that seemed to be the way life goes. You never reach the exact conclusion you wanted, but let's face it, sometimes the conclusion you do reach is the better one. All my life, ever since I was a kid camping out at Rosena Lake, I'd half-seriously wanted to be an Indian. I'd researched Indian culture, memorized Indian terms, tacked posters of long-dead Indian chiefs on my bedroom wall, and studied books about Indian mysticism – all in the hope that old native people like Harriet knew something I needed to know. And maybe my instincts were right, in the sense that I was slowly being cured of a certain foolishness. If we'd climbed up that cliff tonight and pulled the scroll out of its cedar cylinder, its pictographic symbols no doubt would have spelled a different message for each of us. Mine might have said: *You are not an Indian. Why don't you get a life of your own?*

∾

No matter how many times you do it, it's always a lonely experience, coming home in the middle of the night.

It's late, very late. The lights are off and the town is asleep. Minaki Lodge is boarded up and looks like the House of Usher. It's being renovated, and the owners are finding deep-seated problems that are far more serious than anyone expected. The renovation job has stalled, and no one knows when the lodge will open again.

Passing the lodge's black silhouette, I coast down the hill to Murray's Camp, park the Econoline, and sling my knapsack over my shoulder. Welcome home. It's cold and late, and I need a bed. The planks of the dock are wet from late-night dew, and clouds of moths are twirling around the lights. Stepping down into my boat, stowing my knapsack in a dry place up under the bow, I prime the motor and yank the cord five or six times. Finally it bursts to life, coughs and rattles for a while, then settles down into a rough idle. Untying the ropes, I steer out onto the glassy water.

Entering this river on a moonless night is an exercise in faith. It's so dark I can't see the hand in front of my face, so I switch over to the Winnipeg River that branches and forks like a black oak through my memory. The external river, the real one, is of course not perfectly represented by the version in my mind. But I've spent so many years exploring its crooks and limbs that even at times like this, driving blind, I can hypothesize my position with the same kind of approximate accuracy you use in your own home, when you descend a darkened stairway and put your hand out to touch a wall that you assume is still there.

Steering through the serpentine narrows at Orde's Island, I get the boat up and speeding, folding my wool Mackinaw jacket collar over my face to provide some cover from the blast of night air. On either side of the boat, invisible reefs and rocky shoals sprint past like cats in the dark. It's interesting to inhabit a river so intimately that your life depends on your familiarity with it. But in the end, how does that information serve you? Lately, I've wondered if the knowledge I've acquired while living in this country is only taking me farther and farther away from what I actually need in life. As the lights of town recede, there's only blackness all around, and nothing overhead but the cold stars. When I finally pull up to the dark houseboat, I can't help wishing I were returning to the glow of a lantern, and someone curled up in bed, waiting for me to come home.

My driver's licence lists my comical address as "Houseboat, Minaki, Ontario, POX 1J0." Last winter, the enumerator for the Federal Census Bureau arrived at my door wearing snowshoes. I'm supposed to be the sole occupant of this building. But when I walk in the door and throw my knapsack on the bed, I can hear all the little rustlings in the darkness, my room-mates. Living in the city, people get used to being the only living organism in their homes. They get ticked off if they find a spider in their bathroom sink. And if they detect the presence of a skunk under their porch or a raccoon in their attic, it's a cause for war. The last time I was in Winnipeg, my sister saw a mouse in her kitchen and announced that she was selling her house. But here in the bush, the balance of power tips in favour of the critters. Here, they own the place. I'm the visitor.

Lighting a candle, I kick off my jeans and consider rigging up a mousetrap. I killed off all the mice when I left, four or five days ago, but they're such persistent little critters they've probably moved in again. I climb into the soft bed and pull the flannel blanket to my chin. Through my bedroom window, the brightest object in the sky is Mars. It tracks from east to west across the night sky. Right now it's well past the centre of the window, which means it's getting on to two or two-thirty in the morning. People prefer to sleep at night, but animals are most active in the darkness, so this time of night there are always lots of sudden noises. You can lie in the dark and listen to your tenants. A big *clunk* under the floor means that a good-sized animal has just climbed into the flotation. It sounds like the arrival of a flesh-eating swamp creature, but it's just a beaver.

When I first came to the Shield, years ago, I brought along illustrated guidebooks to all the flora and fauna. I was thinking of Nature writ large – the timber wolves, eagles, bears, etc. – and didn't think it would be all that difficult to become an armchair expert on each of them. After all, how many species were on the list? You had your big showy trees, like the white pines, the red pines, the jackpines, the spruces, and your lesser deciduous trees, represented by maybe a dozen hardwoods. You had to learn your birds – your ducks and grouse, which in fact I already knew; your birds of prey, which you had to divide into falcons, buteos, and accipiters. And although the catalogue got a little more confusing when you got down to the insects, dragonflies, midges, and so on, that's what made it challenging. Compared to a tropical forest, the Shield seemed like a stripped-down, minimalist sort of ecosystem. It was like a big three-chord Neil Young ballad that covered half the country. Pine trees and granite, big skies, blue waters. Its beauty was in its simplicity. In total, I couldn't imagine that there'd be more than a hundred species to learn. In fact when I first got here, the bush seemed almost devoid of life.

But just because you can't see things doesn't mean they aren't there. The place was actually teeming with creatures; I just wasn't aware of them. Some animals forage in darkness, and you have to be a bit of a forensic investigator to detect their presence. You might never see the fierce and silent horned owl, although it's very common, but you'll find neat regurgitated packets of compressed fur and bones under a tall tree. Fishers are common too. They're low-slung and serpentine, like a lady's fur wrap sprung to life, and they know a special mongoose-like move that enables them to kill a porcupine without getting jabbed by quills. Fishers are ubiquitous all through the Shield country, but they're so furtive you'll rarely meet anyone who's seen one.

Some predators hunt with their ears, tilting their heads back and forth to focus on the source of a sound. And that makes sense, given that you tend to hear more animals than you see. When I'm lying in bed, the action never ceases. I can hear deer mice skittering up and down the walls, trying to find an entry that isn't plugged with steel wool. Outside the screened window, a soft but distinct *cheep* indicates the aerial passage of a brown bat, issuing its regular echo locator as it zooms around hunting mosquitoes. A loud thump on the roof, followed by a scrabble of claws, means that a flying squirrel has come to visit. It has to be a flying squirrel because it's the only squirrel active at night. They have immense liquid eyes and a kind of furry parachute that folds up into their underarms. Trappers say the best bait for catching them is a red rubber ball.

When I first arrived here most of my neighbours were hiding in plain sight. One day I watched a dragonfly patrol a quadrant of air in front of the houseboat. Her patrol zone was about a hundred feet square, and she went back and forth across it like a NATO helicopter, clipping insects that wandered into it and rushing other dragonflies that violated her boundaries. She was a big one, the common type known as the green darner. Most dragonflies die in the fall but green darners are strong enough to migrate south, like birds. Her labours continued all day, and when evening arrived, she was still zipping back and forth. When I lit the barbecue, I felt that I should be shouting a greeting at her, my neighbour.

Ants have lives too. Most ants are based in a central colony, but each travels up to a mile a day, searching for food. The old horror movies equate brutality with size. We assume that a beast isn't really scary unless it's capable of overturning a police car. But in nature, the downsized world seems the more savage one. Compare solemn and gentle creatures like the whale and the elephant to the bloodthirsty mouse, which thinks nothing of eating its own babies if there are no groceries in the house. Ants, with their mandible jaws and military alliances, end up serving as cannon fodder for some pampered queen. And if you follow a solitary ant for a few hundred yards, across open granite and through heavy forest, you can see that it has to face more dangers than one of the ancient warriors of Xenophon.

I have no idea how many ants live on this island, but they deserve to be on the census, as do the flying insects, whose numbers are legion. In this one houseboat alone, how many paper wasps live in that nest under the eaves? How many spiders inhabit the rafters, the walls, or the crannies along the windows? How many midges hold mating dances around the window boxes, and collapse in furry piles that must comprise tens of thousands? When I first came here I thought I was alone. But on nights like this, lying in my flannel bed, listening to all those scampering feet and tiny wings, I feel like I'm lying on my back in the marketplace of some bustling, alien city.

The world gets more crowded as you descend the food chain. Myriad tiny minnows live under the houseboat, and I've given up trying to identify them. When I tie up the boat and aim a flashlight at the water, they swarm through the down-slanting bomb of light. Some nights there are thousands of them; other nights there are none. I have no idea where they go, or where they've been. They apparently eat tiny shrimp and water bugs, which in turn prey on the zooplankton, which are tiny predators themselves.

Zooplankton hunt at night. They lurk in the depths of the lake until sundown, when they rise to the surface to hunt their cousins, the phytoplankton. Phytoplankton extract energy from sunlight and are simple-minded enough to be considered plants. Even smaller than the phytoplankton are the nematodes – microscopic wormlike creatures that should be counted on the census too. Beneath my bed, in the silt that covers the lake bottom, or in the dark soil that gives root to the bulrushes along the nearby shore, there are swarming colonies of nematodes. Nematodes in turn are massive compared to microbes, which are too numerous to count. In one cup of soil there are more microbes than all the people on earth.

∾

When Charles Darwin published *The Origin of Species* in 1859, he articulated a number of simple and aesthetically perfect ideas. Perhaps the most useful of these, from a layperson's point of view, is that success is determined by adaptability. The earth is covered with various landscapes. If animals succeed in adapting to a landscape, they survive. If they don't, they die. The map of Canada is dominated by the lakes, forests, and rocky outcrops of the Shield. It's a harsh landscape, with very little soil and pro- nounced swings of temperature from one season to the next. Virtually every corner of it is raked by wildfire every few decades, and it's populated by hordes of biting insects that can literally drain the blood from an exposed living body. If you're going to make a living on the Shield, you have to adapt to it. The Shield is not going to adapt to you.

When I lie in bed, listening to the sounds of the night, I often wonder how I'm ever going to fit in here. Ever since I was a kid I've wanted to live here, or at least somehow make a place for myself. But so far, it's been like digging at granite with a wooden spoon. I work as a fishing guide, which is an interesting and quirky sort of job, but no serious person would mistake it for a lifelong career. I have several cardboard boxes full of handwrit- ten, unpublished fiction stuffed under my bed. But I'm only beginning to get a grasp of the novelist's craft – plot development, characterization, and so on. I've been reading books on the architecture of fiction, books like John Gardner's famous text, and I'm beginning to appreciate that my laborious novels are mostly just rambling disconnected stories with no noticeable beginning or end.

I still have my night job at the police station. But that's not a promising career either, and it doesn't have much to do with the wilderness. I came here on a kind of quest. I wanted to learn this country's secrets, or at least engage it in some kind of dialogue. But the country is ignoring me. Lying here, watching Mars inch minutely across the window, I can dispassionately look at my life without vested interest, as a book critic might, and say that the stakes are definitely rising. In conventional novels, the character usually emerges triumphant in the final chapter. But the Canadian backwoods is inherently anti-heroic. Around here, the only thing that's going to emerge triumphant is the landscape.

Tomorrow night is Friday night, which means I'll have two choices for spending the evening – staying home, or going to the beer parlour. The beer parlour sits in the centre of town, luring bachelors like me from far and wide with its glowing windows. To hell with the wilderness, let's get drunk. All the bachelors are hoping to meet a woman, a special woman with a pretty face and a great personality who perhaps has a good job, owns a new pick-up truck, and enjoys a bit of moose hunting. Everyone's head swivels as if on gimbals every time the door opens, hoping it's Miss Perfect, but she never walks in. Like every other Canadian backwoods town, Minaki suffers from a permanent shortage of women. Every autumn, as the north starts to empty out, men outnumber women by a factor of about ten to one. On a typical night at the pub, there might be a dozen people drinking beer and playing pool. And the only woman in the whole place might be Susan, the bartender.

In the beer parlour at night, women are so absent that their absence becomes a kind of presence. Their absence imparts gravity to the most mundane of moments. Standing in the bathroom, washing your hands, glancing in the mirror for a moment to comb your hair, you suddenly realize, I have no one. Playing a game of snooker, working on your fifth ponderous glass of beer, the most banal Elton John ballad seems to have taken on remarkable artistic insight and emotion. Out at the snooker table, or along the sombre rows of men at the bar, there are never any conversations about women. The bachelors don't have to talk about women. Women are already the topic of every conversation they aren't having.

Years ago, a lot of young people came here in search of Utopia. But no one is young any more, and there's a widespread feeling that the party is ending. The community is fragmenting into tribes. The Married Tribe is composed of people who are settling down, building houses, and having children. As much as I grumble about my friends getting old and getting married, I have to admit that my resentment is fuelled partially by envy. Kelly and Sally are building a swanky lodge on the shores of Gun Lake. They've got their pilot's licences and have purchased a float-equipped airplane. Pete and Trout are building a tourist operation with neat cabins they rent out for $1,000 per week. (The resort is known locally as Tax Dodge Lodge.) My friend Dave has become a wilderness outfitter. He likewise flies his own float plane, guides an exclusive clientele of wealthy hunters and fishermen, and is beginning to rack up a collection of true-life adventures, some of which have even been documented in magazines like *Reader's Digest* ("Flight Into Danger!"). For the Married Tribe, moving to this little town in the northern Ontario bush was the best thing they ever did. Instead of soldiering away at some faceless corporation in the city, they're launching remarkable and highly individual lives. They're building splendid homes with floor-to-ceiling windows looking out on the wilderness. They're installing outdoor Jacuzzis on their multi-levelled cedar sundecks and growing their own produce out back. I'm glad they've figured out some perfect formula for unlocking the secret of this country, but I haven't. And I can feel the pressure incessantly rising, as though we were all back at university, in final exams. They've handed in their papers and waltzed out. But I'm still sitting here, stuck.

My comrades are the ones who are left behind: the Bachelor Tribe – a loosely knit group of oddballs, old-timers, fishing guides, carpenter's helpers, away-from-home railway workers, drunks, bush pilots with voided licences, know-it-alls, vagrants, and disheartened puppy-dog police constables who still can't quite figure out how they got posted to this hick town. They tend to gather every night at the beer parlour to commiserate, shoot pool, and tell absurd stories. (One of the new cops, for example, claims he's engaged to Miss Canada.) I like them all well enough. In fact, they're the most entertaining group in town. But I'm not quite ready to develop a serious drinking problem. So I spend most of my evenings at home, reading or writing, listening to the radio. Or else every couple of days, at about four in the afternoon, I dress warmly, load the boat, and cruise out to explore the wilderness, which is why I came here in the first place.

In the autumn, once the water gets cold, the risk of falling overboard and dying of exposure adds a kind of religious zest to boat travel, and I like heading down the river, banging across the charcoal-dark waves into the biting wind. Once I've caught a limit of fish (catching walleyes is easy in the fall), I pull up the boat on the shore and spend the last few hours of the day hunting for grouse. Walking along a forest ridge in some far-flung dead end of the river, you wonder if any human being has ever stepped on these granite hills. The last big thing that happened around here was the Pleistocene ice age, ten thousand years ago. Compared to four and a half billion years of planetary history, ten thousand years is not a long time. And it's not even a long time in human terms. If you consider that an average human life lasts seventy-two years, the ice age ended only 138 lives ago. You could in fact quite easily throw a party that included someone from every generation in human history. You could hold the party in the Grand Rotunda at Minaki Lodge; it would be the ultimate masked ball. Marie Antoinette and Cleopatra would be comparing notes in one corner, while outside, Ernest Hemingway might be watching Turok, the Son of Stone, sketch a giant Pleistocene lion on the patio with a piece of chalk.

These hills are like the halls of time. Environmentalists are worried that the so-called greenhouse effect will trigger a catastrophic increase in the earth's temperature. But a smaller group of scientists argues for a more dramatic and frightening scenario. They've been drilling core samples in the Greenland ice cap and have discovered that ice ages are a normal aspect of the planet's weather cycle. Cold periods last about ninety thousand years; warm periods last about ten thousand years. We're just coming to the end of a ten-thousand-year-long warm period. But that's not the scary part. The onset of an ice age is usually preceded by a pronounced warm spell. The temperature of the planet goes up and down, but it stays within a manageable limit, regulated by ocean currents, which function as the earth's natural thermostats. In the Atlantic the Gulf Stream, which pumps warm air into the northern hemisphere, shuts off if the weather gets too warm. During the 1600s, a prolonged hot dry spell caused the Gulf Stream to slow down, which plunged Europe into its well-documented "Little Ice Age," in which the Thames froze. Over in the Pacific Ocean, the Christ Child or El Niño current functions as a temperature thermostat for much of North America. But that's not the scary part either. What the scientists have discovered is that the onset of an ice age may be much more sudden than we formerly believed. Ice core samples suggest that ice ages are preceded by a steady rise in temperatures, followed by a pronounced correction: a cooling-off period that may actually bring on an ice age within a short period of time. Not millennia, not centuries, but *decades*.

Glaciers never go away. They just retreat. You can look at them on the maps, great packs of them positioned in staging areas across the north. They respond quickly to small variations in weather. Whenever the weather cools down, snow begins to fall. Under falling snow a glacier gathers mass, and its outer edges push outward. You'd think that a glacier's rate of travel would be slow – "glacial" – but once they get moving they grumble and creak like bulldozers, grinding forward at an alarming rate, up to a hundred yards per day. Their undersides are crusted with frozen rock. During the last ice age, the glaciers that covered most of Canada and the northern United States were about a mile thick. Pressed down by such an enormous slab of ice, the raspy undersurface works away granite like a belt-sander works wood. This repeated rasping by glaciers is what creates the undulant granite contours of the Shield. And if you think your own life is a temporary thing, go for an autumn walk in the bush country and you'll be forcefully reminded of the ephemeral quality of all living things. Everywhere on the smooth ground are the glacial striations, long parallel grooves resembling claw marks.

So even though I enjoy walking in the bush more than sitting in the beer parlour, it definitely reinforces the suspicion that time is not my ally. One cool October night I hooked an extraordinarily strong fish. It took five minutes to bring it to the side of the boat, and when I finally scooped it into the net I recognized it as a whitefish, a silvery thing with buggy eyes and clownish lips. I'd never caught a whitefish before and had no idea how to cook one, so I slipped it back into the water. The hook had cut its velvety gills and it was bleeding profusely. I shut off the motor and did a bit of CPR, pumping it back and forth in the numbingly cold water until it finally thrashed its tail and disappeared into the depths. A few minutes later, it floated back up to the surface, trembling, dead.

In the darkness of the autumn evening I carried the fish through town, trying to give it away. It was a big one, a five-pounder. But no one else knew how to cook a whitefish either, and with its overlapping scales it looked vaguely carplike and inedible. Finally I thought of The Prince, a well-liked but impoverished handyman who often strolled around town in a ruined navy blazer and beat-up yachting cap. The Prince was an active member of the Bachelor Tribe and probably needed a girlfriend even more than I did. He was living proof of the fact that men don't do well alone. Women get along fine alone. They somehow acquire a proper place to live, decent furniture, and a nice little imported automobile. But men tend to drop through the floor of the world and keep going.

I knew that The Prince lived on the edge of town in a camper van. Being a van owner myself, I'd always felt curious about his setup, so I walked over to offer him the fish. It was getting dark. I picked my way through the weeds to the back of the community hall, where I found an extension cord plugged into the back wall. By following the yellow cord through the darkened woods, I eventually came to a grassy clearing and a Volkswagen van. Its windows were illuminated with the blue glow of a television, which explained the extension cord.

I knocked on the door and The Prince appeared. He was pleased to accept the fish. ("Well, I'll make use of it for my Thanksgiving dinner! Thank you very much!") He had polish. He had manners and, like many people occupying the lower end of the economy, didn't seem to have a care in the world. He no doubt came from a good community somewhere, where he might have stayed and lived a normal life. But just like me, he'd rolled around the country until he'd wound up here. While I stood there talking to him it occurred to me that I didn't know his real name, and I felt embarrassed by that. What if he died some day? How would we commemorate him? Would we just sharpen his feet and pound him into the swamp? Perhaps no one else knew his real name either. That was the way it was, in this town. If I stayed here much longer, I'd probably lose my real identity too.

We bantered for a few minutes and then he showed me his van. It was small, and I just peered in the doorway. It contained a rumpled bed and a massive Sony television. He'd rigged up a little wood heater in the corner, with a crooked chimney that fed up through a hole in the roof, and it was so hot inside that the side windows were half-open.

I declined The Prince's dinner invitation and wished him luck with the fish. As I walked back out to the road, I glanced back at his campsite. The blue glow of the television filled the wooded clearing. He was back inside the van, and his bare legs were hanging out the window.

ɶ

That autumn, I enrolled in a creative writing class.

On Thursday afternoon, I'd make the long drive into the city with my briefcase full of dog-eared foolscap. The class took place at the University of Manitoba, in a gothic old hulk called the Tier Building. Walking into the Tier Building made me feel sheepish. I was the prodigal son, crawling back home as they always do.

If the highway was slippery I'd get to class a bit late, with snowflakes in my hair and the reek of woodsmoke on my sweater. "Oh good," my classmate Sandra Birdsell would announce, "our token wilderness writer is here."

Some writers feel that you can't learn to write in a classroom. And in truth, the very notion of studying "creative writing" seems to verge on the cornpone, like studying guitar by the Mel Bay Method. But our instructor was Robert Kroetsch, a man who wrote novels and had actually won a Governor General's Award, so I thought I might learn something. At the very least, I'd meet some other writers.

The bearded, frowning Kroetsch was a patient teacher. He listened to our stories and suggested approaches we might take to improve our technique. As soon as he made a suggestion, I usually realized he was right. And that structural problem, or error of syntax, or whatever it was, joined the list of mistakes I resolved to never make again. Just like playing a violin, writing requires arduous work, and it was exciting to learn new tricks.

When class was over, everyone adjourned to the campus pub, except for me. It was a three-hour drive home, and I didn't feel up to tackling a slippery highway after half a dozen beers. This habit of leaving at the end of class turned me, undeservedly, into a man of mystery, and I almost enjoyed teasing my classmates by refusing their invitations. "Can't you come for just one beer?" Kroetsch would ask, scowling with fatherly concern. "Gotta run," I'd say with a smile, lifting my glove in farewell. "Miles to go before I sleep."

I was working on a story called "Two Yellow Pails," a tale about a doomed romance between a white schoolteacher and a young native woman on the reserve north of Minaki. My classmates made some good suggestions for this story and I reworked it, then sent it off to a Toronto literary magazine called *Descant*. A few months later, I got a note in the mail. To my shock, they said they wanted to publish it, and furthermore, they'd pay me $85. It was my first publication, and in fact the first publication in our class. And since it was really my classmates' analysis that had made the story publishable, I went to the bar that night and picked up the tab, which with this hard-partying crew turned out to be more than I was getting paid for the story.

That night in the bar, I sat next to one of the married women in the class. We'd become quite a friendly and close-knit group, and perhaps out of sisterly empathy, she proposed to "fix me up" with one of her friends. This never works out, of course, but my datebook wasn't exactly filled with engagements so I agreed. On our first meeting, at a dinner party at my friend's house, my blind date, whose name was Mandy, didn't show up. She turned out to be sick, and I was glad she was. I knew she wouldn't like me and I wouldn't like her. I'd been on only a couple of blind dates in my life but they'd worked effectively as aversion therapy. During the dinner, my friend did the hard sell, told me what an attractive woman Mandy was. She said Mandy was a divorcée, who before her divorce had lived with her husband in a lovely antique farmhouse near Riding Mountain. "She's very interested in the fact that you live in a houseboat."

The next time, it was my turn to stand Mandy up. My van broke down and I was unable to drive to the city. Then spring came, the class ended, we all moved on with our lives. That summer, I worked again as a guide and spent a lot of time doing renovations on the houseboat. Renovations usually fall into one of two categories – maintenance or improvements. These definitely weren't improvements. They weren't even maintenance. They were last-ditch efforts to keep the place floating. Five or six years of freeze-ups and violent thaws had played hell with my flotation. The sixteen oil drums upon which the houseboat rested – substandard flotation at the best of times – had rusted, cracked, and shipped water. The floor was now only a few inches above the waterline, and the whole building heeled over alarmingly when I walked from one side to the other. I tried pushing long billets of Styrofoam under the deck, but each billet had about eight hundred pounds of flotation force, and it required a lot of planning to get one under the building.

I went to the pub and enlisted the help of four or five buddies. They jammed the nose of the billet under the building and then stood on the foam, trying to weigh it down, gripping each other by the waist, looking like nervous bachelors in a conga line, while I backed off with the boat and gently charged the billet, butting it repeatedly, forcing it under a few inches at a time. This method worked pretty well until the foam billet fetched up against a half-flooded drum. When I butted the billet, it slewed sideways. In slow motion my helpers waved their arms, rolled their eyes, grabbed at each other, then keeled over into the water.

Some of them suggested that I needed to remove the goddamn drums before inserting the foam. The drums still contained enough air to make such removal problematic, so I tried punching holes in them by hand. This was cold and difficult work. Climbing into the cold water, crawling around in the lily pads, I banged on the greasy steel with a hammer and chisel. But the holes didn't do much good if they were above the waterline, and hammering under water is a mug's game. Furthermore, some of the barrels were hidden under the floor, and for these, I had no choice but to blast holes in them with a .308 rifle, fired right through the floor. It wasn't the first time that I was forced to tackle some tricky repair problem with firearms, and although it may sound entertaining, it's actually fairly unpleasant work which calls for a thick towel around the head to preserve the old eardrums.

Attracted by loud gunfire, which even in Minaki was unusual in the middle of town, Larry Willot showed up in the OPP boat and asked me what in god's name I was doing. After I explained the problem, he offered to help out, and drifted down the side of the houseboat and blasted away at the rusty drums with his .38 revolver. Still, the barrels were slow to die. Some of them wallowed free, barely afloat, and I rolled them ashore. In the vacant spaces under the houseboat I jammed in blocks of foam, sawing them to fit. It was a makeshift repair, and by the time September arrived, the water became too cold to work in, and the houseboat was more waterlogged than ever.

I had a vague notion that freeze-up would solve everything. Once the houseboat was locked into the ice, I'd pry it up with hydraulic jacks, lay timbers under it, and lower it onto a fresh new foundation constructed of special marine foam and pressure-treated lumber. Once spring came, the houseboat would descend through the melting ice, and I'd get a few more years out of it.

Eventually I'd build a real house. That was my long-term scheme. You can't live in the backwoods without a scheme. Eventually, I planned to build a log house, which this time would be a real pleasure dome. I'd even selected the property: a handsome peninsula with access by bush road. I'd found out that you could get a government permit to harvest your own beautiful white pine logs. My house would have a huge stone fireplace, big windows overlooking the lake, and a log-buttressed cathedral ceiling with iron chandeliers. I wanted to have stained-glass windows in the bathroom, and I wanted to make them myself. If you lived in a place like that, the girl of your dreams would turn up. She would materialize automatically, as in a science project. Just visualize the scene – a stunning log home with cedar-shingled roof and a wide veranda, a nicely restored red 1956 Chevy pick-up truck in the driveway, a vintage wooden boat, and a Piper Cub float plane tied up at the dock. Now try to imagine the guy who lives in that place not having a great girl-friend. It's just not imaginable. I was quite sure that once I got started on the house, all kinds of chips would fall into place. But before I bought the property and built the house, I needed to raise some money. And I couldn't concentrate on raising money as long as I was dealing with petty day-to-day annoyances like my house going to the bottom of the lake.

My friend Kelly owned a skidder, which is a large insectoid tractor used for hauling logs out of the bush. A skidder is an impressive machine. With its huge wheels and steel claws it will plough through any forest, no matter how dense. The skidder used big inner tubes in its tires. Kelly suggested that I go to Winnipeg and buy some tubes, which could be had for about $25 apiece. Each one of them would float several thousand pounds. "Put one under each corner of the deck," he said. "Pump them up with an air compressor, and Bob's your mother's brother."

This was a perfect Minaki solution: cheap and temporary. I went to Winnipeg on the Thanksgiving weekend, bought some patched-up skidder tubes, and visited my parents. As always, my father wanted to know if I'd seen anything on the way, meaning wildlife. As always, my mother did my laundry and fed me great helpings of roast chicken and mashed potatoes, followed by tea and lemon meringue pie, my favourite. It was always pleasant to come home, eat a hot meal, and pretend to be fourteen years old again, and I'm sure my mother would have been happy if I'd just announced that I was moving back into my old bedroom. But my houseboat was sinking. So I bid them adieu and carried on.

On the way out of town I stopped to see my old friend Douglas. He told me he was going to a party. It was a serious party, with a bluegrass band, and he urged me to come. I wanted to keep moving and get back to Minaki, but I decided to follow the old tried-and-true rule – if there's a party, attend it. The party was at a large fancy house along the river, and there were lots of interesting people there. I ended up staying until two in the morning. When I left, I encountered a solitary woman in the front yard, smoking a cigarette. "Going home already?" she asked, in a deadpan tone.

I said something in return, and we fell into conversation. It was a chilly night, with a big moon above the treetops. She wore fine black leather gloves and some kind of dark woollen cape that made her look like she was on her way to a festival of witches. She had long dark hair and intelligent eyes. When I asked her why she was out here alone, she said she was in a foul mood because it was a full moon, and she missed her home in the country. It turned out, of course, that she was Mandy. And after we had a few chuckles about meeting at last, she grilled me about the houseboat, the country around Minaki, and where she could buy a copy of *Descant*.

After talking at length about Nature, music, wild creatures, the moon, and the effect of coincidence on human affairs, I accompanied her to her car, which was a respectable-looking Volvo four-door with a blue jay feather suspended from the rear view mirror. She climbed in and sat for a moment with the engine running, looking at me through the open window.

I leaned against the car. "Would you like to come and visit me at the lake?"

"When?"

"I don't know, tomorrow?"

"Where would we stay?"

"In my houseboat."

"Hmm. . . ." She pretended to tighten her gloves. She wore a pensive smile, as if considering a smart crack. She was the sort of woman who enjoyed a bit of fencing. "Could we have a fire before bed?"

"We can do whatever we want."

She gave me a direct look. "What time are you picking me up?"

∾

Even before the plane came into sight you could tell it was a Norseman. Like a vintage Indian motorcycle, an old Norseman produces an unmistakable guttural bawl as it flies past.

It was a lovely Saturday afternoon, sunny and warm, with the hills aflame with dying leaves and the glassy river as blue as a flag. Full moons seem to produce this kind of idyllic weather, and I couldn't have picked a better weekend to introduce my little town to someone like Mandy. We stood at the end of the dock at Holst Point and watched the Norseman glide in, bounce onto the water, then come taxiing towards us.

It took several minutes for the plane to taxi up to the dock, and Mandy seemed uncertain as to why we were standing there. I know that many human beings of the female persuasion aren't ordinarily fascinated by flying machines, but the fact is, I needed a few minutes to think.

I was very satisfied, so far, with the progress of our date. We'd had a leisurely drive up here and talked about everything under the sun. Since our arrival, there'd been only one small problem. She hated the houseboat. In my absence, the door had blown open, and the floor was covered with aspen leaves. There were tools all over the bed, sawed-up chunks of Styrofoam protruding from under the deck, and rusted barrels stacked along the shoreline. She didn't even want to go aboard. When we walked inside, the building rolled in such a sickening way that she actually yelped in alarm.

"We can't stay here," she said.

I apologized for the mess and explained that I would have had the place better prepared but I hadn't expected a guest. Whatever the reason, she said she simply wasn't going to spend the night there. And since everything else was going well, I silently forgave her for being fussy, and she probably silently forgave me for living in a shack. We got in my little wooden boat, which she admired, thank God, and went for a cruise down the river. I showed her the majestic and boarded-up Minaki Lodge, which was an even bigger mess than my houseboat. Then I took her for a bite of lunch in the rustic, log-walled dining room at the Point. We didn't mention the houseboat again, which was fine; I just didn't know where we would spend the night.

So I was glad to have a few minutes of silence as we watched the Norseman come sputtering up to the dock. When the pilot climbed out, I was pleasantly surprised to see my old buddy Dave come climbing out after him. Dave greeted us warmly, and I introduced him to Mandy. He said he'd been guiding moose hunters north of the seventh baseline and was glad to have a break and come home for the weekend. He asked us what we were doing that night. He said there was a big Thanksgiving party, and he strongly advised us to come. I told him my houseboat was a bit disorganized, with all the construction work, and we might end up driving back to Kenora and getting a hotel room for the night. "That's stupid," he said. "Use my place."

"Where are you going to stay?"

He said he would stay with his girlfriend. "I was planning to stay there anyway."

This was quite an offer. But for politeness' sake I took a moment or two to think it over. Dave's houseboat was an impressive dwelling. It was the second one he'd built, and it was much nicer than his first. He was a gifted designer, and since his father was a professional woodworker, Dave had access to all kinds of exotic, kiln-dried woods. He'd hand-crafted every detail, and it was beginning to look like it belonged on the cover of *Architectural Digest*. For the last couple of years, we'd moored our houseboats next door to each other out at Virgin Island, and I'd watched him gradually put the place together. He'd done a better job than I had of making a place for himself in this country. He was getting ahead. I was getting nowhere, but still, we were like brothers. Late at night, whoever came home last would swoop past the other person's house at full speed, kicking a big wave into the building and practically knocking the other guy out of bed. During midnight electrical storms, I'd hear a far-off cowboy gee-haw between crashes of thunder. And there were always the minor adventures that come with a life in the bush. One night, for example, a bear started climbing in my kitchen window, so I shooed him over to Dave's place, where he attempted to do the same thing. Some mornings, when it was rainy and depressing and he wasn't home, I'd go over and make myself a cup of tea and just sit in his houseboat. It boasted all the conveniences of a normal house. I could push a button and *Morningside* would issue from the ceiling. I could sit by the hanging plants in the sunroom and look out through the windows at the rainy lake, thinking that maybe some day I'd have a place like this. His houseboat offered an idealized glimpse of what life in this Shield country could be like. So I didn't consider his offer for too long before accepting.

When we arrived at Dave's place we unloaded our gear and got settled. Mandy was impressed with our lodgings, and while I sorted through the music cassettes, she unpacked her bag and laid her nightclothes on the bed. We both knew that we would be sleeping together, and that unspoken understanding imparted a delicious tension to every move we made, every comment. There was only about an hour of daylight left, so we took a walk around the island, climbing the high lichen-encrusted granite ledges. As we climbed the rocks, Mandy wondered aloud if we were walking on ancient "lava." I told her that it was actually igneous granite, the oldest rock on earth. "Certain parts of the Shield are almost as old as the universe," I said.

"How do you know?"

I explained that when I was taking the creative writing course at the University of Manitoba, I often visited the library and borrowed textbooks about botany, geology, and so forth. I explained that I was trying to develop some kind of general comprehension of this country; and not just Minaki, but the Shield country as a whole. "After all, it's our country, and we barely know anything about it."

"And what did you learn?" she asked. She actually seemed interested, so as we walked along through the woods, I told her that, in truth, I hadn't learned much. I'd never been any good at science and could never remember numbers or statistics. But after you read enough geology, you looked at the land differently. It was like removing the wrapper. When you walked these granite ridges you could almost visualize the last ice age, and what the land must have looked like when the glaciers pulled out. There was an old volcanic eruption site about thirty miles southwest of here, and when I drove through the highway rock cuts near there, I found myself picturing the event – the smoking volcano, the flocks of wheeling pterodactyls, and so on. You could never fully separate scientific fact from imagination, and the pictures in my mind were probably erroneous. But at least I was seeing the land in a context. When I was a kid I would have looked at it and thought, Hmm, rocks.

I said that a long time ago, back in Deep Time, 4.5 billion years ago, all the planets and stars had just coalesced, and the earth was an immense globule of molten nickel.

Lighter stuff floated to the top and cooled, forming a membrane like the skin on the surface of a cup of hot chocolate. It grew and thickened into granite, and formed itself into a huge ragged island called Pangea. After quite a while – I didn't know exactly how long – a large part of that super-continent split away and formed into the huge plaque of rock we now call the Canadian Shield. This rocky slab drifted west until it smashed into another immense structure called the Pacific Plate. For a while the two plates butted heads. But the Shield was harder and tougher, and eventually the Pacific Plate began "subducting," or slipping under the larger plate. That subduction process is still happening and causes the earthquakes that shake the west coast today.

In its original form, the Shield had jagged highlands like those we now see on the surface of the moon. They were rasped down by both rain and glaciers. Rain seeped into cracks in the granite and every night, when temperatures plunged, the rock crumbled, producing gravel, which washed off and produced wide alluvial flatlands, which stretched off for thousands of miles, which eventually turned into sedimentary rocks. It's important to realize that the Shield made our continent viable. It's the bedrock upon which North America was built. All the successful continents – Australia, Africa, and the others – have granite Precambrian rock as their foundation. Without a solid foundation of Precambrian rock, a continent can't survive.

I told her that the deeper nickel mines, like the ones in Sudbury, were warm at the bottom. And if you drilled only twenty-two miles down, you'd hit the Mohorovičić Discontinuity, which marked the edge of the planet's core, or if you will, its brain, which is fire. My throat was getting dry from all this talking and hiking, and judging by Mandy's amused silence, she'd heard enough geology for one day, so we walked back to the houseboat, arriving just before dark. We lit some candles, opened a bottle of wine, and went outside to watch the moon come up.

We sat on the slope of the island and toasted the evening, which was perfect. It was calm and warm, there were no mosquitoes, and the lake was a stained-glass window. Even the lunar cycle was perfect. The best night to watch the moonrise isn't on the night of the full moon (when it rises at the same time the sun goes down), but on the evening afterwards, when it comes up forty minutes after nightfall. For perhaps the entire time we sat there – from the moment that the first bulge of light appeared on the horizon, until perhaps half an hour later, when the moon hung like a Jack o' Lantern above the distant trees – we didn't say a word. But Mandy was curled up behind me, like a schoolgirl getting ready to ride a sled downhill, and her breath was soft on my neck. When the show ended I twisted around and kissed her, laying her flat on the rock and slipping my hand into the warmth under her sweater, feeling her heart banging beneath mine. "Are we going to bed now?" she asked. "Or are we going to the party?"

Her voice had that breathy sound of someone wanting to know if it's okay to let the dogs off the leash. If we went to bed now, there wasn't much chance that we'd be going anywhere, and I really wanted her to experience Minaki in its fullness, including a good party with lots of music and laughter. So I suggested we remain resolute and go to the party, at least for a while. "Good idea," she said, standing up and hauling on my hand. "This is going to be fun."

We blew out all the candles. Or at least we thought we blew out all the candles. Then we put on our jackets and headed off. The party was at Pete and Trout Barber's house, alias Tax Dodge Lodge. (Pete, being a scrupulous sort of guy and careful book-keeper, didn't think the name was all that funny.) Pete was a little older than I was, and when I was growing up back in Winnipeg, he was one of those cool guys who ran the school dances and hung out with guys like Neil Young. Now he lived in Minaki, had a pretty wife, lots of business on the go, and was the unofficial mayor of the village. When Mandy and I arrived, fifty or sixty people were already milling about on the back deck and in the party room indoors. The food was a potluck affair, based on a theme of local bounty, and there was lots of smoked fish, venison loin roast, bannock, roast partridge, fresh pickerel, moose casserole, wild rice pilaf, baked lake trout, and mallard à l'orange. Mandy elbowed me in the ribs, embarrassed that we hadn't brought any food. But I reminded her that we hadn't known about the party until this afternoon. And in any case, these people were like family. When you go to a party at your family's house, you don't have to bring anything; you just have to wear a clean shirt.

Later, there was dancing and music. Kelly was playing the saxophone. Dave was dancing with a bunch of women, and Mandy was having a fine time too, working the room without any help from me. It was well past midnight before I finally coaxed her to come outside for a minute, on the ruse of sharing a cigarette. Once we got outside, I gave her her jacket. "Let's go."

"Why?"

"Ssshh . . ." I whispered. "They'll catch us."

"It's a good party."

"It's always a good party." I pulled her behind the bushes and kissed her. Her mouth tasted like wine. She pulled me into the shadow of the house and we necked for a few minutes, grappling and jostling against the wall.

"Okay, you've convinced me," she whispered.

My boat was down the road, parked at the marina. Once we climbed into the cockpit, I told Mandy to close her eyes. "I've got a present for you."

She closed her eyes, and I drove out of Town Bay, past the myriad lights that slurred the surface of the slick water. When the lights of town fell behind us, I shut off the motor and coasted to a stop. "Okay, there it is."

She opened her eyes and murmured in amazement.

High above us, the stars glowed and flickered like a million birthday candles. We drifted in total silence for a few minutes, gazing up at them. I said, "You can see six thousand stars on an average night around here."

"Did you count them?"

"Yes," I lied. "Every single one."

"If I lived here I'd learn the stars too," Mandy allowed. "They're just so bright."

We were both speaking in whispers. With my arm around her, and her head tilted back against my shoulder, we watched the sky slowly rotating above us. She asked me if I'd included astronomy on my home-study course. I said I had, but couldn't remember many of the details. She said, "Give me the Coles Notes version."

I told her that, according to current science, it all started fifteen billion years ago. Fifteen billion years ago there was Nothing. Floating in the middle of this Nothingness was a "cosmic egg." The egg was very dense, because it was packed with all the material in the universe. Abruptly, the egg exploded. Scientists aren't sure why it exploded, but their best guess sounds pretty much like the Book of Genesis:

> Darkness was upon the face of the deep; and the spirit
> of God moved over the waters. And God said: Be light
> made. And light was made.

And a flash of light bigger than any supernova – so big in fact that scientists abandoned all hope of capturing it with elevated language and simply called it "the Big Bang" – sent hot gases flying in all directions. As the burning shrapnel blasted through space, some of it congealed into tiny burning droplets called stars, and the smaller ones cooled down and formed planets.

Here and there, particularly thick clouds of stellar dust formed galaxies. Our galaxy, the Milky Way, contains about two hundred billion stars, give or take a hundred billion.

(Scientists can't count them properly because they can't stand outside the galaxy to get a look.) There are hundreds of millions of other galaxies like the Milky Way, but we can't see them with the naked eye. Back in 1927 the astrophysicist Edwin Hubble determined that the universe is still expanding. And later, two astronomers named Arno Penzias and Robert Wilson discovered that the shock wave of the Big Bang is still out there, rolling away like a thunderclap. With highly specialized measuring equipment, you can hear it.

All the scientists pretty much agree on how the universe started. But they differ on how it will all end. Some hold with fire; others with ice. Some scientists say the universe will keep expanding until it runs out of energy and dies. The fire buffs argue that the universe will eventually slow down, as gravity overcomes the momentum of the Big Bang. Then each star will pause, like a burning arrow at the top of its arc, and begin to rush back towards a terrific pile-up that collapses every wooden boat, highway, mountain, planet, star, and galaxy into one super-compressed tiny super-hot particle. Stephen Hawking says the particle – another cosmic egg – will be about the size of an atom. Then what? Maybe the process will begin again. The cosmic egg may flash to life again with another great bang. Even if we're not around to enjoy it, a fiery rebirth seems like a more encouraging version than a universe that runs out of energy and dies with a whimper.

The only trouble with star-gazing is that it's a bit of a conversation stopper. I'd read every book on this country, gone from the end to the beginning, but I still hadn't figured out the answer to anything. So before we got too chilled and disheartened, I fired up the motor and we carried on. I was looking forward to climbing into bed with Mandy, snuggling under flannel sheets and warm quilts. But when we came around the corner, I saw something. I stopped the boat. A scarf of white smoke was drifting out of Dave's chimney.

"What's the matter?" she said.

"The houseboat is on fire."

"What are you talking about?"

"The house must be full of smoke. Look at the smoke going up the chimney."

I sped up the boat and we carefully approached the door. The windows were black, and we had to be wary of opening the door and causing a backdraft explosion. Standing off to one side, we wrenched the door open and smoke belched out. We ducked inside. The houseboat's interior was like a demonic chapel, dark and smoky, illuminated by a hundred tiny flames. In such a fire, the upper layers of the room fill with carbon monoxide, and if you take a lungful you lose consciousness. So we stayed low, grabbed a couple of plastic buckets from under the sink, and dashed outside. Filling the buckets, we began throwing water on every exposed flame. Fresh air was now coming into the building, and the fire was starting to roll. Mandy and I argued about tactics. She thought I should go and get the fire department. I told her it was too late. She was flinging water like a madwoman and screaming that I should go for help. So I made her promise not to go in the building, then I jumped into the boat and sped for town.

As I burst in the door, the party was still in full swing. Dave and several women were doing the hokey-pokey. I accosted him. "Dave! Your houseboat is on fire."

"Oh sure."

"I'm serious! We need to go! Right now!"

He put his left foot in and his left foot out. "Was it burning when you left?"

"Yeah!"

"Then it's too late."

I got his jacket and pushed him towards the door. He wasn't drunk. He was just refusing to let a little thing like total disaster ruin his evening. We got in the boat and drove across Town Bay. Past the corner of Muncer's Reef the whole sky was lit up with the horrid orange glow of fire. When we arrived at the island the houseboat was encased in a gel of flames forty feet high. I was worried about Mandy, but I could see her standing up on a granite ridge, well back from the heat of the flames. We parked the boat and climbed up to join her. She was crying. Her face gleamed with tears, and gasping wails tore from her throat. Dave stood at my side, slapping me on the shoulder consolingly, as though it were my place and not his.

"Look at her go," he kept murmuring, almost in admiration. The building was cracking and mewing in the terrible heat. He'd built it from Quebec pine, cypress from Florida, and mahogany from Honduras. They were kiln-dried woods and the building burned as fiercely as if it had been soaked in gasoline. There was a sudden explosive boom as the big propane tank on the rear deck blew. Hissing like a huge furious reptile, it spat a dragon's breath of flame twenty feet sideways. Then the roof started falling in. Other boats were now arriving, people climbing the rock to stand here beside us. The women were crying. The men stood there with bottles of beer in their hand. There was nothing to say.

The walls fell in. Soon there was nothing but a burning skeleton on the deck. A barge came steaming around the corner, with its light flashing, and as it drew closer we could see that it was the rescue party – the Minaki Volunteer Fire Department. Assistant fire chief Nick Grogan and about five other volunteers had come to fight the fire. Nick Grogan was a local mechanic, a bachelor who lived quietly in a little house and was probably an alcoholic. At any party, it was about ten minutes worth of entertainment watching him trying to climb a set of stairs. He and the other firemen had all been at the party, and for some reason they'd allowed Nick to drive the barge. As the barge approached, it became apparent that Nick was frozen at the wheel. His eyes were wide, as if mesmerized by the flames, and he held the throttle with a fierce grip right up to the moment when the barge hit the burning houseboat.

It collided at an angle, so instead of being thrown onto the flames, the fire fighters tumbled into the water. The water was shallow enough that they were able to stand up. One of them wallowed through chest-deep water and punched Nick Grogan in the head. Nick snapped out of his daze and returned the roundhouse blow, sputtering and swearing. Soon four of five of them were wrestling and punching each other. Up on the rock, the onlookers barely paid any attention to the donnybrook. In the midst of this sad disaster, it was not only unfunny but too predictable to deserve comment.

That night, Mandy and I stayed at Holst Point. We felt so bad about the fire that we stayed in separate rooms. We probably blamed each other. I suspected that Mandy had left one of her cigarettes on the couch or the bed, and she probably thought I'd done something wrong with the candles. I don't know what she thought, because early the next morning she went back to the city on the train.

Constable Larry Willot came to my room at Holst Point and interviewed me for the police report. I told him we might have left a cigarette or neglected to blow out a candle. Or it might have been a short circuit in the wiring of the houseboat; I just didn't know. He kept nodding in feigned sympathy as he filled out the report. I didn't need any sympathy because I already knew it was my fault. After all, Mandy was just a visitor. And we might have gotten back to the houseboat in time, if I hadn't been holding forth on the universe.

Dave rented a little shack across the road from the bait shop and settled in for the winter. I went to see him to apologize for the fire, but he was annoyed that I even brought it up. "Forget it," he said. "You want a coffee?" The shack was about the size of an ice-fishing hut. It had a plywood table, a Coleman camp stove, and a little closet-type bathroom with a plastic pail for a toilet. The houseboat hadn't been insured, so he had to start all over again. He got a job at a construction site, driving a rock wagon. It was a rough, boring job, driving up and down pot-holed roads all day. But he never said a critical word, not to me or to anyone else, not once.

I would have offered him my houseboat but it would have been an insult. The flotation was so bad that every time I walked to one side it began to tip over. When I fell asleep I dreamed it was turning topsy-turvy, furniture and chairs clattering down from the ceiling, black water pouring in the doors like the end of the world.

Kelly Gibson believed that we could fix the flotation if we pulled the houseboat up on shore with his skidder. Kelly's skidder was an astoundingly rude and uncalled-for sort of machine with immense scarred tires and a winch that was capable of pulling trees out of the ground. Kelly was always entertaining himself with it, and pulling the houseboat up on the beach at Murray's Camp seemed like an interesting experiment. So we wrapped the cable around the base of the houseboat. It was a late October day, very cold. Gusts of wind were tumbling in off the lake like broken sheets of glass, and the ragged steel cable was so cold that our hands kept clenching up into paralytic claws. Finally the jerry-rigged towing harness looked ready, and Kelly climbed onto the skidder. The skidder dug in and spat pieces of lawn. The houseboat screamed as the cable came tight. Most of the building hopped and wiggled onto shore. But a good portion of it remained – a grisly wreckage of rusted drums and broken planks half-submerged in water.

Kelly jumped off and we stood there looking at the mess. The houseboat looked like it had been in a car accident. I knew what he was thinking. We'd been in a lot of adventures together, and I knew he was a proponent of cutting your losses and moving on.

I finally said, "Okay, let's destroy it."

"Where will you live?"

"I don't know."

Kelly climbed back onto the skidder and hauled the building the rest of the way out of the water. He opened the skidder's great mandibles and crushed the walls. Within half an hour the houseboat was reduced to heap of broken lumber. I poured a few gallons of heating oil onto the wreckage and lit the match. We stood there watching, warming our hands on the ripping flames. I kept looking at individual parts of the fire: pieces of shelving that I'd built, a trapezoidal window with melting shards of glass, a window box burning, its soil on fire too. Each tangled object seemed to be creaking and writhing in the heat, giving off hundreds of memories that rose into the flames and tore away on the wind.

By nightfall there was nothing left of the houseboat but a broad scorch mark on the beach. I loaded the van with the things I'd salvaged and headed for the highway. I didn't tell anyone I was leaving. Sometimes it's better to just slip away. It was snowing and flurries hooked sideways out of the darkness and bombed into the headlights. It's wearisome work, driving on snow-packed slippery roads, and I was happy when the storm finally ceased. After three hours of driving I finally saw the city, glowing like a scatter of embers on the horizon.

❧

I rented a bachelor apartment in the Osborne Village and started all over again. My old friend Paul Craft was a contractor, and he charitably hired me to work as a carpenter, a job for which I couldn't have been less qualified. We hammered nails all day, and in the evenings I worked on the latest novel. Writing seemed to be the string of yarn that kept my life intact. My apartment was below ground level, and from my desk I could see bicycle wheels and legs going by. Living in the city made me feel like I'd been exiled from my own country, and all those memories of working as a guide and living in the wilderness lent poignancy to the writing process. I was working on a story that never happened but very well could have. It felt like important work, like recording the lives of people who had never lived. I'd written almost three novels now and amused myself by thinking that I'd eventually become a lesser Kilgore Trout, the unpublished oddball of the Vonnegut novels.

Still, I missed my ducks. On hot early mornings in high summer, when it was already broad daylight at five o'clock in the morning, the wild ducks from the neighbourhood would swim back and forth in the lily pads outside my bedroom, rapping at the wall to request breakfast.

When you're living in the city, it seems like there's time for only a bit of work, a few meetings, and then the day is over. But the island occupied its own time zone. If it was my day off, I'd write in the morning, then do some work outside. There was always decking to be repaired or boat seats that needed varnishing, and it was so silent, on those hot afternoons with no one around, that each single day seemed to go on forever. I often went up on the roof to fiddle with my antennae, trying new configurations to clarify my radio reception, and I liked working up there with my shirt off, feeling the heat pouring up off the asphalt roof, sweating in the afternoon heat, and then walking over to the south side of the roof and stepping off, dropping twelve feet straight down into the water.

Dusk too stretched on. The sun entered the northwesterly horizon at such a shallow angle that it was still twilight at ten-thirty. My bed was like a captain's bunk with an open screen window through which the night air breathed. The antennae on the roof was for maintaining contact with CBC radio, my lifeline to the outside world, and I always listened to *Book Time*, a show that featured readings of great novels, and later on, Big Al McFee, who with his pet mouse finished off the night with music and poetry. During one of those late-night broadcasts I heard someone interviewing the writer Alice Munro. She said that a short story should provide a kind of illumination at its ending, which ideally is one we hadn't expected.

I finally reached a kind of illumination too. Ever since I was a kid, exploring the forests north of Laclu, I'd fantasized about living permanently in the woods. The whole time I lived in Minaki, all I really wanted was a relationship with the wild lakes and forests of the Canadian Shield. I thought it would be like having a summer vacation that never ended. I finally found that relationship, more or less, but it took a few years, and I found it in the last place I would have looked: in the city.

One Saturday morning, I called Larry Krotz and asked him if he wanted to have lunch. Larry was a freelance writer, the only person I'd ever met who actually made a living from writing, and I was so impressed by this that I'd resolved to make him a friend. Larry told me that he couldn't have lunch because he had another commitment, with a woman named Lynn Cunningham. He told me that she was from Toronto, and that she edited a general-interest magazine called *Quest*. Apparently she was travelling across the country, taking the pulse of the nation, and looking for fresh new writers. He said, "Why don't you join us?"

Riding the elevator up to the restaurant, I tried to think up some story ideas. We had a very pleasant lunch. She seemed interested in the fact that I'd worked as a fishing guide. She wanted to hear some stories. I told her about the many characters I'd met, both the good and bad ones. Afterwards, she asked me to write an article about it. "Have some fun with it," she suggested.

I went home. Be careful what you wish for. I'd never written a magazine article before, and now I had to actually do it. But I got busy, and by midnight, I'd completed the piece. I mailed it off in the morning and awaited her reply. There was no reply. A week passed, then a month. Fearing the worst, I phoned her in Toronto and asked if she'd had a chance to look at it. "Of course!" she said. "I loved it. Your cheque should be on its way. Is a thousand dollars all right?"

Apart from publishing my story, she was offering to pay me one-fifth of my annual salary, so yes, it was all right. A few weeks later, I managed to get another piece of short fiction accepted. And that same week, a local publisher phoned me up and told me she wanted to publish my novel. I felt lucky, ridiculously lucky, but I had to remind myself that I'd been working at this for a long time. When my cheque arrived from *Quest* magazine, I told my contractor buddy Paul Craft that I was going to conduct an experiment. I was going to deposit the $1,000 in a separate bank account and for the next three months do nothing else but write. I'd write every morning and every night, and send stories off in every direction. I'd conduct my life as a business. I'd get a bunch of fresh white paper, some new typewriter ribbons, and even a swivel chair.

Three months later, I'd made some withdrawals from the bank account, but I'd also made some deposits, and the principal amount was still hovering around a thousand bucks. At tax time that year, I put "writer" on my tax form and haven't had a job since.

∾

Many years before I mutated into a writer, years in fact before I quit university and hit the open road with that old canoe on the roof, I was cruising down Academy Road one day in a red Triumph sports car piloted by one of my university friends, a good-time Charlie named Glen Harvey.

It was one of those warm, sunny autumn days when the slightest waft of warm breeze sends operatic chords of yellow leaves cascading down from the big elm trees, and you can't imagine being stuck in class or doing anything else that involves being indoors. I was trying to find some music on the radio when Glen suddenly locked up the brakes and we skidded to a stop. "Oh my God," he said. "Did you see that?"

From the panicked sound in his voice I thought he'd just witnessed someone being hit by a car. But as he downshifted into first gear and pulled a fast U-turn, I realized that he'd only spotted a girl. He pulled to a stop at the street corner, where the girl was standing there alone, waiting for a bus. She was a knockout, all right, with long wavy chestnut hair and the sort of large, heavy-lashed brown eyes that cartoonists draw when they want to render some impossibly luscious stereotype of the female face. This wasn't my sort of thing, to hail women at bus stops, so I just sat there and kept quiet while Glen delivered the routine. He was a good talker who wrote his own mottoes in the margins of his schoolbooks ("Never be afraid to ask for the sale"), and to my surprise, she agreed to accept a ride. Moments later, we were speeding along with our new friend somehow jammed into the tiny space between us.

We went to Glen's basement and listened to his new Country Joe and the Fish record, then went to the university pub for a drink. I had my dad's car and followed them over to the campus. It was my assumption that she was with Glen. He was the guy with the patter. But as we sat in the pub, she spent most of the time talking to me, about poetry and stuff, which turned out to be among her interests. Glen's tolerance for heartfelt conversation was minimal, and he soon wandered off. Later that night, when I dropped Carolyn off at her house, I asked her if I could take her to a movie sometime. She informed me that she had a boyfriend, but as she climbed out of the car she kissed me on the cheek and said that she'd enjoyed herself.

Ten years passed. I rented the basement apartment and started a new life as a self-employed writer. Early in the evening, I often walked over to the Safeway to buy my groceries. At about six o'clock every night, the store was busy with stylishly dressed young professionals on their way home from work. One night I bought a platter of chicken breasts, took them home, and discovered they were rancid. Was it worth walking all the way back to the store for a lousy three dollars and fifty cents? I decided that it was the principle of the thing. Back at the supermarket, the manager tried to explain the various ways that the rotten chicken was in fact my fault. I was arguing with him when who should go walking by but Carolyn. In spite of the ten years passing, I recognized her immediately. I chased her and said hello. She was cordial enough, and we chatted a bit. It turned out we were even neighbours. She lived right across the street from me. She didn't, however, share my opinion that this was all an amazing and fortuitous coincidence. I asked her if she wanted to go for coffee, but she declined.

A few days later, I phoned her to see if she'd changed her mind. She hadn't changed her mind, so I gave her a few more days and checked again. Finally, I realized that she didn't want to go for coffee. Several weeks later, in one of those great wheel-of-fate coincidences that seem improbably geared to our lives, Glen Harvey showed up at my door. He was driving a Mercedes coupe and wearing a raccoon coat. He smelled like Giorgio Armani. After planting a big smooch on my cheek, he suggested we go out looking for chicks.

We were no longer teenagers but Glen was still the same. We exchanged a few stories of the old days, and I told him I'd bumped into Carolyn just a while ago. He suggested that I call her, "for old times' sake." I told him I'd already tried that. He badgered me. He urged me to call both Carolyn and her fetching sister, and we'd take them out for drinks. Finally I gave up and called Carolyn, and this time she was annoyed. It was a short, curt conversation, and I hung up wishing that I hadn't done it. Glen swept off into the night.

Minutes later, the doorbell rang. It was Carolyn, looking furious. She shook her finger in my face and asked why I was "harassing" her. I apologized and explained that it was because Glen had dropped over. Glen was the sort of guy it was easy to blame things on. She somehow ended up staying for a cup of tea. She told me that she worked as an RN, and when Paul Craft had been in a bad car accident, she'd taken care of him. When she left my apartment that night, it seemed like we'd agreed to be friends. A month later, she came to the launch party for my first novel. I'd sent her an invitation, but hadn't really expected her to show up. When the party was winding down, I asked her if she wanted to catch a movie sometime. A week later we went to see *Lady and the Tramp*. We got married in the spring, and our daughter was born on Valentine's Day.

We purchased an old three-storey house with big elms in the yard. I organized an office in the porch, and while I tapped at my old IBM Executive, our infant daughter Caitlin would lie snoozing across my knees in her bumblebee pyjamas. When Carolyn came home from work at midnight, she sometimes had just finished wrapping a dead body. All she asked was that I put on a good TV show and rub her feet. There seemed to be a lot of writing work around, and we bought a new apple-red Cherokee. We had lots of friends and enjoyed speeding off to see a movie at the last minute. We had the traffic lights timed so that we could careen downtown, park, and walk into the theatre with our popcorn just as the curtains were opening. We did this at least twice a week. Hollywood couldn't keep up with us. We had a good life. But I'd often lie awake at night, listening to the wind in the trees outside our window, missing the lake country.

One day the phone rang. It was Kelly and Sally, my old friends from Minaki. They said that there'd been a big auction at Minaki Lodge. They'd bought a dismantled building – the old pro shop, a beautifully designed octagonal structure with massive fir beams in the ceiling. They'd intended to make it into a cabin, but changed their minds. Did Carolyn and I want to turn it into a houseboat? I sat down with Carolyn and we discussed the idea. She could see that I needed to do this and agreed to go ahead with it.

I went down to Minaki on the Ides of March, and with the help of Kelly and Dave and a few other guys, we framed it right on the ice, using sixty pieces of foam for flotation. That summer I spent a lot of time in Minaki, finishing the place up. Carolyn didn't always come. She liked the city just fine and didn't feel the same zest for rough backwoods living. I often brought Caitlin though. She was the size of a small tree lemur, and would clamber up onto my chest when she saw something she didn't like. She had her own room in the houseboat, but it was full of dangers. I'd moved the houseboat out to Virgin Island, and during the night thunderclaps would shake the building. Caitlin would climb into my bed, mumbling that there was "a short fat witch" in her bedroom. Then in the morning she would wake up ready to go, eager to go outside and look for minnows.

Just as mysteriously as we had drifted together, her mum and I began to drift apart. You never know why a marriage unravels. You might be attracted to someone because they're smart, funny, sexy, or wealthy, or because it's time you got married and they look like a good person to make a baby with. It's complicated, and doubly so when you blend together two personalities. When a marriage goes sideways, everyone wants to hear a simple explanation, so you come up with something. The truth is, you don't really know what happened, and you never will. After six years together, Carolyn and I decided to split up. We agreed to remain partners in raising Caitlin and expressed our determination to keep our relationship civilized. I found a big old rambling apartment with gleaming woodwork and a fireplace. It had a big bedroom for Caitlin. On weekends and holidays, we headed off to the houseboat, which was gradually turning into the place I'd always wanted, a floating piece of architectural fancy that looks a bit like a Japanese mountain pagoda. Fishermen were always stopping to take pictures of it, and when my tiny niece Helen first saw it, she scrambled aboard and asked, "Is this a fairy house?"

Being single again, or at least single some of the time, I was now free to pursue the mission that had taken me to the Shield in the first place. Being a freelance writer, I found that some publication or magazine was always willing to pick up the tab for my travels, as long as I came back with a good story. I used my freelance journalism work to subsidize the time I spent writing fiction and managed to put out a novel or a book of short stories every couple of years. Life never delivers exactly what we want, but the irony that foils one plan sometimes delivers a better one. When I was growing up, I'd imagined that I'd live in the Shield country and become a hunter-gatherer. As it worked out, I became a hunter-gatherer of stories. My job took me from one end of the Shield to the other, from top to bottom and from east to west. It's a place so full of stories, fabulous scenery, roaring waterfalls, teeming wildlife, self-made people, and heart-stopping vistas of uninhabited wilderness that it would be foolish to try to summarize them. But eventually, I figured out a sort of rough translation of its enigmatic message.

The discovery of the message didn't occur in a dramatic way. And I didn't find it in some far-flung arctic river valley, secreted under a rock. Rather, it just kind of sank in with the passing of the years. Literary critics like Northrop Frye and Margaret Atwood have made the point that the Canadian psyche is shaped by the belief that Nature still prevails. And that's an interesting idea, but it's just an idea. It doesn't sink in until you feel it, and feel it with every step you take.

The old-timers in Minaki knew the truth. Even when they were spinning yarns, it shaped every word that they said. One hot summer night after a long day of fishing I was sitting on the dock with the other fishing guides, and the topic came around to the afterlife. What kind of animal would you like to be?

The young guides voted for all the usual poster animals – the big charismatic creatures with impressive talons and teeth. "I'd like to be a timberwolf," said one. "I'd like to be an eagle," said another. An old Indian named Mitchell Muckle was sitting quietly at the picnic table, with cigarette smoke wafting up from his beat-up hands. He said, "I'd like to be a mouse."

I'd spent all these years trying to develop a big overview of this country. But maybe Mitchell was right. Maybe the mouse, with its sense of smell and its close-up view of every blade of grass, saw the world as it really was. As in any investigation, God is in the details. And although I'd always presumed that you acquired wisdom by acquiring knowledge, I was beginning to wonder if the path to understanding wasn't so much a learning curve as a de-learning curve. The answer wasn't in knowing more, but in knowing less.

One winter afternoon, for example, I wanted to ski over to Virgin Island and visit the houseboat. I wasn't sure if the ice was safe, so I went and visited Jack Stevens, a richly entertaining and hatchet-faced old-timer who was locally known as The Wedge. Jack's trapline included Virgin Island, and he knew more about the ice than anyone. "When is the ice safe?" I asked him. "Never," he said. I'd half-expected him to do this, to bait me with some provocative and playful answer. But he wasn't kidding. "The ice is never safe," he said. "No matter what the weather. And anyone who thinks it's safe is a fool."

He seemed a bit brusque, as though I shouldn't have been asking such a question. He had been travelling and working on the ice all his life. And he'd done it with the terrible knowledge that his life could be taken from him at any moment. We're all travelling on thin ice, of course. But for him the ice wasn't a metaphor; it was real, and walking on it every day had made him a wise man. His point was, nobody knows anything about this country. We're not in charge, Nature is. And it was high time I understood that.

We're lucky enough to inhabit a country where Nature still prevails. In the words of Northrop Frye, the Shield is not merely hostile, but "indifferent to human values." It was here billions of years before we came, and will still be here billions of years after we're gone. It provokes us into admitting that we are nothing. It obliges us to build our own values, invent our own identities. Our country may be a land of snow, a land of chilly lakes, haunted trees, and granite ridges rolling off into the distance like ribs of time, but it makes us who we are.

When my daughter was fourteen years old, she went on a wilderness canoe trip organized by the YMCA. It was an expensive vacation, but her mother and I were convinced that she needed to see the wilderness face to face. The canoe trip turned out to be long and miserable, and the bugs were bad. They dodged bears, waded shin-deep through mucky swamps with heavy canoes and packs on their backs, and paddled so hard their hands bled. It rained heavily, and they slept on the ground in sodden sleeping bags. One night they found a rotted, fallen-down trapper's cabin with skunk turds on the floor and bats crawling around in its broken rafters. But they were as excited as if it was a Four Seasons Hotel. It meant they could sleep on a wooden floor! When they paddled back to camp, the counsellors prepared a welcoming celebration. The girls beached their canoes, kneeled, clasped their sacred paddles to their hearts, bowed their heads, and received the traditional voyageur's benediction. They had left the camp as girls and returned as women.

The Shield has a different effect on everyone who spends time there. For some, it's a tool for growing up. For others, it's a frontier, a place to discard old identities and start anew. In the United States, the cowboy hat and the pick-up truck are symbols of the American heartland. But Canada's symbols are the symbols of the Shield – the beaver, the snowshoe, the checkered jacket, and the float plane. The Shield can be a place that poses an insoluble puzzle, or it can be a place to drink beer at the cottage and relax. God knows there's nothing wrong with that. As one old fisherman told me, "People ask me why I spent so much of my life at the lake. I've thought about it, and decided it's because I enjoyed it." I enjoyed the Shield so much that I tried to live there and proved to my satisfaction that I couldn't. But it's an addictive landscape, and I return to it time and time again.

It's my own unwritten page, a blankness where my own story begins and ends.

One spring night, several years ago, I was staying in the Park Plaza hotel in Toronto, trying to decide whether to go to a birthday party or just stay in my room and watch television. I didn't feel like going to a party. I was listless. It was a rainy night and my immense expense-accounted hotel room was vaguely depressing. But the rule is, always attend the party. So I went, and met Ann, who was alone, like me. She was a smart, attractive blonde, a talented writer, and I'd admired her work for many years. We stayed up late and went back to her house for a nightcap. While she fixed our drinks, I looked at the art in her living room. She owned quite a few landscapes. They were oil paintings, originals, and I was surprised to see A.Y. Jackson's name written in the bottom right-hand corner. "We called him Uncle Alec," she said. "He wasn't really our uncle, but he spent so much time at our cottage in Georgian Bay that he was like a member of the family. When I was a little girl I'd sit on his knee at the table and wipe the marmalade off his sweater. I'd sometimes go with him when he went out sketching."

Ann loved the north country, like me. How could we not love the north country? Summer was coming. We were Canadians. We'd grown up at the lake and we knew how to make love in a canoe. It took some doing, but I persuaded her to be my girlfriend. She came to Minaki and we looked at the stars. I took her out to my old camping spot at Tower Island, which, as always, was like a green cathedral. The moss was soft underfoot and the great pines stirred in the wind.

We drove to Kenora a few days later to buy groceries. On the way, we stopped at Laclu so that I could show her the old cottage. My father had been crippled by a severe stroke and was in a veteran's hospital in Winnipeg. He'd probably never come to the lake again. My mother still came for a weekend when one of my brothers or sisters found the time to bring her, but the cottage was no longer the busy, happy, family meeting place it had once been.

We parked the truck next to the old shed. The lawn was high and unkempt. The front door of the cottage was padlocked, so I couldn't show Ann the interior. But it was fine to walk around outside. My father had planted all these trees when I was a kid, but now they were as tall as the trees in a forest, and busy with hundreds of songbirds. It was nesting season, and the wooded yard was so full of chirping, warbling cries that it was like walking through a Montreal Jazz Festival of birds.

We stopped under a big apple tree to look at one of the decrepit birdhouses that my father had built so many years ago. Then we walked down the hill to look at the water.

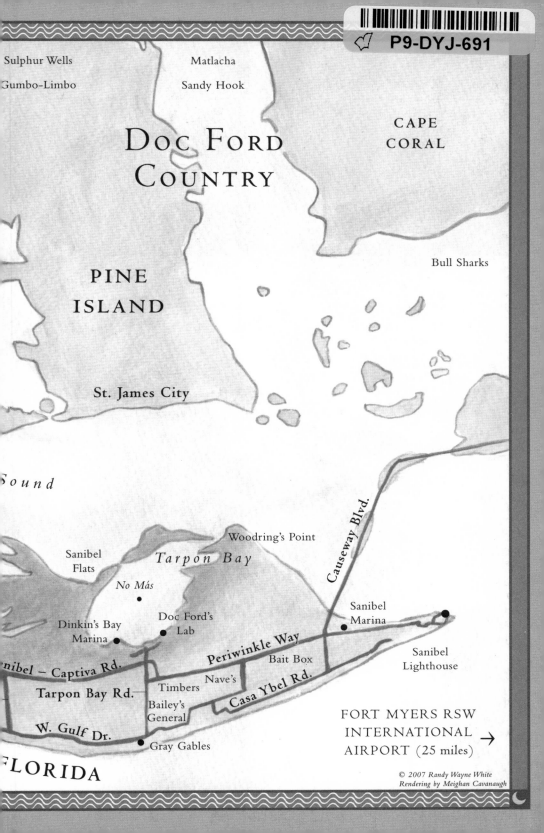

Sulphur Wells

Matlacha

Gumbo-Limbo

Sandy Hook

Doc Ford Country

CAPE
CORAL

Bull Sharks

PINE
ISLAND

St. James City

Sound

Woodring's Point

Sanibel
Flats

Tarpon Bay

Causeway Blvd.

No Más

Dinkin's Bay
Marina

Doc Ford's
Lab

Sanibel
Marina

Periwinkle Way

Sanibel
Lighthouse

Sanibel – Captiva Rd.

Bait Box

Nave's

Tarpon Bay Rd.

Timbers

Casa Ybel Rd.

Bailey's
General

FORT MYERS RSW
INTERNATIONAL
AIRPORT (25 miles) →

W. Gulf Dr.

Gray Gables

FLORIDA

© 2007 Randy Wayne White
Rendering by Meighan Cavanaugh

NIGHT VISION

RANDY WAYNE WHITE

G. P. PUTNAM'S SONS

NEW YORK

G. P. PUTNAM'S SONS
Publishers Since 1838
Published by the Penguin Group
Penguin Group (USA) Inc., 375 Hudson Street, New York, New York 10014, USA • Penguin
Group (Canada), 90 Eglinton Avenue East, Suite 700, Toronto, Ontario M4P 2Y3, Canada
(a division of Pearson Penguin Canada Inc.) • Penguin Books Ltd, 80 Strand, London WC2R 0RL,
England • Penguin Ireland, 25 St Stephen's Green, Dublin 2, Ireland (a division of Penguin Books
Ltd) • Penguin Group (Australia), 250 Camberwell Road, Camberwell, Victoria 3124, Australia
(a division of Pearson Australia Group Pty Ltd) • Penguin Books India Pvt Ltd, 11 Community
Centre, Panchsheel Park, New Delhi–110 017, India • Penguin Group (NZ), 67 Apollo Drive,
Rosedale, North Shore 0632, New Zealand (a division of Pearson New Zealand Ltd) • Penguin
Books (South Africa) (Pty) Ltd, 24 Sturdee Avenue, Rosebank, Johannesburg 2196, South Africa

Penguin Books Ltd, Registered Offices: 80 Strand, London WC2R 0RL, England

Library of Congress Cataloging-in-Publication Data

White, Randy Wayne.
Night vision / Randy Wayne White.
p.   cm.
ISBN 978-0-399-15705-9
1. Ford, Doc (Fictitious character)—Fiction.   2. Marine biologists—Fiction.
3. Florida—Fiction.   I. Title.
PS3573.H47473N54   2011   2010048985
813'.54—dc22

Printed in the United States of America
1   3   5   7   9   10   8   6   4   2

BOOK DESIGN BY MEIGHAN CAVANAUGH

Sanibel and Captiva Islands, and Immokalee, Florida, are real places, faithfully described, but used
fictitiously in this novel. The same is true of certain businesses, marinas, bars and other places
frequented by Doc Ford, Tomlinson and pals.

In all other respects, however, this novel is a work of fiction. Names, characters, places and
incidents are either the product of the author's imagination or are used fictitiously. Any resemblance
to actual persons, living or dead, or to actual events or locales is unintentional and coincidental.

While the author has made every effort to provide accurate telephone numbers and Internet addresses
at the time of publication, neither the publisher nor the author assumes any responsibility for errors,
or for changes that occur after publication. Further, the publisher does not have any control over and
does not assume any responsibility for author or third-party websites or their content.

For my adored partner, Wendy Webb, and our eloquent, gifted
Webb family: Sandy and Jim Phillips, Ben, Sarah, Tom, Janet,
Luke, Jack, Mary, Joost, Jesse, Kelly, Ryder, Layla, and
three ascending stars: Hannah, Phoebe and Zoë Webb

AUTHOR'S NOTE

I learned long ago, whether writing fiction or nonfiction, an author loses credibility if he's caught in a factual error. Because of this, I do extensive research before starting a new Doc Ford novel, and *Night Vision* is no different.

However, a scene takes place in this book for which no research data was available. It concerns bottlenose dolphins that are surprised while foraging beneath mangrove trees, on land, on a starry, moonless night. As the author, though, I can vouch for the scene's accuracy and authenticity because I witnessed a similar event, and the details are as described, although viewed through the eyes of Marion Ford and Tomlinson.

Otherwise, thanks go to experts in various fields. These include Dr. Frank J. Mazzotti, wildlife biologist, and one of the country's foremost experts on crocodilians. Ryan D. Battis, of Laser Energetics, manufacturers of the Dazer Guardian. Peter Deltoro and Dr. Tim S. Sigman, both of whom provided invaluable help to the author.

Special thanks also go to my partner, Wendy Webb, my guardian, Iris

AUTHOR'S NOTE

Tanner, my partners and pals, Mark "Dartanian" Marinello, Coach Marty and Brenda Harrity, my surfing buddy Gus Landl, my spiritual advisers Bill and Diana Lee, my battery and travel mate Don Carman, Stu "The Big Lefty" Johnson, lovely Donna and Gary "Twig" Terwilliger, and Dr. Brian Hummel, the author's intellectual compass and ever-faithful friend.

Once again, the early chapters of this book were written in Cartagena, Colombia, and Havana, Cuba, and I am indebted to friends who helped me secure good places to live and write. My thanks go to Giorgio and Carolina Arajuo for their help in Cartagena. In Cuba, my Freemason brothers Ernesto Batista and Sergio Rodriquez were particularly helpful, as were Roberto and Ela Giraudy, Rául and Myra Corrales and Alex Vicente.

Most of this novel, though, was written at corner tables before and after hours at Doc Ford's Rum Bar and Grille on Sanibel and San Carlos Islands, where staff were tolerant beyond the call of duty.

Thanks go to Col. Raynauld Bentley, Dan Howes, Brian "Boston Blackie" Cunningham, Mojito Greg Barker, the amazing Liz Harris, Capt. Bryce Randall Harris, dear Milita Kennedy, Kevin Filliowich, Kevin Boyce of Boston infamy, Eric Breland, Big Sam Khussan Ismatullaev, Olga Guryanova, lovely Rachel Songalewski of Michigan, Jean, Evan and Abby Crenshaw, Lindsay Kuleza, Roberto Cruz, Amanda Rodriquez, Juan Gomex, Mary McBeath, tattoo consultant Kim McGonnell, the amazing Cindy Porter, "Hi" Sean Scott, Big Matt Powell, Laurie and Jake Yukobov, Bette Roberts and master chef Chris Zook, a man of complex talents.

At the Rum Bar on San Carlos Island, Fort Myers Beach, thanks go to Wade Craft, James Gray, Kandice Salvador, Herberto Ramos, Brian Obrien, lovelies Latoya Trotta, Alexandria Pereira, Kerra Pike, Christine Engler, Stephanie Goolsby, Danielle Gorman, Corey Allen, Nora Billheimmer, Molly Brewer, Justina Villaplano, Jessica Wozniak, Lauren Brown, Kassee Buonano, Sally Couillard, Justin Dorfman, Chris Goolsby, Patric John, Stephen Johnson, Manuel Lima, Jeffrey Lyons, Matthew and Michael Magner, Catherine Mawyer, Susan Mora, Kylie Pryll, Dustin

AUTHOR'S NOTE

Rickards, Brooke Ryland, Ellen Sandler, Dean Shoeman, Jessica Shell, Andrea Aguayo and Kevin "Stretch" Tully.

At Timber's Sanibel Grille, my pals Matt Asen, Mary Jo, Audrey, Becky, Bart and Bobby were, once again, stalwarts.

Finally, I would like to thank my two sons, Capt. Rogan and Lee White, for helping me finish, yet again, another book.

—Randy Wayne White
Casa de Chico's
Sanibel Island, Florida

Everything that has happened, everything that will happen, it all exists in this single moment, endlessly surfacing and submerging; natural order, perfect law. The word "coincidence" is an invention that defines our own confusion better than it describes a unique occurrence.

—S. M. TOMLINSON

One life is all we have and we live it as we believe in living it. But to sacrifice what you are and to live without belief, that is a fate more terrible than dying.

—JOAN OF ARC, 1412–1431

NIGHT
VISION

ONE

ON AN EVERGLADES-SCENTED EVENING IN MARCH, AS I DROVE MY pickup truck west, toward the Gulf of Mexico, my hipster pal, Tomlinson, reached to switch off the radio, saying, "Life is the best thing that can happen to any of us. And it's also the very worst thing that can happen to any of us. Problem is, our luck begins with mom's location when the womb turns into a slippery slide. That's why I self-medicate. It makes the shitty unfairness of it all almost bearable."

We had just dropped my chatty cousin, Ransom Gatrell, at Regional Southwest, and I was eager for a few minutes without conversation. I nodded toward the radio and told him, "Hey, I was listening to that. We can talk later."

"The Guatemalan girl deserves your full attention," Tomlinson reminded me. He leaned back in his seat and stuck his hand out the window, surfing the Florida night. "She's gifted. And she's in trouble."

He wasn't referring to Ransom, although my powerhouse cousin, and my other neighbors at Dinkin's Bay Marina, Sanibel Island, Florida, are a gifted, eclectic bunch.

"Your friends are always in trouble," I said. "Your female friends, anyway. Percentages suggest the problem is *you*, not them."

"Tula isn't a female. She's an adolescent girl," he replied. "There's a big difference. Tula's at that age—a magic age, man—when some girls seem to possess all the wisdom in the world. They're not screwed up by crazed hormones and menstrual periods. They exist, for the briefest of times, in a rarefied capsule of purity. The window is very, very narrow, of course. It's afterward that most women go a little nuts. Hell, let's be honest. All of them."

"Uh-huh," I said.

Tomlinson pressed, "I'm trying to give you the background so you understand what we're dealing with. This girl traveled three thousand miles on freight trains, riding in the backs of semis, to get to Florida. Hell, she even hiked across a chunk of Arizona desert. It's because she hasn't heard from her mother in almost three months. Her brother, two aunts and an uncle are somewhere in Florida, too, and she hasn't heard from them, either. Something's wrong. Tula came here to find out what."

I said, "An entire family goes off and leaves a girl alone in the mountains of Guatemala? Maybe they're not worth finding."

"One by one," Tomlinson replied, "whole villages migrate to the States. You know that. They watch television at some jungle *tienda*. They see the fancy cars, the nice clothes. Meantime, they don't even have enough pesos to buy tortillas and beans. All the volcanic eruptions and mudslides the last few years in Guatemala, how do you deal with something like that? The coffee crop has gone to hell, too. Another revolution is brewing, and there's no work. What would you do if you lived there, and had a family to feed? That's what I meant when I said a person's luck—good or bad—begins with where they're born. Are you even listening to me?"

An instant later, the man's attention wandered, and he said, "Holy cripes, another Walgreens. If they keep piling up the concrete, building more condos, this whole damn peninsula is gonna sink. Just like Atlantis. It could happen."

I downshifted for a stoplight, and I turned and looked at Tomlinson, the odor of patchouli and his freshly opened beer not as penetrating as the magenta surfer's shirt he wore. "Not listening, huh? The girl is thirteen-year-old Tula Choimha from a mountain village northeast of Guatemala City, not far from the Mayan pyramids of Tikal. Did I pronounce her last name right?"

"Choom-HA," Tomlinson corrected, giving it an Asiatic inflection, which is not uncommon in the *Quiché* Mayan language. He spelled the name, then added, "Does it sound familiar? It should. Choimha is mentioned in *The Popol Vuh*. She's the goddess of falling water."

He was referring to a book of Mayan mythology, one of the few written records to survive the religious atrocities of the Conquistadors.

I thought, *Oh boy, here we go,* but I pressed ahead, saying, "Tula just turned thirteen, you told me. Her mother's first name is something unpronounceable, so she goes by Mary. Or Maria. Tula arrived in Florida about eight days ago, and you met her—you *said* you met her— by coincidence at a trailer park the owners are trying to condemn so they can build condos. She lives with five other people in a single-wide."

"Meeting her wasn't coincidental. I would never say coincidental, because I don't believe in—"

I interrupted again. "But you didn't tell me the whole truth, did you? You didn't say that, about once a month, you cruise the immigrant neighborhoods, buying grass or fresh peyote buttons. The illegals smuggle in peyote from Mexico because it's safer than carrying cash they probably don't have in the first place. You used to drive your VW, but lately you've been taking your electric bike. *What?* You think it makes what you're doing less obvious? Just the opposite, pal."

I waited, glancing at the rearview mirror until I saw the man's smile of concession, before I added, "See? I *was* listening."

Tomlinson disappeared into his own brain as I drove west, his right hand still surfing the wind, his left fist cupping a can of Modelo. *Disappeared* is a fitting description. Tomlinson has spent so many nights alone, at sea, he says, that he has constructed the equivalent of cerebral theme parks in his head for entertainment. Books, religion, music, whole communal villages populated, presumably, with Jimi Hendrix and Hunter S. Thompson types. All probably landscaped with cannabis sculptures trimmed to resemble objects and creatures that I preferred not to imagine.

Tomlinson is a strange one, but a good one. His perception of reality has, over the years, been so consistently tinted by chemicals that, my guess is, he has reshaped reality into his own likeness. And it is probably a kinder, brighter reality than the one in which most of us function.

Tomlinson is among the most decent men I know—if you don't count sexual misconduct, which I am trying to learn not to do. He's brilliant and original, something I can say only about a handful of people, and I count him among my most trusted friends—again, his behavior with women excluded. He had come into my little marine lab earlier that day asking for help. And when a friend asks for help, you say yes and save the questions for later.

It was later. Almost ten p.m., according to the Chronofighter dive watch on my left wrist. March is peak tourist season in Southwest Florida, so beach traffic was heavy, both lanes a bumper-car jumble of out-of-state license plates punctuated by roaring packs of Harleys.

After several minutes of silence, Tomlinson's attention swooped back into the cab of my truck, and he said, "This place we're going on San Carlos Island, the trailer park's named Red Citrus. It's not far from the shrimp docks. And, lately, it's become a bitch of a dark space, man. I should have warned you before we started."

I said, "The shrimp docks? That sounds close to your new restaurant."

Tomlinson, the hippie entrepreneur, had opened a rum bar and grille on Sanibel, and another at Fisherman's Wharf, near the shrimp yards, bayside, Fort Myers Beach. I was one of the investors, as was my cousin, Ransom, who also managed both places, along with her two boyfriends, Raynauld Bentley, a Cajun, and Big Dan Howes. So far, Tomlinson's business acumen had showed no damage from his years of chemical abuse, so it had been a wise thing to do.

It was one of life's amusing ironies. Tomlinson, who claims to have no interest in money or possessions, is gradually becoming wealthy, boosted along, perhaps, by his own fearless indifference to failure. I, on the other hand, remain steadfastly middle class *because* of my indifference—not counting a cache of small, valuable treasures I have acquired over the years.

Jade carvings and amulets. Spanish coins of gold and silver. All will remain faithfully hidden away, barring an emergency.

"The trailer park's on the same side of the bay," he replied, "but a couple miles farther east. That's why I used to like cruising Red Citrus, it was close enough. I could moor my boat near the bar and use my electric bike. In the last year or so, though, the whole vibe of the place has changed. The aura, it's smoky and gray now like a peat fire. It's the sort of place that consumes people's lives."

I replied, "Isn't that a tad dramatic?"

He asked, "You ever lived in a backwater trailer park? You've spent enough time in the banana republics to be *simpatico* with the immigrants who live there—that's one of the reasons I asked you to come along. People in that park work their asses off, man, six or seven days a week, picking citrus or doing construction or busing tables at some restaurant. Then they wire half the money—more sometimes—back to their families in Nicaragua or El Salvador or the mountain regions of Mexico. Hell, you know the places I'm talking about, man. These people are always fighting just to survive. That's why the girl deserves our help."

It was true, I am *simpatico*. "These people" included illegals on the run, as well as the "shadow illegals," men and women with green cards and work permits—sometimes forged, sometimes not. They live peacefully and work hard in this country, unlike the drug-fueled minority that gives the rest of them a bad name.

I knew "these people" well because I spent years working in Central and South America before returning to Florida, where I opened a small research and marine specimen business, Sanibel Biological Supply.

The illegals of Central America and Mexico are, in my experience, a gifted people. Strong, tough, smart and family-oriented. All the components required of a successful primate society.

However, *simpatico* or not, I am also pragmatist enough to understand what too many Tomlinson types fail to perceive or admit. In a world made orderly by boundaries, an unregulated flow of aliens into any nation makes a mockery of immigration law. Why wait in line, why respect legal mandates, if cheaters are instantly rewarded with a lawful citizen's benefits?

It is also true, however (as I have admitted to Tomlinson), there is a Darwinian component that must be considered. People who are sufficiently brave, shrewd and tough enough to survive a dangerous border crossing demonstrate qualities by virtue of their success that make them an asset at any country, not a liability.

Long ago, though, I learned I cannot discuss such matters with anyone who is absolutely certain of their political righteousness. So, instead, I listened.

"The undocumented workers have it tough, man," Tomlinson said, as he stared out the window. "They've got to watch their asses from every direction. The only thing they're more afraid of than the feds are their own landlords. Say the wrong word, don't jump when the boss man says jump, all it takes is one vicious phone call. And the dude who runs the trailer park is about as vicious as they come. He's a bodybuilder. A great big bundle of steroid rage, full of grits and ya'lls and redneck bullshit."

I baited my pal, saying, "You're the expert on better living through chemistry," as I slowed and studied the road ahead. We had crossed the small bridge onto San Carlos Island. I could see the ptero-dactyl scaffolding of shrimp boats moored side by side, floating on a petroleum sheen of black water and Van Gogh lights.

On my right were fish markets and charter boats. To my left, a jumble of signage competing for low-budget attention.

As Tomlinson told me, "Just past the gravel drive, take the next left," I spotted a faded wooden sign that read:

RED CITRUS MOBILE HOME PARK
RVS WELCOME!
VACANCY

"A vacancy in March?" I said, slowing to turn. "That tells me some-thing. It's got to be the only place around with a vacancy this time of year."

Sitting up, paying attention now, Tomlinson said, "Doc, I left out a couple of important details. One is that Tula—she's a thought-shaper."

I shot him a look.

"Of course, to a degree, we all have the ability to shape people's thoughts. This girl, though, has powers beyond anything I've ever witnessed."

Thought-shaper. It was another of Tomlinson's wistful, mystic fantasies, and I knew better than to pursue it.

"The second is: People at Red Citrus call her *Tulo*. So just sort of play along, okay?"

I said, "The masculine form?"

"You know how damn dangerous it is for a girl to cross Mexico into the States. Tula wants people to think she's a boy. She's a thought-shaper, remember? And the young ones, the adolescent kids from Central America, have more to fear than most."

I turned, shifted into first and proceeded beneath coconut palms and pines, weaving our way through rows of aluminum cartons that constitute home for many of the one million illegals in the Sunshine State.

When my truck's lights flushed a couple of peacocks, I wasn't surprised. Exotic fowl are common in the low-rent enclaves where migrant workers have adapted to living under the radar. They depend on exotic birds, not dogs, to sound a private alarm when outsiders arrive.

The cry of a peacock is high-pitched. It is a siren whine that morphs into a series of honks and whistles. That's what I thought I was hearing as I parked the truck and stepped out into the summer-cool night.

It was a cry so piercing that I paused, ears alert, before turning to Tomlinson, who was visible in the glow of a security light as he pushed the truck's door closed. His hair was tied back with a red bandanna, which he was retying as we exchanged looks.

The scream warbled . . . paused for a breath . . . then ascended. As if reading my mind, Tomlinson said, "That's not a bird! It's a person—a man, I think!" and then he sprinted toward the source of the sound.

I hesitated, reached behind the seat, then went running after him, struggling to slide a palm-sized Kahr semiautomatic pistol into the pocket of my jeans.

TWO

A FEW MINUTES BEFORE THIRTEEN-YEAR-OLD TULA CHOIMHA heard the screams for help, a huge man with muscles pushed through the trailer door, stepped into the bathroom, then stood for a moment, grinning at what he saw.

The man finally said, "Hah! I knew you was a girl! By God, I knew it the first time I saw your skinny little ass from behind! It was the way you walked."

He paused to stare, then added, "Fresh little peaches up top. Nothin' but peach fuzz down below."

Tula, sitting naked in the bathtub, looked where the man was looking, hoping, as always, to find a miracle. But there was only her own flat body to see.

The girl recognized the man. He was the *propietario* of this trailer park, maybe the owner, too. The man scared her. But the man's wife—or girlfriend, maybe—a woman with muscles and an evil face, scared her more.

Automatically, Tula used her hands to cover herself. But then she took her hands away.

The man had fog in his eyes—most people did—and Tula decided it was safer to be still, like a mirror, rather than behave like a frightened vessel that could be taken by force, then filled.

The man, whose name was Harris Squires, looked at her strangely for a moment. It was almost as if he recognized her face and was thinking back, trying to remember. Then he tilted his head and sniffed twice, nostrils searching. He was a man so large that he filled the bathroom space, his nose almost touching the low ceiling. Squires's nose was flat and wide, like a gorilla's, but he was the palest man Tula had ever seen. A man so white that his skin looked translucent, blue veins snaking out from beneath his muscle T-shirt and tight jeans.

"Know how else I knew you was a girl?" he asked. "I could *smell* you, darlin'. Man-oh-man"—his grin broadened, showing teeth so even that it was as if they had been filed—"I can wind-scent a virgin from seven counties away. What's the word for virgin in Spanish?"

Harris Squires didn't speak Spanish, although he'd learned a few phrases. But his girlfriend, Francisca Manchon—Frankie—spoke bits and pieces of it. She had taught him some things to say. Frankie called male Mexicans *chilies*, or greasers. Women were *chulas*. Harris didn't understand what the last term actually meant, but he guessed it wasn't very nice, knowing Frankie.

"No entiendo," Tula said to Squires. But she did understand. English was her third language. Spanish was the second—and even most Mexicans were unaware that her people, the *Indígena* of Guatemala, grew up speaking Mayan.

Gradually, Tula had acquired Spanish in the marketplaces of Tikal and Guatemala City. English had been learned from nuns at the convent where she and her brother had lived ever since their father was murdered and their mother had been forced north, to the United States, to provide money.

That was four years ago.

Six months earlier, Tula's brother had come north looking for their mother. Now he had disappeared, too.

El Norte—it was the way they spoke of the States in the mountain villages. *El Norte* was always said with a mixture of hope and dread because, in the ancient religion of the Maya, north was the direction of death.

The man stepped closer. "What'd you just say?"

"Yo no comprende," Tula repeated, shrugging her shoulders, feeling the man's eyes on her like heat. Squires leaned in.

He asked, "What's on those necklaces you're wearing? They'd look real nice on Frankie."

She didn't respond, hoping he wouldn't make a grab for the jade amulet and the silver medallion she always wore on leather straps, day and night, no matter what.

Instead, the man reached and began massaging the back of Tula's neck with his fingers. The girl didn't flinch. Instead, she found the bar of soap and began to lather her feet, her movements masculine and intentional, her expressions sullen, like a child.

The man stood, his smile gone. "Bullshit! You speak damn good English, you little liar. You and old man Carlson was spying on me last night, weren't you, goddamn it? You and your special buddy—I snuck back here a few nights ago and heard you two whispering. You was speaking pretty good English, so you can stop your lying right now."

Harold Carlson was one of the few *gringos* who lived in the trailer park. Tula trusted him because she trusted her instincts. Carlson, already an old man at sixty, was also a drunk, probably a paint sniffer judging from the half-moon darkness of his eyes.

But, as Tula knew, the depth of a man's decency could sometimes be judged by the depths of his own despair. People who were kind, after years of being wounded by their own kindness, naturally sought ways to dull the pain.

Carlson was her *patron*. After their first conversation, she had thought of him that way. He would help her, given the chance, because that is what a God-minded person would do. After only eight days in the States, Tula felt confident because she had already acquired two *patrons*.

Her second *patron* was a man as well. He was a strange one, named Tomlinson, who did not have fog in his eyes. Even though he resembled a scarecrow with his straw-bleached hair, Tomlinson was one of the few people Tula had ever met whose kindness glowed through gilded skin.

Tula continued lathering. She had seen what Squires had done last night, but Carlson, the old man, had not. Squires had gone to the bed of a rumbling truck, lights out, and dragged something malleable and heavy across the sand, then down the bank into a little mangrove lake that was surrounded by garbage dumpsters and palm trees.

The sack had sunk in a froth of bubbles, Squires watching, before he returned to the truck.

It was a human body, Tula guessed. Something weighted in a sack. Tula had seen enough corpses being dragged through the streets of her village to know. They were old people who had ended their lives in a gutter usually but sometimes a young man who had died from drinking too much *aguardiente*.

Also, Tula had been old enough during the last revolution to remember corpses drying among flies in the courtyard.

Her father's charred body had been among them.

Tula hadn't intended to spy on Harris Squires last night. She had

13

been sitting in the limbs of a ficus tree, listening to owls speak. There were two big owls, one calling from nearby, the other answering from across the water where the strange boats with metal wings were tied side by side.

The shapes of the boats—their triangular silhouettes—had reminded Tula of the jade amulet she wore around her neck. And also of small pyramids that were covered with vines in the lowlands west of Tikal. These were familiar stone places that the girl often climbed alone in darkness so that she could listen to the great owl voices converse while she stared, unblinking, at a jungle that strobed with fireflies.

The owl voices and the sparking fireflies invited visions into the girl's head. At the convent, Sister Maria Lionza had taught Tula about this phenomenon, and the nun was seldom wrong about such things. Tula had been living at the convent, under the nuns' guidance, learning the healing arts, and also studying the Bible along with her other lessons.

Sister Maria was a fierce woman given to fits of epilepsy and kindness, and she was particularly kind to Tula, who was her favorite.

"My brave little Maiden of Lorraine," Sister Maria was fond of saying. "Our blessed saint spoke of you in one of my visions. And now you are here with us. A messenger from God."

It was only within the last year that Tula had begun to suspect that Sister Maria was actually preparing her to join the nunnery and, perhaps, the *Culta de Shimono*. It was a secret group—a mythical cult, some said—that caused the villagers to cross themselves at night while whispering of wicked nuns who were actually *brujeriás*.

The English word for *bruja* was "witch."

Thanks to Sister Maria's secret teachings, Tula had experienced many visions in the last four years. The most disturbing vision had come into Tula's head three times—all within the last few months—so she knew the vision would come true if she didn't act.

In the vision, Tula could see large white hands choking her mother to death, fingers white around her soft throat. In the vision, Tula's mother was naked. She appeared diminished by her submissiveness, a fragile creature clinging to life, while the big hands suffocated the soul from her body.

It was a difficult vision to endure.

Now, because Tula had yet to answer him, Squires leaned a shoulder against the bathroom wall, getting mad, but nervous, too. Tula could read his eyes.

He said, "Tell me what you saw last night, you little brat! You *were* watching me, weren't you?"

Tula didn't react, but she was relieved. If Squires had known for sure that she had watched him struggling to drag a corpse into the water, he would have killed her. He wouldn't be standing here, asking questions.

Not that that meant he wouldn't anyway. Tula guessed that he would invent some excuse, drive her to a quiet place, then befoul her body, as men did to young girls, and kill her. Or . . . or he would ask someone else to do it. Fog covered the man's eyes, but fog didn't cloud the truth that Tula sensed: Squires was capable of murder—his spirit was already stained with blood, she suspected—but he was also a weak man tainted by the ugliness of people close to him.

Squires's wife, Tula sensed, was a poisonous influence. She had seen the woman only twice, but that was enough. The man called her . . . Frankie? Yes. She was a tall woman with large muscles, but her spirit was withered by something dark inside. Frankie was a man-animal, Tula was convinced, who enjoyed feeding on the weakness of smaller humans.

This man, Squires, was the same in that way.

For the weak, silence is among the few weapons available. Tula was using silence against Harris Squires now.

Squires tried his bad Spanish, saying, "Hear me, *puta!*"

He said it twice, but it didn't cause the girl to look away from her toes, so he returned to English, his voice softer. "I saw you, *chula*— you *know* that. I saw you sitting alone in a tree like a little weirdo. And you saw *me*."

It was true. At first, Tula didn't believe Squires could see her, sitting among branches, listening to owls, but then she realized he could. The man, after dragging the sack to the water, had leaned into the rumbling truck, then stood, holding binoculars to his eye. They weren't normal binoculars, Tula realized, as the man turned in a circle, searching the area, and then suddenly stopped, leaning to focus on the small space she inhabited.

When the man had jogged toward her, yelling, "Who the hell are you? Stay right where you are!" Tula had dropped from the tree and run, vaulting roots, then a wire fence at the boundary of the trailer park property.

Last night, she'd slept curled up on the floor of a bathroom stall, and she had spent most of the day in hiding, too, expecting Squires to appear. Now here he was.

Yes, Squires had seen her. His binoculars allowed him to see in darkness, like a night creature. Tula had heard rumors of such devices from women who lived in widow villages, created by the government after the last revolution for wives who had lost their men. In such villages, they knew about war, and the behavior of drunken soldiers, yet it surprised Tula that a man like Squires would own such a device for he did not look like any soldier she had ever seen.

"Was Carlson with you?" Squires demanded. "You two are buddies, don't try to deny it. The little weasel has been begging me for your mama's phone number the last couple of days."

Tula moved her legs, using the washcloth to hide some parts of her but to reveal others.

For a moment, Squires's expression signaled slow confusion, then he shook it and said, "You know, I just might know where she's living. I bet she's got some pretty little peaches on her, too—I wouldn't mind helping you find the lady. You want that phone number? Play your cards right, *chula*, I'm the man who can give you everything you want and more."

Tula sensed that Squires was lying about knowing her mother, so she ignored him, dipped her face into the water and washed.

Her eyes were closed, but she could feel what was happening when Squires dropped to his knees. His hips were against the rim of the bathtub as he grabbed a fistful of her hair. Then the man pulled her head back, saying, "Answer me, you little brat!"

The girl opened her eyes and sat still, muscles relaxed, letting silence communicate what she wanted the man to hear. Tula waited until he finally took his hand off her.

Slowly, Squires got to his feet and backed away. "What the hell's wrong with you? You a retard or what? You don't look even a little bit afraid. By God, I'll teach you! Just like I'll teach your whore of a mama to jump, once I find her!"

Tula's head snapped around when she heard that. Her eyes found Squires's eyes, and she said, "Don't talk about my mother that way. You have no right!"

That caused the man to smile, taking his time now, because he had finally won this game of silence. "See there?" he drawled. "By God, you speak the language as good as me."

The girl said, "Why be so mean? If you know where my mother is, you should tell me. This is a chance for you to do God's work."

"*God's* work?" Squires said, rolling his eyes and laughing. "You're a damn comedian. You think I keep track of every Mexican spends a few nights in this park? Besides, what do I care? Unless . . ." He paused to give the girl a theatrical smile. "Unless you're willing to give me something in trade. That's the way the world works, sis. Otherwise, why should I bother?"

Squires didn't expect an answer, but he got one.

"Because God is watching us," Tula told the man, looking into his face. It took a moment, but his expression changed, which pleased the girl. "The goodness of God is in you," she continued. "Do you remember how you felt as a child, full of love and kindness? God is still there, alive in your heart. Why do you fight Him so?"

Squires made a groaning, impatient noise. "You got the personality of an old woman. Christ! Save your God-loves-me speeches for Sunday school."

She could feel his anger rising again, and she knew she had to do something because she had broken the silence that protected her. Perhaps she had ruined the spell she was attempting as well.

Tula folded the washcloth, put her hands on the rim of the tub and got to her feet, water dripping. As she did, she looked into the fog that covered the man's eyes.

The man was a foot and a half taller than her, two hundred pounds heavier, but her confidence was returning as she cupped the jade amulet and the medallion in her right hand.

Then, closing her eyes, speaking softly in English, Tula began repeating the phrase that had comforted her these last few weeks, three thousand miles riding atop freight trains, in the trailers of eighteen-wheelers, dodging *Federales* who would have jailed her and the coyote gangsters who could have robbed and raped her.

As if praying, she chanted, "I am not afraid. I was born to do this. I am not afraid. I was born to battle evil, to smite the devil down. I am not afraid. I was born to do this . . ."

They were the words of her patron saint, a powerful spirit who communicated to Tula through the medallion she wore. The saint had died as a young woman, burned at the stake, yet she still came to Tula, sometimes at night in the form of visions, and during the day as a voice that was strong in Tula's head. The voice seemed to come to Tula from distant stars and from across the sea, where, long ago, a brave girl had put her trust in God and changed the world.

If the Maiden could vanquish the English from France, certainly, with the Maiden's help, Tula could now vanquish this mean, weak man from her bathroom.

As Tula prayed, Squires made a sour face. "You was born to do *what*? You was born to be a pain in the ass, that's what I think."

He could feel the heat rising, no longer seeing an adolescent girl standing naked before him but imagining her talking to police, telling them about what she'd seen him do last night.

Squires grabbed the girl's arm and gave her a shake. "Get your duds on. You want to see your mama? We'll get in my truck and go see her now."

The man was lying again. Tula knew it. She could picture herself in the man's vehicle, the two of them parked in some dark place where no one would hear her screams.

Tula switched to *Quiché* Mayan and continued chanting, "I was born to do this . . . I am not afraid . . . I was born to battle evil and smite the devil down . . . ," as the man shook her so hard that her head snapped back, and then said, "Now! Let's go! Stop your goddamn jabbering and—"

He didn't finish. Squires's words were interrupted by a wild, wailing scream, and he let go of the girl's arms.

The man turned toward the sound, listening, then said to Tula as he went to the door, "I ain't done with you, *chula*. Don't you go nowhere!"

The screams came from a person who was terrified and in pain, the voice unrecognizable. But Tula knew instantly who the person was—it was Carlson, the old drunk with the good heart. The girl didn't understand how she knew such things but she did.

Without toweling herself dry, Tula pulled on her jeans, a baggy T-shirt and stepped into her sandals. On the kitchen table, among mole sauce, sodden nachos and an ashtray, was a bottle of tequila. She grabbed the bottle, hesitated, found a flashlight, too, then stuffed a kitchen towel into the back of her pants and went running out the door.

Tula Choimha felt sure and determined, emulating the behavior of the Maiden, who spoke to her now from across the ages. The voice was strong in Tula's head, instructions from a teenage girl who had lived a life of fearless purity six hundred years ago.

The Maiden's voice told Tula to be quick, that she could save the life of her friend. And the girl obeyed, as she always did when under the loving direction of the Maiden of Lorraine.

Tula's patron saint—Joan of Arc.

THREE

FOCUSING ON THE CRIES FOR HELP, I RAN AFTER TOMLINSON, NOT
gaining on him, through an area that consisted of maybe forty
trailers packed tight into an area bordered by a low wire fence. Beyond the fence was a mangrove lake, where a crowd was gathering.
The lake was fringed with coconut palms and a row of garbage
dumpsters.

The place had probably been a homey Midwestern retreat
back in the seventies, popular with Buckeyes who caravanned south
each winter. But now smoldering cooking fires and a sewage stink
communicated the demographic change and a modern economic
despair.

Over his shoulder, Tomlinson yelled to me, "There's someone in
the water!" which I could already see. At first I thought we had stumbled onto a brawl, that the fight had tumbled into the pond.

But the man's screams didn't communicate rage. The sounds he
made signaled terror, an alarm frequency that registers in the spine,

not the brain. His howling pierced the gabble of men and women who were peeking from their trailers, yelling questions and expletives in Spanish, as a dozen or so of the braver residents—several of them children—ventured as a group, not running, toward the water's edge.

In his poor Spanish, Tomlinson yelled, "What's wrong? What's happening?" as I ran past him, hollering in English, "Call nine-one-one. It's a gator. A big one," because I could see details now in the pearl haze of security poles that rimmed the park.

I could see the alligator's tail, slashing water, an animated grayness edged with bony scutes that had not evolved since the days of stegosaurus. I could see the flailing arms of a man as he battled to stay above the surface of the water.

A likely scenario flashed into my mind: The man had stopped on the bank to urinate, or stare at what might have been a floating log—no one in their right mind would go for a swim in that cesspool—and the gator had snatched him.

It happens—not often in Florida—but it happens, and it had happened to a friend of mine only a few years before on Sanibel Island, where I live and run my small marine-specimen supply company. A good woman named Janie Melsek had been attacked while pruning bushes and she had died even though she had fought to the end, just as the man was fighting now. Even though in shock maybe he sensed that if the gator took him under, he would never surface again.

I hadn't been there when a twelve-foot gator took Janie into the water. I hadn't seen what had happened in the following minutes of terror. And things probably wouldn't have turned out any differently if I had. But maybe, just maybe, it was the memory of Janie that caused me to push through the slow phalanx of onlookers, as I jettisoned billfold, cell phone, then pulled the Kahr pistol from my pocket and lunged feetfirst into the water, unprepared for the knee-deep sludge beneath.

Jumping into the lake was like dropping into a vat of glue. My ankles were anchored instantly in muck, so my momentum caused me to slam forward, bent at the waist, face submerged, until I floundered to the surface and fought my way back to vertical.

The man was near the middle of the lake, only thirty yards away, screaming, "Help me! Grab my hand, I'm dying!" so maybe he'd gotten a look at me as I pried one slow right leg from the mud, losing my shoe, and then struggled to pull my left foot free. To do it, I needed both hands, so I pocketed the pistol and went to work trying to break the suction.

Behind me, someone had a flashlight, and he painted the pond until he found the alligator. I'd been right. It was a big one: four or five hundred pounds of reptile on a feed, creating a froth of lichens and trash that washed past me in waves. It was a male. Had to be. Female gators seldom grow beyond ten feet and two hundred pounds.

The animal had its back arched, head high, and I could see that it had a frail-sized man crossways in its jaws, the man's buttocks and pelvis locked between rows of teeth that angled into a reptilian grin.

The alligator's eyes glowed ember orange; the man's face was a flag of white, and, for an instant, his eyes locked onto mine just before the animal slung its tail and rolled, taking him under, then bringing him back to the surface, the animal's eyes not so bright now because the angle had changed but the man still sideways in the thing's mouth.

Because the gator had him by the hips, the roll—a death roll, gator hunters call it—had not snapped his spine.

"*Please*. Take my hand!" The man coughed the words, stretching his arm toward me, his voice pleading as if trying to convince me it would be okay.

I wasn't convinced. I am neither stupid nor particularly brave. But I also know enough about animal behavior to feel sure that I wasn't being mindlessly heroic. There are certain predators—alligators, sharks and killer bees among them—that, once their sensory apparatus has locked onto a specific target, ancillary targets cease to exist.

I have swam at night among feeding sharks so fixated on a whale carcass that my dive partners and I had nothing to fear. I once watched an Australian croc wrestle a feral hog into the water while an infant blackbuck antelope—a much easier target—drank peacefully within easy reach.

This alligator might worry that I wanted to steal the meal it had taken. But it wouldn't abandon a meal in its teeth to waste its time attacking me, additional prey.

I hoped.

I ducked beneath the water, dug at the muck until my left shoe popped free and then I surfaced as someone belly flopped into the pond next to me and began thrashing the water, racing toward the gator.

It was Tomlinson.

I pushed off after him, swimming hard, my head up, focusing on the bright, blurry horror ahead. I passed my friend after only a few strokes, watching as the gator turned and began ruddering toward the far shore.

The man's screams became whistled sobs, similar in pitch to the trumpeting of nearby peacocks, dark shapes that dropped from bushes and sprinted toward the shadows. Behind me, I heard a woman yell in Spanish, "Call for help, someone call the police!" but then heard a male voice hush the woman, saying, "Are you insane? Not the police!"

The gator appeared to be in no hurry now. The animal knew we were in the water—gators possess acute hearing and the night vision of owls—but it didn't seem to care. Even so, it traveled deceptively fast over the bottom, and I was halfway across the lake before I was finally close to enough to make a grab for the thing. Before I did, I rolled onto my side long enough to find the pistol.

I took a couple of more strokes to catch up and then lunged to get what I hoped was a solid grip on the animal's tail. I expected the gator to slash its head toward me, a hardwired crocodilian response. For a few seconds, though, the thing continued swimming, pulling me along—me, an insignificant weight—but then its slow reptilian brain translated the information, and the animal exploded, its tail almost snapping my arm from the socket.

Because I expected the gator to swing its jaws toward me, I ducked beneath the surface, feeling a clawed foot graze my ear. I sculled deeper until my toes touched bottom, took a look toward the surface—it was like being submerged in tar—then swam a couple of yards underwater before angling up, hoping I didn't guess wrong and reappear within reach of the animal's teeth.

I didn't. Instead, I collided with something bony and breathing as I surfaced. The gator's belly, I thought at first. But then I heard a wailing profanity—the voice familiar—and realized I had banged into Tomlinson, who assumed he was being attacked from beneath.

My friend, I could see, had both hands locked on the gator's tail and was being dragged. The animal was swimming faster now, probably convinced we were competing gators, employing harassment, hoping it would drop its prey. It's a common gambit in the animal world, so the thing was trying to get into shallow water before dealing with us.

As I started swimming after them, I heard Tomlinson yell a garbled sentence, words that sounded like "You just scared the piss out of me! Do something, Doc!"

I planned to do something, even though I had no plan. I considered risking a shot at the animal's flank, but there were too many people around, and the slug would skip if it hit the water. No . . . I had to get closer.

It took longer than expected. Despite the gator carrying a man in its jaws and a second man clinging to its tail, I still had trouble catching the animal because I was palming the pistol in my right hand. A pound of polymer and steel is not an efficient fin.

Finally, though, I was close enough to throw my left arm over the animal's back, which wasn't easy because the creature was twice my size. The gator bucked its head at me in warning, its hard belly spasmed, but it kept going. I felt around until I had what I thought was a good grip on the far ridge of scutes, hoping the thing would continue swimming long enough for me to get my right hand up. Next, I would position the pistol flat against the bony ridge behind the gator's right eye.

Alligators have tiny brains, little more than a bulbous junction of nerve cells. However, their heads and jaws are also covered with thousands of bead-sized nodules that serve as remarkably sensitive pressure detectors. That's why a gator can sense a lapping dog, or the splash of a child, from a hundred yards away. Even if the bullet missed the brain, the shock might cause the animal to release its prey and dive or swim for safety.

As I pushed the pistol barrel hard against the gator's head, though, the thing rolled again. I was on the animal's right side. It slapped its tail and rolled to the left. The movement was as abrupt as the slamming of a steel trap, and I was vaulted over the animal, into the air, and lost my grip as I hit the water.

When I surfaced, I had no idea where Tomlinson was. But I

knew the gator still had its prey because I could hear the man coughing water and I could see his dangling legs only a yard away in the
flashlight's beam.

I had come up just behind and to the left of the gator's snout.
Close enough to see the animal's bulging right eye, its pupil dilated
within gelatinous tissue that cast an orange glow.

The gator saw me. No doubt about it, and I wasn't surprised
when the thing slowed and swung toward me, opening its jaws, then
slinging its head to release its prey, now fixated on me. It had been
harassed enough. In the animal's mind, I was attempting to steal its
meal. It had decided to fight.

I grabbed the man's leg with my left hand and pulled, trying to
help him roll free but also using the resistance to lever myself close
enough to throw my right arm over the animal's back. The gator
shook its head again, maybe having difficulty tearing its teeth from
the man's clothing, which provided me with the extra second I
needed to get a grip on the reptilian neck with my left hand.

As its tail hammered the water, spinning toward me, I wrestled
myself atop the gator long enough to steady the pistol barrel flush
behind its right eye. My hold was tenuous, the positioning wasn't
perfect, but I was adrenaline-buzzed and scared. I didn't hesitate. I
fired two quick shots, the report of the pistol heavy and flat, muffled
by the animal's keratin skin.

There was a convulsive, watery explosion that threw me backward. When I surfaced, the gator's tail was vertical, slashing the air
like a wrecking crane, and I had to scull backward to keep from
being hit. A moment later, the animal rolled to the surface, still
thrashing, and then submerged abruptly in a boil of bubbles and
muddy detritus from the bottom.

I wasn't sure if I'd killed the thing or not. Alligators sink when
dead, but they also submerge if they're wounded or feel threatened.

If the bullets had done only minor damage, then the gator could be drifting to the bottom right now, tracking my vibrations as it regrouped. I didn't relish the possibility. To me, a known quantity, however perilous the situation, is much preferred to a vague unknown.

As I turned to search for Tomlinson, I hollered, "Where is he? Did he go under?" meaning the injured man.

I received an answer in the form of another scream. It was a shredded plea in English, the frail man hollering, "Help me! The animal has me again!"

I pivoted toward the sound and started swimming.

FOUR

WHEN HARRIS SQUIRES PUSHED THROUGH THE CROWD OF LITTLE
brown people and realized what was happening, he grinned, thinking, *Awesome!*

Because of his girlfriend, Frankie, it had been a rotten week. But
seeing what he was seeing now made him feel hopeful. Two nights
before, while shooting a homemade skin flick, the idiot Mexican
girl with them had taken too much Ecstasy and stopped breathing
just like that. There was no one around but them, thank God, but
it wasn't until the next morning when Squires finally sobered up
that even he had to admit the girl wasn't going to start breathing
again. Meaning she was dead.

That was bad enough, but it got worse. The girl was a prostitute
who belonged to a Mexican gangbanger named Laziro Victorino.
Victorino was what the illegals called a coyote, meaning that for a
price he would lead groups across the border into the States, then

find them jobs, too—but for a percentage of their pay, which he collected weekly.

Victorino—V-man, his gangbanger soldiers called him—was a wiry little guy but a serious badass who carried a box cutter on his belt and had a teardrop tattoo beneath his left eye, along with a bunch of other gangbanger tats on his arms and back.

Squires was aware that the V-man had made a few films of his own, him and his boys. Snuff films. Kill a man or woman—or just torture them—and get it all on their iPhone video cameras.

Frankie had chided Squires, saying, "Why you worried about some midget Mexican? You're twice that greaser's size. Besides, he's got some new girl with him every time he comes through here. He probably won't even notice she's gone."

Squires doubted that but didn't want to piss off Frankie by voicing his opinion. So he told her he'd never played a role in killing anyone before. And he didn't want to get in the habit of doing it.

That wasn't exactly true, although Frankie didn't know it. No one knew, and sometimes even Squires wasn't convinced it had happened.

Once, only once, alone with a pretty Mexican woman, Squires, naked, had taken the *chula* from behind, lulling her body into a thrashing silence, his hands around her throat, his body finishing and the *chula*'s life ending at a precise, constricting intersection that was euphoric beyond any physical sensation Squires had ever experienced.

He had been too drunk to remember details, though. And by the time he had sobered, the woman's body was already gone—into the lake near his hunting camp trailer, he guessed later—so it was as if he had imagined the whole damn thing.

But it had happened. The event—that explosive physical rush, a sensation of ultimate power—had rooted itself in Squires's brain.

Occasionally, the memory flooded him with a horrifying guilt, which he mitigated by telling himself that it had only been a dream.

When he was blood-drunk on steroids, though, the roots of that memory propagated in the man's head. They snaked deeper into his brain, germinating into a fantasy that had become an obsession.

If he ever got the opportunity, if he ever got just the right girl alone, Squires would make that dream happen again.

Frankie had laughed when he had balked. "We've got nothing to feel guilty about. The stupid little whore did it to herself. It's one less stupid *chula* in the world. Good riddance. No one's gonna miss her and no one's gonna care. Now, do me a favor, clean up around here 'cause I've got that appointment in Orlando tomorrow. Make sure she's gone by morning—and you'd better never goddamn mention it again."

Which meant that Frankie was leaving the dirty work to him. That's just the way the woman was, and Squires had to wonder sometimes if Frankie's love of crazy, wild-sex kinkiness was really worth all her crazy, wild-bitch meanness.

For the first couple of years, it had been a toss-up. But now Harris was tired of the woman—a little frightened of her, too—and he was looking for a way out.

The reason had to do with something else Squires had been wondering about: How had he gotten himself trapped into a relationship with a woman who reminded him more and more of his abusive, bullying mother?

Like his mother, Frankie had a nasty streak in her, particularly when it came to other women. Because of this, it was sometimes hard to tell if some of the things Frankie did were accidental or intentional. For instance, it wasn't exactly true that the Mexican girl had overdosed herself. Frankie had done it.

Frankie had dropped extra Ecstasy tablets into the girl's drink, doubling the dose she usually used when they happened to pick up a Mexican *chula* who was camera-shy and needed some loosening up.

This particular girl was unusually cute, with a sleek, sensuous body. When Frankie's hands were on a girl like that, her face flushed. Her body shook. It was a response that was part passion, part jealousy. It was like she never wanted to let the girl go. So maybe Frankie had decided to keep the *chula* by dropping in those extra tabs.

To Squires, it made what had happened seem less of a crime, the fact that a woman had done it to another woman. But that didn't stop him from going almost crazy with panic when he finally realized the girl was dead. Maybe he had killed that Mexican girl or maybe it was all a dream, but he'd never had to deal with a dead body before. Not sober, anyway.

They had a corpse on their hands. And they had to get rid of the thing without the Mexican gang leader, or the cops, finding out.

Not they, actually. *Him.* Frankie, who was sixteen years older than Squires, and a lot more experienced, would have nothing to do with getting rid of a dead body.

It wasn't the first time that something like this had happened while Squires was around, but it was the first time a girl had ended up dead instead of puking her guts out while Squires tended to her.

That's what really pissed him off when Squires took time to give the subject some thought. When would he learn not to leave Frankie alone with girls that were younger and prettier than her? And even if the stupid *chula* had done it to herself, who was going to believe it?

No one, that's who. Not with at least one eyewitness, maybe two, who had seen him drag the girl's body into the lake.

Now, though, Squires's future seemed to be improving, judging from what he could hear and see, out there on the lake, which was that Fifi had snatched one of the eyewitnesses, old man Carlson, into the water.

Fifi. That was the name of the twelve-foot gator that he and some buddies had trucked in from his hunting camp, east of Immokalee, way back off County Road 858.

Squires could see it happening and he liked what he saw.

The gator had that nosy little turd in her jaws and now looked like she was swimming him back to some dark hole where she could drown him. That's what gators like Fifi did. The ol' girl would probably leave the mouthy asshole underwater to tenderize a bit before finally chowing down.

No way could the cops blame Squires for something an animal did. It was perfect.

Squires wasn't sure if Carlson had in fact been an eyewitness, but, if he was, Fifi was now providing the solution. It had been a smart thing to move the gator here, where she could harass the Mexicans instead of the hunting dogs they sometimes used at his camp.

Squires's hunting camp—well, actually, the property belonged to his mother—was a big place, four hundred acres of cypress trees and saw grass that opened into flats of oaks and pines where feral hogs liked to feed. And where sometimes they'd kill deer and an occasional bear, too.

Once, in that same area, Harris had gotten a clear shot at a panther, but he'd missed.

Harris Squires loved that hunting camp as much as he hated tending his mother's three crappy little RV parks, this one, Red Citrus, being the only one even slightly fun. Red Citrus, at least, had girl tenants who weren't redneck hags with silver hair, big asses and little old titties shriveled like raisins on a vine. Brown girls, true, but at least they were young.

In Squires's mind, the younger the girl, the better—not something he would've admitted to Frankie, who was now in her forties—like the weird little *chula* who'd been pretending to be a boy and called herself Tulo. What was she, twelve, maybe thirteen years old? He'd been pretty down the last couple of days, but surprising "Tulo" in the bathtub had lifted his spirits.

Until that moment, Squires had been confused about how to handle the situation. Seeing the girl's body, though, all water slick and smooth, had changed that. It caused his secret fantasy to bloom bright in his mind.

He'd drive her to the hunting camp and show her around. Just him, alone. At the hunting camp, there'd be no one around to hear or see what he did. Not on a Tuesday night. It was a comfortable spot, private, with a big RV braced up on cinder blocks, generators, a cookshack, a shower and a wide-screen TV for video games and porn. A perfect place for a guy like him to make his fantasy come true with a little wettail.

Wettails, that's what Squires called them. He and Frankie had entertained a bunch of them out there at the camp, which was really more a second home than a camp. The place was comfortable enough to be fun but still wild enough for an ol' boy to get away, spread his wings and do just about any crazy thing he wanted without worrying about some cop or asshole ranger cruising by, asking questions.

Harris Squires hated nosy people. Do-gooders. If he and Frankie wanted to have some fun with a few young wettails, what harm were they doing? But try explaining that to a goddamn do-gooder.

Carlson was a prime example. Now Carlson was getting exactly what the little turd deserved.

Squires nudged a couple of short people out of the way as he edged closer to the lake. He could hear what was happening—Carlson screaming his lungs out, begging for help. It wasn't easy to make out details, though, because the mangrove pond was on the other side of the fence, in shadows cast by palm trees beyond the haze of security lights.

It made him wish he had his night vision binoculars. Those bad boys would've made everything bright as day, but they were behind the seat of his Ford Roush pickup, along with some other gear he usually carried: duct tape, an ax handle, handcuffs, condoms and sometimes a .357 Ruger Blackhawk when he wasn't carrying the gun in the glove box.

The handcuffs was something he carried for Frankie. The woman was crazy for bondage.

Squires turned toward the trailers, seeing kids' bicycles and rusting trucks, now seeing Tula push open her trailer door, then running toward him, carrying something in her hand. Squires squinted to see a . . . bottle of liquor?

What the hell?

Yep, she was carrying a damn bottle of tequila. Well, no one ever claimed that Mexicans were smart. But then he also saw that she was carrying a flashlight, which was exactly what he needed, so he yelled to her, "Over here! Bring me that damn light so we can see what's going on!"

The girl looked in his direction but ignored him. Because of that, Squires was about to yell something else, but that's when a big white guy came dodging through the crowd, speaking in Spanish, saying something that might have been, *"Excuse me, sorry. Let me pass."*

Definitely being polite, as the guy hurried to the lake's edge, kicking off shoes, shirt, then tossing his wallet and cell phone onto the ground before he jumped into the water. A second later, another white guy appeared. He was a skinny scarecrow of a hippie who was doing the same thing, stripping to go in the water.

What the hell were these two white dudes doing at Red Citrus?

Squires yelled to the hippie, "Hey . . . you! What the hell you think you're doing?" but the hippie was busy pulling off his shirt and talking into his cell phone at the same time, before he dropped the phone on the ground, next to his wallet, and then he went into the water, too, but on his belly.

Using his cell phone? The asshole had probably just called 911.

Shit! This was all Squires needed. Fifi was in the process of solving a serious problem, but now here were a couple of solid-looking white citizens messing in his business.

Squires spat, "Goddamn do-gooders!" as he headed after the flashlight Tula was holding, pushing people out of the way.

A moment later, speaking into the hippie's cell phone, Squires was telling the 911 operator, "That's right, cancel the emergency, ma'am. We made a mistake here on our end. I know, I know . . . it's not the first time."

He'd checked PREVIOUS CALLS. When he'd seen 911, he knew he had to do something to stop the cops from showing up.

But then Squires had to whisper "Damn it" as he covered the phone so the operator wouldn't hear Carlson screaming across the water to the big white guy, yelling, "Help me! Take my hand!"

"Sir?" the operator said, raising her voice, "Who's yelling in the background?"

"Ma'am," Squires told her, being sweet, "I understand what you're asking. And at first we thought someone was in trouble. But, turns out, it's just a bunch of Mexican kids playing games. You know how girls squeal when they're running round, playing games at night?"

The woman asked, "Did you place the call? Is your name Tomlinson?"

Squires hesitated, aware that it was sometimes a mistake to lie to the cops before thinking it over. "Yep, that's my name," he said finally.

The operator told him, "We've already dispatched units to that address. Dispatched it to . . . to a Red Citrus RV Park, Guava Street, just off San Carlos Boulevard. That's near Fort Myers Beach, correct?"

Squires was getting nervous and impatient. He covered the phone and yanked the flashlight out of the weird little Bible freak's hand because she kept turning the beam toward the water, where there was now a lot of splashing and swearing going on.

"Damn it," he whispered to the girl, "pay attention!" as the operator asked him again, "Did you hear me? Is that the correct address, sir?"

Squires kept his voice pleasant and easy as he replied, "Well, if you reckon your people need to practice answering ambulance calls, ma'am, there's nothing I can do to stop 'em. I just wanted you to know this one is a false alarm. Everything's just fine here. Our folks are having lots of fun—it's a sort of party going on. So I guess I'm gonna have to apologize to your people again when they show up here for no reason."

The operator asked a couple more questions before Squires covered one ear, listening, until he suspected that the woman was convinced and had canceled the 911 call, no matter what she claimed. Then he hung up, as he swung the light toward the water, wanting to confirm the gator still had Carlson.

Fifi still had the guy, all right. But Squires could see the big white guy was swimming hard to catch up, which caused him to wonder, *Who the hell is that crazy son of a bitch?*

Well . . . there was an easy way to find out.

From the hippie's billfold, Squires removed a wad of cash. It looked like a bunch of crisp twenties. He stuffed the money into his jeans, then retrieved the big guy's billfold. There wasn't nearly as much cash in it but enough. Yep, these two dudes were solid working citizens—plus, there were some other interesting things to see in this second billfold.

Squires's eyes shifted from the pond to what he was holding. He used the flashlight to go through credit cards, business cards and IDs that showed a nerdy-looking guy with a jaw and glasses.

Marion D. Ford, Ph.D.
Sanibel Biological Supply
Dinkin's Bay Marina

Marion. What kind of name was that for a man?

The guy was a damn scientist or something, apparently. What the hell was a scientist doing at a trailer park full of *chilies* and wettails? Squires put one of the man's business cards into his back pocket before he went through the other stuff, paying special attention to a couple of unusual IDs.

Yeah, the dude was a scientist, but there was some other stuff that worried Squires. Could be the asshole worked for the feds, too, because one of the IDs gave this guy, Marion Ford, unlimited access to something called the Special Operations Center at MacDill Air Base in Tampa.

What the hell was that about?

And there was another plastic ID for a military base in Cartagena,

Colombia. But that one was mostly in Spanish, so there was no telling what it meant.

The dude, Ford, Squires guessed, must be some small-time scientist who worked for the feds. But he wasn't really in the military— not according to what Squires was looking at in the billfold, anyway. Just maybe hired by the military, for some reason or another.

Could that mean the hippie and the nerd were actually with the Department of Immigration? Squires gave himself a few seconds to think about it. At first, that made some sense to him. Why else would they come snooping around a trailer park ass-deep in *chilies* and *chulas*?

But then Squires got a sinking feeling. What if the two dudes were actually with the DEA instead? What if they had come here trying to set up some kind of drug bust on the small steroid operation Squires was operating?

Squires whispered "Son of a bitch" as he glanced toward the pond, where he could see the gator rolling in a spray of water, and he thought, *Eat that bastard, Fifi! Kill them both!*

Squires was pretty sure he had seen the hippie, Tomlinson, before, cruising around the park in some shitty old Volkswagen that had to be twenty years old. Sometimes a girlish-looking electric bike, too. Which wasn't that unusual. Dopers often cruised the parks because they knew that the *chilies* arrived from Mexico carrying baggies of weed or peyote buds in their pants instead of cash.

Hell, Squires had bought grass from them himself, although, more often, he just took the shit when he wanted it. Sometimes, he'd yank a guy up by the ankles and shake him, like shaking quarters out of an old pair of jeans. What the hell could a Mexican do about it? Call the cops?

That was one of the good things about managing a place like Red Citrus. No one on the whole goddamn property wanted the cops around, especially Squires and Frankie, so that made it a safe place to be. Which is why, in their newest double-wide trailer, Squires had set up a smaller version of the cookshack they had out there at the hunting camp. It wasn't the sort of cookshack where he actually cooked food. What he cooked up was home-brewed steroid gear like testosterone enanthate, and equine—which was a horse steroid called EQ—plus winstrol and deca-durabolin.

"Gear" was bodybuilder slang for steroids, almost always purchased illegally.

Squires had become good at rendering high-grade veterinarian powders into injectable muscle juice. The kitchen was well supplied with Whatman sterile filters, 20-gauge needles, sesame oil, benzyl benzoate and everything else needed to produce a first-class product.

Squires had started small, producing just enough gear for himself and Frankie, who had, at one time, been one of the top female bodybuilders in the country. Then he began to sell to a few guys he trusted, and that's how they got started.

It was Frankie who noticed how fast the cash was piling up just from selling to friends. So the two of them had expanded the operation, thinking they could make more money dealing gear than they could ever make running his mother's shitty trailer parks or teaching yoga classes, which Frankie sometimes did. They bought vials by the gross. They bought two vacuum machines and a label maker, too.

Turned out, they were right about making money.

Dopers thought a fresh peyote button was expensive? Ask a bodybuilder about the price of a vial of Masteron or high-grade Testosterone-E. Frankie could walk into any gym in South Florida where muscle freaks congregated and make an EQ horsey whinnying noise and that would bring them running.

Juicers knew exactly what the lady was carrying in her gym bag and they were damn eager to buy. Because of the feds, dependable gear was so goddamn hard to get, Squires and Frankie were now making a small fortune, all in cash, selling their home-brewed goodies in kits, complete with pins and syringes if that's what the bros wanted.

Their little organization was becoming so well known, and their products so trusted, that gym rats in South Florida had come up with a nickname for the stuff. They called it Gator Juice. As in, "You tried the Gator Juice Tren? Or the Gator Juice A-bombs? Gator Juice is goddamn grade-A shit. Good to go, man. As in G-*two*-G."

Squires's eyes kept swinging from Ford's billfold to the drama taking place out there on the lake. A couple of *chilies* had come through the crowd carrying a big military-type light called a Golight, so Squires pocketed the scientist's cash, then handed both billfolds to one of the *chilies*, saying to him, "Hang on to these, will ya, *amigo*? Now, give me that goddamn light."

With the Golight, Squires could see that it was getting interesting out there on the water where Ford was doing something that would've been hard to believe if it wasn't actually happening. Ford had his left arm slung over the gator's back while Fifi struggled to swim, still carrying Carlson sideways in her mouth. What Ford was trying to do, Squires realized, was climb onto the gator's back.

Un-by-God-believable!

Into Squires's mind came the image of the big Australian, the crocodile hunter guy who he used to like to watch on TV, which made what was happening easier to comprehend. But once the scientist got onto the gator's back, then what?

Squires placed the big spotlight on his shoulder to steady the thing, then leaned to focus the beam on something the scientist had in his hand.

What the hell was the dude carrying?

A hammer, maybe, that's what it looked like. No . . . not a hammer. It looked like Ford was trying to steady an itty-bitty pocket pistol behind one of Fifi's eyes—which was a stupid goddamn thing to try. At least, Squires hoped it was a stupid goddamn thing to try.

Suddenly, he could feel that sickening feeling in his stomach again, worried the crazy do-gooder was going to find a way to free Carlson and screw up the only good luck Squires had had in a week. But it was pointless, what the guy was trying to do . . . *wasn't it?*

Squires hoped it was true. There was no pussy pistol in the world with enough stopping power to . . .

WHAP-WHAP!

Squires jumped when he heard the gunshots. Then he stood straight, realizing that the man had managed to get a couple of rounds off.

Behind him, the crowd made a collective *Ooohing* noise as they watched the alligator's tail slam sideways, then tilt upward like a crane. The tail stood there for an instant, before the big animal rolled and then sank from sight.

Shit! Where was Carlson?

Squires fanned the light back and forth, searching. Maybe the nosy old turd had gone down with the gator. No . . . no such luck. Carlson was still out there, floundering to stay on the surface while the hippie swam toward him.

Sons a bitches!

Squires felt an acidic surge move from his abdomen toward his head, the signal that he was becoming seriously pissed off. It was a steroid charge that he had experienced many times but seldom as strong as tonight—which would have made sense, if he'd stopped to think about it. Tuesdays and Saturdays were Squires's pin days—"pinning" being bodybuilder talk for steroid injections.

That morning, he had flooded two syringes with testosterone, equipoise, trenbolone and decanoate—all oil-based, veterinarian-strength gear—and injected it into his thighs, but only after heating the oil under a hot spigot to make the sticks faster and less painful.

As a special treat—because it had been such a shitty two days—he had also eaten five tabs of dianabol, a hundred milligrams.

D-bombs, man—nothing else hit Squires quite as hard as dianabol, although he preferred the injectable version. Juice was easier on the liver than pills. But he was out of D-bomb oil until he made his next trip to the hunting camp.

Squires lived for that full-on testosterone buzz. He loved the evening of a pin day, when his blood levels were so hormone drunk that he could track the oil moving through his veins like heat. It caused his muscles to twitch and swell beneath his skin, the fibers feeding so furiously on hormone soup that Squires could feel the mass of his body changing.

"You got your monster face on tonight," Frankie would sometimes say to him as they elbowed for space before their weight-room mirror, Frankie usually posing naked, but Squires wearing a thong because steroid gear shrunk his nuts so small it was embarrassing.

"I love it," the woman would tell him, "when you got your monster face on."

Because of the D-bombs, and because of what was happening, Harris Squires had his monster face on now.

He paused long enough to kick one of the cell phones toward the water, hoping it belonged to the guy named Ford—the damn do-gooder dude who'd just shot his alligator, Fifi. Then Squires batted a couple of *chilies* out of his way, as he began to pace, still carrying the spotlight, waiting for the bastard to make it to shore— if he ever did.

As Harris Squires knew from years of hunting the Glades, big alligators died hard.

FIVE

WHEN I HEARD THE FAMILIAR VOICE YELL, "DOC! HELP ME GET
this guy in!" I spun around to see Tomlinson's silhouette only a few
yards away, but that's all I could see because someone onshore was
blinding me with a powerful spotlight.

I waved my hand and yelled in Spanish, "Get that thing out of
my eyes!"

But nothing happened. So I yelled louder, in English, adding,
"You dumbass!" for emphasis.

For an instant, the light swung skyward, and I could see that
Tomlinson had the injured man in a cross-chest carry, trying to
swim him to shore. He was having trouble, though, because the guy
was fighting him, swinging his fists, trying to get a solid elbow
into my friend's face. The man apparently thought the alligator still
had him.

There was no telling how badly the guy was hurt, but he was
obviously in shock. I swam closer, my head up, got a hand under the

man's arm and pulled his ear close to my lips, yelling in Spanish, "You're safe! Stop fighting!"

I repeated it several times before his head rolled toward me, eyes wide, and he whispered, in English, "Am I dreaming this? Am I dead? This is a terrible dream if I'm not dead."

Yes, he was in shock . . . a small man with a gaunt drunkard's face that was a saprophytic gray in the glow of security lights. His voice was incongruous—he spoke with the rounded vowels of a Virginia gentleman.

I asked him, "What's your name?"

He continued babbling, telling me, "I don't know what happened! I walked down to look at something floating in the water. Next thing I know, something was dragging me in . . . like it was trying to squeeze the guts out of me. I heard something snap . . . something way inside my body."

The man looked at me, eyes blinking, and I heard what he must have sounded like as a child when he asked, "Am I badly hurt? I don't want to die, I really don't."

I replied, "Lay back. Get some air in your lungs. We're taking you to shore." I could see there was an open slash on the man's forearm, and his legs looked as dead as wood, the way they floated on the surface.

As Tomlinson positioned himself to support the man's other arm, he asked me, "Did you kill it?" meaning the alligator, and I could tell he hoped I hadn't hurt the thing.

"Let's get out of here before we catch a damn disease," I told him. "Start swimming, I'll keep his head up."

Truth was, I still didn't know if the gator was dead. Judging from the way the animal's tail had periscoped to the surface, at least one of the bullets had done damage to the neuro system.

Either way, a wounded gator was the least of my worries. The most dangerous animals in Florida's backwaters aren't reptiles. They aren't amphibians or fish. I was more concerned about microscopic animals that, as I knew too well, thrived in stagnant lakes like the one we were in.

The injured man might survive the wounds the gator had inflicted only to die from bacteria that lived in the animal's mouth. Or from a single-celled protozoan that all the commotion had kicked free from the muck below.

The injured man wasn't the only one at risk—Tomlinson and I were in danger, too. There are varieties of single-celled animals that don't need an open wound to slip through a primate's skin armor. The amoeba *Naegleria* can travel through a man's nostrils, into the brain and cause an encephalitis that is deadly. It's rare, but I knew from my professional journals that this same microscopic animal had killed at least four healthy young men in the last few years.

The water temperature of the pond felt warmer than the injured man's flesh. It stunk of sulfur and garbage, and as Tomlinson and I began sidestroking toward shore my fingers noted the water's protoplasmic density. The density was created by microbes and muck held in suspension.

It was a brackish water mangrove lake, not much larger than a baseball field, surrounded by a trailer population that probably used the place to dump all kinds of refuse—natural, man-made and chemical. It caused me to wonder why a quarter-ton alligator would choose such a stagnant, public place to live.

The probability was, the animal didn't live here. More likely, the gator had been traveling cross-country—they often do during the spring mating season. My guess was, the thing had only recently arrived, stopping for a few nights to feed. If a gator that size had been a permanent resident, someone at the trailer park would have reported it to Florida Wildlife cops and demanded that the thing be removed.

Or would they?

I thought about it as we swam sidestroke, Tomlinson on one side of the injured man, me on the other.

Maybe not, I decided. I remembered Tomlinson telling me that the only thing park residents feared more than law enforcement was their own landlord.

That made sense, combined with what I knew about the people who lived in places like Red Citrus. I had spent enough time in Central America, and had lived long enough in Florida, to learn not to underestimate the tenacity of the descendants of the Maya and Aztec. They could endure just about anything with a stoic calm that was all but impossible to read, and just as impossible not to respect.

People like this could live their lives, day by day, next door to an aggressive gator, or next door to a crazed neighbor, and never say a word in protest. Living under the radar meant surviving quietly no matter what.

We were drawing close to shore. The injured man had stopped fighting, but the muscles of his arms remained contracted, his breathing was rapid. To Tomlinson I said, "When we get to the bank, don't try to stand. The bottom's like quicksand."

He asked me, "Do you have shoes on?"

I said, "I was just thinking the same thing. There's probably broken bottles and all kinds of crap on the bottom. We're going to need some help."

To the injured man I said, "What's your name? Can you talk?"

The man groaned, and said again, "Please tell me I'm dreaming this. What happened to my legs? I can't feel my legs."

I thought, *Uh-oh*, and squeezed his arm to reassure him as I looked toward shore. I could see shapes and shadows of several dozen people watching us. But I couldn't see clearly because my glasses were hanging around my neck on fishing line, and also because the spotlight was blinding me again.

In Spanish I yelled, "Take the light away from that person, I can't see! Shine it on the ground. We need some help. Four or five people, hold hands and make a chain so we can pull this man out. But don't come in the water. Stay out of the water!"

I could see people moving toward the bank, including the man who was carrying the spotlight, a huge silhouette capped by blond curls and shoulders in a muscle T-shirt.

It was the landlord. Had to be.

I called to him in English, "Get that goddamn light out of my eyes! I'm not going to tell you again."

In reply, I heard a surly Southern twang shout, "What'd you just say to me, *asshole*?"

The drawl was unmistakably redneck Florida.

Trying to keep it reasonable, I told him, "You're blinding me. We've got an injured man here!"

I saw the man quicken his pace and heard him bellow, "You don't give the orders around here, you do-gooder son of a bitch! I give the orders! Now, get your ass out of my goddamn lake. You're trespassing! What the hell you doin', trespassing in my lake?"

I glanced at Tomlinson. His face was orchid white in the harsh light, and he rolled his eyes. "The landlord," he replied. "He's the jerk I told you about. Something Squires. He's a mama's boy. She's the one with all the property."

Tomlinson had described the guy as all grits and redneck bullshit, plus a full helping of steroids. It matched with what I was hearing.

The water was so shallow now that I was using my left hand to crab us over the bottom, the muck gelatinous between my fingers. It was frustrating. I had no idea how badly that man was hurt, but I knew we couldn't waste time getting him out of the water and treating his wounds. It was impossible to hurry, though. Try to stand, we'd sink to our waists in slime.

"Did you call nine-one-one?" I asked Tomlinson. I couldn't look directly into the spotlight, the thing was too bright, so I was using peripheral vision to keep track of Squires as he descended on us, pushing people out of the way. I noticed that the men who had been attempting to form a human chain scattered from his path.

"We should be hearing sirens by now," Tomlinson replied, "or maybe not. It was only about five minutes ago that I called. But they'll be here." Then he surprised me by calling out in a cheery voice, "Hey! Hey, Tulo, it's me! Tell some of the men we need help getting out of here. We need about five people!"

Tomlinson used the masculine form of the name, but I realized he was yelling to the teenage girl he had mentioned, the girl we had come to help. Tula Choimha.

I saw a slim, luminous figure appear, backlit by the spotlight. The girl had a flashlight, which was pointed at her sandals, and something else in her hand. A bottle, it looked like.

To Tomlinson I said, "Watch the guy's head—he might have a spinal injury."

My pal replied, "Then maybe I should stay in the water with him until the paramedics arrive."

I was thinking about the killer microbes, not the alligator, when I replied, "No, we've got to get him out of here. You, too."

"Dude," Tomlinson muttered, "I don't even want to ask what that tone of yours means." He glanced over his shoulder. "You think the gator might come back?"

I said, "I'll climb up the bank, and we'll try to pull him out without moving his head. These people aren't going to help, they're afraid. Oh . . . and for God's sake, don't even try talking to that landlord. You'll just make him madder. Let me do the talking."

Tomlinson's attention remained on the girl, mine on Squires, who was still shouting threats at us and not slowing as he lumbered toward the water. I knew we had to hurry, but it would be worse to misjudge the situation. Steroid drunks, like pit bulls, are an unpredictable demographic. If the guy was as furious as he sounded, anything could happen.

I laced my fingers into the knee-high weeds that grew along the bank and pulled myself out of the water, hand over hand, trying to time it right. Friends sometimes chide me about my obsessive attention to detail and my hyperawareness of my surroundings—particularly if the environment is populated with strangers.

Sometimes, I am tempted to reply, "I'm still alive, aren't I?" but never do.

Fortunately, my hyperwariness paid off. Again.

Just as I was getting to my feet, blue jeans muddy, a slimy mess, Squires appeared. He took a quick jump step, grabbed me by the left arm and stabbed the huge light into my face as I stood. He was screaming, "Can you see any better now, you son of a bitch! Who do you think you are, coming 'round here, giving orders!"

I pushed the light—a military Golight, I realized—out of my eyes and tried to back away, but the man's hand was like a vise. In an easy voice, I said to him, "Calm down, Squires. We have a guy who needs medical attention."

It didn't help. "Screw you!" the man yelled, his breath hot in my face. "Who the hell died and made you boss, you goddamn do-gooder prick? You're giving *me* orders?"

I kept my voice even. "When the police arrive, what are they going to think when I tell them you tried to stop us from saving this man's life?"

Squires was trembling, he was so mad. He roared, "You're not telling the cops nothin', asshole! How you gonna talk to anybody after I snap your damn head off and use it to feed my gator?"

His gator? It was an unexpected thing to hear, but it told me something.

I was gauging the man's size and his balance. He was about six-five, six-six, probably two-eighty, but weight-room muscle is among the most common cloaks of male insecurity. To test his balance, I rolled my left arm free of his grip. At the same time, I gave him a push with the fingers of my right hand. It wasn't an obvious push. It was more of a blocking gesture, but he didn't handle it well.

Clumsy people have a difficult time with simultaneous hand movements, and this guy was clumsy. The little push turned his entire body a few wobbly degrees to the left. It was all the opening I needed, but I didn't take it.

Now was not the time for a brawl. Besides, Tomlinson and I needed this guy's cooperation if we were going to save the injured man. The illegals who lived in the park weren't going to risk helping us—not if their blustering bully of a landlord disapproved. And I couldn't blame them. They had to live here. I didn't.

I squared my body to Squires's, and said, "This is my last try to be reasonable. We've got an injured man and we intend to help him. Get out of our way and behave like an adult."

That's all it took. Squires screamed at me, "Or you'll do what?" and he jammed the light toward my face again.

I had no choice, I ducked under the light and then drop-stepped beneath the landlord's extended right arm. From the sound of surprise he made, the move was the equivalent of a disappearing act. Where had I gone?

I had disappeared behind him, that's where. Years ago, in an overheated wrestling room, I had practiced hand control and simple duck unders day after day, week after week, year after year. I had practiced the craft of grappling so relentlessly that I had pleased even our relentless perfectionist of a coach, a man named Gary Fries. Fries was a wrestling giant, all five feet seven inches of him, and he would not tolerate mediocrity.

Thanks to that coach, I've never been in any physical confrontation in my life where I didn't feel confident I was in control of the outcome. That doesn't mean I have always won. I certainly have not. But I've always felt as if I *could* win if I picked my shots and made the right moves.

Like now, as I came up behind Squires, saying into his ear, "You've got a big mouth, fat boy," because now his anger could be used to my advantage. I wanted him so mad that he lost control. When the big man tried to pivot, I laddered my hands up his ribs to control his body position and leaned my head close to his shoulder blades so he couldn't knock me cold with a wild elbow.

When Squires realized he couldn't maneuver free, he stuttered, "Hey . . . get your hands off me, asshole!" and tried, once again, to face me.

I was ready because that's exactly what I wanted him to do. I let Squires make half a turn and then stopped his momentum by ramming my head into his back as I grapevined my left ankle around his left shin. An instant later, I locked my hands around his waist and moved with him as he tried to wrestle free.

Our backs were to the mangrove pond. With a quick glance, I confirmed that Tomlinson and the injured man weren't directly behind us—it was a dangerous place to be if things went the way I planned. Then I used my legs to drive Squires away from the water. Instinctively, the man's feet dug in, then his legs pumped as he tried to drive us both backward. Squires was taller, heavier and stronger than I. His energized mass soon overpowered my own.

The timing was important. I waited a microsecond . . . waited until I felt the subtle transition of momentum.

When it felt right, I dropped my grip a few inches lower on the big man's waist. I relocked my hands, bent my knees and then maximized Squires's own momentum by lifting as I arched my back.

I waited another microsecond . . . and then I heaved with all my strength as we tumbled backward.

In wrestling jargon, the move I'd executed was a *suplex*. As I arched backward, I used a two-handed throwing technique, not unlike a Scottish gamesman throwing a fifty-pound rock over a bar. In this case, though, the weight was closer to three hundred pounds. Squires had amassed considerable momentum, and it was his own momentum—not my strength—that sent him flying.

I guessed he would land near the pond's edge, which is why I had checked behind me before setting up the *suplex*. I couldn't have guessed, however, that a man Squires's size would sail beyond the bank and land on his shoulders in a massive explosion of water.

I got to my feet, cleaning my hands on my jeans. I found the spotlight and aimed it at Squires's face when he surfaced. He was disoriented and floundering. I watched him splash to vertical, as he spit water and swore. Mostly, he swore at me, ordering that I get that goddamn light out of his eyes.

I told him, "Come up here and say that, fat boy," and watched the man jam his feet toward the bottom, which is precisely what I hoped he would do.

It was his second mistake of the night.

For a few seconds, Squires stood tall in waist-deep water, as he struggled to find footing. Then he began to sink. The more he struggled, the more suction he created and the deeper he went into the muck.

Squires wasn't a wrestler, and he wasn't much of a swimmer, either. He couldn't manage the delicate hand strokes necessary to sustain positive buoyancy. Soon the man was so deeply mired in mud that he couldn't move his legs. Water was rising toward his shoulders, and it scared him.

"Goddamn it!" he shouted to the migrants watching. "Help me. Get a rope! Somebody go get a rope and pull me out of here."

Drowning was terrifying enough, but then another thought came into Squires's mind. I could tell because of the wild look in his eyes as he glanced over his shoulder, yelling, "Hurry up, before that gator comes back! Does anybody have a gun? Someone break the window of my truck and grab the gun from the glove box. Shit! Hurry up!"

Automatically, my right hand touched my sodden pocket to confirm the Kahr 9mm was still there. It was.

No one moved except for a frail, luminous figure that I recognized. It was the teenage girl Tomlinson had been calling to, Tula. I watched her step free of the crowd, then walk toward me, her eyes indicating Squires as she said in English, "Do you think he might drown?"

I replied, "That's up to him. If he keeps air in his lungs, he'll stop sinking."

I watched the girl, impressed by her articulate English, but more impressed by the way she carried herself and the respect park residents accorded her. When she spoke, even the men watching her went silent.

"Will the animal come back?" she asked me. "Did you kill it?"

I was moving toward the injured man and Tomlinson as I told her, "I wounded it, maybe. I don't know," and was tempted to ask, *Why are you worried about that jerk?*

I listened to the girl tell me, "I used your telephone to call the emergency number. Or maybe it was his."

She glanced at Tomlinson, who was on his knees in the water, cradling the injured man, and then explained, "The angry *propietario* told the emergency police not to come. But they are coming now."

The angry *propietario* was Squires. Apparently, the girl had heard him cancel Tomlinson's 911 call. How else could she have known?

In Spanish, I said to people milling in the shadows, "We need three or four men to help get the injured man out of the water. I think his spine is hurt. We have to take care not to move his head. We need towels and ice and disinfectant . . . and a board of some type for him to lie on. Plywood would work."

As I spoke, I had to raise my voice to be heard above Squires, who was now raging, "Why aren't you people moving? Goddamn it, I need a rope! And one of you bastards fetch my gun! How'd you little shits like to be homeless again? I'll call the feds on your sorry asses if you don't move now!"

The man was panicking in his rage, his attention focused on shadows behind him where the gator might be lurking. As long as he kept his lungs inflated, the muck wouldn't overpower his own buoyancy. But now, I guessed, Squires was hyperventilating, and in real danger. I was considering going in after him myself when the girl called in loud Spanish, "Do what the landlord says. Get a rope, but not his gun! Help him! Would God want you to allow a helpless man to drown?"

God allowed helpless men to drown daily, but her words got

people moving. A couple of guys went jogging toward the trailers, while others moved toward Tomlinson, awaiting instructions. As I approached the bank, I told the men to stay close, we'd need them soon. I was also searching the ground, looking for my shirt, because I wanted to clean my glasses.

Beside me, Tula said, "Use this," and handed me a towel, which she pulled from the back of her jeans. "He's my friend," she added, indicating the injured man. "His name is Carlson, and he has a good heart. When you get him out of the water, I will pray. Will you help me pray to heal his wounds?"

The girl's syntax was odd, I noticed, whether she spoke in English or Spanish. It was formal in an old-fashioned way, which made no sense for someone her age.

Carlson was listening from only a few feet away. He was semiconscious, looking up at the girl, a sleepy, dazed smile on his face.

I said, "My friend will be glad to help you pray. Won't you, Tomlinson?" and handed the towel back to the girl before I told one of the men to hang on to my feet when I gave him the word. Then I got down on my hands and knees and crawled to the water.

It wasn't difficult to lift Carlson ashore. He was all bone and skin, couldn't have weighed more than a hundred and forty pounds. Once we had him on the slick grass, we maneuvered a piece of plywood under him, then sledded him to higher ground.

Through the entire process, I held the man's head steady. From the way he'd described the cracking sound "deep inside him," I guessed the gator had broken his spine. I didn't want to turn a paraplegic into a quadriplegic.

Tula comforted the man as we moved him. She stroked his head, told him he would recover quickly, and also chanted what I guessed to be a prayer in her native language. I can speak only enough *Qui-*

ché Maya to thank the person who brings me a beer, so I had no idea what the girl was saying.

When we had Carlson safely away from the water, I checked his injuries. His forearm showed puncture marks, as did his waist and buttocks, but the bleeding wasn't bad.

His legs, though, had a pasty, dead look that suggested I'd been right about the broken spine. As I took note of the wounds, Tula tapped me on the shoulder and said, "I'll hold his head while you use this." She was holding a bottle of cheap tequila, waiting for me to take it.

Tomlinson had found his sandals and seemed to be looking for something else but stopped long enough to grab the bottle and take a long swig.

"It's not for drinking," the girl told him, her tone communicating disapproval. "It's to clean your wounds."

"That's exactly how I'm using it," Tomlinson replied, then took another long belt, before he said to her, "Tula, while we work on your friend, would you do me a favor? Ask around and find out who has our billfolds. I found the phones, but our billfolds are gone."

But then he told her, "Never mind," as a man approached, billfolds in hand.

Tomlinson thanked the man, saying, *"Muchas gracias, compadre,"* but I could tell that something was wrong as he opened his billfold, then mine.

Tula stared at him for a moment before saying, "Your money is gone. I can see it in your face."

The girl turned toward the water, where Squires was struggling to reach a rope some men were trying to throw him. "He has your money. The *propietario*. No one but him would have robbed you."

In the peripheral glow of the Golight, I looked at the girl closely for the first time. She had a cereal-bowl haircut, and a lean angularity that didn't mesh with the compact body type I associate with Mayan women. Yet there was nothing masculine about her. She was boyish enough to pass for a boy, but her demeanor, while commanding, was asexual. In the truck, Tomlinson had said something that sounded strange at the time but now made sense. He had said, "She's an adolescent girl, not a female," which described her perfectly.

Thirteen-year-old Tula Choimha, I decided, was a child who handled herself like an adult. It was unusual, but probably less uncommon in girls than boys. Besides, the girl had spent the last few years living on her own, without family, which had no doubt contributed to her maturity.

"They're coming to help you," Tula whispered into Carlson's ear as she gauged the direction of distant sirens. She took the bottle of tequila from Tomlinson, soaked the towel with liquor, then dropped to her knees and began to wash the puncture wounds on Carlson's arm and then his buttocks, unconcerned that I had pulled the man's pants down to access his injuries.

"I can't feel my legs," the man told her again. He had said it several times in the last minutes, his reaction ping-ponging between horror and shock.

"Your legs are healing," I heard the girl tell him, her right hand gripping a necklace she wore. "Your wounds are healing now. You must have faith."

I watched her pause, head tilted, and the rhythm of her voice changed. She told him, "Our strength comes from faith. But our faith is sometimes eaten away by little things that God hates. If we lack faith, though there be a million of us, we will be beaten back and die."

I exchanged looks with Tomlinson, wondering if he, too, suspected her singsong syntax suggested that the girl was reciting something she had memorized.

My friend was nodding his approval. Personally, I felt a chill. To me, the robotic passion of the devoutly religious is disturbing. Too often it is a flag of surrender to fear and the exigencies of life. Maybe my assessment is unfair, but I associate religious fervor with pathology. Tomlinson, of course, does not.

"Squeeze my hand and put your faith in God," Tula whispered to the man, as she scrubbed at the puncture wounds on his buttocks. "Remember the godliness that you possessed as a child? It will return to you. God will make your body whole again."

Someone had brought a Coleman lantern, so I switched off the Golight and placed it on the ground. I was looking through my billfold, seeing that someone had rearranged my IDs and credit cards, seeing that all my cash had been taken, as I also watched the girl pour more tequila on Carlson's wounds, then scrub harder with the bloody towel.

"Do you feel this, *patron*?" she asked him. "Can your legs feel the heat of God, trying to enter?"

Once again, Tomlinson and I exchanged looks, as Carlson's eyes widened, and he said, "Maybe . . . maybe I can . . . I'm not sure . . . but something's happening. Wait . . . yes! I do feel it. Yes, my skin is burning! I can feel your hands, Tula!"

"They are not my hands, *patron*," Tula told him, not surprised. "It's the warmth of God's love you feel. He is in your body now. He has traveled from my body into your legs."

The man's face contorted into tears, and I watched him move one pale foot, then the other.

Carlson was crying, "Tula, you're right! I can feel my legs!"

I was pleased to know that I had been wrong about the man's broken spine. Shock, or a damaged nerve, might explain the tem-

porary loss of feeling in Carlson's legs. But my interest in an explanation was short-lived because nearby I heard a man yell in Spanish,
"It is back. The alligator is back. Someone shine the light!"

I swung the Golight toward the lake, where I saw a reptilian
wake, and two bright red eyes riding low in the water.

The huge gator, still alive, still determined to feed, was gliding
toward the bodybuilder, who was already screaming for help.

SIX

SIRENS DESCENDING ON RED CITRUS RV PARK WAS BAD ENOUGH, but when Harris Squires saw red eyes breach the water's surface, glowing twenty yards behind him, he felt a charge of panic beyond anything he had ever experienced, aware that he was about to lose one of his legs, maybe worse.

Squires understood what those eyes meant because of all the nights he'd spent hunting in the Everglades or getting stoned and plinking away at gators in ponds that dotted his four hundred acres.

Fifi was back. The biggest damn gator Squires had ever seen in his life was still alive, watching him, her eyes glowing in the light of a lantern that someone had brought so the two white guys could give first aid to that nosy old drunk, Carlson.

Squires tried to scream, but his voice managed only a high-pitched yelp, as his legs and arms went into hyperflight, trying to free himself from the muck. It was like one of those sweaty damn nightmares he sometimes had when he stacked testosterone and Tren. Nightmares in which he'd try to run, or call for help, but his body was dead, unable to respond.

Mired up to his thighs in mud produced the same sickening terror. He was desperate to run and he was trying . . . he even managed to get his right leg free. But then Squires felt a tearing pain in the back of his leg and realized he'd pulled a hamstring muscle.

The pain brought his voice back, and he yelled to the cluster of men, only a few yards away on the bank, "The gator! The gator's after me! Throw me that goddamn rope again!"

Suddenly, someone on shore turned on the Golight. The dazzling beam confirmed that the gator was swimming toward him, and Squires felt like vomiting, he was so scared.

Four times, the Mexicans had lobbed coils of clothesline to him. But each time the rope wasn't strong enough, or the men weren't strong enough, and the rope had broken or pulled free.

This time, though, a Mexican with some brains had produced commercial-grade nylon with a weight taped to the end. When he lobbed it, the coil went sailing over Squires's head but landed close enough for him to grab the rope before it sank.

As Squires looped the rope around his chest, he risked another glance over his shoulder, and there was Fifi, gliding closer. Her eyes were a ruby pendulum, swinging with every stroke of her tail.

Squires whirled toward the bank and hollered, "Pull, you dumbasses! Don't you see that goddamn gator? For God's sake, pull!" He began to thrash with his arms, trying to help the men tractor him the few yards to safety.

At first, there must have been a dozen Mexicans on the bank willing to help him after the Bible-freak girl had ordered them to do it. When the sirens became audible, however, half of the little cowards had gone scrambling. Now there were only four little men onshore, in jeans and ball caps, all hitched to the rope, and they leaned against Squires's weight.

"Pull! Get your asses moving!" Squires screamed. "Jesus Christ, she's coming faster!"

The first heave of the rope yanked Squires forward. Another heave flipped him onto his back so that his eyes were fixated on the alligator when his left shoe finally popped free of the mud and he began to float toward the bank.

Now Squires's mind returned to nightmare mode, and everything happened in terrible slow motion. He was flailing with his arms, screaming for the men to move faster, while sirens and lights converged overhead, filling his head with a chaos so overwhelming he could barely hear his own voice. The night sky echoed with throbbing lights that were the exact same piercing red as the alligator's eyes.

Fifi was so close now that Squires could see the black width of her head. The animal pushed a wall of water ahead of her that lifted his body as she closed on him, which caused Squires to roll his body into a fetal ball, preparing himself for what was going to happen next.

"Get me out of here, *goddamn you*!" Squires voice broke as he pleaded, and he rolled to his stomach, unable to watch as the gator's mouth opened to take him, the animal a massive darkness only a few yards away.

As he turned, he realized he was close enough to touch the bank, where weeds were knee-deep. He lunged, got a fistful of grass in both hands and tried to pull himself out. He was too heavy, though, and roots ripped away from the earth, causing him to fall back into the water butt first.

As Squires hit the water, everything was still happening in slow motion. He got a snapshot look at three figures running toward him. It was the Bible-freak Mexican girl and the two white guys, the hippie two steps ahead of the guy named Ford. Ford appeared to have stopped for some reason, maybe to fish something from his pocket, but the girl and the hippie were coming fast. But then Squires didn't see anything else because he closed his eyes as he fell backward and landed on Fifi, who felt wide and buoyant in the water.

An instant later, Squires endured a watery explosion beneath him. He floundered for a few seconds, then he felt bony hands on his shoulder and realized someone was trying to drag his weight up the bank but wasn't having much success.

Squires used his fingers to claw at the sand as he crawled out of the water, picturing the gator opening its jaws again to snap off one of his legs, but it didn't happen because then he heard: *WHAP-WHAP!*

Two more gunshots.

Several long minutes later, Squires was on his knees, breathing heavily, aware that headlights of an ambulance and two emergency vehicles now illuminated the area like a stage.

He heard men's voices calling sharp orders, one of them yelling, "Put the weapon on the ground. Step away and show me your hands. Do it now!" Then he heard the same voice, louder, say, "Show me your goddamn hands and walk toward me!"

An asshole cop. It had to be—no one but a cop could mix contempt and authority in quite the same way. But Squires realized they were yelling at the big guy, Ford, not him, which was a relief. It gave him some hope.

The hippie was trying to help Squires to his feet, but Squires yanked his elbow away, saying, "Get your goddamn hands off me!"

but then winced when he tried to take a step. He hissed, *"Shit,"* because the back of his right leg was knotted and hurt like hell because of the pulled hamstring.

The hippie said to him, "Are you okay? Did it bite you? That was damn close, man!"

Squires put some weight on his leg and took a few experimental steps, watching the big guy walk toward a semicircle of cops and EMTs, holding his hands high. Then he listened to Ford say in the distance, "The injured man's over there, he needs attention right away. An alligator grabbed him, I don't know how bad. Then it came back after the big guy. That's why I had to use a weapon."

It had been a bad night so far, but Squires decided this might be a chance to turn things around. He pushed the hippie away and started toward the cops, limping barefooted, straightening himself, trying to look respectable despite his slimy knee-length shorts and muscle T-shirt.

He waited until he was sure the cops were looking in his direction before saying, "I'm the manager, I own this place. I was hoping you boys would show up. That asshole right there"—he pointed at Ford—"almost got me killed, the way he was banging off rounds from that little pistol of his. Hell, maybe he did kill someone. We should have a look around. Check on the units and make sure one of my tenants isn't hurt."

Squires made a point of ignoring Ford, who was staring at him now. For some reason, the scientist had a quizzical expression on his face, not amused, not pissed off, but *interested*, like Squires was some kind of bug.

It was weird the way the man appeared so relaxed, not the least bit worried, despite the guns the cops had now lowered, which caused Squires to remember that maybe Ford and the hippie were part of some DEA sting. Maybe they were even friends with these cops, who might be playing some kind of game.

Cops did shit like that all the time when they had their sights set on busting an underground steroids lab. Or so Squires had read on the Internet bodybuilder forums. It was law enforcement's way of sticking their noses where they didn't belong.

When one of the cops said to Squires, "Stop right there, no closer," Squires did, then listened to the man ask, "What's your name?"

Squires told him, deciding suddenly it was better to be friendly if Ford was DEA, which is why he added, "But I got no hard feelings against the dude. Maybe he was just trying to help me save that poor drunk over there—"

Squires looked toward the bank, where EMTs were already working on Carlson. There wasn't a *chilie* or a *chula* around now, he noticed. They'd all disappeared except for the weird little Jesus freak, who was pestering the EMTs about the old drunk, probably getting in their way.

Behind him, Squires heard the hippie call to the cops, "Why the hell do you have your guns out? Big tough guys—you're afraid of a couple of unarmed men and a little kid?"

The hippie said it in an irritated, cop-hater tone, which, to Squires, was more proof that these guys were working undercover for the feds.

Squires used the opening as an excuse to snap at the hippie, saying, "Shut your mouth, these guys know what they're doing. Let them do their damn jobs!" which might earn him some brownie points with the cops.

Squires hoped so. He felt a welling chemical anxiety inside his head, probably caused by steroids mixing with adrenaline, no doubt the result of that goddamn gator coming so close to biting his ass off. Plus, there was the not-so-small matter of the dead Mexican girl's body somewhere on the bottom of the lake.

Christ, when he remembered the dead body, Squires felt like he might vomit again, he was so nervous.

The bodybuilder stood there, shifting from his bad leg to his good leg, trying to appear as calm as the nerdy scientist. He watched carefully as the cops talked to Ford in a low voice, and then he felt another jolt when Ford not only lowered his hands but then shook hands with someone who stepped out of the shadows. Another cop, maybe, although the man wasn't wearing a uniform.

As the two uniforms holstered their weapons, Squires thought, *Oh shit*, and took a look around. The hippie was walking toward the cops, a pissed-off expression on his face until he saw that the cops had put their guns away, which caused the hippie to relax a little. It gave the skinny dude time to reassess, which is probably why he turned his attention toward Squires.

"What kind of lost soul are you?" the hippie asked, walking to-ward him. "What do you mean, we helped *you* save that man? You didn't do a damn thing but interfere! We just saved your life, and this is how you act?"

The hippie was talking loud enough for the cops to hear if they wanted, but they appeared to be busy with Ford.

Squires decided it was better to deal with the hippie privately before someone started paying attention. So he limped toward the dude, who looked ridiculous, in Squires's opinion, with his droopy surfer shorts, his skinny little muscles and his ribs showing.

When he was close enough, Squires said to him, "Look, I don't want any more trouble here. You play nice, I'll play nice. How's that sound to you?"

A confused expression appeared on the hippie's face as he replied,

"If that's supposed to mean something, man, I don't follow. What the hell you talking about?"

Squires told him, "I'm willing to cooperate," his voice low now. "I know who you are. I think I know why you're here. I'll help set the bust up, if that's the way you want to play it. You think those cops wouldn't like to take down a major supplier? Hell yes, they would. One word from me, it could happen."

Squires was thinking of giving the feds Laziro Victorino, the gangbanger who sold dope on the side, which seemed like a smart way to kill two birds with one stone. Plus, the V-man had shot those snuff films, too, which was a hell of a lot bigger deal than busting a small steroids operation like his.

Maybe the hippie would admit he was DEA, maybe he wouldn't. Squires was watching the man's reaction to see.

The expression on the hippie's face changed from confusion to mild concern. "Who've you been talking to? Did you bully your tenants into giving information about me? Turned them into narcs?"

When Squires didn't answer immediately, the hippie almost lost it. "That sucks, man! It really sucks. There's nothing lower than a damn narc, in my opinion. These people come here with zero money, they need to make a buck, so what's it matter to you? That's really small-time bullshit—and I just helped save your ass. You could be dying right now! Getting your bad-karma ticket punched for hell. Instead, you're threatening me!"

It took Squires a moment to realize what the hippie was saying. He put the words together with all those crisp twenties in the hippie's billfold and started smiling. Squires couldn't help himself. The damn hippie didn't work for the DEA. The dude was worried about getting busted himself!

Suddenly, Squires felt back in control. Well . . . sort of. He still had his girlfriend, Frankie, to worry about, and that gangbanger Victorino. The V-man was scary, but Frankie scared him more. There was no telling the amount of crap the woman would dump on him once she'd heard the cops had been snooping around the lake.

The lake. What lay on the bottom of that lake was Squires's biggest worry. It caused him to look toward the water, where the mangrove trees looked yellow in the bright ambulance lights, the water black as asphalt. What if they wanted to recover the alligator's body and decided to drag the pond?

Squires's smile faded for an instant but then returned. Nope, they wouldn't need to drag the pond. Because now Squires noticed two cops, one of them lying on the bank, trying to get a rope around something that Squires realized was the gator's tail.

Good! Fifi was dead—the fat pig deserved it, after attacking him. Shit, after all the times he'd fed her chunks of pig, once a whole yearling deer? And then the animal turns on him!

The scientist probably couldn't shoot worth a shit, but he'd finally gotten lucky with his little lady's pistol. True, Squires had been counting on the gator to get rid of the dead girl's body, and maybe Fifi already had, which struck him as an encouraging possibility.

At first it did, anyway—until he thought it through.

What if the cops took the gator to the Wildlife people? What if the Wildlife cops opened Fifi's belly to have a look?

Damn it!

Squires hadn't thought of that and he felt sick again. What if the gator had eaten the Mexican girl's body? Or even a few pieces? The cops would come storming back here with search warrants and handcuffs, and that would be the end of him.

Jesus Christ, he couldn't let that happen. Not with the Bible-freak girl still around to testify that she'd seen him drag that heavy sack to the water. If it wasn't for her, it would be easy enough to play dumb and let the cops blame the V-man. Or any one of the hundreds of other drunken Mexicans who lived in the area. That would be the natural direction to go. Wetbacks killed wettails, right? It happened all the time.

Squires took a look around. The girl had disappeared. Where? She had been kneeling by Carlson. Didn't seem the least bit concerned that the cops could ask for her ID, find out she was an illegal and take her skinny ass into custody. Not just illegal but underage at that, which meant she'd probably end up in some state orphanage.

Stupid little Mexican.

Squires felt pressure building in his head again as he fumed about the girl, a nobody wettail who could have him jailed if she decided, maybe even send him to the electric chair. It made him furious to think that one little Mexican had so much power over him.

Squires became even more determined to fulfill his fantasy . . .

A voice interrupted. "Why were you staring at that child? What's going on in the twisted brain of yours?"

Squires realized the hippie was talking to him. He turned, surprised, and a little pissed off. He studied the hippie, seeing the seriousness in the guy's Jesus-looking eyes, also seeing how scrawny the dude was, easy enough to snap the man's body in two if he wanted.

"She's a chick, not a child, you dumbass," Squires said to him, and then enjoyed the guy's reaction.

"You don't know what you're talking about," the hippie said, but in a sort of testing way.

"Bullshit, I don't. You ever seen a boy with pretty little knockers so firm they could poke your damn eye out?"

The hippie took a step toward him. "Why would you even say something so disgusting?"

Squires was loving the look of outrage. "Because it's true," he told the guy. "Tonight, that little girl and me had a nice conversation while she was in the trailer taking herself a bath. That's some tight little ass she's got for a wettail that young."

The hippie said, *"Wettail?"* then started walking toward Squires, the dude's eyes a little crazy. "You lay a hand on that girl, I'll see you in prison. You stay away from her or I'll . . ."

"Or you'll what? Try and scratch my eyes out?" Squires used a *Screw you* smile to make the guy madder, hoping the dude would take a swing at him while there were plenty of witnesses right there watching.

"Have an illegal Mexican girl squeal to the cops?"

The look of frustration on the hippie's face was an awesome thing to see. "Go ahead, tell the cops I was watching the girl take a bath. Let's see how long it takes for them to ship your little pal's ass back to shithole Mexico."

Squires flipped his middle finger at the dude, turned and made a quick trip to his double-wide, where he hid the cash he had stolen from the hippie and the hippie's asshole friend.

He stuck the money under the false bottom of a drawer, with stacks of twenties, fifties and hundreds he and Frankie had amassed from selling Gator Juice. Probably more than fifty thousand there.

Frankie would know the exact amount. Harris Squires seldom had the patience to count it.

An hour later, with all the lights and cameras and Florida Wildlife vehicles arriving, Harris was thinking that killing an alligator was a bigger deal than killing a person.

He had overheard one of the cops telling a reporter that unless it was a life-or-death situation, harming or harassing a gator could mean a year in jail and up to a four-thousand-dollar fine.

Good. He hoped they took Ford away in handcuffs.

It didn't look like it was going to happen, though, the way the cops had been treating the bastard. They'd hauled the drunk, Carlson, away in an ambulance, but not before Carlson had told them that Ford and the hippie had saved his life. Carlson was probably the only witness the nerd needed, but the little Bible-freak girl had seen the whole thing, too. Not that she'd stuck around long after the ambulance left.

Where was she? Squires was getting nervous, thinking that maybe the girl would grab her things and disappear from Red Citrus. Or maybe the cops had taken her away to question her privately.

Damn it! That was a possibility. Could be she was telling them right now what she'd seen Squires doing the night before.

No telling how long before the little brat talked, if it happened. It was something he would have to deal with later, though, because what Squires was doing right now was sitting in the backseat of a squad car, answering questions. There were two cops, a chunky guy in uniform and a Latin-looking woman wearing a white blouse tucked into a dark skirt, a regular professional ball breaker. Squires knew it the moment he set eyes on her.

The woman cop, whose name was Specter, was making notes as Squires told her his version of what had happened. In his version, he had been the hero, not Ford, which didn't get a response from the woman, and that worried him. Had they put him in the squad car to ask about the gator? Or to question him about what he had dumped into the pond the night before? Or maybe, just maybe, one of the nosy cops had taken a peek into his double-wide trailer and seen the steroids kitchen with its propane tanks and chemical jars everywhere.

Squires was feeling twitchy as the woman finally sat back to comment instead of just asking questions. She turned toward the backseat and said, "It's strange—the man the alligator attacked? The victim had no recollection of you being involved in any way, Mr. Squires. Dr. Ford and Dr. Tomlinson both tell stories that are very different from yours. I'm wondering why that is."

The hippie was a doctor, too?

Jesus Christ, Squires thought, *there must be colleges out there giving diplomas away to any idiot who can fill out the forms.*

Squires told the woman, "Let me tell you about that guy, Carlson. He's lived here for more than two years. He's a drunk and a paint huffer. He's out of his mind most the time. You know what a paint huffer is?"

The woman wrote something on a pad before she replied, "We've got another problem. Do you have any idea what that problem might be?"

Squires could feel his heart pounding in his chest. He looked out the window, seeing a tow truck in the bright lights, where a Wildlife cop was taking video as the crane winched Fifi slowly off the ground, all twelve or thirteen feet of her.

Squires was wondering if the back door of the squad car had locked automatically. If not, maybe the smartest thing he could do right now was make a run for it. Hide out for the night, then call Frankie and have her take him to the hunting camp, a place where he could hide and think things over in peace.

Squires put his hand on the door handle, thought about it another few seconds, then changed his mind. Once Frankie heard what had happened, she'd flip out. Hell, the woman would probably turn him over to the cops herself. Besides, how far would he get with a pulled hamstring?

Squires rubbed at the back of his leg and said, "All I know is, if I don't get some ice on my leg, I'm not going to be able to walk tomorrow. How screwed up is that? I help save the life of one of my drunken tenants and I end up crippled for a week. I'm a professional athlete, which I don't expect you to know. I'm training for the Mr. South Florida, which is in Clearwater Beach, this June, so an injury like a pulled hammie can be pretty serious if I don't take care of it."

The woman cop said, "Just a few more questions, Mr. Squires. There's something else I want to ask you about, this problem I mentioned—"

Squires felt himself getting mad, which he knew wasn't smart, but he couldn't help himself from cutting her off, saying, "Miz Specter, we've all got problems. All I know is, I need some ice. I save a man's life, now you're talking to me like I'm some kind of criminal. I don't want to get tough about it, but you're on my private property. And if I need medical attention—a bag of ice, I'm saying—then I should be able to—"

The male cop interrupted, sounding like a wiseass, telling him, "You own a trailer park and you're a bodybuilder. That's a handy combination."

What the hell did that mean?

Squires was telling himself, *Stay cool, don't let the prick make you mad,* as he corrected the guy, saying, "I own three mobile home parks, not trailer parks. A trailer's something you use to haul stuff, not live in. We offer manufactured homes and RV sites. It's what I do in my spare time."

"You're the owner?" the cop asked. "I called the address in, and it came back a women named Harriet Ray Squires owns this place."

"Same thing," Squires replied. "But we're trying to get out of the business, which you can probably understand, seeing the type of shit we have to put up with. Three acres of back-bay waterfront, only a couple miles from Fort Myers Beach. That'll be some serious money once we clear these units off and sell the place."

The cop wasn't done badgering him, though. "So you work for mom when you're not earning a living doing the muscle shows.

What steroids are you stacking?" The cop said it, trying to sound like he knew something about the subject.

The cop continued, "The show you're training for is in June?"

"Mr. South Florida," Squires replied.

The cop said, "Four months away from a show, you're still on your bulking cycle, right? Let me guess, you're doing about a thousand milligrams of testosterone mixed with, what, D-bol? Primo? I hear anavar is big with you guys once you start cutting."

What Squires wanted to do was tell this know-it-all asshole, *Primo is for pussies,* which was true, in his opinion, even if it was one of Arnold's favorite steroids.

Instead, he calmed himself with a familiar lie, saying, "I tried that crap a few years back, but the side effects scared the hell out of me. Plus, they do urine tests now. Steroids are illegal. Or maybe that's just for us professional athletes. I've got no reason to follow it. But, to me, the crap's not worth the risk. I've heard it gave some guys brain cancer. If you've got the right genetics, who needs the shit?"

"A health nut," the cop said, proving he really was a prick, but then the woman took over by silencing the man a look.

"Back to that problem I mentioned," she said to Squires. "Someone robbed Dr. Ford and Dr. Tomlinson. They took almost two thousand dollars from their billfolds. Cash."

That quick, Squires felt like he could breathe again. Hell, he'd almost forgotten that he'd hidden their damn money in his doublewide. Even if the cops had searched him and found the cash in his pocket, it was no big deal. Not compared to a murder rap, anyway, or running a steroids operation.

Squires asked what he thought was a smart question: "Did the guys leave the billfolds in their vehicle? That's not very smart, you ask me. Not around here."

When the woman replied, "No, they tossed them on the ground

before they went into the water," Squires let them see that he was thinking about it.

"I don't want to sound like a racist," he said after a few seconds, "but I've got a lot of Mexican tenants. And the way they are around any kind of valuable property, especially cash money, that's just a fact of life. The little bastards will steal you blind, give 'em a chance. There's something else to think about, too. Or maybe I shouldn't say anything, because I'm not one to stick my nose into other people's business. I hate people like that."

The woman said, "Oh?"

Squires made a show of it, giving it some more thought, before saying, "It has to do with that hippie-looking dude, Dr. whatever his name is. Think about it, that's all I'm saying. A guy who looks the way he looks, carrying that much cash."

"Tomlinson," the woman said. "He and Dr. Ford are from Sanibel Island. You've never met them before?"

"The Tomlinson dude, no, but I've seen him cruising my park plenty of times. About once a month he shows up. Like I said, I don't know the guy, so I'm not making any charges here, but that's another fact of life. The drug dealer types come through my park all the time. They know that the—"

Squires caught himself. He'd almost said *the illegals.*

"—they know that the migrant workers who live here sometimes have grass and peyote to sell. They bring it with them from Mexico when they cross the border. Maybe the guy, Tomlinson, is a drug dealer. Why don't you search their vehicle? You might find something that would surprise you."

That didn't play too well, but Squires didn't care. The cops didn't know about the dead girl's body in the lake. And they didn't know about his steroids kitchen only a block away.

Not yet, anyway.

Harris Squires was looking through the squad car window, seeing the tow truck lower Fifi onto the bed of a truck, its big tires flattening beneath her weight. The vehicle was about the same size as the stake truck he and his buddies had used to bring Fifi to Red Citrus.

Seeing the gator, he couldn't help but worry about what the Wildlife cops might find in the animal's belly. Squires was also thinking, *I've got to get my hands on that little Bible-freak girl before she goes blabbing to the law.*

Half an hour later, when the cops had released him, after he'd showered and iced his bad hamstring, Squires opened a fresh pint of tequila and began to make the rounds.

The little brat wasn't at the trailer where she usually stayed. But that was okay. The girl had left behind her only clean shirt, a ratty little book and a framed photo of what was probably her Mexican family.

She couldn't have gone far.

The bodybuilder took a moment to study the photo. His eyes moved from the girl—who looked about eight or so when the shot was taken—to what must have been the girl's mother, who was wearing an Indian-looking shawl over her head. The angular noses were similar, the line of their jaws.

Why the hell did they both look so familiar?

Hell . . . all Mexicans looked the same, Squires decided. The important thing was to find that damn girl.

SEVEN

AS WE WALKED BENEATH MANGROVE TREES TOWARD MY LITTLE home and laboratory on Dinkin's Bay, Sanibel Island, Tomlinson couldn't help fixating on the subject of Tula Choimha.

It was understandable. The girl had vanished shortly after the ambulance hauled her friend to the hospital and we'd failed to find her even though we had spent more than an hour searching.

"Doc," he said for the umpteenth time, "I know damn well what happened. How often am I wrong when I feel this strongly about something?"

I replied, "You're wrong most of the time, but you only remember the times you're right. Stop worrying about it."

"How can I stop worrying when every paranormal receptor in my body is telling me that Squires grabbed our girl for some reason? She wouldn't have just disappeared like that. Not without saying something to me. Damn it, *compadre*, we should have stayed right there until we found her."

I said, "Do me a favor. Take a deep breath. Then make a conscious effort to use the left side of your brain for a change. Squires is a jerk, but why would he kidnap a thirteen-year-old girl? There's no motivation, he has nothing to gain. It would be the stupidest time possible to crap in his own nest. He grabs the girl when cops are swarming all over the place?"

After a few quiet paces, I added, "We'll check in again tomorrow morning, but we're done for tonight. We did everything we could."

True. After being questioned by county deputies, then Florida Wildlife cops, and after refusing interviews with three different reporters, we had spent more than an hour at Red Citrus, hunting for Tula.

This was after I'd insisted that we both take an outdoor shower and then used the rest of the tequila to kill whatever microbes that might have been searching our skin for an entrance.

At the trailer where Tula was staying, we had found some of her extra clothing—boy's jeans, a shirt—a book titled *Joan of Arc: In Her Own Words*, plus a family photo in a cheap frame. The photo showed a six- or seven-year-old Tula, an older brother, her father and mother standing in front of a thatched hut somewhere in the mountains of Guatemala.

Like Tula, the mother wasn't short and squat like many Guatemalan women—which, to me, suggested aristocratic genetics that dated way, way back. The mother wore traditional *Indio* dress, a colorful *cinta*, or head scarf, and a blue *robozo*, or shawl. The lady had a nice smile in the photo, but there was an odd anxiousness in her expression, too. She was an attractive woman, slim, with cobalt hair and a Mayan nose. Not beautiful but pretty, and looking way too young to have borne two children.

If children had not been in the photo, I would have guessed the mother's age at less than seventeen.

Tula might have gone away and left her clothing, but she wouldn't have left the photo. It suggested that the girl was still in the area. I also found it reassuring that the people with whom she was staying were less concerned than Tomlinson. They were among the few who knew that the unusual boy was actually a girl.

"It is something the maiden does at night," a Mayan woman had told me in Spanish. "She goes to a secret place where no one can find her. She says she goes there to be alone with God. And to speak to angels who come to her at night. Every night the maiden disappears, so tonight is nothing new. Sometimes during the day she disappears, too. We respect her wishes. She is very gifted. Tula is a child of God."

I found the woman's phraseology interesting and unusual. The translation, which I provided Tomlinson, was exact. *Doncella* is Spanish for "maiden." *Hadas* referred to woodland spirits that are common in Mayan mythology, the equivalent of Anglo-Saxon faeries or angels.

It is a seldom used word, *doncella*. In Spanish, "maiden" resonates with a deference that implies purity if not nobility. Again, I was struck by the respect adults demonstrated for the child. It bordered on reverence, which was in keeping with the small shrine the locals had erected outside Tula's trailer. The shrine consisted of candles and beads placed on a cheap plaster statuette of the Virgin Mary.

"Tula has been in the States just over a week," Tomlinson had explained to me, "but already word has spread that a child lives here who speaks with God. Tula didn't have to tell these people anything about herself because she's a thought-shaper. One look at her, her people knew that she's special. Word travels fast in the Guatemalan community. Their survival depends on it."

"In that case," I'd said, trying to get the man off the subject, "park residents will naturally keep track of her movements. They think she's special? Then she'll attract special attention. Someone around here is bound to know where her secret place is."

But no one did. Finally, Tomlinson and I started going door-to-door, but the neighbors were so suspicious of us, two *gringos* asking questions, that they probably wouldn't have told us where the girl was even if they had known.

My guess, though, was, they didn't know.

Now, two hours later, as Tomlinson and I walked toward my rickety old fish house, we discussed what I was going to make for dinner. It was my way of changing the subject. I was hungry, and it had also been several hours since Tomlinson had had a beer. It was an unusually long period of abstinence for the man, so it was no wonder his nerves were raw.

I was relieved to be home. My house and lab are more than a refuge, although they have provided refuge to many. The property, buildings and docks that constitute Sanibel Biological Supply are a local institution, second home to a trusted family of fishing guides, live-aboards and an occasional female guest.

Of late, though, I'd been going through a period of abstinence as well—not the liquid variety. So I was ready for a few beers myself. It had been one hell of a crazy night, and Tomlinson wasn't the only one who felt a little raw.

There are fewer and fewer houses like mine in Florida. The place is an old commercial fish house built over the water on stilts. The lower level is all dockage and deck. The upper level is wooden platform, about eight feet above the water. Two small cottages sit at the center under one tin roof, and the platform extends out, creating a broad porch on all four sides.

I use one of the cottages as my laboratory and office. The other cottage is my living quarters, complete with a small yacht-sized kitchen and very un-yacht-like wood-burning stove that is a good thing to have on windy winter nights.

When we got to the first flight of steps, I paused to turn on underwater lights I had installed near my shark pen. Underwater lights, to me, are more entertaining than any high-tech entertainment system in the world. The drama that takes place between sea bottom and surface is real. It is uncompromising. There is no predicting what you might see.

Tonight turned out to be a stellar example. Even Tomlinson went silent when I flipped the switch, and the black water beneath the house blossomed into a luminous translucent gel.

Simultaneously, a school of mullet exploded on the light's periphery, and we watched the fish go greyhounding into darkness.

Beneath my feet, under the dock, spadefish the size of plates grazed on barnacles that pulsed in feathered ivory colonies like flowers, raking in microscopic protein. There were gray snappers and black-banded sheepsheads, circling the pilings.

In a sand pocket beyond, I noticed meticulous shadowed bars—a small regiment of snook, their noses marking the direction of tidal flow. I also saw a lone redfish, with copper-blue scales, dozing next to a piling, while, above, dime-sized blue crabs created furious wakes as they sprinted across a universe of water, oblivious to the danger below.

"Doc . . . you see that? Over there—see it? There's something moving."

For some reason, Tomlinson whispered the question, and I followed his gaze into shadows of mangrove trees at the shore's edge. My friend's tone communicated curiosity, not danger, so I took my time.

I removed my glasses and cleaned them before replying, "I don't see anything." But then I said, *"Wait,"* and began walking toward shore because I saw what had captured the man's interest.

There was something lying on the sand between mangrove trees and the water. It was a man-sized shape, gray and glistening in the ambient light. Then another shape took form, this one animated and suddenly making a lot of noise as it crashed through foliage.

The shapes were alive, I realized. They were animals of some type.

Red mangroves are also called walking trees because their trunks are balanced on rooted tendrils that create a jumble of rubbery hoops growing from swamp. Whatever the animal was, it was having trouble getting through the roots to the water.

Tomlinson whispered, as if in awe, "My God, Doc—this can't be happening!" Apparently, he had figured out what was in the mangroves, but I still had no clue.

I jogged down the boardwalk as my brain worked hard to cross-reference what I saw with anything I had ever seen before.

Nothing matched.

At first, I thought we'd surprised two stray dogs, from the way one of the creatures tried to lunge over the roots. But no . . . the shapes were too big to be dogs.

Feral hogs? A couple of panthers, maybe?

No . . .

For a moment, I wondered if I was seeing two large alligators. They often strayed into brackish water, and we occasionally even find them Gulf-side, off the Sanibel beach.

Wrong again. Gators don't lunge like greyhounds. And they don't make the clicking, whistling noises I was hearing now.

It was one of the rare times in my life when I wasn't carrying some kind of flashlight, which I regretted, because the creatures began to take form as I got closer. When my dock lights had first surprised them, one of the creatures had been on the bank, several feet from the water. The other had been in the mangroves, many yards beyond.

I watched, transfixed, as first one, then the other animal, finally wiggled its way back into the shallows. Soon, the crash of foliage was replaced by a wild, rhythmic splashing as both creatures hobbyhorsed toward deeper water.

Visibility wasn't good in the March darkness, but I could see well enough now to finally know what we were looking at. Particularly telling were the fluked tails and the distinctive pointed rostrums of the two animals.

From the deck, I heard Tomlinson whoop, *"Wowie-zowie, dude!"* then laughed as he called, "This is wild, man! Have you ever seen anything like that in your life?"

No, I had not.

I had stopped running because I wanted to concentrate on what was happening. I watched intensely, aware that it was one of those rare moments when I knew that, later, I would want to recall each detail, every nuance of movement, in the scene that was unfolding.

The two creatures we had surprised were mammals. But they weren't land mammals. They were members of the family Delphinidae, genus *Tursiops*. They were pure creatures of the sea—at least, I had thought so until this instant.

I watched until the pair of animals had made it to deeper water, where they submerged . . . reappeared . . . then vanished beneath a star-streaked sky.

After a moment, I walked in a sort of pleasant daze to the house, where Tomlinson stood, grinning. He held out an arm so we could bang fists and said in a soft voice, "Bottlenose dolphins. I wouldn't have believed it if I hadn't seen it for myself. Completely out of the water, feeding on dry land."

I was smiling, too. There are few things more energizing than the discovery of something profound in a place that is so familiar, you think all its secrets have been revealed.

Tomlinson was feeling it, too. "My God," he said, his head pivoting from the mangroves to the bay. "How could anyone ever get tired of living on the water? This place is magic, man, it's just pure-assed *magic*. Dolphins foraging beneath the trees while Sanibel Island sleeps. The freaking *wonder* of it all. Wow!"

He paused, both of us listening to the distinctive *Puffffft!* as the dolphins exhaled in synch, out of sight now but their images still clear in my mind.

Tomlinson asked me, "Have you ever in your life heard about something like this happening? Not me. Never ever. And I know *a lot* of devoted druggies who see crazy shit all the time."

Tomlinson was so excited that he was talking too fast, thinking too fast, and I wanted to slow everything down.

I replied, "Hold on a second, I'm trying to think this through. We don't know for sure they were feeding. That's an assumption." My mind was working on the problem, delighted by the challenge.

Tomlinson tried to interrupt, but I shushed him with a wave of my hand.

I said, "Granted, it's the first explanation that came into my mind—that they came ashore to feed. But we need to take a look in the mangroves. A *close* look. And photograph the entire scene, too. If they were feeding, they might have left something behind. I'll get a flashlight."

Tomlinson repeated himself, saying, "In all the literature, in all the crazy dolphin stories I've heard, this is a first. What about you?"

His reference to crazy dolphin stories was an unusual thing for someone like Tomlinson to say, but he was spot-on. Bottlenose dolphins are the unwitting darlings of every misinformed crackpot who has ever yearned for a mystical link between humans and the sea.

That includes more than a few misguided biologists who have credited the animals with everything from paranormal powers to the ability to heal children stricken by disease.

Dolphins—and these were *dolphins*, not porpoises—are brilliantly adaptable pack animals. Intelligent, true, but they are still pack animals, which includes all the ugly mob behavior that the term implies: assault, gang rape, occasionally the attempted genocide of competing species.

Dolphins are brilliantly adapted for survival—and they survive relentlessly, as all successful species do.

I waved for Tomlinson to follow me toward the house as I answered, "In Indonesia, I heard stories, maybe Malaysia, too, from people who claimed to know people who said they'd seen dolphins foraging in the mangroves, feeding on crabs. But it's never been documented—not that I know of, anyway. I just figured it was part of the dolphin mythology. You know, the sort of stories that date back to mermaids—bull dolphins sneaking ashore to have intercourse with virgins. That sort of baloney."

I left the man there and went up the steps, two at a time, to fetch flashlights. Mentally, I was assembling a list of dolphin experts I could call, pleased not only because of what we had just seen but because it had taken Tomlinson's mind off the Guatemalan girl.

When my pal is fixated on a subject, he becomes repetitive and tiresome. I had invited him to dinner earlier in the day, so there was no getting out of it, and I didn't want to have to endure his brooding theories about what had happened to Tula Choimha.

I believed that he was underestimating the girl. She had managed to travel solo, with very little money, from the mountains of Guatemala to Florida on her own with no problems—none I was aware of, anyway. The territory she had crossed included some of the most dangerous country on earth—particularly the migrant trails of

Mexico, where outlaws and warring gangs prey on travelers. Robbery and rape are commonplace.

The fact that Tula had negotiated the trip successfully, and alone, said a lot about her character. But it said more about her instincts. The girl was street-savvy. I thought it unlikely that she would have allowed herself to be victimized in the markedly safer environment of a Florida trailer park, Harris Squires or no Harris Squires.

Inside the house, I grabbed two potent little Fenix LED flashlights, hesitated, then decided, what the hell, first I would change into clean shorts and a shirt. The dolphins wouldn't be coming back, so there was no hurry now.

I leaned outside and told Tomlinson he should do the same. In the lab, I found a 500-milliliter bottle of reagent-grade propyl alcohol. I tossed my clothes outside, doused myself good, ears included, then placed the jug on the deck for Tomlinson to use.

As I changed, I checked my phone messages. One was from a state biologist whose name I had heard, but I'd never met. Her name was Emily Marston.

Emily—common nicknames included Emma, Milly and Em. Probably because it had been a month since I'd had a serious date, I wondered if any fit.

"Dr. Ford, in the morning I'm leading the necropsy on the alligator that was killed tonight. Since we're working at the park station on Sanibel and since you were involved, I thought you might like to join us. But only if you're interested personally. This is not an official request."

I found the woman's voice attractive, and her last sentence an alluring addendum that was, at once, both welcoming and dismissive.

Yes, I was interested.

I made note of the lady's name, her number, the time of the necropsy, then went out the door after slipping a little Kodak point-and-shoot camera into my pocket.

As I did, my mind returned briefly to Tomlinson's assertion that the bodybuilder Harris Squires was responsible for the Guatemalan girl's disappearance. Was there even a small possibility that he was right?

I'm a careful man—particularly when a child is involved and when my own conscience is on the line. I gave it some more thought.

"Every paranormal receptor in my body is convinced that the guy grabbed her," Tomlinson had told me, or something close to that. It summarized his entire argument. Everyone else at the trailer park had told us that she disappeared at night all the time. If they weren't worried, why should we be? But just in case, while I was at the necropsy tomorrow morning, I decided I'd make sure Tomlinson went back to the trailer park to dig around.

EIGHT

WHEN HARRIS SQUIRES TOLD TULA, "YOUR FRIEND, CARLSON, must be in a lot of pain because he wants you to come to the hospital," she knew he was lying, but the voice in her head told her to get into Squires's big, rumbling truck anyway and go with him.

This was early the next morning, several hours after the EMTs had refused to let Tula ride in the ambulance, and after many more hours that she had spent in hiding.

The girl knew it was unwise to linger near the lake, inviting questions from the police. So she had wandered off to her tree to speak with the owls, but the owls were not calling, possibly because of all the noise and flashing lights.

Even so, she waited, sitting alone in the high limbs of the banyan, where she could observe the actions of her second *patron*, Tomlinson, and his friend, the large man with eyeglasses, who was speaking with police.

Tula focused on Tomlinson, who was talking to Squires. She

sensed her *patron*'s good heart and godliness, and also that he was angry about something. He was angry at the landlord, perhaps, who had used God's name to blaspheme them even though they had saved his life.

Yes . . . the man was angry at Squires. Tula had watched Tomlinson walk toward the huge landlord, and, for a moment, she thought he might strike him. Instead, the two men exchanged loud words that weren't always loud enough for her to hear, but she heard enough. Tula knew they were talking about her and she listened carefully.

Soon, she felt ashamed because she realized that the landlord was telling the *patron* about seeing her naked in the bathtub. The girl felt her face become hot, and she felt like sobbing.

No man had ever seen Tula naked before, and very few women. Sitting in the tree, she had vowed to herself that it would never happen again. *Ever.* Not as long as she lived—unless, of course, the voice in her head, the Maiden's voice, told her that she should marry. But that seemed unlikely, and, even then, Tula would not want it to happen.

The Maiden had gone to her death a virgin. Tula knew this was true, just as she knew every detail of the saint's life because, at the convent, Sister Lionza had given her books about Joan of Arc. Tula had read those books so many times that she knew them by heart.

Her favorite book was a simple volume that included only words that the Maiden had written in her own warrior's hand or had spoken before witnesses. Tula loved the book so much that it was one of the few things she had brought with her from the mountains of Guatemala. Its entries spanned the saint's childhood, included her lionhearted testimony at her trial and, finally, her last words as flames consumed her body:

Jesus! *Jesus!*

There was no intrusive scholarship in the book. No third-party guessing about what the Maiden had thought or felt.

That small book was pure, like the Maiden herself. Tula carried it everywhere and had read it so often that her own patterns of speech now naturally imitated the passionate rhythms of the girl who had been chosen by God.

Tula knew that imitating the Maiden's style of speaking caused some people to look at her strangely, but she took it as an affirmation of her devotion. The book had been a great comfort to Tula on the journey from the mountains to this modern land of cars and asphalt by the sea.

Tula had memorized several favorite passages. There were many that applied to her own life:

When I was thirteen, a voice from God came to help me govern myself. The first time I heard it, I was terrified. The voice came to me about noon; it was summer, and I was in my father's garden. I had not fasted the day before. I heard the voice on my right. There was a great light all about.

Soon afterward, I vowed to keep my virginity for as long as it should please God . . .

Tula had not been in her father's garden, of course, when the Maiden's voice first came. Her father had been murdered by the *revolucionarios* as Tula, age eight, watched from the bushes. The memory of what she had seen, heard and smelled was so shocking—her father's screams, the odor of petrol and flesh—that her brain had walled the memory away in a dark place.

Little more than a year later, when Tula began to feel at home at the convent, the dark space in her soul had opened slowly to embrace the Maiden's light.

Another favorite line from the book was: *I would rather die than to do what I know to be a sin.*

When Tula whispered those words, she could feel the meaning

burn in her heart. She had whispered the phrase aloud many times, always sincerely, as an oath to God. The words were clean and un-wavering, like the Maiden's spirit. Tula could speak the phrase silently in the time it took her to inhale, then exhale, one long breath.

I would rather die than to do . . .

. . . what I know to be a sin.

Tula longed for the same life of purity, for it was the Maiden's writing that had first sent her into the trees to seek her own visions. The Maiden, Tula had read, had often sought God's voice in a place called the Polled Wood, in France, where she had sat in the branches of a tree known as the Fairy Tree.

Tula doubted if she would ever see France, but Florida had to be more like Orléans than the jungles of Quintana Roo.

It was strange, now, to sit in a Florida banyan tree so far from home, watching the flashing lights of the emergency vehicles. The Maiden's visions, Tula remembered, were always accompanied by bright light, which caused the girl to concentrate even harder on what she was seeing.

The lights pulsed blue and red, exploding off the clouds, then sparking downward, rainlike, through the leaves. The lights were brighter than any Tula had ever seen, lights so piercing, so rhythmic, that they invited the girl to stare until she felt her body loosen as her thoughts purified and became tunneled.

Soon, Tula slipped into a world that was silent, all but for the Maiden's voice—Jehanne, her childhood friends had called the young saint. Jehanne's voice was so sure and clear, it was as if her moist lips touched Tula's ear as she delivered a message.

It was a message Tula had heard several times in the last week.

You are sent by God to rally your people. The clothing of a boy is your armor. The amulets you wear are your shields . . .

Fear not. I speak as a girl who knew nothing of riding and warfare until

God took my hand. We drove the foreigners away because it was His will. He provided the way.

You, too, are God's instrument. You will gather your family in this foreign land, and free them from their greed. You will lead them home again, where they can live as a people, not slaves, because it is His will.

Trust Him always. He will provide the way for you.

Tula loved the solitude of trees. She loved the intimacy of this muscled branch that was contoured like a saddle between her legs. Once, as the saint's voice paused in reflection, Tula found the nerve to whisper a question with a familiarity that she had never risked before.

"Jehanne? Holy Maiden? I think of you as my loving sister. Is this wrong? I have to ask."

I am the God-light that lives within you, the Maiden's voice replied. *We are one. Like twins with a one soul.*

Sisters? Tula hazarded, thinking the word but not speaking it.

Forever sisters, the Maiden replied. *Even when you leave this life for the next.*

For more than two hours, Tula had sat motionless in the tree as the Maiden spoke to her, providing comfort and the governing voice of God. She was only vaguely aware when her *patron*, Tomlinson, walked beneath the tree, calling her name, followed by the large man with eyeglasses. Whose name, she had learned, was Dr. Ford.

There was something unusual about her *patron*'s friend, she realized vaguely, as the two hurried past. Something solid and safe about Dr. Ford . . . But the man was cold, too. His spirit filled Tula with an unsettling sensation, like an unfamiliar darkness that was beyond her experience.

The girl didn't allow her mind to linger on the subject, and she was not tempted to call out a reply because she was so deliciously safe. Her body and heart were encased by the Maiden. The Maiden's lips never left her ear.

Even when the flashing lights vanished from the tree canopy, Tula continued sitting because Jehanne continued to speak, whispering strong thoughts into Tula's head.

The Maiden's words were so glory filled and righteous that Tula thought she might burst from the swelling energy that filled her body. It caused blood to pulse in her chest, and in her thighs, until her body trembled. It was a throbbing sensation so strong that she felt as if she might explode if the pressure within didn't find release.

You are sent to rally your people. You are sent by God . . .

The first time Tula had heard those words was only seven days ago, her first night in Florida. She had been sitting on this same thick branch, new to the large banyan tree.

Those words had been a revelation.

Tula had come to *El Norte* to find her mother and family, yes. But in her heart she knew there was a greater cause for which God had chosen her. Why else would the Maiden risk guiding her to *El Norte*, the direction of death?

On that night one week ago, Tula had been so moved by the revelation that, as she returned to her trailer, she had stopped to address adults who, every evening, collected around a fire to drink beer and laugh.

It offended Tula the way the adults were behaving because she feared her mother had behaved similarly after she had abandoned her own family. Even so, the girl had stood silently, feeling the heat of fire light on her face, listening and watching.

Gradually, Tula became angry. The Maiden had ordered her soldiers and pages not to drink alcohol or to sin with loose women and dice. She had counseled her followers to pray every day, and to never swear.

These adults weren't soldiers, but they were all members of the same mountain people. They were Maya, they were *Indígena*, like her. And Tula knew it was wrong for them to be living drunken, modern lives so removed from the families they had left behind in the cloud forests.

Tula stepped closer to the fire. She cleared her throat and waited for the adults to notice her. Soon, as voices around her went silent, Tula let the French Maiden guide her Mayan words.

"If your children could see you now," the girl asked in a strong voice, "what would they think? What would your wives and husbands think? I am speaking of the families you left behind in the mountains. Your *real* families. Do you think they are consorting with drunken neighbors, lusting after money and flesh? No. They are asleep in their *palapas*. Their hearts are broken and lonely from missing you."

Tula was surprised by her own confidence, but more surprised by the angry reaction of the adults. Men sat in a moody silence for a moment, then began to jeer and wave her away as if Tula's opinion meant nothing. The women were indignant, then furious. They swore at her in Spanish, calling her a stupid boy who had sex with animals. And the matron of the group—a squat, loud woman— picked up a stick and threatened to thrash Tula unless she ran away.

Tula had stood her ground, looking into the woman's eyes as she approached. Tula was unafraid, for, in that instant, she experienced something strange. She sensed the Maiden melding into her body, bringing with her a heart so strong that Tula felt a profound and joyous confidence that she had never before experienced.

"Sisters?" she had asked the Maiden.

Yes. Even when you leave this life for the next.

Tula had doubted the promise at first but now she knew they were Jehanne's own true words.

As the matron drew near, Tula had smiled, saying softly, "Strike me if you wish, but I will only turn the other cheek. First, though, tell me why you are so angry. Do you hate me for what I said? Or do you hate me because what I said is true?'

The matron had sworn at her and swung the stick in warning but then stepped back because Tula did not flinch. Still smiling, Tula had said to the woman, "Do you remember the goodness of God that you felt as a child? He is still there, in your heart. Why do you fight Him so?"

That stopped the matron, and she listened more closely as Tula told her, "You came to *El Norte* because you love your family. God knows that. It is the same with everyone here, is it not? Only you know how painful it is to be a mother or father who cannot afford food for their children's table.

"But do you also understand how hurtful it is to lose your mother in exchange for a bundle of pesos sent weekly from the United States? Children need their parents more than money or food—that's why I'm here. I have come to lead my family home."

Then Tula had asked the woman, "Who did you leave behind? A son? A daughter?"

The woman's expression transitioned from anger to uncertainty. "What business is that of yours, stupid child?"

Tula was aware of the Maiden inside her, exploring the woman's thoughts, but the Maiden did not share what she was learning.

"You left behind a husband and children," Tula guessed, feeling her own way. "You planned to return, but here you are. How many years has it been?"

It took a full minute before the matron spoke, but she finally did. "Two children," the woman replied, sounding weary now and a little unnerved. "Our first child, she died, so there were three, not two."

The woman looked at the group as she added, "I must stop saying that I have only two children. My third child, her name was Alexandra, but only for nine days. She is with God now. I should have told you this."

Tula had glanced at the man with whom the woman had been sitting and knew he wasn't her husband. The woman was an adulteress, but Tula did not say it. For some reason, she felt kindly toward the woman despite the woman's sins and respected her sadness.

Instead, Tula said, "You are a good women, I feel that is true. It has been several years since you have seen your family, yet you have not abandoned them. I know I'm right, I can see God's own goodness in your eyes. You are a devoted mother. How many times a month do you send money?"

The woman replied, "Every week, I cash my check at the Winn-Dixie, then pay cash to the Western Union clerk at the cigarette counter. At Christmas, I send three checks. In four years, I have never missed a week. Even though my husband has taken another woman, I still send the money."

As an aside to the adults the woman added, "I've heard that my children now call this new woman mother. It is something I have been ashamed to share. I don't know why I am telling you now."

When Tula reached to place her hand on the matron's shoulder, the woman shrugged the hand away, getting angry again—angry not at Tula but because she was so close to tears.

"Leave me alone," the woman said. "We are adults, we've worked hard all day in the fields. Now we are relaxing, what business is this of yours? Go play with your little *penga* instead of harassing good men and women."

"Maybe you know my family," Tula had pressed. "My mother's name is Zabillet. Here, people call her Mary. My brother's name is Pacaw, but sometimes Pablo. He left home six months ago. I have two aunts and an uncle in Florida, too, but I don't know where."

The woman seemed to be paying attention as Tula added, "My mother came to *El Norte* four years ago, when I was only eight. Like you, she sent money every week. There is a phone booth outside the *tienda* in our village, and every Sunday night I was there, waiting, when she called. Two months ago, though, my mother stopped calling. And the number to her cell phone no longer works."

"It's because of the coyotes and the field bosses," a man sitting nearby explained. "They control us by controlling our telephones. Everyone knows that, unless you're stupid. You must be stupid. Why does that surprise you?"

Tula replied, "It doesn't surprise me. Not now. Not since I've learned how the Mexican coyotes cheat us. They charge us pesos to come to *El Norte*. Then they charge us dollars to provide us with work and a place to sleep, and a telephone that they can disable at any time. But when my mother stopped calling, I knew something was wrong."

Sounding impatient, another man said, "We were enjoying ourselves before you interrupted. Now you stand here, asking rude questions. Our *Indígena* sisters and brothers arrive in Florida every day, but we don't ask their names. We mind our own business. If you have lost your mother, go to Indiantown and ask the *Indígena* there. Or go to Immokalee. It is only an hour's drive in a truck.

"If your mother is in Florida," the man continued, "the Maya of Immokalee and Indiantown will know—there are many thousands of us in those villages. Now, please get out of my sight. I did not work all day in the sun to have my beer interrupted by a disrespectful child who criticizes his elders."

Immokalee.

Tula had heard of the town, of course. It was one of the last places her mother had lived prior to her disappearance. Tula had heard of Indiantown, too. Everyone in Guatemala knew of these villages because they were the largest Mayan settlements in Florida. In these places, Tula had heard, the *Indígena* sang the old songs and spoke the ancient language, not the bastard tongue of the Mexicans.

Tula said to the man, "I appreciate your advice, but you are wrong about me being disrespectful. I said what I said, but the words are not mine. You do not understand who I am. Look at me closely, perhaps you will."

"The nerve of this *mericon*!" one of the men chided. "He is a dirty little faggot. See how he poses and struts, as if he is more important than his elders?"

"Doubt me if you wish," Tula said in a firm voice, "but I will not listen to your profanities. Look at me. Don't just use your eyes, use your heart also. I have been sent here by my patron saint. I am unworthy, just a stupid child. But I am also an instrument of God. So be careful how you speak to me."

There! She had finally said aloud what she had never had the courage, or conviction, to share with anyone. Tula was afraid for a moment how the people would react.

She could feel the adults looking at her, their faces suspended above the fire as brown as wooden masks worn at festival time in the Mayan mountains. As the men and women stared, Tula felt her body transforming as she stood erect, chin angled, and she wondered if the adults would correctly perceive the changes that were taking place within her.

It was something that Sister Lionza had been teaching Tula at the monastery, the art of projecting thoughts—the first hint that the nun was preparing her for membership in the *Culta de Shimono*.

Thoughts are energy. Our thoughts are sparks from God's eyes. Devote your thoughts to an image. Picture that image with all your heart. Soon others will see, with their eyes, the image that lives in your mind.

In Tula's mind, as she posed by the fire, she envisioned a precise picture of herself the way she *yearned* to look. Her jeans and ragged shirt were armor molded to her body by firelight. The amulet and medallion that she clutched were now a glittering shield.

Yes, Tula decided. The adults saw that her body had been transformed. A few of them, anyway. It was in their eyes, both respect and wonder. She felt sure enough to say, "I'm only a child from the mountains, but I have been transformed by my patron saint. Don't be uneasy, don't be afraid of my strange dress. The Maiden speaks to me and she speaks through me. She provides me words for you that I believe are words from God."

Voices around the fire muttered, asking about the Maiden—what did the name mean?—while Tula continued speaking.

"The Maiden has told me that this land will never be our home. Our home is in the cloud forests of the mountains. It is in the jungles where our ancestors built pyramids that rivaled the greatness of Egypt. She has told us to think back and remember our home. And the love we have for it. It is true that we do not have shiny red pickup trucks in our yards. Or televisions with large screens. But what good is a red truck when it cannot drive you to your family?"

Tula sensed emotion in the people her words touched just as she could also hear the whispered grumblings of those who did not see or believe—men mostly, but also a few women who got to their feet, speaking insults and a few whispered profanities.

The matron, however, was not among them. She had stared at Tula with glistening eyes.

"You speak to God?" the woman asked. "How do we know you are not lying?"

Jehanne had been asked this same question many times by her inquisitors, so Tula used the Maiden's own words to answer.

"I do not speak to God. He speaks to me. Any other way would be improper. Who am I? I am a poor, stupid child. The voices that direct me come from Him. I believe this truly in my own heart. I am his instrument; only a messenger instructed by the words of my patron saint, the Maiden."

The woman, near tears, replied, "I don't know why I believe you, but I do. It must be true, for you looked into my heart and told me what I was feeling. I miss my children. I miss my village, and the cooking fires and the odors of my girlhood. What did you say to us about God being in us as children? I can't remember your exact words—"

"I asked you to remember how you felt as a child. When you felt the goodness of God inside you. God is still there, alive in your heart. I asked, 'Why do you fight Him so?'"

From the shadows beyond the fire, a man's voice chided Tula, saying, "Next this boy will be telling us that he also speaks to the goats who bugger him! Why is he wasting our time. Go away, little turd, or I will bugger you myself!" Grinning, the man had stood and pretended to unsnap his belt.

Tula was surprised that only a few people laughed at the insult, and she was comforted by the realization that very few of these people would ever laugh at her again.

When Tula had finally left that fire circle, seven nights before, some of the adults had watched her in a silence that was a mixture of fear, awe and longing. On that very same night, someone placed a statuette of the Virgin Mary outside her trailer.

The next evening, after the day's work was done, the matron and two neighbor women appeared at Tula's trailer, seeking to speak privately.

The next night, a small line formed outside Tula's door. Each night afterward, the line was longer. Some people came from as far as Indiantown, Miami and Immokalee to speak with the child who was said to be an emissary from God.

News of the unusual child traveled at lightning speed through the cheap cell phones of the Guatemalan community.

Sometimes, women and men wept as they asked for Tula's guidance and advice. Many attempted to kneel and kiss her hand, but Tula refused their adulation, just as the Maiden had refused the worshipping gestures of her own followers six hundred years before.

"We are sisters?" Tula had questioned Jehanne, hoping desperately that it was true.

Even when you leave this life for the next, the Maiden had promised.

Tula was now more determined than ever to be equal to the honor of being chosen by Jehanne.

To every person who came to her, Tula challenged them with the same parting question: "Do you remember the goodness of God that was in you as a child? He is still there, in your heart. Why do you fight Him so?"

Much had changed since Tula had spoken to the fire circle a week before. The respect with which her neighbors treated her was beyond her experience, yet she handled it comfortably and exercised her new power only for good—to spread the word that she was searching for her family, and, tonight, to order the adults to help save her *patron,* Carlson, and also the landlord, Harris Squires.

Something else that had changed, Tula realized, was that she had lost her anonymity. The eyes of her neighbors followed her everywhere she went. Which is why she had waited long after the ambulance and police cars had left to finally climb down from the tree and retreat to her trailer.

She didn't stay long, though, because the memory of Harris Squires's words scared her. She knew the giant man would come looking for her soon. So she had gone to the public toilet, curled up in a stall and had tried to sleep.

Too much had happened, though, for Tula's mind to relax. She fretted about Carlson—would he live?—and also regretted not speaking with the strange man, Tomlinson, who Tula barely knew but who she had immediately accepted as her second patron and protector.

Early that morning, still unable to sleep, Tula had returned to her tree to speak with the owls and watch the sunrise, she told herself. But it was really to invite that pulsing, trembling feeling into her body. As she straddled the limb, which Tula thought of as a saddle, the Maiden had floated into Tula's body almost immediately, but only for a short time.

Suddenly, then, without farewell, the Maiden's voice was gone. It was replaced by the distant inquiries of morning birds—the owls had remained silent—and then the sound of approaching footsteps.

Tula had been weeping, as she always did when the Maiden left her, yet she was crying softly enough to hear the crack of twigs and then a man's voice say, "Lookee, lookee, what I see. It's getting so I know where to find you. What do you think you are, *chula*? Some kind of bird?"

Tula looked down to see Harris Squires staring at her through the strange binoculars that allowed him to see in the night like an animal.

It wasn't until the giant had grabbed Tula, clapping his hand over her mouth to silence her, that the Maiden's words returned to comfort the girl, saying, *Stop fighting, go with him. You are in God's hands. God will show you the way.*

———————

Now, sitting beside Squires in his oversized truck, Tula said to the man, "What do you call these bracelets on my wrists? They're hurting me. Will you please take them off?"

Squires made a noise of impatience as he drove. He had been trying to focus on his sex fantasy, but the girl kept talking.

"Why don't you answer me?" the girl said, irritated. "I have every reason to be angry at you. Instead, I am speaking to you politely. You should at least answer when I ask you a polite question."

Squires made another groaning sound.

She didn't stop. "If I had wanted to run from you, God would have given me the strength. Instead, He told me to come with you. That's why I am here. There's no need for you to chain my hands."

Squires was aggravated, but also surprised by the girl's calm voice, her matter-of-fact manner.

"They're called handcuffs," he told her, because it was obvious that she wouldn't shut up until he answered. "It's a safety precaution. If you did something stupid, like open the door and jump, who'd you think would get the blame?"

"I just told you," the girl replied, "God wants me to be with you. God must care about you or He wouldn't have told me to save you from the alligator last night. I wouldn't be with you this morning. Do you remember me ordering my people to help you?"

Her people? Who the hell did she think she was?

The girl had something wrong with her brain, Squires decided. Maybe she was some rare variety of retard—he had seen things on TV about kids like that. Or maybe just crazy. It had to be one of the two because of course Squires remembered the girl yelling at the crowd of Mexicans, ordering them to help him. He also remembered the little flash of hope the girl's voice had created in him as that big goddamn gator swam toward him fast with those devil-red eyes.

Why would the little brat try to help him? It made no sense for her to save his life after he had forced his way into the bathroom, then played around with her while she was naked.

Crazy. Yeah. She had to be.

As Squires drove, he looked at the girl, who was fiddling with the handcuffs, acting like they were hurting her skinny wrists. Close-up, she was a tiny little thing, her fingers long and delicate with dirt beneath the nails. The vertebrae on the back of her neck were visible beneath the Dutch-boy hair, like something he'd see on skinny dogs.

Compared to Squires's own bulk, the girl was a sack of skin and bone, which Squires found galling. The weirdo was nothing but a worthless little *chula*, yet there was also something oddly big about her, too, the way she handled herself, full of confidence. It was disconcerting.

In a bar, Squires could flash his shit-kicker monster face as fast as any other brawler, but, truth was, he'd never felt confident about anything in his life. Not compared to the way this little kid acted, anyway.

What really burned his ass, Squires realized, was that all the women in his life were the same way. Frankie and his ball-busting witch of a mother both had that same know-it-all confidence.

No . . . not exactly the same, because the girl didn't use the same nasty-mouthed meanness that his mother and Frankie both used to make him feel like a pile of shit most the time. But even though the girl was different, in her way, she was just another bossy female.

Tula said to him now, "You *do* remember that I helped save you. I can tell. Just now, you were thinking about the big alligator coming to eat you. But it didn't eat you because we all helped you. So you should trust me. I'm not going to run away. I'm here because God wants me to be with you. Perhaps He wants me to be your protector every day, not just last night. It's possible."

"My protector!" Squires laughed. "Take a good look at me, *chula*. Why the hell would I ever need your help?"

He glanced away from his driving long enough to touch his right bicep, which he was flexing. "You ever seen another man in your life built like me? Not down there in some Mexican shithole, you never did, I'd bet on that. I don't need protecting from nobody because there's not a goddamn thing in the world I'm scared of."

A moment later, he said, "Okay, in a minute or so I'm going to pull up to a garage and I want you to do what I tell you to do."

They were in East Fort Myers now, bouncing down a long driveway toward the river, horses grazing in a pasture to their right.

The giant man continued, "We're gonna switch vehicles—it's where my mom lives, but the bitch isn't home. She's off on some cruise someplace with one of her boyfriends. But if you see someone coming down that goddamn driveway, you honk this horn, understand? I'll leave the truck running until I get it in the garage."

No one came. Leaving Tula chained in the truck, Squires even took some time to go inside the house, make a protein shake and pack a bag of ice for his sore leg. He also found a pint bottle of tequila, which he kept on the seat next to him.

Soon they were on the road again, but in an older truck with huge tires that smelled of dogs and beer and the tequila the man was nipping at. His hunting buggy, Squires called the vehicle, which had an even louder engine than the truck they had left behind hidden in his mother's garage.

Tula knew that Squires was lying about taking her to the hospital to see Carlson. But what she had told the giant was true. Even though the man had forced her into the truck—leaving her few possessions behind at the trailer park—she wasn't going to attempt to escape. Not unless the Maiden ordered her to.

The handcuffs were heavy on her wrists, though. And Tula felt vulnerable, sitting on the floor with her hands bound, unable to see out the window. The man was a fast driver, weaving through morning traffic, braking hard for red lights. Or maybe it just felt as if they were going fast because she was on the floor and Squires had the windows open, the roar of the truck's mufflers loud in Tula's ears.

This was even more frightening than climbing onto the top of a freight train, riding exposed to wind and rain through the mountains of Mexico. On the train, at least, Tula had been able to watch for dangers ahead.

But not here, riding on the floor. She was unaccustomed to this kind of speed and she feared a collision. Tula imagined impact, then being trapped, unable to use her hands, especially if there was fire.

Fire terrified the girl. She had watched her father die in flames, smelled his clothes burning, heard his screams, and the vision still haunted her.

Even the Maiden had feared fire. In the little book Tula had left back in the trailer were Jehanne's own words:

Sooner would I have my head cut off seven times than to suffer the woeful death of fire . . .

Tula bowed her head and began to pray, speaking in English loudly enough to be sure that the giant landlord heard her, hoping to irritate the man into action.

"Dear Lord my God, I ask in Jesus' name all blessings on this man who is driving too fast and drinking liquor at the same time. I ask that he look into his heart and understand that he's scaring me, the way he's got my hands locked. Even though the police might stop us at any time and arrest him and take him to jail! Make him know

I am not going to run away because I am his friend. And a friend does not leave a friend . . ."

The girl went on and on like that.

The louder the girl prayed, the bigger the gulps Squires took from the tequila bottle. After a while, even liquor didn't help, and Squires couldn't stand it anymore. He glanced down at Tula, then turned on the radio, wanting to drown out her voice. It was AC/DC doing "Black Ice," but it only caused the girl to pray louder.

Shit. The little brat was maddening.

Squires found all her talk about God disturbing, an upset he felt in his belly. Truth was, he didn't want the girl to talk at all. Even if he didn't make his fantasy come true by raping her, he still had to kill her when they got to the hunting camp—what choice did he have? And the more she talked, the more girlish and human she seemed, which Squires didn't like.

It irked him that she had brought up the gator attack to make him feel guilty. She was just making it harder for him, using guilt like a weapon, which is the same thing that Frankie and his mother did on a daily basis.

The realization that this little girl was no different provided Squires with a sudden, sweet burst of anger that immediately made him feel better about driving her to the hunting camp, where he was going to get her drunk, get her clothes off and have some fun.

"Why can't you just sit there and shut up," he said to the girl as he screwed the top back on the bottle. "Do you want to see your drunken friend, Carlson, or not? I'm trying to do you a favor! So instead of whining about your wrists and asking God for a bunch of stupid favors, you should be thanking me for going out of my way to help you."

"But what will the policemen say if they stop us and see what you've done to me?" the girl replied, sounding more like an adult than a girl. "Or if we get in a wreck and the ambulance comes? They'll see that you've handcuffed me and take you to jail. How will God be able to help you in jail?"

Squires said it aloud this time—"Shit!"—as he turned hard onto a shell road, then parked behind some trees in a chunk of undeveloped pasture, where he removed the girl's handcuffs.

It was probably a smart thing to do, because it was midmorning now, he had to pee, and if the girl was going to try to run an empty pasture was better than a 7-Eleven or some other place where strangers could see.

But the girl didn't run. When Squires returned to the truck, he yanked Tula up onto the seat beside him, and said to her, "There! Happy now? You got no more excuses for whining."

It didn't shut her up, though.

"You should wear your seat belt," the girl reminded him when they were on the road again. "God cares about you. You keep forgetting. And if you got hurt in a crash, what would happen to me? I have no money and no extra clothes."

"Do you ever think about anyone else but yourself?" Squires snapped.

A few seconds later, he said, "God cares?" and managed to laugh, although it wasn't easy. The suggestion that anyone cared about him was idiotic. His head ached from too much tequila, last night and already this morning. And Frankie was pissed at him—yet again. Someone must have called her from the RV park last night when the cops arrived because the woman had left five messages on his cell between ten and two a.m. The last message was a rant so profane that Squires had deleted it before getting to the end.

"I ask you to do one simple thing and you completely fucked it up—as usual," Frankie's message had begun, and then it got nasty from there.

Well . . . that was enough of Frankie's bullying ways, as far as Squires was concerned. He had had it up to *here* with the woman's bullshit. That's why before leaving Red Citrus he had cleaned out all the important stuff from their double-wide just on the chance he could summon the nerve to leave and never see that bitch again.

The important stuff included bags of veterinarian-grade pills and powder that were in the locked toolbox in the bed of his hunting truck. And also about sixty thousand cash from steroid sales, which was in a canvas bag bundled with rubber bands along with the Ruger revolver. The whole business was under the driver's seat, safely inside a hidden compartment that he had made himself using hinges and a cutting torch.

Frankie was mad now? *Christ.* The woman would go absolutely apeshit when she realized the money was missing.

Squires was also worried about Laziro Victorino, the badass Mexican with the box cutter and teardrop tattoo under his eye. If cops found a piece of a woman's body inside an alligator from Red Citrus, the V-man would know instantly it was one of his prostitutes and he was going to be pissed. Someone would have to pay, because that's the way it worked with the Mexican gangs.

You kill one of them, they killed two of you. That's why Victorino made snuff films. To remind people.

First person the V-man would suspect was him and Frankie because everyone knew they had a thing for videoing Mexican girls, sometimes as many as three at a time. They were videos that Frankie posted on her porn website but also sold to Victorino's gangbangers, which was another way she made money when she wasn't dealing gear. Not that Squires and Frankie ever appeared on camera. No, the videos were for profit but also a way for Frankie to have fun behind the scenes.

Mostly, though, Squires was worried about the dead alligator. What would cops find in her belly when they cut the thing open? That would probably happen this morning, from what he had over-heard the Wildlife cops saying. That reminded Squires to switch the radio from AC/DC to a news station.

In Florida, a dead alligator that had eaten a girl would be big news.

Even with the radio loud, it was hard to think his problems through. It was because the weird little Bible freak never shut up. She asked questions about the truck's air-conditioning. And the CD player, then about his iPhone, which was plugged into its cradle next to the gearshift. It was like the stupid kid had never been out in the world before.

The girl also kept giving him updates from God.

This God talk was getting old.

"Think back to when you were a child," she was telling Squires now as she sat upright beside him, looking at something near the gearshift—his iPhone, maybe. "Do you remember how safe you felt? Do you remember the love and goodness you felt? That was God's presence inside you. And He is still there, so why do you fight him so?"

They were on Corkscrew Road, driving east through bluffs of cypress trees, past orange groves and grazing cattle, toward Immo-kalee, the gate to his hunting camp only half an hour beyond that little tomato-packing town.

Because of what the girl was saying, Squires's mind slipped back to when he was young—he couldn't help himself even though he tried—and he was surprised to realize that the noisy little brat was right.

Truth was, he really had felt *different* as a child. He had felt safe and full of kindness, unless his witch of a mother was screaming at him, calling him a "worthless little bastard" or saying, "You're even stupider than your faggot father!"

It was strange how things had changed since he was a kid. Maybe because of the tequila, or maybe because of the guilt the girl had caused him to feel, the realization struck Squires as important. He took a swallow from the bottle and let his mind work on it until he thought, *I'll be goddamned. What the brat says is true.*

Somehow, the world and his life had become mean and dangerous and dirty.

How? When had it happened?

That was a complicated question that took some time. The man wrestled with the issue as he drove. Had it started when he'd first discovered tequila and weed? Up until then, he'd been kind of a quiet, shy kid.

No . . . no, that wasn't the reason he felt as shitty as he did right now. His life had really taken a turn for the worse when he met Frankie. That was almost four years ago, him being twenty-two at the time, Frankie thirty-eight but still with a body on her. And the woman was a regular hellion when it came to games in bed.

Sex—Frankie was addicted to it, and not plain old regular sex, either. The woman liked it rough, sometimes violent enough that Squires's nose and lips would be bleeding when they were done— once even his dick, which was having problems enough of its own because of the way steroids affected it.

The woman liked hurting her partners, especially if they were female.

Yes, it was when he'd met Frankie that things had really begun to change. That's when his life had switched from living a hard-assed guy's life, hanging out with other bodybuilders, to living a life that was small and mean . . . yes, and dirty, too.

It was strange thinking about stuff like that now while driving to his hunting camp, where, until that instant, Harris Squires had fully intended to punish this noisy little freak by raping her.

But *damn* it. Now all this talk about God was deflating his enthusiasm, not to mention his dick. Worse, it was adding to his gloom. It threatened to bring back the withering guilt that kept welling up about accidentally murdering that Mexican woman.

Trouble was, unlike with the Mexican woman, Squires had no choice about the girl. She was an eyewitness. She had to go.

Because it made him mad thinking about what he had to do, he said to the little brat, "Do you have any idea how crazy you sound? You're in the United States now, *chula*. In Florida, they'll throw you in the loony bin for saying crazy crap like that."

Reaching for his iPhone for some reason, the girl replied, "Where are we going? I know you're not taking me to the hospital. You can trust me, so why not tell me? It's always better to tell the truth."

"Why, because God is watching us?" Squires laughed, pushing the girl's hand away. The time on his iPhone, he noted, was 10:32 a.m. They still had to get through Immokalee, another hour of driving ahead of them.

"If God really is watching," Squires told her, sounding both angry and serious, "the dude had better perform one of his miracles pretty damn quick. Or it's out of my hands, *chula*. Hear what I'm telling you?"

Because of the caring, wounded expression that appeared on the girl's face, Squires added, "No one can blame me. What happens next, I can't control. And that is the *truth*."

NINE

THE NEXT MORNING, I WAS UP BEFORE SUNRISE, 6:30 A.M., because I was supposed to meet the necropsy team at eight a.m. sharp. I wanted to get a quick workout in first, though.

Lately, I had been nursing a sore rotator cuff, but was still doing PT twice a day, taking only an occasional Monday off. I knew I'd feel like crap if I didn't get a sweat going and have a swim. When a man gets into his forties, he has two choices—invite the pain required to maintain his body or surrender himself to the indignity and pain of slow physical decomposition that, in my mind, would be worse than death.

I wanted to make this one fast but tough.

I punished myself with half an hour on a brutal little exercise machine called a VersaClimber. HIT—high-intensity training. Thirty seconds climbing the machine at sprinter's speed—about a hundred feet per minute—then thirty seconds at a slower pace. Over and over, nonstop, after a five-minute warm-up.

I couldn't use the pull-up bar, so did a hundred sit-ups, a hundred push-ups, then jogged Tarpon Bay Road to the beach. The swim out to the NO WAKE buoys and back was painful, but it didn't hurt as much as the mile-and-a-half run home.

When I lumbered, huffing and puffing, down the shell road, Mack, who owns Dinkin's Bay Marina, was having a meeting with Jeth, Nels and the other fishing guides. So I stuck around long enough to tell them about the dolphins we had seen in the mangroves—I knew they wouldn't believe Tomlinson—then headed for the shower. Tomlinson himself was already on his way back to Red Citrus.

An hour later, I was standing over the remains of the alligator I had killed. The thing was stretched out, belly-up, on a tarp beside dissecting trays, a lab scale, and an assembly of knives, jars and a single stainless-bladed saw.

It was not something I felt good about, looking down at the dead gator. This inanimate mass only hours before had been a tribute to the genius of natural selection and the animal's own survival skills. The rounds I'd fired had put an end to a life that had probably spanned sixty years.

Emily Marston's team consisted of herself, a sullen man who didn't offer his name and a graduate student from Florida Gulf Coast University who was assigned to document the necropsy on video.

The sullen man, I soon decided, had been romantically involved with the woman biologist, but the relationship had ended recently and unpleasantly.

It wasn't a guess and it wasn't intuition.

The situation was easily read in the tension between the two, the curt questions, the man's surly tone and the woman's defensive body language.

Judging from his age, the man might have been one of Marston's professors a few years back. In the field sciences, it's not unusual for female students to bond with male teachers—ironic that the romantic habits of scientists often mimic the behavior of the animals they study, but it is true.

Emily Marston certainly wasn't icy to me. She was warm and deferential. The way her eyes sought to communicate with mine caused me to wonder if her invitation to the necropsy had been more than professional courtesy. We probably had a few mutual, peripheral friends, but we'd never met. I wondered why.

"Dr. Ford, I've read so many of your papers—some of them a couple of times," Marston had said, greeting me as I'd stepped from my truck. "I guess you'd call me . . . well, a sort of fan. Except now you'll just think I'm an even bigger nerd than I am."

She was a large woman, late twenties, with an angular Midwestern face that suggested the automotive crossroads of Michigan—part German with a touch of Pole and Irish, I guessed. She struck me as the librarian type: a woman who camouflaged her body beneath baggy, masculine clothing that only served to emphasize a busty, long-legged femininity.

Right away, I was interested in the woman physically. I couldn't help myself. I prefer the closet beauties, the private, introspective types who share their physical gifts only with a few. But I also reminded myself that, by Dinkin's Bay standards, I had been abstinent for a long, long time. And seducing women who are on the rebound from a relationship is a repugnant behavior employed only by the lowest form of predatory male.

Even so, I noticed that incidental physical contact between us was more than occasional. It seemed accidental, though it seldom is. Shoulder bumps shoulder, elbow brushes breast. It is the oldest form of human cipher, the secret language of females and males, a language that no one acknowledges but every man and woman on earth employs and understands.

Like now as I stood next to Marston, who had changed into rubber boots, gloves, safety goggles, coveralls and a heavy lab apron that she pretended to be having trouble tying.

"Do you mind," she asked, touching fingertips to my arm before turning her back to me.

"Sure, happy to help," I said, and tied the thing, aware of the nasty look her former lover was giving us.

When I was done, I managed to make the situation worse by letting my hand linger on the woman's shoulder as I told the little group, "This my first necropsy. For an alligator, anyway. You know Frank Mazzotti, the saltwater croc expert? I almost had the chance to watch him work, but I had to leave the country for some reason. I really appreciate the invitation."

"Well," the woman replied, sounding a tad breathless, "it's always nice to be the first at something in a person's life. Paul"—she looked at the sullen man—"did you read his paper on filtering species in brackish water environments? It was in the *Journal of Aquatic Sciences*, wasn't it, Dr. Ford? Really an excellent piece. Your writing style reminds me of the late Archie Carr, the turtle master. Formal, very orderly, but readable. No bullshit academic flourishes when clear, concise sentences will do the job."

I told the woman I wasn't in Carr's league and meant it. Then added, "Let's make a deal. Call me Ford. Or just plain Doc—which is a nickname. It has nothing to do with what I do. Having a degree, I mean."

I tried not to sound like a self-satisfied jerk, but I bungled that, too.

Now I felt like an even bigger ass as I let the woman pat my shoulder while she continued speaking to Paul. "In the article, he referenced a necropsy on a manatee that had died during a severe red tide. Wasn't that at Dinkin's Bay where you live, Doc? He was the first to make the association between dinoflagellates and toxicity in sea-dwelling mammals."

"How nice for Dr. Ford," Paul said, ignoring me—not that I blamed the guy. I really didn't, although he was pushing the limits when he added, "And let's not forget that we also have Dr. Ford to thank for providing us with a dead alligator to work on this morning. Very, very thoughtful of you to kill such a beautiful animal. What did the police report say?"

The man looked at a clipboard, before reading, "'The alligator was subdued by four shots at point-blank range from a nine-millimeter Kahr handgun.'

"Subdued," the man continued, sarcasm creeping into his voice. "I guess that's police jargon for slaughtered."

He looked up from the clipboard and spoke to the graduate student. "I've never understood why some men feel inadequate unless they're carrying a gun. I'm not talking about you, of course, Dr. Ford," he added, his sarcasm undisguised. "It's the rednecks and hicks I'm referring to. The right-wing bumper-sticker types. I'm unfamiliar with handguns. Is a Kahr one of those famous pistols that heroes use in the movies? Maybe you're carrying it now concealed somewhere in your pants. I bet Emily would love to see it."

I had been watching the woman's face color, but the guy had finally crossed the line. She snapped, "Paul! Enough! Stop what you're doing right now! Dr. Ford's my guest, and I won't allow you to—"

The man cut her off, saying, "Your days of telling me what I can and can't do are over, Milly dear. The courts took care of that, remember? It was your decision, not mine. And, frankly, I couldn't be happier. Didn't we come here to work? I have other things to do."

Which, from Marston, earned the man a chilly "Don't we all

have better things to do, Paul? You're the one who insisted on coming along."

"I volunteered to help. And, of course"—for the first time the man looked directly at me—"I wanted to see why you were so determined to meet the famous Dr. Marion Ford. I thought maybe I'd understand once I saw him. But, sorry, I just don't get what the fuss is all about."

I had taken a step back to remove myself from the conversation. Long ago, I learned not to participate in quarrels between lovers—particularly if I happened to be one of the lovers. So I stood there, feeling embarrassed for both people, as they argued, Drs. Paul and Emily, two intelligent people who had once been in love.

It went on for a while. The barbs they exchanged exhibited a practiced familiarity that proved these two people had become expert at hurting each other. But it ended abruptly when the woman finally called a truce, saying, "Paul . . . Paul, I'm sorry, Paul! I was wrong to let you come. It was mean of me. It was thoughtless, and I'm sorry. I truly am."

The man, Paul Marston, Ph.D., I would learn later, responded by throwing his apron and clipboard on the ground as he said, "Yes, your behavior has been very mean and thoughtless. For once we agree. And how refreshing to have you finally admit it, for a change."

Then the man turned, strode to his Subaru and drove away.

"Damn it," Emily said when he was gone. "I'm so sorry you two had to witness that. Paul isn't like that. Not really. And neither am I. But we signed our divorce papers less than two weeks ago, so it's an emotional time. I'd hoped we could continue our professional relationship, but clearly . . ."

The woman allowed silence to trail off.

The grad student, who had pretended to be busy organizing her camera gear, spoke for the first time, saying, "I think they both be-haved like jerks, Dr. Marston. What is it about men?"

It took me a moment to realize that the girl had included me. What the hell had I done besides allow myself to be used as a foil? Even so, I decided it was time to try to reverse the dark momentum on this pretty spring morning.

"There's a lesson for ladies everywhere," I said to them both. "The male of the species is equipped with a prick for reasons that exceed the demands of basic human reproduction." I looked at Mar-ston. "If you come up with an explanation, I'd like to be among the first to hear it."

I was hoping to see a pair of smiles. It took the grad student a moment—maybe we both shared the same physical awareness of Emily Marston.

Finally, though, the girl gave in.

Fifteen minutes later, I was saying to Emily, "I'm particularly inter-ested in seeing what's in the animal's stomach."

She was wearing a digital headset. She nodded and said, "An animal this age, you never know what you're going to find." She nodded again to the grad student as a cue, touched the POWER button on the mini-recorder, selected a knife and then began dictating as she started the necropsy.

"The specimen is an adult male alligator. Length and weight have already been noted. Scutes at"—she was looking at the ridges on the animal's back—"scutes seven and ten show distinctive scarring, but I judge it to earlier injuries. There is no evidence the animal has ever been tagged or documented. We'll begin by making a standard Y-cut from the animal's sternum to its cloaca."

The woman looked at me, adding as an aside, "There's no scalpel big enough for something like this. So I use a Gerber Gator Serrator. Really. That's the name of the knife. I found it at some outdoors store and couldn't resist."

The tool in her hand looked like an oversized pocketknife, and it was sharp. I watched her saw through the dense scale work of the gator's belly as the grad student moved to a better angle with her video camera.

Marston was good. She worked with speed and a minimum of wasted effort. I watched her remove and weigh, in precise order, the animal's heart, its liver and other vital organs, before she said, "Next we open the stomach. As I told Dr. Ford, you never know what you're going to find, particularly with an animal this age."

She looked at the grad student with concern before adding, "How are you doing? I know, the smell can be tough to deal with. Are you okay?"

The student had gone a little pale. "Maybe if I get a bottle of water," she said, "that might help. Mind if we take a short break?"

With Marston's permission, the girl hurried off to the shade, where there was an Igloo filled with ice and drinks.

The smell of the alligator didn't bother me. I found it heavy and distinctive. There was a musky sweetness that reminded me of the way a fresh tarpon smells—a delicate, vital odor that was mixed with an acidity that I presumed to be cavity fluids and blood.

I said, "Do you mind if I use that extra pair of gloves and help you with the stomach when you get it open?"

"Sure," the woman replied. "You sound more than casually interested. Are you looking for something in particular? Last night . . . the person the gator attacked, he didn't lose any—"

"No," I said. "The man still has all his parts. Just puncture wounds."

She was nodding. "That's what I thought or the police would have insisted on being here. Or EMTs would've opened the belly last night."

I said, "What I'd expect to find is the stomach empty. Or almost empty. We're only, what, a month or so away from their dormant season?"

"The last real cold front was in January," Marston corrected me. "This animal has certainly eaten since then."

"Even so," I said, snapping on a surgical glove, "he had to be pretty hungry to attack a full-grown man. Not only that, he came back and tried to attack a second man, even though I had already wounded the thing. What I'm interested in finding is those rocks I've read about. The ones you find in a gator's belly. Gastroliths? I've never seen one."

"How's the man doing?" the woman asked, meaning Carlson. "I haven't heard anything since last night. In fact, I'd love for you to tell me the whole story sometime—if you ever have time. I've been studying alligators for seven years and I can't imagine anyone jumping into the water at night and wrestling around with something this size. I certainly wouldn't have tried it. That takes a very unusual man, in my opinion."

I caught the friendly implications. I also sensed that the woman was providing me with an opening to ask her out. It was in the airy way she said it—something I would act upon but later. In reply, I told her I hadn't gotten an update on Carlson and turned the conversation back to gastroliths.

"We still don't know for certain that alligators swallow rocks for ballast," the woman told me, sounding more relaxed and in charge now. "But I can't think of any other reason they'd bother. In an animal this size, I would expect to find quite a few. They don't look like much until you clean off the patina. But then some of them can be quite interesting."

She was right. With the grad student filming, Emily slit the animal's stomach lining, then held it open as I fished my hands in. At first, I thought there was nothing to find. But then, closer to the intestines, I found several hard, globular objects. I removed one that was about the size of a baseball and handed it to Emily. She appeared pleased.

"This is one of the larger gastroliths I've seen," she told me as she used the knife to scrape part of it clean.

I used a paper towel on my glasses, then knelt beside her to see. I'm not a geologist, but there was no mistaking the crystalline facets of the rock, soon glittering in the morning sunlight. It was a chunk of gypsum.

Marston caught the significance immediately.

"This is very strange finding a stone like this," she said softly, studying the thing.

"That's what I was thinking."

The grad student had zoomed in on the rock. "I don't understand what you're talking about," the girl said. "It's pretty—sort of. But what's so special about a rock?"

Emily asked me, "You found this animal in a pond on San Carlos Island, right? It's really is quite surprising."

I told her it was a brackish lake, only a few miles from Fort Myers Beach, before telling the grad student, "In Florida, the only gypsum I know of comes from the highland regions in the north and central parts of the state. Alligators travel, I understand that. But is it possible this thing could have crossed a hundred miles of swamps, then crawled through cities, across highways, this far on its own?"

The woman was thinking about it, lips pursed. She was wearing safety goggles, and I liked the nerdy dissimilarities of her elegant jaw, the sweep of autumn-shaded hair. Only a male biologist is capable of undressing a woman with his eyes and then completing the fantasy by projecting how she would look naked, sprawled on white sheets, all the while kneeling on a tarp beneath buzzing flies, his hands slick with gastric fluids.

That's exactly what I was doing. But then my conscience intervened by reminding me that this woman had been divorced for only a couple of weeks. No matter how confident Emily Marston appeared, she was vulnerable, probably an easy target for just about any decent-looking, unprincipled jerk who came along. Although I am, admittedly, an occasional jerk, I do embrace the conceit that I am a jerk with at least a few principles.

I listened to the woman say, "If the gastrolith was a lot smaller, and when you consider how old this animal must be, I wouldn't have a problem with the distance. Over a period of thirty or forty years, yes, it could have traveled a hundred miles on its own. But my guess is, only a large alligator would ingest a rock this size, which suggests to me that someone may have transported the animal—"

The grad student, still filming, interrupted, saying, "Maybe a dump truck hauled a load of gravel to the beach. You know, from around Lake Okeechobee, as fill or something. That would explain a chunk of gypsum being this close to the Gulf of Mexico."

I smiled at the girl, pleased by her quick reasoning, and I told her exactly that as I fished my hands into the gator's stomach again.

I removed several more gastroliths. Then I found a chunk of what appeared to be a turtle skull. Then several more bones, bleached white from acid, that were not so easily identified.

Not at first, anyway. It wasn't until I had placed the bones on the tarp in an orderly fashion that I began to suspect what we had just found. Collectively, they resembled the delicate flange of a primate's hand—not necessarily a human hand, because feral monkeys are common in Florida

I became more certain they were primate bones when I added a radius bone and pieces of what might have been metacarpal bones.

"My God," Marston said, voice soft, "I think we need to call the police. This isn't fresh, obviously. It has to have been in the gator's stomach for at least a few months, but even so . . ."

I told the woman, "Wait. There's something else."

I had been holding my breath while I felt around in the animal's stomach and started breathing again as I leaned into the stomach, then placed yet another bone on the tarp.

This one was unmistakable. The grad student stumbled for a moment, almost dropped the camera, but then she leaned to zoom in on what we all could identify.

It was a wedding ring. Cheap and brassy, but set with a minuscule stone that may or may not have been a diamond The ring had been crushed, probably by the gator's teeth, so that it was crimped into the bone of what had once been a human finger.

"A woman's hand," the female biologist said, and had to work hard to keep emotion out of her voice.

"A woman's ring, anyway," I replied, holding the bone close to my eyes, seeing what might have been a bit of inscription. "The medical examiner will know."

At sunset, I was on my back porch, lathering beneath the outdoor shower, when I felt the vibration of unfamiliar footsteps. Tomlinson was in the house, probably guzzling the last of my beer. Plus, the snowshoe slap of his big bare feet is distinctive. It wasn't him.

The person approaching was decidedly female. Wearing hard-soled shoes, I guessed, possibly high heels.

With a bar of soap, I attempted to cover what I could cover as I turned to see Emily Marston, although I didn't recognize her at first. True, I wasn't wearing my glasses. True, I only got a glimpse before the lady sputtered an apology, then ducked behind the corner of my house. Still, I did not associate the long glossy hair and a white tropical suit with the boot-wearing biologist I had worked with that morning.

When I heard the woman call, "Sorry! I'm really . . . sorry," I recognized the voice, though.

My reaction was immediate and adolescent—which is to say, I did what most men would do under the circumstances. I made a quick visual survey of my personal equipment, hoping I had been enhanced, not diminished, by the sun-warmed water in the rain cistern overhead.

First impressions are important. Particularly in the primate world, where proportions are emblematic.

Not bad, I decided. Not bad at all. Yet I attempted to deepen my voice as I called to the lady, "The house is open, go on in. Make yourself at home. There's a bottle of red wine, maybe some beer—if there's any left."

She would discover, soon enough, that I had company.

I reached for a towel, then my clothes, taking my time at first until I remembered that every minute I lingered was another minute that Emily Marston would be alone inside with Tomlinson.

It was a risky combination. A divorcée on the rebound and my randy pal.

Even sober, my boat-bum friend has the sexual discipline of a lovebug. By now, seven p.m., he was already a six-pack and a couple of joints into this balmy March evening. Stoned, there are no depths to which the man will not sink in hope of luring fresh prey to his sailboat and, at the very least, getting the lady's bra off.

As Tomlinson is fond of saying, "There are few experiences in life more satisfying than unveiling a pair of fresh breasts."

Speaking of women as if they were festively wrapped presents— a metaphor that, for Tomlinson, made every new day a potential Christmas morning.

As I came into the house, though, Emily was sitting primly at the galley table, looking elegant in a copper blouse and white linen jacket, while Tomlinson talked about the phenomenon we had witnessed the night before—the two dolphins we had seen charging out of the mangroves. That was probably a good thing because he had been obsessing about the Guatemalan girl, who had yet to reappear. He had called me earlier that day to report no luck and that he was coming back. I wasn't sure what else to do, but we had decided to keep the problem running in the backs of our heads to see if something came up.

"Sorry to show up uninvited, Doc," Emily said as I knelt at the refrigerator, looking for a beer. "I should have yelled. Or rang the bell . . . or something. But I did knock—"

"I had my earbuds in," Tomlinson explained, motioning to some kind of miniature device that played music. "I was listening to a new download. A four-hertz theta frequency, trying to get my head straight."

Emily looked at him, interested, as she continued speaking to me, saying, "So I walked around to the back of the house because I could hear someone humming—"

Tomlinson interrupted, "Doc was humming?" as if he didn't believe her.

I said, "Isn't that what people do when they shower? Sing, hum. I was showering."

Emily said, "Yes, you were," sounding as if she approved, her eyes locking onto my eyes. "I hope you aren't pissed—and you certainly shouldn't be embarrassed. I was restless tonight—we had ourselves quite a day, didn't we?"

Yes, we had. Emily and I had spent all morning together, waiting for the county forensic team to arrive, and then most of the afternoon answering questions, first from the authorities and then from a couple of reporters.

I avoid media types. It's an old habit. Putting my name or face out for public scrutiny is unwise when you've lived the life I have lived. When a guy has determined enemies, he protects his privacy with determination.

The woman, though, didn't have a problem with it. She had handled the reporters politely and with just the right amount of professional reserve. I was impressed.

"That's why I had to get out and go roaming tonight," she was explaining now. "I decided to risk surprising you to see the amazing Dinkin's Bay"—she smiled—"where bottlenose dolphins walk by moonlight."

The woman glanced at Tomlinson, and I could tell that she hadn't expected me to have company—for good reason. I had dropped more than a few hints during our hours together, telling the lady that I lived alone, wasn't dating anyone special, and that I usually worked late in the lab—if she ever happened to be in the area.

Not that I had anything sexual in mind.

Right.

Now here she was, and her uneasiness was palpable.

Tomlinson has an uncanny ability to read people. He helped the woman relax by making her laugh, saying, "Know what the weird thing is? When I tell people about the dolphins, they don't believe me. But the moment Doc says it, it's like gospel. I just don't get it."

He leaned toward Emily. "From what I've heard, you're an educated woman. Any insights into how some people can be so damn misguided?"

Emily laughed, then asked if we'd take her outside to see the area where the dolphins had come ashore. She was wearing hard-soled shoes, not heels, but I told her it was a bad idea.

"It's all muck and mangroves," I explained. "Your clothes would be a mess. Plus, the mosquitoes. It's no place for a lady at night."

That earned me a smile and another potent look. "Thanks for noticing. After the way I was dressed this morning, I went out of my way to look like a woman tonight."

For an instant, I wondered if the woman wasn't being a little too obvious, then decided it was okay. I liked her, she liked me and was letting me know it. Nothing wrong with that. "You succeeded," I told her.

"Then I've already had a good night," she replied. She held my gaze for a moment, then turned to Tomlinson. "Doc told me that you found pieces of crabs' legs and carapace when you checked the area. But, to him, that wasn't enough proof the dolphins were feeding. What do you think?"

Tomlinson had been doing some staring of his own, and I was relieved to hear him say, "I always defer to Doc in matters that require a brain but not much heart. But what I really think is, I need to get going. It's sushi night at the Stone Crab. And Rachel told me they just got in some fresh conch from Key West."

"But wait," Emily said as she watched him get to his feet. "You mentioned something I wanted to ask about. Were you practicing deep theta-wave meditation? I wanted to hear more."

Now she definitely had Tomlinson's attention. "It sounds like you know something about the subject."

"At home, I've got a few four-hertz theta tracks. But I prefer the higher frequencies." She included me in the conversation with a look. "The higher frequencies are associated with brighter colors, feelings of well-being. After what we found in that gator's stomach, I went straight home, showered and put the headsets on."

Tomlinson was smiling, and I could sense that his determination to exit courteously had been replaced by a growing interest in Emily.

"Biofeedback and brain harmony," he said. "We are chemical-electric beings, grounded only by spirituality. Kindness and passion in most of us. Lust in a few cases, too. Quite a few, from what I've seen in this part of the world."

I said, *"Lust?"* aware that Tomlinson was an expert at planting subliminal suggestions into the heads of unsuspecting females.

Emily was laughing, a smart lady who apparently had pretty good antennae of her own because she took control of the conversation, saying, "I'll discuss the subjects of passion and lust with Doc—*if* he's interested. But not in mixed company, thanks. The thing I wanted to ask about is, if you were listening to a theta track, I'm guessing you're upset about something. Doc told me a little bit about what happened last night. The gator attack and the girl disappearing. Not everything, of course. He's a hard one to get to open up. He mentioned he had a best friend. That's you, I take it."

Tomlinson grinned, and said, "It requires someone who's forgiving. And not easily bored."

"Then it is you. How do you get him to talk?"

Tomlinson came close to winking at me as he replied, "I fed him psychedelic mushrooms once—by accident, of course. And once I got him stoned on some very fine weed—same thing, by accident. At best, even when high I would describe him as vaguely chatty. But in a very careful way."

Emily was having fun with this, but I felt like they were teaming up when she asked, "You don't smoke, Doc? Or is he kidding?"

I had opened a Diet Coke because all my beer was gone. Compliments of Tomlinson, of course. I shook my head slowly, *no*, took a sip and listened to Emily talk.

"I guess I'm surprised—that's not a judgment, by the way. Personally, I can't believe it hasn't been legalized. It makes me feel all loose and relaxed. I laugh a lot. And act stupid. I think it's good for people like us to act stupid sometimes. Don't you . . . Doc?"

Now the expression on Tomlinson's face was telling the world *I'm in love*, which is why I spoke up, saying, "You mentioned sushi night at the Stone Crab? They close at nine, don't they? You've only got two hours."

The restaurant was only five minutes away on a bike. He knew exactly what I was telling him.

Tomlinson countered, "We could all go. I could tell Emily about Tula. Maybe later we can even drive across the bridge to Red Citrus and have another look around. I like this woman, Doc. What's your last name?"

"Marston," Emily said, watching my friend's face. "Emily Marston. Or Milly. Or Em. Or whatever you want."

Tomlinson let that settle, retreating into his brain to think about it. "Marston, that's not very tribal-specific. You have olive eyes . . . no, gray-green. Polish, maybe, which tells me Chicago, or maybe Detroit. A bit of Irish, too, plus some German? Doc," he said to me, "this person is intuitive. She has a gift. I think she can help us find the girl—after I fill her in."

Once again, the woman took charge, making me her ally by saying, "Nice try, but Marston isn't my maiden name. Another night, maybe. Until then, Doc can fill me in just fine. We have a lot to talk about."

"*Well* . . . all righty, then," Tomlinson said, aware that he'd just been dismissed. His inflection, though, suggested a truce but not capitulation.

"Doc could use some downtime," Tomlinson offered, getting to his feet. "The dude has been pretty restless himself lately. He doesn't have to say anything. Everyone at the marina can tell. He spends time looking at maps and listening to foreign news on his shortwave. He works out harder, he drinks fewer beers. The one sure sign?" Tomlinson gave me a knowing look. "His lab begins to smell of a very specific kind of oil that folks like me don't associate with fish and boats."

"Oil?" Emily said, confused, then sniffing. A moment later, I was taken aback by the look of recognition on her face. *"Oil,"* she said. "Yeah, I can smell it. Very faint, but it's there."

I stood and opened the screen door. "If you think of it, you might stop by the 7-Eleven and buy some beer. See you in the morning— but not too early. *Okay?"*

Tomlinson was laughing as he headed out the door but turned to say to the woman, "Or maybe I'll see you two at the Rum Bar later. We just got in a shipment of twelve-year-old Fleur de Caña from Nicaragua. Really superb stuff."

I was heartened by Emily's green-eyed gaze and by her response: "It's entirely Doc's call. Whatever he's up for, I'm with him."

Whatever concerns I had about Emily Marston's vulnerability were set free when she slipped her arm through mine as we walked toward the marina and she told me, "I didn't divorce Paul because I was unhappy with him. I did it because I was unhappy with myself. Oh, I pretended it was his fault. Came up with all sorts of reasons why we had to end the relationship and move on. He'll always be the professor. To him, I'll always be the student. And another big problem was . . ."

I waited through several seconds of silence before I told her, "Talk about it or don't, that's up to you. I was impressed by the way you stood up for him, after your argument this morning. That was nice. Unusual for an ex-wife or -husband to do."

It was as if she didn't hear me because she picked up the thread, saying, "For some reason, I want to be honest with you about what happened, Paul and me. One of the problems was, he doesn't enjoy physical contact—not really. Not with me, anyway. But not with anyone, I think. I'm amazed at how many people dislike being touched. Aren't you?"

No, but I didn't say it. Instead, I walked and listened, giving the woman time.

It took a while. Finally, she asked, "Know what I was doing, Doc? I was making excuses. I was using a device that doesn't make me look very damn nice at all. I blamed Paul to justify what I did. The truth is, I ended the marriage because I wasn't happy and I wanted out. Blaming him was a way of getting what I wanted."

I replied, "I think it's common for the species Sapiens to do whatever it takes to justify pleasure by manipulating our own guilt. Don't be so hard on yourself."

"But that doesn't make it right," Emily countered. "Seriously, I'm not trying to punish myself. For me—and it drives me nuts sometimes—for me, the way my mind works, it's important to get the facts straight. My dad used to say something that was cute at the time, but now it makes sense. He'd say, 'You lie to your friends and I'll lie to mine, but let's not lie to each other.' I try not to lie to myself, Doc. I think that's maybe what he meant."

I smiled and said, "The age difference between you and Paul wasn't a factor?"

"Fifteen years is just about perfect," she replied. "It puts the male and the female at about the same level of maturity."

"You're not joking."

The woman said, "Maybe twenty years. It depends on the guy," but didn't hit it too hard, which told me the subject was unimportant to her.

We were walking through the shell parking lot, toward the marina docks, after stopping to admire the lady's new car. It was a mid-sized Jaguar, black and tan, that didn't mesh with her occupation or her probable income. Now I could see boats moored in rows, windows glowing, and an American flag at the end of the dock, flapping in a star-bright breeze.

I said, "Are you always this frank?" letting her know that I appreciated it.

"Doc," she replied, "I'll be twenty-eight in October, and I plan on living to be a spry and very active ninety. I don't want to live a screwed-up, unhappy life. Or a selfish life. We receive peace in exchange for helping others. I really believe that." Then she grimaced and said, "Jesus, I didn't mean that to sound so naïve and girlish. Did it?"

"You have it all planned out," I said.

"It's not being selfish," she replied, "to take responsibility for our own lives. And that's the only plan I have. This morning, when you laid that poor woman's bones on the tarp and I saw that ring, I felt so goddamn sad I wanted to cry. Did it show?"

I lied. "No."

Emily said, "It was my wedding ring I was looking at. That's the way it felt. *My* ring finger, and I had been swallowed by something as predatory as any alligator that's ever lived."

"Predatory?" I said.

"By fear," she said. "I think fear rules unless we fight it. But not many people do, you think? We just go with the flow, doing what's expected. Letting our lives drain right down into the gator's belly."

"Some, maybe" I said. "I'm in no position to judge."

"Well, that's not for me. I'm going to try my damnedest to live a life that matters. Cut the safety net and throw it away. Which sounds idyllic, but it's actually scary shit when I think it through. That's what I plan to do, Doc. In fact, I'm already doing it. Starting two weeks ago." She leaned her breast into my arm. "If I have regrets later, it's not because I was afraid to, by God, try something new."

I patted the lady's hand and steered her past the bait tank, toward the bay, where dock lights were tethered to black water, golden shards roiled by wind. The fishing guides were in, their flats skiffs rocking in a buoyant line, and a whisper of big band music seeped from one of the sleeping yachts, out of sync with the tapping flagpole halyard.

It was a little after seven p.m. on a Wednesday. A quiet time at Dinkin's Bay.

I was feeling good. The decision that Emily would come to my bed had just been made without even discussing it—an exchange made via silent subtext. The unspoken dialogue that takes place minute to minute between fertile males and females, generation after generation.

This female had not only said yes. She had fronted the wordless invitation. She had also put me at ease by allowing me to fish for answers to unspoken questions.

Was she emotionally stable? *Yes*.

Did the age difference matter? *No*.

I was enjoying the moment, aware that it was among the rarest of transitional times. I would soon undress this woman. "Unveil her," in Tomlinson terms, for the first time. And there would never be another first time for Emily and myself.

There was no rush, no need for more complicated sexual maneuvering. I could luxuriate in what was to be. I'm no romantic, but I do love women. Hidden beneath a cotton blouse, bound by elastic, what would Emily's breasts look like unveiled in the back-bay light of my bedroom? Her hips, her thighs . . . and what subtleties of layered coloring in the lady's shadowed triangle?

"Did you hear what I said, Doc?" Emily asked, nudging me. "You just disappeared on me. Where'd you go?"

I noted the lady's intuitive smile, which told me she knew full well where my mind had gone—probably because her mind had been there, too.

Yes, I was right, because she turned to a subject that had all the freeing implications of seeing the bones of a dead woman's hand. The bawdiest of sexual behavior can be excused—even celebrated— by reflecting on unexpected tragedy, the inevitability of death.

As I had told Emily: *People do whatever it takes to justify pleasure by manipulating our own guilt.*

"I was thinking about the Guatemalan girl," she said. "I asked if you'd read the story in the *Naples Daily News* last week. It was about human trafficking. I'm interested because I joined the Florida Coalition Against Human Trafficking. I've been to only two meetings, but I'd like to get a lot more involved."

I said, "A biologist doing social work?"

"I can't think of a better cause."

I said, "When I put that together with you new car, it suggests to me you're wealthy. Isn't that an oxymoron? Wealthy biologist?"

"Normally about now," she smiled, "I would get very self-righteous and ask what money has to do with a social conscience.

But you guessed right, our family has money. My father did well for himself. Maybe I should have mentioned it. He's an ornithologist."

I replied, "A wealthy bird-watcher. Another oxymoron."

"Oh, that is the least of the mysteries about my dad," the woman said, giving my a searching look. "He gets a big kick out of telling people that bird-watching was an inexpensive hobby—as long as you had a passport and your own private jet."

I was struck by the mix of her inflections. Emily said it in a joking way, but she also seemed to be baiting me with information that invited further investigation.

Because I couldn't discern her purpose, however, I dodged the temptation. "So your paternal family has money," I said.

Emily replied, "My grandfather left me a trust fund when I turned twenty-one. Not a ton of money but enough. Paul had a problem with that. He's a nice man. He really is. But he has ego issues. Would you have a problem if your wife had a lot more money than you?"

I found the word "wife" startling so shrugged and dodged that question, too. "The human-trafficking thing," I said, "I've always had an interest. Probably because I worked in Central America for several years. I spent some time in Africa, too. Tell me what you know."

A moment later, I had to ask, "Why are you smiling?"

"Because you're funny," Emily said. "The way you guard your secrets by asking questions. Your interest is real, though—that's makes it okay for some reason. You care about people. I can tell. By the way, you left out the time you spent in Southeast Asia and Indonesia and a bunch of other places, too."

Before I could reply, the woman told me, "I know more about you than you realize—including all the traveling. I already told you, I've read your research papers. In your writing, the really interesting stuff is always between the lines. Like when Tomlinson mentioned the smell of oil in your lab. I recognized it. I know what kind of oil it is. Do you want me to tell you?"

It was gun oil and specialized solvent. Tomlinson had surprised me by mentioning it. He had never mentioned it before.

"The pumps and aerators in my lab require special lubricants," I said. "There's no mystery about that."

Emily replied, *"Really?"* to let me know that she was aware that I was lying. "You became sort of a hobby of mine, Dr. Ford. Paul embarrassed me so bad this morning when he mentioned it—which was precisely what he intended to do. Not that there's a lot out there about you. Only two photos. That's all I could come up with on the Internet. And I'm pretty damn thorough when I get on a research binge. Does *that* bother you?"

"Money and the attention of a beautiful woman," I said, turning to face her. "Why would that bother anyone?"

"I'm not beautiful," Emily said, her face tilting suddenly downward. "You don't have to say that. We're both pragmatists. People like us prefer the truth. I might be handsome on a really good day, but I'm not beautiful. I never have been. So there you are. I came to terms with it long ago."

I replied, "I'll be the judge of what's beautiful and what isn't. If you don't mind."

The woman hesitated, wondering if I was going to kiss her. She gave it a moment, looking into my face, then she took my hand and tugged. Suddenly we were returning to my stilt house, walking faster than before.

After a minute or so, she was talking again, back on a safe subject. "Trafficking is big business," she began. "A lot bigger than the average citizen realizes." Because I was momentarily confused, she explained, "You asked, so I'm telling you what I know. More than a thousand undocumented workers, men, women and children, arrive in Florida daily. They're smuggled in by Mexicans, mostly. And a lot of the smugglers are Latino gang members. Coyotes—that's what they're called in the trade. But you know about all this. Of course you do."

I was thinking about recent headlines that detailed the gang wars now going on in Mexico and California. Mass murders, men, women, and children pulled from their beds and shot in the back of the head execution style. Eighteen near Ensenada. A dozen gangbangers killed the same way in Chiapas. "Ceremonial-style murders," as one survivor had described it.

I replied, "I've never learned anything in my life while my mouth was open. Keep going. You just filled in a couple of blanks."

"Okay," she said. "If that's what you want. Coyotes are usually in the drug business, too. It's a natural. Prostitution and pornography, those are the other primary sidelines. The people they screw over . . . it makes me furious to even talk about it because the people they use have nowhere to turn for help. They're slaves by every definition of the word. The way coyotes and their gangs abuse women and children is beyond despicable."

Emily started to continue but then hesitated. "I'd rather not go into some of awful things they do. It's really upsetting to me. Not if you already know."

Along with the news stories, I had also read Florida Law Enforcement reports that detailed how traffickers recruited sex slaves and controlled them. Fear was the common weapon. One gang, the Latin Kings, had videoed a live vaginal mutilation. They showed it to new recruits to keep them in line. There had been at least one ceremonial beheading, the perpetrators all wearing bandannas to cover their faces, their tattoos hidden by long-sleeved raincoats.

Cell-phone video cameras. It was what they used.

"No need for details," I told Emily. "Keep it general."

The woman let her breath out, relieved. "I'm not going to tell you why I appreciate that, but I do. Okay . . . so come up with the very worst punishments you can imagine and that's the daily reality for a lot of small brown women and boys. These are people we see every day working in the fields, riding their bicycles, hanging out at the supermarket and cashing their checks to send money home."

I said, "That's why Tomlinson's so worried about the girl. Me, too."

"Tula Choimha," Emily said. "Is that how you pronounce it?"

I said, "The girl . . . she's a very different sort of thirteen-year-old. Religious, but religious to a degree that borders on hysteria. You know what I mean? For the wrong sort of egotistical asshole, she'd be an inviting target. Humiliate the saintly little Guatemalan girl. There's a certain breed of guy who'd stand in line to do that."

"That's a volatile age. For girls especially it can be a nightmare," Emily said, sounding like she had lived it. "Fantasies range from sainthood to whoring. A scientist from Italy published a paper that gives some credence to what's called poltergeist activity. You know, crashing vases, paintings falling from the walls—all caused by the turbulent brain waves of adolescent girls. Which all sounds like pseudoscience to me, but who knows? Maybe there's a grain of truth."

I had stopped tracking the conversation when Emily mentioned poltergeists. I was reviewing what Tomlinson had told me earlier on the phone. He had returned to Red Citrus, but Tula was nowhere to be found. Her few personal possessions were still in the trailer, untouched since the night before. But it looked as if her cot *had* been slept in.

Tomlinson had called and asked me to join in the search. But, at the time, Emily and I were stuck at the necropsy site, waiting for the medical examiner's investigator. So he had driven his beat-up Volkswagen, hopscotching from one immigrant haven to another searching for Tula, but no luck.

"Did he stop at churches?" Emily asked me now, regaining my attention.

"Tomlinson didn't mention it. You're right, that would've been smart. Maybe the girl was afraid of something. Or someone. And ran to the nearest Catholic church for protection. She couldn't risk turning to the authorities."

The woman said, "Please tell me your friend contacted the police, right? Her safety's more important than her damn legal status."

"Of course," I said. "I called, too. Tomlinson insisted."

"Because he was afraid the police wouldn't take him seriously?"

I said, "It wouldn't make any difference. The state has a whole series of protocols that go into effect when a child is reported missing. Illegal immigrant children included. There's a long list of agencies, from cops to the Immigrant Advocacy Center, that get involved. Tomlinson thinks they're going to issue an AMBER Alert tonight, if they haven't done it already. It's the best system in the world for protecting kids. But it's still an imperfect system."

I continued, "The problem is that people at her trailer park—the family Tula lives with?—they don't believe the girl's missing. At least, that's what they told the cops as recently as this afternoon. They say she goes off by herself for hours at a time. Police will do more interviews tomorrow. We may not like it, but that's the way it is for now. An AMBER Alert, of course, if it happens, will change everything."

Emily asked, "Do you think she was kidnapped? It's a possibility, I hate to say it. The coyotes, the things men like that do to young girls and boys . . . I don't even want to think about."

I said, "She left behind a family photo that she'd carried for three thousand miles. That bothers me. There was a book we found, too. And some clothing. So, yeah, I think something happened."

"A book?" Emily asked.

"Not a Bible," I said. "It's a book of quotes from Joan of Arc. I took a close look. A lot of dog-eared pages and fingerprints. Some underlined passages. She kept it with her for a reason."

"Joan of Arc," the woman nodded as if that somehow made sense to her.

I gave it some more thought. "A church could be the answer," I said. "It's plausible. She got scared and ran. There were cops all over the place, so she probably scooted off to the nearest church so she wouldn't be questioned."

I wasn't convinced, though, and neither was Emily. Why hadn't church authorities contacted state authorities if they had a runaway girl on their hands?

"Doc?" Emily said. "If you're going back there tomorrow to check the churches—let me come with you. My Spanish is pretty good. Your friend was right. I think I can help."

I found it interesting that she seemed to intentionally avoid using Tomlinson's name. Was it to reassure me that she had no interest? Whatever the reason, I found it endearing.

From my pocket, I took a little LED flashlight. I clicked it on, took Emily's hand and led the lady down the mangrove path to the board-walk that crosses the water to my house. When we got to the shark pen, I switched off the underwater lights and pocketed the flashlight.

We stood for a moment in the fresh darkness, listening to a wa-terfall of mullet in the distance, seeing vague green laser streaks of luminescence thatch the water.

"Enough talk about coyotes and kidnappings, and every other dark subject," I said, putting my hands on the woman's shoulders.

I felt Emily's body move closer, her face tilted toward mine. She was ready and smiling. "Is that why you turned off the lights? To brighten the mood?"

"No," I said as I slid my hands down to her ribs. I took my time, stopping just beneath her breasts, my index fingers experimenting with a warm and weighted softness.

"I was starting to wonder if I'd have to make the first move," Emily Marston said—said it just before I kissed her.

TEN

LATE WEDNESDAY AFTERNOON, LAZIRO VICTORINO WAS SITTING
at Hooters in Cape Coral with a tableful of wings and low-level
Latin King brothers when the news lady came on the television,
reporting from a swamp near Fort Myers Beach, about a dead alligator that had a human hand in its belly.

Probably a woman's hand because they had also found a wedding ring.

Victorino recognized the place immediately. It was Red Citrus
trailer park. Hell, most of the *Indígena* who lived there, he'd personally arranged for their transportation to Florida and jobs, which
meant that he *owned* those people.

He'd probably also owned the woman the hand had belonged to.

Victorino wasn't the only one paying attention to the news lady.
One by one, his Latin King *pandilleros* turned to look at him, not
staring but letting him know they weren't stupid.

In the last few months, Victorino—the V-man—had mysteriously lost three, maybe four, *chulas*, and, goddamn it, it had to stop. Next, his homeys, his *pandilleros hermanos*, would do more than just stare at him. They would be laughing behind his back, making jokes that the *jefe* had lost his balls.

Victorino had suspected for months who was stealing his girls. Maybe selling them, maybe starting a prostitution business, maybe killing them, too—not that he cared, not really. There were always plenty of immigrant girls to choose from. But he couldn't tolerate a public display of disrespect, and the bony hand of one of his dead *chulas* on the six o'clock news was as public as it could get.

This bullshit had to stop. Laziro had worked too hard building an organization, recruiting soldiers, disciplining his *Indígena* girls, sometimes even his *pandilleros* when a soldier got out of line.

Yes, it had to stop. And Victorino knew exactly who to see to make that happen.

He stood, dropped a fifty on the table from a turquoise money clip, then threw his homeys a hand sign before pushing his way to the door—two fingers creating devil horns. He paused for a moment to confirm the nods of deference he deserved. Then he drove his truck to Red Citrus trailer park, where he expected to find Harris Squires. The *gringo* giant was all muscle but no backbone. V-man had bullied the shit out of the dude more than once, so no problem. He was looking forward to cutting this white boy down to size.

Instead, he found the dude's hard-assed lady. Victorino had done business with her, but he had never tried to push her around because the *puta* was pretty scary herself.

The woman's name was Francis-something, but everyone called her Frankie. The woman was old, which was intimidating to begin with. Probably early forties, and she had muscles like a man from shooting up all that gear shit the couple made to sell. She had a hoarse steroid voice like a man's, too, but everything else was all woman, particularly her store-bought double-D *chichis*, which she showed off braless, wearing muscle T-shirts and tube tops, probably trying to look like the muscle-magazine covers she'd posed for ten or fifteen years ago.

Mix the lady's *chichis* with a body covered with tats, dyed scarlet hair, pierced tongue and her nasty attitude, it was no wonder that even Latin King soldiers watched their behavior, and their asses, around Frankie. Harris Squires probably believed they showed the lady respect because of him and his muscles. But the dude was wrong.

Frankie was the scary one, which is why even the V-man had never crossed her. How you gonna win, crossing a *gringa* ballbuster who was six feet tall with biceps the size of his own calves?

That was about to change.

Standing outside a new double-wide, Victorino got up on his toes, looking through a bedroom window into Squires's private trailer. The place was a mess. Closet and drawers ransacked, clothes on the floor, a suitcase lying open on a bed that hadn't been made, so at first the V-man thought, *Shit! They're already gone.*

It made sense they'd run off, and not just because of the six o'clock news. There were cops all over the place, which is why Victorino hadn't turned into Red Citrus. Instead, he had parked his truck at the shrimp docks down the road near a rum bar. Then he had walked through what reminded him of a boat graveyard and jumped the fence, saw a squad car and two unmarked SUVs waiting by the garbage dumpsters, where, he guessed, they would soon be dragging the lake, looking for more pieces of the dead girl. Or maybe dead girls.

Three of Victorino's ladies had gone missing, so the timing was about right. It was a year ago that Squires and Frankie had started shooting porn up there at their fancy hunting camp, small-time at first, but then with a special video room with lights, a water bed and all kinds of weird black leather contraptions hanging from the ceiling.

Neither Squires nor the redhead had appeared in any videos that Victorino had seen. But he'd heard they both got off behind the scenes, enjoying all kinds of kinky shit. The couple had taken a special interest in the V-man's girls once they got seriously into the business. They'd hired more than a few *Indígena* as talent, and several Mexican cuties, too.

About ten months ago, Victorino's first *chula* had disappeared. After that, about every three months, he'd lose another one. The V-man had suspected them for a while, but bones inside the belly of that redneck asshole's pet alligator was the final proof he needed. His *pandilleros* realized it, which is why they'd given him those looks at Hooters.

Maybe the cops suspected, too. No wonder the pair had split before police started asking questions, so the V-man figured he'd missed them. But then he saw Frankie walk into the room, carrying an armful of folded clothes, a joint between her lips, curling smoke, and he felt better about the situation. The woman hadn't finished packing, so maybe Harris was still here, too.

No . . . the white giant was gone. Victorino confirmed it when he circled the trailer and saw that the dude's big V-8 Roush Ford monster truck was gone. Squires wasn't smart, but he wouldn't have loaned that sweet ride to nobody.

Victorino checked a couple more windows, then went to the door where a sign read NO ENTRY! in Spanish and English. He tested the knob and was surprised to find the door unlocked.

A moment later, he was standing inside, seeing a big-screen TV and stereo equipment, then a kitchen that didn't look like most kitchens, but that was no surprise to the V-man. On the counters were four big gas-burner plates, each with its own canister of propane. The shelves were lined with a mess of medical-looking shit, bottles of oil and chemicals, and measuring beakers that looked like they belonged in a lab. Which was exactly what this place was—a lab for cooking steroids.

Jesus, just a spark, the whole place would explode like a bomb— maybe not a bad way to handle the situation, Victorino decided, if he could get Frankie and her muscle boy into the trailer at the same time.

Victorino had seen a kitchen like this before, only a lot bigger. It was at Squires's hunting camp, where Victorino and his *pandilleros* had partied themselves on a couple of occasions. They weren't invited often, but, when they got the call, the V-man and a few of his boys made an appearance because it was a mutually beneficial business association.

Squires and Frankie ran three trailer parks, which provided handy instant housing for newly arrived illegals. On the side, they shot porn, which the Latin Kings also made and marketed as a sideline, and that put money into everyone's pocket.

Victorino's soldiers pedaled the videos to dumb little *Indígena* dudes, who'd probably never seen a naked woman in their pathetic little lives. The *gringo* couple needed girls for their movies, of course, which meant they also needed weed and blow, which put cash right back into the V-man's pocket.

Not that Victorino trusted the *gringos*. No way. It was business, nothing more. The couple treated him like just another wetback. To them, there was no difference between him, a Mexican stud and some scrawny little *Indio* from Guatemala or El Salvador or some Nicaraguan *pendejo*.

A wetback was a wetback, to most *Americanos*. That's how clueless they were. But the V-man never let it show that it bothered him. When he looked into a *gringo*'s eyes and saw the contempt or indifference, all he did was smile his great big gold-toothed smile, pretending to be their Mexican *amigo*. But he was really thinking how goddamn stupid they were.

These two especially, an old woman with wrinkles on her muscles and her redneck boyfriend, the two of them acting like big-money hotshots until the cops finally took them down.

Which would happen. If the V-man didn't get busy and take them both out first.

The V-man wasn't smiling now as Frankie came into the room, stumbling because he surprised her, then yelling at him in her deep voice, "What the hell are you doing in my home?"

Then she caught herself because she recognized Victorino as the V-man yet didn't sound any friendlier when she added, "Oh. It's you. What the hell are you doing in here without knocking? I'm in a hurry. We don't need any more grass or shit today. Get out. Get out of here right now."

Victorino let the woman watch him react slowly, making her wait as he turned his back to her. He made sure the door was closed but unlocked in case he wanted to get out fast. He pivoted to face her, then snapped on the surgical gloves he had brought along for effect.

First the left glove. Then the right.

Then he surprised the woman again by flashing the box cutter he was palming and asked, "You don't want any smoke or blow—but what about girls? You don't need any more of my pretty little *chulas*? The way you been killing my girls off, I thought you'd be in the market by now."

The V-man expected the woman to squat right there and piss her panties, she should have been so scared, seeing the rubber gloves and the razor. Instead, it was the woman's turn to surprise him.

Frankie balled her hands into fists and took a step toward him, shouting, "I'm trying to figure out just how goddamn stupid you are! You come in here, cops all over the place, looking like a faggot or a fucking serial killer, with those gloves, your bandanna and your pissy little knife. I should slap the shit out of you right now, then tell the cops you tried to rape me."

Victorino had to smile at the woman's *cojones*.

"Me?" he said easily. "I'm the stupid one? They found pieces of one of my girls in your bigass alligator today. What you call that fucking lizard, Fifi or something? On *your* property. It was just on TV, bitch, and you're calling *me* stupid?"

He bounced the razor in his hand, not believing how the *gringa* was handling this. No wonder his soldiers were spooked by the woman.

The woman's face changed. "You're kidding me, on television news? You've got to be shitting me. What did they find?"

Victorino told her. "Bones of a human hand. You pretend you don't know that? Had a fucking ring on the finger! A woman's hand."

Now Frankie's resigned expression read *Sooner or later, it was bound to happen*.

"Half an hour ago," Victorino continued, "I was sitting at Hooters, enjoying some chicken wings with my boys. Why you think I hurried over here, leaving behind all that fine food?"

He held up the box cutter. "You better listen to what I'm saying, *chinga*. You and your jelly-boy boyfriend disrespected the V-man. All the times I was nice to you both and this is how you thank me? Now I got no choice but to leave a few marks on that body of yours. As a warning to other dumbasses. Cut off an ear, then slice my initials into your face, that might get my point across. Or maybe cut one of those big titties and listen to the air leak out."

He pointed the razor at her, wanting the woman to pay attention to the blade. But she didn't. Instead, Frankie was suddenly preoccupied, thinking about something else, acting like the V-man wasn't even in the room.

Victorino raised his voice. "You hear what I just said to you . . . *puta*?"

The woman made a waving motion with her hand. "Quiet," she said. "I'm trying to figure out how to handle this." After a moment, she added, "And don't fucking call me a *puta*."

Jesus, this wasn't going the way things usually went when Victorino waved a blade in a girl's face. He was staring at the woman and he couldn't believe that her face showed no fear. Instead, when Victorino reached to grab her elbow, the woman yanked the elbow away and got madder.

"Keep your greasy hands off me. Haven't you got any damn sense?"

Victorino took a step back, his grin fading, then moved between the woman and the door, thinking she might run for it. Hoping she'd make a move, actually, which would give him an opening. He'd forgotten how goddamn big Frankie was, so he might have to tackle her, get her on the ground, then stuff something into her mouth before going to work with the box cutter.

But the woman didn't run. She returned to her packing, throwing clothes into the suitcase. "You have any idea how much shit I have to do?" she said. "The cops are bringing in equipment to drag the pond, you dipshit. Two or three hours at the most, the boat, or whatever it is they use, gets here. Next thing, they'll be banging on this door. One of your idiot whores OD's, falls in the water, who you think they're gonna blame? They're gonna blame *you*, dipshit. And I'll be here to give them your name unless I can get this cook-shack cleaned up and get our shit out of here. So leave me alone!"

Jesus. This woman had balls. Hell . . . maybe she really *did* have balls. Hard to tell with the sweatpants she was wearing. Victorino had never thought about getting a look at the lady's goodies before, but now it crossed his mind.

He stood there, thinking about it. Two or three hours before the cops went to work dragging the lake?

They had some time.

He let the woman see him retract the razor and put the box cutter into his jeans. "Where's your asshole boyfriend?" he asked. "That jelly boy should be here helping you, not letting you do all the work."

Frankie said, "Don't even mention that prick's name to me." Then she nodded toward the hallway and told him, "Out there in the main room, I've got two more suitcases. Go get them. And hurry up."

Victorino didn't like that. A Latin King captain didn't take orders from some *gringa*. Even for her to try to give him orders was offensive. On the other hand, it wasn't likely that an old white woman knew crap about the respect a *pandillero* captain deserved. And the woman did have nice-looking *chichis*.

"Did you hear me?" she said. "Run and get those suitcases."

"Hey, you about to get your face slapped, lady," Victorino replied. "You want a favor, you ask the V-man nice. You say 'please' and you say 'thank you.' Or you can kiss my Mexican ass."

"Okay . . . *please* get my goddamn suitcases. And be quick about it—unless your Mexican ass wants to go to jail."

When Victorino returned to the room carrying the suitcases, he asked about Squires again, saying, "When's your boyfriend coming back? Does he know the cops are here? That would piss me off, my man running away with all this shit going down."

"That asshole isn't a man—he's an overgrown mama's boy," Frankie snapped. "You know what he did? He ran out on me early this morning. He stole fifty-nine thousand dollars cash from our box and packed his shit. Then the dumbass stuck around long enough to take some little teenage brat with him."

Victorino said, "Teenage?" not following but very interested in the cash the lady had just mentioned.

"Some underage little bitch!" the woman yelled. "I know because some state asshole officials were nosing around here an hour ago, asking about a missing kid. Harris figured the cops were going to arrest him, so he ran and took along something to play with. But I'll find him. I know exactly where he's going and I'll catch him there."

Victorino was trying to unsnap one of the suitcases but having a tough time. "A white girl?" he asked, curious because he had heard that Frankie enjoyed *chulas* a lot more than the redneck.

"No, some little Mexican brat who everyone thinks is a boy. But not me. I knew better—even Harris didn't believe me when I told him. She's probably not even thirteen yet, but you know what a perverted asshole Harris is. So he apparently figured it out."

After thinking about it for a second, the woman sounded fairly perverted herself, adding, "Her name's Tulo-something. You remember her? Kind of pretty, with a Dutch-boy haircut with bangs, and always quoting the Bible. But a cute little ass on her."

Victorino said, "A girl, you sure about that?"

Frankie ignored him, too busy packing to listen.

Victorino said, "Maybe I know the one, a skinny kid, got here 'bout a week ago. Kinda tall, for a Guatemalan, and real quiet. Had a fucked-up haircut, like someone used a bowl on his head."

"Not a he, a *she*—a sneaky little tramp of a girl," Frankie said. "I knew it right away."

The V-man was employing his thoughtful-businessman expression. "A little *chula*, huh? I'll be go-to-hell. That Guatemalan *puta* lied to me. I'm gonna have to do something about that."

The woman made a snorting noise.

"And Harris, too. The way I've been losing *chulas* lately?" the V-man said. "I've got to cut someone's balls off for this, then stuff them down his goddamn throat! My homeboys will be laughing behind my back, wanting to steal my shit, everything I've built. I take this personally."

Folding a blouse, Frankie told him, "I don't give a damn how you take it. You're gonna have to wait in line if you want to kill Harris and that little wettail." Then she stared at the bed for a moment before saying, "You haven't figured out how to open that goddamn suitcase yet?"

The V-man was doing his best, getting frustrated with the cheap-assed little gold snaps, as he replied, "I won't kill the little bitch. But I've got to find her and make an example. I'm a businessman. Killing a girl that age, where's the profit?"

Frankie slapped Victorino's hands away from the suitcase, saying, "A regular genius, that's what you are. A regular Wall Street tycoon," as she popped the locks with her black fingernails, then returned to her packing.

The V-man was thinking, *Smart-ass white bitch,* but pretended to be unruffled, not pausing as he continued, "Wall Street or Main Street, business is still business—when you get to be a man in my position. You say she's, what? Twelve, maybe thirteen? That means

I own her for four or five more very profitable years. It's sort of like owning a fine racehorse, understand? Or a nice limo you rent out."

Frankie said to the V-man, "You mind moving your ass?" then pushed by him to get to the closet. No . . . a table, where she found a lighter, then stood tall in front of the window and relighted a joint that the bitch didn't bother to offer him.

From the smell of the smoke, the V-man guessed it was shit his *pandilleros* had sold her. Fine Mexican weed laced with cocaine. Yes, the woman was inhaling deeply, smoking what the homeboys called a *banano*, so no wonder she was so jazzed.

The V-man kept talking, saying, "I start her out by selling her virginity five or six times to some of my best clients. Top dollar. Dudes down here from New York, Chicago, real-money players who the V-man deals with only *personally*. Then put the *chula* to work, doing private parties. Buy her some clothes, show the bitch how to use lipstick and protective condoms 'cause pregnant *chulas*, they very hard to market. Maybe next year, on the street. Or six months, depending on how she holds up. Unless one of my clients wants to rent her full-time as a maid or a cook—I'm still making money on that."

The woman stood and looked at Victorino for a moment as if an idea had just come into her mind. "Do you know who that dead hand belonged to?"

"The one in the alligator?" Victorino said. "It was one of my *chulas*. Had to be."

Frankie asked him, "What makes you so sure?"

"Three of my ladies went off, left their shit, their money," Victorino said. "Hell, they even left their *shoes* and never came back. Not all at once, of course, but I ain't dumb. Went off and left their fuckin' *shoes*, I'm saying. Even a crazy woman wouldn't go off and leave her shoes. Why you think I come straight here when I finally got me some proof? You two been fuckin' around with my *chulas*, everyone knows that. But I figured you was selling them on the street—"

"Harris killed them," the woman interrupted.

Victorino stopped talking and tried to read the woman's face. Was she telling the truth?

"You got my attention," he said slowly.

"I just told you, Harris murdered all three. Maybe more—I was never around when he did it. He'd get screwed up on blow or triple his testosterone dosage by accident—he's always forgetting his needle days—and that just makes him even crazier. Or he'll drop a handful of D-bombs, which makes him even worse."

The woman continued, "You want to cut someone's balls off for disrespecting you? Harris Squires is the guy you're looking for—if you can find his balls. Because of all the juice he shoots, he's got a dick the size of a Vienna sausage."

Victorino enjoyed that so much, he had to smile. He found it encouraging, just the two of them alone, suddenly sharing secrets, in this brand-new double-wide that smelled pretty good, like carpet, marijuana smoke and fresh vinyl.

He said to the woman, "All three, huh? You sure of this?"

"I just said it. Pay attention, I don't make a habit of repeating myself."

"He fed 'em all to that bigass alligator?"

The woman said, "Harris and some buddies loaded that stinking animal into a truck, drunk as hell, playing Crocodile Hunter one night, and brought the gator here to scare your wetbacks. We planned to sell this place to developers once his asshole mother dies—if she ever does. All the legal bullshit from pissed-off renters would have slowed things up. To Harris, the boy genius, it seemed like a smart thing to do."

Victorino was giving it some thought as he said, "That *pendejo* snuffed out three of my ladies, huh?" not loud, letting the woman know that he was angry but cool about it, a professional boss man who knew how to deal with situations such as this. "How'd he do it? Use a gun? He don't have the balls to take his time and make it enjoyable."

The woman said, "He's got a thing for rough sex. It's the only way he can get off. He'd load their drinks with Ecstasy, then choke them while he was banging them. Or maybe they just OD'd on their own. How would I know?"

That's exactly what Victorino was thinking: How could the woman know these details unless she was involved?

It also crossed his mind that a woman her size, with all those muscles, she might even be talking about herself, not about her boyfriend. He had heard the rumors that Frankie liked doing women even better than men. It was because of all that steroid shit she shot into her body.

Victorino motioned to the kitchen. "That shit you cook up, it makes a dude's thingee shrink?" Because the woman ignored him, he decided to add, "Think it would bother you watching me cut Harris's little thingee off?"

That got the *gringa*'s attention. Frankie Manchon gave the man a weird look like she'd love to watch him cut Squires's nuts off.

Man, this was one scary lady. But kind of sexy, too. It was the way her blue eyes got a real shiny, eager glow. . . .

Sexy, yeah, the V-man decided, in a real dirty way, which might be fun. Victorino was thinking maybe he should take a few seconds and lock that outside door so the two of them could enjoy their privacy.

That's exactly what he did.

But then she spoiled it.

"Take off those fucking rubber gloves," she told him. "They make you look like a janitor."

That did it. This woman needed to learn some respect.

He said, "You say your jelly boyfriend drugged three of my ladies and killed them? You think that's a big deal? Like he's a badass or something?"

Frankie tried to interrupt him, probably with some smart-ass remark, but Victorino kept talking, saying, "I'm a fucking Aztec, *chinga*. You understand what that shit means? One time, I cut a dude's heart out, the thing still beating in my hand. That's the last thing this dude saw—his eyes wide open, staring at his fucking heart. That was before I cut the dude's neck open. Cutting his neck was my way of being *kind* to the dude, understand? Because he had been my loyal brother up until an unfortunate thing he did. But I got no personal relationship with you and your redneck boyfriend. You hear what I'm telling you?"

The woman was listening now, looking at him with her shiny blue eyes, but not showing much.

"But when some woman disrespects me, what I do is I start cutting pieces off her body until she begs me to stop. Then I feed those pieces to the damn dogs and make her watch them eat her ears, her fingers, maybe a chunk of her tongue if the fool has a big mouth like you.

"Rednecks use alligators? My boys and me, we prefer dogs. Pit bulls we keep for the fighting ring. And it's been a while since any of them got some white meat. Do you know what I'm saying?"

The woman took a moment before she replied, "Yeah, you're a hardass and you like talking about it. You made your point."

Victorino wasn't so sure, so he pulled up his left sleeve to show the woman his Diablo tattoo, eight teardrops beneath it, six blue, two red. "Know what these are? These are my stripes. In the Kings, you don't wear this paint, *chinga*, unless you earned it. Take a look for yourself."

For some reason, that impressed the woman, and Victorino realized that she wanted to prolong this talk of killing. It made her breasts stick out, her breath coming harder, as she took a step to get a better look at his arm.

"Why the different colors?" she asked. "I don't think I've ever seen sloppier tats in my life. You want some good work, I've got a man in Key West who's an artist."

Frankie touched Victorino's arm, her black stiletto fingernails with glitter on them denting his skin. "These tattoos, they look like your guy used a sewing needle and Easter-egg dye."

The V-man jerked his arm away, saying, "That's 'cause I did 'em myself! The blue is for six dudes I wasted, two in Chicago. Both of them Crips—but here I am."

He tapped at the red teardrops. "These the ones you need to pay attention to. One of my girls doesn't obey me, I give her one warning only." And he took out the box cutter.

Yeah. Frankie was impressed now, her chest moving faster, her blue eyes bright. She came closer, her arm lifting toward him, and then—*Whap!* The slap caused Victorino to drop the razor, he was so surprised, and the next thing he knew the woman was on him, trying to claw his eyes out with her fingernails. Yelling at him, too, saying, "You think you're man enough to get my panties off? Do you? Huh? *Do you*, you skinny little shit? It took three of my cousins my first time—and they were Vermont studs, not wetbacks."

She kept repeating it as she flailed at him, her voice low and hoarse, breathing fast, as Victorino got behind her, then spun her down on the bed.

And for a while, that was all Victorino remembered.

An hour later, 6:30 p.m., the V-man was in his pickup truck, following the woman's Cadillac convertible to Harris Squires's hunting camp, where she'd promised they would find the redneck, the money and the pretty little girl who'd been pretending to be a boy.

Before leaving, Frankie had unpacked a bottle of Crown Royal and a baggie of grass that one of Victorino's soldiers had sold her. In their vehicles, they each had a plastic cup and a joint—sweet-smelling *bananos*, fine weed laced with coke. By now, they were both feeling good.

Victorino certainly was. The woman was a goddamn animal in bed. He'd never experienced anything like it in his life. No other woman had come close to doing what Frankie had done to him. And, *man*, Victorino had, by God, gotten off on it, feeling crazy wild afterward.

Already, the V-man was ready for more. He had heard old women were best in the sack 'cause they were so damn appreciative, but it was more than that with Frankie. The woman had a monster in her. Something black and glossy with claws that lived inside her head, looking out through those blue eyes of hers.

"I want to watch when you use that razor blade on Harris," Frankie had said to him, her voice still flushed.

"Sure," Victorino had replied, meaning it. It would be a chance for him to show off a little and also prove to his *pandilleros* he was still a hardass. He had decided to invite some of his brothers along and maybe video the whole thing.

Not sure all this was going to take place, though, he then had to ask Frankie, "But what you got planned to do with your boyfriend's body once we done? That can be a problem. That big lizard of yours, she's dead now."

The woman noticed Victorino looking at the row of propane tanks in the kitchen as she replied, "You just stick to your business and let me do the thinking." Then added, being even more serious, "But the little girl—you can't touch that girl. I want you to promise me that."

Giving a Latin King captain orders again, but it was okay. It was pretty clear to Victorino what Frankie wanted. She wanted that little girl-boy virgin for herself.

But that was okay, too. The *gringa* woman, being the way she was, she'd probably get off a couple of times on her own and then invite the V-man to join the party.

ELEVEN

EMILY MARSTON AND I WERE TAKING A BREAK, CURLED UP NAKED, spooning on my narrow bed, when I heard Tomlinson trotting up the boardwalk, the distinctive slap of his feet telling me he had something important going on. Why else would he be in such a hurry?

As Emily stretched and yawned, I turned my wrist to see the glowing numerals of my Chronofighter watch. It was still early, only 9:30 p.m.

"The house is shaking again," she joked. "My imagination?"

I leaned to kiss the woman's cheek, then behind her ear, feeling a welling sensation within my chest that was not unknown to me but so rare and long ago that I was startled. I was also dubious, instantly on alert.

That same thoracic response is probably why sappy poets associate the heart with love. I had just met this woman, knew very little about her. To feel what I was feeling, after only a few hours together, was irrational. Not that love is ever rational.

"It's Tomlinson," I said. "Something must be wrong."

There was.

"Tula sent me a text," Tomlinson told me as I pushed aside the bedroom curtain, shirtless, buckling my belt.

I noticed that his hand was shaking as he combed fingers through his John Lennon hair. "He's got her, Doc. Harris Squires, I was right. And the goddamn cops told me they're already doing everything they could. Those *assholes*!"

Adjusting my glasses, I took his cell phone, saying, "Maybe if you lived in a country where there were no cops, you might have a little more respect."

Tomlinson began to pace, his ribs showing, now shirtless, wearing red surfer baggies. "If you called downtown, it might be different," he said. "You know a lot of guys on the force. We've got to do something, Doc!"

The text was in English. I sat next to my shortwave radio, turned on the lamp and read, "Safe, in his truck. In God's hands. 22 miles from Im."

I said, "I don't doubt it's from her, but are you sure? Where did a Guatemalan kid learn how to use a cell phone?"

"It's the first thing they learn when they get here," Tomlinson replied, sounding impatient. "That, plus the best food is always at Taco Bell."

I said, "She didn't finish the message, so okay . . . yeah, of course it's from Tula. I remember you saying she had your number in case of emergencies."

"She sent it from Squires's phone," he said, chewing at a strand of hair. "I called and recognized his voice. I didn't say anything. Do you think I should have? He wouldn't have let her send me a text, and I was afraid I'd set him off, make him suspicious. So I just hung up. You know, like a wrong number."

"Did he call back?"

"No . . . Jesus! If he sees that text she sent, I'd hate to even think what a guy like that would do to Tula."

On a pad of paper, I copied Squires's number, then spun the swivel chair to face Tomlinson, who was now leaning into the refrigerator, moving stuff, then saying, "Jesus Christ, Doc, don't you ever go to the store? We're out of beer again. What a night to be out of beer!"

I said, "Tula was in the middle of writing 'Immokalee.' I-M— what else could it be? Twenty-two miles from Immokalee, but she was interrupted."

Tomlinson used his hip to bang the refrigerator door closed as I added, "Which means she saw a road sign—the distance is precise. Unless Squires told her, which seems unlikely. Why would he tell the girl where she is? She's only been in Florida for a week, so she couldn't have guessed the distance from landmarks. But why would he take her to Immokalee?"

Tomlinson replied, "Everyone in Guatemala has a relative living in Immokalee. Or Indiantown. Or maybe the guy has a place down there, who knows? Rednecks have hunting camps sometimes."

I was trying to project a reason why Squires would drive Tula Choimha to a Guatemalan stronghold. I said, "He could be taking her there to look for her mother, but that makes no sense. I don't associate acts of family kindness with Harris Squires."

"The girl's a thought-shaper," Tomlinson reminded me. "She can get people to do things they normally wouldn't. Tula can project ideas in a way that makes people think they came up with it on their own."

I ignored him, saying, "He might do it if money was somehow involved. Or sex and money—the world's two most powerful motivators. A thirteen-year-old girl and her mother. There's no money in that combination. Which leaves—"

I left the sentence unfinished as I returned my attention to the girl's text to see if there was more to learn from the few words she had written.

Listening, Tomlinson used his heel to shut the fridge. He was carrying a tumbler filled with ice toward a bottle of Patrón tequila on the counter as I continued, "They've done some traveling, that's obvious. Maybe he stopped at a 7-Eleven or something and left his phone in the vehicle. That gave her an opening to use the phone, but Squires interrupted Tula before she could finish the text. And her hands aren't tied—they're not taped, anyway. That's a positive. But why not call you instead of type a message?"

Tomlinson had already figured it out. "Because she couldn't risk holding the phone to her ear. You're right, probably a 7-Eleven. Someplace he could keep an eye on her through a window. So she hid the phone in her lap and texted. That would have been safer. And there's less chance of him checking for texts, then checking recent calls. Tula's very smart, I already told you."

"Do you know what kind of truck he drives?" I was leafing through my private phone book, many of the names written in my own form of code. As I picked up the phone to dial a police detective friend of mine, Emily appeared from behind the curtain, combing her auburn hair with a brush, wearing one of my baseball jerseys buttoned down to her thighs.

"We meet again," she smiled, looking at Tomlinson. "I was just getting acquainted with your best friend. Your timing could be better, you know. But . . . it also could have been a lot worse."

Tomlinson stopped chewing at his hair long enough to say, "It looks to me like someone just finished touching all the bases."

The woman had a nice smile, ironic and tolerant. "A baseball metaphor," she laughed, tugging at my jersey. "It works, but not entirely accurate. I was counting on extra innings."

As Emily said it, she moved past me, trailing an index finger along my shoulder. I saw the way Tomlinson's eyes followed her, focusing first on the abrupt angle between breasts and abdomen created by the baggy baseball jersey, then on her long hiker's legs, calf muscles flexing.

Clearing my throat, I burned my pal with a look that read *Don't even think about it.*

Emily noticed, which caused her to grin, charmed apparently by our adolescent sparring. Then she rewarded me with a look that read *You've got nothing to worry about.*

That thoracic glow again. It was in my chest.

On the telephone, a detective acquaintance, Leroy Melinski, was telling me, "I've got the report up on the screen right now. Thirteen-year-old Tulo Choimha, an undocumented Guatemalan national. He, uh . . . he was reported missing last night, but it didn't get official until a couple of hours ago when a full AMBER Alert went out. So maybe your beach-bum pal's pestering did some good. Is he still the strung-out cop hater I remember?"

Looking at Tomlinson as he came through the door with two quart bottles of beer—I'd remembered there was beer stowed on my flats skiff—I said to Melinski, "If anything, he's worse. I think the man's personality evaporates as he ages. It's causing his weirdness to condense right before my very eyes."

"Personally," Melinski replied, "I don't think cop haters are funny. I'd slap the shit out of that hippie prick if he gave me a reason."

The bitterness in that caused me to raise my eyebrows, and I said, "As entertaining as that sounds, I called to talk about the missing child."

"The kid," Melinski said. "I know, I know. But there's another piece of news first I think you'll find interesting. Our guys finished dragging that lake this afternoon. Where you shot the alligator?"

As I listened, I signaled Tomlinson to pay attention. "You found more bones?" I asked.

"No, they found a different body. A fresh one. Another female. Latin, probably mid-twenties, but both of her hands were right where they belonged. The only thing missing was the girl's life. Someone put her in a garbage sack, then used wire and concrete blocks to sink her. Dead two or three days at the most, according to the guys on the scene. Which is a guess, of course, but they've seen enough floaters to come close. No obvious injuries, so no telling how she died. We're still waiting on the medical examiner's report."

To Tomlinson and Emily I said, "It's official, there's an AMBER Alert out on Tula. And they found another dead girl—unrelated to the bones we found in the gator. They finished dragging this afternoon."

Tomlinson threw his head back, fists against his temples—a silent scream—while Emily shook her head, smile gone.

To Melinski I said, "That hand belonged to someone. They found nothing else down there that was human?"

"I was told they did a pretty thorough search, but maybe they'll try again tomorrow. One of the medical examiner's guys told me the bones you found might be a month old or a year old. Maybe more. But it definitely wasn't a fresh kill—assuming the victim died. And they're not sure it's female, despite the wedding ring. They're trying to narrow it down. That's a job for the forensic lab."

I said, "Which means it's even more important to find that missing kid. The killer—that's the guy we think abducted her, Leroy. He's a steroid freak. With a real nasty temper."

I had already given him Squires's name, his number and told him about the text Tomlinson had received. The detective had passed the number along to his staff, and we were awaiting confirmation that the cell phone belonged to Squires.

"You don't need to convince me about hurrying," Melinski said. "When a kid goes missing, there's a forty-eight-hour window. I don't have to tell you what usually happens if the search goes longer than two days. Problem is, this morning the family the kid lives with told officers that he wandered off by himself all the time but he'd show up. He always did. So it wasn't considered a priority until this afternoon. No father, no mother to push for a search, which I'd like to say hasn't happened before. But it has."

I corrected him. "You must have misheard, Lee, this is a girl we're looking for. Tula, not Tulo. She's been pretending to be a boy since she left Guatemala because she's smart. You know how dangerous that border crossing is. The family she lives with knows the truth. And probably a few others but not many. I'd consider it a personal favor if you called out the cavalry on this one. Like I said, the guy she's with is a chemistry freak. He goes from cold to hot real fast."

I could picture the detective reading through the computer files as he replied, "If that's true, then this whole damn report's wrong. If the family knew it was a girl, why didn't they say something? He . . . *she* was reported as a suspected abductee late this afternoon. The AMBER Alert went out at twenty hundred hours. All the missing-child protocols are in effect, but our people have been looking for a damn teenage boy, not a girl."

"Last time I saw her," I told him, "she was wearing jeans and a baggy blue T-shirt, so most people couldn't tell the difference." Then I gave the man the best physical description I could, pausing to pass along details that Tomlinson provided as he paced back and forth.

I could hear Melinski's fingers tapping at a keyboard as he said,

"That's something to go on, at least. The problem is—and this is a good example—people in these kinds of places, the immigrant trailer parks, they're scared to death of our guys. So some of the state agencies, the Immigrant Advocacy people, will be sending people around asking questions. Maybe they're on it now. Christ, I hope so. We have almost no information on the kid."

I could hear his frustration as he added, "For more than an hour, we've been looking for a boy. Who knows, maybe some cop stopped them, then turned her loose, not knowing."

I said, "But at least you can narrow down the search area. Maybe they're in Immokalee by now. Or somewhere close."

Melinski said, "You said she didn't type out the whole word. She wrote: I-M."

I replied, "What else could it be? Did anything come up on Squires?"

I listened to Melinski typing as I watched Emily busy herself in my little ship's galley of a kitchen. She was listening, eyes moving from the teakettle to me, the concern showing on her good-looking face, that jaw and nose, autumn-colored hair swinging loose.

"There are thirteen Harris Squires in this state," Melinski said after a moment, "but there's only one whose mother owns trailer parks. A rich kid, from what I'm seeing. A rich mother, anyway. She owns three mobile home parks . . . a house on the beach . . . taxes almost thirty grand a year. And four hundred–some acres of undeveloped land in the Everglades east of Naples."

Immokalee was northeast of Naples about thirty miles. Tomlinson's remark about rednecks liking hunting camps came into my mind.

"Any houses or cabins on that property?" I asked, thinking a hunting camp would be a good place to disappear with an abducted girl.

"Uhhh , nope . . . I don't see anything here. Nothing that's been permitted, anyway," he replied, then began to read from Squires's file.

"He got bumped once for possession of marijuana, no conviction, back when he was a kid. Get this"—Melinski paused, and I could picture his face in front of a computer screen as he read—"'The informant regarding the minor in question was the minor's mother, Mrs. Harriet Ray Squires. Mrs. Squires had to be restrained by officers when she confronted said minor the morning after his arrest.'

"Christ, Doc," Melinski laughed, "the guy's own mom narced him out. If he's one of those crazies who only goes for young girls, maybe it's because his mom was such a hardass. He looks for women he can control."

I said, "That's the only thing on his record?"

"No," the detective said, "but he's not what I'd call real dirty. Not compared to most of the losers who come through here. There's a DUI arrest, which his lawyer somehow got tossed out when he was nineteen. Then about five months ago he was banged for speeding—doing a hundred and ten on I-75, Pinellas County. If this is the guy we're after, he's got a vehicle that can do that and more. It's an almost new Ford Roush pickup truck. That's one of those tricked-out specials. Big engines and big tires for guys with egos and—"

I interrupted, "What's the license number? And the color?" I was leaning over a notepad, making notes.

There was a pause before Melinski let me know how patient he was trying to be, saying, "Doc, come on, now. You know I'm not allowed to do that. Even if I was allowed, I wouldn't do it because the last thing we want is some civilian playing detective, upsetting people and probably getting his ass into trouble. Meaning you. Frankly, you've got a history of it. No offense."

I said, "It was just a question, Lee."

"A few months back, you were the suspect in a murder rap, Doc. So excuse me for being careful. I shouldn't even be talking to you."

I said, "I called because I want to help, not get in the way."

"Please tell me you don't plan on looking for this guy, Doc. There's an AMBER Alert on the kid, what more do you want? What can you do that a state full of trained professionals can't?"

I said, "I know . . . you're right, but—" then listened to Melinski say, "From what you said, this guy Squires is a bad actor. Driver's license has him listed at six-six, two forty-five, and he has a concealed weapons permit. No weapons registered to him, but that doesn't mean diddly-squat. In this state, you can buy freaking grenades if you know who to talk to. Why risk inviting that kind of trouble? What's this girl to you?"

I was looking at Emily as I told him, "Like you said, the girl has no parents around. No one to act as her advocates. I've spent a lot of time in Guatemala. I speak the language and I like the people. So why not? The point is, I don't give a damn about Squires—arrest him or don't arrest him, that's your business. But I care about the girl. If I can help find her by asking around, talking to people in the Guatemalan community, what's wrong with that?"

Melinski said, "Hang on a second," sounding impatient. A moment later, he said, "Okay, here it is. The number that sent Tomlinson the text? It's his phone, Harris Squires's. As of now, every cop in the state will be looking for that fancy-assed truck of his. And we'll find him. I can guarantee you that."

To Tomlinson and Emily I whispered, "It was Squires's phone," as Melinski continued, "My next move is to contact our hostage-negotiation guys and ask them how we deal with this. Risk calling Squires and asking him if he's got the girl? Then try to talk him down, convince him the smartest thing he can do is turn himself in. Or keep everything under the radar until we locate the truck.

I'm not the officer in charge of this, but I know who is, and she'll listen to me."

I said, "If you have the right kind of person talk to him, someone trained—definitely not the tough-guy type—it could work."

"But what if it *doesn't*?" Melinski asked me, sounding angry or frustrated—a man who had been in a tough business for too long. "Jesus Christ! A thirteen-year-old girl a thousand miles from home. No family to look after her, and some steroid freak jerk grabs her. These Latin American kids, man-oh-man, Doc. The undocumented girls, particularly, they're the easiest targets in the world—you're right about that one.

"Some of these gangbangers," he continued, "the Mexican coyote types. To them, snatching female illegals is like a sport. Like hunting rabbits or doves—something soft and harmless that can't bite back. And the sad thing is, hardly anyone even knows this shit takes place every day. Let alone cares."

To Melinski I said, "I don't envy you guys the choices you have to make."

I meant it.

"Doc," the detective said, "I'll give you my cell number, if you want. And I'll call you the moment we get anything new. But I don't want you nosing around, asking people questions about that girl. And I don't want you messing with this Harris Squires dude. Give me your word?"

I replied, "I have no interest in finding Squires. I don't ever want to see the guy again. I'll promise you that."

A few minutes later, we were in the lab, discussing ways to help find the girl, which, of course, meant finding Harris Squires. Try as I might, there was no separating the two.

My lab is a wooden room, roofed with crossbeams and tin sheeting. The place smells of ozone and chemicals, creosote and brackish water that I could hear currenting beneath the pine floor as Tomlinson lectured us.

My friend was trying to hurry us along, doing his best to sound rational and reasonable, telling me, "It's not even ten yet, and it takes less than an hour to drive to Immokalee. Faster, if we knew someone who had a big fancy car. We could be there way before bar closing time. Right on Main Street there's a good barbecue place, too, that stays open. I wouldn't suggest it, but they have a salad bar."

He turned to give Emily a pointed look, obviously aware that her Jag was parked outside the marina's gate. But if the lady noticed, she didn't react. She was going through a file I had started years ago, a file on bull sharks that inhabit a freshwater lake one hundred and twenty-seven miles from the sea in Central America.

We had gotten on the subject of sharks earlier in the evening when I was showing the lady a gadget I was testing that might repel attacking sharks. Laser Energetics of Orlando had sent me the thing, a palm-sized tactical light called a Dazer. Its green laser beam was hundreds of times more powerful than a legal laser pointer and could drop a man to the ground with one blinding blast. A test victim had described the pain as "like a screwdriver in the eye," which is why a special federal license was required to possess it. If the Dazer affected sharks the same way, it might save sailors, pilots and divers who found themselves in a bad spot.

On the file Emily was holding I had written in ink *Sharks of Lake Nicaragua*.

"You have some fascinating stuff here," Emily told me, looking at a black-and-white photo of a fisherman I had interviewed a few years back. He was missing a scarred-over chunk from his right thigh. Attacks in Lake Nicaragua are not uncommon. Water is murky, private bathing facilities are rare and backwater bull sharks have the feeding instincts of pit bulls. Males of the species, *Carcharinus leucas*, have a higher concentration of testosterone in their blood than any animal on earth.

In the background of the photo, tacked to a wall, were several sets of shark jaws. The largest of them was opened wide enough to cut a man in half.

The fisherman I'd interviewed had lost his thigh as a kid and had dedicated his adult life to getting even. The fact that Japanese buyers paid top dollar for shark fins only made his work sweeter—until he and other fishermen had all but depleted the landlocked shark population. The man was dead broke when I met him but still thirsty for revenge. By then, though, a rum bottle provided his only relief.

I know a quite a bit about Central America and the varieties of sharks that thrive there—finned predators and two-legged predators, too. For several years I had lived in the region, traveling between Nicaragua, Guatemala and Masagua during the endless revolutions. I was in the country doing marine research—a fact that I made public to anyone who asked because I was also working undercover on assignment for a clandestine agency composed of a tiny, select membership.

By day, I did collecting trips, wading the tide pools, and I maintained a fastidious little jungle lab. By night, I shifted gears and did a different type of work. I attended village celebrations and embassy functions. I wore a dinner jacket and went to parties thrown by wealthy landowners. I wore fatigues and trained with a counterinsurgency group, the *Kaibiles*. Less often, I roamed the local countryside on the hunt for gangster "revolutionaries" who, in fact, were little more than paid bullies and assassins.

On those occasions, I carried a weapon for a reason.

I've spent my life doing similar work in other Third World countries—Indonesia, Southeast Asia, Africa, Cuba. The study of marine biology has served me well in my travels, both as my primary vocation and as a believable cover. When a stranger inquires about local politics, residents are instantly suspicious, and for good reason. But when a stranger asks about the local fishery—where's a good place to catch sharks?—he is instantly dismissed as just one more harmless, misguided fisherman.

I've never really confided in Tomlinson, but he's perceptive, so knows more about my background than most. And he probably suspects that I'm still involved in that shadow world of hunter and hunted—which I am. But he doesn't know the truth and he never will.

No one ever will.

I was looking at Emily, thinking about the complications my sort of life brings to a relationship, as Tomlinson intruded again by saying with exaggerated patience, "I don't expect your full attention. You both have the same rosy glow, which tells me you've had yourselves a really fabulous first date, so congratulations. But have you heard even a single word I've said?"

Emily looked up from the folder, her expression empathetic. "I know you're worried about the girl. I don't even know her and I'm worried. But I'm going to follow Doc's lead on this. Something tells me he's got better instincts than most when it comes to these things."

She looked at me as she added, "Trust me, I understand what it's like to have a family member go missing."

Tomlinson gave her a curious, questioning look, as if trying to decipher the implications. Then he got back to business, saying, "Okay, I agree with Doc. If every cop in Florida is looking for Tula, what good can we possibly do? It's a valid point. But here's another fact that's valid: Cops aren't welcome in immigrant communities. How many times have we talked about this? Why not at least go to Immokalee and have a look around? An hour in a car together—a four-beer drive, depending on traffic, and traffic shouldn't be bad on a Wednesday night that far inland. Hell, it could be fun."

Emily was studying my face, her expression now asking me *What do you think?*

She had dressed, but looked less formal in her white slacks, copper blouse, because her jacket was still hanging in my bedroom closet. I hoped it would stay there for the rest of the night—along with the woman—if we could manage to get rid of Tomlinson.

The trouble was, Tomlinson was right. Guatemalans would probably talk to us, but they would vanish the moment police appeared. If Squires had indeed taken Tula to Immokalee, someone would have noticed a big *gringo* with an *Indio* child. Why he would risk doing something so stupid, I had no idea. But if he had, the locals might trust us with the truth, which we could then pass along to police.

I said to Tomlinson, "It's been a while since I've been to Immokalee, but I remember it being farther than an hour."

Tomlinson was sitting at my desk computer. He'd been doing a lot of typing and printing as I showed the lady around the lab, enjoying her reaction to rows of aquaria that contained sea anemones, snappers, filefish, sea horses, scallops with iridescent blue eyes and dozens of other brackish-water creatures that I had collected from the grass flats around Dinkin's Bay.

"Immokalee seems like a long way to you because your truck's so slow," Tomlinson replied, not looking up from the keyboard.

"Have you ridden with this guy yet?" he asked Emily. "Like an old lady, he drives—no offense to old ladies, don't get me wrong. I love women of all ages. But top speed in that old Chevy of his, it might be sixty. Not that he's ever pushed it that hard. I keep telling him to buy a new vehicle, but he's too cheap. In that truck of his, he's right. It would take us forever."

I asked Emily, "Have you ever been there?" meaning Immokalee.

I got the impression she had, but the lady shrugged, open to fresh information.

"It's inland, southeast of Sanibel—saw grass and cattle country. Tomatoes, citrus and peppers, too—all crops picked by hand. It's only forty-some miles, but you have to take back roads because it's off the tourist path. The town's not big, maybe twenty thousand people, and the population is mostly Hispanic."

I looked at Tomlinson, expecting him to correct me, as I added, "Back in the nineteen eighties, a Mexican crew chief brought in a truckload of Kanjobal Maya from Guatemala to work in Immokalee's tomato fields and another place, Indiantown, which is north. That began the connection. Now those two towns have become sort of the Mayan capitals of Florida. That's where all the Maya head when they're looking for family. Or if they get into trouble."

Tomlinson did correct me, saying, "It was nineteen eighty-two, I've got it right here on the screen. Now half the population of Indiantown is Mayan. This article doesn't say how many Guatemalans live in Immokalee, but the Latin population is almost eighty percent, which means there has to be ten or fifteen thousand *Indios* in Immokalee—which makes it bigger than most of the cities in Guatemala.

He continued, "I don't blame those people for not wanting to be documented. They're mostly political refugees, on the run from their government because they did something or said something to piss off the big shots in Guatemala City. Their government still uses firing squads, don't they, Doc?"

The man said it in an accusatory way as if I were somehow responsible.

"Up against the wall, asshole," he added, shaking his head, "which is typical of a bunch of right-wing Nazis."

Right wing, left wing, it made no difference in Central America . . . nor anywhere else, for that matter, because the power hungry all gravitate toward the same dangerous interstice on the political wheel.

Even so, I said nothing as Tomlinson continued paraphrasing from what he was reading on the computer.

"In the seventies, Guatemalan exiles tried building a little village just across the border in Mexico. But their own army had a bad habit of sneaking across and shooting the *Indígena* on sight. Finally, Guatemalan military wiped out the whole village.

"Florida was a whole ocean away, and the really desperate refugees decided this was a safer choice. Now about thirty thousand Maya live in south Florida, which historically makes for a very nice symmetry, when you think about it."

I saw that Emily had missed the connection, so I explained, "He's talking about the original inhabitants of Southwest Florida. It was a major civilization. They were contemporaries of the Maya, a people called the Calusa."

I suspected that the woman knew Florida history, but she listened intently as Tomlinson told her, "The Calusa and the Maya had too much in common for it to be accidental—in my opinion, anyway. The Calusa built shell pyramids and courtyards. They were led by ancestral kings, not chiefs—just like the Maya. They were here thousands of years before the Seminole."

He studied the woman long enough to confirm she was inter-ested before confiding, "Some nights, I anchor off one of the islands near here—Useppa Island—where the shell mounds look like small mountains. I smoke a doobie or two, and those pyramids come alive, man. People march around the mounds in wooden masks, carrying torches. Cooking fires burn, babies cry—real live vignettes. Teen-agers screwing in the bushes, old men taking dumps knee-deep in water—scenes like that. When the wind's just right, I can hear hard men talking war. It's a very heavy connection for me. The Calusa are still here, man, when moonlight chimes the right notes."

Emily was smiling, charmed by Tomlinson's childlike sincerity. No surprise there. I had seen that smile on the faces of hundreds of women, maybe thousands, in the last ten years.

My pal continued, "Archaeologists may call them by a different name, but the Calusa were Maya. They were oceangoing people who got around. It's sad but kinda funny now that the Mayan peo-ple are considered illegal immigrants even though they've been on this peninsula five thousand years longer than anyone else."

Tomlinson looked up from the computer screen, done with his monologue, and glanced at his watch, eager to get going, a familiar stoned smile on his face. It had been fifteen minutes since I had told Detective Leroy Melinski that I would not search for Harris Squires, but now we were planning to do just that.

But then something unexpected happened. I watched my pal focus on Emily, studying her face, and then the smile faded as he looked at something that had just appeared on the computer screen. Whatever it was troubled him.

After a moment, the man motioned toward me as he said to Emily, "You're serious about this guy, aren't you."

It was a statement, not a question.

Confused, then amused, Emily replied, "What a strange thing to say. I'm not in the habit of picking up strangers at alligator necropsies. Maybe the average girl does, but not me. I wouldn't be here if I wasn't interested."

Tomlinson's expression changed, a look that was all too familiar. I call it his Sorcerer's face. His eyelids drooped, his eyes appeared glazed by what he was seeing, the details he was absorbing, his attention focused laserlike on Emily Marston.

"What I'm saying is, you've been interested in Doc for a while. In your head . . . in your brain, there's a whole little room devoted to Dr. Marion Ford, isn't there? That *is* unusual."

Emily's smile hardened, a defensive posture, but she continued listening.

Tomlinson's eyes were almost closed now as he said, "You've done a lot of thinking about this guy. I can sense the vibes, it's becoming very clear. But it took you a while to find a way to meet him. A proper way to meet him, I mean. Someone told you about Doc a long time ago, maybe. Someone who was. . . . who was *important* to you."

He took a breath, his eyes open now as he asked, "Am I right?"

Emily turned to me. "Does he guess weights and birthdays, too?" She laughed the words, but her discomfort was visible.

I understood why. After we had made love for the second time, I had taken her out in my flats skiff, a twenty-one-foot boat. We had drifted from Woodring Point almost to the marina, lying on the deck, looking up the late-sunset sky. I'd learned a lot about the woman by the time we'd returned to my stilt house an hour later and made love yet again.

As I knew, Emily was uncomfortable because what Tomlinson had just said was all too close to the truth. She had heard about me a couple of years before from her own father, whom she adored.

Had Emily told me her maiden name, I would have made the connection much earlier.

The highly regarded amateur ornithologist who could afford to travel to Third World places had mentioned my name several times to his daughter—usually when she was dating some guy her father didn't deem worthy.

I could admit to Emily that I knew that man, but that was as far as I could go. She willingly shared her secret, I could not.

I became even more uncomfortable when she told me that her father had disappeared thirteen months ago. I had met the man only twice—under circumstances that are still classified—so I knew without doubt that bird-watching was to him what marine biology is to me. It was an effective cover story for the dangerous intelligence work he did.

From past experience, I also suspected that Emily's father was dead. If I ever disappear from Dinkin's Bay, the same will be true of me.

It was a strange situation to be in. In a way, I knew things about Emily's father that she would never know. She described him as "sweet, sensitive and generous."

I didn't doubt that was true, but I also knew the guy had to have a dark side or he would not have survived as long as he had in the business. I covered my discomfort with a silence that communicated an interest in the woman's past. My interest was genuine.

Now Tomlinson had pried into our private conversation with yet another of his uncanny guesses. What irritates me is that he always does it in a way that gives the impression he possesses supernatural powers, which, of course, he does not.

It took me a couple of years, but I finally figured out how he does what he does, although I may never understand how he does it so well. Tomlinson is extraordinarily perceptive. He has a genius for reading nuances of speech, body language and facial expressions. He then ties all those tiny bits of datum together to make plausible and often accurate projections.

It requires an intellect of the first magnitude, yet it is still a magician's trick.

I said, "Knock it off, Tomlinson. She has to work tomorrow. We can take my truck or your VW. Either way, we've got a long drive. If we're going, let's go."

Emily stood, neatening papers to return to my *Sharks of Lake Nicaragua* file. "We'll take my car," she said. "He's right, my Jaguar's fast. As in, scary fast. I'll call my office in the morning. I can take a personal day if we don't make it back tonight. Is there a hotel near this place we're going?"

I said, "Yes. Sort of," remembering a Bates Motel–looking place at the edge of town called Sawgrass Motor Court. I felt like I should offer her another chance to beg off but didn't want to risk it. Instead I said, "Immokalee's only an hour, maybe forty minutes, in a decent vehicle. Don't worry about it, we'll be back here before one-thirty in the morning. Probably earlier."

"Or we could stay at my cottage," she offered. "It's not Sanibel— but what is? You'll like it, though. It's an old Florida Cracker house"—she was looking around my lab—"sort of like this. All yellow pine. Wood so hard, you can still smell the turpentine sap when you drill. I have two bedrooms, and it's close to the Interstate—on the river, near Alva."

Tomlinson was standing at the printer now, waiting for something to finish. His eagerness to get on the road, all as his nervous energy, was suddenly gone.

He handed me several printouts. One was a map of Immokalee, churches and restaurants marked. Another was a Google Earth satellite photo. It took me a moment to realize it was the four hundred acres that Melinski had mentioned. According to tax records, it was owned by Harris Squires's mother.

I was using a magnifying glass on the satellite shot, seeing what might have been an RV hidden in the trees, as Tomlinson said, "Doc, can I talk to you for a minute? Alone."

I replied, "If it has something to do with Emily, go ahead and say it." Then I had to wonder why my normally talkative pal suddenly went very quiet.

It took several seconds before Tomlinson finally said to Emily, "I don't want to upset you, but I get premonitions sometimes. That's why I was asking you about Doc. I wanted to see if your karmas are connected."

Emily said, "Our karmas?" as if she didn't understand but was willing to listen.

"I'm a psychic sensitive," Tomlinson told her, pouring himself another shot of Patrón. "An empathetic, too. In fact—and this is something I don't share this with many people—I was employed by our own damn government as an expert on what they called remote viewing. I'd have never done it if I'd known who was paying me. Ask the good doctor if you don't believe me."

I nodded a confirmation. While still in college, Tomlinson had worked for the CIA during a time in history when the Soviets and the U.S. had recruited people who, after completing a very bizarre military test, were believed to have paranormal powers. The CIA called the project Operation Stargate. Stargate was fully funded by Congress until 1995, when wiser heads prevailed.

Tomlinson was looking at the woman, his voice soft, as he continued, "I just found something that gives me a very bad feeling about Emily making this trip. For Doc and me, it doesn't matter. We've lived and died a dozen times. But you . . . you're fresh, you're new. I've got a feeling something bad's going to happen tonight if you go to Immokalee. It's because of your karmic linkage with Doc and me."

"Are you stoned?" Emily asked him, serious.

"I was," he replied, giving it some thought. "*Cannabis interruptus*— the girl's disappearance has completely screwed up my schedule. On a lunar scale, I'd say I'm closer to the Sea of Crises than the Sea of Tranquillity. We can share a spliff if you want—but later. Right now, I'd like you to take a look at this."

Emily's expression asked me *Is he for real?* as she reached for a photo he was handing her, something he'd just printed from the Internet. I intercepted the thing and took a look. It was a pen-and-ink drawing from the time of the Spanish Inquisition. A Mayan pyramid in the background. In the foreground, a woman, tied to a ladder, was being tilted toward a roaring fire by Conquistadors.

I passed the drawing to Emily as I asked, "What does this have to do with her, for Christ's sake? You're getting her upset for no reason."

"Look at the face," Tomlinson replied, voice calm now but concerned. "I don't know why it caught my eye, but it did. There's a connection. I'm not sure what, but I don't think Emily should go with us."

"You think this woman looks like me?" Emily asked. "I'm flattered, I guess. We're both dressed in white, is that what you're saying? If it wasn't for the gown, she could be a nice-looking boy."

After a moment, she added, "Our cheekbones, I guess, are similar, and . . . she has a sort of plain face, like mine. But don't most women have plain faces? And the hair's completely different."

The image of the adolescent girl, Tula Choimha, came into my mind. I wondered why Tomlinson didn't make the association, it was so obvious. But why lend credence to a preposterous assertion by asking a pointless question?

Emily handed the drawing back to me as she said to Tomlinson, "It's sweet of you, but, come on, be serious. I don't believe in this sort of thing. If you don't want me tagging along, just say so. All of that pseudoscience nonsense—precognition, astrology, clairvoyance, numerology. Sorry, I've never been able to take that sort of thing seriously."

The woman put her hand on my shoulder. "Doc, talk some sense into him, would you?"

Tomlinson replied, "It's called tempting fate when we ignore our own instincts."

He turned to me. "I really don't think she should go, man. Something bad's going to happen. I can feel it. If you want, stay here with her, I'll go to Immokalee on my own. It has something to do with fire, I think."

He took the drawing from my hands, giving it serious thought. "That's what came into my mind when I saw this. Fire . . . and pain. Something terrible. Why risk it?"

I felt ridiculous, caught in the middle. Emily was waiting for me to agree with her—we were both scientists, after all. Tomlinson, my pal, was asking me to respect his instincts.

To me, it was more than that. Intellectually, I knew there could be no rational linkage between a random drawing and what might or might not happen to Emily on this very real Wednesday night in March.

Logically, it was absurd. Emotionally, though, I couldn't let go of the fact—and it is a fact—that Tomlinson's intuition, although often wrong, is also more than occasionally right.

As I took the drawing from Tomlinson's hands, saying, "Let me see that again," Emily gave me an incredulous look that said *You can't be serious?*

I looked at the thing, paying no attention to the details because I was carrying on an argument in my head. Debating Tomlinson in the comfort of the lab, or sitting over beers aboard his sailboat, is one thing. But human certitude is an indulgence that can be enjoyed only in a cozy and safe environment.

It irritated me to have to admit it to myself, but, wrong or right, Tomlinson had asked a reasonable question: *Why risk it?*

As I placed the drawing on the dissecting table, Emily said to Tomlinson, "We're not being fair to Doc. I can almost see his mind working. Choose between his best friend or agree with a woman he's just met? That's not something he'd do to us, so I'll make it simple. I withdraw. I'll see you guys tomorrow evening for drinks, if you want. You can fill me in."

I thought I noted some mild sarcasm until the woman slipped her hand beneath my arm and gave a squeeze. I thanked her by placing a hand on her hip and pulling her closer. Truth was, she had a point. Would I back a lady I'd just met? Or remain loyal to an old friend?

I backed Tomlinson, of course. Sort of.

"Here's what I think," I said, looking at Tomlinson. "Three *gringos* driving an expensive car will attract too much attention in Immokalee. In a place that small? Especially at this hour. My Spanish is better than yours, and I speak a little *Quiché*. Emily's not dressed for barhopping. And frankly, Tomlinson, you wouldn't be an asset, either. There are some cowboy types down there in Immokalee who aren't real fond of hippies."

I felt a perverse jolt of pleasure at the surprise on the man's face. I interrupted as he tried to protest, telling him, "You say Emily is in danger tonight? It's not rational, but I'm not going to argue. Which means she should stay here. Either that or you should follow her home just to make sure she gets back safely. I'm going to Immokalee by myself."

Tomlinson appeared nonplussed, his expression asking me *Is this some sort of test?*

In reply, I smiled and said, "If I can't trust my best friend to look after a lady in danger, then who can I trust?" To emphasize my point, I stood and squeezed his scarecrow shoulder almost hard enough to make him wince.

"But I have to go!" he said. "I'm worried sick about that little girl."

"Then drive your VW back to Red Citrus and have another look around," I told him. "Splitting up makes more sense, anyway. We can stay in touch by cell phone. But *after* Emily is safely home. If I hear something, I'll call. You do the same."

Giving me a look of approval, Emily said to Tomlinson, "Sounds like your pal has made up his mind. Any objections to me coming here tomorrow after work? This is an interesting little marina you have. I bet you two have some stories."

I said, "I'm counting on it," as Tomlinson took a square of paper from his breast pocket, unfolded it to reveal a pencil-thin joint.

He said, "You've gotta love this guy, don't you? The freaking earth could be wobbling off its axis, anarchy loosed upon the world. But good ol' Doc will still be trying to do the right thing, in the most rational possible way, wanting the best for all concerned."

He held the joint so Emily could see it. "In the meantime, us *human* humans have time for a couple of hits. Care to join me outside for the pause that refreshes?"

I was a little surprised that Emily nodded her head. Tomlinson was baiting me, that was apparent, so I ignored them both.

As I went out the screen door, down the steps toward my shark pen, I was already busy deciding what equipment to take just in case I got lucky and got a lead on the missing girl. The odds were slim, but that was okay. The fact was, it would be a relief to be on the road alone. No more talking, no more debates.

That feeling stayed with me, even after I had kissed Emily good-bye and I was bouncing down Tarpon Bay Road in my old pickup truck, a canvas backpack sitting square and heavy beside me, traffic sparse.

In the bag was a Sig Sauer 9mm semiauto pistol, plus the pocket-sized Kahr that is fast becoming my favorite handgun. There was an odd assortment of other gear that I usually carry only when outside the country: gloves, a black watch cap, a handheld GPS, a Randall attack/survival knife and a MUM night vision monocular mounted on a headband.

Just for the hell of it, I had also included the tactical laser light, the Dazer. I hadn't done enough testing to have confidence it would work on feeding sharks. But the company that made the thing, Laser Energetics, had invested years, and a lot of money, to prove that a small, blinding laser beam could disable a human attacker.

Had Emily been along and gotten a peek into that bag, she might have been shocked.

Or would she?

It was something to think about as I drove across the causeway bridge, the Sanibel Lighthouse strobing to my right, a black fusion of water and stars to my left.

Maybe not, I decided, judging from who her father was . . . or had once been. The man couldn't have confided even in his daughter, but it was possible that Emily had been inquisitive as a girl and had done some snooping.

As I passed beneath the tollbooth onto a fast four-lane, I checked my watch. It was 10:05 p.m. on this Wednesday night. Tula had been under the steroid freak's control for at least twelve hours.

It was an unsettling fact.

Unless somehow related, grown men kidnap young girls for only one reason. Once their sexual fantasy is satiated, they usually panic and choose murder as a way to obliterate their lesser crime. The only variable is how many hours before the kidnapper has had enough?

One thing was certain: In twelve hours, the girl had already been victimized.

But was she still alive?

TWELVE

JUST BEYOND A SIGN THAT READ IMMOKALEE 22 MILES, HARRIS
Squires locked the gate to his hunting camp behind him, then
banged the truck into four-wheel drive, telling himself, *Shoot the girl
in the back of the head. Stop thinking. Get it over with.*

After what he'd just heard on the radio, about cops finding human
bones in the dead alligator's belly, he had no choice but to do it.

And he would.

It was almost noon on Wednesday. The craziness of the previous
night—the alligator, the flashing police lights—seemed like a month
ago, which might have had something to do with the pint of Cuervo
Gold Squires had killed on the ride. Mixed with Red Bull and a
Snickers bar, he should have had a good buzz going. But instead his
brain felt raw and skittish.

Beneath his seat, in the hidden compartment, Squires had the .357
Ruger Blackhawk revolver in a canvas bag that was also packed full
of cash money.

The gun was the long-barreled model, chrome with black grips. The cartridges were as thick as his pinkie finger. They were hollow points that would blow the back side out of a watermelon after neatly piercing its rind.

An unsettling image of the girl's head came into Squires's mind of how her face would look after the bullet exited. Skin without a shell and lots of blood. But this wasn't pretend, there was no going back. Fifi may have missed her chance to kill him, but that fat toad had found a way to totally screw up his life.

Squires had felt dizzy as the radio announcer's voice drilled the details through his skull. Then he'd felt physically sick, a nauseating panic deep in his chest that made him want to jump out of the truck and run screaming into the cypress shadows that lay ahead.

The bones had to belong to the *chula* Frankie had killed. The one he had bundled into a garbage bag, weighting the body with wire and cement before dragging it to the lake. Squires kept telling himself that, even though he knew there was a chance that the gator had eaten a different dead girl months earlier. The Mexican girl from his sex dream—if the sex dream was real. Which could prove to cops that he was the murderer, not Frankie.

If it had really happened.

It was a dream, Squires told himself now, because that's what he wanted to believe. *I didn't do anything wrong. Or I would remember dragging a body to Fifi's pen. The Mexican girl probably ran off while I was asleep.*

That made Squires feel a little better. That goddamn Frankie was entirely to blame for this mess. Her with her love for kinky sex, the way she got off on using and abusing Mexican girls. It was some kind of sick power trip . . . or maybe Frankie's way of punishing younger, prettier women for the saggy way her own body was aging.

Squires realized that he had never allowed himself to acknowledge just how dangerous the woman was. If he did, then he'd have to admit to himself that the dead *chula* he had sunk at Red Citrus probably wasn't the first girl Frankie had killed. There might be at least two others, maybe more.

It was just a guess, Squires couldn't prove it because, until they had trucked Fifi out of the hunting camp, Frankie had handled all her personal *chula* problems on her own.

Frankie might be getting up there in years, but that woman was still big and strong as hell. She could have stuck a dead *chula* under each arm and carried the bodies down to Fifi's pen, no problem.

That's why Harris Squires had stayed out of the woman's way and didn't ask questions. In his mind, if he ignored the shit Frankie did, it was like it never happened. Plus, on the rare night when a girl disappeared, he was always so screwed up on tequila, grass and crank that it all seemed blurry and unreal, anyway. Sort of like his sex fantasy dream . . .

Until now. Everything in Squires's life had changed as of last night, and this morning. Now he'd probably go to jail—even the electric chair—because of all the sick and nasty shit Frankie had done.

Tula had been listening to the radio, too, and paid close attention to how the giant man beside her reacted. She saw Squires's face mottle, then go pale. It was a rancid color, like the faces of sunbaked corpses she had seen on village streets as a child. That caused her to think of her father, the way he had been murdered, and Tula had placed her hand on the giant's hand, her first instinct a desire to comfort Squires rather than abandon him to the misery of his own fear.

Tula had felt real fear before. Not the common everyday sort that everyone feels but the variety of fear that sweeps people over the abyss, then sucks them downward. It was while sitting in a tree near the convent, reliving her father's death, that she had experienced a wave of panic so dark that Tula felt as if her heart might explode. Immersed in the memory of what she had witnessed, of what she had lost, it was then, her brain numb with fear, that Tula heard the Maiden's voice for the first time.

That moment had changed everything.

No matter what happened to Tula in the future, the girl felt a serene confidence that fear of that magnitude could never overwhelm her again. The scars from that night were like armor. Thanks to the Maiden, Tula believed she was now immune.

"You should breathe into your belly," she had told Squires as he switched off the radio. "It sometimes helps."

After studying the man's face for a moment, she had added, "God is with you if you need Him. Ask and He'll come into your heart. The goodness that was in you as a child is still alive inside you. Just ask God and He'll help you."

When the girl touched him, Squires had yanked his hand away, drawing it back to slap Tula, but something stopped him.

"Just shut your damn mouth—" he said, biting off the sentence. "Don't you say another word to me. Understand? Not another damn word or you'll be sorry!"

Squires found the girl's calm demeanor infuriating, and he almost did slap her when she replied, "There is no sin so terrible that God won't forgive you. Two nights ago, when I watched you at the lake, I knew what was in the bag that you put into the water. I knew it was the body of a dead person. But, even so, I prayed for you."

Squires could barely speak, he was so incredulous, but managed to ask, "You *admit* that you saw me?"

"Of course," Tula replied, and then repeated a familiar phrase: "I would rather die than to do something I know to be a sin. I will never lie to you. It's an oath I have made to . . . to someone important. On the radio, the man said the bones they found were probably from a woman's hand. Because of the ring she wore. Why would you murder a young woman?"

Squires couldn't believe what he was hearing. She would rather die than tell a lie? Jesus Christ, the girl was *begging* for it.

"I didn't kill her!" Squires yelled, leaning toward Tula. "You hear me? I didn't goddamn kill her! All I did was get rid of the body! So why did you have to be there, snooping around?"

Tula said to him calmly, "Why do you use such terrible words—taking God's name in vain? That's a sin. I won't listen to you anymore if you use profanity."

Squires pushed his face toward the girl, his eyes glassy as he bellowed, "Kiss my goddamn ass! Do you realize what this means, you idiot? Why'd you have to be there watching? Now I got no goddamn choice! Do you even understand what I'm telling you?"

As Tula began to answer, the man drew his hand back again to slap her and roared, "I'm warning you for the last time! Shut your mouth!"

Tula could see that Squires was crazy with anger, and she sensed that he was on the brink of an emotional explosion. The man appeared near tears.

When she tried to comfort Squires, though, by patting his knee, it only caused him to moan in frustration, then swear at her, using a word Tula had never heard before but she assumed was profane.

By then, they were at the gate.

Now Squires was wrestling the truck over a rutted trail that tracked for a half mile through pine flats, cypress and myrtle to where an RV and his steroid cookshack were anchored with hurricane stakes, the building hidden beneath trees near a cypress pond that looked cool and inviting to Tula.

Focusing on the cypress trees helped keep Tula from weeping—

that's how badly she felt for the man. She was also beginning to feel frightened for herself. During the hours since they had left the trailer park, the Maiden had not come into Tula's head to speak with her or to calm her.

Tula knew that the Maiden would not abandon her. There was no possibility of that. But where was the Girl of Lorraine now when Tula sensed so much danger?

I must find a tree, Tula thought. *If I can sit peacefully in a tree and breathe into my belly, the Maiden will return and tell me what I should do.*

Tula could think of only one reason why the Maiden would order her to travel with this giant, angry man who might also be a murderer. It was the Maiden's way of providing Tula with a vehicle and a driver to go in search of her mother. Tula had became convinced of this when she saw the sign that read IMMOKALEE 22 MILES. But how could she make Squires understand that the Maiden wanted him to help with the search?

Yes, Tula needed guidance. It seemed unlikely that the man would react kindly if she asked to be left alone in a tree. Not until he calmed down a little—then, perhaps, Tula could reason with him, and possibly even win him over as a friend.

So instead of asking to be allowed to walk into the cypress grove, Tula said, "Why have we come here? You should eat some food, it's no wonder your body is trembling. We haven't eaten all morning. And I have to use the bathroom."

Squires had pulled into the shade of a tree near a medium-sized trailer, white with green trim, its paint fading. Unlike the trailers at Red Citrus, this trailer was also a motor vehicle, with tires jacked off the ground on blocks and a windshield covered with shiny aluminum material. There were also a couple of wooden structures that looked homemade, one of them with locked shutters and a heavy door.

Squires switched off the engine and said to Tula, "Get out of the truck and shut up. I don't want to hear nothing else out of you. Just do what I tell you to do. We're going for a walk."

There was something strange about the man's voice now. It was a flat monotone, all of the emotion gone out of it. Tula could smell the alcohol on his breath, but his eyes looked dead, not drunken.

"Walk where?" she asked, trying to be conversational. "It's very pretty here. There are trees down by the water that look good for climbing. And lots of birds—egrets with white feathers, I think. Do you see them up there?"

The man's face colored, but he got himself under control before saying, "I'm going to tell you one more time and I want you to listen. No more talking. You've got nothing to say that I want to hear, so shut up and follow me. That's exactly where we're going, to look at all the pretty birds."

"But I need a bathroom," Tula insisted as she watched Squires lift the driver's seat and then open what appeared to be a hatch in the floor. He removed a canvas bag that was heavy, judging from the way he handled it.

Squires turned and began walking toward the cypress pond where Tula could see white birds suspended like flowers among the gray limbs, some on nests in the high branches.

"Get moving," he said without looking at the girl. "And I'm warning you—I don't want to hear another goddamn word out of you."

Tula got out of the truck and realized that her legs were shaking. Staying calm when the man was angry had not been easy, but this different voice, so flat and dead, was scaring her. She walked around the back of the truck, wondering if she should risk telling the man that her bladder was so full that she feared wetting herself. But Tula stopped after only a few words when her voice broke, afraid that she would start crying.

The Maiden had never cried, even when tortured by her tormentors. Even as flames had consumed her, the brave saint had not wept, but, instead, had called out the name of her Savior.

"Jesus," Tula whispered now, her right hand clutching her amulets, as she followed Squires toward the trees. "Please protect and keep me, Jesus," she said in Mayan, and continued repeating the phrase as they walked along the edge of a pond that was cooled by cypress shadows and moss. The giant kept walking, far into the tree shadows, so far that Tula's abdomen began to cramp because of the pressure in her bladder.

Finally, Squires stopped beside a tree at the edge of the pond, where water black as oil was flecked with leaves, white-feather down and long-legged insects that skated on the surface beneath cooing birds. For a time, the man stood with his back to her, and Tula realized that he was taking something from the canvas bag.

"Turn around and look at the water," Squires said to her in the same flat dead voice. "Do it now."

"Can I please go to the bathroom first?" Tula asked the man, frightened but also angry at herself because tears had begun streaming down her face.

Squires was looking over his shoulder at her. "No. Just do what I tell you to do. This won't take long. Turn your back to me and look at the water. Hurry up."

Tula could see that Squires had something in his hand. She got a look at it when she pivoted toward the pond.

It was a large gun, silver with chrome.

Tula had seen many guns during the fighting in the mountains, but she had never seen a gun so shiny before. The metal was hypnotic, it was so bright, which scared her.

Tula's chest shuddered, and she couldn't help herself. Urine dribbled down her leg as she began crying, but silently, keeping her weakness to herself as she sensed the giant walk up behind her, the gun in his hand that was soon a silver reflection on the black water, the man on the surface huge, the size of a tree.

"Get down on your knees, child," said a voice in Tula's head, and Tula obeyed instantly, overwhelmed with relief, because it wasn't a man's voice. It was the Maiden. The Maiden had returned to her in her moment of need, and Tula knew everything would be okay now.

Get down on your knees, the Maiden counseled, *and pray.*

Behind Tula, as she whispered a prayer, the giant stood in silence. A minute passed. Then two minutes, then three.

In the water's reflection, Tula could see that Squires was pointing the pistol only inches from the back of her head. Occasionally, he would lower it, but then he would raise the pistol again. But Tula was no longer frightened.

Once again, she felt a serene immunity from fear. The amulets she clutched in her hand provided strength. What happened would happen. She was with God and she was content. The Maiden would not allow her to suffer pain, and, ultimately, Tula would be re-united with her mother, her father and family again, which was something the girl wanted more than anything she had ever wanted in her life.

Be at peace, child. I am with you always, the Maiden said, speaking as softly as the muted light inside the girl's head.

For another minute, Tula waited, her head bowed. She felt so confident and content that she decided to help the man along by saying, "If this is what you must do, then I forgive you. If it is God's will, then you are doing the right thing. Don't be afraid."

Tula waited for so long in silence that she had resumed praying before the man spoke to her, "It's what I have to do. I don't have a damn choice, and it's your own fault. You'll tell the police what you saw and they'll arrest me. Even though I didn't kill that girl, they'll charge me with murder. Do you understand?"

His voice wasn't so empty of emotion now. It gave the girl hope, but she was inexplicably disappointed, too. She had felt so peaceful and free kneeling there, waiting for it to end.

Tula considered turning to look at the man but decided against it. Looking into the barrel of the silver gun might bring her fear back, and she didn't want that to happen. She didn't want to risk crying or losing control of her bladder again.

"I understand," she said to Squires. "I'm sorry I saw what I saw. I didn't mean to be in the tree watching you, but I was."

Tula glanced at the water's mirror surface and saw that Squires was leaning toward her now. Then she felt the barrel of the gun bump the back of her head as the man said, "You told me yourself you don't lie. Even if you promised me you wouldn't tell the cops, I wouldn't believe you. Do you understand now why I have to do this? Unless you promise me—I mean, *really* promise me—and mean it."

The man's voice was shaking, and Tula knew he was going to pull the trigger. She closed her eyes, pressing her chin to her fingers, as she replied, "I can't promise you, I'm sorry. If the police ask me, I will have to tell them the truth. I won't lie to you and I won't lie to them. It's because of another promise I have made."

In Tula's ear, she heard a metallic *Click-Click* and she knew that the man had pulled back the revolver's hammer. On her cheeks, she felt tears streaming, but she wasn't afraid. She was ready for what happened next.

What happened next was, in the high cypress limbs above them, there was a squawking, cracking sound. Then the fluttering of wings as a bird tumbled from the tree canopy and thudded hard on the ground nearby. Tula looked up, surprised. Then she was on her feet and running toward it without even thinking, tucking the jade amulet and silver medallion into her T-shirt as she sprinted.

"It's a baby egret!" she cried, kneeling over a thrashing bird that looked naked because its feathers hadn't come in yet. "I think it broke its wing."

Carefully, the girl cupped the fledgling in her hands, using her thumb to try to steady the bird's weak neck. And she stood, saying over her shoulder to Squires, "That must be her mother up there. See her?"

Tula motioned to a snowy egret that was hovering overhead, its yellow feet extended as if to land, excited by the peeping noises the baby bird was making.

"Yes," Tula said, "its wing is broken. At the convent, we took care of many sick animals. We can help this bird, I think." Then she looked at Squires, adding, "I can't stand it anymore. I have to go to the bathroom now."

Then she stopped because of what she saw.

Harris Squires was sitting on the ground. He was rocking and crying, his hands locked around his knees, making a soft moaning sound in his misery. If the gun was somewhere on the ground nearby, Tula didn't see it.

The scene was even stranger to Tula because, the way the man was sitting, slope-shouldered and huge, reminded her of a bear she had seen begging for peanuts at the zoo in Guatemala City.

The bear had struck the girl as being very sad, an animal as repulsed with itself as it was humiliated by its captivity. The scene was even stronger in Tula's mind because her father had taken her to the zoo the day before he was murdered.

Slowly, the girl walked toward Squires. She was embarrassed for him and sad in the same way that she had felt sad for the bear. She placed the little bird a safe distance away, in case the big man moved, and then hesitated before touching her fingers to Squires's shoulder.

Tula patted the man gently as she might have patted the bear, given a chance. And then said to him kindly, "I must go behind a tree and use the bathroom. I can't stand it anymore. *Please*. But promise me something. It's important. Promise me you won't look. I know that you have seen me without clothes. But I don't want a man ever to see me that way again. Do you promise?"

Rocking and sobbing, the giant nodded his head.

Tula said to Squires, "My mother had a little doll like this. She wore it pinned to her blouse. Even the same color, bright orange and green, instead of blue like most of them. They're called worry dolls in English. At night, you tell your worries to the doll and put it under your pillow. The next morning, all your worries are gone."

The girl sniffed the doll, knowing it couldn't be her mother's—not way out here, so far from where a woman could get work cleaning houses or mopping floors in a restaurant—but, then, Tula had to wonder, because the odor of raw cotton was so familiar.

Maybe it seemed familiar because everything else inside this man's trailer was so foreign.

Squires had started the generator, and they were inside the RV that smelled sour and stale like the ashes of a cold cooking fire. Tula had found the doll, only an inch tall, mounted on a brooch pin in a strange room where there was a camera, lights on tripods and a bed with a strange black leather contraption hanging from the ceiling.

The doll was on a table piled with photos of naked women. The women were frozen in poses so obscene that Tula had looked away, preferring to focus on the miniature Guatemalan doll in traditional Mayan dress.

The photos were of Mexican women, judging from their features, but a few Guatemalan women, too. Tula didn't linger over details and closed the door to the room behind her, feeling as if the ugliness of that space might follow her.

Squires was sitting in a recliner, looking dazed, eyes staring straight ahead as he drank from a pint bottle of tequila. He had found the revolver, which was now lying in his lap, and Tula sensed that he was rethinking what had happened out there in the cypress grove. She had witnessed his breakdown and he would begin hating her for it soon, the girl feared, if she didn't get his mind on something else.

After pinning the worry doll to her T-shirt, Tula went to the kitchen, where she found cans of beans and salsa and meat but no tortillas. There was a can opener, too, and plates, and a cheap little paring knife with a bent blade, but sharp.

"You need food, that's why you feel so tired. I'll cook something," Tula said to Squires as she carried a pan to the stove. A moment later, she said, "We have a gas stove at the convent, but I can't get this one to light. Unless I'm doing it wrong."

Squires blinked his eyes, seeming to hear her for the first time. It took a while, but he finally said, "You're a nun?"

"Someday, when I'm older," Tula replied. "I am going to dedicate my life to God and to helping people. My patron saint is Joan of Arc. Have you heard of her?"

After a few beats of silence, Tula added, "I am modeling my life after the Maiden. That's what the people of France called her, the Maiden. But to her friends, she was called Jehanne."

"The gas isn't on," Squires said to the girl but didn't get up from the chair. His indifference suggested he didn't care about food. But he did appear interested in the convent Tula had mentioned because, after several seconds of silence, he said, "You live with nuns?

No men around at all, huh? That's got to be weird. Not even to fix shit?"

"The convent is where I live and go to school. I work in the kitchen, and the garden, too. That's how I learned to speak English and to cook using a stove."

Tula had been twisting the dials for the burners without success. Now she was searching the walls, looking under the stove, hoping the man would take the hint and make the gas work. He needed food, not tequila, and Tula wondered—not for the first time—why so many men preferred to be drunk and stupid rather than to eat hot food.

The giant took a sip from the bottle and told her, "I was raised Catholic. I used to be, anyway. But then all that stuff about priests cornholing little boys—and the goddamn Pope knew about it 'cause he was probably screwing boys himself before he got old. Little boys are in big demand in the Catholic religion. That's probably the problem with you. You've been brainwashed by all that sick Catholic bullshit. Why else would you pretend to be a boy?"

Tula wondered if Squires was trying to upset her, give himself a reason to get angry again and shoot her. So she changed the subject by saying, "I've been thinking of a way to solve your problem. I don't want you to go to jail. There's another way, I think, to keep the police from arresting you."

That surprised the man, Tula could see it, so she added, "I believe you when you say you're not a murderer. Just looking into your face, you couldn't do something like that—not by yourself, you couldn't. I don't want to tell the police what I saw. That's why I've been thinking about this problem."

"My guardian angel," Squires said in his flat voice, not bothering to attempt sarcasm. "I forgot. You were sent by God in case I get into trouble. Lucky me."

He took another drink, and Tula could feel the anger building in the man.

Getting irritated herself, the girl turned away from the counter where she had the salsa open and had used the sharp paring knife to cut the meat into slices. "Listen to me!" she said, frowning at the giant. "I want to find my mother and brother. That's all I care about. I want to go home to the mountains. If I'm home in the mountains, your policemen can't ask me questions. That's why I've been thinking of a way to help you."

That made Squires snort, a sound close to laughter. "What do you want me to do, buy you a plane ticket?" he asked. "Drive you to the airport and wave good-bye? That easy, huh? I don't think so, *chula*."

Tula felt the Maiden flow into her head, giving instructions, which is why she calmed herself before crossing the room, where she placed her hand on the giant's curly blond head. "You may not believe it, but it's true," she said. "I wouldn't be here unless God wanted me to help you. He loves you. He wants you to come back to Him. You can believe me or not believe me, but you can't deny the goodness that's in your heart."

The girl didn't say it, but her recent words came into Harris Squires's mind. *Do you remember the goodness that was in you as a child?*

The girl patted the man's head as he stared down into the tequila bottle. Tula could feel Squires's brain fighting her, but she continued, "The Maiden has told me how to help you. We must go to Immokalee and ask the people there about my mother and my brother. I have two aunts and an uncle somewhere, too. When we find them, I want you to come home with us to the mountains. In your truck, you can drive us."

Tula looked around the room, seeing the stained walls, the carpet, a peanut can filled with cigarette butts, sensing in the next room the obscene photos staring up at the ceiling tiles.

She said, "This place has sin and ugliness all around. It's no wonder you're unhappy. You should leave this dirty life behind while
you still can. You would like the mountains. We live closer to God
in the mountains. It is cool there, even in summer, and the rains will
begin soon. You can stay a week or a month. Maybe you will like
it and want to build a home. The police won't find you if we leave
Florida. They can't ask me questions."

"Drive you clear to Mexico?" Squires said like it was a stupid
idea. But at least he was thinking about it. Tula could see that his
mind was working it through.

"Guatemala, not Mexico," Tula corrected him. "It's much more
beautiful than Mexico. And the villages aren't so dirty. Most of
them, anyway."

Yes, Squires was giving the idea some consideration because he
asked, "Where's Guatemala? Is it farther than Mexico? Mexico's a
hell of a long way."

"I'm not sure of the exact distance," Tula said, coming as close to
lying as she could allow herself.

"But it's farther than Mexico, that's what you're telling me."

Tula replied, "What does distance matter when there are roads
and you own a truck? You can drive the whole way. Or take a train,
once we're across the border. I hear the coaches are nice. I've never
been inside a train, but I rode on the top of boxcars from Chiapas
to San Luis Potosí. Three different train lines, I had to board."

"You're shitting me. You climbed up and rode on the top of a
train when it was moving? Christ, what do those things do, fifty,
sixty miles an hour?"

Tula replied, "One night, an old man told me we were traveling
almost three hundred miles an hour, but I think he was drunk. It's
the way even adults travel if they want to come north. Sometimes,

riding on top of the train was nice. We could pick green mangoes if the trees were close enough, and it only rained once.

"In Chiapas, though, it was dangerous. There are a lot of Mexican gangs there that wear bandannas and tattoos. At three stops, they robbed some of the men. And I think they attacked two girls who were on one of the cars behind me."

Tula started to add that she hadn't seen it happen, but she had heard the girls screaming. Her voice caught, and she couldn't continue with the story.

Mentioning gangs and tattoos reminded Squires that the police weren't the only ones looking for him. Laziro Victorino would be cruising Red Citrus the moment he heard about the alligator with a dead girl's bones in its belly. Victorino was a little guy, but he was all muscle and attitude, a scary little shit who enjoyed killing people. Cutting them up with that box cutter of his or shooting them behind the ear and feeding them to his dogs.

Squires had heard the stories and he had seen a couple of the V-man's snuff films. The teardrop tattoo beneath the dude's eye was so weird it was scary.

What Squires hoped was that Victorino would run into Frankie, who might well kick the shit out of that vicious little wetback. Or vice versa. Either way, it was okay with Squires. He hoped he never saw either one of them again in his life. He was sick of the whole goddamn business.

A question formed in Squires's head as he reviewed his predicament: Why the hell did he have to stay in Florida?

The answer was simple: He couldn't think of a single goddamn reason.

Not the way things were now. Almost everyone he knew was an asshole or a drug dealer or a crackhead killer like the V-man. The girl, Tula, was a weirdo Jesus freak, but she had hit the nail on the head when it came to the life he was living. It was a dirty life. It made him feel dirty—Squires could admit that to himself now that he was on the run from a murder rap. So why not make a change before it was too late? Maybe going to Mexico wasn't such a bad idea.

He said to the girl, "I drove to New Orleans once and it took me twelve hours. How much farther is the border? I think you have to drive clear across Texas, too."

Squires placed the tequila bottle, then the revolver, on a magazine stand, and sat up a little as he tried to picture the geography of the southern United States. In his mind, everything south of Texas was just a hazy design, with curves and bulges bordered on both sides by oceans.

"First," Tula reminded him, "we must go to Immokalee and ask about my mother. I'm not going home without my family. People call her Mary. Mary Choimha. Or Maria sometimes, too. She lived at your trailer park for a while, that's why I went there first."

"Every *chula* in Florida is named Mary or Maria," Squires said. "I can't keep track of everyone who rents at my place. You Mexicans are always coming and going."

Tula said, "Then you lied to me. You said you had met her, that you could take me to her. You told me that at the trailer park last night."

Squires shrugged. "So what? We're not all perfect like you."

"You would remember my mother," the girl insisted. "She's very beautiful—much prettier than me. Carlson said, last year, he saw your wife talking to my mother. That she gave my mother a cell phone . . . or maybe you gave it to her, Carlson wasn't sure. But the phone stopped working two months ago, which is why I came here. My mother would have called me if her phone was working."

Squires told the girl, "I don't have a wife, especially not the bitch you mean," as he leaned back to think about what he'd just heard.

The information was disturbing. All kids thought their mothers were pretty—Squires all too aware that he was a rare exception, because his mother was a chain-smoking witch. But why would Frankie give Tula's mother a cell phone unless Frankie had something to gain?

Squires had given dozens of cheap phones to Mexicans, the cell phones that charged a flat fee with a limited number of minutes. Usually, he gave them to men who were good workers—and it was always for selfish reasons: It was a way of controlling the guy, make him indebted, and a little scared, too, that the phone would be taken away or the service canceled.

Christ, Frankie had run so many Mexican girls through the hunting camp and their double-wide at Red Citrus, he would have needed a calculator to keep track.

Was it possible that this kid's mother was one of the *chulas* Frankie had used? Squires considered the girl's age, which would put the mother in her mid- to late twenties, Mexican girls being prone to marrying young.

The possibility was too upsetting, though, and Squires decided that it wasn't something he wanted to think about. He stared at the girl intensely for a moment, then looked away, suddenly aware there was something eerily familiar about the girl's eyes and high cheekbones.

"Why would you listen to that crazy old drunk, Carlson?" Squires said to the girl. "I don't want to hear any more about your mother. Understand?"

Aware of the man's sudden mood change, Tula said, "Let me fix you some food while we talk. You need to eat for strength if we're going to drive to Immokalee."

The man laced his fingers together—Tula had never seen hands so huge—and sat up in the recliner. He was trying to remember how many Marys and Marias he or Frankie had screwed or used one way or another. But then felt a withering guilt descending, so he stopped himself. Instead, he let his mind shift back to the girl's idea about leaving Florida.

Squires had thought of traveling to Mexico many times. Most of the big steroid manufactures were there because it was legal to make and sell gear. Hell, the place was bodybuilder heaven. In fact, Squires's first supplier, before he got into the business, was an Internet place called mexgear.com. Mexgear's shit was good to go, and they had good prices. Squires had bought Test C, Tren, EQ and Masteron from the online Mexicans there for less than fifty bucks a vial, and they'd always thrown in some extra gear if it was a big order.

The fact was, he didn't need Frankie to continue his steroid operation. He could set up an underground lab just about anywhere, plus he spoke English, unlike the Mexgear guys, which always made it a pain in the ass to deal with them.

Speaking English was definitely to his advantage, Squires decided, even in Mexico. Most bodybuilders were Americans or lived in Europe, so it would be a smart way to expand and maybe make a lot of money. He couldn't wait forever for his rich mother to die.

"Go to Mexico for a few months," Squires said aloud, testing the idea on his ears.

He looked toward the little kitchen as if he'd just awakened from a doze. "I don't need any food. Not now. But I could us a little pick-me-up. Come with me—I'm not taking my eye off you for a second. If you want to cook, that's up to you. Here, I'll show you how to turn on the gas."

Tula watched the giant get down on his knees and open a cabinet beneath the sink. He told her, "There's a red knob under here and an emergency-cutoff switch. But first check and make sure you turned the burners off or one spark and this whole place could go up."

Squires stood, the trailer creaking beneath his weight, and Tula followed him out the door, past the peeping baby egret that she had placed in a box after feeding it water and a few drops of condensed milk with an eyedropper. Squires had refused to help her catch and mash up minnows from the pond, which is what Tula believed that baby egrets ate, but maybe later he would.

Or maybe the mother egret, which was still flying around, occasionally landing near the box, would figure it out and bring the fledgling some food.

A few seconds later, Squires removed two padlocks from the homemade-looking wooden building. He lifted a steel bar, and soon Tula was inside a dark space that smelled of chemicals and propane.

When her eyes adjusted, she saw a row of gas burners on a counter that were connected by hoses to tanks beneath. It explained the propane smell, just as shelves filled with bottles and stacks of paper filters explained the odor of chemicals.

"What do you make here?" the girl asked Squires.

"You ask too many questions. Forget you ever saw this place, that's my advice to you," the man replied as he touched a switch, neon lights flickering overhead. That done, Squires took a pack of syringes from a drawer, then opened two small boxes that contained rows of unmarked vials.

Out here, the propane burners had steel manual lighters, like lanterns the girl had used. She stood against the wall, out of the way, as the man put a pot of water on, flame low.

"I always heat my vitamins first. It's cleaner, plus it shoots smoother," he told the girl as he loaded a syringe with oily-looking liquid from three different vials, then dropped the syringe into the water.

"I got a shot once," Tula said, pleased they were having a conversation. "A doctor came to our village. He was British, I think, but still a nice man. The needle was a vaccine for mosquito bites, he said, not vitamins."

"Vitamins keep me strong and healthy," Squires replied in a tone that told Tula he was lying about something, she wasn't sure what.

Fascinated by what she was seeing, Tula watched as the man stripped off his shirt, then rubbed what smelled like alcohol on his left shoulder. Never in her life had she seen such huge muscles. Squires really was a giant. He looked as if he had been carved from stone, gray stone, the sort her ancestors had used to build pyramids.

"I saw a movie once in Guatemala City," Tula told the man, aware of a strange feeling in her chest. "My father took us, my brother and me. The movie was about Hercules, the strongest man in history. He was so strong that he pulled down marble columns and defeated the Centurions who killed Jesus. But I think you are stronger than him. You are much larger."

For the first time since she had met Harris Squires, a pleasant smile appeared on the man's face. In that instant, Tula could see how the giant must have looked as a little boy. He had been a sweet child, probably, maybe a little shy. It caused the girl to wonder what had happened in this man's life to make him mean and to do dirty things such as take photographs of naked women.

Squires replied, "Hercules, no shit? Well, it's all about living clean and using the right vitamins," as he plunged the needle into his bicep and emptied it.

He wasn't done. He used two more syringes—one to load the steroids, a second needle to inject—and pinned a darker oil into the cablelike muscle that angled from his neck to his shoulder.

"Dianabol," Squires said, sounding dreamy and satisfied, rolling his shoulders. "By God, I love a big hit of D-bomb. I don't need any food now, I'm good to go."

Tula watched the man, wondering what that meant as he added, "It's twenty-some miles to Immokalee, but I don't expect there to be much action on the streets. Not on a Wednesday. But if that's what you want, let's do it."

Tula felt a thrill as the Maiden came into her head again, instructing the girl what to say next.

"We'll go to the churches," she told Squires. "On a Wednesday night, people will be praising God and singing. We will find people there who might know about my mother."

Squires was shaking his head. "Where do you come up with this crazy crap? People don't go to church on Wednesday nights, not even Catholics. Unless it's to play bingo or some kind of shit. At least, they didn't back when they made me go."

"The Maiden speaks to me," Tula told him, interested in the man's reaction. "If she says it's true, then it will happen."

Saying it, the girl felt as if she was sharing a secret with Squires, something that increased the weight on her chest and gave her an odd sensation in her abdomen. It was a warm feeling, standing close enough to the giant now to touch her head briefly against his elbow just to see how he reacted.

This time, he didn't yank his arm away. So Tula took another chance by placing her fingers on the man's huge wrist as she told him, "We can trust the Maiden. Whenever I need guidance, she is always there for me."

It felt strange to the girl, her fingers on a man's skin, but Tula decided that she liked it.

Squires turned off the burner, then the lights, before padlocking the door closed. As they walked toward the RV, he said, "The

Maiden . . . ? You mean that saint you mentioned? Don't ever tell a shrink what you just told me. They'll throw you in the damn loony bin. Which is probably where you belong."

"Joan of Arc is my patron saint," Tula said, her voice firm. "She *does* speak to me. Usually at night—that's when the visions come to me."

Irritated, Squires said, "Night visions, too. You're even screwier than I thought. Listen, I don't want to hear every damn detail. You talk too much."

"But it's true," the girl said. "I see things that will happen in the future. Sometimes I see things during the day, too. But it's better if I'm alone. For me, sitting in a tree is a nice place."

Remembering that the girl had spied on him from a tree caused Squires to feel the dianabol he'd just injected accelerate to his temple, vessels throbbing. It created a blooming chemical anger in him, and he clenched his fists as he reconsidered what was happening.

Why the hell was he being nice to this crazy little *chula*? He brought her out here expecting to strip the girl's clothes off, then have some fun. The little brat could send him to Raiford Prison if she wanted. At the very least, he should kill her.

It's not too late. I can take her out to the pond, shoot her in the back of the head, then drive to Mexico on my own. I don't need her. Why put up with any more of her crazy talk?

But from the sick feeling Squires got just thinking about it, he knew he couldn't do it. Maybe later but not now. The reasons had to do with the girl's irritating kindness . . . and also the haunting familiarity of her face.

Even so, it pissed him off the way this know-it-all wettail kept chattering away, so Squires decided to shut her up by saying, "I don't want to burst your bubble, *chula*, but that Joan of Arc bullshit, it's all just fairy-tale crap. You're talking about the girl who carried a sword and dressed like a dude? It's total bullshit."

Instead of waiting for the girl to answer, he continued, "She's a goddamn cartoon character, for Christ's sake. Like Santa Claus and the Easter bunny. The Disney World people probably came up with that Joan of Arc stuff. What in the hell ever convinced you that she talks to you?"

Tula was a couple of steps behind Squires as they walked toward the RV, but she hurried ahead and grabbed the man's wrist, which caused Squires to stop and peer down at her.

"Don't ever say that again," Tula told him, her expression fierce. "The Maiden is real. I can show you in the history books! She led King Charles's army, carrying her banner and sword. She forced the English sinners out of France. At first, even the king didn't believe that she was sent by God, but the Maiden proved it to him."

Tula gave the man's wrist as shake. "She was a great leader and her soldiers loved her. The Maiden lived a *pure* life. She died a virgin, as a woman without a husband should. Have you committed so many sins that you don't want to believe such a good person could exist?"

Squires didn't know what to say. He felt ridiculous, allowing himself to be lectured by this skinny little teenager with her boy's haircut, breasts just beginning to blossom.

"And something else," the girl continued, giving the man's wrist another shake. "Stop calling me a *chula*. My name is Tula. Please show me respect. And no more profanity! It hurts me when you use those words. Why do you intentionally hurt me when you know I care for you? I want to help you to be happy again, but then you say such awful things!"

Harris Squires got a funny feeling in his throat when the girl said that. It was stupid to react that way, he knew it, but there it was.

He stood silently as he watched the girl march off toward the truck, then turn with hands on her hips before saying to him, "If we're going to Immokalee, let's go. But you can't go like that—not into a church. You have to change your clothes."

Squires growled, *"What?"* He was carrying his shirt in his hand, wearing baggy shorts and flip-flops.

The girl didn't back down. "If you hadn't thrown me into your truck this morning without even asking, I would have brought my extra shirt. But you have clean clothes hanging in the trailer. I saw them."

Squires thought about arguing, maybe even threaten to slap the girl's face to let her know who was in charge. But then he thought, *The hell with it.*

The little brat was exhausting. Besides, it wouldn't kill him to get cleaned up a little. It might even make him feel better, because his shirt was soaked with sweat—he could smell its hormonal stink—and he hadn't showered since almost having his ass eaten off by Fifi the night before.

"You mind if I take a little nap first?" he said to the girl, being sarcastic, but he meant it. He was suddenly very tired despite the fresh D-bomb juice and testosterone pulsing through him.

"Will you put those steel things on my wrists again, the hand-cuffs?" the girl asked. It made her nervous, the idea of being alone with the man in the trailer. He might start drinking again. Drink himself into a different mood, and Squires might even try to force her into his bed—Tula would have preferred a bullet in the head to the horror of a man's hands on her body.

But then she studied the giant's face, seeing how empty and tired he looked, and decided no, he would not hurt her. Not now, at least. So the girl added, "If you think you have to chain me, I won't fight you. If it will allow you to sleep for a little while, I think it's what you should do. I won't mind."

The Maiden had been imprisoned in chains, and Tula felt an unexpected thrill at the thought of sharing the experience. It was exciting, the prospect of being locked up alone, but safe with God and Jehanne in her head, while the giant slept nearby.

But the man disappointed her by saying, "If you promise to shut your mouth for a little bit, I don't care what you do. Run off and get eaten by panthers, that's your decision. Just stop your damn talking for a while. My ears are starting to hurt."

Four hours later, when Squires exited the trailer wearing slacks and a polo shirt instead of shorts and flip-flops, his hair wet and slicked back, Tula tried to compliment him by saying, "You look very nice. Blue is a nice color, it shows your eyes. When you were sleeping, you looked so peaceful, I hated to wake you. But it's getting late."

The girl was nervous because Squires was carrying the iPhone she had used an hour ago to type a quick message to her *patron*, Tomlinson, while the giant slept. She had done it just to let him know that she was safe and not in trouble. It was the first text Tula had ever attempted and she had hit the SEND button accidentally before she was done.

Would the big man notice?

Tula watched Squires glance at the phone, then held her breath as he looked at it more closely.

"That's weird," he said, swiping his fingers over the screen. "Usually, I don't get service out here at the camp, but it looks like someone called. No message, though—probably because of the shitty reception."

Tula relaxed a little when the man swore again softly, adding, "It was Frankie, I bet. I bet she is one pissed-off chick. If I'm lucky, I won't never see her again."

As they approached the truck, the redheaded woman with muscles was still on Squires's mind because he asked the girl, sounding serious, "Tell me something. At Red Citrus, you ever talk to Frankie? Did she ever try to get you off alone?"

"I saw her at the trailer park twice," Tula said. "I had a bad feeling about her, though. So I stayed away from her."

Squires was interested. "A bad feeling? What do you mean by that?"

"A feeling that there is something dark in the woman's brain. That's the only way I can explain it. She scared me. I'm glad you don't want to see that woman again. I think she is a bad influence for you. And she's too old, anyway. A man who looks like Hercules could choose any woman in the world. You should marry a nice woman. A young girl who cares about you and can cook you food."

Realizing how that sounded, Tula threw her hand over her mouth, embarrassed.

But Squires didn't appear to notice. Sounding like it was hard for him to believe, the man said, "That surprises me. Frankie never said even a single word to you?"

"Her eyes watched me when she saw me," the girl replied. "I could tell she wanted to speak with me, but I didn't give her the chance. Her eyes are very blue. I felt like she was trying to see through my clothing. And that there might be something bad inside her. Maybe evil, I'm not sure. So I stayed away."

The man appeared satisfied, maybe even relieved. "Good," he said. "That was real smart of you. Never ever let that bitch get you alone."

Squires grunted as Tula, getting into the truck, tried to buoy his spirits by saying, "There's no need to worry about the redheaded woman now. The Maiden is my protector. Now she is your protector, too."

"Sure, yeah, right," the man replied. "Whatever you say, sis. But if you really want to impress me, try shutting that mouth of yours for a while."

"You'll see," Tula insisted. "Jehanne is right about the churches tonight. We will find people there who can help us. And that woman—Frankie? Even if she is evil, you and I have nothing to fear."

By the time they'd spent a couple of hours in Immokalee, with its Circle Ks, tomato-packing warehouses and migrant housing, Squires had stopped trying to figure out how the weird little Jesus freak had gotten so famous among all these Mexicans who came out of the woodwork to see the girl, once word got around that she was in town.

Squires knew that the *chilies* back at Red Citrus had built some kind of voodoo-looking shrine to Tula. Why? He had no idea. But how did these Mexicans know about the girl way out here in cattle-and-tomato country, sixty miles from the Gulf beaches and his trailer park? Christ, Tula had been in Florida for only a week or so. Now here she was with strangers fawning over her like she was some kind of damn rock star.

Something else that surprised the man was that the Maiden—whoever the hell *she* was—was right about churches being open on a Wednesday. Not all, but a couple.

More likely, though, credit went to the strange little girl who heard voices but sat quietly, hands in her lap, during the twenty-mile drive from the hunting camp to this city linked to the outside world just by train tracks and a winding road.

The only time Tula had stirred was once when they passed a state trooper's car going the other way. When the girl saw Squires's knuckles go white on the steering wheel, she stroked his forearm and said, "If a policeman stops us, don't worry, I'll tell them you're my friend. And that we're looking for my mother. They'll believe me. Know why? Because it's the truth."

Squires had tried to catch the news on the radio, hoping for an update on the dead woman they'd found. It was also in his mind that Tula could have been reported missing and that the cops might make the connection.

Hell, for all he knew, Frankie had blown the whistle on him herself, once she discovered that all their cash missing. Blame the dead girl's body on him, that would be easy enough for Frankie to do—and maybe even try to prove it, the bitch was such a good liar.

But no luck with the radio—there were only FM stations out here in the boonies. So Squires decided, screw it, he would just go with the flow and stick with the girl. He couldn't make himself kill his crazy little eyewitness, so maybe he was better off joining her. For now.

At the edge of the Everglades, the open highway became Main Street, with palm trees and gas stations, and lots of small brown people, some of them woman, wearing what looked like colorful blankets. And lots of scrawny, bowlegged Mexican men, too, wearing straw cowboy hats.

At a supermarket named Azteca Super Centro, Squires turned right past Raynor's Seafood & Restaurant, then drove backstreets, zigzagging through a residential area, because that is what the girl told him to do.

The man had never been in a town so small with so many wetback churches. Iglesia Bautista Jesucristo. Pentecostal Church of God. Evangelica Redimidos por la Sangre de Jesus. Amigos en Cristo.

It was like being in a foreign country, the names were so strange. A lot of Spanish praying went down on this plateau of asphalt and lawns bleached brown by the Florida heat, the entire city opened wide to an Everglades sky above.

Not all of the churches were busy, but a couple were, with parking lots full—pickup trucks and rusting Toyotas—church doors open, with people inside singing hymns or shouting out wild words in Spanish.

Squires could hear all this, as they idled along in his truck, windows down. A few blocks later, they came to an adobe-colored brick building with a tin roof, Iglesia de Sangre de Cristo, and the girl told him to pull in. She'd start here.

"I'm staying in the truck," Squires said, giving Tula a look that told her *Don't bother arguing.* "But remember this: If you try running out on me, there'll be hell to pay. That ain't a profanity, it's a promise."

Tula stared at him a moment, the door open, her wounded expression asking the man *When will you ever learn?*

Then she jumped down to the ground, a girl not much taller then the truck's tires, saying, "If the priest will let me, I'm going to talk to the congregation. I would like you to come in and listen. I wouldn't feel as nervous if you were with me. Please? I can speak in English for you. Most of them will understand."

Squires shook his head, and kept his eye on Tula until she was inside. After half an hour, though, he did get out and peek through a window, because it seemed strange the way people off the street were suddenly hurrying across lawns to get to the church. The place was already packed, but more people kept coming, some of them chattering on their cell phones, excited expressions on their faces, as they jogged along.

What Squires saw through the window caused him to wonder if Frankie had slipped some Ecstasy into his fresh batch of steroids, the stuff he'd just injected.

That's how surreal the scene was.

What he saw was Tula, the skinny little girl dressed like a boy, standing at the altar, speaking Spanish in a strong voice, as the priest—a fat little dweeb with no hair—looked on adoringly. Which caused Squires to think maybe the asshole really believed Tula was a boy. But the priest wasn't the only one giving the girl his full attention.

Sitting squashed together on wooden pews, some of the women were bawling silently into hankies, moved by what the girl was saying. And a line was forming near the altar, Mexican men with farmer's tans, short little women—some on their knees—apparently waiting to meet the girl when she was done speaking.

But why? Squires moved to a window that was closer to find out.

It made no sense, but what the people wanted to do, he discovered, was kiss the girl's hand, or hug her, or maybe ask her to say a prayer for them, which Tula appeared to do several times, touching her hand to a person's head while she muttered words toward the ceiling.

My God, even the priest got in on it, hugging the girl while she touched his dweebish bald head and said something that Squires was close enough to hear but couldn't understand.

Dumbass, the man thought to himself. *Why the hell didn't I ever learn Spanish?*

It was frustrating hearing but not understanding, especially because he was trying to figure out why the girl commanded such respect from so many adults, all of them strangers.

Maybe Tula sounded smarter in Spanish. That might explain it, which caused Squires to spend some time weighing the possibility. It had to be true, he finally decided. In English, the girl came off as pretty damn strange, maybe even nuts. In Spanish, she must have sounded a lot smarter.

Right or wrong, it gave Squires a funny feeling to witness how famous the girl had become. He guessed it was something to be proud of, hanging out with a celebrity, even if the girl's fans were all Mexicans.

What he was witnessing was impressive, Squires had to admit it. Being with a celebrity was new in his experience, unless he counted Frankie, which he didn't of course. Fifteen years ago, Frankie had been a minor bodybuilding star—Miss South Florida U.S.A. once and Miss Vermont Bodybuilder three times in a row—which the bitch never stopped reminding him when they got into arguments over which steroids were best for different kinds of cycles.

But being with Tula, the strange little Jesus freak, was an entirely different experience. Squires had never seen anyone look at Frankie the way these adoring people kept their eyes glued to that little girl.

Yeah, sort of proud—that's the way he felt. And he would have continued watching if a few tough-acting Mexicans—or were they Guatemalans?—hadn't slipped out the church door to give him their hard-assed beaner glares.

"What you lookin' at, man?" one of the *chilies* said to Squires as they walked toward him, all three taking out their gangbanger bandannas, he noticed.

Squires turned to gauge the distance to his truck where he'd stored the Ruger Blackhawk beneath the seat. Not that he needed a gun to deal with these little turds—even with a pulled hamstring—but it was good to know he had options.

He waited until the trio was closer before he said to them, keeping his voice low and confidential, "Hey, I gotta question for you boys. What's that little girl in there saying that's so important? Man, even the priest is hanging on every word. How'd she get so famous?"

Squires was trying to be friendly, strike up a nice conversation with these hard Mexicans. But no luck.

The head *chilie* was easy to pick out. He was the one tying on his blue colors, low over the eyes, as he said something that sounded like, "Choo tryin' to be funny or what, man? 'Cause choo ain't funny," his Mex accent strong.

Not quite so friendly now, Squires told the dude, "You'd be laughing your ass off if I wanted to be funny, douche bag."

The two beaners moved closer to the head gangbanger, standing shoulder to shoulder, as their leader replied, "We know who you are, man. We know all about the shit goes on out there at your damn hunting camp, too. So get the hell out of here, back to your trailer park that smells of *mierda*. This here's a damn church, man. Why you wanna bother us here with your presence?"

Squires was surprised, at first, that the Mexican knew so much about him, but then he wasn't. Hell, maybe all three of these dudes had lived at Red Citrus for a while. That wouldn't have surprised him, either, because most of the illegals sooner or later showed up at one of his parks.

"Let me offer you some friendly advice," Squires said to the men, motioning for them to lean closer. "Pay attention or I'll rip your ears off and stick 'em up your ass. I asked you a polite question. I expect a nice answer. That girl in there is a friend of mine. Why's the priest letting her stand up there and talk to the whole audience?"

"Right-t-t-t," one of the *chilies* said, feeling around for something in his pocket. "That girl in there, if you say you know her, you lying *coño*. She's a saint, man. So you better behave yourself with respect or we'll run your white ass outta here."

"Is that what she claims?" Squires asked.

"She talks to God and God answers her back," the Guatemalan replied, sounding defensive, but pissed off, too. "What proof you want? God is telling her we should return to our homes in the mountains. And not put up with *gringo* assholes like you. For what? Live in a shithole trailer park like yours? Drive a fancy truck that takes half my pay every month?"

The word "mountains" registered in Squires's memory, which caused him to say, "I hear it's pretty nice where some of you Mexicans come from. Even in summer, I heard it's nice 'n' cool up in those mountains. That true? What's a big house and a few acres sell for?"

"A jelly boy like you moving to Guatemala?" the *chilie* said to him. "Man, don't even think about it. We don't want your kind dirtying up our home." He took a step. "You say you a friend of this girl? I think you full of bullshit, man."

Squires was looking through the church window again, trying to gauge how pissed off Tula would be if he caused a disturbance outside. No, he decided. He wasn't going to do it. The girl had already gotten mad at him once today, giving him a look that had made him feel sort of low, like he'd disappointed her. Once was enough. He didn't want to have that feeling again.

Squires held up his hands, palms out. "Stay cool, *amigos*. Only reason I'm here is to help the girl find her mama. Ya'll just run along before the little saint in there makes you come back and apologize to me. Because when she was talking to God, the big guy didn't send her to *you*. God sent her to *me*."

Smiling, Squires limped back to his truck and waited. The three gangbangers looked at one another for a moment, their faces unfocused, then they obviously decided *Fuck it!* and went inside the church.

While he was messing with the radio, trying to find some decent news, his phone rang once, but no one was there when Squires answered, saying, "Hello . . . *hello?*" during a long silence.

A wrong number, he decided. It had to be.

An hour later, a little after eleven p.m., Squires and the girl were back at the hunting camp, walking from his truck toward the RV, as frogs chirred from a spatial darkness that was bordered by cypress trees and stars. He had been feeling pretty good about things up until then, but, suddenly, Squires didn't feel so good anymore.

Shit!

Frankie was at the trailer, waiting for them. Laziro Victorino, too, along with some of his gangbanger soldiers, who came out of nowhere so fast they had their hands on Tula before Squires had time to do anything about it.

Up until then, though, it had been the best night he'd had in a while. The big man had been feeling better and better about helping the strange little girl instead of shooting her in the back of the head. And Squires had never seen the girl so happy.

On the drive from Immokalee to the hunting camp, she had sat in the passenger seat, chattering away, sounding excited because she had found out where her aunts and brother were living. Maybe her mother, too. Or so she thought.

But when Tula told Squires about it, he wasn't so sure.

"Aunt Vilma and Isabel are working on a tomato farm in a city called Ocala!" Tula had exclaimed as she exited the church, waving a piece of paper. "I have Aunt Isabel's phone number. And my brother, he picked oranges this winter. He was always so lazy, but it must be true."

As they drove down Main Street, Immokalee, out of town, the girl was laughing, telling Squires, "Pacaw has moved around a lot, but he might be living outside a city that is named Venice. He had trouble finding work because he's younger than me, only twelve— but he acts older. Everyone I met at the church thought he was at least sixteen. The people I met tonight, they are wonderful."

Squires had to ask. "Did they say anything about me? Some tough Mexican dudes came outside and gave me some of their tough-taco shit. But you were . . . you know, in the middle of your speech. I didn't want to cause no trouble."

The big man said it expecting the girl to appreciate his thoughtful-ness. Maybe she did, but he had hoped for a more positive reaction.

Squires gave it some time before he glanced at the girl and asked a question that had been on his mind: "You could have run out on me tonight, sis. You could've had your new friends call the cops. Why didn't you? I was sitting here in the truck, wondering about it."

The girl had looked at the giant, shaking her head, and didn't bother to speak the words her affectionate expression was tell-ing him.

Instead, she said, "I'm very hungry. One of the women—she was so sweet. She asked for a lock of my hair but didn't have any scissors. She told me there is a very excellent restaurant not far. It's called Taco Bell. You must be hungry, too."

They used the Taco Bell drive-through, and Squires listened to the girl chomp down about half her weight in junk food as he drove—Tula, beside him, eating like it was the best Mex she'd ever had in her life.

Squires had the taco salad and an unsweetened iced tea. He was an athlete, for Christ's sake. In his business, diet was everything, even during a bulking cycle. The perfect male body wasn't built in the weight room, it was sculpted in the kitchen—Squires had read that someplace.

Ten miles from the hunting camp, the girl had gotten onto the subject of her missing mother, a conversation that Squires had tried to postpone because he already suspected where it was going.

"I keep trying to tell you the best news," the girl had said to him. "My mother was working in restaurants and cleaning houses. But then she went to work for a very rich man and has been traveling a lot—which is probably why I haven't heard from her. She didn't tell anyone the man's name. But she told someone's niece that the man's company makes movies. That she was going to become an actress! This was about two months ago, which is probably why she had to get a new telephone. My aunts or brother will know more when I talk to them. Didn't I tell you that my mother is beautiful?"

Squires thought, *Uh-oh* . . . understanding immediately why Tula's mother hadn't told anyone her employer's name. Either no one had revealed the name to her or the woman was too ashamed to admit it. Every Mexican in Florida knew that Laziro Victorino was a badass gang leader and the only films he had an interest in were porno and snuff films.

That gave Squires a sick feeling in his belly. She *could* have been talking about some other guy who made movies—but he strongly doubted it.

Tula's mother must have been damn hard up for money to make such a decision, which wasn't unusual for Mexican women who sent money back home. But to go to work for the V-man? It had to be more than just needing cash, Squires decided. Maybe she'd gotten hooked on crank or crack. No telling, but a lot of Mexican girls did after getting into porn or prostitution.

Squires remembered the little girl sniffing the little doll she'd found and saying her mother had one just like it. It didn't prove the girl's mother had been entertained by Victorino or Frankie, sitting in their trailer, drinking margaritas laced with Ecstasy. But it sure made it a strong possibility.

There was also an even more disturbing possibility, but just thinking about it made Squires feel queasy. That he'd been the one who'd entertained Tula's mother—the Mexican *chula* in his sex dream. So Squires had changed the subject by handing Tula his iPhone, saying, "Call your aunt what's her name. Tell her you're okay. Where'd you say they're living? Do it now because we're going to lose reception the moment I turn off the road to my camp."

"We're not going back to the trailer park?" the girl asked, surprised. "That's what I told the priest. That's what I told everyone, that we're returning to Red Citrus." She hesitated. "I would feel better if I could sleep on my own cot and get my things. I have a book there I read every night before I turn off the light."

Squires shook his head. "The camp's closer, and I need a drink. We'll get your things tomorrow."

Guessing what the girl was worried about, he added, "Don't worry, you'll have your own bed. And all the damn privacy you want—as long as you promise to stop talking so much. What about calling your aunts?"

As Tula giggled in her seat, excited to be dialing her aunt, Squires thought about details. He wasn't good at geography, but he'd done bodybuilding shows all over Florida. Tula had mentioned Ocala and Venice. They were both north, off Interstate 75, which was right on the way if they were driving to Mexico.

Damn . . . it was a big decision. Leaving the country had seemed like a smart thing to do earlier when he'd been drunk and scared shitless. Now, with the girl laughing and chattering in Spanish to her aunt, it suddenly seemed all too real. Like the idea was closing in and smothering him.

How would he feel riding with a bunch of wetbacks all that distance? His truck was a double cab, so there'd be enough room. Hell, Mexicans were like folding chairs. You could pack twenty of them into a Volkswagen. And it wasn't like he'd be breaking any laws, since he'd be driving a load of illegal immigrants back to where they belonged. Still, the prospect seemed so foreign to him that he began searching for an alternative.

But no matter how Squires viewed his situation, he couldn't get around the fact that if the cops questioned Tula about the dead Mexican girl, they'd arrest him for something, probably murder. Laziro Victorino was in the back of his mind, too.

Then Squires thought about the way the girl had described her village. It was quiet and clean, she'd said. A place that was high in the mountains where it was cool, and closer to God.

Squires told himself he didn't care anything about God. But he was sure sick of Florida, where he'd been doing stupid, illegal shit, always feeling guilty—*a dirty life*, Tula had described it, and the girl was right.

All his problems would be solved, though, if he took Tula and her family to Mexico. No more murder rap, no worrying about cops busting his steroid business, no more of Frankie's bullying, and of her sick, twisted ways.

Squires reminded himself that he had around sixty grand in cash—plus a few grand more he'd stolen from the two white guys last night. That was more than enough money to kick back at some Mexican beach resort for a month or two.

And if he liked the place, maybe he'd invest some of that money in starting up a first-class steroids lab—a place where it was legal to use and make gear. Hell, he could hire Tula and her family to keep the place clean and do office work. The girl was strange, but at least he knew that she'd never steal from him or lie to him about the books.

Okay, Squires thought to himself, *Mexico it is.*

Goddamn, that felt good! He'd finally made a decision. It put a little smile on his face until Tula handed him his cell phone as if the thing was broken, telling him, "I can't hear what my aunt Isabel is saying anymore. She was right in the middle of telling me something important when we got cut off."

"I told you, we don't have good reception out here," Squires replied.

"But I wanted to hear what she was telling me!"

As the man slipped the phone into his pocket, he paid attention because the girl sounded so serious, which is why he asked her, "What'd she say that's got you so riled up?"

Tula replied, "My aunt said an important woman called her tonight. A woman who works for the government helping immigrants. She was very worried because she said the police are looking for you and me."

Squires felt his heart begin to pound. "Your aunt said that?" he asked.

"No, that's what I'm trying to tell you. The woman said they've been talking about us on the radio and television all night. Some kind of special alert for children. It has a color in the name."

Squires whispered, "Shit! An AMBER Alert."

Reacting to the expression on the man's face, Tula added quickly, "Yes—but it's okay, don't worry! The first thing my aunt will do is call the woman and tell her that you are my friend. She's probably talking to the woman right now. Telling her that I'm very safe and happy. My aunt promised."

Squires said, "Jesus Christ, an AMBER Alert. What next?" but was listening, wanting to hear better news.

Tula told him, "Then my aunt will call the church and speak with the priest—she knows him very well because she picked tomatoes in Immokalee for a season. His name is Father Jimenez, and she will ask him to telephone the police tonight and tell them the same thing."

"Talk slower," Squires said. "Tell the cops what?"

"That I'm with you because I *want* to be with you. So no one will be worried. My aunt was so relieved to hear my voice, she was crying. But she promised me, so I know she will do it."

Tula held up the paper she was carrying. "In the morning, I will call the woman myself. I have her number here, too."

Squires took a deep breath, letting it out slowly, before he said, "Maybe you should call the immigration woman now. I can back up. Usually, reception doesn't go to hell until I get to the gate."

But then he realized that turning around, driving toward Immokalee, might be a mistake. The woman from state immigration would want to know Tula's exact location. That would bring the cops, asking questions.

The girl made up his mind, saying, "The police will believe Father Jimenez. A priest? Of course they will believe him. Plus, I told Father Jimenez that you are a wonderful man. He wanted to meet you, but I told him you are shy about coming into churches."

Squires liked it when Tula said that. He began to relax a little and feel at ease as the girl added, "Do you now believe that the Maiden is watching over us? When you do God's work, good things happen to you!"

By then, they were at the gate to the hunting camp.

Squires began to suspect trouble when he realized there was a light on inside his RV, the vehicle sitting up on blocks in the darkness. He and Tula had just gotten out of the truck, which was when the big man placed his hand on the girl's shoulder, stopping her.

"Hold it, sis," he said as he stared at the light. He knew he'd switched off the generator before leaving just in case he and the girl didn't return. Plus, he would've heard the little Honda engine running if it was on.

That meant that someone inside had a flashlight. Or had lit a candle, or an oil lamp maybe. But where was the person's truck?

Squire's head pivoted from the mountain of cypress trees to the west, then to the east, where there were shadowed pine flats and a distant halo glow that was Lauderdale.

There had to be a vehicle somewhere. No one in their right mind would hike cross-country through the Everglades, not this late. Not half an hour before midnight . . . unless . . . unless they had parked their vehicle behind the RV. Which was possible. But how could they have gotten through the gate? The gate had been locked when he and Tula had arrived just as he'd left it.

Thinking that gave Squires a prickly feeling along his spine. Frankie had the only other key.

Squires reached out, patted Tula's arm and whispered, "Hang on for a second, sis. Something ain't right about this."

He took a few slow steps toward the trailer, favoring his right leg, but then stopped abruptly when he saw what might have been a person moving in the shadows behind the trailer.

Squires couldn't be sure. He had left the truck running, lights on, so he could see to unlock the door to the generator shed. He didn't have a flashlight, so all he saw was a blur of movement like someone ducking for cover.

Squires was thinking about hurrying back to the truck and opening the hidden compartment to get his revolver and night vision binoculars. That's when Tula whispered, "There's someone here. I smell cigarette smoke. And perfume, too."

Squires thought, *Shit. It's Frankie.*

Yes, it was. The large woman appeared, standing in the RV's doorway, shining a flashlight in his eyes, then focused the beam on Tula. Squires was shielding his eyes when he heard Frankie say, "Well, well, look at what we have here. Harris, you dumb pile of shit, I don't know what to do first—have some fun with the pretty little wettail you brought me or call the cops and hope there's a reward for turning in a kidnapper."

The woman was very drunk and probably stoned. Squires could tell by the way she slurred her words. Frankie had to grab the railing as she started down the steps, adding, "Either way, I want the goddamn money you stole from me. Sixty thousand dollars in cash, you son of a bitch. You really thought I'd let you get away with it?"

For a woman, Frankie had the lowest voice Squires had ever heard. It was from using too much primobolan and shooting testosterone, which the woman lied about, too. But there was no disguising what steroids had done to her voice—and the female parts of her body, too.

Squires waved and called, "Hey, sugar babe, I was hoping you'd be here!" like he was glad to see the woman, but then he nudged Tula toward the truck, leaning to whisper, "Get in and lock the doors. Don't come out 'til I tell you."

Tula yanked her arm away, though, being stubborn, and said, "I'm not leaving you! You're afraid of her, I can tell. I'm staying with you."

Frankie, on the grass now, wearing tight jeans, her breasts ballooning out of a tank top, was close enough to hear the girl, because she laughed, saying, "Now, isn't that sweet! You found yourself a loyal little *chula*. A cute young one, too. Harris, know what that tells me? It tells me you haven't screwed her yet. Even if she's a virgin, she wouldn't still be hanging with you. She'd be ready for someone bigger and better by now."

In a chiding voice, Frankie spoke to Tula, saying, "I'll bet you're still pure as the snow, aren't you, *niña?* Then this goddamn piece of white trash comes along and kidnaps you. But you don't have to be afraid of him now. Come here to Frankie"—the woman was patting her thigh as if calling a dog—"I'll make sure you're safe."

Squires felt Tula move close to him, throwing an arm around his bad leg for protection.

He wasn't afraid of Frankie—he'd never admitted it to himself, anyway—Tula was wrong about that. But the woman did make him nervous, particularly when she was as drunk as she was now.

Nervous, yes, that's the way Squires felt, but he could also feel a testosterone heat moving to his ears.

"You shut your mouth about this girl," Squires said to Frankie in a warning tone as he stepped in front of Tula. "She's not used to your garbage talk. And stop your damn swearing in front of her. This little girl's religious."

Frankie laughed, *"Priceless,"* as Squires continued, "You go on back inside the trailer. If you want to talk to me, I'll get the generator going and we'll talk. But you leave this girl alone."

Squires was lying about the generator. The moment Frankie closed the trailer door, he'd load Tula into the truck and they'd get the hell out of there.

Go where, though? Frankie knew what she was talking about when she'd mentioned kidnapping. Even if the priest told the cops that everything was okay, a call from Frankie might put them back on the alert. The woman would drop the dime on him the moment he left, Squires was sure of it.

Or would she?

Mismatched details were going through Squires's mind as he tried to view the situation clearly. Maybe Frankie didn't have so much leverage over him after all, he decided. Once he was in jail, how could the woman force him to give back the money he'd taken? She'd have to admit to the feds that they'd piled up a ton of cash selling steroids. They hadn't paid a dime in taxes, either.

No, Frankie couldn't risk that.

The woman was drunk. She was a vicious twat, but she was smart. She'd realize that getting the sixty grand was the most important thing, once he reminded her. It caused Squires to wonder if maybe he should offer the woman some kind of deal . . . which is when he heard an engine start in the distance.

A second later, a truck loaded with men came fishtailing out from behind the trailer, the truck's lights blinding him and the girl. In the same instant, a Mexican voice from behind Squires said, "Hey there, jelly boy! You stand real still or I'll blow your damn head off.

Squires turned.

Christ! There was Laziro Victorino, grinning at him with his gold teeth. And pointing a shotgun at him—a Browning Maxus 12-gauge that Squires had kept locked in the trailer gun closet.

Victorino and Frankie together?

It took Squires a slow, stunned moment to realize what had happened. Yeah . . . it had to be. Frankie and the gangbanger had teamed up. That was the only explanation. Frankie had somehow hooked up with the V-man, probably today at Red Citrus. After the woman had discovered the money missing, she would have been in the perfect mood to seduce someone like Victorino, a guy who could help her get what she wanted.

Even so, this surprised Squires, because Frankie was the most racist person he'd ever met. But here it was, staring him right in the face. And the two of them had been at it for a while, sharing some fun together, judging from the confidential looks Victorino and Frankie were now exchanging. Both of them drunk and probably cocaine crazy.

Squires had seen the woman like this many times. And the V-man was no different, he guessed—probably worse. Drunk as they were, neither one of them gave a damn about what they did or the consequences. They wanted the cash. But the V-man probably wanted Tula more or he wouldn't have wasted his time—a girl Tula's age was worth a lot more than sixty thousand to a business shark like him.

And they would kill him, Squires realized. They had to. Use the shotgun, but, more likely, Victorino's box cutter. He'd do it slowly to impress Frankie, a woman probably twisted enough to video the whole thing.

That made Squires feel sort of queasy. Then he felt worse when he realized that, no, Victorino and his gangbangers would be the ones to video his murder. Get it all on their iPhones and add another snuff film to their collection.

This was all shocking information for Squires to process. He didn't expect loyalty from Frankie, but he didn't expect her to help a Mexican dude murder him, either. He and the redhead had spent more than four years together, most of it either screwing or screaming at each other, but they'd had some good times, too. Could Frankie let go of all that so fast?

Squires got his answer when Frankie called to Victorino, "Don't shoot him now, dumbass! Get them in the cookshack, I've got the camera all set. Hurry up, it's almost midnight!"

Cameras in the steroid shack—this was another surprise to Squires. Why not the trailer, where they had already built a porno set complete with lights and a computer?

The V-man was wagging an index finger at Tula as he pointed the shotgun at Squires, saying something in Spanish to the girl—probably ordering her into the steroid shack—before telling Frankie, "What's the rush, now? Bring some duct tape. I'll hold the gun on your boyfriend while you tape him."

The woman replied, "The greaser genius giving orders again," sounding sloppy drunk now. But still sober enough to remember that Victorino enjoyed killing women, because she added, "Duct tape. Check. I'd love to tape that worthless piece of shit."

Squires watched the redhead walk toward the RV but then stop near the steps, where she reached down into a box. When he heard Tula scream, "Don't you touch that!" he remembered the fledgling bird the girl had saved. Could the thing still be alive?

Yes, it was. The egret was squawking and flapping its bare wings as Frankie held the bird up in the light. The woman was grinning as she said to Victorino, "Do you Mexicans like to eat squab? I think we've got a bottle of champagne around her someplace." Before the man could reply, though, the woman said, "Ouch! The little bastard just bit me!" and hurled the bird hard against the aluminum siding of the RV.

Tula gave a little shriek and swung her head away, but Victorino thought it was pretty funny, the hard-assed redhead getting bit by a bird.

Staring at Squires, the V-man grinned as he said to Frankie, "See? We're having ourselves some fun now. What's the hurry? Come back with the duct tape, then we gonna have more fun making movies. Hell, this dumbass probably has the money on him, maybe stashed somewhere inside his truck. It won't be hard to find."

As Tula sobbed, Squires was thinking, *The hell it won't.*

He'd built the hidden compartment himself, using a cutting torch and the help of a magic mechanic friend of his. Frankie didn't know about the compartment, because while she sometimes drove his Ford Roush, she never messed with his hunting truck.

More pressing on Squires's mind was the fact that Victorino and Frankie had planned this out together. Cameras and duct tape? Those were the principal props in the few snuff films that Squires had seen. They were sickening things to watch, although he'd never admitted that to Frankie, who always had a glassy, heated look on her face by the time one of those videos ended.

Thinking about it caused Squires's heart to pound, a slow fury building in him. Victorino would use that shitty hardware-store knife on him. He felt certain of it. And then he and Frankie would have more fun together by raping the girl, probably filming that, too.

Then an even worse scenario flashed into Squires's mind: They would video what they did to Tula first, just to piss him off. Make him watch the whole sick business before they got around to killing him.

Again the question came into Squires's mind: Why the cookshack, a room that was all chemicals and propane tanks but no bed?

A moment later, Victorino's gangbanger buddies were jumping out of the truck—a Dodge Ram—as it skidded to a stop, running toward Squires and Tula. The V-man took a few quick steps, his eyes still fixed on Squires, and scooped the girl up in his left arm.

Tula screamed for help, yelling, "He has me, make him let me go!"

Squires took a step but then stopped, frozen by the gun and what was happening.

Now the girl was hollering to her invisible friend, "Jehanne! I need your help, Jehanne!" as she slapped at Victorino with her hands. Then the skinny girl shot a heartbreaking look into Squires's eyes, pleading, "Don't let him hurt me. All I want is my mother!"

Without even thinking about it, Squires began limping toward the V-man. Slow at first, then faster, taking long strides despite his bad hamstring.

Squires knew that the shotgun was loaded with bird shot, which was what he and his buddies used to hunt dove and quail. Little tiny pellets half the size of match heads. Hell, he'd been hit by more than a few of those pellets when he and his drunken buddies shot at birds in a cross fire. They didn't hurt much, and it took almost a direct hit to break the skin.

Not that it mattered, because inside Squires's brain something had snapped. He felt an invincible cerebral combustion surging through him. It caused the steroid oils, and the D-bombs he'd swallowed, to engorge his monster face with blood.

Laziro Victorino screamed a warning as Squires moved toward him, dragging his right leg with every step. The gangbanger screamed again as he hurled the girl to the ground, pointed the shotgun and this time pulled the trigger.

Squires jolted, grunting at the stinging impact. But that didn't matter, either. The giant stumbled, regained his balance and kept coming.

Arms outstretched, Harris Squires was hell-bent on getting his fingers around the V-man's neck because now the little saint was calling for his help again, screaming, "Please, *please*, Harris! Don't let these men take me away from you!"

THIRTEEN

THE REASON I TURNED EAST, TOWARD WHAT TURNED OUT TO BE Harris Squires's hunting camp, was because after touring Immokalee, seeing a helicopter and a half dozen cops parked outside a church, I decided that my detective friend might be wrong when he told me that Squires and Tula had left Immokalee and were now on their way back to Red Citrus trailer park.

It was 11:20 p.m. when Leroy Melinski called my cell to give me what he believed was the good news. I had cruised Immokalee's slow streets and then headed out of town, occasionally glancing at the satellite aerial that showed Squires's four hundred acres of what was probably saw grass and cypress trees.

"The girl wasn't kidnapped," the detective explained when I answered. "She told a bunch of people—including a priest and one of her aunts—that Squires volunteered to drive her around and help her find her mother. So there you have it, Doc. Turns out your kidnapper is just being a Good Samaritan."

The reception on my phone was fuzzy, so I said, "You've got to be kidding. Say that again."

Melinski told me, "Harris Squires and the girl stopped at some church, a pretty big one, so there's confirmation on all this. A couple hundred people listened to her give a speech or a sermon, whatever you call it. Squires got out of his truck to listen, but he didn't come inside."

I said, "People on the scene told you this?"

The detective said, "Squires even made nice with some gangbangers who gave him a hard time. Not Latin Kings. Probably MS-13 from Guatemala, who are bloodthirsty little shits. But even they must have been convinced."

I told him, "This just doesn't mesh with what I know about Harris Squires," as Melinski talked over me, saying, "I know, I know, it's hard to believe, but I've heard enough to be convinced. So you can relax, okay? Go back to your test tubes or have a beer. I'm going to bed."

I said, "Some minister lets a thirteen-year-old girl, a stranger, get up in front of the whole congregation? Why?"

"It happened," Melinski replied, sounding impatient, "that's all that matters. I talked to the priest myself. He's worked in Immokalee for nine years, which means he's heard every possible combination of bullshit story. According to him, the girl walked in and said she had something important to say, so he let her talk. He described her as happy and relaxed, which is not the way a kidnapped kid acts."

"The priest," I said.

"Along with several local women, too. They offered her a place to stay, but the girl refused. Squires may have something to do with the dead body we found, who knows? But the girl's with him because she wants to be with him. End of story."

I said, "Harris Squires wouldn't lift a finger to help anyone—not unless he expected to get something out of it."

Melinski told me, "We'll find out more when they get back to the trailer park. The girl told the priest that was their next stop, so we've got some uniforms there waiting."

I had to ask, "Did your hostage-rescue people call his cell?"

"That's the only part that bothers me," Melinski told me. "They tried but no answer. Reception's bad around Immokalee, which could explain it. The priest said, at first, he didn't like the idea of a Guatemalan girl being with a *gringo* guy that age. He tried to talk her into staying, but the girl was so sure of what she was doing, he decided it was okay. At least for the hour or so it takes them to get back to the trailer park. Red Citrus? Yeah, Red Citrus. Maybe a little longer because the girl told the priest they might get something to eat first."

"What time did they leave?" I asked. "I hope you have cops checking the local restaurants."

Melinski told me, "They pulled out at little before eleven, so they should be at the trailer park in half an hour or so." With exaggerated tolerance, he then added, "Have you heard anything I said? You can stop worrying. The priest told me some pretty wild stuff about the kid. So, finally, I maybe understand why you've taken an interest. You didn't tell me the Latinos consider her some kind of saint or something."

"The priest said that?" I asked.

"The guy sounded a little in awe of the girl, in fact. He said there were women crying, people waiting in line to ask the girl's blessing. 'God has taken the girl by the hand'—this is the priest talking, not me. But the man was serious. So there's no need to worry, according to him. The priest's exact words almost, and more than nine years he's been working with immigrants."

I said, "If God took missing girls by the hand, there would be a lot fewer missing girls. Please tell me you're not buying into this baloney."

I was relived that Tula and Squires had been spotted. But I was also feeling too restless to allow myself to be convinced. I didn't admit this to Melinski, of course, and pretended to be satisfied when he promised to call when he got word the girl was safely back at Red Citrus.

After I hung up, I checked the luminous face of my dive watch: 11:25 p.m. I was approaching the intersection of Immokalee Road and what I guessed was Route 846, where Squires owned the four hundred acres. Continue straight and I would take yet another lap through Immokalee, then north to home—or maybe Emily's place, if I could get her on the phone. Make a right, I would have to drive at least forty miles, round-trip, out of my way—and probably for no reason.

In my mind, though, I suddenly pictured the Mayan girl looking through the window of Squires's trucking, seeing a sign that read IMMOKALEE 22 MILES, then texting the information to Tomlinson, a man she trusted. The image was so strong that I actually shook my head to get rid of it.

As I neared the intersection, I hesitated, my intellect telling me one thing, my instincts telling me something else. Normally, that's seldom a cause for indecision—which is why I was a little surprised when I found myself following my intuition. I turned right onto the narrow two-lane that vectored eastward into the Everglades.

Something else my intellect and instincts argued about was whether I should call Tomlinson. If he had gone to Red Citrus, as expected, I should tell him to wait there to make sure Tula arrived.

It only made sense that I call him, but I had settled into a comfortable cocoon of solitude, focused laserlike on finding the girl. For me, that cocoon is a place rarely enjoyed when I'm Florida and I didn't want to leave it.

It had to do with my shadow life. Solitude is what I enjoy most about it. I travel alone to Third World countries, to Everglades-dark places, and I find people. I then track those people. I become familiar with their schedules, their habits.

For the period of a week—sometimes two, depending on the importance of the assignment—I charted the subtle movements and interactions of a stranger's life. I did it invisibly, with a laboratory precision that in the end allowed me to segregate that person from his surroundings as effectively as using tweezers to remove a bee, undetected, from its colony.

That was my specialty—my genius, Tomlinson might have called it, had he ever learned the truth. What I do, however, doesn't demand genius. I have no illusions about my own gifts, other than to acknowledge that, since I was very young, I have had an obsessive need to identify, then define, orderly patterns in what most would dismiss as chaos.

We all have our quirks.

That's my job when out of the country: to discern order in the chaos. To create a precision target. As creator, I am also tasked with finding the most effective method of displacing that target from his surroundings.

I am good at it.

After wrestling with the decision for a mile, I decided I wasn't in the mood for a conversation with Tomlinson. Instead, I pulled over long enough to send a text:

Tula and Squires to arrive at Red Citrus by midnight, cops waiting. Let me know. If you're drinking, stop now. Don't piss off cops!

After a moment of thought, I added, *Is Emily safe?* then sent the text with a slow *Whoosh!* that told me reception was getting worse.

I got out of the truck long enough to urinate, then got back in, but left the dome light on. Out of long habit—or, perhaps, just to reestablish my focus—I took inventory of my equipment bag. First, I popped the magazines of both pistols to make certain they were loaded, although I knew they were.

I am not a gun fancier or collector, but the precision tolerances of fine machinery appeals to the same sensibilities that cause me to linger over a fine microscope. It was true of my Sig Sauer P226 pistol. The Sig was one of the first issued after the Joint Service Small Arms test trials of 1985, and I have trusted my life to it since that time. I had recently purchased a new magazine that held fifteen rounds instead of only ten. I had also added Tritium night sights, which I had yet to try on a range.

I held the Sig's magazine in my hand, testing the mobility of the rounds with my thumb, the odor of Hoppe's No. 9 gun solvent spreading a lingering sweetness through the cab of my truck. It reminded me of Tomlinson's crack about smelling gun oil in the lab whenever I felt restless. An inside joke? Or was it a veiled reminder that, one way or another, my relationship with Emily was doomed as long as I continued to live my shadow life.

Whether a dig or a warning, what he'd said was true: When I get restless, it shows. After a month or two without a new mission, I find myself studying maps. I find myself at night sitting within easy reach of my Trans-Oceanic Radio, recleaning my weapons as if that private ceremony was an incantation that would bring a call from my handler.

After inspecting the Sig Sauer, I took the much smaller, lighter Kahr pistol in hand. It was black-matte stainless, comfortable to hold. After so many years trusting the Sig, it was tough to admit that this was now my weapon of choice. It wasn't as tiny as another favorite—a Seecamp .380—but the Kahr slipped just as easily out of the pocket. And it could be hidden almost as completely in the palm of my hand. Firing the Kahr, though, was a pleasure, and it had more stopping power than the Seecamp.

Like the Sig, the Kahr was loaded with federal Hydra-Shok hollow points. But the Kahr had the added advantage of a built-in laser sight that was activated whenever I gripped the thing to fire.

Unlike the high-tech Dazer Guardian, also in the bag, the laser sight was red, not green.

It was unlikely that I would use any of these weapons, just as I knew there was very little chance now that I would stumble onto Harris Squires and the Guatemalan girl. He and Tula were on their way to Red Citrus while I was out here wasting time on back roads east of Immokalee.

It didn't matter. I was in a certain mood. To rationalize wasting time, I told myself this was training, a way to stay sharp.

I leaned to roll down the passenger window, and drove on.

Tomlinson is right. I'm not a fast driver. I slowed even more whenever I switched on the dome light and checked the satellite aerial. My pal had used a highlighter to square off the boundaries of Squires's property, but it still wasn't easy to pick out landmarks. I was driving through a shadowed mesa of cypress that I guessed was Owl Hammock. It meant I had at least fifteen miles to go.

Thus far, I hadn't passed a car. Not one.

Alternately squinting at the aerial, then accelerating, my headlights tunneled through a starry silence, toward a horizon abloom with the nuclear glow of Fort Lauderdale, eighty miles to the east.

I passed through the precise geometrics of tomato fields and citrus orchards. Then more cypress domes that exited into plains of myrtle and saw grass. My eyes moved from the road, to the satellite aerial, then to my watch.

11:45 p.m.

Training exercise or not, my mind wandered back to Emily. My reaction to her had been a surprise. A shock, in fact, and now it was a new source of restlessness that was pleasure mixed with angst.

I had left Tomlinson alone with Emily for a reason—a deceit that Tomlinson had guessed correctly. It was a test. He suspected it, I knew it. I was subjecting myself, my new lover and my old friend to yet another of my relentless personal evaluations.

"Why do you set traps for people you care about when you're the one who is inevitably hurt?" a smart but troubled woman had once asked me.

I had no answer then. I had no answer now.

It was a uncomfortable truth to admit, but that was balanced by something I believed with equal honesty: Emily Marston could be trusted. There was no rational explanation for why I trusted her, but I did. Attraction is commonplace. A visceral, indefinable unity is not. The chemistry that links two people is comprised of elements too subtle to survive dissection, too complex to permit inspection.

It was unlike me to ponder the exigencies of romance, but that's exactly what I was doing as the miles clicked by. My mind returned to the bedroom, where I had used every gentleness to follow Emily's physical signals, then fine-tuned what I was doing to match her respiratory and moaning guidance. Our rhythms escalated until, finally, she had tumbled over a sheer apex, crying out, then sobbing, a woman so disoriented even minutes later that she seemed as vulnerable as a creature newly born.

I'd like to believe I am a competent lover, but I knew my skills did not account for an eruption of such magnitude. It was Emily, uniquely Emily, her physical release so explosive that it was as un-mistakably visual as it was audible—a jettisoning fact that only made her sob harder, and voice her embarrassment.

"That's why I've always been so careful about men," she had whis-pered. "I can't help how my body reacts, and it's goddamn embar-rassing. It creeped Paul out, I think, so I almost never really let myself go. Tonight, *Christ*! I got carried away, I guess. I'm so sorry."

Sorry? I had just experienced one of the most sensual couplings of my life. I did my best to reassure her and succeeded, apparently, because half an hour later it happened again.

To equate sexual release with trust was as irrational—or as sen-sible—as any other aspect of love play between male and female. But there it was. It was the way I felt.

Just by thinking it through, I felt better about coming to Immo-kalee alone. After only a day together, I had no right to expect fidel-ity from the woman nor a reason to demand trust. If Tomlinson or anyone else could lure Emily away, so be it. I would be disap-pointed. *Very* disappointed. But I also knew that I would be secretly relieved. Discovering the truth tonight might spare me a more pain-ful surprise down the road—no doubt the reason why I set such traps in the first place.

It was refreshing to be able to admit that to myself. Freeing, in its way. So I closed a mental door on the subject and focused my attention on what I was doing.

A good thing, too.

By then, in the lights of my truck, I could see a curvature of tree line that indicated a bend in the road. According to the satellite aerial, it was where County Road 846 turned north as County Road 857—and marked the midway point of Squires's acreage. To the south was saw grass and swamp. To the north, more of the fertilized geometrics that define Florida agriculture.

I slowed enough to poke my head out the window and checked an east-facing road sign that drifted past. I was not surprised by its message. It was the same sign I'd seen in my odd vision of the girl.

IMMOKALEE 22 MILES.

Almost concurrently, two Hispanic-looking men on the Everglades side of the road caught my attention. They were standing by a gate, smoking cigarettes, no vehicle in sight. The gate was chained, I noted. I also noted the way the men turned their faces away from my headlights, shielding their identities, as I drove past.

They were spotters, I decided. They were standing watch. If Squires had indeed driven Tula Choimha home to Red Citrus, why were these two guarding the gate to his Everglades acreage?

It suggested to me that I had indeed seen some kind of structure beneath the trees in the aerial photo. It suggested to me that Squires and the girl were nearby.

Slowing to a crawl, I gave the men a mild wave. In response, one of them flipped his middle finger, then turned his back. His reaction was more than just aggressive. It was stupid. Why would he invite a confrontation down here in redneck country, where a lot of pickup trucks still had gun racks?

I decided the guy was either drunk or he was aggressive for a reason. Was there something happening beyond that metal gate he couldn't risk anyone seeing or hearing?

I shifted into neutral, letting the truck coast, as I picked up my phone to call Leroy Melinski. It was the reasonable thing to do even though I didn't want to do it. Perversely, I hoped there was no reception or that I got the man's voice mail. Leaving the detective out of the loop would allow me to remain invisible.

I liked the potential of that. Neither Melinski nor anyone else knew where I was. The two men at the gate had no idea who *I* was.

I could talk to the men or slip by unnoticed and search the area alone. Do it right and no one would ever know I had been there.

I got my wish. No reception.

I lifted my gear bag onto the passenger's seat as I shifted into reverse and swung the truck around. By the time I got to the gate, both men were standing in the road, dark bandannas now covering their faces like bank robbers in a TV western, their body language communicating a rapper's insolence. The bandannas and the tattoos told me they were members of a Latin gang—*pandilleros*, in Spanish slang.

Should I stop? Or should I park a mile up the road and jog back?

I foot-flicked my high beams on long enough to convince myself that neither man was palming a weapon. It gave me a reason to stop, which is exactly what I wanted to do—another perverse preference. I can tolerate stupidity because it is a biological condition. Ignorance and arrogance are choices, though.

I got out of the truck, engine running, lights on and my gear bag within easy reach if I needed it.

Beside the bag was the palm-sized laser I'd brought along, the Dazer Guardian. Because I had demonstrated the weapon to Emily earlier, I'd already overridden the twenty-four-hour security timer, which meant the weapon was operational, ready to use at the touch of a button.

I gave the thing a long last look, then almost stuck it in my pocket before I swung the door closed. But then I reminded myself I had never tried the light on a shark, let alone a couple of two-legged gangbangers, and now was not the time to risk a disappointing first test.

I felt confident I wouldn't need it, or any of the other weapons in my bag.

I was wrong.

———

Because both men assumed I didn't speak Spanish, I listened to them exchange nervous and profane assessments of me as I walked toward them.

I was a homosexual cowboy who had lost his hat as well as a horse that I abused anally. I was a drunken Gomer—a welfare redneck—who was too poor to buy a truck that was not inhabited by rats.

Hearing that caused me to take a closer look at the lane beyond the gate, wondering about their truck. It was all tree shadows and darkness, but my headlights were bright enough that I should have seen reflectors on their vehicle.

I did not. It confirmed what I had suspected: The dirt road led to a cabin or some sort of area where these two had parked.

Maybe Squires and the girl were there now. If not, someone else was there, because I heard radio static and then watched one of the men pull a little VHF from his pocket, saying in Spanish, "Don't bother us now. We got a visitor. Some white Gomer—he's probably pissed because Dedos just flipped him off."

Latin gang members use nicknames. Dedos was appropriate. It meant "Fingers."

The radio crackled in reply, a voice saying, "Tell that *pendejo* to stop causing us problems! A white dude? Jesus Christ, get rid of him! What kind of car? You call me back if there's any trouble, you hear me, Calavero?"

Calavero—another graphic nickname.

"A truck. An old redneck piece of shit, don't worry about it," Calavero said, looking at me now as he shoved the radio into his pocket. Then he said in pretty good English, "What you doing way out here, Gomer? You lost or something? Hell, man, my homey, he was just using his finger to point to the best direction for you to go. Straight up, unless you want to drive through a bunch of cow shit."

The man laughed, glancing at his partner, Dedos, then used his chin to motion toward me. It was a signal to separate, possibly, because Calavero started moving to my left as Dedos took a couple of steps toward the truck's passenger side.

I had stopped midway between the men and my truck, a hazed silhouette to them because of my headlights. If they hadn't separated, I would have continued to assume they weren't armed. But movement was all the warning I needed. So I maximized my Florida accent, saying, "I'm lookin' for an ol' boy named Harris Squires. You boys know where I can find him?"

That stopped them. I used their momentary surprise to take a long step back, then leaned a hip comfortably against my truck, close enough to get to the door fast if I needed to.

Calavero was the talker, and I listened to him reply, *"Amigo,* we can't even see your face 'cause of them lights. How we supposed to answer a question like that? I suggest you get back in your truck and get the fuck outta here, man."

I planned to. But not yet.

"It's a pretty simple question," I said. "He's a great big guy, Harris Squires. I met him last night. He's not the one who said it, but I heard he has something for sale out here I might want to buy. Why don't you call him and let him know I'm here?"

I could only guess at what Squires might have to sell, but the *pandilleros* knew.

In Spanish Dedos said to Calavero, "He wants to buy steroids from jelly boy this time of night? Or maybe the V-man's right. Maybe they been running our girls outta here. Call Chapo, tell him we got to speak to the V-man right now."

Chapo—the voice on the radio and another nickname. *Shorty.*

It didn't tell me everything I wanted to know, but it told me enough—enough to get a rough estimate of how many people I was dealing with. Also, that there was an established pecking order. There were at least two more *pandilleros* beyond the gate, including a boss man named V-man. Plus Squires and, hopefully, the Guatemalan girl.

I had also learned that Squires wasn't a friend of the gang—perhaps he was even their captive. It was unlikely but a possibility. Referring over the radio to a man the size of Squires as "jelly boy" required a controlled environment or some firepower to back it up.

It was time for me to get going, I decided. Time to drive fast to an area where there was phone reception because I'd walked into something bigger than I had ever anticipated. This situation required the police—a whole squad of pros, including a chopper. In another country where there were fewer laws, maybe, just maybe, I would have tried to handle it on my own. But not here. And not when there was a chance that Tula Choimha was alive and still in danger.

Because I didn't want the men to know what I'd learned, I said, "I don't have time to stand around listening to you boys talking Mexican. If you see Squires, tell him I stopped by. But don't blame me when he gets pissed off 'cause he didn't make a sale."

I stood and turned my back to them, paying close attention as the two bickered about whether they should let me go or not. Because the exchange was in Spanish, they believed there was no need to keep their voices low. Dedos was the violent one, but Calavero was the boss.

"Stab him with a knife, that's just stupid!" he hissed at Dedos. "For what, to rob him? He don't have any money, look at his goddamn truck! We gonna have enough bodies to deal with!"

I almost stopped when he said that but forced myself to keep moving.

Dedos's response: "Man, we can't just let him go—the Gomer

knows Squires! Call the V-man. The dude could bring the cops the moment he's out of here. Then what's the V-man gonna say?"

It wasn't until my hand was on the open door, my foot on the running board, that I allowed myself to risk a glance over my shoulder.

My timing could have been better.

Dedos was fast and quiet. He had closed the distance between us, suddenly only one long stride away from the truck. His arm was extended, something in his hand. A cell phone, I thought at first, but his partner was yelling, "Don't shoot him, you idiot!" so I knew that I was mistaken.

I threw my hands up, a defensive response, as I dived into the cab of my truck. At the same instant, I heard a percussion-cap *BANG!* then a brief whistling noise. A microsecond later, I felt a dazzling impact of something metallic that glanced off my left shoulder, then clanged hard against the truck's cab.

It took me a moment to realize I'd been tasered with an electroshock weapon. The thing produced a crackling burst of pain that radiated through my spine, down the sciatic nerves of my legs. Zapped by several thousand volts, my brain flashed with what might have been the white schematic of my own cerebral synapses.

Then the wild sensation was gone.

My body lay immobile on the seat for an instant, as my brain worked it through. Dedos had used an older taser, with a steel dart attached to a wire. But the dart hadn't hit me squarely. It had plowed a furrow of blood across my left shoulder, then skipped out, hitting the truck, steel on steel.

Now Calavero was calling, "Grab him, *pendejo!* We got no choice now!" as he also yelled into the radio, calling for help, but didn't seem to be getting a response.

I was dazed, my glasses hanging by fishing line around my neck, as Dedos grabbed me by the ankles, trying to pull me out onto the road. I kicked back hard . . . missed . . . then kicked again and heard the man make an encouraging *Woofing* sound that told me I had connected with his groin.

I got my left hand on the steering wheel and was pulling myself into the truck when Calavero joined the attack. He used his boots to kick my calves and thigh muscles numb as he ordered Dedos, "Get on your feet, you drunken fool! Use the radio, tell them we need help 'cause you did something stupid again."

My equipment bag was in the middle of the seat, not quite within reach. The palm-sized laser was close enough, though. I grabbed the thing as, once again, I felt my body being dragged out of the cab.

I had experimented enough with the laser to know that the rubberized cap was an instant-on switch, much like a flashlight. But the system was far more complex. There was another switch that cycled through various ranges of effectiveness, from one yard to almost a quarter mile.

To impress Emily, I had dialed the thing to three hundred yards and then painted distant mangroves with its luminous green beam—"searchlight mode," according to the literature. Stupidly, I hadn't taken the time to switch the laser back to close-quarters-combat range. Would searchlight mode have any effect on men only a few yards away?

Calavero had a gun in his hand now, I realized. A little chrome-coated derringer, with sizable over-under barrels that told me it was heavy caliber. He was using the butt of the gun to bang at my knee, looking for an opening to put a bullet into me. My truck was about to become a killing field, and all I wanted to do was get the hell out of there and start over.

Probably because I have never been shot in the stomach or chest, an odd, slow thought moved through my mind, oblivious to the panic I felt. *Pain or impact?* Which would I feel as a bullet splintered my ribs?

I tried to kick my legs free so Calavero couldn't get a clean shot. It caused him to pocket the weapon long enough to concentrate on his grip. As he pulled me from the truck, my head banged hard on the running board, then I landed, back first, on the asphalt.

I fumbled the Dazer upon impact but managed to recover as Calavero gave me another numbing kick to the thigh. My glasses were still around my neck, but I could see well enough to know he was reaching for the derringer again. If I didn't disable the man soon, he would shoot me, then keep shooting until I was dead.

I used the laser.

When I brought the Dazer up to fire, I told myself, *Keep your finger off the damn switch until you've aimed!*

I had been told that surprise was an important aspect of the laser's effectiveness. So I waited . . . waited until I had the weapon in both hands, leveled at the man's face. I was sighting down the little metal tube as if it were a gun when I touched the button.

When contact was ignited, I got my answer about the Dazer's effectiveness. The *pandillero* was stunned.

In Calavero's corneal reflection, I saw a bolt of green fire that flared like a welding torch. There was an instant of shocked silence, Calavero's eyes wide, his face contorted, then a scream as he released his grip on me and tried to claw his eyes free of the pain.

I jumped to my feet, hearing Dedos yelling, "Pull him out from behind the truck, I'll shoot him!"

The partner was armed now, I realized. I couldn't deal with both men at the same time, so I ducked low behind the door, holding the

Dazer like a roll of quarters. I drew my arm back and swung hard from the hips, hitting Calavero twice in the ribs with my fist, hearing the distinctive *pop* of thin bones breaking.

Making a grotesque wheezing noise, the man collapsed beneath my left arm, blind and unable to take a full breath. To make sure he was disabled, I gave his eyes another laser burst, his scream not so loud this time because he was semiconscious.

It took a moment to balance Calavero's body against my chest, then get the Dazer positioned correctly in my right hand. When I was ready, I dragged Calavero away from the door, using him as a shield, until I had a clear view of his partner, Dedos, who had taken a few steps back.

The man was crouched in a shooter's stance, hands gripping a black semiauto pistol. Its laser sight created a smoky red beam that I realized connected the pistol with a dot that painted my forehead. I ducked lower, closer to the door, as the beam bounced, then searched for me.

Dedos's hands weren't steady. He was probably spooked by how easily I had disabled his partner. Yes . . . that was the reason, because he decided to bargain.

"Man, I don't want this kind of trouble," he called to me. "Tell you what. You throw that green-light thing you got on the ground, I'll do the same. I promise, man. You can stand up now—*seriously.* You want, I'll count to three. I count to three, we both throw our shit on the road at the same time. How about that?"

From behind the door, I said, "I don't want to have to kill you. Put your weapon on the ground and put your hands behind your head. Show me your hands, you won't get hurt."

The man answered with a forced laugh, saying, "You sound like a cop, the way you say that. But you ain't no cop. You just a cowboy redneck, talking big."

I didn't respond. Instead, I switched the Dazer's range to close-quarters combat, then took a second to check Calavero's pockets. I found an ornate pocketknife and the VHF radio—lucky for me because I realized that the volume had been turned low. I adjusted the volume so I could hear the *pandilleros'* friends if they called, then jammed the knife and the radio in a pocket of my fishing khakis.

A moment later, Dedos hollered, "Kill me with a light, man? How dumb you think I am? A light can't kill nobody, man!"

I'd kept my left arm locked around Calavero's throat. To keep him from responding, I squeezed his windpipe closed as I replied to Dedos, saying, "Then why's your friend dead? You tell me."

Calavero's body thrashed briefly until I reduced pressure, listening for his partner's quiet feet. I heard nothing, so I risked a look.

With one eye to the driver's-side window, I watched Dedos take another nervous step backward before he yelled in Spanish, "Calavero, hey! You okay? *Answer* me."

I watched until I saw that Dedos had lowered his weapon just enough for me to make a move. Using the door as a shield, I stood, aimed the Dazer at the man's face and pressed the button. As I did, I averted my own eyes, but not until I witnessed Dedos's face contorted by a searing, ocular virescence. It was simultaneous with his shrill scream.

The pistol went flying as Dedos covered his eyes. It didn't help because I kept the laser beam focused on his face, using the door to steady my aim. Dazer literature claims that green is four times more visible to the human eye than other colors. It claims that a laser of this wattage could pierce human flesh, including finger and eyelids.

"It feels like a knife through the orbital socket," one of the Dazer techs—who had experienced the pain—told me. At the time, I had assumed it was a mild exaggeration to get me interested in testing the company's product.

I believed the tech now, particularly when Dedos began to roll on the ground. After a few seconds, he gagged and then vomited. Nausea is a common reaction to being blinded by the laser, according to what I had been told.

I felt confident enough to take a quick look at my shoulder. The dart had plowed a small furrow of flesh. It was bleeding but not badly. Next, I switched off the Dazer long enough to crawl into the truck and grab my equipment bag. In those few seconds, I formulated a plan. I needed information *now*. Where was Tula Choimha? If the men didn't volunteer that information, I would have to force it out of them.

And I knew exactly how to make that happen.

Bag over my shoulder, I dragged Calavero to the front of my truck, positioning his head under the bumper. Alternately, I zapped both men with the laser even though they showed no readiness to fight back.

Next, I kicked Dedos's pistol away, then dragged him near his partner, but closer to my truck's right front tire. When he saw where I'd positioned him, the man became combative. To quiet him, I hammered my elbow into his nose. After one blow, Dedos pretended to be unconscious.

Then I stood and looked far down the road, first to the west, then to the east. How close would a driver have to be before he noticed the two men?

Not very close, I decided, which told me I needed to get moving When the *pandilleros* had first attacked me, I'd desperately hoped a car would turn down this remote road. Not now. An eyewitness was the last thing I wanted. Unless I was willing to detain an innocent passerby, the plan forming in my head would have to be abandoned.

I didn't want to risk making that decision. Not that I was incapable of eliminating an eyewitness—I have done it before in my life. But I have never taken the life of a wholly innocent witness. Not knowingly, anyway. And never, ever in my own country.

"What have you done to my eyes?" Calavero moaned as I used duct tape on his ankles, then his wrists.

"Maybe this will help," I replied, then stripped off more tape and wrapped it around his head as a blindfold.

When I had both men bound, I repositioned them so they could both feel next to their faces the tread of my front tires. My truck was still running, which scared them. Even though they lapsed into a machismo silence, their expressions were easy enough to read in the headlights.

I knew that what the *pandilleros* were imagining was far more terrifying than what they would have experienced had I not taped their eyes. Which was all part of the plan.

I had set up a variation of an interrogation technique that, unlike waterboarding, is unknown to the public. I had been with a special ops team years ago in Libya when I witnessed just how effective— and fast—the technique was at extracting information from an enemy.

I knelt between the men and spoke in English, saying, "I'll give you one chance to answer questions. Refuse, get smart with me, I'll crush your heads with the truck. If you lie, same thing. You're road-kill. I'll leave you here for vultures."

"Don't tell him anything," Calavero said to his partner in fast Spanish. "His voice is different now, hear the difference? The accent. He *is* a cop. But he's not going to hurt us. Cops aren't allowed to hurt people in the States, you'll see."

Dedos didn't sound convinced when he answered, "My nose is broken, man, I could strangle on my own blood if he doesn't let me sit up." Then in English he added, speaking to me, "We don't know anything! But what do you want to know? Hurry up, I'm dying here!"

I asked the men about the girl. I asked about Harris Squires. I asked how many more of their gangbanger friends were waiting down this rutted drive?

Their reply was a smug silence that infuriated me. Two punks, secure in the rights guaranteed by their adopted country, were playing hardass. Two bottom-feeders who profited from the misery of others, dealers of drugs and flesh.

I zapped them both with the Dazer, but the duct tape mitigated the pain. I leaned closer and lasered them again, but they only squirmed and thrashed their heads in response.

"Why is this asshole doing this to us?" Dedos yelled in Spanish, getting mad. "I'm going to die, I'm choking! Even if he is a cop, how's he know so much about Squires and the little virgin?"

Voice steady, Calavero replied, "Shut up. The V-man will have us out of jail by morning. Tell him anything, you're dead, *pendejo*."

Dedos's words, "the little virgin," answered one of my questions. It told me that Tula Choimha was here and maybe still alive. Or had been, the last time these two saw her. Which couldn't have been long ago. According to Melinski, Squires and the girl had left Immokalee a little before eleven p.m.

I checked my watch. *Midnight.*

I was tempted to drag the two into the ditch and get moving, but I had to have more information. How many *pandilleros* and how were they armed? Was Squires a captive or working with the gang?

Calavero was telling Dedos, "My ribs are broken, you don't hear me whining, you pathetic woman—" when I interrupted him, saying in English, "No more talk. You have five seconds to answer my questions."

I began counting as I squatted to confirm the heads of both men were positioned directly in front of my tires.

"Why are you doing this? Who *are* you?" Dedos wailed, coughing blood as he tried to sit up.

With my foot, I forced the man to the ground. Then gave it a beat before I told them both in Spanish, "No more time. You assholes have no idea who I am. But you're about to find out." To convince them my Spanish was good, I added an insult that's common in Mexico.

I heard Calavero swear, groaning, "The Gomer understood us. Everything we said!" as I swung into the truck, limping a little because my leg muscles were beginning to knot from being kicked.

As I positioned myself behind the wheel, the VHF radio beside me crackled, and I adjusted the squelch to hear, "Calavero! Get your fingers out of your ass. Why haven't you called?"

I hit the button and replied, "I tried. Where were you?"

"Don't give me your shit. What happened to the Gomer? That's all I want to know."

I kept the radio a foot from my mouth and tried to make my voice higher and hoarser, to imitate Calavero. "Dedos is an idiot, but the white guy is gone. How much longer?"

I didn't want to risk his suspicion by saying more.

The man—Chapo, I guessed—was suspicious anyway.

"What's wrong with your voice? You sound different."

I snapped, "I'm bored shitless, I'm thirsty. Maybe you'd rather talk to Dedos."

The voice paused . . . more suspicious now? Even when the man laughed, saying, "Dedos is an asshole. What else is new?" I wasn't convinced.

I kept an eye on the wooded road, expecting Chapo, or his partners, to come and check things out for themselves.

The interrogation technique we'd used in Libya is called the Spare Tire Switch, although I have never heard the term again as it relates to intelligence gathering. It was called that by CIA officers running the operation—presumably CIA, because such information is never offered.

A spare tire, handled by two quiet men, is bumped against the head of a blindfolded enemy. A third team member sits next to them in a truck, engine running, that alternately accelerates, then decelerates, as the spare tire rocks in sync, as if attempting to climb over the enemy's face.

The interrogation subject, of course, doesn't know it's a spare tire. He's convinced he is lying under the truck. It is a powerful motivator.

My variation worked well.

When I got my truck into first gear, I accelerated slowly forward until I felt the first hint of resistance. It was accompanied by a duo of howls from Dedos and Calavero.

Instantly, I shifted to neutral, then stepped quietly out of the truck.

Using my left hand on the doorframe, my right on the accelerator, I began to rock the truck forward and back. With my hand, I added more gas with each forward thrust. The terror the two men endured—and the pain they imagined—was caused by the engine noise that grew progressively louder. It was the noise that convinced them their skulls were about to crack like eggs.

After just a few seconds of this, Calavero was begging me to stop.

"Anything," he pleaded, "I'll tell you anything."

He did, too. But he wasn't nearly as eager to share as Dedos, who I had to threaten just to shut him up.

"Crazy with fear" is just a cliché—until you have actually interacted with someone whose brain has been addled by terror. They weep, they slobber. Their sense of time and balance has been scrambled.

"Sick with fear" is another cliché, yet it accurately described the visceral dread I felt after what the two men confessed to me.

They were members of the Latin Kings. The Kings were killers and proud of it. Members were holding Squires and the girl captive at a hunting camp that consisted of an RV and a couple of outbuildings, half a mile away through the woods. There, a man named Victorino—a Latin King captain—and a woman called Frankie were filming a sex video, using Tula Choimha as their victim.

It made no sense to me when Dedos explained that the woman was Squires's girlfriend, but I didn't press for details. I grabbed the radio after a moment of indecision, pressed the transmit button and called, "Chapo! Stop everything! I think maybe the cops are here. Chapo?"

I waited . . . called again, but no reply. It was maddening.

Dedos referred to the girl as *la chula virgen*. The Mexican slang he used to describe how she would be raped was particularly disgusting: *Romper el tamor con sangre.*

His boss was going to bust through the girl's screen in search of blood.

Equally disgusting was the indifference with which Dedos offered details. He wasn't referring to a teenage girl. He was discussing a worthless object, a young Guatemalan, no better than an animal.

It was not uncommon in the racial hierarchy of Mexican gangs. He mentioned Tula, in fact, as an unimportant aside after Calavero had told me about Harris Squires.

"This person—we call him jelly boy—he disrespected the reputation of our organization," Calavero said. "For this, he is being punished. How, I do not know. That is up to our *jefe*. Now, stop this bullshit! Arrest us, if you want. We'll be out by tomorrow, what do I care? I'm not guilty of anything but being too stupid to kill you when I had the chance."

Calavero was lying about Squires, and I knew it. When I threatened to put them under the truck again, Dedos was more forthcoming. Squires was to be the victim in a snuff film, he said. With a camera rolling, Squires would be murdered—"Slow, like a kind of ceremony," Dedos said—then his body would be burned.

"If he's still alive," Dedos added. "He attacked the V-man, so the V-man shot him in self-defense. With a shotgun, but I don't know how bad. When they sent us out to watch the road, jelly boy was still alive. He was bleeding from the face and chest, but the man is big as a mountain, so who knows? I only do what I am told. I have nothing to do with anything that happens at the hunting camp."

It was then that Dedos told me about the girl.

That's when I tried the radio. Then again.

Nothing but static.

I felt a panicked need to hurry even though I was unclear about the timing. Had Tula already been raped or was it happening now? More threats didn't make it any clearer, and I couldn't waste any more time.

Shock affects different people in different ways. Into my mind came an analytical clarity: I had to do whatever was required to help the girl—do it in a way that didn't risk my future freedom, if possible, but saving the girl came first.

There is a maxim that applied. At least, I wanted it to apply, because it excused the extreme behavior that might be required of me. An old friend and I had pounded out the truism together long ago in a distant jungle:

In any conflict, the boundaries of behavior are defined by the party who cares least about morality.

The Latin Kings cared nothing of morality. They'd made that clear.

I gave myself a second to review. No one knew I was here. The *pandilleros* had no idea who I was. They wouldn't expect a hostile visitor, particularly someone with my training and background. And, tonight, there were no rules, no boundaries of behavior.

Thinking that transformed my strange, restless mood into a resolute calm. I had made the decision to act before giving it conscious thought. The decision tunneled my vision. Thoughts of legalities and guilt—even my fears for the girl—vanished. They were replaced by the necessity of operating in the moment. Of acting and reacting with an indifferent precision.

It was a familiar feeling, a cold clarity that originated from the very core of who I am. I might have been in North Africa or the jungles of Central America. Nothing existed but my targets—threats which I must now find and neutralize.

There were three targets, according to Dedos, not counting Squires or the woman named Frankie, whose role was still unclear. Two fellow gangbangers plus their boss, Victorino—or the V-man, as they called him. All men were armed with handguns and knives. Two carried fully automatic weapons—"T-9s," Dedos told me.

He was referring to one of the cheapest machine pistols on the market, a Tec-9. Cheap or not, the thing could spit out twenty or thirty rounds in only a couple of seconds, then fire again with the quick change of a magazine.

Daunting. But yet another reason not to hesitate when my targets were in sight.

I was hurrying now, but methodically. From my equipment bag,

I took a pair of leather gloves and put them on. The night was warm, but I pulled on a black watch cap, too. Roll it down, it became a ski mask.

I looked at my leather boat shoes. The tread was distinctive, so I found rubber dive boots in my truck.

When I had changed shoes, I tried calling Chapo on the radio again—nothing but static. Then I frisked Dedos and Calavero more thoroughly.

Dedos had pointed a .45 caliber Glock at me, fifteen rounds in the magazine, one in the chamber. Because Glocks have no safety—and I don't trust the weapon, anyway—I chose not to slide it into my belt.

That would come later.

Calavero's derringer was a .357. The recoil had to be horrendous, but it was a manstopper at close range. I slipped it into my back pocket.

I found a key to the gate and keys to what Dedos said was a Dodge Ram pickup hidden in the trees fifty yards down the hunting camp road. Because a priority was getting my own truck out of sight, I opened the gate, backed my truck into the shadows, then jogged back to Calavero and Dedos. I used my Randall knife to free their ankles—but not their hands—then ripped the tape from their eyes.

"Get up, get moving," I told them, pointing Dedos's Glock at them. If I was going to shoot someone, I wanted the medical examiner to find rounds from a gangbanger's gun, not mine.

"Show me you where you parked your truck," I ordered them. "You can lay in the back while I look for the girl. Or stay here if you want. Let the ants eat you, that's your choice."

It was a lie. They were going with me.

From my equipment bag, I removed the night vision monocular, then hid the bag behind the seat of my truck. The monocular is fit-ted on a headband that holds the lens flush over one eye.

When I flicked the switch, the gloom of the woodland ahead vanished. I was in an eerie green daylight world, details sharp. My right eye is dominant, yet I prefer to shoot using natural night vi-sion, which is why I wore the monocular over my left eye. It is a personal preference that wouldn't have held true were I carrying a rifle or a full automatic.

As we jogged toward the hunting camp—I had to literally kick both men in the butt to get them going—I stayed behind them off to the side. Because I couldn't get Chapo on the radio, I had no choice now but to go into the hunting camp fast and hard.

Twice, I told Calavero to shut up, stop talking, but he continued to goad me. Breathing heavily, he made threats about what the V-man would do when I found him, then said, "When our lawyer gets you in court, man, how you gonna explain to the judge about my broken ribs? Dedos's fucked-up face? You going to jail, faggot. Police brutal-ity. We got lots of Latin King brothers in the joint, they'll love meet-ing you. Man, those brothers gonna have some *fun!*"

That caused him to laugh, imagining what they would do to me.

By then, I could see the grille of their Dodge hidden in trees. To silence Calavero, I considered hammering him in the back of the head with the Glock but didn't. Pointless demonstrations of power—like anger—is for amateurs.

Instead, I timed his steps, kicked his right foot into his left ankle, then brought my knee down hard, between his shoulders when he fell. I taped his mouth, then pulled the man to his feet. As I forced Calavero to lean his head against the fender of the truck, I told Dedos, "You seem like the smart one. Keep your mouth shut until I tell you to speak."

Dedos nodded eagerly, his face through the night vision lens a misshapen montage of silver eyes and glittering blood.

Dedos got his chance to speak sooner than expected. As I forced Calavero, then Dedos, into the passenger side of the Dodge, the radio squelched with a muffled voice. Pulling the radio from my pocket, I heard a man say, "Calavero, you there, man? Come in."

It wasn't Chapo's voice.

I touched the transmit button and replied, "Hang on a minute. Talk to Dedos."

Then I pressed the radio to my chest and told Dedos, "Tell him cops just busted through the gate. In a truck. Tell him to leave the girl where she is and run. But"—I slapped him behind the ear for emphasis—"*listen* to what I'm telling you. If you screw this up, if they hurt that girl, I'll kill you. I'll shoot you in the back of the head."

To make my point, I touched the Glock to his temple, mildly amused that, beside him, Calavero leaned toward the dashboard so he wouldn't be hit if the bullet exited his partner's head.

Dedos looked at me as if I were crazy. "You kidding, man. The *truth*? That's what you want me to say to my boys?"

I replied, "Do it!" then held the radio up to Dedos's mouth.

Dedos was so frightened, his voice had a hysterical edge, the pitch of nervous laughter.

"The hell you talking about?" the *pandillero* replied. "Stop with your joking. V-man is sick of that little virgin, so we need something in the truck. The chain saw. Check, make sure it's there."

I took a deep breath, steadying myself. As I did, the man spoke again, saying, "Wait a minute. You serious? Put Calavero on. You're joking about cops, right?"

I ignored him, thinking it through. If they needed a chain saw, it was to dismember Tula's body. And if the girl was already dead, I was better off going in quietly. It was safer, cleaner. Take the men by surprise, one by one. Or just wait for them to finish up and jump them as they left the camp.

But what if they were killing her *now*?

I held the radio to my face for a moment, undecided. Then I touched the transmit button and said in English, "If you hurt that girl, you're dead. Understand me? Tell Victorino. Tell him to stop everything and throw your weapons on the ground. We're coming in. You've got three minutes, then you're going to jail."

There was a shocked paused before the man responded in English, saying, "The fuck you talking about? Who *is* this?"

Hoping the gangbangers would abandon the girl and scatter, I told him, "We've got your names, we know where you live. We'll come to your houses if you run. But don't hurt that girl—or you'll be sitting on death row."

The pandillero was replying as I sprinted around to the driver's side, saying, "I don't know nothing about no girl, man! We having a party, that's all . . . ," but I didn't listen to more.

I tossed the radio into Calavero's lap as I started the Dodge, put it in drive, then transferred the Glock to my right hand. Because I knew I might need the emergency break, I tested it to make sure it worked. Then I floored the accelerator, fishtailing toward the hunting camp.

Dedos was hollering at me, calling me crazy, saying, "I can't see nothing, man! You're gonna kill us all!" because I drove with the lights off.

I could see fine. Through the night vision lens, my world was sharp and clear. It was, to me, a familiar world, where shadows are unambiguous, a place without shades of gray.

Dedos was right about one thing, though. If Tula Choimha was dead, I would kill them all.

FOURTEEN

WHEN THE MEXICAN MAN WITH GOLD TEETH SHOT HARRIS Squires with a rifle, Tula Choimha collapsed on the ground, in shock for a moment, regressing back to the child that life had never allowed her to be.

The lone exception: the night she had watched her father die in flames.

Tula screamed, drawing her body into a fetal position, as her eyes continued to watch what was happening. She screamed again when she saw that blood peppered the giant's face and chest. But when the big man stumbled . . . almost fell . . . then somehow found the strength to keep moving forward, toward the man with gold teeth, Tula's hysteria was displaced by her concern for Harris Squires.

The girl got to her feet, yelling in Spanish, "Stop hurting him! Don't shoot him again!" Then she ran toward the Mexican, her fists clenched.

The Mexican was laughing at Squires, taunting him. He was motioning with his hand for the giant to keep coming. With every step, though, the Mexican took a step backward, staying just out of the giant's reach.

Behind Tula, the redheaded woman was enjoying herself, calling, "V-man . . . Hey, Vic! Try to shoot him in the balls. See what kind of marksman you are!"

The rifle the man carried, Tula noticed, had two barrels. So maybe the rifle was a shotgun, although Tula wasn't sure of the difference. Was the V-man carrying the gun in the crook of his arm because both barrels had been fired with one shot?

If so, Tula believed the giant might survive because his spirit was still strong despite the blood that now soaked his pretty blue shirt. The girl could tell because Squires was saying to the Mexican, "Is that your best shot, *chilie*? That the best you can do, douche bag?" his voice flinching with pain at each step but his eyes aflame, focused on the V-man.

Suddenly, it was as if the Mexican was done having fun, because he took two fast steps backward. Then he pointed the shotgun at Squires's pelvis, saying, "I want to do this slow, jelly boy. Maybe shoot off your *penga*, that'll make you smile for the camera. *Then* I'll use the knife."

Still grinning, the V-man looked toward the redhead as if seeking her approval . . . but then his expression changed. His attention shifted to Tula, who, still running and only a few strides away, screamed, "No-o-o-o!" a word that she had transformed into a sustained shriek.

The resonance of a young girl's scream is fine-tuned by eons of adaptation to repel attackers, particularly human males. The V-man winced, his ears aching, and his awareness of Harris Squires was momentarily jammed. Then he had to stick a hand out to stop Tula, who crashed into his thigh, her fingernails flailing, as she tried to sink her teeth into the man's arm.

Victorino's Latin King soldiers had been pillaging the RV. But two of them were now sprinting to help as the V-man hollered, "Ouch, goddamn you!" Then: "Get this little bitch off me!"

Victorino swung his open hand at the girl's face but missed. "Damn brat!" he hissed, then swung again and connected hard. Tula went sprawling, her nose bloody.

An instant later, the V-man's attention returned to Squires, who was suddenly towering over him, his right fist drawn back. Victorino noticed just in time to roll his face away from the sledgehammer impact, a glancing blow that would have crushed his face. Instead, Victorino backpedaled several steps, still holding the shotgun, then went down hard on his butt.

Squires kept coming, the grin on his face grotesque because of the blood. But then the giant wasn't grinning anymore because the V-man's soldiers, Chapo and Zopilote, tackled him from behind.

Chapo had a small crowbar in his hand—he'd probably been looking for a secret stash inside the RV. And he began hammering at Squires's back and butt with the bar to immobilize the man.

Victorino was dazed but still coherent enough to yell to Chapo, "Cripple him, but don't kill him! Leave him for me!"

Then, standing, testing his balance, Victorino had to yell again, warning Chapo, "Watch out for the little cougar!" because the girl had a rock in her hand and was sprinting to help Squires.

Frankie intercepted the girl, though. She did it on the run, even with a drink in her hand, sweeping the skinny child up with her muscles, then swinging her around as if playing a game.

The redhead was still in a playful mood, the V-man could see it, which provided him an optimistic boost. So far, tonight hadn't been nearly as much fun as he'd hoped. On the drive to the hunting camp, he'd pictured how it would go in his mind, first impressing the redhead by killing Squires with a flourish, then the two of them getting it on in front of the camera, being real sexy-dirty with the cute little *chula*.

But this *chula* was a street cat, not a whimpering child like most. And jelly boy had proven he had balls after all, almost humiliating him in front of Frankie.

Shit—Victorino was looking at his wrist where the girl had bitten him to the bone—the *puta* would have to pay for this. He'd make an example of her. Not kill her—a girl her age was too valuable— but maybe tie her up and use a razor like the Muslims did. Cut her body so she'd never be able to enjoy a man even when she was old and not getting paid for it.

Yeah, get it on camera. Victorino was wiping blood on his jeans as he pictured how it would go. Give the redhead a private warning by letting her watch him use the box cutter on the girl, then show the video to new *chulas* when they arrived in Florida desperate enough to do anything for money.

Tell the new girls: *See what happens when you disobey the V-man?*

But that would come later. *After* he and the redhead had enjoyed themselves a little, just as planned.

It would happen.

Victorino felt his confidence returning as he watched Frankie touch her fingernails to the little virgin's throat and whisper something into the girl's ear.

The *chula* had been screaming but instantly stopped, her face paling as if she was about to be sick.

It caused Frankie to beam at the V-man and brag, "You're an idiot when it comes to girls, know that? To make a spoiled brat behave, you have to understand it's all an act. Screaming, not putting out, whatever. It's because they *want* something. Figure out what it is, then threaten to take it away. That's how you handle a *puta*. Just about any girl, if she's cute at all. They're all the same."

Frankie laughed into the *chula*'s face, adding, "Aren't you, darling? *Aren't* you?" Then looked at Victorino, smiling. "I think the two of us are gonna get along just fine. You ready to have some fun?"

Spooky, the V-man decided, the way the redhead said that. *They're* all the same. But kind of sexy, too, like Frankie was different from other women.

And maybe she was. But the bitch was already insulting him in front of his soldiers, calling him an idiot in her superior way. Which had to stop.

Victorino watched Frankie brush the girl's hair back very gently as if playing with a doll, then he turned his head and told Chapo and Zopilote in Spanish, "Tie up jelly boy, we'll deal with him later. Then search his truck. The tall *gringa* and me want some privacy for maybe an hour, with the girl. Find the money wherever jelly boy hid it. Then get the gas cans out, soak everything so the whole fucking place goes up when we're ready. Afterward, I'll give you the redhead as a present."

In reply to their surprised expressions, he added, "*Seriously.* Have yourselves some fun with those big *chichis* of hers tonight because tomorrow, maybe next day at the latest, I'm cutting them off."

What Frankie whispered into Tula's ear was, "Listen, you spoiled little bitch. If Harris dies tonight, it's *your* fault. So shut your mouth . . . or God's gonna blame you for killing your new sweetheart."

It shocked Tula that a woman with eyes as black with fog as Frankie's could speak of God in such a knowing, confident way.

And also that the woman was able to look into Tula's heart and recognize the sudden affection she felt for Squires.

Never in her life had a man done so much to protect her. Not since her father had died. The giant had not only tried to save Tula, he had continued to fight for her safety even after having been shot, then beaten. It squeezed the girl's heart now, seeing him lying on the ground, bleeding and humiliated, after risking so much to help her. She wondered how many bullets were in his body and if he was dying.

He is our warrior, the Maiden said into Tula's mind when she stopped struggling against the tall woman's muscles. *He is our knight. You must do whatever you can to help him.*

As if reading Tula's thoughts, the redhead surprised the girl again by saying, "Harris is kind of cute, isn't he? Like a big stupid animal who's eager to please. Trust me"—the woman laughed into the girl's face, her breath foul with smoke and alcohol—"I know exactly what you're thinking."

Into Tula's mind flashed the image of the sad bear in the zoo as Frankie swung her toward the RV, bragging, "Know how I do it? I understand how women think. All their sneaky, catty ways. Plus, we're a lot alike, me and tomboys like you. The first time I saw you, I could tell. *A boy, my ass.*

"Difference between us, you're still hiding behind God. Me, I got smart quick and joined the other side. That's where the fun is and the power. It's all about power, *niña.* Power and money-money-money."

Then the woman stumbled, slurring, "*Shit*—you spilled my drink! Look at what you did. And your goddamn blood's all over my new tank top!"

They were at the door to the RV now, and Tula was looking over the woman's shoulder, seeing two men use tape on the giant's wrists as the Mexican with gold teeth watched, holding the shotgun over his shoulder like a soldier who was tired of marching. In the lights of the pickup truck, Victorino's face appeared swollen, misshapen, which reminded Tula of her own throbbing nose.

She pushed herself away from the woman and said, "I can't breathe, please put me down. I need to blow my nose because the man hit me."

The woman dropped Tula without warning—like a practical joke. When the girl's head banged the steel steps to the trailer, it evoked a snort of laughter from Frankie.

"Good," she said. "Knock some sense into you."

The woman had found a tissue in her jeans and was rubbing at the blood on her shirt, her balance unsteady, getting madder as she smeared the blood. Then she gave up and hurled the tissue at Tula. "Stop fighting me! If you don't, I'll tell that Mexican to kill your boyfriend. How'd you like that?"

Tula was on her feet, sniffling, trying to stop her nose from bleeding, but her eyes were focused on Squires, who was still on his back, hands folded across his belly like a corpse because of the tape. The two men had the doors to the giant's truck open. They were leaning inside, throwing things out onto the ground, while the Mexican with the gold teeth walked toward the RV, a bandy-legged man trying to appear taller than he was.

Frankie looked away from Tula long enough to grin at the V-man, who was close enough for her to call, "Does my Mexican stallion need a drinkie?"

Then the woman stabbed her fingernails under the girl's chin, lifting Tula's face, and whispered, "How's a little saint like you gonna feel? Murdering your sweetie when God knows you could've stopped it."

Tula could barely hear the woman's words because, suddenly, the Maiden was in her head, voice firm, telling her what to do, what to say. The girl's heart was pounding, but she wasn't afraid—not for herself, anyway—but she ached for Squires, who lay on the ground, breathing fast, shallow breaths. She watched him turn his head to the side and cough, something bubbling out of his mouth and nose.

Blood, Tula realized.

Inside the girl's head, the Maiden's voice warned, "He has a bullet in his lungs. To save him, God will forgive you for anything you must do. I lied to my Inquisitors. *Remember?*"

Tula remembered. Jehanne had even warned the vigilante priests that she would mislead them, if necessary, to spare her warrior knights. It was in the book Tula had left back at the trailer park.

I would rather have you cut my throat than betray my knights by telling you the truth, the saint had vowed.

Lying to an enemy wasn't a lie—it was a weapon. And it made Tula furious to see the giant lying on the ground, vulnerable and in pain. It caused her to remember that she had weapons of her own.

You were born to do this, the Maiden whispered over the noise of Frankie's voice. *You were born to fight evil, to smite the devil down.*

Evil. This woman, Frankie, *was* evil. Tula had known it from their first meeting. In Harris Squires, the girl had recognized the scars of the redheaded woman's sins. A wickedness so pervading that it had clouded the man's goodness. It clung to him like an odor.

That odor filled the air now, stronger than Frankie's drunken breath, as Tula looked into the woman's face and said, "I'm sorry . . . I don't want you to be mad at me. I'm sorry about your blouse— you're so beautiful, it's a shame. Because of the way you look, a woman so tall and pretty, it scares someone like me. That's why I tried to get away."

The woman appeared startled. It took her a drunken moment to process what the girl had said. "You're goddamn right you should be sorry. But maybe the stains'll come out if I don't let it dry. I've heard if you use warm water—"

Abruptly, Frankie stopped, as if she'd just realized something. She had been looking at her tank top, pulling it away from her breasts, but then grabbed Tula by the hair and tilted her face upward. "Hey! Where'd you learn to speak such good English? Don't get the idea you can fool me, you're not smart enough."

The girl stared at Frankie, wanting the redheaded woman's eyes to concentrate on her, only her. At the convent, Sister Lionza had taught her that focus was required if she hoped to influence a person's thoughts.

Tula winced because the woman was hurting her but maintained eye contact, saying, "I don't blame you for being suspicious, but there's something you don't understand." The girl lowered her voice as if to whisper a secret. "I've never had anyone say the things you just said to me. It's like you were inside my mind. You understand my thoughts. Do you really? It would be nice to know that someone really understood. I feel guilty sometimes—and alone."

Slowly, the woman released Tula's hair, looking at her, her expression puzzled. She watched the girl's posture change, noting the girlish cant of hips, the innocent dark eyes, before asking, "What I said about not killing Harris, you mean? Or about the tomboy thing?"

By then, Victorino was close enough for Tula to glance at the man, then say to Frankie, "Maybe later we can talk—just us together? It's . . . it's not easy for me to trust anyone, but you seem . . . different than other women."

Victorino arrived, throwing his arm around Frankie's waist, asking, "What's the problem with the little bitch now?"

The woman disentangled herself from the man and gave him a shove, demanding, "Where's the money? Did you find it?"

The V-man couldn't believe what he was hearing, the woman mad at him again for no reason. "You been watching the whole time," he said. "What the hell you think? My boys are doing that job right now, stop worrying. I give them an order, you can bet they gonna do it."

"Priceless," the woman muttered, "a regular genius," as she placed her hand on Tula's shoulder. When the girl felt Frankie's fingernails on her skin—their questioning pressure—Tula walked her hand across the small of the woman's back and leaned her weight against Frankie's thigh despite the welling disgust inside her.

Tula was concentrating on Squires, sending the giant strong thoughts, telling him, *Stay alive . . . stay alive . . . stay alive,* as Frankie said to V-man, "Tell me something—why'd you have to slap this girl? You're so goddamn dumb, I'd slap you myself if your face wasn't already such a mess."

The man thrust his wrist out, saying, "The bitch bit me, what you expect?"

Frankie didn't even bother to look. She leaned her nose toward Victorino, standing on her toes, Tula noticed, to tower over the man. "Big tough Mexican stud," she said loud enough for everyone to hear. "Harris almost kicked your ass, that's what really happened. So you went and did *this*." The woman nodded toward Tula.

"A girl with a face as cute as hers, now I'm going to have to take her inside and get some ice. Why'd you do it? It make you feel like your dick's bigger to bloody up some defenseless girl? Well, it hasn't done much for you so far, *amigo*."

Victorino was glaring at the woman, pretending not to notice that one of his soldiers had stopped to listen, while the shorter one—Chapo—held a VHF radio to his mouth, talking to someone.

As Frankie took the girl's hand, turning her toward the open door, Chapo called to V-man in Spanish, saying, "Hey! Calavero says some white dude stopped, he's asking for jelly boy. A redneck in a truck."

Tula's attention vectored, thinking, *Tomlinson?*

The girl shook her hand free from the woman, senses probing the darkness beyond the silhouettes of trees. Her mind was alert for the aura of godliness that accompanied the strange man with long hair. Instead, she discerned an unexpected force—something cold out there beneath the stars. It was a focused energy, dispassionate, moving her way. And human . . . Or was it?

Tula tilted her head, hoping the Maiden would provide confirmation, but received only a vague premonition of violence.

The V-man had his back to Tula and Frankie, relieved to be conversing with Chapo. A *gringo* stranger was easier to deal with than the redhead's nasty attitude. Victorino called in reply, "The Gomer asked for jelly boy by name? What's a redneck dude want, coming out here this time of night?"

Frankie, Victorino realized, had stopped at the top of the steps for a reason. Probably waiting until Chapo was done talking so she'd have everyone's attention before insulting him again. Victorino was so pissed off by the shit the woman had said, he considered walking over and kicking Squires in the ribs—blow off some steam—then demand to know if jelly boy had told anyone that he'd be at the camp tonight.

Chapo spoke into the radio again, then called, "Dedos flipped the Gomer the finger, I guess. Pissed him off. So maybe the white dude's a local and that's why he turned around."

Victorino said, "Turned around?" but then realized what Chapo meant. He said, "Don't waste your time worrying about rednecks. Tell Calavero don't bother us unless he's got a real problem. Search jelly boy's truck, then get to work doing the other shit I told you to do."

Chapo nodded, forgetting that the woman didn't speak Spanish. He'd already been told the V-man didn't want her to know about the cans of gas they'd brought and the bag of rags so they could torch the hunting camp.

Frankie, still watching, waited as Victorino changed his mind, saying, "No. First you two help me drag jelly boy in there . . ." With his chin, he indicated the wooden steroid shack. Then changed his mind again, saying, "Shit, you haven't found the money yet? You two drag his fat ass by yourselves. *I'll* search the truck."

The woman turned to confirm that Tula was inside the RV, doing something in the kitchen—looking for a towel because of her nose, she guessed. Frankie swung the door closed, stepped down onto the sand and wiggled her index finger, motioning Victorino closer.

"The hell you want?" The man took a couple of careful steps toward the RV, expecting the redhead to take a swing at him or launch into another tirade.

Instead, Frankie produced a joint, lit it, then offered it to the V-man, her *chichis* sticking out because she was holding her breath after taking a big hit.

Man, that *banano* grass smelled good. A couple tokes of coke-soaked weed, that's exactly what he needed. Victorino leaned so Frankie could put the cigarette between his lips.

"The girl has a thing for me," the woman finally said, exhaling and keeping her voice low. "She wants me to be her teacher—sort of sweet, really. You wouldn't understand. But all the signs are there."

Victorino said, "Probably because you talk to her so sweet," being sarcastic.

The woman shook her head. "Don't take it personally. I said all that nasty shit to convince her I'm on her side. But I knew you were smart enough to figure it out. I'd have made a hell of an actress, huh?"

The expression of confusion on the Mexican's face. *Priceless.*

Frankie grinned, holding her hand out impatiently for the joint as Victorino replied, "Then we still gonna do it, huh? In front of the camera?"

"Don't worry. You'll get your share."

Victorino took a second hit of the *banano* as he watched the body-builder's head disappear into the shack, the two *pandilleros* dragging the man by his feet. He said, "What about jelly boy? Do him later or after you have your fun?"

"Get his clothes off him—at least his pants." Frankie said, taking the joint from Victorino's hand. "You meant what you said, didn't you?"

Cut the man's nuts off.

The V-man replied, "A dude disrespects the Latin Kings—I got no choice in the matter." He was studying the woman's face, hoping to see that hungry look again. And there it was: Frankie flicking her tongue to moisten her lips, eyes bright.

The V-man couldn't help himself. He kissed the woman, enjoying how she exhaled the last of the *banano* smoke into his mouth. Frankie let him slip his hand under her bloodstained shirt, too, then drew back and said, "I just wish you made better movies. Last one, you taped the girl's mouth—you couldn't hear her scream! What's the point of that?"

Now the know-it-all woman was being nasty again, telling Victorino that he sucked at making movies, too.

The V-man was thinking, *This is one very crazy* gringa. High from smoking coke and grass, and probably thirsty for more Crown Royal, the woman's mood swings were really pissing him off.

In that instant, Victorino decided he was done with Frankie. As of tonight. Wait any longer, he realized, and she would want part of the sixty grand, once they found it. No . . . she would want it all.

The realization made Victorino want to smile. He was picturing himself using the box cutter on Frankie, too, but only after reminding her why it was better if he didn't tape her mouth.

You're the one told me how to make movies, he would tell the woman. No . . . he'd say, *I could make it easier on you, but I don't want to disappoint my audience.*

But the V-man kept that to himself, playing it cool, even when Frankie asked him, "What are you grinning at? You look like the cat that just ate the bird."

Whatever the hell that meant.

She started to walk to the RV. "I'm going to see the girl. Get started on Harris. When I hear him screaming, I'll know it's time to come out and play."

Tula was inside the RV, rushing to follow the Maiden's instructions and also trying to come up with some ideas of her own. She had to escape and save Harris Squires. But how?

It was dark inside the trailer, even with the lights of the truck tunneling through the curtains, so first Tula found three candles, lit them, then got busy. Everywhere she went, everything she did, she ran. There was no telling how long Frankie would be out there talking to Victorino. Soon, the woman would come inside, expecting the girl to share her secrets—and her body, too.

Tula had known from the start what Frankie wanted. The same with Victorino, with his vicious gold teeth. The two of them were plotting together, probably outside right now, forging an agreement about who would take her body first.

It made Tula queasy, the thought of Frankie or the Mexican touching her. But she was now aware that she might have to allow it to happen. Jehanne had already promised Tula God's forgiveness. Whatever was required to win the redheaded woman's protection, and her help, was permissible.

The thought of submitting herself to Frankie, though, was disgusting. But her feelings no longer mattered. Tula was resolved to do whatever was necessary to save Squires and find a way for the two of them to escape. It was what the Maiden was telling her to do.

However, the Maiden's written words were also strong in the girl's mind: *I would rather die than to do what I know is a sin.*

Tula had repeated the phrase so often that it was part of who she was. She believed she could endure anything rather than disappoint God. But those words, even when whispered as a vow, did not apply to the life of another human being. Allow Harris Squires to die just to spare herself embarrassment and pain?

Tula couldn't do that. If she could save the giant by surrendering her body to evil, she would. In the meantime, her brain was working hard to devise another way.

The RV door had a tiny window, and the girl stood on her toes long enough to confirm that Frankie and Victorino had moved away from the RV so no one could hear them. The woman was just lighting a marijuana cigarette, which suggested that she was in no hurry. Tula knew that it was marijuana because many people smoked *mota* in her village, even married women if they were suffering cramps during their periods. That's what the women claimed, anyway, although the girl was dubious.

Tula thought about locking the door, then decided against it. Frankie had believed her lie about wanting to speak privately. It would only make her suspicious. So the girl hurried to the kitchenette to search for weapons.

Help yourself, and God will help you, Jehanne had written. *Act, and God will act through you,* she had counseled her knights.

Tula was looking in cupboards, opening drawers, hoping to find an ax or a large knife, or even a gun. Although she had never fired a weapon, the girl was willing to try. But could she kill another human being? Tula tried to imagine how it would feel, as the Maiden reminded her, *These are our enemies. You must fight.*

That was as true, and as real, as the revulsion Tula felt for the redheaded woman. Still . . . to sin against God by hurting another human being. It was a difficult decision to make.

But then Tula reminded herself that the Maiden had carried the equivalent of a gun—a sword she had found behind the altar of a church and carried into battle. Jehanne had told her inquisitors that her sword had never shed blood, yet she had also warned that she would lie to them, if necessary. And there were witnesses who swore the Maiden had used her sword to kill Englishmen, and also to punish prostitutes.

Tula pictured herself stabbing Frankie . . . then imagined the woman lying on the ground, dying, as the evil inside her bled out onto the sand.

If it meant saving herself and the man who had fought for her, the girl told herself that she would have to do it. Even so, she still wasn't convinced she actually could.

Tula didn't find an ax, or a gun, but the paring knife she had used earlier was in the sink, the blade bent but sharp. The girl wrapped a dishrag around the blade and hid the thing in her back pocket.

Squires's wrists and ankles had been taped. She would need a knife to free the man—if she could invent an excuse to be alone with him. But why would Frankie or Victorino allow such a thing?

Thinking about it was discouraging, until the Maiden's voice spoke again, telling the girl, *God is with you. He will show you the way.*

Cupping a candle in her hands, Tula trotted down the hall to the bedroom. There, a steel locker had been broken open—Victorino's men had done it, she guessed—but there were only boxes of shotgun shells, no weapons.

Next, reluctantly, she checked the strange room with the bed and mirrors where there had been a video camera and a stack of obscene photos.

Victorino's men had been there, too. The camera was gone. The photos were scattered across the floor, dozens of them. Tula tried not to look at them as she searched under the bed, then a tiny closet, but she didn't want to step on the pictures, either—it was like walking on someone's grave.

As she moved through the room, Tula winced at each new obscenity. The eyes of unknown women peered up at her, communicating a secret agony that was as apparent to Tula as the grotesque poses the women affected for the lens. They were young girls, some not much older than herself, each brown face forever trapped in a frozen silence from which Tula perceived screams of pain, of fear, of desperation.

Then, suddenly, the girl's legs went out from under her, and she found herself sitting on the floor, weeping, holding the candle in one hand, a photo in the other.

From the photograph, despite the woman's nakedness and despite her leering mask, a familiar face stared back at Tula. In disbelief, the girl turned away from the picture, then looked at it again, hoping to discover that she was wrong.

No . . . her eyes hadn't tricked her. What Tula saw was a loving likeness of herself, the girl's own first memories of home and kindness and safety.

It was her mother.

Still pinned to Tula's shirt was the miniature doll that she had found earlier. The girl touched her fingers to the doll as she studied the photograph, her mind trying to ignore her mother's shocking nakedness by focusing on the face she loved so much. Familiar odors came into the girl's mind, then memories of her mother's touch. Tula had been crying softly, but now she began to sob.

How had this happened?

Tula remembered the woman at the church in Immokalee saying her mother had gone to work for a man who made movies. But her mother never would have consented to something like this. Trade her dignity . . . her very soul . . . for money? No, impossible. Even more impossible because, also in the photo, a man's reflection was visible in a mirror—not his face but his naked anatomy.

Not since Tula's father died had the girl witnessed anything more painful. In a way, this was even more traumatic because her mother had encouraged by example Tula's devotion to God and the Church. Never had there been such a good and loving women—even the villagers said it was true. To Tula, she represented all that was godly and clean, a woman who had vowed to be forever faithful to her husband even though he had been dead for a year when Tula heard her make the promise.

It was beyond the girl's ability to comprehend. Here, though, was the truth—an obscene infidelity that seemed to debase the children of all loving mothers and mocked Tula's deepest convictions.

The Maiden came into Tula's head, then, reminding her, *Only God's eyes know the truth. The truth is lasting but often hidden from us. Even though we see, we remain blind.*

Jehanne had written those words centuries ago, but it was if they were intended to comfort Tula at this very moment. The words were true. This photograph represented only a moment in time. It proved nothing other than it had happened.

But *why* had it happened?

Her mother had been forced to participate in this profanity, Tula decided. In fear for her life, probably. It was the only explanation that made sense. Perhaps the naked man in the photo was holding a gun. Or the man behind the camera. Only minutes ago, Tula realized, she herself had made the decision to submit to sin if it meant saving herself or the life of Harris Squires.

Gradually, the girl felt her faith returning. Her mother had been the victim of threats and violence. The girl felt certain of it now. Her mother would confirm the truth of what had happened when Tula found her. Or . . . should she even mention the photo when they were finally face-to-face?

No, Tula decided. She would never speak of it. Not to her mother, not to her family, not to anyone. It would only add to the humiliation her mother had suffered. Her mother had given Tula life—like God. And like with God, Tula knew, she would never doubt her mother's goodness again.

This photo . . . it felt so light and meaningless between the girl's fingers now. Yet it was a final justification for the mission on which God had sent her—to rescue her family, to lead her people home from this terrible sinful land.

Then, as she held the photo, another realization came into the girl's mind, but not as shocking. Her mother had been *here*, at the hunting camp. The photo had been taken in this very room. Tula confirmed it by comparing the background with the bedroom's walls and the mirror hanging above the bed.

Harris Squires, she realized, hadn't lied about knowing her mother. It had only sounded like a lie because the man honestly didn't remember meeting her. Tula felt certain of it, just as she felt sure the giant would have remembered her mother if she had worked for him.

No . . . Harris hadn't forced his mother to do this. He might have played a small role, he might even have been aware that it was happening—but only because he was under the spell of someone more powerful. Someone evil.

Tula could hear her pulse thudding as her thoughts verified what she had sensed from the beginning: Frankie was to blame for this. The drunken woman with her man's voice, her tattoos, her viciousness. Carlson had seen her giving Tula's mother a cell phone how many months ago?

The girl couldn't remember, but she now knew in her heart the truth of what had happened. The redheaded woman had victimized her mother. Only one of many. Frankie's many sins lay scattered on the trailer floor, these profane photographs like discarded souls. The woman was *evil*.

Her body shaking, Tula got to her feet, aware that Frankie could return to the RV at any second. She had to get herself under control. For Tula to allow Frankie to see her weak and in tears would only give the woman more power over her.

She couldn't allow that to happen. She *wouldn't* allow it to happen.

Tula considered tearing the photo of her mother into tiny pieces. Instead, she folded it and put it into her back pocket, while, inside her, the revulsion she felt for Frankie was transformed into hatred, then rage. She had never experienced the emotion before. It created inside her a determination and fearlessness that was unsettling because, in that instant, Tula understood why soldiers in battle were so eager to kill.

As the girl hurried down the hall toward the kitchenette, it was difficult to keep her hand off the paring knife. She wanted to use the knife now. She wanted what she had imagined to happen: Frankie on the ground, the evil bleeding out of her.

Which was when the Maiden's voice surprised Tula by saying, *What about the stove? The giant showed you how to turn the gas on.*

The girl was confused for a moment. To be so passionately focused on one subject, it was difficult to concentrate on anything else. But she tried, wondering, *The stove?* Of what use was the gas stove now?

Then she understood. Frankie had been smoking a cigarette. If the woman was still smoking when she walked into a room filled with propane, she would die.

For a moment, Tula was excited. But the Maiden rebuked her, telling the girl that the stove was better used as a diversion, because it was smarter.

The girl was disappointed, but she understand. If the RV caught fire, Victorino's men, and Frankie, would be so surprised they might forget about Harris Squires for a few minutes. Maybe they would leave the giant alone long enough for Tula to free him, then they could escape together down the lane to the road.

No . . . not the dirt lane. Tula remembered that Victorino had sent two men to watch the road, so she and the giant would have to escape through the woods.

But escape without confronting Frankie? That seemed cowardly after what that evil woman had done to Tula's mother.

The Maiden entered the girl's head and comforted her, saying, *God will judge her. Can there be anything more terrible than His wrath?*

Tula wasn't convinced. As always, though, she obeyed. Equipping herself for a hike through the woods, the girl put matches, two candles and a bottle of mosquito repellent in her pockets. Then she knelt beneath the sink and turned the gas valve until it was wide open.

At the stove, however, the girl hesitated. She had extinguished the candle she was carrying, but there were still two burning candles in the room. Secretly, she wanted to blow out the candles and hope Frankie was still smoking a cigarette when she opened the door. But there were no secrets with the Maiden, who told Tula, *Hurry . . . the woman's coming. Do it now!*

Tula opened both valves on the stove, then ran down the hall, pulling doors shut to isolate the propane, including the door to the bedroom she entered, maybe slamming it too hard, but it was too late to worry now.

On the far wall was a window. Tiny, but big enough to wiggle through. Tula bounced over the bed to the wall, then flipped the lock, expecting the window to open easily.

It didn't. The window frame was aluminum. Maybe it was corroded shut. Tula used all her strength, pushing with her legs, then tried cutting around the edges of the window with the paring knife.

It still wouldn't open. As the girl stood there, breathing heavily, she could smell propane gas seeping under the door. She would have been less surprised by smoke and flames. Had the candles gone out, extinguished by the doors she had slammed? Or did the concentration of gas have to be higher before the candles would ignite it?

Tula didn't know. She knew only that she had to escape from the trailer before Frankie came in, smelled the propane and realized that a trap had been set for her.

Next to the bed was a lamp. Tula grabbed it and swung the base of the lamp against the Plexiglas window, expecting it to shatter with the first blow. It made a sound like a gunshot, but the glass didn't break.

Panicked because she had made so much noise, Tula began hammering at the window. Finally, it cracked, but the girl had to pull the Plexiglas out in shards, piece by piece, before the window was finally wide enough for her to crawl through.

She draped a towel over the opening so she wouldn't cut herself, then dropped to the ground, feeling an overwhelming sense of relief to be free.

The feeling lasted only a few seconds.

As Tula got to her feet and turned toward the shack where she'd last seen Squires, a low voice from the shadows surprised her, saying, "You sneaky little slut. What did you use to break the window, a damn sledgehammer? I didn't even have to go inside, it was so obvious."

Frankie was standing at the corner of the RV, a towering shape silhouetted by headlights. Not smoking now but a pack of cigarettes in her hand.

Tula's fingers moved to her back pocket, feeling the lump that was the paring knife. An edge of her mother's photograph was sticking out, too.

"It's because you scare me," the girl said, trying to sound reasonable. "What I told you was true. I want to talk to you, tell you things I've never been able to tell anyone. But my body's afraid because of the way you look. Why would someone as beautiful as you waste time helping someone like me?"

With her deep voice, the woman said, "Liar! The whole time, you were lying," sounding furious but undecided as if she wanted to be proven wrong.

Tula focused her eyes on the woman's black eyes, hand inside her back pocket, saying, "We should go inside and let me wash your blouse. I know how to get bloodstains out. Where I lived in the mountains, that was one of my jobs, washing clothes."

In her mind, Tula was picturing Frankie pausing at the steps of the RV to light a cigarette, then opening the door.

The woman was staring back, perhaps feeling the images that Tula was projecting because, for a moment, the woman's anger wavered. But then the woman caught herself, visibly shook her head as if to clear it and yelled, "What the hell's *wrong* with me? You're lying again! Don't tell me what to do!"

Then the big woman charged at Tula, whose hand suddenly felt frozen, unable to draw the knife from her pocket, so the girl turned and ran.

Frankie sprinted after her, yelling, "Come back her, you lying brat! Just wait 'til I get my hands on you!"

For a woman her age and size, Frankie was quicker than Tula could have imagined. After only a few steps, the girl felt a jarring impact on the back of her head. Then she was on the ground, Frankie kneeling over her, using a right fist to hit the girl so hard that Tula didn't regain full consciousness until she awoke, minutes or hours later, in the cookshack.

Woozy and dreamlike—that's the way Tula felt when she opened her eyes. Nauseous, too. It took the girl several seconds to organize what she was seeing as her eyes moved slowly around the room. Overhead were bars of neon light. The sound of a motor running confirmed that the generator had been started. There was a strong odor of gasoline, too.

Tula wondered about that, making the distinction between the smell of gasoline and the smell of propane, which struck her as important for some reason.

Tula lifted her head to study her body, then lay back again, eyes closed. She was tied, unable to move, her wrists taped to the legs of a heavy table. They had used short pieces of rope on her ankles, securing her legs in a way that suggested they intended to cut her jeans and shirt off next. The owl-shaped jade amulet and her Joan of Arc medallion were missing, she realized, but the girl could still feel the shape of the paring knife hidden in her back pocket. Even so, in her entire life, she had never felt so naked and defenseless.

Could this really be happening?

Yes . . . it was as real as the blood Tula could now taste in her mouth. The girl strained against the tape again. The table moved a little, but her legs were spread between a stationary counter. Freeing herself was impossible, so she lay back to think, her mind still putting it all together.

Frankie and the Mexican with gold teeth were standing nearby but not looking at her. The woman was concentrating on a camera mounted on a tripod, angry about something—impatient with the camera, Tula decided. Then Frankie spoke to Victorino, muttering, "I told you the battery was in wrong. Stupid wetbacks, if it's anything more complicated than a knife, you can't deal with it."

A moment later, though, the woman swore, and said, "This battery's no good—probably because of the way you did it. In the RV, I've got a camera bag full of shit. Send one of your pals to go get it."

Tula's brain was fogged, but mentioning the RV was of interest to her. She had just escaped from the RV, she remembered, where she had left the stove valves open to fill the trailer with propane.

Slowly, the girl's attention shifted to Victorino, who was wearing surgical gloves for some reason. The gloves and the man's wrists were stained with blood. He was glaring at Frankie with dead, drunken eyes, and seemed too preoccupied to respond.

It was because of what a second Mexican had just said to Victorino. Even before Tula had opened her eyes, she had heard the man speaking Spanish, but her mind had not translated his words yet his phrases lingered. What the man had said was important for a reason, Tula was sure of it, yet her brain had yet to unravel his meaning.

Poli—she had heard him use the word. *Poli* was Mexican slang, the equivalent of "cop." If so, then it *was* important. But why had the man mentioned police? Tula strained to recall. She squeezed her eyes closed, her brain scanning for details.

Yes . . . it was coming back to her. The man had said something that sounded like *The cop said don't hurt the girl. They're coming in.*

Words close to that. "The girl" referred to her. It had to . . . didn't it? *Don't hurt the girl.* It suggested to Tula that the police were coming to save her.

Tula wanted to believe it, but what was happening around her was so surreal that she didn't trust her judgment. Hope was such a tenuous, flimsy thing, after the photograph she had found in the RV, after what she was now experiencing.

The Mexican who had mentioned police was standing in the doorway, holding a radio. He sounded worried. "We dumped all the gas just like you said. Why don't we torch the place now and go?"

Gasoline . . . it explained the odor, which Tula filed away as the man, getting very serious, added, "The redheaded witch, she doesn't understand a word of what we're saying, right? So leave her here with the girl. Get the woman's fingerprints on your box cutter and let the cops arrest her for jelly boy. Hell, maybe they'll think they got into a fight or something. Cut jelly boy free, too—he's not going anywhere. You know, a steroids war. Let the cops figure it out."

The man was referring to Harris Squires. Tula had momentarily forgotten about the giant, but events were flooding back now. But arrest the woman for what? What had happened to Harris?

Confused, her mind working in slow motion, Tula moved her eyes to where the Mexican was looking. He was staring at something to her left. But to see, she would have to move her head and risk alerting Frankie that she was conscious.

Into the girl's mind, the Maiden spoke, saying, *Be fearless. You were born to do this! I have not forsaken you!*

To hear Jehanne's voice at such a moment caused the girl's eyes to flood with tears. Because she was crying when she turned her head, she was unable at first to decipher what she was seeing. A massive pale shape was lying next to her. Tula squinted tears away, and the shape acquired detail. Even then, it took her several seconds to understand what she was seeing.

It was Harris Squires. After what they had done to the man, Tula didn't want to believe it was actually the giant. His body appeared shrunken, deflated. Harris was naked, legs tied wide, just as they had tied her legs. His chest was peppered with shotgun BBs, his ivory skin patched with blood.

Beneath the giant's hips, the blood had pooled like oil. Tula didn't want to look any closer but she forced herself. Her brother was the only male she had ever seen naked, so it took the girl a moment to understand what had happened

Victorino had mutilated the giant.

Tula grimaced and turned away, comforted only by the fact that Squires was unconscious, no longer in pain, and also that he was still breathing.

When the girl opened her eyes again, Frankie was standing over her, staring down. The woman smiled and said, "Well, well, well! My sleeping cutie is finally awake."

Then, turning to Victorino, she asked, "What are you two yapping about? What's wrong?"

Victorino was ripping off the rubber gloves, suddenly in a hurry, as he asked the Mexican man in Spanish, "Where's my Tec-9? Chapo's got the other one—is he ready? Goddamn it, he should've been in contact! We got to be ready for anything anytime!"

The Mexican took a boxy-looking gun from the bag on his shoulder and handed it to Victorinio, saying, "It bothers me that we haven't heard a word from Calavero or Dedos, either. Dedos, he's probably passed out. But Calavero, if the cops grabbed him—"

Victorino interrupted, "That's what I'm *telling* you," as he ejected the magazine from the weapon, checked it, then slammed it back.

"Shit," he said, "for all we know, it's not the cops. It's some *La Mara* bangers from Immokalee. Why would cops call and warn us they're coming? You know, Guatemalan punks talking English because they figure we're so rich, we got lazy and stupid."

In Guatemala City, Tula had heard of the street gang, *Mara Salvatrucha*. *La Mara*, for short, or MS-13. It was a murderous gang, always at war with Mexican gangs. She lay back, taking in details, as the V-man asked Frankie, "You and jelly boy ever do any business with *La Mara*? Maybe that's who it is."

Frankie got taller on her toes again as Victorino slipped by her, the woman yelling, "What kinda shit are you trying to pull now? I don't know anyone named *La Mara*! You and your greasers found the money, *didn't you*? Now you're feeding me some bullshit excuse about why you have to run."

Holding the box cutter in his hand, the V-man leaned over Squires for a moment, then pushed the razor toward Frankie, saying, "Cut his hands and legs free. Someone finds him, we want them to wonder what happened."

Tula remembered what the Mexican had said about fingerprints. Frankie took the knife in her right hand and, for a moment, Tula thought the woman was going to stab the blade at Victorino. The man took a step back, thinking the same thing, which was when the Mexican warned Frankie from the doorway, saying, "Don't even think about it, *puta*. It'll be like shooting balloons at the fair. Like back when I was a kid."

The Mexican was pointing a pistol at Frankie, holding the weapon steady until the woman muttered, "A couple of big tough wetbacks, that's what you are," then dropped the razor, too unconcerned to watch where it landed.

Tula was watching, though. She kept her eyes on the razor even as Frankie collected her cigarettes and pushed past the Mexican, outside, pausing only to tell Victorino, "I need a drink. Either of you disappear while I'm getting it, I'll have *your* nuts!"

Then, without waiting for a reply, she was walking toward the RV, hips swinging. Tula could see the woman plainly through the open door. The girl focused her eyes on the back of Frankie's head, then pictured the woman on the RV steps. Tula was telegraphing images, thinking over and over, *Light a cigarette . . . Light a cigarette.*

Tula could also see Victorino standing in the doorway, the weapon in both hands, his concentration intense. Maybe he hadn't heard the woman's insult. No . . . he'd heard, because as his eyes swept the darkness he called after the redhead, "You can burn in hell, for all I care—" but then stopped abruptly and crouched.

A second passed, then another, before he whispered to the Mexican, "Hey—there's a vehicle coming down the road. See it? No lights, but it's headed this way. How the hell they get past Calavero and Dedos?"

The Mexican started to say, "Our two guys—maybe that's who it is. See them through the window?" then stopped talking as he watched the truck fishtail, then drift into a slow spin.

Now on his knees, the V-man was yelling, "Shit—that's our Dodge! Those aren't cops. They stole our goddamn truck!"

Beside him, the Mexican tried to mention Calavero and Dedos again but was interrupted by two consecutive gunshots, *WHAP-WHAP!* very close.

Victorino ducked his head back, hissing, "Shit, they firing on us, man! Shooting at us from our own truck!" Then he took a quick look out the door and decided, "We've got to get to jelly boy's truck. Four-wheel drive, we can drive through the goddamn swamp if we need to."

The Mexican sounded dubious, saying, "I don't know, man, that shit's wet out there."

"Our goddamn truck's got the road blocked, man!" Victorino said, getting mad. "You don't got eyes in your head? Plus, they probably got more dudes waiting for us as we leave. We gotta take jelly boy's truck and get the hell out of here." The man peeked out the door again, asking, "You ready with the thing I told you about?"

The Mexican showed Victorino the lighter in his hand, saying, "You want me to wait until the *gringa* is inside the RV? Unless you think we don't have time."

Smiling, the V-man replied, "I warned the bitch. You heard me warn her. Let's go!"

Both men took off running, the Mexican firing three shots at something, then Victorino opening up, his weapon making a continuous ratcheting sound, loud, but not as loud as the pistol.

From outside came the sound of more gunshots—maybe Victorino's men. Maybe someone else.

Tula's mind was too busy thinking to notice or care.

Sensing the room's sudden emptiness, Tula lay back for a moment, concentrating on breathing into her belly to calm herself. Then she attempted to communicate with the Maiden.

They poured gasoline, I can smell it. This building might catch on fire. Please don't let me burn.

Jehanne didn't reply, but into Tula's head came words Joan of Arc had written, words the girl had committed to memory: *Help yourself, and God will help you. Act, and God will act through you.*

Tula raised her head. Through the open doorway, she could see that Frankie was on the steps to the RV but crouched low because of the gunshots. Maybe the woman would seek cover inside the trailer and light a cigarette later to calm herself. Revenge wasn't a priority in Tula's mind now, though.

Her eyes moved to the razor Frankie had dropped. The box cutter had landed only inches from Harris Squires's right hand. The giant no longer reminded the girl of Hercules or polished stone. Only a few hours ago, the veins of his body had resembled blue rivers, tracing the contours of his biceps, the muscles of his chest and calves.

Now the rivers had been drained. The giant appeared shrunken inside his own skin, a mountain of pale, dead flesh, although the man's chest continued to move.

Tula watched Squires's chest lift and fall, his breathing shallow. As she stared at him, the girl focused all of her attention on the man's unconscious skull, seeking the spirit that lived inside.

Open your eyes. God will save us. Open your eyes. You are the strongest man I have ever met, open your eyes . . .

For more than a minute, Tula repeated those phrases, but then was stopped by more gunshots, then a *Woofing* detonation that shook the floor beneath her. It was a firestorm explosion so close that it sucked air from the room, replacing it with heat so intense that it felt like needles on the girl's face and arms.

Through the doorway, Tula saw a wave of fire rolling toward her, the flames so wild and high that the RV was screened from view.

Had the trailer exploded?

The fate of the redhead seemed unimportant now, and Tula threw her head back, screaming, "Jehanne? Jehanne!" then strained to use her teeth on the tape that bound her wrists. The table to which her hands were tied moved a few inches with each effort, but the angle was impossible.

As the girl convulsed her body, trying to tear herself free, the memory of her father's last moments came into her mind, an image so stark, so sobering, that it caused Tula to stop screaming long enough to hear a voice calling to her. When she tilted her head to listen, the voice summoned her again, a soft voice, barely audible.

Tula became motionless, head up, eyes wide, listening for what she expected to be the Maiden offering advice . . . or, at the very least, comfort.

Instead, she heard a man's voice beside her say, "Sis . . . Sis! Shut your mouth long enough to answer me. Are those assholes gone?"

Tula turned to see Harris Squires looking at her, his eyes two dull slits. On his face was an inexplicable smile that gave the girl hope even though she knew it was because the man was in shock, probably delirious, he was so near death.

Tula began crying, she couldn't help herself, and talking too fast as she replied, "Harris! I am so sorry they hurt you. But you'll get better. I will take care of you myself. I will take you home to the mountains and make sure no one ever hurts you again. I promise!"

No . . . the giant wasn't delirious. He was alert enough to look toward the door, see the fire, then say, "Shit! This place will go up like a bomb. I've got to get you out of here!"

That possibility stayed with the man for a second, but then he realized the hopelessness of what was happening. Squire's face contorted, then he slammed his head back and began to sob. "Did you see what those sons of bitches did to me?" he moaned. "I fought and fought, but I couldn't stop them. I'm sorry, I'm so sorry. I'm no good to anyone now."

Tula yelled, "Harris, *stop it*, you're wrong!" to snap the man out of his misery. Then she used her head to motion toward the box cutter, telling him, "We have a knife, Harris! If I can pull myself close enough, maybe you can cut the tape on my wrists."

Squires opened his eyes as the girl added, "Don't leave me again,

Harris. Stay strong, *please*. God will help us—but we have to help ourselves first."

The giant appeared to be fighting unconsciousness, his voice barely audible as he replied, "My guardian angel, I forgot." Then, gaining focus, he asked, "What knife?"

Because of all the blood on the floor, Tula wondered how the man found the strength to open his fingers and take the box cutter into his huge right hand.

Inch by inch, Tula dragged the table closer to the giant. He held the razor, fighting unconsciousness as he waited. Two minutes passed, then four minutes. From the doorway, the girl could hear the roaring energy of combustion as the fire drew closer, feeding itself on gasoline fumes and grass. Soon heat and smoke made it difficult to breath, but the girl continued to fight the weight of the table.

Squires watched her, struggling to remain focused after losing so much blood. Every minute or so, he would awaken himself by telling Tula, "Don't give up! Just a couple more!" These were phrases he had spoken so many times in weight rooms while spotting partners that he repeated the words by rote.

Even so, the giant's determination was an inspiration to Tula, but his terrible wounds also caused the girl's heart to ache.

When Tula realized the roof of the wooden shack had caught fire, she began to lose hope. She was dizzy from breathing smoke and her arms ached. For a few seconds, the girl paused to rest, and also to gauge the distance remaining before Squires might be able to cut the tape on her left wrist.

Two feet . . . a little less. The wooden building was burning so ferociously, though, it might as well have been two miles.

Tula closed her eyes and summoned the Maiden, resigned now that she and her warrior giant were probably going to burn to death. No . . . the smoke would kill them first, the girl reminded herself.

In books she had read about Joan of Arc, witnesses all agreed that the saint had died from smoke inhalation before flames despoiled her flesh.

In a way, Tula found the recollection comforting, but she wasn't ready to give up. Before yanking at the table once again, she spoke to her patron saint. A request.

Give us time. Just a few more minutes. If not, please grant me just one wish. Spare this good man from more suffering and pain.

FIFTEEN

THROUGH THE NIGHT VISION MONOCULAR I SAW TWO MEN KNEEL-
ing in the doorway of a wooden shack, guns drawn, as I steered the
Dodge truck, headlights off, toward an RV where a tall woman was
approaching the steps, presumably about to enter.

Isolated beneath a macrodome of Everglades stars, the detailed
images of the woman, the men and both structures were as sharply
defined as if looking through a well-focused microscope.

The men heard our truck approaching, then singled us out in the
darkness. The woman did not. She appeared oblivious, standing
with her back to the road, patting her pockets for something, probably looking for a flashlight or maybe cigarettes.

Beside me, Calavero, his mouth taped, made grunting noises of
disapproval while, beside him, Dedos told me, "*There*—that's the
redhead bitch. It was all her idea, her and that asshole bodybuilder."

Because the truck's windows were closed, air conditioner on, the
man didn't have to raise his voice to be heard. It also guaranteed that

his fellow gangbangers wouldn't hear him if he decided to call a warning or yell for help.

For the last half mile, Dedos, my new best friend, had been supplying me with information as we bounced through the woods at forty miles an hour, the heads of both men banging off the ceiling more than once.

I had only slowed long enough to transform my wool watch cap into a full-faced ski mask, then fit the night vision monocular over it.

I had also experimented with the vehicle's cruise control. It worked fine at twenty-five mph, but I needed more speed to skid the truck into a combat turn—which is what I intended to do. On pavement, I would've needed to be doing at least sixty. On this dirt lane, though, forty would work—even with the Dodge's antilock brakes.

Antilock brakes have become the bane of tactical driving schools worldwide. I've been through enough of those schools to know.

As we closed on the hunting camp, I noted a redneck-looking pickup truck, off to the left. The doors were open, junk strewn all around, which made no sense. But it was the sort of truck a guy like Harris Squires would drive and it gave me hope that he and Tula Choimha were still here.

I kept my eyes focused on the men in the doorway, paying close attention to the orientation of their weapons. One man held a pistol—a long-barreled revolver, it looked like. The other, a fully automatic Tec-9 that Dedos had mentioned. Maybe he was the gang leader—V-man, they called him, or Victorino—but that was too early to confirm. If Dedos had told me the truth, the math was neither difficult nor comforting. One gangbanger was missing. So was a second Tec-9.

Where?

Time for careful observation was over. We were speeding toward the clearing, and I had to make my moves fast and clean. In preparation, as I drove, I opened my door and held it open with my left foot. Because I had already switched off the truck's dome light, the cab remained dark.

With cruise control locked in at forty, I was free to move my right foot to the emergency brake. Pointing the Glock at the men in the doorway, I waited . . . waited until I saw one of the men stand, bringing his weapon up to fire, and that's when I jammed the emergency brake to the floor.

The cruise control disengaged instantly, the wheels didn't lock, but the truck had enough momentum to bounce into a skid, then do a slow-motion right turn as I guided the wheel. My left foot was already searching for the chrome step to the ground when the door flew open.

A "modified boot-turn," is the tactical term. The turn is used to effect a hasty retreat from roadblocks or a trigger-happy enemy. The technique dates back to the days of bootleggers.

Crouched low, I waited as the truck skidded. Then, as it slowed, I closed the door quietly and stepped off the running board while the Dodge was still moving. For a second or two, I trotted along behind the truck, using the bed to screen me from sight.

By the time the Dodge had come to a stop, I was several paces into the woods. In the doorway of the shack, both men were on their feet now. The temptation was to take a wild shot at them. For an expert marksman, eighty feet was manageable. But I am only a competent shot with a handgun, plus I was using a stranger's weapon, the Glock. I wasn't going to risk giving away my location to a man carrying a full automatic.

Besides, I had already committed myself to an extraction plan and

I was determined to stick with it. It was the simplest plan I could devise, and it didn't include engaging gangbangers in a running gun battle.

I had whittled the strategy down to three priorities: If possible, I wanted to block the exit to the road so they couldn't pack Tula into a vehicle and run. Next, I would locate and mobilize the girl. Finally, I would have to eliminate witnesses who might be able to identify me later.

As far as Dedos and Calavero were concerned, the last priority came first. They had seen my face, they could ID my truck. I could have killed them myself. Later, I would do just that *if* they survived the scenario I had just contrived. Surprise, panic and confusion—these are all linking elements in the majority of deaths from friendly fire. Using the gangbangers' own radio and vehicle, I had combined the elements into a volatile combination.

Kneeling behind a tree, I provided what I hoped was an effective catalyst. I took aim and fired two shots, targeting the Dodge's rear tires. Maybe the tires ruptured, maybe they didn't, but I didn't stick around to confirm that I had or had not temporarily immobilized the truck and blocked the exit to the road.

Instantly, I was on my feet and running. The structures which comprised the hunting camp were luminous green through the night vision monocular. They flickered past, bracketed by trees, as I gave careful attention to each building. As I ran, I did a hostage assessment, trying to determine the girl's most likely location. That's when the men in the doorway opened fire.

I dropped to the ground and remained motionless for a moment. Then I lifted my head, hoping to confirm that they were firing at the Dodge.

They were. The Tec-9 sounded like a fiberglass machine gun

firing plastic bullets. The report of the revolver was flat and heavy. Combined, they created a chorus of breaking glass and punctured metal as slugs hammered through the Dodge.

In less than five seconds, the men had fired twenty, maybe thirty rounds. Then there was an abrupt silence that left the night sky echoing with the squawks of outraged birds and the trilling of indifferent frogs.

I crawled toward the Dodge, then lifted my head again. I could see only the back of the truck. The silhouettes of Dedos and Calavero were no longer visible through the shattered rear window. It seemed impossible that they hadn't been hit, but that was something I would have to confirm later. Judging from the vehicle's tilted angle and the steam spiraling from the engine, the blockade I'd hoped to create was now solidly in place.

I got to my knees, my attention on the two gangbangers. They weren't heading for the safety of the RV as I'd assumed. They sprinted past the trailer, indifferent to the woman cowering near the steps, and I watched as one of the men took something from a bag and handed it to the man carrying the Tec-9.

A fresh magazine, I realized.

As the two men slowed to reload, I heard one of them holler, "Chapo! Where are you? Chapo, get your ass over here now! We're going!"

The woman looked unsteady as she got to her feet, one hand on the stair railing. She screamed, "What the hell is happening?" then added a string of profanities, calling the men cowards for leaving her. Her language became more graphic as she demanded money they owed her.

She mentioned a figure: sixty thousand cash.

Interesting, but my mind was on Chapo, the missing *pandillero*.

His was the voice I had heard on the VHF. Presumably, he was the gangbanger carrying the other Tec-9.

Was he in the RV, guarding Tula Choimha? Or in the shack? Until proven otherwise, I would have to handle myself as if either could be true.

The man carrying the Tec-9 was the V-man, the gang's leader, I decided. I was sure of it when he summoned Chapo again, yelling, "You better get your ass in gear, man, 'cause we're leaving now!"

The men didn't wait for an answer and neither did I. As they took off running, I shadowed their pace, keeping trees between us. They were headed for what I assumed to be Squires's truck. It was a massive vehicle, built for the swamps, with deepwater tires, an industrial winch and banks of lights mounted overhead on a roll bar. A mudder, Floridians might have called it, a swamp buggy, to uninformed outsiders.

I had a head full of adrenaline, and my first instinct was to disable the truck so the men couldn't escape. A vehicle that size could bulldoze the Dodge aside, then make a clean break for the road.

Ahead was a tangle of swamp tupelo, then a stand of bald cypress, the trees wide enough to provide cover and thick enough to shield me from bullets. It was a marshy area. I knew it even before I was ankle-deep in water, but the trees gave me an ideal angle, a clean side view of Squires's truck. The Glock held fourteen more rounds. I was tempted to put a couple of slugs into the tires, then a few more into the engine. Do it right, have some luck, and the gangbangers wouldn't be going anywhere. Not fast, at least.

As I pressed myself against one of the trees, though, my training and experience took over. An emotional response is for amateurs. Anger is a liability that signals a lack of discipline.

Priorities, I reminded myself. *Stick to the plan.*

Engaging an enemy with superior firepower was not only dangerous, it was a waste of time. And pointless. So far, these two gangbangers had not seen me. Killing them—or even stopping them from escaping—was unimportant.

In certain circles, there was a maxim that has saved many lives and taken more than a few.

Keep it simple, stupid.

That's exactly what I intended to do.

I shifted my focus to one objective and one objective only: Find the girl, then get her out safely.

My second priority was also important—leave no witnesses—but it was still a secondary consideration. If the V-man and his partner made it to the road, that was a problem for the police. Dedos and Calavero were a different story, but they weren't going anywhere. If they weren't dead, they were at least wounded and could be dealt with later.

The girl was foremost in my mind. I had to find the girl. I might also have to deal with Chapo, I reminded myself, the man who carried the second Tec-9. Or the tall woman who Dedos had accused of orchestrating Tula's abduction and rape. In my lifetime, I have encountered at least two women who were as dangerous as any man. Maybe this woman was as dangerous or maybe she was just a masochistic freak. If the time came, I would find out. The fact that she was female would not save her if circumstances required me to act.

Shielded by the cypress tree, I knelt and took a closer look at Squires's truck. It was a supersized model, and all four doors were open, dome light on. So much junk lay scattered around the truck,

I got the impression that it had been ransacked. The woman's reference to sixty thousand dollars came into my mind, but I didn't linger on the implications.

I wanted to be absolutely certain that the girl wasn't being held captive in the truck. I could see clearly enough through my night vision to confirm she wasn't in the cab. But what about the bed?

The truck bed wasn't covered, and it seemed unlikely the gang-bangers would have left her there. To be sure, I watched both men closely as they approached the truck. It took a while. They appeared worried about what was hidden in the trees behind them, close to the smoking Dodge.

Finally, it was V-man, carrying the Tec-9, who told me what I needed to know. As he approached the driver's side of the truck, he didn't bother to glance into the open bed. Same with the man carrying the revolver.

Had Squires or the girl been lying there, they would have at least taken a quick look to make sure their captives were still secured. Instead, the men climbed up into the truck, then the engine started.

Surprisingly, as I watched, the gang leader didn't turn toward the exit road as expected—maybe he didn't want to be slowed by the disabled Dodge or possibly because he feared an ambush. Instead, he accelerated fast over ruts and through tall sedge, the truck's headlights bouncing northwest toward what to me appeared to be swamp, judging from the hillock of cypress trees in the distance.

Maybe Victorino was familiar with the area and knew of a lumberman's trail not visible on the satellite photo. I had studied the photo pretty thoroughly, though, and was doubtful. But the fate of the gang boss and his partner was no longer my concern.

The girl wasn't in the truck, that's all I needed to know. It told me that Tula was being held in the RV or the wooden shack—unless they had already killed her and disposed of her body someplace in the woods.

I turned and began retracing my steps toward the Dodge, studying the two buildings, but also keeping an eye on the tall woman who was still watching the truck as if hoping the gangbangers would change their minds and return. She had been yelling a stream of profanities and threats even as the men drove away, but now she punctuated it all by screaming, "Come back here, you assholes!"

After a few moments of silence, as the woman cupped her hands to light a cigarette, a man's voice surprised both of us, calling, "Don't worry, Señorita Frankie! They comin' back right now. I just talked to the V-man."

I recognized the voice, the heavy Mexican accent, and began trotting faster toward the disabled truck. Because of the rubber dive boots I wore, I moved quietly, using night vision to pick the cleanest, shortest path. I had the Glock in my right hand, my gloved index finger ready, resting parallel to the barrel. In my left hand, I carried the Dazer.

It was Chapo's voice. Finally, I had located the man armed with the second Tec-9. He had played it smart, I realized. Instead of panicking, he had remained in the shadows, trying to figure out what was happening before making a move. It was a sensible thing to do. Chapo had a VHF. He knew that Victorino or his partner had a radio, too. So why should he risk making his position known?

My brain assembled all of this data automatically, then warned me that dealing with this man might require special care.

Startled by Chapo's voice, the woman shouted, "Jesus Christ! You scared the hell out of me!" Then she stood taller, exhaling smoke, and searched the darkness before calling, "Where are you? What was all that shooting about? No one tells me shit around here!"

To the northwest, I noticed, the truck was already turning—but having some trouble from the way it looked, rocking back and forth in what might have been mud. I allowed myself only a glance, though, because I was still moving fast.

I changed my heading slightly when I heard Chapo reply to the woman, saying, "I wanted to be sure of something before getting V-man on the radio. Now I'm sure. You better go on inside the trailer 'til you can come out."

The woman was drunk, I realized. She puffed on the cigarette and took a couple of careful steps in the direction of the truck before Chapo stopped her, dropping his pretense of politeness. "No closer, *puta*—you'll get yourself hurt. I'll shoot anyone, they get too close. Do what I say. Get your ass inside that trailer until it's safe to come out."

The woman hollered back, "For Christ's sake, at least tell me what's happening! Is it the cops?"

I was zeroing in on the man's hiding place, deciding maybe Chapo wasn't so smart after all because he continued to respond, saying, "We got us a visitor, *señorita*. He's around here somewhere. Hell, maybe he's got a gun pointed at you right now."

Chapo laughed, then tried to bait me by adding, "But it's no big deal. It's only a dumb redneck—sorta like jelly boy. And you saw what happened to jelly boy. V-man and us will take care of this Gomer. I bet he can hear me right now!"

No, Chapo had his shrewd moments, but he wasn't smart. He had just provided me with important intel. Jelly boy? He was referring to Squires, I decided. They had ransacked the bodybuilder's truck, probably looking for money, then they had killed him. Or tortured him at the very least. Chapo had also let it slip that Dedos or Calavero had told him about their visitor. Maybe just before they had died . . . or maybe both men had survived.

If so, their minutes were numbered because now I was close

enough to the Dodge to see where Chapo had hidden himself. The *pandilleros* hadn't told him I was wearing night vision, apparently . . . or the man wasn't aware that he'd done a bad job of concealing his feet.

Just as his nickname suggested, Chapo was a little man. The first thing I spotted were his two child-sized cowboy boots. He had positioned himself under the truck, feet visible beneath the passenger's side, the barrel of the Tec-9 and a portion of his head protruding from beneath the driver's side. It provided him a panoramic view of the buildings and the clearing while the truck's chassis protected him on three borders.

Or so he thought.

As I approached, I considered yelling to get his attention, then using the Dazer. A bad idea, I decided. Even bat blind, a man with an automatic weapon can cover a lot of area by spraying bullets.

Instead, I got to my knees, then to my belly. I crawled for a short distance but then stopped. I was approaching from the back of the truck, which wasn't ideal. It gave me a decent shot at the man's lower body, but that's not where I needed to hit him.

I had to try something different and I had to make up my mind fast. Unless the gangbangers had mired Squires's truck up to the axles, they might soon return, although I thought it unlikely.

Peripherally, I was aware that the woman was now on the steps of the RV, reaching for the door, when I decided to surprise Chapo by doing the unexpected. I bounced to my feet, already running, and reached the bumper of the Dodge after three long strides. When I dropped down into the bed of the truck, I could hear Chapo yelling, "Hey! Who's up there?" his question nonsensical because he was so startled.

I was looking down at the man, seeing the back of his head, holding the Glock steady in both hands. Only because it might provide me a larger target, I answered the man, hoping he would turn. I told Chapo, "Up here, it's Gomer. Take a look."

He replied, *"Who?"* maybe trying to buy some time as he tilted his face to see but also attempting to aim the Tec-9 upward without shooting himself in the chin.

Twice I shot Chapo: Once above the jaw hinge, although I had aimed at his temple. And once at the base of the skull.

A moment later, I heard Dedos's frail voice call from inside the cab, saying, *"Amigo!* I need a doctor, I'm hurt!"

I looked to confirm that Chapo wasn't moving, then I knelt to peer through the shattered back window. The truck was a chaos of glass, debris and blood.

Dedos was staring at me from the front seat, his hands somehow free, maybe from broken glass or possibly Chapo had cut the tape. When the man realized who I was, he thrust one arm toward me, palm outstretched, a classic defensive response when a man sees a gun aimed at his face.

Dedos spoke again, saying, "It's me, *amigo.* I helped you. Remember?" His voice had a pleading quality but also an edge of resignation that I have heard more than once.

Speaking to myself, not Dedos, I replied softly, "This is necessary—I'm sorry," a phrase I have spoken many times under similar circumstances before squeezing a trigger or snapping a man's neck.

We are a species that relies on ceremony to provide order, yet I have never allowed myself to explore or inspect my habit of apologizing before killing a man.

When I fired the Glock, the round severed a portion of Dedos's hand before piercing his forehead. I shot him once more, then turned my attention to Calavero, whose body was splayed sideways between the front and back seats.

Through it all, the man hadn't moved. Maybe Calavero had died more quickly because his mouth was taped. I didn't know—or care. If Calavero was still alive, though, he would be able to identify me later. I couldn't risk that.

Because I was aware that this would soon be a crime scene that demanded close inspection, I knelt, placed the Glock next to my feet, then took Calavero's own .357 derringer from my back pocket. When the medical examiner recovered slugs of different calibers from these bodies, it would suggest to police that there had been more than one shooter.

Recent headlines had inspired the crime scene I was now manipulating. Eighteen people killed, execution style, by a gang in Ensenada. A dozen in Chiapas forced to kneel, then shot in the back of the head. It was not something a respected marine biologist from Sanibel Island would be party to.

I had to lean through the back window to position myself closer to Calavero. I wanted to get a clean angle, close to the man's left ear. Because the gun was so small and the caliber of the cartridge so large, I anticipated the terrible recoil. When I pulled the trigger, though, I was the one who felt as if he'd been shot.

It wasn't because of the derringer's recoil. Simultaneously, as I pulled the trigger, there was a thunderous explosion to my left. I was thrown sideways, the derringer still in my hand, aware there were flames boiling in the sky above me.

I landed hard on my shoulder but got quickly to my feet, holding the Glock again, unsure of what had happened. Nearby—close enough to feel the heat—what had once been a recreational vehicle was now a mushroom cloud of smoke and fire. Flames were radiating outward, toward where Squires's truck had been parked, and also toward the wooden shack, traveling in a line like a lighted fuse.

Someone had poured a gas track, that was obvious. It was arson. But what had caused the explosion?

I remembered the tall woman standing at the door to the RV, a cigarette in her hand. RVs, like many oceangoing vessels, use propane. It was all the explanation I needed

Then, as if to confirm my theory, the women suddenly reappeared from the flames. She was screaming for help, slapping wildly at her clothing even though her clothes didn't appear to be on fire. I watched her spin in a panicked circle, then sprint toward the cooling darkness that lay beyond the inferno. Soon, she disappeared into a veil of smoke that separated what was left of the RV and the wooden shack.

If Dedos hadn't told me the woman had orchestrated the Guatemalan girl's abduction, I might have gone after her. Instead, I tossed the derringer into the cab of the Dodge, then vaulted to the ground.

Running hard, I headed toward the flames, yelling Tula's name.

To my right, the wooden structure hadn't caught fire yet. It soon would, but I had to check the RV first because, as I had already decided, it was the most likely place to keep a captive girl.

There was a light breeze out of the northeast. It was enough to change the angle of the flames and channel the flow of smoke, so I had to circle to the back of the trailer before I could get a good look at what was left of the structure.

There wasn't much. The westernmost section of the trailer, though, was still intact. I noticed two small windows there— bedroom windows, perhaps—that had been shattered by the explosion. The darkness within told me flames hadn't reached one of the rooms yet, so I ran to take a look.

As I got closer, the heat was so intense that I had to get down on the ground and crawl. It seemed impossible that anyone inside could still be alive, but I had to make sure. I took a deep breath, put both gloved hands on the frame of the windows and pulled myself up to take a look.

Smoke was boiling from the plywood door, the floor was a scattered mess of photographs, some of them already curling from the heat. There was an oversized bed and so many shattered mirrors that I would have guessed the room had been used to film pornography even if I hadn't noted the tiresome, repetitive content of the photos. A camera tripod lying on the floor was additional confirmation.

Tula had been in this room. I sensed it—a belief which, by definition, had no validity. Yet, I also knew intellectually that if the tall woman and her gangbanger accomplices had planned to rape the girl, this is the place they would have chosen.

I screamed Tula's name. I tried to wedge my shoulders through the window and call for her again.

Tula!

The window was too small fit my body through, the heat suffocating, and I was finally forced to drop to the ground just to take another full breath.

I squatted there, breathing heavily, trying to decide what to do. I told myself the girl couldn't possibly be alive, yet I pulled myself up to the window for a final look.

There was a closet, but the door was open wide enough to convince me the girl hadn't taken refuge inside. I called Tula's name over and over, but when I smelled the stink of my own burning hair I dropped to the ground, then jogged away in search of a fresh breath.

I was furious with myself. It was irrational anger, but to come so close to saving the girl's life only to fall short and lose her to fire was maddening. I also couldn't delude myself of the truth: I probably could have forced my shoulders through the window and made a more thorough search of the RV had I really tried.

The fact was, I was afraid.

Like the other primary elements wind, air and water, fire can assume an incorruptible momentum that is a reality—and a fear— hardwired into our genetic memories over fifty million years of trying to domesticate nature's most indifferent killer.

That's what I was thinking as I ran toward the wooden building, my attention focused on the building's roof that was now ablaze, instead of noticing what was going on around me—a mistake. With my night vision system, I owned the darkness, yet instead of looping around through the shadows I stupidly sprinted straight toward the burning building—in plain sight of Victorino and his partner, I soon realized, as Squires's truck skidded to a stop only thirty yards to my right.

Because of the fire's combustive roar, I hadn't heard the engine approaching. Nor had I been listening for it. My last memory of the two men was of them bogged in mud, trying to escape.

That all changed when I heard a gunshot, then the telltale sizzle of a bullet passing close to my ear. It was an electric sensation punctuated by a vacuum of awareness—a sound once heard, never forgotten.

I ducked and turned, seeing one of the gangbangers using an open door to steady the gun he was holding. Thirty yards is a long distance for a revolver, but the man had come close. I was already diving toward the ground when he fired a second round.

I was shooting back at him with the Glock even before I hit the ground, squeezing the trigger rapid-fire, my rounds puckering the door's sheet metal, then shattering the glass window.

I heard the man bellow as he ducked from view, but I kept firing, while my left hand searched for the Dazer that was in my back pocket. I didn't aim, I shot instinctually, letting muscle memory control my right hand. Nor did I count the rounds—something I always do—because I had been taken so totally by surprise, and also because I had allowed myself to panic.

There was a valid reason to be afraid. I could see Victorino behind the diver's-side door, slapping at the Tec-9, getting ready to open fire. Maybe he hadn't seen me until his partner had drawn his weapon and fired. Or maybe the Tec-9 had jammed—they are notoriously undependable.

Whatever the reason, I knew that if he got the machine pistol working, I was dead.

When Victorino's partner suddenly reappeared, he was beneath the passenger's-side door on his back, chest pulsing a geyser of blood. At least one of my rounds had hit him.

Because there was no cover nearby, I got to my feet and charged the truck. I had the Dazer in my left hand, the Glock in my right. It seemed impossible that the gun's magazine had more than one or two rounds left, and I was tempted to dump the weapon and reach for my Kahr 9mm—the pistol I had used to kill the gator. It was in my hip pocket, fully loaded.

Victorino was bringing the Tec-9 up to fire, though, his head and shoulders framed by the driver's-side window. A wasted second would have killed me. I was pointing the Glock at the man, screaming, "Drop it! Drop it!" as I squeezed the trigger.

Instead of a gunshot, I heard *Click*.

Absurdly, I tried the trigger again. *Click-Click-Click*.

The Glock was empty.

Victorino had ducked involuntarily when he saw me sprinting toward him, aiming the pistol. But now that he realized I was out of ammunition, I watched the man appear to grow taller as he stepped away from the truck. He was taking his time now, grinning at me with what might have been gold teeth, the machine pistol held at chest level.

I had stopped running. The Glock was useless, so I dropped the thing at my feet, hoping the man was egocentric enough not to shoot me immediately, which is what a professional would have done. Maybe he would offer some smart-ass remark, provide me with a few seconds to think while he gloated over his triumph before killing me.

As if surrendering, I thrust my hands in the air, as Victorino took charge, his ego on display. He told me, "The flashlight, too. Drop the flashlight, jelly boy. Who the fuck you think you are, coming in here causing so much trouble? And take off that goddamn ski mask!"

I was holding the Dazer in my left hand, my thumb on the pressure switch. My heart was pounding. Even if I had the laser aimed accurately, even if I blinded him instantly, the man would still be able to fire twenty or thirty rounds in the space of a couple of seconds. It was my only hope, though. Drop the Dazer without at least trying, I would be dead.

Victorino took a step toward me and yelled, "Do it now, *cabrón!*"

As I reached to remove my watch cap, I mashed the pressure switch and collapsed to my knees. My aim was off only slightly, and I saw a shock of green light pierce the man's eyes. In sync with Victorino's shriek of surprise, I rolled to the ground, anticipating a long volley of gunfire. Instead, a three-round burst kicked the sand nearby, then the gun the went silent while the man continued to howl, trying to shield his eyes with his left hand but still jabbing the machine pistol at me with his right.

The Tec-9 had jammed again, I realized.

I took a long, deep breath and got to my feet, still aiming the laser. Until the weapon's fouled chamber had been cleared, the thing was probably harmless, yet there was also a possibility that Victorino had somehow activated the safety—a mistake he might correct at any moment.

Holding the laser in both hands, I kept it focused on Victorino's face as I dodged out of his probable line of fire. I was yelling, "Drop the weapon, get down on your belly!" repeating the commands over and over as I approached. But the man was in such obvious pain, I doubted if my words registered.

When I was close enough, I slapped the machine pistol out of Victorino's hands. When he tried to take a blind swing at me, I grabbed him by the collar, kicked his legs from beneath him, then pinned the man to the ground.

I had one knee on Victorino's chest as I jammed the Dazer hard into the socket of his left eye. The laser's megawattage was radiating heat through its aluminum casing that even I could feel despite my leather gloves.

I held the gang leader there for several seconds, ignoring his screaming pleas, his wild promises, until I was certain he had had enough. Then I switched off the laser, pressed my nose close to his and said, "Tula Choimha. The Guatemalan girl you abducted—where is she?"

Victorino started to tell me, "I don't know nothing about no—" but I didn't let him finish.

I speared the Dazer into the socket of the man's right eye and held the pressure switch, full power, as he tried to wrestle away. Even when he had stopped fighting me and was screaming, "I'll tell you anything! Anything!" I kept his head pinned to the ground. I held him there for another few seconds before switching off the laser, then I tried again.

"Where's the girl?" I asked the man. "Did you kill her?"

In the stark light of the inferno, Victorino was crying now—perhaps an involuntary ocular response to the laser or because he was afraid. The teardrop tattoo beneath his left eye glistened with real tears. The irony might have struck me as vaguely amusing had I been in a different mood.

I placed a finger on Victorino's Adam's apple, my thumb on his carotid artery. As I squeezed, I said, "I'm not going to ask you again. Where is she?" and then I lifted until the gang leader was on his feet.

He didn't try to fight me. "You blinded me, man," he said. "I can't see! How the hell you expect me to answer questions when I can't see nothing?"

When I squeezed his throat harder, though, Victorino opened his eyes and blinked a few times before telling me, "Okay, okay. Everything's real blurry, man. And my eyes fucking hurt, man. It's like you stuck a knife in my brain. You got to give me a minute."

I gave him a shake and said, "Tell me where you have her—the girl. And what happened to Harris Squires?"

I released the man long enough to confirm his partner was dead. Beside the body was a .44 Smith & Wesson, a small cannon that caused my pants to sag when I stuck it in the back of my belt.

My attention had shifted to the wooden building, flames shooting out the door now. It caused Victorino to turn his head, and I felt myself cringe when he finally answered my question. "Last time I saw that little girl," he said, "she was in there."

I got behind the gang leader and shoved him toward the flames. If Tula Choimha was still alive, she wouldn't last long.

We had to hurry.

I slapped Victorino in the back of the head, then pushed him harder toward the building, yelling, "The girl might still be alive. Run! Help me get her out, I won't kill you!"

The man replied, "You serious?"

When I pulled my hand back to hit him again, Victorino took off running.

Together, we sprinted toward the wooden structure, the heat from the burning RV so intense that we had to circle away before angling toward the door of the shack. As we ran, I took the Kahr semiautomatic from my pocket, already aware that Victorino was faster than I and he might decide to keep running.

That's exactly what he had decided to do—until I stopped him by skipping two rounds near his feet.

"Goddamn it, man!" he yelled. "I'm not escaping, I'm trying to get to the back side of this place. I think there might be a window there."

Victorino had long black hair. I grabbed a fistful, then used it like a leash to steer him, saying, "We check the door first. Get as close as you can and take a look."

I gave the man a shove toward the opening as my brain scanned frantically for a better way to clear the building. For a moment, I considered the possibility of ramming one of the walls with Squires's truck—but that might bring the blazing ceiling down on the girl, if she was still alive inside.

But Tula wasn't alive. She couldn't be. I knew it was impossible, as my eyes shifted from the truck to the building that was now a roaring conflagration of smoke and flames.

Twenty feet from the door, Victorino dropped to his belly because of the heat. He yelled, "There's something you don't know, man! This place"—he gestured toward the building—"it's a cookshack for steroids. It's got a bunch of propane tanks all lined up. Any second, they're gonna start—"

There was no need for him to continue because that's when the first propane canister exploded. Then three more followed in staccato succession, each shooting a fireworks tapestry of sparks into the night sky.

When Victorino got to his feet and tried to sprint to safety, I caught him by the hair again and yelled, "We check that window next. I'm not giving up until I'm sure."

From the expression on the gang leader's face, I knew there was no window. He had been lying. Even so, I herded him to the back of the building, where a small section of the wall had been blown outward. From a distance of thirty yards—that was as close as we could get—I could at least see inside the place.

I was positive then. No living thing could have survived that fire.

For several seconds, I stood there numbly, taking in the scene. Had I arrived a few minutes earlier, spent less time interrogating Dedos and Calavero, maybe I could have saved the girl. It wasn't the first time my obsession for detail had thwarted a larger objective. But it was the first time an innocent person had died because I could not govern what secretly I have always known is a form of mania— or rage.

Obsession *is* rage, a Dinkin's Bay neighbor had once told me—a man who also happens to be a Ph.D. expert on brain chemistry and human behavior.

The fact was, I was doing it now—obsessing—and I forced myself to concentrate. Later, I could wallow in the knowledge of my inadequacies. Tonight, I still had work to do.

There were a lot of unanswered questions. Unless I was willing to risk prison, I had to understand what had happened here. Obsessive or not, details are vital when manipulating a crime scene.

I asked Victorino, "Is Squires in there, too?" The wooden building, I meant.

I knew the man wasn't telling me the whole truth when he replied,

"I think so. Him and that woman, Frankie, they did some weird, kinky shit. But she got pissed off at him. That Frankie is crazy."

I watched Victorino's head swivel. "Where the hell that woman go? She's the one you ought to be hammering on, man. Not me."

When I told him the woman had been in the RV when it exploded, he did a poor job of hiding his reaction—a mix of relief and perverse satisfaction.

Victorino and Frankie had been sexually involved at one time, I guessed. Hatred is often catalyzed by the pain of previous intimacies—or infidelities.

I asked, "Were his hands tied? His feet? What about Squires?"

I was trying to assemble a better overview of who had done what to whom. Before crime scene police could understand who the bad guys were, I had to understand it myself.

Victorino replied, "Man, I had nothing to do with that shit." When he saw my expression change, though, he added quickly, "But, yeah, I'm pretty sure Frankie had them both tied pretty good. She was getting ready to do a video deal, you know? So later she could have fun watching herself do shit to the girl, and her old boyfriend, too. A freak, man. I already told you."

The truth of what had happened was becoming clearer in my mind despite Victorino's dissembling. As the man continued talking, inventing details, I was studying the portion of wall that had been blown open. It was a narrow section of planking wide enough for me to see inside, if the angle was right, but not large in comparison with the rest of the structure.

It bothered me for some reason. What I was seeing didn't mesh with my knowledge of explosives and the complex dynamics involved. At that instant, as if to illustrate, another propane canister exploded, and we both ducked instinctively, watching a column of red sparks shoot skyward.

Victorino was telling me, "My boys and me, we sold them grass, coke, whatever. Sometimes moved some of the muscle juice shit they made—strictly business, you understand. That's the only reason we come out here tonight. Then this shit happened."

What bothered me about the hole in the wall, I realized, was that the boards had shattered geometrically, yet it was a random displacement of matter in an otherwise solid wall.

What I was seeing made no sense. An explosive force creates a rapidly expanding wave of pressure slightly larger than the volume of the explosive. It expands with predictable symmetry—a three-dimensional sphere capped by a matrix of superheated gases and particles. The matrix created by the exploding propane takes was rocketing upward. Why had this small space been blown *outward*?

But then I decided that the anomaly could be explained in many ways. A weakness in the structure, an absence of bracing because the hole had once been a window or a door. The shack looked homemade, sturdy but inconsistent. What I was doing, I realized, was fishing for hope—hope that the girl and Squires had managed to crash their way through the wall and escape.

The fire had started so suddenly, though, the heat and flames so intense that the pair would have had very little time to knock a hole in what had been a very solid wall. And they had both been tied, hands and legs.

"The bitch *invited* us," Victorino told me. "She told me they had a new batch of muscle juice. Only reason my boys and me were here tonight. And we got certain security procedures we follow. Two guards at the gate, two of my best men with me riding shotgun. A dude they don't know shows up, they're trained to take certain steps. It was nothing personal. You understand."

I waited, watching Victorino's eyes move from the fire to the shattered windows of the Dodge pickup, aware that at least two of his men were dead inside. The truck appearing animated in the oscillating light. I wondered if the man would have the nerve to ask what he was aching to know. He finally tried.

"Maybe you know something about the steroid trade yourself?" I watched Victorino grin, showing his gold teeth. He wasn't a bad-looking guy, actually. He had a good chin, a strong Aztec nose and cheeks. Had the man made different decisions—or been born in a different setting—he might have succeeded in a legitimate business.

Staring into the fire, I said, "Her name was Tula Choimha—the surname dates back to the time of the Maya. She was thirteen years old, two thousand miles from home, and the girl had no one to protect her from scum like you. That's why I'm here."

Victorino chose not to respond.

Slowly, I backed away from the heat. Victorino backed away, too, but he was gradually creating more distance between us, I noticed, until I hollered at him to stop. I used the pistol to wave him closer, before telling him, "Let's get in the truck and get the hell out of here. You drive."

It surprised the man. He replied, "Both of us you mean?" unsure if he had less to fear or more to fear.

"A plane or a helicopter's going to spot the flames," I told him. "Cops and firefighters will be coming soon. Maybe park rangers— we're close enough to the Everglades. I don't want to be here when they show up. How about you?"

I had taken off the night vision headgear, and Victorino jerked his head away when he realized I was going to remove the ski mask, too.

Mask up—but not off—my face pouring sweat, I told the man, "It's okay. You can look."

Victorino was three steps ahead of me, facing the truck. I could see his mind working, wondering what was going on.

The man stood frozen for what seemed like several seconds. Perhaps because I began to whisper to myself, repeating a private liturgy, he finally turned to look at me.

When he did, I asked, "Where's the money? Sixty thousand dollars cash." I didn't know if the drunken woman was telling the truth, but I was thinking about Tula Choimha's determination to lead her family home to Guatemala. They would need money.

Victorino's eyes revealed the money's location, but I waited until he lied to me, replying, "Money? What money?" the staged look of confusion still on the man's face when I shot him in the chest. A few seconds later, I shot him at close range in the back of the head.

His partner's .44 Smith & Wesson made a thud when it landed on the ground beside Victorino's body.

I wasn't going to invest much time searching for the money—if it existed. What I had told Victorino was true. The hunting camp was in one of the most remote regions in Florida, yet a fire of that magnitude might still attract attention.

I found the cash in a canvas gym bag on the floor of Squires's truck, along with a .357 Ruger Blackhawk revolver. The temptation was to get behind the wheel of the truck, and drive as fast as I could back to the main road. But then I remembered that the Dodge blocked the exit. Bulldozing the thing out of the way would take time and would make a lot of noise. It would also prove that at least one of the shooters had escaped.

It was safer, cleaner, if I returned on foot.

To add further confusion to the scene, I tossed the Blackhawk under the truck, then took off, jogging toward the darkness, gym bag over my shoulder, as I repositioned the night vision monocular over my left eye.

I had learned my lesson. Until I was close enough to my truck to risk stepping into the open, I would stay in the shadows. To me, darkness—and open water—have always represented safety.

I am a stubborn man, though. Because the anomalous hole in the wall still bothered me and because it would be the driest route back to my truck, I chose to run past the burning shack before turning into the woods. There, the topography was upland pine. Plenty of cover but lots of open ground, unlike the swamp to my right. It would be a hell of a lot easier to parallel the hunting camp road before angling to the gate where my truck was hidden.

There was a third reason: I also believed that if Squires and the girl had managed to escape, they would have had to travel a similar path to safety. It was unlikely that they had survived, but it would satisfy my mania for thoroughness while also providing an ironic last hope that my obsessiveness hadn't cost a young girl her life.

It happened.

Fifty yards into the woods, north of where the shack was still burning, I heard a mewing sound. It was soft, rhythmic, a noise so similar to the sound of wind in the pine canopy that I would have dismissed it as a feral cat had I not been wearing night vision.

After only a few more steps, I could discern the source of the noise. It was Tula Choimha. She was kneeling over a massive shape that I soon realized was the body of Harris Squires.

I had been moving so quietly, the girl hadn't heard me. I didn't want to frighten her, but I also realized that I couldn't allow her to see my face. I lowered the ski mask, readjusted the monocular, then knelt before calling to her softly, "Tomlinson sent me. Don't be afraid. Your friend Tomlinson wants me to help you."

It was as if I had spoken a secret password. Instead of being startled, the girl jumped to her feet and ran to me, sobbing, then threw herself into my arms. Only when she noticed my strange headgear did she recoil, but I patted her between the shoulders as I held her and spoke into her ear, saying, "I'm taking you home. Please don't ask me any questions. Okay? But it's true, I'm taking you home."

Through the lens, the girl's face was as radiant as phosphorus, but I could also see that her nose was swollen, her face bruised. She stared at me for a moment, and I sensed she knew exactly who I was, although she had only seen me briefly after the alligator attack at Red Citrus.

"You're Tomlinson's friend?" she asked, but there was a complexity to her intonation that signaled she was asking far more than that simple question.

"I'm taking you home," I repeated. "That's all I can tell you. But first I need to know how badly you're hurt. Someone hit you in the face, I can see that. But were you burned? It's important that you tell me the truth."

My mind was already scanning our options. If Tula needed emergency attention, the decision was easy. I would call 911 and risk the fallout—claim to have found her wandering in the woods, which was true. If she was okay, I would park in the shadows at Red Citrus and not let her out of my truck until Tomlinson had arrived and found her "officially."

But the girl replied, "I have a headache, that's all. Some of my hair got singed. The only reason I'm not hurt is because"—her head pivoted toward Squires—"because the giant saved me. I have never met a man so strong—stronger than Hercules, even. We were in a building, there was a fire, so he picked me up like a bear, then we both crashed through a wall."

Carrying the girl in my arms, I walked toward Squires. What I saw was unexpected. The man appeared to be badly burned on his

333

shoulders, yes, but he had also been peppered with a shotgun and castrated. It caused me to remember what Victorino had said about the woman I had seen running from the RV, batting at imaginary flames.

"That Frankie is crazy," he had told me.

It was a rare nugget of truth from the gang leader.

"Please," the girl told me after several seconds. "You shouldn't look at Harris anymore. He's not covered. God is with him now, but we still need to show respect. I'll come back later. I'll pray for Harris and then cover him with a shroud."

I wasn't surprised that Tula was in shock. But I also wondered if she was delusional—something I had suspected from the first—because she leaned her mouth close to my ear as if to whisper a secret, saying, "Jehanne already told me that you were coming. That you would be wearing a helmet like a knight. I expected it to be made of steel"—the girl touched her fingers to my ski mask—"but this is the armor that Jehanne spoke of. I understand now. You are the warrior knight God sent to save me. That's why I understand I cannot ask you questions."

"Jehanne," I said gently even though I had never heard the name. "Yes . . . that was good of her. I'm glad she told you because I didn't want you to be afraid."

Cradling the girl in my arms, I turned and began walking in the direction of my truck. Tula laid her head against my shoulder and began to cry. After a few steps, though, she pulled away and plucked at an oversized polo shirt that covered her like a dress, saying, "Normally, I'm not so weak, but I can't help myself. It's hard for me to leave Harris all alone because he fought for me so hard. He even gave me his shirt to wear. And he found my amulets—my shields."

The girl was cupping what looked like a necklace, as she continued, "Once I was wearing my amulet, I thought everything was going to be okay, that God would heal him. That we would live in the mountains together, where I could take care of him. But then . . . but then . . ."

I felt the girl's body shudder, and I expected her to say that it was then that Squires had died.

Instead, Tula turned to look at something I hadn't yet noticed. It was an elongated form lying in the distance, difficult to decipher details even with night vision. I began walking toward the shape as I listened to the girl explain, "But even God can't control evil. The power it has over people—a giant like Harris, it makes no difference. I wonder sometimes if even Jehanne understands."

The girl nodded toward the shape, her expression fierce, then turned away before telling me, "Evil. That's what killed Harris— even though I fought to save him just like he fought for me. She came out of the darkness, screaming profanities, and running. It surprised us. Both of us. I fought back. But Harris lost his strength and died."

Carefully, I placed the girl on the ground, her back turned, and I walked to the body of the woman I had seen fleeing the RV. It was Frankie, I realized

I knelt, then risked moving the woman's arms to assess her injuries as best I could. To be certain, I even used a small LED light to check her legs, her face, a portion of her abdomen.

The flames might not have been imaginary, but Frankie's body had only minor burns. Some blistering on her arms and a head of singed red hair. Maybe the explosion had blown the woman clear of the fire—possible, if she had been standing in an open doorway when a cigarette ignited the propane.

I knew from what I'd witnessed that the woman was already drunk. Alcohol could have contributed to her hysteria, so Frankie had assumed the worst, panicked and sprinted into the woods. Maybe the woman had tripped and fallen. Or collapsed from exhaustion—but only after surprising the Guatemalan girl and her injured body-builder protector.

What my careful scenario didn't explain was the blood that soaked the woman's tube top . . . and the paring knife protruding from Frankie's throat.

"She was evil," Tula said to me, her back still turned. "She wanted to kill Harris and she finally did. But not his goodness. That's what I was trying to save."

My mind was working fast, already anticipating the questioning the girl would have to endure. Tula Choimha needed an out. Some-thing real. Something she had witnessed with her own eyes so she could speak honestly of it later.

I said to Tula, "I want you to watch something. It won't be pleasant. Later, though—when people ask you about what happened—you'll be able to tell them honestly what you saw. Other things . . . things that happened earlier tonight . . . you'll probably want to forget."

I waited until I was certain that the girl had turned to look. Then I used the paring knife on Frankie—several times—before leaving the knife just as I had found it, in her throat.

We walked in silence then, the girl in my arms. It wasn't until we were almost back to my truck that Tula looked up into my masked face and said, "Do you remember the goodness that was in you as a child? God's goodness, I'm talking about."

I replied, "Sure. Everyone does," because I thought it might make her feel better or reassure her at the very least.

I had underestimated the Guatemalan girl's strength, however, and her maturity. It was Tula who then provided me with a more tangible form of reassurance, saying, "That doesn't mean warriors shouldn't lie to protect other warriors. Joan of Arc did it many times to protect her knights. The Maiden has promised me it's true—Dr. Ford."

EPILOGUE

ON THE SECOND SUNDAY IN MARCH, WHICH IS WHEN DAYLIGHT savings adds an hour of light to winter's darkness, I drove my truck to the West Wind Inn, a mile from Dinkin's Bay, and was on the beach in time to watch the sunrise.

It was 6:43 a.m. The sun had not yet appeared above the Sanibel Lighthouse, but clouds to the west were fire laced, tinged with pink and edged with turquoise from a sky that melded blue with the green of an old morning sea.

I had just taken possession of a custom surfboard, designed by surf icon Steve Brom and shipped from the Florida Panhandle by YOLO Boards of Santa Rosa Beach.

It was Tomlinson who had discovered the fledgling company, perhaps charmed by the YOLO acronym: *You Only Live Once.*

As my friend pointed out, the name didn't mesh with his convictions about reincarnation or life after death, but, as he explained, "You gotta love the kick-ass spirit it represents."

I was unmoved until I had tried one. The next afternoon, I spoke to Brom and ordered a board specifically for my needs. After discussing what I wanted, I then provided the man with my height and weight.

Amused, the California surf guru had told me, "I don't expect to see you on the pro circuit anytime soon. But this might be my chance to create a board that even a gorilla could use, maybe even learn to shred."

Funny guy.

The board—a stand-up paddleboard, by definition—had arrived yesterday, a Saturday, just as I had finished separating a new batch of specimens, sea horses and filefish in one tank, two dozen anemones in another. After I had unboxed the board, I had leaned it against the outside wall of my lab, then trotted down the steps to get a better view from the deck.

There is something iconic about the shape of a surfboard. It gave me pleasure just looking at it. The body was laminated bamboo, rails classically arched, the bottom painted deuce-coupe yellow. The board was more than eleven feet long, the ends symmetrically rounded, and I amused myself by deciding it would have appeared equally at home on Easter Island, guarding a seaward bluff, or sliding down a North Shore wave.

Waves. That's why I had come to the beach. It's why I had done only an abbreviated morning workout, then headed straight to the West Wind after checking the weather report.

Sanibel Island isn't known for its surf, but this morning was different. Wind was blowing low over the Gulf, rolling waves from the southwest, their crests finally peaking as they soldiered toward the beach after a five-hundred-mile journey from the Yucatán, Mexico.

Just beyond the second sandbar, fifty yards from shore, a translucent green beach break was curling with a symmetry so consistent that I realized my hands were shaking a little as I strapped the leash around my ankle, then carried the board to the water.

To my left, to my right, there were early-morning beach strollers and shellers and young honeymooners walking hand in hand. Decade after decade on the islands, the faces differ, but the beaches continue to provide a safe conduit to the infinite, narrow galleries of sand that illustrate relentless change.

The surf line, though, was as empty as the horizon.

Waves were waiting. And so was something else I needed: solitude. I craved it. Craved it so intensely that, since I had rescued the Guatemalan girl eleven days earlier, I had been avoiding people. It is the same when I return from an overseas assignment. I view it as decompression time, a period of slow reacclimatization after surfacing from the depths.

At the gate to my boardwalk, I had hung the NO VISITORS PLEASE sign. I retreated to my lab, ignoring e-mails, refusing phone calls, and I had even skipped Dinkin's Bay Marina's traditional Friday-night party.

I worked out every morning and afternoon, then spent most of the day in my flats skiff or in my little trawler, dragging nets. My only companions were the sea creatures that inhabited my aquaria, my telescope and the marina's self-important cat, Crunch & Des, who spent an unusual amount of time gifting me with an unusual amount of attention.

Two people I made a special effort to avoid were Tomlinson and Emily Marston.

The only person I spoke with daily—almost daily, anyway—and visited whenever I could, was Tula Choimha. I had wrestled with the possibility that interacting with the girl might cause police to be suspicious. As I got to know her better, however, and because I paid close attention to how law enforcement types reacted when I was around, I was soon convinced that the opposite was true.

More important, I was convinced of something more compelling: Tula could be trusted. We never discussed what had happened. The girl was savvy enough to understand that any mention of that night could mean years in jail for me.

Instead, we spoke of her brother and her aunts and how eager she was to return to Guatemala. Her mother, though, was never mentioned. I didn't pry because of something Tula had shared with me that night during our long drive. "My mother is dead," the girl told me. After several minutes of silence, she explained, "Harris confessed something to me that I can never speak of again. I love them both and I forgive them both. Because I love them, the truth of how my mother died will die with me."

A safer topic for our daily talks included the hundreds of Central Americans who visited the girl's hospital daily, waiting patiently and offering prayers, even though they knew they would not be allowed to see the patient they revered.

It required special patience for me to pretend to accept Tula's explanation. "They're aware that God has sent them a message through me. My people don't belong here. No amount of money is worth the homes and families they abandoned. On their cell phones, I know they probably exaggerate what I suffered—some of the crazy stories the nurses have told me! But the fire was real, and so was the evil. God wants me to keep spreading His message. And I will."

What transpired the night I rescued Tula was on my mind hour after hour, day after day. From it sprouted additional worries and realizations. I had saved the girl. It made me responsible for her in some ways. I also felt a growing affection for Tula that was beyond anything I had anticipated. It matched my admiration for Tula's intellect, her maturity and her decency.

In the bag I had taken from Squires's truck, I had counted out more than fifty-three thousand, mostly in hundreds, fifties and twenties. Cash of that amount would invite scrutiny, and I was still investigating the best way to create an account in Tula Choimha's name.

Responsibility is a petri dish of worry.

But now as I waded into the Gulf, then paddled toward the surf line, my earth-linked worries faded, becoming incrementally smaller with every freeing stroke.

Nine days after the missing Guatemalan girl made headlines by suddenly reappearing at Red Citrus RV Park dazed and injured, she was released from the hospital with the blessings of the Florida Department of Law Enforcement, but only after several interrogation sessions plus four days of medical tests and psychological evaluations.

"The child is suffering from shock and what may be post-traumatic amnesia," a department spokesman was quoted as saying. "But she is a resilient child, very brave, and the information she has provided is so detailed that we believe we have a firm grasp on the facts regarding how she disappeared and the murders she may have witnessed."

Because of the girl's age, thankfully, the reports never revealed Tula's name.

Unlike Tomlinson, who is a *New York Times* junkie, I avoid newspapers. Reading a litany of human outrages, I believe, is a damn dark way to start what in Florida is usually a consistently bright day. Because I had a personal stake in how the investigation unfolded, however, I spent those ten days paying close attention.

Especially nerve-racking were the afternoons that I knew Tula was being interrogated.

At any moment, day or night, the police could come tapping at my door. Paranoia isn't irrational when fears are well founded or when guilt is the burden of someone who is truly guilty. It was a new experience for me—while living within the normally safe borders of the United States, anyway—and not pleasant.

Not that I suffered from pangs of guilt. I didn't. If a shrink somehow learned the truth about my life, if he was provided details of some of the things I have done, he might conclude that I am a sociopath, incapable of remorse or guilt.

The shrink would be wrong. I am sufficiently objective to acknowledge that I am less affected by emotion than most people, yet I suffer guilt and regret on a daily basis just like everyone else. I am aware that too many times I have behaved thoughtlessly, stupidly and childishly. I have hurt people I care about and I have said words that will forever make me wince.

The difference between myself and a sociopath is this: When I executed those five men, I did it while in full control of my emotional and intellectual facilities. I didn't pull the trigger because I wanted to do it. I killed those men because it was *necessary*—required, in fact, by the circumstances and the exigencies of their own violent behaviors. Pyromania is to arson what murder is to assassination.

"Strictly business," Victorino might have explained it, and the man would have been correct for once.

When I replayed the events of that night in my mind, I felt no guilt for the same reason I felt no perverse thrill or any emotional satisfaction. Even so, what had happened was on my mind constantly. So I followed the news reports.

The St. Pete *Times* referred to the incident as *The Immokalee Slay-*

ings, which for that excellent newspaper was an understandable hedge because Immokalee was the nearest town and also because three of the seven victims resided within the city limits.

Laziro Victorino, I was not surprised to learn, had chosen upscale locations—a riverfront home in Cape Coral and a condo near Tampa.

"Police believe the homicides are gang related," one of the stories read. "Mass killings have become commonplace in Mexico, and the ceremonial nature of the Immokalee slayings suggests that gang violence has finally arrived in South Florida. Four victims were shot execution style. The body of a fifth victim was mutilated, although authorities refuse to provide specific details."

Because police had found steroid-manufacturing apparatus at Harris Squires's hunting camp and also a small facility at his Red Citrus double-wide, the news reports implied what police had yet to confirm: The killings had something to do with a turf war over the sale of illegal steroids.

"Such turf wars date back to the days of Prohibition," one newspaper editorial read. "Illegal drugs spawn murderous behavior. To members of a warring gang, killing an enemy is viewed as a right of passage."

Six consecutive days the slayings dominated headlines, but the few known facts didn't vary much. It wasn't until the ninth day that some enterprising reporter hammered away at an obvious question until some unknown source provided an answer. How exactly did a teenage Guatemalan girl escape the carnage only to be found forty miles away, wandering the shrimp docks near Tomlinson's rum bar, bayside, Fort Myers Beach?

According to a source familiar with statements made by the abductee, the reporter wrote, *the girl was rescued by a person she described as a "Spanish-speaking man who drove a truck."*

Because the man wore a ski mask, the girl was unable to provide a physical description of her rescuer, although she described him as "kind and gentle" in at least two of her statements. In a third statement, the girl told investigators that the man's truck must have been almost new because it was so quiet that she was able to fall asleep as the masked man drove.

The story continued, *Although it cannot be confirmed, at least some investigators believe the man may be a member of one of the warring gangs whose conscience would not allow him to execute a young girl. A Collier County psychologist, often consulted in homicide cases, has suggested the man may be the father of a girl who is of similar age. Police are cross-referencing the information in search of the suspect, although investigators believe that most, if not all, of the warring gang members were killed on the night the incident occurred. The exception, of course, is the man who drove the girl to safety.*

A Spanish-speaking masked man. Tula had found a way to effectively distance me from the case by providing her interrogators with very specific truths.

After five days, heartened by the reactions of police and the news report I read, I began to enjoy a tenuous confidence that I had manipulated the crime scene convincingly. After seven days had passed, the only cop who had bothered to contact me was my detective friend, Leroy Melinski. And the only reason he called was to congratulate me on Tula's rescue.

Well . . . to congratulate Tomlinson. Not me.

"I've got to give your crazy hippie friend credit," Lee had said. "All night, our guys had been staking out that trailer park, but it's your pal who happens to find the girl wandering the streets and brings her in. 'Psychic intuition,' he told our guys. He claimed that's how he knew where to find her. The first thing they did, of course, was check his vehicle for weapons and a ski mask. And he also had a very solid alibi—he'd spent the entire evening with a woman biologist that Tomlinson claims you know. So maybe there's something to that mystic bullshit after all."

I didn't comment on Melinski's reference to Emily, although I was tempted to tell him he was right about the bullshit but wrong about the rest of it.

Tomlinson's "psychic intuition" had nothing whatsoever to do with him finding Tula.

Truth was, Tomlinson was so drunk and stoned by the time I reached him on his cell phone that I judged him incapable of driving to Red Citrus. Because I couldn't depend on him, I hung up without mentioning that Tula was with me.

I was disappointed in the guy, of course, but I wasn't shocked. I *was* shocked, however, when I dialed Emily Marston as a backup and suddenly I was talking to Tomlinson once again.

For a moment, I was confused. Had I or had I not dialed Emily's cell phone?

Yes, I had.

"Ms. Marston is temporarily indisposed," Tomlinson answered formally, unaware he was speaking to me. Because he tried hard to sound sober, he only sounded drunker when he added, "May I help you? Or you can wait for Emily—she's a pretty quick little spliff roller."

By then, Tula and I were only twenty minutes from Red Citrus. I had driven the distance with particular care for obvious reasons, and now the girl was asleep, her head in my lap. So as not to wake her, I had to move my right arm gently to get a look at my watch.

1:30 a.m.

My best friend, it turned out, was still guarding the safety of my new lover, Emily, the quick little spliff roller. The temptation was to nail Tomlinson with a very valid question: What in the hell, exactly, was going on?

Instead, I remained calm. I had to because I needed his help. Someone had to be close to Red Citrus, waiting, when I dropped off the girl. Someone I trusted. Not inside the park because cops might still be posted. If police saw the exchange, if they suspected I was the one who had driven Tula to safety, they would search my truck and correctly associate me with the murders I had just committed.

Phone to my ear, I took a slow breath and said, "Tomlinson, if you care anything about our friendship, please don't say a word. Just listen."

The instant he tried to respond I stopped him, saying, "I'm warning you, this is serious. And please don't use my name—or tell Emily it's me."

After a reassuring silence, I told him, "I need your help. I'm counting on you." Because it was true, I added, "You're the only person I trust with my life."

During another long pause, I imagined the man's mind trying to rally. Tomlinson claims that his brain conceals what he calls "a sober lifeguard twin" who comes to his rescue in demanding situations no matter how wasted he happens to be. He claims his ever-sober twin has saved him from suspicious cops and freak storms at sea.

Because of my tone, I suspected that Tomlinson was summoning that lifeguard now.

Finally, he said, "Anything you want. You can count on me."

As he spoke, I could hear Emily in the background, asking, "Is it for me? Why are you using my phone?" The woman, at least, sounded sober, but I wasn't going to entrust her with what had to happen next.

As I spoke to Tomlinson, I used short sentences. I kept my directions concise. Lifeguard twin or not, the man still sounded slobbering drunk.

Half an hour later, I sat in my truck in the shadows of the boatyard that adjoins Tomlinson's rum bar. The bar's party lights and its underwater lights were still on, but the place was closed.

Twice, cop cars cruised past, probably changing watches at Red Citrus, I guessed. Each time, as my knuckles whitened on the steering wheel, I felt Tula pat my arm, trying to calm me.

When a Yellow Taxi finally appeared, pulling beneath the security light near Hanson's Shrimp Yards—exactly as I had instructed Tomlinson—I leaned, kissed Tula's singed hair and told her, "You're safe now. Tomlinson's waiting. He won't ask you any questions. He promised me—and I trust him."

Then I sat back and watched the girl run toward the security light into my pal's waiting arms.

Aside from a few accidental meetings at the marina—"awkward" would describe our exchanges—it was the last time I saw the man until that early Sunday morning when I noticed two familiar figures appear from the strand of sea oats that separate the West Wind Inn from the beach.

I was a hundred yards from shore, waiting for a good wave. I watched the figures stop . . . scan the water . . . and then both people waved.

It was Tomlinson, looking absurd in a pink sarong. Emily was beside him.

I had been avoiding the couple, it was true. But I waved in reply, anyway, because petty demonstrations of anger are, in my opinion, the equivalent of cancerous little cells that eat away at the quality of a person's life.

Why not? I was feeling pretty good because I'd already had some fun. Waves had tumbled me and humbled me, confirming, with supreme indifference, that I still had a lot to learn about paddleboard surfing.

My ego is still sufficiently adolescent, though, that I became determined to make my final ride to the beach stylish enough to impress Tomlinson and, more important, Emily.

Maybe I tried too hard. That's probably what happened. Only a few seconds into the ride, the board nose-dived, then pearled. I went flying.

Because I deserved it, I expected both Emily and my pal to be laughing as I carried the board to the beach. Not derisive laughter. The variety that comforts a friend after he has looked foolish.

Instead, they both appeared oddly serious as I approached. It became more serious—and confusing—when the woman marched toward me, then took my face in her hands. She stared into my eyes for a moment before saying, "This is an intervention! That's why we're here."

More confused, I said, "Huh?"

The woman explained, "An *intervention*. It's a sort of last-resort tactic that's supposed to work on alcoholics and habitual gamblers. So we decided that maybe, just maybe, it would work on someone as obsessively stubborn, bullheaded and downright dumb as you."

I replied, "*We* decided?" moving my head to look at Tomlinson.

The man rolled his eyes and shrugged as if to distance himself from what was happening. "I wouldn't call Doc dumb," he said. "The rest of it's true, yeah. Especially the 'obsessive-stubborn' deal. But 'dumb,' that's taking it a little too far."

I replied, "*Thanks*, pal," and broke away from Emily's grip long enough to place my board on the sand.

A moment later, though, she was cupping my face in her hands again. There were tears, I noticed, welling in her eyes, so I stood quietly and paid attention.

"We both know what you've been thinking about Tomlinson and me, and you're wrong," the woman said. "I've called you more than a dozen times. I sent you e-mails, trying to explain. I came to the marina twice, but each time you were off somewhere doing God knows what on your boat. It's been more than ten days, damn it!"

Emily's hands dropped to her sides and formed fists to illustrate her frustration. "I thought you cared about me, Doc! I wanted to talk with. No . . . I *needed* to talk with you! The night you called my cell phone, the night Tomlinson answered, why didn't you at least have the courtesy to explain to me that you were in trouble? If you'd told me you the truth, that you were in trouble and needed help, I would have been there for you, damn it!"

I tried to remain expressionless as slowly, very slowly, I shifted my attention to Tomlinson. My throat was tight as I asked the man, "You *told* her about what happened that night?"

Even when he's stoned, Tomlinson has wise old eyes, a prophet's eyes, some say. He stared back at me now, though, with clear eyes, his gaze steady. "I didn't tell her the specifics," he replied. "Just enough so she would understand."

I said, "Well, discretion has never been your strong suit," not caring now if Emily realized that I was suddenly furious.

Sounding unflappable, Tomlinson continued, "I figured it would be okay. So I explained that your truck broke down in Immokalee and a couple of the rednecks were giving you a hard time. But I didn't mention the cops—or the drunken waitress at the barbecue place."

Emily said, "What drunken waitress?" as I studied the man's face in surprise, wondering how any human being could lie so effortlessly.

I exhaled a slow breath, very relieved. "It was an ugly scene," I told Emily. "There was no reason to get you involved."

I expected the lie to calm the woman. Instead, it made her madder. Emily put her hands on her hips and leaned toward me, saying, "No, the truth is, you thought your buddy and I had something going on that night. Didn't you? Just because he answered my phone at one-thirty in the morning. That we both got stoned and jumped in the sack or something—like I'm some sort of easy tramp. That's why you didn't want me to help you. That's why you've been avoiding both of us. Tell the truth, Doc."

Glancing at Tomlinson, I did tell the truth. "It wouldn't be the first time that it's happened," I said.

Smiling, Tomlinson was walking toward us. "I explained that to her, Doc," he said. "I'm a sinner, God knows it, and now Emily knows it. But what you need to understand is that my premonition of fire almost came true. That's why I was still there at Emily's house. Trust me, she couldn't get rid of me fast enough."

The woman was protesting, "That's not *exactly* true," as Tomlinson continued, "Remember that old drawing I showed you, the woman falling into a wall of flames? I followed Emily back to her place just like you told me. Just as I was pulling away, she came running out, saying maybe she smelled smoke."

To Emily I said, "Is he serious?"

The woman replied, "I told you about the house I own, out near Alva. It's built of old Florida pine. It took us a while to figure it out, but one of my electrical breakers was bad, just starting to spark. If we'd gotten there a few minutes later, the whole place would have gone off like a bomb."

"There's nothing more calming than a bud of Captiva-grown weed," Tomlinson added. "That's what we were doing when you called. I was already shit-faced, of course, but her"—Tomlinson nodded his chin toward the woman—"she was as about as loose as a nun at a Viagra convention. Because I was there after midnight, though, I don't blame Doc for assuming the worst. Later, I tried to explain to her why you don't trust me and probably never will."

To survive the awkward silence that followed, Tomlinson looked around, saw the waves, then focused on my new surfboard. "Very cool," he said. "An eleven-six? Really sweet rockers."

I was staring at the man, tempted to ask if he remembered what I'd said to him eleven nights earlier about trusting him with my life. Not actually say the words but just jog his memory in case he'd been too sloshed to remember.

Instead, I put my arm around Emily. It seemed a wiser, safer choice. As Tomlinson leaned to study the YOLO graphics, I touched my lips to the woman's cheek, then suggested that we walk back to my stilt house, where I could apologize in private.

"But what about your new surfboard?" she asked, trying to look over her shoulder as we walked toward the sea oats that fringed the beach.

I replied, "Don't worry, Tomlinson has it. Sooner or later, he would've taken it, anyway."

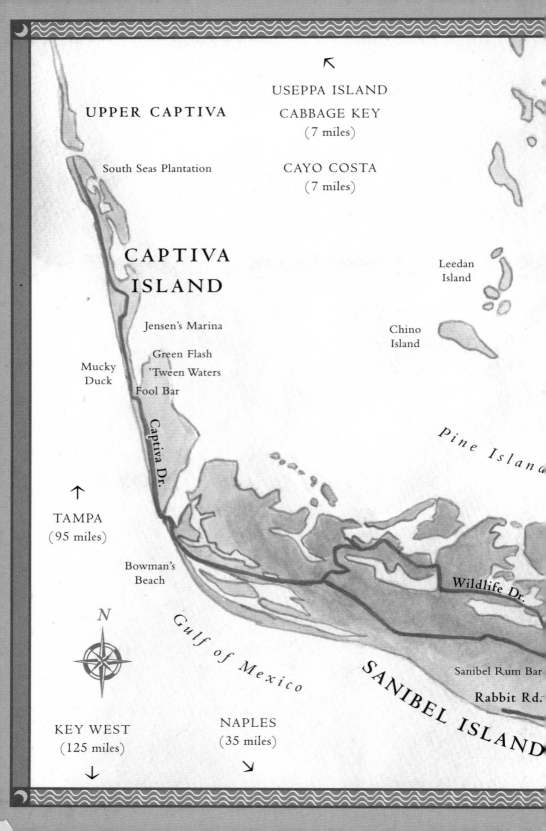